Litigation
and Trial Practice
for the
Legal Assistant

Third Edition

Litigation
and Trial Practice
for the
Legal Assistant

Third Edition

Roderick D. Blanchard

West Publishing Company

St. Paul   New York   Los Angeles   San Francisco

Composition: Parkwood Composition
Copyeditor: Laura Beaudoin

Library of Congress Cataloging–in–Publication Data

Blanchard, Roderick D.
    Litigation and trial practice for the legal assistant / Roderick
D. Blanchard. — 3rd ed.
        p.   cm.
    Rev. ed. of: Litigation and trial practice for the legal
paraprofessional. 2nd ed. c1982.
    ISBN 0-314-56995-2
    1. Civil procedure—United States. 2. Trial practice—United
States. I. Blanchard, Roderick D. Litigation and trial practice
for the legal paraprofessional. II. Title.
KF8840.B53   1990
347.73'7—dc20
[347.3077]   89-24976
                                                              CIP

To my wife, Mary

68934

Contents

Chapter 2 Lawyer and Client Relationships   15

Chapter 3 Causes of Action and Remedies   27

Chapter 4 Affirmative Defenses   71

Chapter 9   Gathering the Evidence   129

Chapter 10   Investigation   137

Chapter 11   Interrogatories   153

Chapter 12   Expert Witnesses   165

Chapter 13   Oral Depositions   177

Chapter 20 Evidence 259

Chapter 21 Fact Brief 287

Chapter 22 Trial Preparation 295

Preface

The civil justice system exists to resolve controversies which arise out of transactions and occurrences, whether between persons, corporations, state governments or the federal government, or any combination of these legal entities. These controversies usually involve injury to a person, damage to property, or a loss of money or profits. The party who has experienced the alleged loss contends that the harm was caused by another person's wrongful act or omission. There must be a rational means of resolving the controversy so that the resolution comports with a common sense of what is fair and just. The remedy provided must be fair in light of the loss actually sustained and the remedy must be just in light of the parties' conduct. The objective of the civil justice system is to resolve parties' "private" disputes so that the parties do not have to resort to self-help to obtain justice, revenge, or some other means of satisfaction.

Our state and federal governments have provided civil courts to resolve private disputes. The courts have developed a large body of law, called the "common law," to guide them in their decision-making process. Of course, the common law is subject to changes and limitations made by legislative law. The courts also developed rules of procedure which the parties must follow when they bring their controversies to the courts for determination. Much of our study will be concerned with the current rules of procedure, which control how a case is put into suit, brought to trial, and brought to a judgment to finalize the parties' legal rights and obligations.

No tribunal has worked so well for so long as the English courts, after which American courts are patterned. It is interesting, therefore, that so many laypersons have only a vague understanding of how civil litigation is conducted and what it involves. Most judges and lawyers who serve the judicial system are convinced of its irreplaceable value. The lack of *informed* criticism of the system is cogent evidence that the system does work well. The ever-increasing workload and responsibilities which government and society place upon the courts is testimony to their success and acceptance as a means of resolving controversies. The judicial system continues to grow in importance.

Lawyers are an integral part of the civil justice system. They are officers of the courts in which they practice. They must honor and protect the courts they serve. At the same time, they are advisers and representatives of their clients. Lawyers must be knowledgeable about the substantive law, which determines the parties' legal rights and obligations. Also, they must be conversant with the Rules of Evidence and the Rules of Procedure, which control how civil cases are prepared for trial and presented in court.

In England, the legal profession is divided into two branches. One branch is composed of solicitors, who act as the client's agent in preparing documents and in handling transactions. The other branch is composed of barristers, who prepare and present cases in court. Only barristers may become judges. There is no such dichotomy for lawyers in the United States. As a practical matter, however, lawyers are becoming more and more specialized. As in England, litigation is becoming a field of specialization. Indeed, many lawyers are becoming so specialized in litigation that they handle only certain types of cases. For example, some very able trial lawyers choose to handle only business litigation. They do not feel comfortable handling personal injury cases, with all of the associated medical problems and human emotions. And some lawyers who handle personal injury cases prefer not to handle litigation involving complicated accounting, business, and tax problems.

All lawyers must follow the same rules of law and the same court procedures, adhere to the same professional and moral standards, and strive for the same objectives for their clients. To be an effective professional, a paralegal must understand the reasons for assignments and appreciate how his or her efforts fit into the overall representation of the client. A paralegal's education in the profession does not end upon completion of school.

Several years ago I started teaching a course in civil litigation for paralegal students. It was a new course in a new college program. There were no textbooks available and not even an established format for the course. After a good deal of thought and discussion with other lawyers, I concluded that the course should focus on educating paralegal students about the objectives of civil litigation and the role lawyers play in handling civil cases. This book is predicated upon the belief that the more understanding a paralegal has about the legal system and lawyers' functions, the better a paralegal can help the clients and lawyers with whom he or she works. A course in civil litigation for paralegals should not be limited to a study of office procedures and legal forms. These skills can be quickly learned on the job if a paralegal has a good understanding of the legal system and procedures.

The work performed by paralegals in civil litigation can be interesting and exciting. The field is growing, because paralegals have shown that they provide valuable assistance in handling civil cases. Each case is a new challenge, and there are great opportunities for personal pride and satisfaction in doing important work well. Certified paralegals are able to take a major role in gathering and organizing the evidence for proving a client's claim or defense. Paralegals are becoming involved in all phases of trial preparation such as interviewing clients, locating and interviewing witnesses, analyzing and preserving evidence, and preparing litigation documents. The variety of the problems makes civil litigation a fascinating area of the law.

Lawyers can assign many responsibilities to paralegals and maintain or even improve the high quality of service for which nearly all lawyers strive. If a lawyer has the assistance of one or more paralegals, there is a good possibility that the client's problems will receive attention more promptly and more thoroughly. What is more, the paralegal services may permit somewhat lower legal fees with the improved service. The entire legal system benefits from the help of competent paralegals.

I hope that this book will contribute to a greater appreciation of the judicial system and the legal profession that helps it to work so well. It is difficult to convey the full drama and excitement of civil litigation. I wish that each principle of jurisprudence, each rule of procedure, and each rule of evidence could be illustrated by examples—especially actual experiences. I have tried in this third edition to provide more illustrations of legal principles and the operation of the rules of law and procedure. It is my hope that professors will supply more examples and expand upon the matters covered. The glossary provides a convenient reference for many of the technical words used in this book. The glossary definitions and explanations are educational in themselves and deserve study.

Introduction to Civil Litigation

Parties to a dispute should try to settle their differences between themselves; however, there are many reasons why parties look to the judicial system for help in resolving their differences. The parties may not be able to agree that a wrong has been committed or that the claimant has sustained a loss or what would be fair compensation or adequate restitution. The parties may disagree about the terms of their own agreements. Sometimes the party against whom a claim is made refuses even to discuss the matter. If government did not provide a means for compelling the parties to communicate about their dispute and resolve their dispute, the party claiming a loss would likely seek self-help and, perhaps, resort to violence.

Civil litigation provides a means to force parties to communicate about their dispute. When a suit is commenced the parties become subject to the power of a court, which is really the power of the government. In our society the courts have been given the ultimate authority for determining and declaring parties' legal rights and obligations. Through litigation private controversies may be fully and finally resolved according to fairly objective standards which generally have good community acceptance. Courts determine what the law is and how the law applies to the facts in each case. Courts occasionally create rules of law so that they are able to resolve controversies for which there is no established law or precedent.

Civil litigation necessarily involves many areas of the law. Where there is a dispute between two or more parties, a lawyer must first look to the *substantive law* to determine what the parties' rights and obligations are. The substantive law has three main categories: contracts, property, and torts, with many subcategories. Each field of law melds into other areas of law. A lawyer must call upon all of his or her education, training, and experience to handle civil litigation. Lawyers must follow *procedural law* to determine how the parties' substantive rights can be established in a court of law. Litigation involves the whole field of law—substantive law, procedural law, and the law of evidence. Law schools do not teach civil litigation as a separate course because it encompasses too much.

Our study is principally concerned with procedural law used for preparing cases for trial, with an emphasis on those areas where paralegals may assume major responsibilities. The procedural law dictates the methods, manner, and means of gathering evidence to present at trial and of conducting the trial. Lawyers must carefully follow the prescribed procedures in the prosecution and defense of civil actions. The procedural laws mandate certain activities and prohibit other activities. A thorough study of the legal procedures is necessary to avoid wrongful conduct which could embarrass or otherwise harm the client.

Since there are innumerable opportunities for lawyers to do mischief when handling clients' important matters, a Code of Professional Responsibility has been created to guide lawyers and protect clients. Ethical considerations apply to every procedure employed by a lawyer in the prosecution of the client's cause. Therefore, paralegals must become familiar with the professional standards and ethical considerations by which lawyers are bound.

Most cases involve a dispute on the facts which must be resolved before the rules of law can be applied to determine the parties' legal rights. In a trial, the jury's verdict establishes the facts. "Verdict" means "to speak the truth." The ultimate determination of the parties' respective rights and obligations is the court's decree or judgment. The final step in handling civil litigation is the enforcement of the judgment for the benefit of the prevailing party. If the parties do not have any dispute concerning the facts, the controversy may be resolved as a *matter of law* by the judge. Juries do not determine or resolve issues of law. Juries only decide fact issues. Questions of law, whether substantive or procedural, are always decided by judges.

Unlike lawyers, judges cannot select the types of cases they want to handle. They must handle whatever cases come before them. No one can possibly know all of the law. Consequently, judges often must look to the parties' lawyers to supply the applicable law and precedent which applies to a particular controversy. Judges have a right to expect the lawyers to be forthright about the applicable law. Often there is room for disagreement about the meaning or application of statutes and precedent. But a lawyer's argument on the law and use of authorities must be made in good faith.

The terms "lawyer" and "attorney" are often used synonymously, and that will be true in this book; however, "attorney" may refer to a person who is authorized to transact business for another person. Therefore, sometimes the term is enlarged to "attorney-at-law." The term "lawyer," however, always refers to a person who is educated and trained in the law, who is licensed to practice law, and who may represent clients in court.

Many of the procedures which, historically, have been performed only by lawyers may be done by paralegals who have a good basic understanding of the judicial system. The purpose of this book is to describe and analyze the structure of civil lawsuits and to explain the procedures used in civil litigation. The emphasis is upon litigation as it is conducted in the federal district courts. A vast majority of the states have similar, if not identical, rules of civil procedures. So a study of the federal rules really has a double value. We will examine the relationship between lawyers and clients involved in litigation. We will also examine the relationship between lawyers and the courts they serve. Students may even gain an appreciation for *legal analysis*, which is one of the primary objectives of an education in the law.

Criminal procedures differ significantly from the procedures used in civil litigation. The two branches of the law are quite distinct, so do not assume that the rules and procedures discussed herein carry over into the field of criminal law.

The student must have access to a current publication of the *Federal Rules of Civil Procedure for the United States District Courts*. Most of the forms and documents contained herein are from actual court files. The names, dates, and places have been changed, however, even though the matters are of public record. The forms in the Appendix are supplemental to the official forms found in *Federal Rules* and are intended to be illustrative of documents used in litigation. They should be referred to while studying the text. The glossary should be helpful, but frequent use of a good law dictionary, such as *Black's Law Dictionary*, will be necessary. Students should strive to become familiar with the language of the legal profession to increase their abilities to communicate effectively with lawyers and other paralegals.

Throughout the book are references to *The Federal Rules of Civil Procedure*. These are Rules 1 to 86. There are also references to the *Federal Rules of Evidence*, which are numbered 101 to 1103.

Most of the examples used in the text come from accident cases; however, most of the rules and principles apply equally to cases arising out of business dealings, real estate transactions, and other kinds of transactions. Accident cases have been chosen to illustrate problems and solutions primarily because most of us can readily relate to them.

There is some repetition in the text. For example, discussion concerning preparation of a client for a deposition is also relevant to, and discussed in, the sections concerned with preparation of a client to testify at trial. Discussions of evidentiary problems and procedures appear in the sections on evidence, discovery, and trial. The repetition is necessary to show the interrelationship of the various rules and procedures.

The civil justice system is a good system. It works about as well as a human institution can. It has inherent checks and balances which help to reduce errors and which provide the opportunity to correct errors. There are a few dissident voices who urge abandonment of the jury system for some more efficient method of establishing the truth in civil lawsuits. Great Britain has eliminated juries for most, if not all, civil actions. The advocates of jury abolition in the United States would undertake such a drastic change not because the present system does not work well but for the purpose of obtaining "substantial" justice more economically. "Substantial justice" is something less than *justice*. "Substantial justice" is a term used to describe administrative hearings and arbitration procedures which seek compromise solutions rather than determining who is correct in fact or what law actually is determinative. The advocates of "substantial justice" see it as an acceptable compromise to obtain economies—as long as it is someone else's rights that are in controversy. I strongly believe in the present system and the traditional adversary method of handling civil litigation. It is imperative that the jury system continue in civil litigation. The checks and balances in our judicial system should not be forsaken for economy or expediency. There are ways in which the present system could be improved to make litigation more economical and speedy, but the basic premises upon which the present system is founded are sound.

Litigation and Trial Practice for the Legal Assistant

Third Edition

1 Principles of Litigation

Our judicial system and court procedures have evolved out of centuries of experience. The premises upon which the system is based are valid. The procedure utilized for ascertaining the truth and applying the law have proven to be very effective for peaceably resolving controversies. The judicial system is based upon logic and reason, but its success is largely due to the fact that it takes into consideration the strengths and weaknesses of human nature. It contains inherent checks and balances and numerous safeguards to help insure that justice is accomplished according to law. The system may not work perfectly, but it does work exceedingly well.

When a person's legal rights have been violated, causing injury or loss, litigation provides a means for identifying the rights, proving the violations, establishing the nature and extent of the loss, and providing a remedy—usually in the form of monetary compensation. Money awarded as compensation is usually referred to by lawyers as "money damages" or simply "damages."

Where a person believes that another person has wrongfully caused him or her to suffer a loss, there should be no reason for a person to feel forced to resort to violence or self-help to obtain justice. If the judicial system were too complicated, too expensive, or too unpredictable in the administration of justice, parties would avoid using courts and resort to self-help. Therefore, the procedures for instituting a lawsuit and prosecuting it have been kept relatively simple. The cost of litigation to the parties is only a fraction of its actual cost. For example, the current fee for the plaintiff in a federal district court is one hundred dollars. There is no filing fee for the defendant. If parties were forced to bear the entire cost of their litigation, such as the cost of the courtroom and court personnel, the parties might be forced to forego valuable rights, or accept obligations which they do not owe. Courts should be available to everyone who needs them, and, generally, they are.

Considering the number of courts and the enormous amount of important litigation they handle, it is amazing that they work so well. Most lawyers who regularly appear in court have the utmost respect for the system and confidence in the ability of courts to make just determinations.

The Authority of the Courts

When a controversy is put into suit, the parties call upon the government to use its personnel, facilities, and power to bring about a resolution of the problem. A court provides the forum in which parties state their claims and present their evidence in an orderly manner. Through the court's subpoena power, parties may require witnesses to appear in court to testify and produce any tangible evidence in their possession. Parties to a pending lawsuit may be compelled to comply with court orders and procedures through the court's power to impose sanctions and penalties. The prevailing party is awarded a judgment in his or her favor, which is enforceable against the losing party through the power of the executive branch of the government. Courts have power to litigate controversies between individuals, corporations, governmental agencies, states, the federal government, and other legal entities.

Cause of Action

When should a person resort to litigation as a means of resolving a controversy? Obviously, not every dispute is a proper subject for litigation, nor can the courts always provide the ideal remedy or even a satisfactory remedy; however, anyone who has a claim that can be formulated into a cause of action may put that claim into suit—usually with the help of a lawyer. A cause of action arises only when a person acts contrary to law and the wrongful act or omission causes an injury or other loss to another. The wrongful act may be the breach of a contractual duty, a statutory duty, or a duty established by common law. But ordinarily, no cause of action will lie unless a real loss or an actual injury has resulted from the unlawful act or omission.

A party may not "split" a cause of action. If a party has several items of loss all arising out of the same transaction or occurrence, all claims must be included in one lawsuit. For example, an automobile accident may cause a party to suffer automobile damage, personal injuries, a loss of income, medical expenses, and a loss of personal property such as clothing. All of the party's losses must be included in one lawsuit. If any item is omitted, even inadvertently, the party is precluded from recovering damages for the loss in another suit. Likewise, if a plaintiff has a claim in negligence and a claim for breach of warranty against a defendant—both arising out of one occurrence— he or she must sue on both theories in the one lawsuit. Any claims not asserted are waived. Any defense not duly asserted is waived. A defendant cannot obtain a new trial or a second trial on the grounds that he or she inadvertently overlooked a defense that might have been available if duly asserted. Various types of causes of action are discussed in chapter 3.

Stare Decisis

The law must be consistent and predictable; otherwise, parties would never know what their legal rights and obligations are. Therefore, once a rule of law has been propounded by a court, that rule is adhered to by that court and all other lower courts in that jurisdiction unless and until the precedence of that rule is overruled. A court may overrule its own decisions, and a court-made rule of law may be overruled by another higher court. For example, the United States Supreme Court can overrule a rule of law adopted by any federal court. The principle requiring courts to follow established rules of law is called stare decisis. Trial courts must follow the precedent of the appellate courts. Appellate courts may overrule their own previous decisions thereby establishing new rules of law.

Jurisdiction

Jurisdiction may be thought of as the authority or power of a court. A court that undertakes to determine a controversy must have jurisdiction over the parties and jurisdiction over the subject matter of the case, otherwise its judgment is unenforceable—a nullity. Jurisdiction over the plaintiff is never a problem, because when the plaintiff files a complaint, he or she thereby submits to the court's jurisdiction. Jurisdiction over the defendant can be obtained only if he or she is within the territorial limits of the court or has some special contact with the jurisdiction such as doing business there. A court obtains jurisdiction over the defendant through service of process (summons and complaint) upon the defendant. Once the defendant submits to the court's jurisdiction—even if inadvertently—the defendant cannot avoid the court's authority.

Jurisdiction over the subject matter depends upon the powers granted to the court by the authority that created it. The parties cannot give the court jurisdiction over the subject matter. As soon as a court becomes aware of any jurisdictional defect, the case must be dismissed.

A judgment obtained in one jurisdiction is readily enforceable in another jurisdiction. The procedure is quite simple. The foreign judgment is made the subject of a lawsuit in the new jurisdiction. An allegation is made that the judgment was duly obtained in the other court and an authenticated or exemplified copy of the judgment is filed with the new court. The only basis for the defendant (judgment debtor) to avoid the judgment is to prove that the court that rendered the judgment lacked jurisdiction over the defendant or lacked jurisdiction over the subject matter. Since state courts must give full faith and credit to other state's judgments, the burden of proof is on the judgment debtor to prove a lack of jurisdiction. Assuming the judgment debtor fails in proving a lack of jurisdiction, the local court renders its own judgment, which may be enforced like any other judgment within that jurisdiction.

Remedies

Sometimes courts are able to restore to a party the very thing that he or she lost through the wrongful conduct of another person. Included in such things may be real estate, personal property, documents, and, to a certain extent, intangibles such as a job or a reputation. Where restoration is not feasible, the law attempts to provide fair compensation for injury, damage, and losses through an award of "money damages." Money seems to be the best common denominator.

Through a civil suit, a party may be able to prevent (enjoin) an individual, government, or corporations from pursuing a course of conduct that is harmful to a person or property. Courts have the power to issue restraining orders and injunctions to prohibit wrongful conduct. On the other hand, courts seldom are able to compel a party to perform services. Regardless of the specific remedy sought, the procedures used for preparing and presenting a claim and defense are much the same.

Multiplicity of Suits

Multiplicity of suits is impermissible. Courts will not allow a plaintiff to sue the defendant in two or more courts on the same claim. If a claim is sued in two courts, the defendant has the right to make a motion for dismissal of one of the cases. If the defendant notices (schedules) a motion for dismissal on these grounds, the plaintiff should decide which forum he or she prefers and voluntarily dismiss one of the cases. Multiplicity of litigation wastes the courts' time and imposes an economic hardship on the parties.

One might wonder why the plaintiff's lawyer would ever start more than one suit. The answer is that, on occasion, the plaintiff may experience difficulty obtaining jurisdiction over one or more of the defendants in one jurisdiction, so he or she starts as many lawsuits as is necessary, wherever necessary. Also, the plaintiff may start a lawsuit in one jurisdiction to keep the statute of limitations from running out while trying to obtain service on defendants in another jurisdiction.

Res Judicata

A controversy may be litigated only once. When the parties have had their controversy determined by a court of competent jurisdiction, they cannot relitigate the matter. If the loser attempts to raise the same issues in a new case, the prevailing party has a complete defense by merely showing that the issues were already determined. The second court will not litigate the same issues a second time. The second court won't even litigate issues which should have been determined in the first trial but were not. The principle is referred to as res judicata, which means the subject matter has been adjudicated. Neither party may go to another court and contend that the first court reached the wrong result, except through established appellate procedures. If, however, the first determination was made by a court that lacked jurisdiction, that court's judgment or decree is a nullity. For a court's judgment to be effective and binding, the court must have jurisdiction over the parties and the subject matter. Therefore, the judgment debtor may contest the first court's jurisdiction when the judgment creditor tries to enforce the judgment in a new (foreign) jurisdiction. If jurisdiction was lacking, the judgment cannot be enforced.

Collateral Estoppel

An accident may give rise to a cause of action in favor of the plaintiff against two or more persons. If the plaintiff sues only one person and the court determines that the plaintiff did not sustain a loss, or that the loss was caused solely by his or her own wrongful conduct, that determination is a bar to any claim the plaintiff may have against other persons not sued in the first case. The principle is called collateral estoppel, or estoppel by verdict. The rationale is that the plaintiff presumably tried the case as well as he or she could and presented all of the available evidence. The adverse result should be the same in a second trial against a different defendant. Courts should not be bothered by piecemeal litigation. The plaintiff should join in one action all persons who are liable to him or her. But suppose the jury in the first trial finds that nonparties were responsible. Collateral estoppel would not prevent the plaintiff from bringing a new action against those other persons, because such an action is not inconsistent with the determinations made in the first trial.

Real Controversy

There are fundamental limitations on the kinds of controversies which courts may handle. A controversy must be real, as opposed to hypothetical. It must arise out of an actual transaction or occurrence. Parties could conjure up all kinds of interesting fact situations for which they would like a court's "advisory opinion." But people are not permitted to use the courts to resolve their hypothetical questions. This principle of jurisprudence has some very practical applications. For example, if one party to a contract believes that the other party is going to breach the contract, it might be nice to have the issue litigated before the breach actually occurs. But, there is no controversy between them that permits either party to invoke the power of the courts. For another illustration, suppose that during the course of a trial the parties are able to reach a settlement so that their controversy is, in fact, resolved; it would be considered a fraud upon the court for the parties to continue with the case just to see how it would have been decided. Their settlement ended the dispute. They cannot impose upon the courts.

Real Party in Interest

A lawsuit must be brought in the name of the person who owns the cause of action. As stated in Rule 17: "Every action shall be prosecuted in the name of the real party in interest." The defendant has an absolute right to deal with the party who owns the cause of action. If it appears that the plaintiff is not the real party in interest, the action must be dismissed by the court. Suppose that Johnson loans Smith five hundred dollars on a promissory note and Smith defaults. Johnson considers the note as almost worthless because Smith has no ability to pay at the present time. But Jones decides to buy the promissory note from Johnson for fifty dollars on the basis that someday Smith will pay or can be compelled to pay. Who owns the cause of action? The real party in interest is Jones in an action on the note. Contract claims are assignable. The point with which we are concerned is that the lawsuit must be prosecuted in the name of the real party in interest.

As a general rule, personal injury claims cannot be assigned or transferred. This principle tends to discourage intermeddlers from fomenting personal injury litigation. Nevertheless, there is a growing list of exceptions to the prohibition against assignment of injury claims. For example, if a medical insurance policy has paid an accident victim's medical bills, the insurer may have a right of subrogation against the tortfeasor. Some courts have indicated a willingness to permit the insurer to pursue its subrogation claim even though it is part of the insured's personal injury claim.

Necessary Parties

If a plaintiff fails to include a person who ought to be a party to the lawsuit, either as a plaintiff or defendant, the action is subject to dismissal for failure to include a necessary party (Rule 19). On the other hand, the defendant may elect to bring an action against the person who should have been a party originally. The additional necessary person may be made an "involuntary" plaintiff or a third-party defendant. Court procedures encourage, and even require, joinder of all claims into one lawsuit to facilitate the ends of justice and to minimize the number of cases and trials. For example, suppose that Smith and Jones are co-owners of a parcel of real estate that they claim was damaged by a trespasser. The action against the trespasser must be brought in the names of both Smith and Jones so that the entire claim can be resolved in one action and one trial. The action could not be maintained by only one of them. Obviously, the owners face a potential dilemma if one is opposed to bringing suit against the alleged trespasser.

Judges and Juries

The trial judge determines all questions of law and procedure that arise during the course of a trial. The judge controls the courtroom and the people in it. Lawyers, witnesses, parties, and even spectators may be held in contempt of court for disruptive conduct and be summarily punished. This plenary authority is necessary for judges to insure respect for their courts.

The physical features of the typical courtroom promote the authority and dignity of the court. Of course, the judge personifies the court, so everything centers upon the judge. At the same time, however, the judge is sequestered from everyone else. The judge enters the courtroom through a separate entrance. The judge sits behind a large bench which is elevated above everything else in the courtroom. The size, height, and position of the bench give the appearance and feeling of physical dominance. The bench provides a physical barrier between the judge and the rest of the courtroom. The judge's robes set him or her apart and provide an air of classic dignity. The robes are always black, emphasizing the solemnity of the proceedings. The work area of the courtroom is directly in front of the judge's bench, so that the judge can control all activity. Most courtrooms still have a bailiff to maintain order and to protect the judge when necessary. If the lawyers need to talk with the judge at the bench so that the jury cannot hear them, the lawyers must obtain permission from the judge to "approach" the bench. Spectators are excluded from the court's work area by a railing or "bar". The lawyers work inside the area which is barred to the public. Hence, lawyers are often referred to as "members of the bar".

Courts have extensive power that is limited primarily by the courts' own self-discipline. The ability of courts to control themselves is strengthened by a hierarchy which places trial courts under the control of appellate courts. Appellate courts are subject to scrutiny by the other branches of government and by the public: their acts and decisions ordinarily must be published in opinions which explain the reasons for the courts' decision or action. Professional ethics require lawyers to support the dignity of the courts by always being respectful of the judges, even during moments of acute disagreement. A lawyer would be subject to disciplinary action if he or she were to publicly criticize a judge for the handling of a case. A lawyer must use the procedures within the system, such as the appellate process, to obtain correction of judicial abuses. The judicial system is not a democratic process, and it is not supposed to be subject to political manipulations.

With experience, a judge acquires knowledge and understanding helpful to the handling of his or her responsibilities. But experience may also cause a judge to acquire prejudices for or against certain lawyers, parties, and types of litigation. Even though judges consciously endeavor to keep their personal feelings from affecting their decisions, the potential for problems exists. The real danger of prejudice lies in the subjective determination of controverted facts, a biased evaluation of witnesses and bias toward their testimony. It is common for certain witnesses to appear in court quite often. For example, certain physicians, appraisers, and policemen appear in court on a regular basis. It is very easy for a prejudice acquired in one case to carry over to another case. Since jurors are exposed to only a few cases during their term of service, it is unlikely that they will develop strong, fixed attitudes about a lawyer or a party or certain types of cases. Trial by jury provides one of the important checks to help balance our judicial system.

Appellate Courts

Appellate courts, such as the United States Supreme Court, are primarily concerned with determining questions of law. Only after a controversy has been fully presented to a trial court and a determination made by the trial court does an appellate court become involved. Appellate courts depend upon the trial courts to resolve disputed issues of fact, so that the law can be applied to established facts. Appellate courts are concerned with both matters of substantive law, which determines the parties' rights, and procedural law, which determines how the case must be prosecuted.

Appellate courts have inherent power to change court-made rules of law. On occasion, an appellate court determines that an old, established rule of law must be set aside. This is done by issuing a decision and written opinion that expressly overrules all prior decisions which are inconsistent with the new holding. The case in which the change is made is given the benefit of the change. Usually the new rule affects only future cases. In that event, all causes of action arising out of transactions or occurrences before the date of the new decision are governed by the old rule of law. But all causes of action arising thereafter are governed by the new rule of law. If an appellate decision does not expressly state that the new rule is to be given prospective effect only, its effect is retroactive as well. Then the new rule applies even to pending cases but not to cases already adjudicated or settled.

Courts Are Neutral in an Adversary System

Civil litigation is an adversary proceeding. Each party is required to gather and present his or her own evidence. The trial court remains entirely neutral. Judges are permitted to ask clarifying questions of witnesses during the course of a trial, but, when this is done, the judge usually explains to the jury that they should not give any greater or lesser weight to the testimony elicited through those questions. In federal courts, a trial judge may comment on the evidence after instructing the jury concerning the applicable law. Most state court judges avoid doing that. If the judge's comments are adverse to the party who subsequently loses, it makes the party feel that he or she did not have a fair trial.

When a judge elects to comment on the evidence at the end of the trial, he or she should remind the jurors that they are the exclusive judges of the facts. They must determine the truth solely from the evidence presented during the course of the trial. They should not be influenced by what they think the judge wants the verdict to be. A judge usually instructs the jury that his or her comments are not intended to indicate what he or she thinks the outcome of the case ought to be. A judge usually tells the jury, at the end of the trial, that if he or she has said anything or done anything that would seem to indicate such an opinion, the jury is to disregard it.

There are a few situations in which a judge may affirmatively act to protect one party. For example, judges do intercede on behalf of minors and incompetent persons to make sure that their rights are protected. Courts always make sure that guardians are appointed to represent minors who are involved in civil litigation whether as plaintiffs or defendants. If the plaintiff is a minor who is desirous of settling the claim, the proposed settlement cannot be binding upon the minor unless the settlement is approved by a court. The court must inquire into the circumstances of the occurrence or transaction that gave rise to the defendant's liability, as well as the nature and extent of the minor's injuries or other losses. The defendant's ability to pay may be a factor. The judge must evaluate all the facts to determine whether the settlement is prudent from the minor's standpoint. Only if the judge decides that the settlement is truly in the minor's best interests should the judge give approval. This is one of the few instances in which judges take a role other than that of a neutral. It should be noted that if the judge refuses to approve a proposed minor's settlement and the defendant is unwilling to pay more, the case must go to trial. If the jury finds in favor of the defendant, the minor plaintiff has no recourse against the judge for not approving the proposed settlement. He or she must abide by the verdict.

Representatives

In cases involving a person who is incompetent to manage his or her own matters, such as a minor, the court must see to it that a guardian is or has been appointed for the purpose of protecting that person's interests in the litigation. This is true whether the incompetent is a plaintiff or a defendant. A guardian who is specially appointed to represent a litigant is called a *guardian ad litem*. The guardian will be discharged by the court upon conclusion of the litigation. His or her duty in the litigation is to protect the incompetent's interests and carry out the court's orders. If a guardian has already been appointed by a probate court, ordinarily that person is a proper representative to handle the incompetent's litigation. Then a guardian ad litem is not necessary.

The parties' status in the case is indicated in the title of the action:

> John Jones, as guardian ad litem of
> Mary Jones, a minor,
>   plaintiff,
>   vs.
> Robert M. Smith, and
> John Jones,
>   defendants.

The complaint usually contains a separate paragraph alleging that the representative was duly appointed to act in a representative capacity. Rule 9(a) specifically states, however, that such an allegation is not essential.

Assignment of Claims

The owner of a claim (cause of action) for money damages has the right to prosecute the claim in court. The purpose of proving or establishing the claim in court is to have the mere claim reduced to an absolute right that is enforceable against the party who is liable. This absolute right is established by a judgment that declares the parties' rights and obligations. A cause of action that is subject to being assigned to another person is sometimes referred to as a "chose in action." The phrase means that it is an unperfected right. Though unperfected, the right is identifiable and has value. Though it is not property, as such, a chose in action can be bought and sold or assigned. For example, if a dispute arises between a seller and buyer of goods, and the buyer refuses to pay for the goods, the seller's alleged right to payment could be assigned or sold to another person or company who could bring suit to recover on the claim. As part of the cause of action, the assignee would have to prove a valid assignment.

A trespass to real estate could cause damage. The owner of the damaged property may want to sell the property before he or she can bring suit against the trespasser. The buyer may be willing to take an assignment of the cause of action against the trespasser. The value of the assignment is quite subjective and is usually negotiable between the assignor and assignee. The assignee's recovery is often limited to the amount paid for the assignment, but not always.

As a general rule, personal injury claims cannot be bought and sold or assigned. There is no commercial necessity for such assignments. The rule effectively prevents lawyers and others from speculating in personal injury claims. Suppose Jones sustains injuries due to the tortious conduct of the defendant. Jones is the only person who is permitted to sue the defendant to recover money damages for those injuries. If the law were otherwise, Jones might be inclined to sell his cause of action to another person. It is not too difficult to imagine some well-to-do individual or company speculating in personal injury lawsuits. Some injured parties would be willing to sell their claims for an inadequate sum of money to obtain payment immediately; the buyer might be able to turn a handsome profit on a subsequent settlement or jury verdict. But profit making is contrary to the objectives of civil litigation.

Also, such dealings tend to shortchange injury victims who are in need. The plaintiff's lawyer must not permit the plaintiff to become a party to such a scheme.

Indemnification for a loss by the plaintiff's own insurer may complicate ownership of the claim. For example, if an automobile is damaged by the defendant in an accidental collision, the automobile owner may elect to receive payment for the loss under the collision coverage of his or her own automobile insurance policy. The insurance company has a right to an assignment of the automobile owner's claim against the **tortfeasor.** Most automobile insurance policies provide that the insured must bear the first one hundred dollars of the loss. If the insured retains a partial interest in the claim because of a deductible clause, he or she remains owner of the cause of action and is the real party in interest to bring the claim. If the insured succeeds in making a recovery against the tortfeasor, the insured's contract with his or her insurer requires a reimbursement to the insurer out of the recovery. The insured holds the funds in trust for the insurer.

If an insurer pays the full amount of its insured's loss pursuant to the terms of a direct-loss (not liability) insurance policy, the insurer becomes the real party in interest to bring an action against the tortfeasor who caused the loss. The insurer owns the cause of action; the action must be brought in the insurer's name. For example, suppose that the insured's automobile was destroyed by a fire caused by the defendant's negligence. The insured may elect to obtain payment for the loss under the automobile policy. The loss comes under the "comprehensive" coverage, which does not require the insured to pay any portion of the loss—no deductible. In that event, when the insurer pays its own insured for the loss, the insurer is subrogated to the claim against the defendant. The insurer becomes the owner of the cause of the action and is the real party in interest. Suits against the defendant tortfeasor must be brought in the name of the insurance company. The insured has no right to control the litigation. The insured's contract with the insurance company requires the insured to cooperate in the prosecution of the lawsuit.

Whenever a cause of action is properly assigned, it must be prosecuted in the name of the assignee. The maximum amount of money damages that the assignee can recover is, ordinarily, the amount paid for the assignment. Proof that the assignment was duly consummated is part of the cause of action. The assignee must plead and prove the assignment as part of the case.

Commencement of Lawsuit

A lawsuit is very easy to start. The first step is to prepare a complaint, which sets forth the plaintiff's claim against the defendant. A complaint sets forth the basic facts and alleges that the defendant breached one or more legal duties owed to the plaintiff. In federal court the action is commenced by filing the complaint with the clerk of court. The clerk then prepares a summons directed to the defendant. The summons instructs the defendant that he or she must answer the complaint or be held liable by default. There is no actual limit to the number of persons who may join together as plaintiffs to bring an action against the defendant. Nor is there any limit to the number of defendants who may be named and sued in any one case. For example, if a lawsuit concerned a parcel of land owned by ten individuals in common, all ten should be named as parties, whether as plaintiffs or defendants.

There are several methods by which the summons and complaint may be served upon defendants. The traditional method is to have the United States marshal serve it by delivering a copy of each to the defendant personally or by delivering it to the defendant's residence by leaving a copy with a person who resides there also. The person with whom the summons and complaint are left need not be related to the defendant, but the person must be of suitable age to understand the importance of the event. Many states now authorize service of the summons and complaint by mail. Notwithstanding this step toward liberalizing the requirements, the service is not effective until the defendant decides to accept service by signing an acknowledgement. The defendant returns the signed acknowledgement to the plaintiff's lawyer by mail. Some types of cases, such as automobile accident cases, allow service of the summons and complaint upon a state official, such as the secretary of state. Under some circumstances, service of process may be made by publication in a legal newspaper. These methods of service are discussed in greater detail in chapter 6.

Counterclaims and Cross-claims

A defendant is required to assert, by way of counterclaim, all claims that he or she has against the plaintiff arising out of the same transaction or occurrence. If the defendant fails to assert his or her claims against the plaintiff, the claim is waived. The defendant is barred from bringing the claims in another lawsuit at another time. The entire controversy should be determined once in one proceeding. It is more economical for the parties and the court to resolve the entire matter in one trial.

Where there is more than one defendant, they may resolve claims between them by serving cross-claims; however, cross-claims are not compulsory. A cross-claim has the effect of establishing adversity between the defendants. The existence of adversity has some important procedural effects. For example, the lawyer for one defendant may be able to cross-examine a co-defendant if there is adversity between the defendants.

Third-party Claims

If a defendant determines that he or she has a right to indemnity or contribution from a person who is not yet a party to the case, the defendant may commence a third-party action to obtain indemnity or contribution. A claim for indemnity is a claim for complete reimbursement. For example, in accident cases, the defendants who have liability insurance are entitled to indemnification by their liability insurers for any obligation the defendant has to the plaintiff. An action for indemnity is sometimes necessary when a dispute arises between the defendant and his or her own liability insurer as to whether the plaintiff's claim is covered by the insurance policy. A third-party claim is limited to the claims arising out of the plaintiff's alleged loss. The defendant cannot use a third-party action as a basis for obtaining compensation for the defendant's own loss.

A claim for contribution looks for a sharing of liability and responsibility. For example, if two automobile drivers are negligent so as to cause injury to the plaintiff but the plaintiff brings action against only one of the drivers, the driver who was sued could bring a third-party action against the driver who was not sued to obtain contribution for any award that the plaintiff may obtain.

Declaratory Judgment Actions

Courts may resolve controversies requiring the interpretation of statutes and documents. A lawsuit brought for this purpose is called a declaratory judgment action. The court judgment determines the meaning and effect of the statute or documents in dispute. For example, if the parties have a disagreement over the meaning of their contract, it is possible for either party to start a declaratory judgment action to have a court interpret the contract for them even though the contract has not been breached and no loss has been sustained. The court declares the parties' rights and obligations. The controversy must be real or the action will be dismissed. Declaratory judgment actions are given special treatment by Rule 57. Through declaratory judgments, parties are also able to establish legal status concerning employment, marriage, property ownership, and right to government benefits.

Civil Penalties

Rarely is civil litigation concerned with penalizing a wrongdoer. An award of money damages is for the purpose of making the plaintiff whole. The financial obligation imposed on the defendant, if found liable, is merely incidental to the objective of providing compensation. Courts do not concern themselves with whether or not the defendant can afford to pay or whether the plaintiff can afford to absorb the loss. There are a few exceptions, though. Many states have legislation imposing a civil penalty recoverable by a plaintiff employee if a defendant employer wrongfully withholds the employee's wages. The employee may be awarded treble the amount of wages wrongfully withheld. In addition, the employee may be allowed interest from the date the wages were due. Similarly, in some states a trespasser who takes crops or lumber from the land of another is subject to paying three times the value of the property taken. Obviously, the purpose of treble damages is to deter the wrongful conduct.

One other area of civil penalties deserves mention here. Many states allow plaintiffs to recover punitive damages—a penalty assessed against the defendant in addition to compensatory damages in cases where the defendant intentionally inflicted injury. For example, an intentional battery with a knife, gun, or even a fist may be the basis for imposing punitive damages. Punitive damages are recoverable regardless of the degree of injury or other harm—as long as there is some harm. The measure of punitive damages depends upon the character of the wrongful conduct and the financial worth of the defendant. The term "exemplary damages" is sometimes used for punitive damages because the award is held out as an example to others to discourage wrongful conduct. If the award is really going to penalize the defendant, the size of the award must take into consideration the defendant's ability to pay—at least that is the rationale. Consequently, in those cases where punitive damages are allowable, the defendant's financial worth may become part of the evidence in the case.

There is considerable and growing opposition to allowing punitive damages in civil actions. Its opponents argue that punitive damage awards subject the defendant to double jeopardy. Civil procedures lack the safeguards of criminal cases. For example, the burden of proof is less in civil cases. They argue that only the state should impose fines for criminal conduct. Where more than one claim may result from a tortious act, the imposition of multiple penalties can have ruinous consequences for the defendant. A claim of punitive damages injects the defendant's financial worth into the case, which could adversely influence the jury on other issues and be a personal embarrassment to the defendant. The merits and future of punitive damages is not a subject for this book, but it is a matter of concern to anyone interested in jurisprudence.

Expense of Litigation

Each party to a civil lawsuit must bear most of his or her own expenses, including investigation costs, most witness fees, and lawyers' fees. There are few exceptions to the general rule. The exceptions generally involve special remedies provided by statute where the monetary loss may be relatively small, but the principle at issue is important. Such legislation makes the courts more readily available to those who have been the victims of some form of official harassment or discrimination. The prevailing parties in such lawsuits are usually allowed to recover all their expenses, including lawyers' fees. In most cases taxable costs are limited to the filing fee, subpoena fees, United States marshal's fees, and some small portion of expert witness fees.

Settlements

When parties negotiate a settlement of a claim, they may take into consideration many factors that have no actual relevancy to their legal rights and obligations—such as the effect of the dispute on friends, business associates, or relatives. A defendant's lack of insurance or lack of financial responsibility may be an important factor inducing the plaintiff to accept a compromise or reduced settlement. A party might be constrained to settle because of the cost of litigation or the unavailability of witnesses. But legal rights and duties do not turn on the availability or unavailability of insurance or the effect of litigation on personal relationships. If the parties are unable to reach a settlement, they have to set aside all collateral considerations and rely solely upon the factors that are material to an action at law. The parties must evaluate the strengths and weaknesses of their respective positions in light of rules of law and the procedures by which courts apply those rules of law.

In various ways, the judicial system encourages parties to settle their own disputes. But when the parties cannot reach an accord or agree upon a settlement, the person who wants to force a determination may obtain a judicial determination and a judicial remedy through litigation. It is necessary, though, that the controversy be one that can be stated as a cause of action. This is another way of saying that the controversy must be one over which courts have jurisdiction, one that can be determined by law, and one for which the law provides a remedy.

Professional Ethics

Lawyers are subject to a strict Code of Professional Responsibility, which limits and directs how they are to conduct civil litigation. A lawyer's violation of the Code subjects the lawyer to disciplinary action, which may result in a loss of license to practice law. The Code dictates the obligations that lawyers owe to their clients, to the courts, to opposing lawyers, and even to persons with whom they do not have any direct contact or relationship. One feature of the Code of Professional Responsibility is that if a lawyer violates the Code, he or she is subject to disciplinary action even if the violation does not cause any actual harm to anyone. The Code assists and guides lawyers in dealing with apparent conflicts in their loyalties and obligations. These apparent conflicts may develop between a lawyer's duty to the court and duty to the client. Or, a lawyer may develop apparent conflicts between clients. A lawyer is subject to disciplinary action for violating professional ethics even if the violation does not cause any actual harm to the client or to the court.

An unethical act committed by a paralegal is the ethical responsibility of the lawyers who employ the paralegal. In other words, a lawyer could be censured for the mistakes or misconduct of a paralegal who has acted within the course of his or her employment. Ethical considerations which govern lawyers' conduct will be discussed throughout the book. Paralegals must avoid being involved in any conduct that violates the Code. It is doubtful that paralegals could be censured and punished in the same way that lawyers can be sanctioned by the courts and by the Boards of Professional Responsibility. Nevertheless, any violation of the Code by a paralegal must be considered to be a matter of the gravest concern.

2 Lawyer and Client Relationships

Qualifications to Practice Law

A lawyer is granted the privilege of practicing law within one or more states upon meeting the requirements established by each state's highest court. No one has a constitutional right to practice law. An applicant for a license must demonstrate that he or she meets established minimum requirements for knowledge, ability, and moral character. Most states require an applicant to be a graduate of an accredited law school and to pass a state bar examination. Also, each applicant is screened to determine whether there is any evidence of poor moral character, which could be a basis for withholding or revoking a license. No one may practice law in any state without a license. Any individual who attempts to do this is subject to disciplinary proceedings by the court just as though he or she were a lawyer and may be subject to criminal prosecution. Paralegals are not authorized to practice law—just as paramedics may not practice medicine. They may work with and assist lawyers, but a lawyer must assume ultimate responsibility for advice given and representation of the client in legal proceedings.

Only after being authorized by a state's highest court to practice law in the courts of that state is a lawyer allowed to apply for admission to practice in the federal district courts in that state. A petition for admission to the federal district courts must be supported by affidavits of two other lawyers who have been admitted to practice in the court. The affidavits must affirm that the petitioner is a competent lawyer and of good moral character. No additional examination is required. In a similar manner, lawyers are admitted to practice in the federal circuit courts of appeals and the United States Supreme Court.

Professional ethics require lawyers to handle legal matters in a competent manner. This means that lawyers must have the education, knowledge, and skill necessary to handle the cases they undertake. Equally important, lawyers must thoroughly prepare for each matter whether it is a motion, deposition, conference, or trial.

Professional Responsibility

the act of baseness, vileness, or depravity in private & social duties which man owes to his fellow man

A lawyer is subject to disbarment for any conduct that constitutes moral turpitude. Of course, this does not mean that misdemeanors or ordinance violations would necessarily result in disbarment. The privilege of practicing law is valuable and cannot be taken away at the "pleasure" of the court. A lawyer is entitled to a hearing to controvert any charges that may affect his or her privilege to practice law.

Some states have integrated bars, which means that membership in the bar association is a prerequisite to obtaining a license to practice in that state. The bar association is given an official status and has the initial responsibility for determining whether an applicant may be admitted to practice.

An integrated bar association also has responsibility for conducting disciplinary proceedings against lawyers who are found guilty of unethical conduct. In those states which do not have integrated bars, the highest court in the state has the authority to discipline and disbar delinquent lawyers. The court ordinarily performs the investigation and prosecution functions through personnel appointed by the court. Nevertheless, the authority remains with the court, and it must make the final decision on admissions, disciplinary action, and disbarment.

Lawyers may represent clients in state courts, federal courts, and other official bodies that conduct hearings affecting legal rights. They are authorized to advise laypersons concerning legal problems and may prepare legal documents and instruments for clients such as contracts, wills, deeds, mortgages, patent applications, and, of course, legal process used in civil litigation. Such documents may be prepared by anyone for his or her own use, but laypersons are not allowed to prepare legal documents for another person or for a company. That would constitute an unauthorized practice of law. There is often little difference between the functions performed by lawyers and the activities of real estate brokers, tax advisers, and certified public accountants. Indeed, certain accountants are authorized to appear on behalf of clients in tax courts. Just what activities are the exclusive domain of lawyers is far from clear. But the law makes a very important distinction between the communications of a client with a lawyer and the communications of a client and other professional business advisers. Only the communications with lawyers are privileged.

Lawyers must abide by the client's wishes concerning the objectives of the litigation. If the client wants to settle a claim on terms less favorable than what the lawyer honestly believes is fair and obtainable, the lawyer must accede to the client's preference. If the client wishes to forego a valid claim or dismiss a meritorious claim, regardless of the reason, the lawyer must comply. The lawyer may consult and advise the client against an improvident course of action but, ultimately, must accept the client's decision concerning the objectives of the litigation.

Lawyers have the responsibility and authority to choose the means and procedures for obtaining the client's objectives. Nevertheless, in making "technical" decisions concerning the methods and means, a lawyer must consult with the client and be guided by the client's decision regarding costs. If other persons could be adversely affected by the means recommended by the lawyer, the client has a right to reject and overrule the lawyer's recommendations.

Lawyers' Conflict of Interests between Clients

Lawyers must not represent one client against another client or against a former client. In that regard, the relationship between a client and a lawyer lasts forever; notwithstanding the general rule, a lawyer may represent a new client against a former client if the former client expressly consents. If a lawyer undertakes to represent two clients who are potentially adverse to each other, the nature and potential consequences of the conflict must be fully explained to the clients. If the lawyer proceeds with the joint representation, the lawyer may be compelled to forego both cases when the conflict materializes. For example, it is unethical for a lawyer to represent both an injured automobile driver and a passenger against the driver of the other automobile with which they collided. The passenger has a potential claim against both drivers. But, suppose that the passenger is the driver's wife and the wife does not want to obtain money damages from her husband. A lawyer could undertake to represent both if the lawyer fully explains the possibility that the passenger (wife) may not obtain any damages, unless she brings an action against her husband. The lawyer's explanation and the clients' consent should be reduced to writing. As a further precaution against criticism, a lawyer could advise one or both of the potential clients to talk with another lawyer about the desirability of separate representation.

Multiple representation also raises a problem when the parties have any opportunity to settle the case with an aggregate amount. A lawyer is in a very poor position to recommend acceptance or rejection and cannot advise concerning the proper allocation between clients. Using the preceding husband and wife example, where both were injured and both have a claim against the other driver, suppose that the other driver has a $25,000 liability insurance policy, which the driver's insurer is willing to pay to settle *both* claims. The insurer doesn't care how they allocate the money, but there is no additional money available. If the clients agree on the allocation, there is no problem. But if they are unable to agree, their lawyer must not counsel them. Each of them may need to consult with another lawyer concerning the division.

Fiduciary Responsibilities

person holding the character of a trustee

A lawyer is considered a fiduciary of the client's properties and monies. As a fiduciary, a lawyer must exercise the highest degree of care in handling a client's monies, properties, papers, and confidential communications. The fiduciary relationship does not terminate upon the conclusion of the client's business. It lasts forever! For that reason, a lawyer is precluded from representing new clients against a former client unless, of course, the former client expressly consents.

Agency

A lawyer is considered to be an agent of a client in handling that client's legal matters. Other parties may deal with the lawyer on the basis that he or she has authority to act for and bind the client. Notices directed to a lawyer as a representative of a client are binding upon the client. A lawyer's authority is limited to the particular matter for which he or she has been retained.

There are some very important limitations on a lawyer's authority in handling a client's litigation. A lawyer must not start a lawsuit for the client without the client's permission nor dismiss a lawsuit without the client's express authority and direction to do so. Settlement negotiations may be conducted for the client, but a lawyer is not allowed to accept or reject a proposed settlement without securing authority to do so—even if the settlement is clearly in the client's best interest.

A lawyer's authority and responsibility to a client go beyond an ordinary agency. He or she has implicit authority to do whatever is reasonably necessary for the preparation and conduct of a trial. A lawyer may prepare interrogatories, schedule depositions, attend calendar calls, attend pretrial conferences, and make representations to the court about the state of readiness of the case. He or she may enter into stipulations with opposing parties concerning the evidence and trial procedures as well as agree or object to the admissibility of evidence. Of course, he or she may consult the client about such matters but is not required to do so. A lawyer has the ultimate *responsibility* for handling the litigation but is always subject to the client's ultimate *authority*.

Officers of the Court

Lawyers have dual roles in the judicial system. They are officers of the courts in which they practice, but they are also representatives of their clients. Lawyers are required to act in their clients' best interests and give advice that will benefit clients in the conduct of their legal matters. But lawyers are also required to protect the courts from frauds and abuse. The success of the judicial system is absolutely dependent upon the ability of lawyers to serve their clients' needs and the courts' interests without compromise. Consequently, a very stringent code of professional ethics has been established to guide lawyers. Any violation of the code of ethics hurts the legal profession and contaminates the entire judicial system.

The Code of Professional Responsibility was adopted by the American Bar Association in 1969. The Code provides guidelines for resolution of various ethical problems. Many states have adopted the Code and the Disciplinary Rules as standards of conduct, which, if violated, provide the basis for imposing sanctions—including disbarment.

The Preamble to the Code of Professional Responsibility states the importance of the ethical considerations.

PREAMBLE

The continued existence of a free and democratic society depends upon recognition of the concept that justice is based upon the rule of law grounded in respect for the dignity of the individual and his capacity through reason for enlightened self-government. Law so grounded makes justice possible, for only through such law does the dignity of the individual attain respect and protection. Without it, individual rights become subject to unrestrained power, respect for law is destroyed, and rational self-government is impossible.

Lawyers, as guardians of the law, play a vital role in the preservation of society. The fulfillment of this role requires an understanding by lawyers of their relationship with and function in our legal system. A consequent obligation of lawyers is to maintain the highest standards of ethical conduct.

In fulfilling his professional responsibilities, a lawyer necessarily assumes various roles that require the performance of many difficult tasks. Not every situation which he may encounter can be foreseen, but fundamental ethical principles are always present to guide him. Within the framework of these principles, a lawyer must with courage and foresight be able and ready to shape the body of the law to the ever-changing relationships of society.

The Code of Professional Responsibility points the way to the aspiring and provides standards by which to judge the transgressor. Each lawyer must find within his own conscience the touchstone against which to test the extent to which his actions should rise above minimum standards. But in the last analysis it is the desire for the respect and confidence of the members of his profession and of the society which he serves that should provide to a lawyer the incentive for the highest possible degree of ethical conduct. The possible loss of that respect and confidence is the ultimate sanction. So long as its practitioners are guided by these principles, the law will continue to be a noble profession. This is its greatness and its strength, which permit of no compromise.

Although the Code of Professional Conduct is directed to lawyers, it applies, at least by implication, to any person who assists lawyers, whether as an investigator, secretary, or certified legal assistant.

The Disciplinary Rules were developed from ethical considerations. They help to define ethical considerations and specify their application to problem areas. If accused of a violation of professional ethics, a lawyer is entitled to a hearing that meets all of the requirements of due process of law. A lawyer has a right to know the charges against him or her, to present evidence in defense, and to be heard by an impartial tribunal.

A lawyer must not direct or encourage a client to engage in conduct that is unethical for the lawyer. The client must not be allowed to violate the lawyer's oath by falsely answering interrogatories, by testifying falsely, by procuring the absence of witnesses, or by suborning perjury. Whatever is forbidden to the lawyer is forbidden to the client as well. If a lawyer discovers that a client is guilty of some such impropriety, he or she must take affirmative action to correct the wrong. Some of the considerations and alternatives are discussed below.

Lawyers are forbidden to engage in activities that foment litigation. It is not difficult to imagine a situation where a lawyer finds that business is a little slow and is tempted to examine public records to find a problem with the title to a parcel of real estate for the purpose of obtaining a client. Similarly, unscrupulous lawyers could research articles in newspapers and magazines to find potential libel suits. By such conduct, lawyers create problems solely for their own financial gain. Similarly, lawyers are in a good position to encourage accident victims to pursue litigation rather than drop a claim or settle out of court. Such practices are degrading to the profession and could flood the courts with petty, unnecessary, and unwanted litigation. Any lawyer who creates that kind of business should not be practicing law. Society's interests should be served, not damaged, by lawyers and civil litigation.

A lawyer who incites litigation is subject to disciplinary proceedings and possible disbarment. Paralegals, too, must avoid instigating litigation. That is not to say that a paralegal must avoid recommending a good lawyer when and where one is needed, but a paralegal should not create a controversy where none exists.

Champerty

A lawyer is not permitted to provide financial support for a client by paying the client's living expenses during the pendency of litigation. The practice of advancing monies to a litigant on the basis that the "loan" will be paid out of the verdict or settlement is known as champerty, and it is unethical. At first, it would appear to be considerate, even charitable, for a lawyer to provide a means of support for a client until the case is concluded, especially if the client is disabled and unable to work due to injuries. But if lawyers were to provide financial aid to clients with the expectation of being repaid through the court award or settlement, they would soon find themselves personally involved in the clients' financial affairs and personally interested in the outcome of the case. The danger is much too great that a lawyer's professional judgment could be affected by personal interest in the litigation. The lawyer might be inclined to recommend for or against a settlement in light of his or her own needs rather than those of the client. Good advice is rarely rendered by a person who is personally involved in the matter. There is also the problem that financing clients could become an expected practice; and most lawyers would find that to be an impossible burden. Lending money is better left to banks and other financial institutions.

If a lawyer were to become financially involved in a client's case, there is the possibility that before the case is over, the client could end up "assigning" the claim to the lawyer. Assignment of personal injury claims is contrary to public policy. It is permissible to assign causes of action arising out of transactions such as contract matters, but in personal injury cases, there is, again, a real danger of *maintenance* through the device of assignments. A lawyer must not pay the client's litigation costs or provide financial support to the client during the pendency of the litigation. A lawyer is permitted to advance, on behalf of the client, various expenses incurred in connection with the litigation, but this may be done only on the basis that ultimately the expenses will be paid by the client, regardless of the outcome of the case.

Solicitation and Advertising

Historically, lawyers were forbidden to advertise their services. They could not even permit others to advertise on their behalf. The prohibition was based, in part, on the concern that advertising would foment litigation and lawyers would unduly impose themselves on prospective clients at unpropitious times. The profession is currently in a dilemma over advertising. Advertising is considered to be degrading, but perhaps it is necessary if the public is to be fully informed about the availability of lawyers' various services and the charges for services. There are many people who are not personally acquainted with any lawyer and who are unaware of the types of services that lawyers can provide.

Today advertising is permitted on a limited basis. The limitations are not concerned with the amount of advertising but with the methods of advertising. Advertising is justified on the basis that the public benefits from dissemination of information about the kinds of services which lawyers provide, the cost of legal services, the background and experience of lawyers, and where and how to locate lawyers.

Lawyers may advertise in public media, including newspapers, television, billboards, radio, and directories. However, lawyers may not advertise by direct solicitation, whether in person or by telephone. Lawyers may not pay or reward other persons for recommending them to handle legal matters. They may include in their public advertisements information about themselves, such as age, date admitted to practice, law school attended, offices held in bar associations, teaching positions held, and certification in any specialties in the law. The information must be accurate and factual. For example, it would be unethical for a lawyer to advertise that he or she graduated from Harvard if he or she did not obtain a law degree from Harvard. The advertisement would be considered misleading.

A public advertisement may state the lawyer's address and telephone number and describe the basis for charges. For example, an advertisement may state flat rates for certain types of representations such as adoptions and uncontested divorces or hourly rates for defending against a drunk driving citation. An advertisement may state that the lawyer will handle civil litigation claims on a contingent fee and advance court costs. An advertisement must be so worded that it does not create unjustified expectations about the results the lawyer will obtain. For example, it would be unethical for a lawyer to advertise that the lawyer "wins most" cases he or she tries.

Lawyers may permit their names to be listed in professional directories. These directories are particularly useful to lawyers who need to refer clients to other lawyers in other communities. The principal such directory is *Martindale–Hubbell,* which is published in several large volumes each year.

Lawyer-Client Privilege

The lawyer-client relationship is established whenever a lawyer permits a client to seek his or her professional advice. If the client discloses information, believing it to be under the protection of the lawyer-client privilege, that is sufficient to establish the relationship. A lawyer is forever precluded from using such information to the detriment of the client and from disclosing it to others. The communications are privileged whether written or oral. Only the client may waive the privilege.

A lawyer's records prepared from communications with a client are similarly privileged. The privilege belongs to the client, not to the lawyer. The privilege applies to written communications as well as oral communications. The client may waive his or her privilege either intentionally or inadvertently. All that is needed for a waiver to occur is for the client to relate to some third person the substance of an otherwise privileged communication. In other words, the privilege must be carefully protected.

There is a fundamental difference between confidential communications and privileged communications. A matter that is kept secret between two or more persons would be considered confidential. Most businesses are desirous of keeping their customers' matters confidential. Banks, lending institutions, credit card companies, and department stores all strive to keep their records from getting into the hands of the curious. They avoid publicizing information in their possession about their customers. Nevertheless, a court of law could compel a company to produce its records if the records were relevant to a controversy in suit. But if a communication is privileged, no person and no court can legally compel a disclosure of the communication for any purpose.

The reason a client's statements to a lawyer are privileged is that the client is able to obtain good, competent legal advice only by "telling all" to the lawyer. If the client labored under the fear that statements to the lawyer could be used against him or her as admissions, the client might be inclined to hold back vital information. The privilege applies whether the client discusses marital problems, business problems, criminal matters, preparation of tax returns, etc. It does not matter what the subject is as long as the client is seeking professional legal help or advice.

The law makes an important distinction between advice sought by the client for the purpose of determining legal rights and advice sought for the purpose of evading the law, either in a current or future activity. For example, if a client were to consult a lawyer for the purposes of working out a plan to illegally evade taxes, the communications would not come within the privilege. Indeed, under those circumstances, a lawyer would be duty bound to try to persuade the client to comply with the law. If that failed, the lawyer could be required to inform the proper authorities of the client's scheme. The lawyer could even be compelled to testify against the client concerning the scheme.

For a long time, the privileged status of a communication was lost if the subject matter was voluntarily disclosed to any third person, even the lawyer's secretary. Most courts now recognize that lawyers must act through others, such as private secretaries and legal assistants. Consequently, the privilege has been extended in most jurisdictions to include lawyers' agents. Courts should recognize that it is desirable and necessary for lawyers to disclose privileged information to paralegals assisting them. Of course, if the privilege is enlarged in this manner, it is necessary for paralegals to be subject to the same close controls that courts have over lawyers and be subject to the same rigid professional ethics.

In several recent cases news reporters have attempted to establish a rule that their "confidential" news sources should have privileged status. In the past, reporters could be punished through contempt of court proceedings for their failure or refusal to divulge sources, assuming there was a good and sufficient reason for litigants to know the identity of the sources. The issue presented to the courts in these cases is whether the need for privileged news sources outweighs the need for identification of witnesses who have important evidence relevant to criminal and civil lawsuits. The question also arises whether any item is newsworthy if the identity of the source is not subject to disclosure. Some reporters who have challenged the law have been forced to spend time in jail for refusing to comply with court orders directing them to testify. Their incarcerations were punishment for being in contempt of court.

If a client were to file an ethics complaint against his or her lawyer or commence a negligence action for malpractice, the client cannot claim the attorney-client privilege in an effort to keep the accused lawyer from using records and communications as defense. The privilege is intended to be used as a shield for the client and never as a sword. A lawyer may use all of the client's records and communications, whether written or oral, as defense.

Duty to Court

A lawyer is an officer of the court and must conduct himself or herself in a professional manner at all times, showing respect to the court even when seriously disagreeing with the presiding judge. A lawyer's zeal and desire to serve a client must not lead to misuse or abuse of the court. A lawyer's highest duty is always to the court. If a lawyer believes that a judge has acted improperly in any matter, the lawyer has the right and duty to bring that fact to the attention of the proper authorities. He or she must not insult or cast aspersions on the court in public.

Though a lawyer owes complete fidelity to a client and ordinary care in the handling of the client's litigation, a lawyer's highest obligation is to the courts, which the lawyer serves. Therefore, a lawyer must not perpetrate a fraud upon a court by producing false testimony or otherwise abuse the judicial process for any purpose. For example, if a lawyer learns that a client has attempted to bribe a witness or juror, his or her first effort should be to urge the client to confess the wrongdoing to the other party in the action with the hope that the matter can be resolved. If the client refuses to do so, the lawyer's only recourse may be to inform the court of the wrongful act. Some authorities argue that, under such circumstances, a lawyer may withdraw from further representation of the client and should make no disclosure to the court. This position is based on the premise that the criminal act—the fraud—has already occurred without the lawyer's knowledge. At this point, the client is in need of legal advice because of the problem, just as for any other crime. Most courts have rejected this argument.

·There should never be a direct conflict between a lawyer's duty to a client and duty to the court. The Code of Professional Conduct helps lawyers to determine where their primary obligations lie and how to avoid or resolve apparent conflicts.

Collateral Profits from Relationship

If a lawyer handles a client's legal matters in such a way as to realize a profit, aside from a proper legal fee for services, there is a presumption that the profit was obtained by undue influence or fraud. This is particularly possible in the field of estate planning, business planning, and real estate transactions. If the client or client's representative (such as a guardian or administrator) brings a claim against the lawyer, the lawyer has the burden of showing that the transaction was fair and otherwise proper. For example, if a lawyer prepared a will for a client and included himself or herself as a beneficiary, the heirs would be in a good position to challenge the bequest. The lawyer would have the burden of proving that the bequest was in accord with the testator's wishes, that the testator was competent, and that the testator was not subjected to any undue influence.

Termination of Relationship

A client may discharge a lawyer at will. The relationship is considered to be so personal and so dependent upon the client's trust that a client cannot be compelled to continue using a lawyer whom he or she does not want. A client does not even need a good reason for terminating the relationship. A lawyer, on the other hand, may have a little more difficulty terminating the relationship. For example, if a lawyer is handling a case that is very near trial, the lawyer's withdrawal from the case could impose a hardship not only on the client but also on the court. Consequently, some courts have special rules and procedures that lawyers must follow to withdraw from a case. Some courts have determined that a client's inability to pay a fee for legal services is not grounds for a lawyer to withdraw. This is especially true in criminal cases. Consequently, lawyers may feel constrained to obtain a substantial retainer at the outset.

A lawyer is permitted to withdraw from a case if the client refuses to follow court orders or other legal requirements. If a lawyer learns that the client is using his or her services to perpetrate a fraud, the lawyer is under a duty to withdraw. Lawyers must be careful not to prejudice their clients' rights or interests by withdrawing. This means that a lawyer must provide reasonable notice to the client so that the client can obtain a replacement lawyer and meet all deadlines.

Malpractice

A lawyer, of course, is required to exercise due diligence and ordinary skill in handling a client's legal matters. If a lawyer is negligent and fails to measure up to the standards of the profession, he or she is liable to the client for any loss proximately caused by the negligence. Negligence in rendering professional service is commonly called legal malpractice. Due care does not mean that lawyers handling litigation must win their clients' cases. Theoretically, lawyers will "lose" half of the cases they try. The standard of ordinary care or due care does mean that trial lawyers must possess the knowledge and skill ordinarily possessed by lawyers handling civil litigation. Lawyers must use due care in gathering evidence and exercise ordinary ability in trying cases. The same skill and knowledge must be applied in the preparation of legal documents and in giving legal advice. As a group, the largest problem that lawyers seem to have is not being sufficiently diligent. It is very easy to wait too long before giving necessary notices, commencing an action, or otherwise actively pursuing matters—especially if the matter seems to lack substance or merit. With the help of paralegals, lawyers may do a better job of keeping current.

If a lawyer withdraws from a case, the lawyer should document the withdrawal. The letter should be sent to the client by registered mail, and a copy should be filed with the court if there is an action pending. Otherwise, if problems develop with the case, the client may try to excuse himself or herself on the basis that the lawyer was still acting on his or her behalf. The lawyer would be in trouble with the court and might face a malpractice action. A letter or formal notice of withdrawal helps to protect against such problems. If a lawyer is handling litigation that is actually pending in court, a formal *notice of withdrawal* must be filed with the court. In some states, a lawyer may need the court's permission to withdraw.

Occasionally, a would-be client discusses with a lawyer the merits of a potential claim, but the lawyer advises that the claim has no merit or for other reasons refuses to take the case. Before the would-be client talks to another lawyer, the statute of limitations "runs" against the claim. The client decides to pursue the claim but cannot because it is barred. The would-be client may contend that he or she thought the lawyer was working on the case and should not have let the statute of limitations run out. To protect against this kind of scenario, the lawyer should make sure that the would-be client is told and understands that (1) the lawyer is not going to handle the case, and (2) the date on which the statute of limitations will run against the alleged cause of action. The best procedure is to provide this information in a letter to the would-be client to reduce possibility of a misunderstanding. It is also a good idea to establish proof of delivery of the letter.

Lawyers' Fees

A lawyer's compensation for services is a matter of negotiation between a lawyer and client. Fees may be an agreed sum for a particular undertaking or based upon an hourly rate. A lawyer's hourly rate is usually based upon his or her experience and the complexity of the particular legal problems. When a lawyer represents the plaintiff in civil litigation to recover money damages, the lawyer's fee may be based upon a percentage of the monies recovered. When the fee is based upon a percentage of monies recovered, it is contingent upon an actual recovery, which means the lawyer receives a fee only if compensation is actually collected for the client. Contingent fee percentages range between 20 percent and 50 percent. The percentage ordinarily depends upon the size of the case, the possibilities of an appeal, and the likelihood of obtaining a recovery. Disciplinary Rule 2-106 prohibits "clearly excessive" fees. A client is always free to choose another lawyer if the proposed fee arrangement is unacceptable.

When a lawyer undertakes to represent a client, he or she may be precluded from representing certain other persons or companies and, consequently, from obtaining other business. That kind of limiting effect on a lawyer's business opportunities is another consideration that may be taken into account in setting fees. In some types of cases, the amount of the fee or percentage may be limited by statute or court rule. For example, court rules may prohibit a lawyer from charging over a certain percentage when representing a minor. In certain types of cases, such as class actions, the lawyer's fee is subject to court approval for reasonableness.

If discharged, a lawyer is entitled to be paid for services rendered. Payment may be based on the value of the services received by the client. The lawyer may not necessarily be entitled to recover fees on the basis of the original retainer agreement. Of course, one indicator of the value of such services is the original retainer agreement. If the client refuses to pay, the lawyer may file a lien with the court in which the action is pending. The lien gives the lawyer a claim upon any recovery of money obtained by the client. The priority of the lawyer's claim depends upon state law. The amount of the lien is subject to determination by litigation if the parties are unable to agree upon the amount. A lawyer always has the right to bring an action in court for payment of a fee. Otherwise, lawyers would be at the mercy of unscrupulous clients.

Attorney Pro Se

A person may choose to represent himself or herself in a civil action. The law does not require individuals to hire lawyers. If a person elects to represent himself or herself, he or she is referred to as an **attorney pro se.** Usually, judges try to discourage laypersons from representing themselves, because they can become lost in the maze of procedural and substantive law. The attorney pro se has probably consulted with several lawyers who have advised that the claim is not valid but wants to proceed anyway. If the claim is too large for the small claims court, it probably warrants the expense of a lawyer's help.

3 Causes of Action and Remedies

One of the functions of our state and federal governments is to maintain domestic tranquility. Peace among citizens would not be possible without a means of resolving the controversies that naturally occur among citizens. Therefore, government must provide the means for resolving private controversies. It is not enough for the courts to decide who is right and who is wrong. In addition, government must provide remedies that satisfy most litigants. The remedies must be in proportion to the loss and comport with a generally accepted sense of reason and fairness. The means of obtaining a remedy must be economical, fair, and reasonably calculated to bring about a just result based upon the truth. The obligation created by available remedies must be consistent with what obligors reasonably can be expected to afford. Furthermore, the obligations must not exceed what society can afford. The responsibility to provide a system that can meet these criteria has been entrusted to the courts, both state and federal. Civil litigation complements the criminal law but does not and cannot replace it. There is an apparent trend in the criminal law to require restitution, where that is possible, as part of a criminal's punishment.

The Essentials to Causes of Action

The law strives to afford a suitable remedy to every person who has suffered an actual loss caused by the unlawful conduct of another. The word "unlawful" is used to describe conduct that is in violation of common law standards or standards established by legislation. The task is momentous. There seems to be no limit to the types of controversies that can develop between people. Courts cannot undo every wrong, nor can they provide a remedy for every loss and inconvenience. With several centuries of experience, the courts have determined that only certain types of wrongful conduct should be actionable, and only certain kinds of losses should be redressed. If the claim is one that courts consider to be actionable, for which a remedy can be provided and the loss compensable, the claim constitutes a *cause of action.*

Every cause of action requires the plaintiff to prove that (1) the defendant breached a legal duty owed to plaintiff; (2) the plaintiff sustained an injury to person or property loss recognized by law; and (3) the defendant's breach of duty was the proximate cause of the plaintiff's injury or property loss. Each cause of action is predicated upon a particular legal duty protecting persons and/or property. Each cause of action affords the plaintiff with a particular remedy. Much of a lawyer's education and training is devoted to obtaining an understanding about causes of actions, their elements, and their applications. There are many, many causes of action. Duly alleging and proving a cause of action is the means by which a litigant can obtain a judicial remedy.

When a lawyer considers handling a case for a plaintiff the lawyer must first determine whether the client has a valid cause of action. If any of the elements necessary to a cause of action are missing, the courts cannot provide a remedy. Litigation cannot be used to resolve the parties' dispute. If a lawsuit were commenced, as soon as the court determined that one or more of the elements of the pretended cause of action were missing, the court would be constrained to dismiss the case. Any time, effort, and money spent to prove a claim that does not fulfill the requirements of a cause of action are simply wasted. If the plaintiff does not have a cause of action, he or she should be told that as soon as possible. Rule 12(b) provides that the case must be dismissed if the complaint fails to state a claim upon which relief can be granted. Another way of saying this is that the case must be dismissed if the complaint fails to state a cause of action.

The investigation efforts, discovery procedures, and trial preparation of all parties are influenced by the legal issues, and the legal issues are largely determined by the elements of the cause of action. For example, if the claim is based upon common law negligence, the plaintiff must obtain evidence to prove that (1) the negligent act or omission was a breach of a legal duty owed to the plaintiff; (2) the defendant failed to use due (reasonable) care in light of the foreseeability of harm to plaintiff; (3) the plaintiff sustained a compensable injury or property damage; and (4) the negligent act or omission was a proximate cause of the injury or loss. If any one of these elements is missing, the claim does not meet the requirements for a cause of action in negligence.

If the claim is based on breach of contract, the plaintiff's lawyer must obtain evidence to prove that (1) the parties were legally competent to enter into a contractual relationship; (2) a contract was made through a valid offer and acceptance; (3) legal consideration was exchanged between the parties; (4) formalities were met if the alleged contract is of the type that must be in writing and signed; and (5) the defendant's alleged breach of the contract caused the plaintiff to suffer an actual loss. If any one of these elements is missing, the claim does not constitute a cause of action for breach of contract.

The defendant can defeat the claim, whether in tort or contract, by disproving any one of the elements necessary to the plaintiff's cause of action. But the burden of proof is upon the plaintiff to establish all of the elements of the cause of action. The burden is not on the defendant to disprove the claim. The customary burden of proof is to establish the claim by a fair preponderance of the evidence.

A client may feel that he or she has a claim for breach of contract, but on analysis, the lawyer may determine that the only cause of action is for fraud, which involves different elements and a different *measure of damages*. Or, a client may want to sue for an alleged trespass to real estate to recover money damages, but upon reducing the facts to their basic elements, a lawyer may determine that the proper claim—or only claim—is for an injunction to abate a *nuisance* created by the defendant's conduct. A nuisance, in this context, is any wrongful conduct that substantially interferes with or disturbs the occupant's use and enjoyment of his or her real property. Nuisance is a cause of action for which courts provide a remedy at law.

[handwritten margin note: Nuisance — wrongful conduct interferes with real property use and enjoyment]

For each cause of action, certain *affirmative defenses* may be available. An affirmative defense usually arises out of some wrongful conduct on the part of the plaintiff—but not always. Each affirmative defense has certain elements which the defendant must prove. Proof of an affirmative defense totally defeats the plaintiff's cause of action or, in certain cases, reduces the amount of recovery of money damages. The defendant must prove affirmative defenses or the defenses are disallowed. Ordinarily, the burden of proof is by a fair preponderance of the evidence.

A paralegal is not ordinarily expected to know about all causes of action and all affirmative defenses. But when working on a particular case, a paralegal should be familiar with the elements applicable to the particular cause of action and the affirmative defenses raised. Lawyers should be pleased that paralegals indicate an interest in the technical aspects of the case. As stated earlier, the more knowledgeable a paralegal is about the law and legal procedures, the more effectively he or she can handle assignments in litigation. But it is beyond the scope of this book to discuss causes of actions and affirmative defenses in depth.

Breach of Contract

In its simplest form, a contract is merely a legally enforceable promise. The parties ordinarily enter into a contract voluntarily, expecting that each will benefit from the commitments it creates and imposes. The benefits may be monetary profit or the acquisition of something desired, such as land, personal property, or even an idea. The type of remedy afforded by law depends, in part, on the purpose of the contract, the parties' objectives, and their reasonable expectations. If the defendant has breached a contract, he or she is subject to an action for breach of contract. The most common remedy is the award of money damages compensating for loss of the benefits of the bargain.

When undertaking a case involving an alleged breach of contract, a lawyer's first effort must be to determine whether there is a contract. An action for breach of contract presupposes a valid, enforceable agreement. Contracts may take many forms and may come about in numerous ways. Some contracts are in writing, signed by both parties; some contracts are entirely oral; some are implied by the parties' conduct; and some are implied by operation of law. Notwithstanding the many types of contracts, there are certain elements that are essential to all contracts. An enforceable contract requires: (1) that the parties be legally competent to enter into a contract; (2) a valid offer and acceptance which results in a meeting of the parties' minds concerning the subject of their contract; (3) the exchange of legal consideration; and (4) compliance with particular formalities imposed by statute for certain types of contracts. A purported contract is not enforceable if the object of the contract is unlawful.

The parties must have the capacity to contract. Otherwise, the contract is void or voidable at the election of the party who lacked capacity. A person is not capable of making a contract if, at the time the purported contract is made, he or she is a minor, under a guardianship, insane, or intoxicated. A company that is not incorporated has no separate legal existence and cannot contract for itself. An unincorporated company may contract only through its owners as individuals or authorized agents. Partnerships are legal entities that may contract through one or more authorized partners.

The plaintiff who sues on a contract has the burden of proving that the contract was made; that all technical requirements were met; that he or she has performed all conditions precedent; and that all conditions of the contract have occurred. (A condition precedent must occur before the contract becomes effective even though all the terms and conditions have been agreed upon. A common example of a condition precedent is when a buyer agrees to purchase a new house or the condition that his or her own house sells.) The plaintiff must prove that the defendant breached the contract. There is no need to show that the breach was willful or the result of fault. Culpability is not a consideration or an issue. The plaintiff must prove the nature and extent of the loss resulting from the breach of the contract. The proof on all elements must be by a fair preponderance of the evidence.

The contract offer ordinarily contains the substance, terms, and conditions of the contract. Acceptance of the offer must be effectively communicated to the offeror in compliance with any conditions imposed by the offeror. If the acceptance is qualified, or changes one or more of the essential terms of the offer, the acceptance may actually be a counteroffer, which does not create a contract unless duly accepted by the original offeror.

A contract is made only if the parties reach a meeting of the minds concerning the subject matter. For example, if the seller offers to sell an automobile to the buyer, it is essential that they have in mind the same vehicle or a valid contract cannot result from their negotiations.

A contract requires the exchange of consideration. A simple promise—even if made under oath—is not a contract and cannot be enforced at law. Unless a consideration is given for the promise, there can be no contract. The most common consideration is the payment of money; but, even a mere promise exchanged for another promise may be legal consideration, which will support a contract. If a contract recites that a consideration has been paid but, in fact, it was not, the alleged contract is defective and unenforceable.

The following pleadings are illustrative. They are based upon hypothetical disputes, but they are true to life.

COMPLAINT: Breach of Contract

Comes now plaintiff, and for its cause of action against defendant alleges:

1. (Jurisdictional Allegations)
2. On August 2, 1989, defendant contracted to sell and deliver to plaintiff ten tons of newsprint-quality rolled paper.

3. That the terms and conditions of said contract between the parties were reduced to writing; a copy of said written contract is attached hereto and incorporated by reference as Exhibit A.

4. That said written contract was duly signed by defendant's representative at the time and place specified in the contract.

5. That plaintiff paid to defendant the sum of three thousand dollars as the initial partial payment as recited in the written contract.

6. That all conditions precedent of said contract have been performed or have occurred.

7. That defendant did not deliver said newsprint paper to plaintiff as required by the terms of said contract, and defendant is in default.

8. That plaintiff has necessarily sought and obtained other newsprint paper to meet its needs and requirements.

9. That as a direct consequence of defendant's failure to perform on said contract plaintiff has suffered damages as follows:

    a. Plaintiff is entitled to recover the three thousand dollars initially paid to defendant as a down payment, together with interest at the rate specified in the written contract (or the legal rate provided by law).

    b. Plaintiff's printing business was necessarily interrupted for a period of ten working days, causing plaintiff to suffer a loss of profit in the amount of ten thousand dollars.

    c. Plaintiff was required to purchase similar newsprint from another supplier at an additional cost of six thousand dollars.

Wherefore, plaintiff prays for judgment against defendant in the sum of nineteen thousand dollars, together with plaintiff's cost and disbursements herein.  ← prayer for relief

Plaintiff demands trial by jury.

(date)

_____
Attorney for Plaintiff

ANSWER

Comes now defendant, and for its answer to plaintiff's complaint:

1. Denies each and every allegation, statement, and matter in plaintiff's complaint, except as hereinafter expressly admitted or alleged:

2. Admits the allegations of paragraphs 1 through 8 of the complaint.

3. Admits that defendant is liable to plaintiff in the amount of three thousand dollars for money had and received, but <u>denies defendant is liable for interest thereon.</u>

FIRST DEFENSE

Alleges that paragraph 9(b) of the complaint fails to state a claim upon which relief can be granted.

SECOND DEFENSE

Alleges that on August 7, 1982, defendant's entire plant and warehouse were destroyed by fire through no fault of defendant, and that the loss of the plant and warehouse made impossible defendant's performance of the contract.

Wherefore, defendant prays that plaintiff take nothing by reason of its alleged cause of action, and that defendant have judgment for its costs and disbursements.

(date)   _____
                                       Attorney for Defendant

Certain contracts must be in writing and signed to be enforceable. The state statute that identifies contracts that must be written and signed is commonly referred to as the Statute of Frauds. The statute specifies what kinds of contracts must be in writing and the necessary elements to each written contract. If a contract is required to be in writing but is not, the contract is not enforceable. The Statute of Frauds provides the defendant with a complete defense.

There are other bases upon which the defendant may properly seek to avoid a contract that was duly made. If the plaintiff breached the contract, the breach provides the defendant with a complete defense. But the defendant has the burden of proving that the plaintiff also breached the contract. If the contract was obtained through fraud by the plaintiff, the contract is voidable by the defendant, but the defendant must allege and prove the fraud. If the parties made a new agreement to replace the old one and fully performed the new agreement, the old one is a nullity and unenforceable. The new agreement and its performance are called an accord and satisfaction. An accord and satisfaction is a complete defense. The defendant has the burden of proving the defense. If the plaintiff does not sue within the time provided, the statute of limitations provides the defendant with an affirmative defense. The defense must be raised in the defendant's answer or it is waived. The defendant must prove the facts making the statute of limitations applicable. Once in a while, after a contract is made, circumstances develop making performance of the contract impossible. Impossibility is a defense that the defendant must plead as an affirmative defense. It is a complete defense.

In most instances, contracts are mutually beneficial. When a breach occurs, the parties may elect to continue performance of the remainder of the contract. That may be the only realistic choice in some cases. If a party elects to proceed with the contract knowing the other party has breached one of its terms or conditions, the election to proceed may constitute a waiver of the breach. It would be unfair for the plaintiff to sue on the contract after waiving a breach. Of course, the parties may formalize the waiver by preparing a writing in which the extent of the waiver is described and the consequences of the waiver stated. Ordinarily, a waiver is a complete defense, which the defendant must allege in the answer and prove to avoid the plaintiff's cause of action.

There are other affirmative defenses which may be available in contract actions. A partial list of them appears in Rule 8(c).

Specific Performance

In some breach of contract actions, the award of money damages is clearly an insufficient remedy. In those cases, a court of general jurisdiction has the authority to require a party to perform the contract. The remedy is called specific performance. Courts are frequently asked to decree specific performance of contracts involving the sale of land. The law views each parcel of land as unique. Therefore, money damages are not adequate to replace the land. That is not to say that every breached contract for the sale of land is enforced by an action for specific performance. Another example is a contract for the sale of a piece of art that is unique. The buyer may force the seller to deliver the artwork and title by an action for specific performance.

Courts may enjoin (command) parties to perform certain activities or not to perform certain activities. For example, a court could order a union not to strike or not to picket. A court may order a corporation to undertake negotiations to settle a labor dispute. Actions to enjoin conduct may involve use of *restraining orders, temporary injunctions,* and *permanent injunctions.* On the other hand, courts cannot order an individual to perform personal services, which would constitute involuntary servitude and be unconstitutional.

COMPLAINT FOR SPECIFIC PERFORMANCE

Comes now plaintiff and for his cause of action against defendant alleges:

1. (Jurisdictional Allegations)
2. That on or about August 3, 1981, plaintiff and defendant, through his duly appointed agent, entered into a written contract by which defendant agreed to sell and plaintiff agreed to buy certain specific real estate. A copy of said contract is attached hereto as Exhibit A.
3. That as provided by said written contract plaintiff duly tendered to defendant the purchase price for the land as provided for in Exhibit A.
4. That defendant wrongfully refused to accept tender of the purchase price.
5. That defendant wrongfully refused to convey title of said land to plaintiff.
6. That plaintiff is ready, willing, and able to perform on the contract and hereby offers the full purchase price to defendant.
7. That plaintiff cannot obtain similar land similarly situated that would meet plaintiff's requirements.
8. That all conditions precedent have been performed or have occurred.

Wherefore, plaintiff prays that court issue its decree ordering defendant to perform the contract by providing plaintiff with a warranty deed to said land.

If specific performance is not granted, plaintiff prays for judgment against defendant in the sum of fifty thousand dollars as damages for defendant's breach of contract.

Plaintiff further prays for his costs and disbursement herein.

(date) _____
Attorney for Plaintiff

ANSWER

Comes now defendant and for his answer to plaintiff's complaint:

1. Denies each and every allegation, statement, and matter in said complaint contained, except as hereinafter expressly admitted or alleged.
2. Admits that he is the owner of the land described in Exhibit A.
3. Denies that he executed the contract identified as Exhibit A attached to the complaint.
4. Denies that any person had authority to sign said contract for him or to act on his behalf concerning said land.
5. Denies that he received any consideration for the alleged contract.

Wherefore, defendant prays that plaintiff take nothing by reason of his pretended cause of action and that defendant have judgment for his costs and disbursements herein.

(date)   _____
                                          Attorney for Defendant

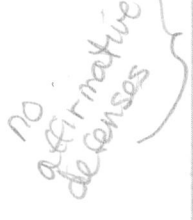

no affirmative defenses

Fraud and Misrepresentation

Some kinds of misrepresentations give rise to an action in tort against the persons who made the misrepresentations. Misrepresentations that are actionable fall into either of two categories: fraud or negligent misrepresentation. The law recognizes that many people make many statements, both written and oral, that are not true or only half true, but no legal liability should result. If a person regularly understates his or her age by five years, should that misrepresentation create a cause of action? Of course not. But if a person misrepresents his or her age on an application for a life insurance policy and the insurer relies upon the misrepresentation to its detriment, the misrepresentation may be actionable as a fraud. If the owner of an automobile claims that the automobile gets thirty miles per gallon of gasoline, but it actually delivers only fifteen miles per gallon, the misrepresentation is reprehensible but it is not actionable. In contrast, if the seller of an automobile makes a similar misrepresentation to a buyer, a cause of action for fraud may accrue in favor of the buyer.

Suppose the seller of a house misrepresents to the buyer that the neighbors are nice people when he or she knows that the neighbors are cantankerous, difficult people. Does the misrepresentation create a cause of action for fraud in favor of the buyer against the seller? Suppose the seller of a house represents that the house has never had a wet basement. But soon after acquiring possession of the house the buyer discovers water in the heating ducts under the basement floor, which was unknown to the seller. Does the seller's statement constitute a misrepresentation? Did the statement create a duty on the part of the seller to know that there was or was not water in the heating ducts? Answer: No. Was the seller's statement only a representation of the seller's own knowledge and experience with the property? Answer: Yes. If the seller has not misrepresented his or her actual knowledge, are there grounds for fraud? Answer: No.

Suppose an art dealer misrepresents a certain painting to be an original and the painting is purchased by a knowledgeable collector who knows that it is not an original. Does the collector have a claim for fraud? Should the party who claims damage because of the misrepresentation have to show that he or she in fact relied upon the misrepresentation? Answer: Reliance is essential to an action based upon fraud. Does it make a difference whether the misrepresentation is made in good faith? Answer: The misrepresentation must be made with the intent or expectation that the other party will rely upon the statement to be actionable for fraud.

Fraud is a tort. A tort is wrongful conduct that violates the rights of another person and causes harm to that person or his or her property. The law provides a remedy to the victim of tortious conduct. The objective of the law of torts is to compensate a party for his or her loss without providing profit. Whereas in contract law, the parties voluntarily enter into an agreement for the purpose of profit. If one party breaches the contract, the loss of the anticipated profit flows naturally from the breach. The law allows a recovery of loss of profits in contract actions.

At common law certain factors must be present before a misrepresentation becomes tortious and, therefore, actionable as a fraud. The elements have been listed in various ways by courts and legal scholars. The following list of elements has been used by more than one court and provides a rather detailed analysis of the factors relevant to actions for fraud and misrepresentation.

1. There must be a representation.
2. The representation must be false.
3. The misrepresentation must have to do with a past or present fact.
4. The misrepresented fact must be material to the contract or transaction.
5. The representation must be susceptible of knowledge.
6. The representor must know the representation to be false or in the alternative must assert the fact as of his or her own knowledge without knowing whether it is true or false.
7. The representor must intend to have the other person induced to act or the other person must be justified in acting upon it.
8. The other person justifiably acts in reliance upon the representation.
9. The other person must suffer damage by reason of reliance upon misrepresentation.

A statement of mere opinion is not usually actionable. On the other hand, if the opinion is rendered by an expert concerning a matter within the scope of his or her expertise, an erroneous opinion may be actionable on the basis of fraud or negligent misrepresentation. For example, a lawyer's statement of opinion about the law and its application could possibly be actionable against the lawyer but not against a layperson. Ordinarily, a representation concerning future events is not actionable as fraud. Of course, there are exceptions. By way of illustration, if the seller of a parcel of land knows that an aircraft flight pattern will be established over the land in the near future, a representation to the contrary may constitute a fraud even though the event is to take place in the future. The fraud occurs because the defendant has present knowledge of established plans for action. Otherwise, prognostication is similar to rendering a mere opinion—not actionable as a fraud.

The defendant must intend or expect that the plaintiff will rely upon the misrepresentation, and the plaintiff must, in fact, rely upon it. If the vendor of a parcel of land represents that the parcel is 200 feet deep, but before the sale the buyer measures the length and determines it is only 190 feet deep, the buyer cannot later sue for fraud, because he or she did not rely upon the alleged misrepresentation. Reliance is essential to any action for fraud.

The plaintiff must prove that the misrepresentation that was relied upon caused him or her to suffer actual damage or a loss. Suppose that the seller of a used automobile misrepresents that it is a 1988 model knowing that it is a 1987 model; suppose that 1988 models have an average value of three hundred dollars more than comparable 1987 models; suppose further that the buyer ends up paying no more for the automobile than he or she would have paid for a 1987 model. In other words, suppose the buyer received full value for what was paid but believed he or she was getting a better bargain than was obtained. Has the buyer really sustained a loss because of the misrepresentation? By contract standards, the answer would be yes. Certainly there was a breach of contract and maybe a breach of warranty. The buyer received less than he or she bargained for. But by tort standards, most courts would say that the buyer did not sustain a loss. The answer to whether or not a loss occurred depends upon whether the parties are in a state that follows the *loss-of-the-bargain rule* of damages or the *out-of-pocket rule* of damages for fraud.

In the preceding automobile example, the buyer is not out-of-pocket any money. He or she has not actually lost anything but merely lost an expectation. If the state allows damages for a loss-of-the-bargain, the buyer's damages are three hundred dollars.

In most states, an action for fraud lies if a person makes a statement as a positive assertion, not knowing whether it is true, and, nevertheless, intends the statement to be relied upon. For example, suppose a real estate agent shows a house for the owner and a prospective buyer asks the agent whether the basement has a water problem, and the agent, without knowing one way or the other, says no. If the basement does have a water problem and the buyer relied upon the statement, an action for negligent misrepresentation may be brought against the agent.

Rule 9(b) requires that the plaintiff plead fraud and misrepresentation with particularity. This means that, unlike most causes of action, the specific facts supporting each element of the cause of action must be set forth in the complaint. The following is an example:

COMPLAINT: Action in Fraud

Comes now the plaintiff and for his cause of action against defendant alleges:

1. (Allege facts showing jurisdiction.)
2. That on or about June 1, 1990, plaintiff and defendant entered into an agreement by which defendant agreed to sell to plaintiff a certain 1985 Buick automobile, and plaintiff agreed to buy said automobile.

3. That the parties' agreement was reduced to a writing, and copy thereof is attached hereto as Exhibit A, and is incorporated herein by reference.

4. That defendant represented to plaintiff that said automobile had a "new" engine, as appears more fully in Exhibit A.

5. That defendant intended plaintiff to rely upon said representation, and plaintiff did so rely.

6. That said representation by the defendant was false; the engine is not new, and the original engine was never replaced or overhauled before the sale.

7. That plaintiff paid to defendant the sum of Seven Thousand Five Hundred ($7,500.00) Dollars for said automobile in reliance upon defendant's false representation.

8. That the cost of a new engine for said automobile is One Thousand Five Hundred ($1,500.00) Dollars, and the fair market value of the automobile without a new engine is not more than Seven Thousand ($7,000.00) Dollars.

9. That plaintiff has sustained a loss due to a defendant's fraudulent misrepresentation in the amount of One Thousand Five Hundred ($1,500.00) Dollars.

Wherefore, plaintiff prays for judgment against defendant in the sum of One Thousand Five Hundred ($1,500.00) Dollars, together with his costs and disbursements herein.

(date)

_____
Attorney for Plaintiff

ANSWER TO COMPLAINT IN FRAUD

Comes now defendant and for his answer to plaintiff's complaint:

1. Denies each and every statement, matter, and thing in said complaint contained, except as hereinafter expressly admitted or alleged.

2. Denies that the court has jurisdiction over the subject matter of plaintiff's claim and that the controversy exceeds the threshold requirements of ten thousand dollars.

3. Admits that the parties did enter into a sales agreement for the sale of an automobile about the time and place specified in the complaint.

4. Specifically denies that the automobile engine, referred to in the complaint, was misrepresented, and puts plaintiff to his strict proof of the alleged misrepresentation.

5. Denies that plaintiff did not receive full value for the purpose price of said automobile.

6. Alleges that Exhibit A, attached to the complaint, is incomplete and does not set forth the full agreement of the parties.

Wherefore, defendant prays that plaintiff take nothing by reason of plaintiff's pretended cause of action, and that defendant have judgment for his costs and disbursements herein.

(date)   _____
                                        Attorney for Defendant

Of course, this answer does not undertake to raise all possible defenses to an action in fraud. It merely purports to illustrate a proper way of alleging denials and defenses.

There is also a cause of action known as fraudulent concealment. The claim is based upon the defendant's failure to disclose facts under circumstances where there is a legal duty to disclose. The cause of action is primarily relevant to business transactions.

Trespass

A person who is in possession of real property has a right to the quiet, peaceful possession of the property. The right to possession may be based upon ownership, lease, or easement rights or through adverse possession. Any unauthorized entry on the premises constitutes a trespass. The occupant may sue for damages resulting from the wrongful entry. For example, suppose that a lessee of a farm has remained in possession of the property after the lease expired. If a stranger enters upon the land without permission, the stranger is a trespasser, and the tenant may bring an action in trespass against the stranger for any damage the trespasser caused. If the trespasser did not cause any discernible damage, he or she is still liable for nominal money damages and, possibly, punitive damages—depending upon the purpose for entering the premises. The law presumes some damage (such as a bending of the grass). On that basis, the law is able to affirm the possessor's right to exclusive, peaceful occupancy. The occupant is able to protect those rights by bringing a civil action against anyone who violated the occupant's right to exclusive occupancy.

A trespass occurs whenever an entry is made without consent of the possessor or without legal authority. In the preceding example, even though the farmer-tenant is in possession, his or her possessory rights are subject to the higher or superior right of the owner to recover possession upon expiration of the lease. The holdover tenant cannot sue the landlord who enters the land to take back possession in accordance with the requirements of local law. Historically, the common law permitted the landlord to use reasonable force to eject the holdover tenant. Many states have enacted laws against self-help and require the landlord to use the services of the state by bringing an action for unlawful detainer or action in ejectment against the holdover tenant. Such actions enable the landlord to obtain possession within thirty days or less.

The trespasser is liable for the damage caused by his or her entry. The wrongful entrance upon the premises may be intentional, such as when using the property or removing material from the premises such as water, trees, crops, or mining minerals. A trespass may be involuntary, as when a ship is forced ashore or into a dock by a storm when an airplane crashes on the land. Or a trespass may result from negligent conduct on the part of the defendant. For example, if a drunken person drives a car off the road and into a house, the unpermitted entry is a trespass. The driver is liable for damages in trespass. On the other hand, an entrant is not liable in trespass if the entry was caused by the wrongful conduct of another person. For example, if the alleged trespasser was driving an automobile that was struck by another vehicle, thus forcing it off the road onto the plaintiff's property, the entrant is not a trespasser. Of course, the negligent motorist who caused the accident and wrongful entrance may be treated as a trespasser. A trespass may be committed by throwing articles upon another's land or across the land. For example, the wrongful placement of utility lines over property may constitute a trespass.

If an entry upon real estate is without legal right, or without the occupant's consent, the entry is wrongful and is a trespass. The trespasser is absolutely liable for any damage caused—even if the entry was unavoidable. For example, if an airplane crashed upon another's land and caused damage to the land, the entry is a trespass. The pilot is liable for the damage caused by the trespass even though he or she was not negligent and could not have prevented the accident.

A trespasser may acquire ownership and title to real estate by wrongfully occupying it for a statutorily specified number of years, such as ten or fifteen years. The occupancy must be open, notorious, and contrary to the rights of anyone else in the property. This is commonly referred to as adverse possession. A tenant cannot acquire title from the landlord through occupancy because a tenant's occupancy is not hostile to the rights of the landlord.

If the trespasser enters for the purpose of stealing crops, trees, or minerals, he or she is liable for the value of the materials taken or for the diminution in the value of the real estate. For example, if a trespasser cuts down an ornamental tree for the wood or as a matter of spite, the damage to the land (diminution in value) may exceed the worth of the tree or cost of a similar tree. On the other hand, the trespasser may wrongfully remove a mineral such as gravel, and the value of the gravel is worth more than the amount the land has diminished in value. The occupant may elect to recover the value of the gravel. In many states, the occupant is allowed by statute to recover three times the value of the property wrongfully damaged or taken by the trespasser. Treble damages in such cases is a civil penalty for the benefit of the victim. The penalty is to act as a deterrent.

According to common law, the occupant of real estate is allowed to use such force as is reasonably necessary to eject a trespasser from the premises. The occupant owes the trespasser a duty not to intentionally injure him or her. The law places a higher value on "life and limb" than on the protection of real estate. Therefore, a trespasser does not subject himself or herself to being intentionally shot or injured just because he or she is trespassing. Nor may the occupant set a "trap" for trespassers without being liable in tort for compensation for injuries the trespasser sustains. Of course, the occupant of land does have a common law right to self-defense. The occupant's best alternative, when practicable, is to call upon the local authorities to remove trespassers.

The occupant's consent to an entry upon the premises and authority to enter that is implied by law are complete defenses to an action in trespass. The defendant has the burden of proving consent or authority. They are defenses that must be pleaded in the answer. Consent may be expressed orally or in writing or implied by the circumstances. Authority is implied by law when the entrant has a legal duty to enter. A police officer or fire fighter who enters upon the property in the line of official duty has implied authority to enter. They are not trespassers.

COMPLAINT: Action in Trespass

Comes now plaintiff and for his cause of action against defendant alleges:

1. (Jurisdictional Allegations)
2. That at all times material herein plaintiff was and is the owner and in possession of Lots 1–5, Block 4, Townsend Addition, Clay County, State of Iowa.
3. That on August 4, 1981, defendant wrongfully entered and trespassed upon said premises and damaged plaintiff's buildings, removed gravel from the premises, and destroyed three trees all to plaintiff's damage in the sum of twenty-six thousand dollars.

Wherefore, plaintiff prays for judgment against defendant in the sum of twenty-six thousand dollars together with his costs and disbursements herein.

(date)

_____
Attorney for Plaintiff

ANSWER

Comes now defendant and for his answer to plaintiff's complaint:

1. Denies each and every allegation, statement, and matter in said complaint contained except as hereinafter expressly admitted or alleged.
2. Admits the allegations contained in paragraph 2 of the complaint.
3. Admits that defendant entered upon said premises on August 4, 1981, but specifically denies that the entry was wrongful or a trespass.
4. Denies that defendant caused any damage to plaintiff's buildings and put plaintiff to his strict proof of same.
5. Admits that defendant cut down three trees which had been located upon the premises, but denies that said trees had any value to the premises.
6. Alleges that defendant entered the premises with consent of the owner and or possessor of the premises and that he was duly authorized and directed to remove the trees from the premises.

Wherefore, defendant prays that plaintiff take nothing by reason of his pretended cause of action, and that defendant have judgment for his costs and disbursements herein.

(date)

_____
Attorney for Defendant

Assault

An assault is any intentional threat of bodily harm or death that puts the victim in fear of physical harm. An assault gives rise to an action for compensatory damages in favor of the person who has been put in fear of bodily harm or death. The threat of injury or death may come from a mere physical gesture, with or without words. It is not necessary that the tortfeasor use a weapon to threaten the victim. The wrongful conduct must cause the plaintiff to be put in fear of immediate bodily harm or there is no assault. An assault does not require any physical contact. If a contact does occur, then there is a battery.

The defendant perpetrator must have a specific intent to cause the victim to be fearful or apprehend immediate harm. The defendant commits an assault if he or she puts the victim in fear while unsuccessfully trying to commit a battery. For example, if the defendant intentionally shoots a gun at the plaintiff but misses, an assault has occurred if the defendant was put in fear of being shot. The apprehension of injury must occur while the defendant is in a position to cause harm, not subsequently. If the plaintiff did not know that the defendant had tried to shoot him or her with a gun but found out about the event later, no cause of action will lie for assault.

There are some people who are fearful of even innocuous or ordinary conduct. But the victim's apprehension of injury is judged on the basis of whether the ordinary, reasonable person would feel threatened. Stated another way, the plaintiff must have been put in fear, and the fear must have been reasonably justified. Mere swear words or foul language uttered in the presence of the victim or uttered at the victim do not constitute an assault. The words must convey a threat of harm with an apparent ability to do harm. An assault may be by a gesture, such as a "cocked fist" held close to the victim's face.

A cause of action for assault accrues when the victim experiences apprehension. Consent to an assault is an affirmative defense. When people voluntarily enter into some games and athletic contests, they impliedly consent to conduct that under other circumstances would constitute an assault. Or the perpetrator may have a privilege to conduct himself or herself as an authority figure, such as when a parent disciplines his or her own child or a police officer makes an arrest.

Battery

A battery involves an impermissible physical contact of an injurious nature or a physical contact that is offensive to ordinary sensibilities. Ordinary physical contacts incidental to living in a society are considered permissible and not actionable. Some examples of common batteries include an intentional punch in the face, an intentional shooting, intentionally tripping someone, spanking, rape, a tackle in the course of a basketball game, and a surgeon operating on the wrong part of the body. The contact must be intentional to be actionable as a battery.

Some contacts are batteries, not because they are harmful, but because they are offensive to most people. An allegedly obnoxious contact is not actionable unless the plaintiff actually experiences emotional distress. Mental suffering is not presumed. The most obvious example of a battery without any actual physical harm is contact which is sexually oriented, such as an unwanted kiss. Merely touching a person with a knife in a threatening manner would constitute a battery. Maliciously throwing a pail of water on an individual could give rise to an action for a battery. All too often practical jokes end up being batteries.

A cause of action for battery requires proof of a contact, that the contact was without actual or implied consent, and that the contact was intentional. The intent to make contact may be implied from the nature of the contact and surrounding circumstances. Compensatory money damages are allowed for any physical injury and emotional distress resulting from a battery. Punitive damages are allowed in many states where the battery is malicious, that is, where there is an intent to cause harm as a result of the impermissible contact.

COMPLAINT: Assault and Battery

Comes now plaintiff and for his cause of action against defendant alleges:

1. (Jurisdictional Allegations)
2. That on August 6, 1981, in the city of Smithville, Ohio, defendant assaulted plaintiff by pointing a rifle (weapon) at plaintiff and defendant verbally threatened to shoot plaintiff.
3. That plaintiff was put in great fear for his life and was fearful of severe bodily injury.
4. That defendant struck plaintiff with a blunt portion of his rifle thereby breaking plaintiff's jaw and rendering plaintiff unconscious.
5. That as a direct consequence of the battery, plaintiff suffered severe and painful injuries that may be permanent in nature.
6. That plaintiff incurred medical expenses, will incur future medical expenses, has suffered a loss of income, and will suffer a loss of earning capacity as a direct consequence of the battery.
7. The assault and battery perpetrated by defendant upon plaintiff was intentional and malicious.
8. That plaintiff is entitled to recover punitive (exemplary) damages from defendant.

Wherefore, plaintiff demands judgment against defendant in the sum of fifty thousand dollars for compensatory damages and ten thousand dollars as punitive damages, together with plaintiff's costs and disbursements herein.

(date)

_____
Attorney for Plaintiff

ANSWER

Comes now defendant and for his answer to plaintiff's complaint:

1. Denies each and every allegation, statement, and matter in the complaint, except as hereinafter expressly admitted or alleged.
2. Admits the allegations of paragraphs 1, 2, 3, and 4 of the complaint.
3. Alleges that defendant is without sufficient knowledge or information upon which to form a belief concerning plaintiff's claims of injuries and damages and, therefore, puts plaintiff to his strict proof of same.
4. Alleges that plaintiff trespassed upon defendant's premises and entered defendant's dwelling for the purpose of burglarizing the dwelling.
5. Alleges that when defendant discovered plaintiff in defendant's home, plaintiff was armed with a knife and carrying off personal property belonging to defendant.
6. Alleges that defendant then and there arrested plaintiff and held plaintiff until the police could be summoned.
7. Specifically denies that defendant used more force than appeared necessary to protect himself, his property, and to effectuate the arrest.

Wherefore, defendant prays that plaintiff take nothing by reason of his pretended cause of action, and that defendant have judgment for his costs and disbursements herein.

(date)

_____
Attorney for Defendant

Negligence

Negligence is failure to use reasonable care. Reasonable care is care that a reasonable person would use under like circumstances. Negligence is performance of some act that a reasonable person would not do, or the failure to do something that a reasonable person would do, under like circumstances. In the case of a child, reasonable care is care that a reasonable child of the same age, intelligence, training, and experience would have used under like circumstances. A cause of action in negligence lies against a person who causes damage or destruction of property or injury to a person through negligent conduct.

To understand the basis for a negligence action, it is necessary to understand the underlying legal duty of "due" or "reasonable" care. Every person owes a duty of reasonable care not to injure others or damage others' property. The duty is to act reasonably considering the foreseeability of harm to others. The law does not demand perfection. What is reasonable care depends upon existing circumstances that are known or should be known. The test is, what risks of harm are foreseeable, and is the act or omission in question reasonable in light of the foreseeable dangers? A person's conduct is not judged on the basis of hindsight. Adults are charged with knowledge ordinarily possessed by members of the community and knowledge of natural laws such as gravity. A higher duty is imposed upon common carriers such as airlines, railroads, and bus companies. They must exercise the highest degree of care for the protection of their passengers.

Some states recognize degrees of negligence such as ordinary negligence, gross negligence, willful negligence, and wanton negligence. But these characterizations of negligence have lost their original significance in most states. In the hierarchy of culpability, the next level is *reckless* misconduct. Reckless misconduct can be described as conduct that is intentionally perpetrated in the face of substantial and obvious danger to other persons or property without specifically intending to injure anyone. For example, driving on a crowded city street at a speed slightly over the speed limit is negligence, but driving on a city street at eighty miles per hour is reckless.

The relationship between persons may be critical in determining whether a duty of care exists at all. Some examples may be helpful to understand the concept of a duty and the basis for a duty.

1. Suppose a person sees a neighbor using a metal ladder very near an uninsulated electric power line and recognizes that the neighbor is in danger of being electrocuted. Does this person have a legal duty to warn or stop the neighbor? No. Failure to warn or stop the neighbor would not result in legal liability to that person if injury did occur. The law does not require ordinary individuals to act to protect fellow citizens, whether or not they are neighbors, from injuring themselves.

But if a homeowner has an acquaintance on the premises helping with house painting and sees that person on a metal ladder near a power line, the homeowner has a duty to stop the dangerous activity or is considered negligent for violating the duty. The duty arises out of the relationship.

2. Suppose an individual comes upon a trench in the road and realizes that motorists may not be so fortunate to discover and avoid it; if a vehicle were to run into the trench, it would be damaged and its occupants injured. Does the individual have a legal duty to warn motorists of the danger or to stop motorists, or to fill the trench? Is that person negligent toward the motoring public for failing to take these precautions? The conduct may be reprehensible, but there is no breach of a legal duty. Therefore, no action in negligence will lie against the individual. However, the person who excavated the trench or failed to erect barricades is negligent. By creating the "trap" in the public highway, the excavator breached a legal duty to members of the public using the highway. Suppose that the trench exists in an area of highway under the control of a construction contractor. The contractor may have a duty to protect the public from the trench, even though he or she did not create the trench. The duty arises out of the contractor's contractual relationship with the government to protect the public in the construction zone. The state may be negligent for failing to discover the danger and for failing to eliminate it.

3. Suppose a woman invites people to her home for a social gathering. She knows that most of the guests will use the front sidewalk but is unaware that several bricks in the sidewalk are dangerously loose. One of the guests trips on a loose brick, falls, and is injured. A negligence action may lie against the woman as the occupant of the premises. She owes a legal duty of reasonable care to make the premises reasonably safe. The duty of reasonable care includes an obligation to conduct reasonable inspections to discover potential dangers to guests and to take preventive action such as to give warnings or correct the danger. Conversely, the laws of some states provide that the occupant of a house does not owe a legal duty of inspection to mere social guests, that is, there is no duty to prepare the premises for them. The only duty is to correct *known* defects or hazardous conditions or to warn social guests of *known* dangers. So, if this hostess was unaware of the loose bricks, she is not liable in negligence to the injured social guest, because she did not have a legal duty to inspect and prepare the premises for her guests. In all states, however, the law imposes a legal duty on the part of a business to inspect and prepare the premises for business invitees or customers.

4. Suppose a man dug a hole in his backyard to plant a tree. During the night a thief entered the premises to steal an outboard motorboat engine. As he was leaving the premises with the engine he fell in the hole and was injured. Is the property owner liable to the thief for negligently leaving the hole unguarded? Does the thief's malevolent purpose insulate the property owner from liability? In most states, thieves are treated as trespassers. They have no right to be on the premises, and the property owner owes them no duty of care. Nonetheless, the property owner must not use more force than is reasonably necessary to eject the trespasser. Nor may the property owner set traps for the purpose of catching or injuring trespassers.

In negligence actions it is always necessary to determine whether there is a relationship between the injured plaintiff and the proposed defendant. This determines whether there is a legal relationship that creates a legal duty on the part of the defendant to avoid injuring the plaintiff or to actively protect the plaintiff from injury.

So-called malpractice cases are really just actions in negligence. They are claims against professional people based upon their alleged failure to comply with the standards of their professions. Of course, the substandard performance or conduct must have caused some harm to the plaintiff for an action to lie. Malpractice actions may be brought against physicians, lawyers, nurses, accountants, pharmacists, engineers, architects, etc. The gravamen of the claim is that the professional failed to have the necessary education or skill to practice in the profession or to perform the particular function in question. Or, the professional may be negligent for failing to exercise due care in the performance of the service or function. In either event, it is the standard of the profession that dictates the minimum standard of care and performance.

Juries are presumed to be constituted of laypersons. Laypersons are presumed to be unfamiliar with the duties and standards of the professions. Consequently, the law requires that persons active within the profession, who are familiar with the professional standards, testify to establish the applicable standards. This is done through "expert testimony," that is, testimony of members of the profession. Expert testimony may also be necessary to determine whether the standards have been violated. An untoward or disappointing result from a professional's services is not, in itself, sufficient basis for maintaining or proving a malpractice action in court. It is for this reason that a patient who sues a physician usually must find another physician who will testify that the treating physician's conduct deviated from acceptable professional standards. Otherwise, the patient's case must be dismissed for failure to prove a prima facie case.

The preceding examples illustrate that even though the concept of negligence is simple enough, its application is often very difficult. To make the whole subject more difficult, the law of negligence is constantly changing. The study of tort negligence involves a study of the interrelationships among people, public institutions, and governments. Each relationship creates a different duty. For example, a bus driver must exercise the highest degree of care for the protection of passengers but only reasonable care for the protection of other motorists or pedestrians using the roadways.

Many legal duties are established by statute. A violation of a statutory duty is negligence. There can be no excuse of justification for noncompliance with a statute enacted to protect a particular person or class of people or properties. A violation of a statute is commonly referred to as *negligence per se*, which means that the violation is, in itself, negligence. For example, a statute forbids merchants to sell guns to minors. A gun is sold to a minor, who accidentally shoots another person. The vendor's illegal sale is negligence per se. The statute was enacted to prevent exactly that kind of an occurrence.

Some statutes, by their terms, provide that a violation is not negligence per se but merely *prima facie evidence of negligence*, which means that a violation is merely evidence of negligence. The application of such a statute is illustrated in the following typical jury instruction: If the statute was violated, the violation is negligence unless the jury finds evidence tending to show reasonable excuse or justification or evidence from which a reasonable person, under the circumstances, could believe that the violation would not endanger any person entitled to the protection of the statute. If the statutory violation were not limited to prima facie negligence, the violator would not be permitted to show excuse or justification.

Most state highway codes provide that traffic violations are merely prima facie evidence of negligence and not negligence per se. A technical violator may be excused or justified. A violation is to be judged on the basis of all the other circumstances surrounding the accident, including the known risks and those that reasonably should have been anticipated and the reasons for the violation. A jury has the task of weighing the reasons for the violation against the gravity of the violation and the foreseeability of harm resulting from the violation. In the absence of any reasonable excuse or justification, a judge would have to determine that the violation was a negligent act or omission. Could a jury be justified in excusing a father's unlawful speed if he is driving his seriously injured child to a hospital to obtain medical care? Perhaps. Suppose he collides with a car that violated a stop sign—the father being on a through street. The jury would be entitled to weigh the reasons for the violation against the reasons for the statute.

In a negligence action, the plaintiff must prove that the defendant's conduct was negligent and that the negligence was a *proximate cause* of the occurrence or accident. If the negligence is not a proximate cause of the accident, the defendant is not liable for the accident. The term *direct cause* is sometimes used instead of proximate cause. The subject of causation is just as esoteric as the concept of negligence. A proximate cause is a cause that has a substantial part in bringing about the accident either immediately or through happenings that naturally follow one another. For example, suppose that a motorist parks an automobile two feet from the curb when local law requires that the automobile be parked within one foot, and another motorist runs into the back of the parked automobile. It is unlikely that the technical violation (of parking two feet from the curb) was the actual cause of the accident. Suppose that a motorist is traveling ten miles over the posted speed limit and is struck by another vehicle, which went through a stop sign. The excessive speed is merely coincidental and not a proximate cause. The cause of the accident was the stop sign violation, because the violation would have caused an accident even if the motorist on the through street had been traveling within the speed limit. Speed did not, in this illustration, cause the accident or induce negligence on the part of the other driver. Usually, the issue of proximate cause is a question of fact for a jury to decide. Unfortunately, the illustration is an oversimplification. Suppose the motorist is traveling twenty-five miles over the speed limit. It is reasonable to believe that the passenger's injuries will be greater because of the excessive speed. One of the reasons for speed limits is to reduce the severity of injuries, as well as prevent accidents. Still the question arises, did the excessive speed *cause* the accident?

There may be more than one proximate cause of an accident. When the effects of negligent conduct of two or more persons actively work at substantially the same time to cause an accident, the conduct of each may be a proximate cause of the accident. If two defendants contribute toward a loss, they are jointly and severally liable for the entire loss. For example, if two motorists collide in an intersection because both failed to keep a proper lookout, their concurrent negligence makes both of them liable for their passenger's injuries.

Another facet of the law of causation is the concept of the *efficient intervening cause*, or *superseding* cause. A superseding cause relieves all prior negligent conduct of any liability for an accident. But the requirements of a superseding cause are very specific. For a cause to be a superseding cause, its harmful effects must have occurred after the original negligence and the superseding cause must not have been brought about by the original negligence. For example, if the driver of an automobile sees a truck unlawfully stopped on the highway ahead and has sufficient time to avoid a collision but negligently fails to do so, the automobile driver's negligence is a superseding cause of the collision. The superseding negligence of the driver insulates the owner of the stopped truck from legal liability for the collision though the truck driver created the dangerous condition.

A party who claims another party was negligent must prove negligence by a fair preponderance of the evidence; or, said another way, negligence must be established by the greater weight of the evidence. The mere fact that an accident occurred does not, in itself, necessarily mean that someone was negligent. If there is a deficiency in the evidence so that negligence is not proved, the court must direct a verdict against the party who has the burden of proof. A directed verdict means that the claim or defense is disallowed by the judge because there are insufficient facts to support the alleged cause of action.

Historically, there were two affirmative defenses frequently asserted in negligence actions: *contributory negligence* and *assumption of risk.* Contributory negligence is not a special kind of negligence or a special quality of negligence. It simply designates the negligence on the part of the plaintiff. The old rule was that if the defendant was able to prove by a fair preponderance of the evidence that the plaintiff was negligent, that negligence defeated the plaintiff's claim. Similarly, if the defendant could prove by a fair preponderance of the evidence that the plaintiff assumed the risk of injury, the plaintiff's assumption of risk constituted a complete defense to the plaintiff's claim in negligence. Where these affirmative defenses are (were) established, the defendant would prevail even though the plaintiff was able to show that the defendant was negligent.

Historically, the law was not at all concerned with any comparisons of fault between the parties. Negligence and causation were considered absolutes. Any causal negligence was sufficient to create a claim or a defense. Similarly, the assumption of risk by the plaintiff provided the defendant with a complete defense. The plaintiff assumed the risk if he or she voluntarily placed himself or herself in a position to chance a known hazard. To prove assumption of risk, the defendant must prove that the plaintiff had actual knowledge of the specific risk; that the plaintiff appreciated the risk; that the plaintiff had a choice or opportunity to avoid the risk; that the plaintiff voluntarily chose to chance or incur the risk; and that the risk assumed materialized to cause the plaintiff's injury or harm.

As an example of an assumption of risk, suppose that a cook in a restaurant negligently permits the sink to overflow and soapy water spills on the floor, making it slippery. A janitor is summoned to clean up the water but slips and falls on the floor because of the soapy water. The janitor knew of the risk and appreciated the danger of the slippery floor, but it is the janitor's job to deal with such conditions. By proceeding with the clean-up work, the janitor voluntarily chose to incur the risk and has no claim against the cook or cook's employer because of the assumed risk. Before the days of workers' compensation, employers were able to use the assumption of risk defense very effectively in many of the personal injury cases brought by employees.

The law of contributory negligence and assumption of risk has evolved in most states into the law of *comparative negligence.* The law of comparative negligence is a so-called equitable approach to tort litigation. The doctrine is justified by its proponents as more fair. The objective is to obtain some compensation for the plaintiff even though he or she was also negligent and contributed to the loss. When a case is tried pursuant to the law of comparative negligence, the jury is required to evaluate each of the parties' causal negligence and apportion their negligence on a percentage basis.

There are two principal forms of comparative negligence. In those states adopting *pure comparative negligence,* recovery of money damages by the plaintiff is reduced by the amount or percentage of his or her casual negligence. For example, if the plaintiff is found to be 20 percent causally negligent, the damages award is reduced to 80 percent of the amount awarded by the jury.

If the plaintiff's causal negligence was 75 percent of the total negligence causing the accident, the damages award is reduced to 25 percent of the amount awarded by the jury.

Other states with ordinary comparative negligence similarly reduce the plaintiff's award by his or her percentage of causal negligence, but if the plaintiff's causal negligence is greater than the defendant's causal negligence, the plaintiff is not permitted to recover any damages against the defendant. Where ordinary comparative negligence applies, a plaintiff who is 51 percent at fault cannot recover any compensation. In states with comparative negligence, the defense of assumption of risk is treated as a form of comparative negligence.

In states that apply the law of contributory negligence, each defendant who is liable for the plaintiff's injury or loss is liable jointly and individually for the whole loss and entire award of compensatory damages. They are equally liable to each other for one-half of the award made to the plaintiff. In states with comparative negligence, the codefendants are also jointly and individually liable for the amount of damages recoverable by the plaintiff. But between the codefendants, each is liable only for his or her percentage of causal negligence. For example, if the jury determines that the plaintiff was 20 percent at fault, defendant A was 10 percent at fault, defendant B was 30 percent at fault, and defendant C was 40 percent at fault, and the amount of money damages awarded to the plaintiff is $10,000.00, the plaintiff's recovery will be $8,000.00. The plaintiff cannot recover any damages from defendant A, who was less negligent than the plaintiff. Defendants B and C are liable to the plaintiff for the entire $8,000.00. Between defendant B (30 percent) and C (40 percent), their obligations for the $8,000.00 award is proportional. Defendant B would be obligated for $3,428.57, and defendant C would be obligated for $4,571.43. The proportionate amounts are easily calculated by converting the 30 percent to 30/70 or 3/7 and converting the 40 percent to 40/70 or 4/7.

$$3/7 \times \$8,000.00 = \$3,428.57$$
$$4/7 \times \$8,000.00 = \$4,571.43$$

COMPLAINT ALLEGING ACTION FOR NEGLIGENCE

Come now the plaintiffs and for their cause of action against defendants allege:

1. (Allege Facts Establishing Jurisdiction)
2. That plaintiffs are and at all times material herein have been husband and wife, and they reside in the state of Wisconsin.
3. That defendant Shawn and Associates, Inc., is and at all times material herein was a Wisconsin corporation having its office and principal place of business in Spencer, Wisconsin.
4. That the defendant Drake Apartments, Inc., is and at all times material herein was a Wisconsin corporation having its office and principal place of business in Spencer, Wisconsin.
5. That the defendant Barton & Associates, Inc., is and at all times

material herein was a Minnesota corporation having its office and principal place of business in Madison, Minnesota.

6. That on or about July 19, 1987, Shawn and Associates, Inc., contracted with Drake Apartments, Inc., the owner of premises located in 724 South 5th Street, Spencer, Wisconsin (hereinafter the job site), to act as general contractor for the construction of an addition to said premises, and in connection therewith Shawn and Associates, Inc., agreed to assume responsibility for providing a safe place to work for all persons working at the job site, including all subcontractors and their employees.

7. That on or about October 26, 1987, Drake Apartments, Inc., entered into a contract with Barton & Associates, Inc., whereby Barton & Associates, Inc., agreed to provide certain services, including architectural services, to Drake Apartments, Inc. On or about July 28, 1987, Shawn and Associates, Inc., as general contractor, entered into a contract, attached as Exhibit A, with the Johnson Construction, a subcontractor, for the erection by Johnson Construction of the structural steel frame for the addition to said premises. In connection therewith Shawn and Associates, Inc., agreed to assume responsibility for providing a safe place to work for Johnson Construction and all Johnson Construction employees at the job site, and Johnson Construction agreed to indemnify Shawn and Associates, Inc., from all claims for damages and injury in connection with the work.

8. That plaintiff John Doe at all times material herein was employed by Johnson Construction as a steelworker.

9. That Drake Apartments, Inc., negligently and in violation of its legal obligations failed to employ a competent and careful contractor to do the work and to perform the duties which Drake Apartments, Inc., owed to third persons, including the plaintiffs, and to take precautions against risk of physical harm to persons on the premises.

10. That prior to and on February 7, 1988, defendants negligently and in violation of federal and state OSHA standards and in breach of their contractual obligations failed to provide plaintiff John Doe with a safe place to work at the job site, failed to use proper construction procedures, failed to supervise the work at the job site properly, failed to inspect the job site properly, failed to correct unsafe conditions, failed to erect proper barricading to protect plaintiff at the job site, failed to adequately warn plaintiff of unsafe conditions and hazards existing at the job site, and failed to fulfill its nondelegable contractual and legal responsibilities with respect to working conditions at the job site.

11. That defendant Barton & Associates, Inc., negligently and in breach of contractual duties to plaintiff failed to provide general administration of the construction contract, failed to properly represent the owner, failed to determine, in general, if the work was proceeding properly and in accordance with contract documents, and failed to advise and consult with Drake Apartments, Inc., regarding safety on the job site.

12. That on February 7, 1988, as a direct consequence of the negligence of the defendants, and each of them, plaintiff John Doe, while working at the job site, fell in a stairwell at the job site and suffered permanent injuries and permanent disability.

13. That because of his injuries, plaintiff John Doe has been prevented from transacting his business and has lost wages in the approximate amount of $50,000; he has incurred expenses and obligations for medical attention, hospitalization, and related care and miscellaneous items in the approximate amount of $100,000; he has been and will in the future be totally physically disabled and totally dependent upon others for his care; he has lost all future earning capacity and will lose all future wages; he will incur substantial medical expenses and additional living and miscellaneous expenses in the future; and he has suffered and will in the future suffer great pain of body and mind.

14. That due to the injuries sustained by John Doe, plaintiff Jane Doe has been and in the future will be required to provide care for her husband; she has permanently lost the services of her husband; her comfort and happiness in society and his companionship have been permanently impaired.

Wherefore, the plaintiffs, and each of them, demand judgment in their favor and against the defendants, and each of them, jointly and severally, as follows:

1. Money damages for plaintiff John Doe in the sum of $150,000.
2. Money damages for plaintiff Jane Doe in the sum of $50,000.
3. Reimbursement for plaintiff's costs and disbursements herein.

(date)

_____
Attorney for Plaintiff

ANSWER TO COMPLAINT IN NEGLIGENCE

Comes now defendant Drake Apartments, Inc., and for its answer to plaintiff's complaint:

1. Denies each and every allegation, statement, matter, and thing in said complaint contained, except as hereinafter expressly admitted or otherwise alleged.

2. Admits that plaintiff John Doe sustained injuries about the time and place mentioned in the complaint, but specifically denies that Drake Apartments, Inc., was negligent.

3. Alleges that this answering defendant does not have sufficient knowledge or information upon which to form a belief concerning plaintiffs' claims of injuries and damages; therefore, plaintiffs are put to their strict proof of same.

4. Alleges that plaintiff John Doe was negligent so as to cause his alleged injuries and damages.

5. Alleges that plaintiff John Doe assumed the risk of his alleged injuries.

> Wherefore, defendant Drake Apartments, Inc., pray that plaintiffs take nothing by reason of their pretended cause of action, and that this answering defendant have judgment for its costs and disbursements herein.
>
>
> (date)   _____
>   Attorney for Defendant, Drake
>   Apartments, Inc.

The answer admits the occurrence of the accident but denies liability by denying negligence. Plaintiffs are put to their proof to establish their damages. The answer raises two affirmative defenses: contributory negligence and assumption of risk. Jane Doe's claim is based upon a derivative cause of action. Therefore, her claim is defeated by any affirmative defense that defeats her husband's claim.

Products Liability

Products liability law includes a number of causes of action that are available to persons who are injured by defective products. A little history is helpful in understanding products liability law. Historically, the injured consumer had to prove an action in negligence against the product manufacturer or vendor to recover money damages for any injury caused by a defective product. The consumer had to prove that the product was defective, that the defect was the result of some negligent conduct on the part of the vendor against whom the claim was made, and that the defect was the proximate cause of the injury. A product is considered to be defective if it is unreasonably dangerous for use in the ordinary manner. A product may be unreasonably dangerous because of its design, the materials used, poor fabrication or assembly, a failure to provide adequate instructions for its use, or failure to provide adequate warnings about dangers in its use. In a negligence action the manufacturer is not liable for defects if the manufacturer acted with reasonable care. Often it is difficult for the plaintiff to prove a prima facie case of negligence against the vendor.

The next step in the evolution of products liability law was the creation of implied warranties, which arose out of the contract between the seller and buyer. The law had long recognized the right of the parties to create express warranties concerning the quality and fitness of goods sold. As the marketplace became more structured, the law began to impose implied warranties that the products were of *merchantable quality* and *reasonably fit for the purpose* for which the goods were sold. Even so, implied warranties benefited only the immediate buyer because the cause of action is predicated upon the contract between the buyer and seller. The law made "privity of contract" a condition to maintenance of the action. Therefore, the retail purchaser could not bring an implied warranty action directly against the manufacturer. The purchaser could only make the warranty claim directly against the retail vendor. In turn, the retailer could seek indemnity from the vendor from whom the retailer had purchased the product. Also, the purchaser's claim could be barred by failure to give notice to the seller of the defect and injury within a "reasonable" period of time.

Gradually some of the restrictions on implied warranty actions were abrogated by court decision and statute. For example, the privity of contract was relaxed so that members of the purchaser's family could sue on the contract for breach of implied warranty. Nevertheless, vendors were often able to avoid liability by including warranty disclaimers as part of the sales contact. Also, the common law recognized various common law affirmative defenses to the implied warranty actions such as contributory negligence and/or assumption of risk on the part of the user. A feeling developed among legal scholars and writers that the law should make compensation for the harm caused by defective products as a cost of doing business. They reasoned that most products in modern society are manufactured and marketed by large, well-established companies that could easily spread the cost of damage claims by simply increasing the cost of their products.

This rationale lead to the creation of a relatively new cause of action commonly known as **strict liability in tort.** Now all states have adopted this cause of action in one form or another as an additional means of providing compensation to persons injured by defective products, whether or not the injured person was a purchaser of the particular product. All that the injured person has to prove is that the product was defective at the time it left the vendor's possession and the defect was the proximate cause of the injury. A cause of action for strict liability in tort lies against manufacturers, distributors, wholesalers, and retailers. But no action will lie against a seller of a product who is not in the business of selling that kind of product. In other words, implied warranty actions and strict liability actions can be maintained only against merchants of the particular product.

Privity of contract is not necessary to strict liability actions. As originally conceived, contributory negligence or comparative negligence and assumption of risk were not defenses to strict liability tort actions; nevertheless, the current trend is to allow comparative fault as a basis for reducing the plaintiff's recovery of damages, just as in ordinary comparative negligence actions. The need for such an approach became manifest from a whole line of cases that showed consumers grossly abusing the products—using them in ways which were totally improper. The vendor had to prove that the product was not being used for its intended purpose or was being used in a dangerous manner that could not reasonably have been foreseen by the vendor. Once the courts recognized "product abuse" as a defense to strict liability claims, it was relatively easy to move to the comparative fault concept for allocating damages in product cases. It should also be noted that strict liability became a cause of action before "comparative fault" came into vogue as basis for obtaining compensation for personal injuries. The concept is now being carried into products litigation.

Today, a claim may be based upon negligence or breach of warranty or strict liability in tort. Sometimes the facts permit the plaintiff to pursue all three legal theories (causes of action) at the same time. The theory upon which recovery is sought determines what facts must be proved, what evidence is necessary, and even what damages are recoverable. Defenses applicable to a negligence action may not apply to a warranty action or to a strict liability action. And defenses that apply to a warranty action may not apply to a negligence action. The amount of damages recoverable under one theory may be significantly more than under another theory. Therefore, the plaintiff's lawyer must choose the cause of action or actions carefully. In many cases, all three causes of action will be pleaded against the vendor. In some states, the plaintiff is required to elect between a negligence claim and strict liability claim before the case is submitted to the jury. This development has occurred because, on occasion, some states have found that the submission of both theories in the same case leads to inconsistent verdicts.

With regard to negligence actions, manufacturers owe to purchasers and users a duty to use reasonable care to make their products reasonably safe for ordinary use. Said another way, manufacturers must use due care to make their products so that they are not unreasonably dangerous when used in the ordinary manner for a proper purpose. But manufacturers are not liable for the consequences of a product's failure if the manufacturer used ordinary care in making the product. For example, if a manufacturer builds an automobile with a defective axle and the defect could not have been prevented or discovered by the exercise of reasonable care, the manufacturer is not liable to the purchaser or occupants who are injured in an accident caused by the broken axle. The retail vendor of the automobile would not be liable either. Very often, reasonable care is looked upon as the care that the industry use in making similar products, as there may be occasion to compare with the conduct of other manufacturers of similar products.

Let's use the same example but apply a breach of implied warranty theory for recovery. An automobile with a defective axle is not of merchantable quality and certainly is not fit for use as a motor vehicle. Therefore, in the above example, a recovery in favor of the purchaser and members of his or her family may be possible under a breach of implied warranty theory. But passengers who are not members of the purchaser's family could not maintain a warranty action—at least not in some states. The law permits the vendor to qualify and limit implied warranties. Indeed, the contract of sale may exclude all warranties by making the sale "with all faults" or "sold as is." Furthermore, contracts often limit the time during which a warranty may be claimed. Assume for purposes of this example that the axle broke twenty-five months after the automobile was purchased and the contract eliminated all warranties after twenty-four months. The sales contract effectively negated the implied warranties.

The owner and occupants of the automobile in this example could maintain an action in strict liability in tort for their personal injuries caused by the defective axle. They would need to prove that the axle was defective when it left the manufacturer's hands. One might wonder why a negligence action is ever pursued in a products case in light of the fact that a strict liability case is easier to prove. But there are cases in which a jury has determined that the product in question was not defective but that the vendor's negligence caused the accident in question. See *Bigham v. J. C. Penney Company*, 268 N.W.2d 802 (Minn. 1978).

Each vendor in the chain of sale is liable to the plaintiff consumer for the full amount of damages. But each vendor whose liability is based upon mere warranty or strict liability in tort is entitled to obtain indemnity from the preceding vendor(s) in the chain of sale; whereas a negligent vendor is precluded from obtaining indemnity but may be allowed to obtain contribution from other negligent vendors in the chain of sale.

COMPLAINT: Strict Liability in Tort Complaint

Plaintiff for her complaint against defendant alleges as follows:

1. (Jurisdictional Allegations)

FIRST COUNT

2. At the times herein mentioned, defendant Dawn Co., Inc., was engaged in the manufacture of a chemical oven cleaner called "Sparkle." Said cleaner was manufactured for sale to the general public.

3. During the month of February 1989, plaintiff purchased a can of defendant's oven cleaner identified by the marking "5M142D," which was manufactured and sold by defendant for retail sales to the general public.

4. At all times following the purchase of the oven cleaner, plaintiff reasonably and properly handled the product.

5. Defendant sold and delivered said oven cleaner to retailers knowing that in the regular course of business it would be resold to a customer for use as an oven cleaner.

6. Defendant failed to provide plaintiff with a warning concerning the hazards of using said oven cleaner.

7. Said oven cleaner was negligently designed, manufactured, tested, and inspected by defendant; and the oven cleaner was dangerous to the physical health of users when the product left the defendant's control or possession.

8. Defendant was negligent in failing to provide adequate instructions for its use and failing to warn of the product's dangers.

9. On March 12, 1989, plaintiff used said oven cleaner for the first time and in accordance with the printed instructions on the can for the purpose of cleaning her oven in her home located at 5606 Lawndale Lane, Spencer, Illinois.

10. Defendant's negligence directly caused plaintiff to suffer severe itching, swelling, dizziness, restricted breathing, and an anaphylactic reaction all to plaintiff's general damage in the sum of thirty thousand dollars.

11. Plaintiff incurred expenses for medical attention, hospital, and medicines in the sum of five hundred dollars.

SECOND COUNT

12. Plaintiff realleges paragraphs 1 through 10 of first count as if those allegations were set forth in full in this count.

13. In marketing the oven cleaner product, defendant impliedly warranted that the product was of merchantable quality and fit for the purpose for which it was intended.

14. In fact, the product was not of merchantable quality and was unsafe and unfit for the purpose for which it was sold, purchased, and used.
15. Defendant's breach of said implied warranties caused plaintiff to suffer serious bodily injuries.

THIRD COUNT

16. Plaintiff realleges paragraphs 1 through 14 of Counts One and Two as if those allegations were set forth in full.
17. Defendant expressly warranted that the oven cleaner contained no caustic or choking fumes or chemicals to irritate eyes or nose.
18. Said oven cleaner did not conform to the express warranties made by defendant and printed on the product container.
19. As a result of defendant's breach of the express warranties, plaintiff suffered serious bodily injuries.

FOURTH COUNT

20. Plaintiff realleges paragraphs 1 through 18 of Counts One through Count Three as if those allegations were set forth in full.
21. The oven cleaner manufactured and sold by defendant was unreasonably dangerous for use in the ordinary manner and, therefore, was a defective product.
22. Plaintiff used the product in the intended manner for the proper purpose.
23. As a result of the defective and injurious character of the oven cleaner, plaintiff suffered injuries as described previously.
24. As a result of the defective condition of the oven cleaner, defendant is strictly liable in tort to plaintiff for the injuries she sustained and losses suffered as described previously.

Wherefore, plaintiff prays for judgment against defendant in the sum of twenty-five thousand dollars and her costs and disbursements herein.

(date)

_____
Attorney for Plaintiff

ANSWER

Comes now defendant and for its answer to plaintiff's complaint:

1. Denies each and every allegation, statement, matter, and thing in said complaint contained, except as herein after expressly admitted or alleged.
2. Admits the allegations of paragraphs 1 and 2 of the complaint.
3. Alleges that defendant is without sufficient knowledge or information upon which to form a belief concerning plaintiff's claims of injuries and damages, and therefore, puts plaintiff to her strict proof of same.

4. Alleges that if plaintiff sustained injuries and damages as alleged in the complaint, they were caused by the negligence of the plaintiff.
5. Alleges that plaintiff did not serve defendant with notice of breach of warranty as required by law.
6. Alleges that plaintiff assumed the risk of injury. (It is not necessary to allege that plaintiff misused the product, and that was the cause of injury, because "misuse" is not an affirmative defense even though misuse by plaintiff would prevent plaintiff from recovering money damages. The plaintiff has the burden of proving that the plaintiff used the product in the ordinary intended manner.)

Wherefore, defendant prays that plaintiff take nothing by reason of her pretended cause of action, and that defendant have judgment for its costs and disbursements herein.

(date)   _____
                                    Attorney for Defendant

Liquor Vendors' Liability

It is a well-known and accepted fact that the use of intoxicating liquors often causes or contributes significantly to accidental injuries and property damage. Historically, vendors of intoxicating liquors were not liable for the accidents caused by inebriated customers, because the inebriated person's wrongful conduct was considered the sole proximate cause of the accident. The consumer was held responsible to know when he or she had enough alcohol. The vendor was not the consumer's guardian. In recent decades, a concern grew that vendors ought to be responsible if they were to make an illegal sale of intoxicants and the illegal use contributes to cause harm to others. Most or all states have adopted *dramshop* legislation, which creates a civil action against liquor vendors and in favor of persons, other than the inebriate, who suffer harm as the result of an illegal sale of intoxicants.

In these dramshop actions, the illegal sale or bartering does not have to be a proximate cause of the accident. The law only requires that the illegal sale contribute to the occurrence of the accident. For example, it has been determined that an illegal sale of intoxicants may have contributed to a man's suicide, so the vendor could be liable to the man's surviving spouse and children for loss of support. Courts have acknowledged that intoxication probably did not cause the person to commit suicide but the jury could properly find that the intoxication contributed to the suicide.

The plaintiff must prove that the defendant vendor made an illegal sale. The two most common types of illegal sales resulting in liability are sales to minors and sales to persons who are already *obviously* intoxicated. Such sales are prohibited by law. In addition to the illegal sale, the plaintiff must prove that the intoxication contributed to the wrongful conduct and that the intoxicated person caused a loss or injury.

The alleged intoxicated person (AIP) does not have any claim against the vendor for injuring himself or herself. Nevertheless, if the intoxicated person is injured and becomes disabled for a period of time, the spouse and children of the intoxicated person have a claim against the vendor for loss of support. Of course, if the intoxicated person dies, the claim for loss of support may be very substantial.

Most states recognize **complicity** as an affirmative defense. Complicity describes the victim's conduct if the victim participated in the illegal sale or effectively brought about the inebriant's intoxication. Complicity is an affirmative defense that the liquor vendor must allege and prove. Complicity is a complete defense even in those states that have comparative fault statutes. For example, two men spend several hours in a liquor establishment buying each other intoxicants, and they become obviously intoxicated. An illegal sale of liquor is made to them, and one of the intoxicated persons attempts to drive his car with the other intoxicated man as a passenger. They have an accident, which was contributed to by the driver's intoxication. The passenger's complicity in the illegal sale is a bar to his claim against the liquor vendor, who illegally sold liquor to the driver. Similarly, if the plaintiff acts with complicity in the sale of intoxicants to a minor and is injured as a result of the minor's intoxication, he or she cannot recover compensation from the liquor vendor who made the illegal sale.

Dramshop statutes require the plaintiff to give notice of the illegal sale, occurrence, loss, and intent to make a claim. The notice must be given to the liquor vendor within a specified number of days after the occurrence. A typical period for giving notice is 120 days. Failure to give the statutorily mandated notice bars any action against the vendor. The reason for the notice requirements is to give the vendor an opportunity to investigate and evaluate the claim before the evidence disappears. If a notice is required by state law, the plaintiff must allege in the complaint that he or she complied with the notice requirement. If the allegation is denied, the burden is on the plaintiff to prove that he or she duly gave or served notice. The plaintiff's lawyer must be careful to establish and preserve proof of service of the notice.

Unless specified in the dramshop statute, negligence on the part of the injured plaintiff is not a defense to the liquor vendor. On the other hand, the law seems to be moving toward application of comparative fault principles to these cases. If comparative fault or negligence is applicable, the plaintiff's recovery of money damages is reduced by his or her percentage of causal negligence.

DRAMSHOP COMPLAINT

Come now the plaintiffs above named and for their claim and cause of action against defendants, and each of them, herein complain and allege as follows:

COUNT I

1. (Allege Facts Establishing Jurisdiction)
2. Joy Peterson is the administratrix for the estate of James William Peterson.

3. That on June 1, 1989, defendant Kenneth Roberts was operating his motor vehicle on Constance Boulevard at or near the intersection of Highway 65 in Tampa, Florida.

4. That at said time and place, James Richard Anderson was operating his motor vehicle on Highway 65 at or near the intersection with Constance Boulevard in Tampa, Florida.

5. That plaintiffs Christine Peterson and James William Peterson were passengers in the automobile owned and operated by James Peterson.

6. That at the above time and place defendant Kenneth Roberts and the intestate James Anderson operated their respective vehicles in such a negligent, careless, and unlawful manner that they caused their vehicles to come into violent collision.

7. That as a direct result of said collision, Christine Peterson and James Peterson suffered serious and permanent injuries and were prevented from transacting their business, sustained great pain of body and mind, and have incurred and will in the future incur expenses for medical attention and hospitalization in the sum not presently known but believed to exceed fifty thousand ($50,000.00) dollars.

8. That as a direct and proximate result of defendants' negligence, plaintiffs Christine Peterson and James Peterson have each sustained and will sustain in the future a loss of earnings and loss of earning capacity in a sum not presently capable of determination.

COUNT II

Plaintiffs reallege all paragraphs set out in first count as if fully set forth herein.

9. That on May 31 and June 1, 1989, defendant Happy Hour tavern illegally sold, furnished, and/or bartered intoxicating liquors to Kenneth Roberts in violation of (Statute) and by this violation of statute and by the illegal sale, furnishing, or bartering, caused and/or contributed to the intoxication of Kenneth Roberts.

10. That on May 31 and June 1, 1989, defendant Happy Hour Tavern illegally supplied, furnished, or gave alcoholic beverages to defendant Kenneth Roberts, thereby causing or adding to the intoxication of said Kenneth Roberts.

(In most states an allegation of a negligent sale of intoxicants would not state a cause of action.)

11. That as a direct and proximate result of the illegal selling, furnishing, or bartering (or negligence in supplying) on May 31 and June 1, 1989, Kenneth Roberts collided with a motor vehicle owned and negligently operated by James Anderson in which plaintiffs Christine Peterson and James Peterson were passengers, thereby causing severe and permanent injuries to Christine Peterson and James Peterson as alleged previously.

12. That as a direct and proximate consequence of said collision, plaintiffs Christine Peterson and James Peterson suffered injuries of which they herein complain.

13. That as a further, direct, and proximate consequence of said collision plaintiffs Christine Peterson and James Peterson have incurred hospital expenses and medical expenses and they will require medical attention in the future.

14. That plaintiffs Christine Peterson and James Peterson have been damaged in their ability to earn income and will suffer said inability into the future.

Wherefore, plaintiffs, and each of them pray for judgment against the defendants, and each of them, in the sum of fifty thousand ($50,000.00) dollars, together with their costs and disbursements herein.

(date)   _____

                          Attorney for Plaintiffs

ANSWER

Comes now defendant, Happy Hour Tavern, and for its separate answer to plaintiff's complaint:

1. Denies each and every allegation, statement, matter, and thing in said complaint contained, except as hereinafter expressly admitted or alleged.

2. Alleges defendant is without sufficient knowledge or information upon which to form a belief concerning plaintiff's claims of injuries and damages and, therefore, puts plaintiffs to their strict proof of same.

3. Alleges that plaintiffs failed to serve notice of claim upon defendant as required by law.

Wherefore, defendant prays that plaintiffs take nothing by reason of their pretended cause of action, and that it have judgment for its costs and disbursements herein.

(date)   _____

                          Attorney for Defendant

Nuisance

The owner of real estate and the occupants of real estate are entitled to the comfortable use and enjoyment of the property without being subjected to disturbing odors, noises, or activities. The law protects the occupant against the loss of use and enjoyment of real property by allowing the occupant to bring an action for *nuisance* to recover money damages as compensation for interference with the occupant's use and enjoyment of the property. The interference must be substantial in nature and duration. If the nuisance is likely to continue, courts have the power to enjoin a nuisance, that is, order that the nuisance be abated.

Courts must weigh the value of the activity complained of and the character of the area against the effects on the use of the premises. For example, if the defendant establishes a creosote plant near an established residential area, the smell and fumes may be too much for the residents. They may have a cause of action for damages in nuisance and grounds for obtaining an injunction to abate operation of the plant. But suppose the plaintiff buys a house that is near a commercial or government airport and in the path of aircraft landing and taking off. Excessive noise may constitute a nuisance that is actionable. But the necessity of having the airport where it is and the utility of the activity justify some impairment of plaintiff's use and quiet enjoyment of the property. Of course, there is also a tendency on the part of the courts to protect the existing character of the area, so if the airport, railroad, sanitary landfill, or paint factory was in the area first, fairness suggests that the newcomer should expect that he or she may have to put up with the status quo; however, being there first is no guaranty of prevailing in a nuisance action.

An action to recover damages caused by a nuisance does not require proof of fault or wrongful conduct. The plaintiff must prove that the alleged nuisance has created a substantial interference in the use and enjoyment of the property; the utility of the nuisance does not justify its continuance. A distinction between an action for trespass and an action for a nuisance is that the former is an act against the property; the latter is against the use and enjoyment of the property. In both instances, the person in possession is ordinarily the real party in interest, as opposed to the interest that an owner or remainderman may have.

NUISANCE COMPLAINT

Comes now plaintiff and for his cause of action against defendant alleges:

1. (Jurisdictional Allegations)
2. That at all times material herein plaintiff was the owner and in possession of the premises commonly known as 3908 East Ninth Street, Bakersville, Ohio.
3. That plaintiff occupied said premises as his homestead with his family.
4. That during the period of June 1, 1989, to the date of the commencement of the preceding entitled action defendant has occupied and used the premises at 4000 East Ninth Street, Bakersville, Ohio, as a meat-cutting plant and the preparation of various meats for sale in commerce.
5. That during said period of time defendant has allowed meat products, meat by-products, and various chemicals to create toxic and offensive smelling fumes and odors.
6. That said fumes and odors significantly reduce the use, comfort, enjoyment, and value of plaintiff's said property.
7. That prior to commencement of this action, plaintiff notified defen-

dant of the adverse effect that defendant's activities have had on plaintiff's premises.

8. That defendant's activities could be conducted in a manner so as not to endanger and impair the use of other properties in the area.

9. That defendant's present activities create and permit the noxious and toxic odors and fumes that damage plaintiff's property and impair its use.

10. That plaintiff has suffered damages in the amount of fifteen thousand dollars for the loss of enjoyment and impaired use of his property.

11. That unless defendant is enjoined from continuing to create the noxious fumes and odors, plaintiff's property will continue to suffer damage.

Wherefore, plaintiff prays for judgment against defendant permanently enjoining defendant from creating toxic and noxious fumes and odors that escape from defendant's premises to adjoining properties, and further prays for damages in the sum fifteen thousand ($15,000.00) dollars, together with plaintiff's costs and disbursements herein.

(date)

_____
Attorney for Plaintiff

ANSWER

Comes now defendant and for its answer to plaintiff's complaint:

1. Denies each and every allegation, statement, and matter in the complaint contained, except as hereinafter expressly admitted or alleged.

2. Admits the allegations of paragraphs 1, 2, 3, 4, and 7.

3. Specifically denies that defendant's use of defendant's land has created a nuisance.

4. Alleges that defendant is without sufficient knowledge and information upon which to form a belief concerning plaintiff's alleged damages, and puts plaintiff to his strict proof of same.

5. Alleges that defendant's plant and operations have been conducted in essentially the same manner for twenty-five years and that the plaintiff acquired his premises knowing the existence of defendant's facilities.

6. Alleges that defendant purchased an easement from plaintiff's predecessors in interest that easement and covenant runs with the land and that binds plaintiff precluding plaintiff from suing defendant for the alleged nuisance.

7. Alleges that plaintiff's pretended cause of action is barred by laches.

8. Alleges that plaintiff's pretended cause of action is barred by the easement and covenant, a copy of which is attached hereto as Exhibit A and incorporated by reference.

9. That plaintiff's cause of action is barred by the applicable Ohio statute of limitations.

Wherefore, defendant prays that plaintiff take nothing by reason of his pretended cause of action, and that defendant have judgment for its costs and disbursements herein.

(date)

_____
Attorney for Defendant

Replevin

If a person wrongfully obtains possession of personal property or wrongfully retains possession of personal property, the rightful owner may bring an action in *replevin* to recover possession of the property. Courts use their power to restore the property to its rightful owner or custodian. The gravamen of the action is the right to immediate possession.

Sometimes the plaintiff can obtain possession with commencement of the action through use of an order to show cause, which requires the defendant possessor to show cause, if he or she can, why custody of the property should not be given to the plaintiff or kept by the court while the action is pending. The plaintiff may be required to post a bond protecting the defendant in the event the case is decided in favor of the defendant. The bond is intended to compensate the defendant for his or her loss of use of the property and even for the value of the property in the event the defendant defeats the claim for replevin.

A party obtains an order to show cause by making a motion to the court with supporting affidavits that show that the moving party has a right to immediate possession of the property. Upon making a prima facie showing of the right to immediate possession, the court usually issues an order compelling the defendant possessor to appear before the court and show good cause why the property should not be turned over to the moving party. The procedure is commonly called procurement of an *order to show cause*.

Ultrahazardous Activities

A person who engages in ultrahazardous activity is strictly liable for damage caused by the activity. An activity is ultrahazardous if it is incapable of being conducted without a significant likelihood of damage to property or injury to persons. A person engaged in an ultrahazardous activity is liable even though he or she conducts the activity with great care. Culpability is not an issue. Nor is the utility or necessity of the activity an issue. The only real question is whether the activity is appropriate for the area in which it is conducted.

Some examples of ultrahazardous activity should be helpful. Very often, heavy construction work requires pile driving in urban areas where the resulting vibrations may cause substantial damage to nearby structures. Even though the pile driving is necessary, the contractor is liable for its consequential effects on surrounding properties. Dynamiting is another similar ultrahazardous activity. A contractor using dynamite would be absolutely liable for damage caused by vibrations and debris that damages surrounding properties. Of course, the flying debris might also be grounds for an action in trespass.

Activities do not have to be as inherently dangerous as dynamiting and pile driving to be ultrahazardous. For example, construction of a dam that stores a large quantity of water may be an ultrahazardous activity. The owner of the dam could be absolutely liable to other properties damaged by percolation of water through soil. If the dam should break, the owner could be absolutely liable for harm to persons and property caused by the escaping water. Keeping a wild animal, as opposed to a domestic animal, is an ultrahazardous activity. The owner is absolutely liable for any injury caused by a wild animal that escapes the owner's premises. Crop spraying with chemicals that can cause damage to other foliage on surrounding properties is an ultrahazardous activity. If some of the chemical escapes onto neighboring properties and causes damage, the person applying the chemical is absolutely liable for the damage caused. Conversely, a contractor who sprays crops is not absolutely liable to the customer for damage to "other" foliage on the customer's property. Liability to the customer would depend upon the contract or an action in negligence. In each of these examples, the defendant has acted reasonably to promote his or her own business or other legitimate interest. In each instance, the party to be held liable acted for a proper purpose. But, because the activity is considered to be ultrahazardous, the actor is strictly liable for harm caused to others.

Intentional Infliction of Mental Suffering

Most states now recognize a cause of action in tort for the intentional infliction of mental suffering. The cause of action requires a specific, subjective intent on the part of the defendant to inflict suffering upon the plaintiff. Mere negligence, that is, failure to use due care, does not support this cause of action. The mental suffering may be inflicted by words, conduct, or by a combination of words and conduct. It is difficult to imagine a situation where the cause of action would lie and words were not used. Not only must the defendant intend the plaintiff to experience mental suffering, the conduct to accomplish it must be outrageous in character. The conduct must be of a type that is utterly intolerable in a civilized society. Mere insults, swearing, foul language, or even verbal threats do not give rise to the cause of action. The jury must find an actual, wrongful intention on the part of the defendant to cause the plaintiff to suffer. It is not enough for the jury to find that the defendant should have known that his or her conduct could cause mental suffering. Of course, the plaintiff must prove that the wrongful conduct was the proximate cause of the suffering. It is not necessary for the plaintiff to show physical symptoms manifesting the mental suffering, nor is medical treatment a necessary element to the damages.

This cause of action may be available in situations where actions for assault and defamation would not lie. But, the actions certainly could overlap. An example should be helpful to show application of a cause of action for intentional infliction of mental suffering. Suppose the defendant maliciously tells the plaintiff that the plaintiff's spouse has just been killed in an accident at work. In fact, there is no truth to the statement. The sole motive for defendant to utter this false statement is to upset the plaintiff, and the plaintiff does suffer a severe emotional breakdown because of the statement. These facts would give rise to an action for intentional infliction of mental suffering. An action for defamation would not lie, because the statement, even though false, is not damaging to the plaintiff's reputation. An action for assault would not lie, because the plaintiff was not put in fear of bodily harm. A cause of action would not lie for invasion of privacy, because the statement has not been made public, and other elements are also missing.

The cause of action accrues when the plaintiff experiences the mental suffering. In the preceding example, the cause of action would accrue when the statement was made to the plaintiff.

False Imprisonment

False imprisonment involves the intentional confinement of the plaintiff to a specific area without authority in law to do so. The confinement must be real and significant. The plaintiff must be aware of the confinement. It is not sufficient for the plaintiff to discover, after the alleged confinement, that he or she would not have been permitted to leave the premises had he or she wanted or attempted to leave. On the other hand, the cause of action does not require physical restraints such as walls or a fence. For purposes of the cause of action, the defendant can effectively confine the plaintiff through mere threats of force or false assertions of authority. The defendant may be liable for a false imprisonment where the defendant forces the plaintiff to accompany the defendant. There is a fundamental difference between confining a person and preventing a person from entering a restricted area. For example, a cause of action for false imprisonment will not lie against a theater for not allowing certain customers to enter.

The defendant must intend to *confine* the plaintiff by limiting or controlling freedom of movement. Parents have legal authority to limit their children's freedom of movement. A parent may delegate such authority to a baby-sitter or neighbor under some circumstances and for some purposes. The confinement must be intentional and not merely inadvertent or even negligent. For example, if a storekeeper closes and locks the store for the night and a customer is accidently locked in the store, the customer does not have an action against the storekeeper for false imprisonment. But that would not necessarily preclude an action in negligence.

The cause of action accrues as soon as the plaintiff becomes aware that his or her freedom of movement has been wrongfully restricted. No actual mental or physical injury is required. Of course, the plaintiff could recover damages for consequential damages, such as pain and suffering, which might result from such wrongful conduct.

The defendant can defeat a claim of false imprisonment by proving actual authority to confine or restrain the plaintiff or that the plaintiff consented.

Malicious Prosecution

The tort of malicious prosecution involves the improper use of criminal court proceedings, without justification, for an improper purpose. For example, a person would be subject to an action for malicious prosecution by filing a criminal complaint against another person for the purpose of damaging the other's reputation or of causing the latter to experience the inconvenience of being arrested or for the purpose of causing the other to experience an emotional upset. To be liable for malicious prosecution the defendant must have instituted the criminal proceedings against the plaintiff or wrongfully caused the proceedings to continue. The criminal proceedings must have been resolved in the plaintiff's favor by dismissal or verdict. As part of the plaintiff's cause of action, the plaintiff must show that the defendant lacked probable cause to believe that the criminal proceedings were justified against the plaintiff. In other words, it must be proved that the defendant acted out of malice against the plaintiff, and not for the purpose of serving the ends of justice.

The plaintiff is entitled to recover money damages for loss of time spent in defending against the criminal proceedings, for the expenses he or she incurred in the defense, for loss of income, and for damaged reputation and mental suffering. A cause of action for malicious prosecution accrues when the criminal proceedings have been terminated in the plaintiff's favor. There are no special affirmative defenses applicable to this cause of action. The defense is usually based upon the defendant's reasonable belief that the plaintiff had committed a particular crime or the defendant's lack of malice.

Abuse of Judicial Process

This cause of action is somewhat similar to malicious prosecution, but it involves the unjustified use of civil procedures for a wrongful purpose. The plaintiff must prove that the defendant was motivated by an improper purpose. Again, the cause of action does not accrue until the plaintiff obtains a dismissal of the underlying action. The burden of proof is difficult, and the plaintiff must prove actual damages.

Defamation

An action for defamation arises out of an utterance and publication of a false, defamatory statement. A statement is defamatory if it would cause the plaintiff to suffer a loss of esteem in the eyes of those who know him or her. In other words, the cause of action is concerned with protecting the plaintiff's reputation. The law gives the plaintiff the opportunity to hold the defendant accountable for publishing such statements and a remedy in the form of money damages for the harm to the plaintiff's reputation. A defamatory statement is uttered when it is spoken or written; it is published when it is communicated to some third person, that is, someone other than the plaintiff. Unless there is a publication to another person, there is no cause of action, but publication to only one other person is sufficient. In other words, an action will not lie where the defendant tells the plaintiff that he or she is a "crook". It does not matter how much the plaintiff's feelings are hurt by the statement; no cause of action will lie, unless the statement is heard by another person. The plaintiff cannot create a cause of action by telling other persons what the defendant said to him or her. However, the defendant is liable for any republications.

The law of defamation has two primary subdivisions: libel and slander. Libel concerns the publication of defamatory statements through any medium such as a letter, memorandum, article, photograph, motion picture or painting. Slander involves the publication of defamatory statements through oral communication. The dichotomy exists because the different methods of publication have different consequences. In the eyes of the law, libel is somewhat more serious because of the tendency of people to believe statements which are in writing. Furthermore, defamatory statements in documents appear more calculated and have potential for greater distribution. Generally speaking, the recovery of damages is easier to obtain and the damages are greater in amount in actions for libel.

There are several areas which are commonly looked upon as being obviously defamatory. They include allegations of criminal conduct, sexual misconduct, professional incompetence, and affliction with a contagious or loathsome disease. But any statement may be considered defamatory if it would tend to cause other people to lose confidence in the plaintiff's abilities, trustworthiness, or reliability.

Some statements may be defamatory only because of the plaintiff's particular circumstances, position, or relationships. For example, it could be defamatory to say that the plaintiff is inclined to have an alcoholic drink on occasion if the plaintiff is a leader in a church which has abstinence as one of its tenets. Statements which merely reflect the defendant's *opinion* about the plaintiff are not considered to be defamatory. Such statements are understood to reflect upon the defendant as much, or more, than upon the plaintiff. But the distinction between fact and opinion is sometimes very difficult to ascertain. Again, it is clearly defamatory to call someone a "crook." A person could not avoid being liable for defamation by having qualified the statement in this way—"In my opinion, the plaintiff is a crook."

In determining whether a statement is defamatory, the words are to be given their ordinary meaning. However, the plaintiff has the right to prove that the words used by the defendant contained an innuendo which, when taken in context, are understood by others to be defamatory.

An action for defamation cannot be brought on behalf of a deceased person for the benefit of the deceased's reputation or to assuage the feelings of the survivors. A corporation can be defamed, but only if the defamatory statements reflect adversely upon the corporation's honesty, integrity, or credit. A corporation is not defamed by a statement that its products or services are bad.

The plaintiff has the burden of proving the utterance and publication to another person and consequential harm. However, in libel actions and certain slander actions the law infers *some* harm even if no specific damage can be shown.

No matter how derogatory the statement is, truth is a complete defense. For example, if the defendant stated that the plaintiff is a "crook," the statement is obviously defamatory. If the defendant can prove that the plaintiff committed the crime, the defendant's proof defeats the cause of action. The proof need only be by a fair preponderance of the evidence. Even if the plaintiff was previously tried in a criminal action and found innocent, the defendant in the libel action has the right to try to prove that plaintiff is, in fact, a "crook."

The defendant may avoid liability for defamation by showing that the publication was subject to a privilege or qualified privilege. Statements made by officers of the court and by parties in pursuit of proper legal proceedings are clothed with a privilege. Therefore, statements made in pleadings or testimony in depositions, testimony at trial, and legal opinions are clothed with a privilege. Legislators acting in their official capacity are clothed with an immunity. Newspapers and other publishers are given a qualified privilege which allows them to print information about public persons when newsworthy, provided the publisher acts in good faith. The plaintiff must prove that the newspaper, television station, or other publisher acted out of malice; otherwise, the cause of action will fail. A member of the news media may mitigate damages by printing a retraction.

Invasion of the Right of Privacy

An unauthorized intrusion into the plaintiff's privacy that discloses private matters to public scrutiny without social justification gives rise to a cause of action for invasion of the right of privacy. The intrusion must be to a significant degree. The publication must be to many people, not just to one or two. This is one of the features which distinguish the action from defamation. Courts look to the reason or purpose for the publication. If the publication was motivated by malice or by a desire for commercial profit, a breach of duty is more readily found.

Truth is not a defense. It is not even necessary for the plaintiff to show that his or her reputation was damaged by the publication. Indeed, the publications which constitute an invasion of privacy might actually engender sympathy for the plaintiff. Only living individuals may bring an action for an invasion of privacy. The plaintiff does not have to prove any monetary loss in order to be able to recover money damages for his or her mental suffering, embarrassment, and humiliation.

The defendant may avoid liability by proving that the plaintiff is a public figure and that the matters publicized are not private or should not remain private. For example, suppose a man is running for high office and a newspaper reporter discovers that the candidate is involved in an extramarital affair and publishes the facts. The candidate's right to privacy has probably been invaded. But by becoming a candidate for public office, he has opened up his private life to public scrutiny. The defendant may also avoid liability by showing that the plaintiff consented to the publication. For example, if a person posed for a photograph for commercial use, there is a presumption that the person consented to its publication. Of course, the best evidence and defense would be to have a contract reflecting the person's consent.

There are many, many other causes of action providing various forms of relief. A few of the remaining causes of action include actions for dissolution of marriage, actions for dissolution of a partnership, actions for damages caused by domestic animals, actions for damages for United States patent infringements, actions for damages for unfair competition, and actions for violation of civil rights. Each action has its own specific requirements or elements and is subject to certain affirmative defenses. A paralegal may wish to increase his or her understanding of the law by studying causes of action. *Corpus Juris Secundum* and *American Jurisprudence Second* are treatises on the law which provide concise statements about causes of action, their applications, and their limitations.

4 **Affirmative Defenses**

There are two basic approaches to defending against a cause of action in a civil lawsuit. One approach is for the defendant to dispute and challenge the plaintiff's claim and evidence. In other words, the defendant resists the plaintiff's efforts to prove the claim. The second approach is for the defendant to allege in the answer and prove one or more affirmative defenses which counter and defeat the plaintiff's cause of action. An **affirmative defense** has the effect of defeating the plaintiff's claim, even if the plaintiff is able to prove conclusively the cause of action against the defendant. Of course, the defendant's strategy might include both approaches. They are not necessarily inconsistent. For example, the most basic affirmative defense in contract actions is the defendant's claim that the plaintiff breached the contract before the defendant's alleged breach occurred.

The first approach, which is to deny the merits of the plaintiff's claim, is based upon the premise that the plaintiff must prove all of the elements to the plaintiff's cause of action to establish the defendant's liability. Each element must be proved by a fair preponderance of the evidence. The defendant's theory or strategy is simply to prevent the plaintiff from proving the cause of action. For example, in a breach of contract action, the defendant may challenge the plaintiff's claim that there was an enforceable contract by *denying* that the parties actually exchanged consideration, so there is no valid contract in the first place. (In some cases, the elements may have to be proved by clear and convincing evidence. The degree of proof varies depending upon the type of cause of action being prosecuted.) If the plaintiff cannot prove a valid contract, the claim of breach of contract necessarily fails.

The first approach has several variations on the same theme. The defendant's strategy may be merely to object to the plaintiff's evidence or argue that the evidence is not convincing. Or, the defendant may take a more active approach and introduce evidence that contradicts the plaintiff's evidence on the material elements to the plaintiff's cause of action. The defendant's strategy may be to persuade the judge that one or more of the necessary elements to the plaintiff's cause of action are missing. If the defendant is successful in that effort, the judge is required to dismiss the case, because the plaintiff has not established a prima facie cause of action. Even if there is sufficient evidence to make out a prima facie case, that does not mean that the evidence has necessarily been persuasive on all of the elements necessary to plaintiff's cause of action. So the defendant's strategy may be directed at creating doubt about one or more of the elements to the plaintiff's cause of action. If the jury decides that the necessary facts have not been proved, the jury must find for the defendant. Of course, these strategies are usually made part of a grand defense strategy.

The second approach involves the presentation of one or more *affirmative defenses* which have the effect of defeating the plaintiff's cause of action. Any legal theory that has the effect of avoiding or defeating plaintiff's claim, even though the claim is true and proven, is considered to be an affirmative defense. All causes of action are subject to one or more affirmative defenses. The Rules place the burden upon the defendant to plead all affirmative defenses in the answer and to prove the affirmative defenses by a fair preponderance of the evidence, just as the plaintiff must prove the elements to a cause of action. Some affirmative defenses, like causes of actions, may require proof of evidence that is **clear and convincing.** For example, proof of a *mutual mistake*, which is grounds for reforming a written contract, must be established by evidence that is clear and convincing. Even then, the burden of proof is somewhat less than "beyond a reasonable doubt," which is the government's burden of proof in prosecuting criminal actions. A partial list of affirmative defenses appears in Rule 8(c). The list is not all-inclusive, but it does mention the most frequently used affirmative defenses.

Pleading an affirmative defense is much like pleading a cause of action. The defendant's failure to plead an affirmative defense in the answer results in a waiver of the defense. Each affirmative defense should be pled in a separate paragraph for clarity and convenience of the parties. It is usually sufficient for the defendant simply to allege the legal conclusion or the affirmative defense by name. For example, the defendant's answer may allege: "Plaintiff's cause of action is barred by plaintiff's assumption of risk." The material time and place are already sufficiently stated in the plaintiff's complaint, so there is no necessity that they be reiterated in the defendant's answer. However, if the affirmative defense relates to a new transaction or occurrence, it must be fully identified by time and place. For example, if the defendant pleads a *release* as an affirmative defense, the time and place at which the release was made must be alleged, along with the terms and effect of the release. Usually the terms are stated by attaching a copy of the release to the answer as an exhibit. Some of the more common affirmative defenses are discussed in this chapter. They should be studied for their essential elements in order to gain an understanding of their uses and limitations and the kind of evidence necessary to prove them.

Accord and Satisfaction

The first affirmative defense mentioned in Rule 8(c) is accord and satisfaction. This defense may be thought of as a type of release. It arises out of the parties' decision to replace their former agreement (contract) with a new agreement, which is then fully performed. The new agreement is called an accord. Performance of the new agreement operates as a satisfaction of the old agreement. An accord and satisfaction provides a complete defense to an action on the original contract. The defendant must offer evidence to prove that the parties had a bona fide dispute over the terms or application of their original agreement and that the new agreement was consciously made as a compromise on both sides. The existence of the bona fide dispute and compromise provides the necessary consideration to make the accord an enforceable contract. Proof of the satisfaction (payment) or other performance by the defendant is essential to the defense. If the defendant has defaulted on both the old agreement and the new accord, the plaintiff may elect to sue on either.

When a dispute arises out of a transaction, it is common for a person to tender a check in a reduced amount as "payment in full." If it is made clear that the check is offered to resolve a disputed claim—not an admittedly valid obligation—and if the check is accepted by the payee, the disputed obligation is fully discharged. The acceptance and negotiation of the check constitute an accord and satisfaction. The purpose of the tender must be manifest. The payee must accept the tender according to the stated terms or return the check uncashed.

Arbitration and Award

If the parties to a dispute agree to submit their controversy to a third party or tribunal for determination and resolution, and the matter is decided by the arbitrator, the disappointed party cannot subsequently litigate the controversy in court. The prior determination is binding as an arbitration and award. Only if there was fraud or some other defect in the arbitration procedure may the losing party dispute the award. Arbitration is frequently provided as the primary means for settling disputes under insurance policies, construction contracts, and labor agreements. The arbitration procedure may be specified by the agreement in question or the parties may adopt the provisions of the Uniform Arbitration Act, which has been adopted by most states. Parties may agree to arbitrate questions of fact and/or questions of law. They must agree on the scope of the submission, and that should be in writing. The scope of submission determines or limits the arbitrator's authority, usually to specific matters.

On occasion the parties to an arbitration agreement may have a disagreement over the scope or application of an arbitration award. It may take a judicial decree to resolve the *new* dispute. Sometimes the parties to an arbitration agreement find that they are in disagreement concerning the permissible scope of the arbitration. This is sometimes referred to as the *scope of submission*. The general rule is that the arbitration tribunal is not authorized to determine disputes concerning the scope or extent of its power. The issue must be submitted to the courts for determination.

The popularity of arbitration seems to be increasing as an alternative method of dispute resolution. Paralegals can expect to become involved in various aspects of arbitration. An understanding of civil litigation procedures will make learning arbitration procedures very easy.

Statutes of Limitations

The purpose of a statute of limitations is to bar old, stale claims. For example, suppose two motorists were involved in what seemed to be a very minor accident, it would be unfair for one to sue the other ten years after the accident, claiming the accident actually caused grievous bodily harm. In all probability, the passage of time would impair (prejudice) the defendant's ability to gather evidence to defend against the claim. The same is true for contract actions. So the legislatures have established time periods in which claims must be sued or the claims are barred. Each state has a compendium of statutes of limitations that vary with the causes of action and remedies claimed. Any cause of action is subject to being barred by a statute of limitations.

In some states, the applicable statute may be as short as one year for a particular type of action. In other states, the same cause of action may be subject to a much longer statutory period, maybe as long as six years. Medical malpractice actions generally are subject to relatively short statutes of limitations. Medical cases often present unique problems in preserving evidence, so there is good reason for treating them separately.

A statute of limitations begins to run against a claim when the injury or loss occurs. For example, in an automobile accident case, the cause of action accrues (and the statute of limitations begins to run) the day of the accident. If the time period allowed by the statute of limitations is one year, the time period would be counted beginning from the following day. The day of the event is not counted. In this regard, there is an analogy to computing time as provided by Rule 6. In a products liability case, the statute of limitations begins to run when the defective product causes an injury. An action for breach of contract accrues and the statute of limitations begins to run when the breach occurs, even though the actual damages may not be realized until later.

If the plaintiff's cause of action is based upon fraud, the cause of action does not accrue until the fraud is discovered or should have been discovered. If the defendant acts to conceal the fact that the plaintiff has a claim against him or her, the statute does not begin to run until the plaintiff discovers that he or she has a claim. In other words, the defendant's fraud keeps the statute of limitations from running, but, once the fraud is discovered, the statute does begin to run.

States differ in their use of the statute of limitations in medical malpractice cases. In these cases, the cause of action accrues when the injury occurs. However, the statute of limitations does not begin to run against a medical malpractice case until treatment for the condition in question terminates. In some states, the statute does not begin to run until the patient discovers the malpractice and consequential injury. States which take that approach have what is commonly called the "discovery rule." Postponement of the running of the statute of limitations in medical malpractice cases is justified on the basis that the time limitation is relatively short and the physician has a fiduciary relationship to the patient that allows an inference of fraud or concealment if the patient is not told about the problem when it occurs.

A statute of limitations does not run against a minor during his or her minority. A minor plaintiff is always allowed the time designated by the statute. If that time runs out during the plaintiff's minority, the plaintiff is still allowed another year after reaching legal age to bring the action. For example, if a six-year statute of limitations applies to a negligence action and the plaintiff is sixteen years of age at the time the cause of action accrues and the plaintiff attains majority at age eighteen, the statute runs against his or her claim when the six-year period expires. The statute would run against the claim during the plaintiff's twenty-fourth year. But if the minor plaintiff is only ten years old when the cause of action accrues, the six-year period would end during the plaintiff's sixteenth year. But the law provides that the statute of limitations is "tolled" during the plaintiff's minority. The minor has one more year after his or her eighteenth birthday in which to assert the claim. In this example the statute runs against the minor's claim when the minor reaches nineteen. A statute of limitations is also tolled by legal disabilities such as insanity.

Assumption of Risk

Assumption of risk is a defense that applies to actions in negligence generally and breach of warranty claims in products cases. The defendant must prove that the plaintiff's loss (injury or property damage) was the result of a danger or risk that was open and apparent to the plaintiff; that the plaintiff appreciated the risk presented by the condition or activity; that the plaintiff voluntarily chose to incur the risk; and that the injury resulted from the risk assumed. A typical application of the defense is where the plaintiff knowingly proceeds to walk on a sidewalk or floor that is obviously slippery. But if the defendant's slippery sidewalk is the only practicable means that the plaintiff has of going to his or her destination, can it be said that the risk was *voluntarily* incurred? Most likely not.

Spectators at baseball games should know that there is a likelihood that some baseballs will be hit into the stands. That is a normal occurrence and one for which some of the spectators hope. If a spectator has the opportunity to sit in a protected area but voluntarily chooses to sit in an open area, the spectator can hardly complain about getting hit by a "home-run" ball. The spectator chose to be where the action is. Even though the ball park could have provided more protection for more spectators, the ball park is not liable if the spectator assumed the risk of being hit by the ball. A football player assumes the risk of injury from a hard but fair tackle. However, a football player does not assume the risk of being assaulted by a disgruntled opponent.

If an individual voluntarily chooses to ride with a drunk driver, that person must know that there is a great risk that they will have an accident. The same is true if someone elects to ride in an automobile driven by another in an illegal race on a public street. The passenger assumes the risk of injury that arises from a danger that is apprehended and voluntarily incurred.

One more example may be instructive. Suppose that a man purchased a new electric appliance. After using it a couple of times, he discovers that it has a short. If he continues to use the appliance, he assumes the risk of injury or loss that results from the electrical short. He would also be contributorily negligent. Often the two defenses overlap. To successfully prove the assumption of risk, the defendant would have to prove that the plaintiff fully understood that the short was dangerous and likely to cause harm. Whereas the defendant could establish negligence on the part of the plaintiff by proving that the plaintiff was aware that something was wrong and that he or she should have investigated the problem. This is an example of where the plaintiff *should have known* of the danger and was negligent for not preventing the harm.

With the advent of comparative fault, some states have abolished assumption of risk as a defense, which is separate from contributory negligence or comparative fault. In those states assumption of risk is looked upon as being merged with negligence.

Contributory Negligence

Contributory negligence is negligence on the part of the claimant (usually the plaintiff) that bars his or her claim against another party. For example, in a negligence action where the plaintiff and defendant have sued each other, the parties' contributory negligence would prevent either from recovering against the other. Contributory negligence is not a defense to an action based upon strict liability in tort; nor is it a defense to a claim under the Dramshop Act against a liquor vendor.

The defense of contributory negligence has been abolished by those states that have adopted the law of comparative negligence or comparative fault.

Discharge in Bankruptcy

Federal laws provide that individuals and corporations may voluntarily declare bankruptcy if they cannot meet their current obligations. Three creditors can force an individual or corporation into involuntary bankruptcy. The effect of the court's determination that the petitioner is bankrupt is to discharge him or her from all declared debts as of the date of the petition. The creditors must be given notice of the petition for bankruptcy so that they have an opportunity to challenge the petition and to share in the debtor's existing assets. Defects in the proceedings, such as a failure to give a creditor notice, preclude the debtor from being discharged.

Certain kinds of debts are not dischargeable in bankruptcy. They include those created by the petitioner's fraud, willful conversion (theft) of property, and intentional tortious acts which cause injury to persons or damage to property.

Duress

A promise that is otherwise legally enforceable is not binding if it was exacted from the promisor by duress. Duress is the threat of death, bodily harm, or damage to property.

Estoppel

Estoppel is an esoteric concept that has a variety of applications to actions in tort and to actions in contract. It originated in equity, but it is now firmly recognized as a legal defense. The defense of estoppel precludes the plaintiff from recovering money damages for a loss that resulted from the defendant's mistake, that is, the defendant's mistake was induced by the plaintiff's wrongful conduct in the first place. For example, if a corporation were to replace its outstanding stock certificates with new certificates but failed to collect the certificates from one shareholder who subsequently sold the old certificate to a bona fide purchaser, the corporation could be estopped from denying the validity of the old stock certificates. The purchaser would be entitled to dividends and to have his or her ownership recorded on the stockholders' register. Where an insurance company holds out an agent as authorized to sell its insurance policies, it cannot subsequently avoid a policy on the grounds that the agent was not properly licensed. The insurer could be estopped from denying the agent's qualifications.

If the plaintiff were to represent to the defendant that the plaintiff's camera was owned by another person, who had possession of the camera, and the possessor sold the camera to the defendant, the plaintiff could be estopped from denying that the third person was the owner. The law would give effect to the sale because of the plaintiff's misrepresentation on which the defendant reasonably relied.

Waiver

Waiver is an affirmative defense that has application to actions in contract and tort actions. Waiver is the intentional relinquishment of a known legal right under circumstances where the defendant would be prejudiced if the plaintiff were allowed to reassert the right. For example, suppose that an automobile insurance application and policy provides that the policy shall be void if the applicant has had an accident within the year preceding the application. Suppose that the applicant misrepresented on the application that he or she had no accidents, but the insurer learned about the misrepresentation within a month after the policy was issued and did nothing about canceling the policy. The insurer's failure to take steps to revoke or cancel the policy in good season after discovering the misrepresentation could result in a waiver of the right to cancel.

Suppose that a store lease provides that the landlord may terminate the lease if the tenant sells liquor on the premises, and that, to the landlord's knowledge, the tenant does sell liquor for a couple of years and then stops. The landlord's acquiescence in the tenant's conduct could constitute a waiver of the right to claim a violation of the lease.

Fraud

Fraud and its elements are discussed in the preceding chapter as a cause of action in tort, which gives rise to a claim for money damages. The same elements will give rise to an affirmative defense to actions in contract and in tort.

Consent

Consent is an affirmative defense to actions for battery, actions for trespass to real estate, and actions for conversion of personal property. In an action for battery, if the defendant can prove that the plaintiff consented to the physical contact in question, the consent is a complete defense. For example, if the plaintiff sues the defendant in battery for personal injuries, claiming that the defendant wrongfully punched the plaintiff in the nose, the defendant may avoid civil liability by proving that the plaintiff agreed to fight. When boxers enter the ring they consent to be battered. Consent is not the same as assumption of risk. Consent requires actual agreement to the defendant's conduct.

A civil action to recover money damages for rape is an action for a battery. Other than the statute of limitations, the only viable defense to such an action is consent. Consent must be proved by a fair preponderance of the evidence.

Consent does not have to be express to be effective. Consent may be implied from the circumstances. For example, if the defendant asks the plaintiff for permission to use the plaintiff's automobile, and the plaintiff responds by pointing to the keys lying on the table, and defendant picks up the keys, gets into the automobile and drives away, permission to use the car would be implied from the circumstances. Suppose that while the defendant is using the automobile a collision that totally destroys the automobile occurs. Suppose further that the defendant was not negligent in the operation of the automobile. The plaintiff would not be able to maintain an action in negligence against the defendant for loss of the automobile. However, the plaintiff would have a right to damages from the defendant if the defendant wrongfully **converted** the automobile. The plaintiff's cause of action for conversion of the automobile may be defeated by the defendant's proof that the plaintiff actually consented to its use. Perhaps this example seems a little too elementary and obvious. Suppose that the plaintiff expected that the defendant would just drive a few blocks away, but the accident occurred two hundred miles away. Now, is there a conversion? Is there consent to the use of the automobile? Some courts would find that the defendant did convert the automobile.

Ethical Considerations

Lawyers are subject to disciplinary action for asserting a claim or defense that is frivolous. A claim or defense is frivolous if there is no apparent basis in fact or law for the claim. This is another important difference between criminal law and civil law. In criminal law a defendant and his or her lawyer may put the state to its burden of proving every element of the crime, even though they know the defendant did what he or she is accused of doing. They know that there is no defense; nevertheless, they may put the state to its proof.

In addition to professional ethics, Rule 11 provides that a lawyer's signature on a pleading is the lawyer's certification that the lawyer has made reasonable inquiry into the matter and believes that the claim and defenses alleged in the pleading have basis in fact. A lawyer also certifies that the claim or defense is not being asserted for an improper purpose, such as harassment or delay.

5 Jurisdiction and Court Organization

Jurisdiction

A court's authority over individuals, corporations, property, other branches of government, and political subdivisions is limited to the court's *jurisdiction*. Indeed, in this context, the terms "authority" and "jurisdiction" are essentially synonymous. In other words, if a court acts outside of or beyond its jurisdiction, it acts beyond its authority and beyond its power. The government, which creates the court, establishes the nature and extent of the court's jurisdiction. Jurisdiction may be limited by the types of cases which the court may handle, the territory in which it may operate, and by the persons who are subject to the court's authority. All of the courts in the United States, state and federal, are subject to some limitations in jurisdiction.

We ordinarily think of the courts as one of the three separate branches of government—part of the marvelous system of checks and balances built into our system of constitutional government. In the federal government, however, only the United States Supreme Court is entirely separate, with its foundation in the Constitution. Since it was created by the Constitution, the Constitution establishes and defines its authority. Its power cannot be abridged or expanded by Congress. On the other hand, the federal district courts and circuit courts of appeals were created by acts of Congress. Congress determined their organization, function, and the scope of their jurisdiction. Though separate and independent, the three branches of government must work together. A healthy spirit of cooperation was manifested by the Congress when it recognized that the lower courts should operate pursuant to rules established by the Supreme Court and enacted enabling legislation that authorized the Supreme Court to promulgate the Federal Rules of Civil Procedure—an important part of our study in this book.

The legislature, which creates a court and defines its functions, may modify those functions by subsequent legislation. As an example, by statute the

United States Congress adopted the Federal Rules of Evidence, as propounded by the Supreme Court, to be used by all federal district courts. The codification of the rules of evidence replaced a system of common law rules of evidence used by the federal courts for two centuries. Federal judges must follow and apply the new rules even if they happen to prefer the old common law rules.

It is necessary to look to the authority by which each court was created to determine the scope of the court's jurisdiction. State legislatures may change the structure and functions of state courts through legislation. For example, a state legislature may add more judges, may redefine districts in which courts function, courts may be merged, or an intermediate appellate court may be created by legislation.

When a lawyer obtains a new case, one of the first considerations is to determine which court or courts have jurisdiction in the matter. For purposes of this book, jurisdiction may be divided into three basic categories: (1) jurisdiction over the person; (2) jurisdiction over the subject matter of the litigation; and (3) geographical or territorial jurisdiction. A court does not have jurisdiction over a case unless the court has obtained jurisdiction in all three areas.

The parties may give a court jurisdiction over their persons. When the plaintiff commences a civil action, whether in a state or federal court, the plaintiff thereby submits to the jurisdiction of that court. The defendant may voluntarily submit to personal jurisdiction of a court. Indeed, the defendant must allege in the answer the court's lack of jurisdiction over his or her person; otherwise, the defendant waives the right to challenge the court's jurisdiction later in the case. A court obtains jurisdiction over the defendant through service of a summons upon the defendant in the manner provided by law and the court's rules of civil procedure. If the summons or service of the summons is defective for any reason, the court fails to obtain jurisdiction over the person of the defendant. (Service of process is discussed in greater detail in chapter 6.) Since the insufficiency of service of process affects only the court's jurisdiction over the person of the defendant, the defect may be waived intentionally or inadvertently. Conversely, the defendant cannot do anything to give a court jurisdiction over the subject matter of the case. Subject matter jurisdiction may be challenged at any time, even after entry of judgment.

Jurisdiction over the *person* refers to jurisdiction over parties whether the parties are individuals, corporations, governmental subdivisions, or other legal entities. For example, state courts do not have jurisdiction over the United States government or any of its agencies. All civil actions involving the United States must be brought in federal district courts. A state court does not have jurisdiction over civil actions against another state. One state may obtain jurisdiction over another state only in a federal court. Jurisdiction over the *subject matter* refers to the type of case and the subject of the case. For example, federal courts do not have subject matter jurisdiction over divorce cases, adoptions, registration of real estate, or probation of a will. Subject matter jurisdiction also refers to the dollar amount for money judgments that courts may award. Jurisdiction over the *territory* refers to the geographical limitations on a court's authority. For example, state courts do not have authority to determine ownership of real estate located in another state. A federal district court cannot subpoena a witness who is located in another state.

The most obvious and pragmatic limitation on a court's jurisdiction is the geographical or territorial limitation. With few exceptions, a court has no authority beyond its designated territorial limits. The limitation arises out of very practical considerations. For example, if a judgment debtor and his or her property are within the territorial limits of the court, enforcement of the judgment is a relatively straightforward procedure. However, one can imagine the difficulty that a court in Massachusetts would have enforcing its judgment in Texas. Texas probably would not look kindly upon Massachusetts' officious conduct. The Massachusetts court simply could not have enough personnel to handle extrastate activities. Similarly, a Massachusetts court would have practical difficulties trying to determine title to real estate located in Texas and even more difficulty trying to enforce a judgment affecting title to property in another state.

The territorial limitation on a court's jurisdiction becomes a little vague in accident cases. For example, suppose two acquaintances from California are traveling in an automobile through Minnesota when they are involved in a collision, and the passenger desires to bring a negligence action against the driver to recover money damages for personal injuries. Must the lawsuit be brought in Minnesota? Suppose the driver and passenger return to their native California? Do they have to return to Minnesota to litigate their dispute? Causes of action arising out of occurrences (torts) usually are "transitory." This means that the cause of action accrues in the territory where the accident occurred but also follows the parties (at least, it follows the defendant). Consequently, the plaintiff can sue the defendant driver in any state where the defendant can be found and serve that individual with a summons and complaint.

In this hypothetical situation, the action could be brought in Minnesota, whether or not the defendant driver can be found in Minnesota to be served with a summons and complaint. The Minnesota court's authority exists under the state's nonresident motorist statute, which provides that a nonresident motorist impliedly appoints the Minnesota Commissioner of Highways as the motorist's agent to receive service of process for any motor vehicle accident that occurs within the state. All states have such statutes. The plaintiff passenger must serve the summons and complaint upon the Minnesota Commissioner of Highways. The plaintiff must also mail a copy of the summons and complaint to the nonresident motorist at that person's last known address. Through this procedure, the Minnesota courts obtain jurisdiction over the nonresident driver.

The manufacturer of a defective product that is shipped into another state for resale and use submits to personal jurisdiction of the courts in the state where the product causes injury if the manufacturer has significant business contacts in that state. A few decades ago it would have been necessary for the consumer to bring the lawsuit in the state where the manufacturer was incorporated or where it conducted its business operations. In recent years, the concept of due process of law has been expanded to permit states to enact so-called long-arm statutes for protection of their citizens in cases such as this. The cause of action is considered to have its origin in the state where the injury occurred. Service of process may be made upon the foreign corporation by serving the secretary of state where the injury occurred. The plaintiff must promptly mail copies of the summons and complaint to the foreign corporation at its registered office or principal place of business. The foreign corporation will have to defend itself in the state where the consumer's injury occurred. If the plaintiff consumer moves to another state, the cause of action does *not* follow. The suit must be brought in the state where the injury occurred or the state where the defendant manufacturer conducts its business as of the time of service.

A corporation is subject to personal jurisdiction in the state where it is incorporated whether or not it does business in that state. A cause of action in tort or for breach of contract follows the defendant to another jurisdiction but does not follow the plaintiff. However, if the plaintiff follows the defendant to another state and brings the action there, the defendant can counterclaim against the plaintiff for any claim the defendant has that arises out of the same transaction or occurrence. Whenever the plaintiff elects to sue in a particular court, he or she submits to the jurisdiction of that court during the pendency of the suit.

The amount of money damages claimed in the complaint determines whether certain courts have jurisdiction to handle the case. Small-claims courts usually cannot award money damages for more than a few hundred dollars. The exact amount varies from state to state. If a plaintiff has a claim for $350, but the jurisdictional limit of the small-claims court is only $300, the plaintiff must give up $50 of the claim in order to use the small-claims court. On the other hand, all federal district courts have a jurisdictional requirement in "diversity of citizens" cases that the amount in controversy *exceed* $10,000. (Diversity suits authorize a citizen of one state to sue in federal court if the defendant is a resident of a different state.) Federal district courts do not have jurisdiction to handle diversity cases involving lesser amounts. The parties cannot avoid the jurisdictional requirement by agreement or otherwise. If the amount in controversy is $10,000 or less, it would be a fraud on the court to feign a larger amount for the purpose of trying to give the court jurisdiction.

A court of *general jurisdiction* has authority to grant all remedies available in law and equity. In addition to awarding money damages in unlimited amounts, they can issue decrees for adoption, divorce, injunctions, specific performance, change of name, and judgments determining title to real estate. (Some of these remedies are discussed in chapter 3.) Courts of limited jurisdiction are unable to provide some of these remedies.

Federal Court Organization

The United States Constitution provided for the establishment of the United States Supreme Court. It is an independent, separate branch of our federal government. The Constitution also authorized Congress to establish such inferior courts as the Congress deems appropriate. Through that power, Congress has created a United States federal district court for each state and for certain United States territories. Federal lawsuits are commenced in these courts and the cases are tried in them. Congress also created thirteen United States circuit courts of appeals. Parties may appeal to a circuit court of appeals to obtain a new trial or reversal of the district court's judgment if the district court committed prejudicial error in handling the case. The circuit courts of appeal deal with procedural errors and substantive errors. Each of the thirteen circuit courts serves the district courts in a designated area.

The statutes that created the district courts and the appellate courts also established the jurisdiction of each. So there are three principal levels of courts in the federal system. The jurisdiction of each district court is limited to the geographical boundaries of the state or territory it serves. Each state's district courts have been subdivided into divisions for each of administration. The jurisdiction of the district court in each division is statewide.

The federal district courts are courts of *original jurisdiction*. This means that cases originate in the district courts. Cases are tried in the district courts and the original decisions are made there. The federal district courts are also courts of limited jurisdiction. They are limited to certain types of cases. Only certain persons may bring actions in our federal district courts. For example, two Texans who are involved in an automobile accident in Texas and who decide to sue each other for personal injuries cannot bring their actions against each other in the Federal District Court of Texas. On the other hand, if one of the Texans moved to another state, even after the automobile accident, then there would be diversity of citizenship, which would permit an action in federal district court, assuming the amount in controversy exceeded ten thousand dollars. Effective in 1989, the controversy must exceed fifty thousand dollars for the federal district courts to have jurisdiction in diversity cases.

Federal law provides that certain types of cases must be brought in federal court, such as cases involving United States patent infringements, regardless of the amount of money in controversy. Any actions against the United States government or its agencies must be brought in a federal district court. In addition, federal district courts may be used to bring actions against a foreign government, against the government of another state, or against a foreign corporation. A corporation is considered to be a resident of the state of its incorporation. Even though a diversity of residency exists, however, if the claim is for the sum of ten thousand dollars or less, a federal district court does not have jurisdiction. This is a limitation imposed by federal statute, not the Constitution. (Note: in 1989 the law changed so as to require that the amount in controversy exceed $50,000.)

A large body of law has developed concerning diversity of residency (or diversity of citizenship) as a prerequisite to federal jurisdiction. If the case is not subject to federal jurisdiction, the plaintiff must resort to the state courts— an unsatisfactory alternative to some litigants in some cases.

Usually there is no great problem determining whether or not a controversy involves more than ten thousand dollars in cases arising out of transactions, such as an action on a contract or promissory note. Conversely, cases that arise out of a personal injury and property damage claims are more difficult to evaluate for purposes of jurisdiction. As a rule of thumb, courts and parties look to the amount of special damages and the seriousness of the injuries. (Special damages are out-of-pocket expenses that the claimant has incurred because of the alleged wrongful conduct of the defendant.) If there is medical evidence of a significant permanent disability, federal courts usually accept jurisdiction; however, federal district judges may differ on how stringently they apply this limitation. If a case goes through trial and the jury determines that full compensation should be less than ten thousand dollars, the court allows entry of judgment for the lesser amount. The monetary limitation does not cause the court to lose jurisdiction retroactively.

Each state has one federal district court. Each district court is subdivided into a number of divisions. Each division of the court is located in a separate major city. There are times when two or more federal district courts, each in a different state or territory, have jurisdiction. The case should be brought in the court where the venue is proper. There are a number of rules that determine the proper venue. When a lawyer refers to venue, with regard to federal courts, he or she may be referring to the district as a whole or to a particular division within a district. Generally speaking, the proper venue is the one that is most convenient to all the parties and witnesses.

Federal district courts are courts of record. That means a complete record is kept of all proceedings in the courts. When testimony is taken everything that is said is recorded by a court reporter. When a lawyer makes an oral argument to the court, the argument is recorded. A transcript may be obtained by a party or even a nonparty who has any need for the information contained in the record. A transcript of the record may be obtained by a party to show an appellate court that an error occurred at the trial court level, but a transcript is not made from the stenographer's notes unless it is specifically ordered. The person who orders a transcript must pay for it.

When a party believes that prejudicial errors occurred in the trial, that party may appeal from the judgment. An error is considered "prejudicial" if it had the potential for actually affecting the outcome of the case. An error must be prejudicial to be appealable. The appeal is taken to the circuit court of appeals for the area in which the trial court is located. Cases do not originate in the appellate courts. There are thirteen federal judicial circuits which include the District of Columbia Circuit and the U.S. Court of Appeals for the Federal Circuit. The location of each circuit is shown in the map following Appendix VIII.

The United States Supreme Court is an appellate court. It is not a court of original jurisdiction. (Article III provides in part: "In all cases affecting ambassadors, other public ministers and consuls, and those in which a state shall be party, the Supreme Court shall have original Jurisdiction. In all other cases before mentioned, the Supreme Court shall have appellate jurisdiction, both as to law and fact, with such exceptions, and under such regulations as the Congress shall make.") Trials are not conducted in the court. Relatively few cases are appealed to the Supreme Court. Most cases that do reach it are appealed on a petition for a writ of certiorari. This is a procedure by which the appellant requests the Supreme Court to issue an order allowing him or her to appeal. If the Supreme Court deems the issue to be appealed significant to society or the law in general, it may grant the application by ordering the lower court to "send up" its file for review.

State Court Organization

Each state has a system of courts that have general jurisdiction, usually described as district courts. Each district court has the power to hear almost any kind of case involving any sum of money and to grant all forms of judicial remedies. Each district court has statewide jurisdiction, that is, their subpoenas, orders, and decrees may be enforced anywhere within the state and even against its citizens who are outside the state. Each district court operates within a specified territory, usually a county or group of counties. As a general rule, a cause of action should be brought in the district court located in the county in which the cause of action accrues. Ordinarily, that is the proper venue for the action. As mentioned, a district court's jurisdiction is ordinarily statewide—not limited to a county.

A cause of action in tort accrues in the jurisdiction and venue where the tort and injury occur. If the tortious conduct occurs in one state and the plaintiff's injury occurs in another state, the cause of action accrues in the state where the injury occurred. In a contract case, the cause of action accrues in the county where the contract was performed. If the contract was not performed at all, the cause of action may accrue where the contract was formed. In a real estate case, the cause of action accrues in the county where the real estate is located. Usually the proper venue is the most convenient place for the case to be tried. Venue also refers to the territory from which the jury is selected. Factors which determine jurisdiction and the proper venue may be the same, but the two terms involve quite different concepts.

The plaintiff selects a venue when he or she commences the action by filing the complaint. If the defendant believes the plaintiff selected the wrong venue, he or she must make a demand for a change of venue within the time specified by law—usually before the answer is due. Otherwise, the defendant waives the right to have the case heard in the proper venue. In other words, the right to a change of venue is waived by a failure to seasonably object. If for some reason the preferred venue is not convenient, the action is ordinarily brought in the venue where most of the defendants reside.

Each state has various other courts of limited jurisdiction. Most cities have small-claims courts. These courts exist for the speedy, inexpensive handling of small claims that involve nothing more than the award of money damages. They handle a tremendous volume of property damage claims, claims for wages, claims for breached contracts, collection of rent, collection of delinquent accounts, and even small personal injury cases. The jurisdiction of small-claims courts may be as large as one thousand dollars, or even more, depending upon the needs of the community. Lawyers are allowed to appear on behalf of clients, but the system tends to discourage lawyers' participation. The amount in controversy usually does not warrant the expense of legal representation. The procedures are kept informal so that a lawyer's guidance is not necessary. The rules of evidence are not followed closely. The parties are encouraged to simply tell their stories in their own words with as few interruptions as possible. The judge or referee asks such questions as he or she deems necessary. Of course, companies and corporations cannot appear in person, so they often send lawyers to appear on their behalf along with the necessary witnesses. These courts have subpoena power, but subpoenas are seldom used.

Service of process in small-claims courts is kept very simple and inexpensive. The usual procedure is to have the plaintiff prepare a sworn complaint in the clerk of court's office. The complaint contains a short, narrative statement of the plaintiff's version of the facts. The clerk of court usually tries to assist the plaintiff in framing the allegations. The filing fee is nominal, generally one to ten dollars. A copy of the complaint is mailed by the clerk of court to the defendant at his or her last known address. A notice is sent with the complaint directing the defendant to appear in court at a specified time to defend against the allegations, and if the defendant fails to do so, a default judgment will be taken against him or her. If the last known address proves to be incorrect, that would be grounds for setting aside any default judgment obtained against the defendant. The defendant is not required to prepare and serve an answer to the complaint.

Cases are usually heard within six weeks from the date of filing. Twenty or more cases may be scheduled for hearing in the course of a morning or afternoon session. After the judge has heard the narrative testimony of the parties and their witnesses, he or she takes the matter under advisement. Obviously, he or she must make a decision right away because it would not be possible to keep all the cases in mind for very long, but rendering a decision in open court might lead to a courtroom altercation. Also, it might upset the other parties, who are waiting for their cases to be heard, and cause them to change their "stories" to fit the judge's pronouncements.

Notwithstanding the informality of small-claims courts, their decisions should be rendered according to law rather than the judge's personal sense of equity. For example, if the plaintiff sues on an oral contract, which is unenforceable because it comes within the statute of frauds and should have been in writing and signed to be enforceable, the decision should be for the defendant. The judge should explain to the losing party that the decision is controlled by rules of law, and why. The explanation usually can be given without pronouncing the court's decision in open court. Using this approach, the court helps the party to understand why he or she lost. If the decision were announced in court, there is danger that the parties might become violent towards each other. The losing party may not be quite as angry against the system when he or she receives the formal notice of decision in the mail. Most judges are acutely aware of the importance of making the parties feel that the system is working properly. This is especially true in small-claims courts, because parties do not have lawyers to explain the problems to them. The judge never comments on the credibility of the witnesses. That would only cause problems.

Small-claims courts are not courts of record. The only documentation of the trial is the court's order for judgment. If a litigant is disappointed in the outcome, he or she cannot appeal directly to an appellate court. Usually, the procedure is to appeal to the next higher court of original jurisdiction—probably a municipal court or a county court. There the parties receive a new trial, which is called a "trial de novo." This time the case is tried with all of the usual court formalities. Of course, the appeal must be taken within the designated period of time and in the manner prescribed by the small-claims court's rules. Notice of the decision and judgment usually contain the information necessary for the losing party to appeal and obtain a trial de novo.

In some communities, certain "smaller" civil cases are tried by a local justice of the peace. A justice of the peace is usually not a lawyer and may not have formal training in the law. His or her income probably depends directly upon the litigation handled. "Justice courts" lack some of the safeguards that characterize courts of law. Consequently, these justice courts seem to be disappearing.

Municipal courts and county courts handle a large volume of litigation even though they are courts of limited jurisdiction. They cannot render judgments in excess of a specified amount, such as ten thousand dollars; they are courts of original jurisdiction; and they are courts of record, so a transcript of the proceedings is available. An appeal may be taken directly to an appellate court from a municipal or county court. The parties have a right to trial by jury just as if the matter were brought in a court of general jurisdiction. Usually, the rules of procedure for municipal and county courts are very similar to the district court's rules. There is considerable value in keeping the rules of procedure uniform in all courts throughout the state. For the same reason, many states have adopted rules of civil procedure that mirror the Federal Rules of Civil Procedure. The limitations on a municipal court's jurisdiction prevents it from handling suits for divorce or for determining title to real estate, granting injunctions, or rendering other types of equitable relief.

Courts of general jurisdiction can handle any type of civil lawsuit. There is no maximum amount of money damages that they can award; there is no minimum amount required for jurisdiction. Their judgments and decrees may be enforced anywhere within the territorial limits of the state. They are always courts of record, and the losing party may appeal directly from the court to the appropriate appellate court. A court of general jurisdiction has authority and powers through the state supreme court that the legislature cannot take away. For example, the legislature could not provide in a statute that the district courts shall not have jurisdiction to determine that a particular statute is unconstitutional. Some district court rules provide that if the plaintiff is the prevailing party but recovers a judgment for an amount of money within the monetary jurisdiction of a lower court, the losing party may "tax" his or her costs against the prevailing party. The purpose of such rules is to encourage parties to use the lower courts if at all possible and to save the courts of general jurisdiction for the more significant cases. Taxable costs may include the filing fee, witness fees, and the cost of service of process.

Appellate Courts

Appellate courts do not have original jurisdiction of lawsuits. That is, cases are not commenced in the appellate courts. Their function is to supervise the trial courts and make sure that trial courts act within the law, follow prescribed procedures, and do not abuse their discretionary powers. Appellate courts make the final determination of all questions of law. The trial courts still have primary responsibility for resolving disputed facts.

Appellate courts reverse trial judges for abuses of discretion only when the abuse is manifest. For example, trial judges have broad discretion in determining whether a person qualifies as an expert witness. When a trial court's ruling is challenged on appeal, it is common for the appellate court to state in its published opinion that it might have ruled differently than the trial court, but the holding is affirmed because the trial court's ruling was not clearly wrong. The same is true where an appellate court is asked to pass judgment on a trial court's order that affirms or disallows the amount of money damages awarded by a jury.

Appellate courts never take testimony to resolve issues before them, that is, witnesses are never allowed to testify. An appellate court's rules may or may not provide for oral argument by lawyers concerning issues of law that have been appealed. Motions to the appellate courts are always made in writing, not orally. The established procedures are quite technical and discourage laypersons from attempting to prosecute their own appeals. Appellate court decisions are published so that other litigants may obtain guidance by the precedents established. The fact that appellate court decisions (opinions) are published is another check within the judicial system to keep courts responsible to the parties and all citizens.

6 Introduction to Federal Procedure

The structure of a civil lawsuit is largely established by the Federal Rules of Civil Procedure. The Rules prescribe the methods for commencing lawsuits, serving other parties, conducting discovery, making motions, conducting the trial, and perfecting appeals. If a paralegal is to understand what lawyers do when handling civil litigation and how they do it, a good understanding of the Rules is essential.

Commencement of a Lawsuit

A lawsuit is easy to start, and it should be. Parties who have valid claims should not be discouraged from using the courts to resolve those claims. If a person has a meritorious claim, that person's first step should be to consult with a lawyer to determine whether or not the claim is one that can be formulated into a cause of action. If a lawyer concludes that the claim has probable merit, a complaint that sets out the necessary allegations to establish the client's cause of action is prepared. Rule 11 requires the lawyer to sign the complaint. If no lawyer has been retained, the complaint must be signed by the plaintiff. The complaint is not a verified document, that is, it is not notarized. The lawyer's signature on the complaint is his or her personal certification that there are good grounds for the claim and that the action has not been brought for the purpose of harassment, embarrassment, or delay. A lawyer does not have to browbeat the client to determine whether or not the claim has merit, but for the client's sake, and the lawyer's own protection, he or she ought to comply with the spirit of Rule 11. A violation of this Rule 11 subjects the lawyer and client to sanctions.

Before the Federal Rules of Civil Procedure were adopted in 1938, the complaint had to set forth, at length, all the facts that gave rise to the claim. The form and language of the complaint were as important as the substance. If the complaint failed to state sufficient facts to establish a cause of action, it was subject to being summarily dismissed upon demurrer (motion) filed by the defendant. The complaint provided all of the information about the plaintiff's claim that the defendant needed to either admit liability or to defend against the suit. The Rules have reduced the technical requirements for drafting complaints; nevertheless, a complaint still has the function of informing the court and defendant of the basic facts that give the court jurisdiction and informing the defendant of the nature of the claim, the remedy sought, and the amount of the claim.

Conciseness has become a hallmark of a well-drafted complaint. As provided in Rule 8(a)(1): A complaint shall contain a "short and plain statement" of the claim showing the pleader is entitled to relief. "A pleading that sets forth a claim for relief, whether an original claim, counterclaim, cross-claim, or third-party claim, shall contain (1) a short and plain statement of the grounds upon which the court's jurisdiction depends, unless the court already has jurisdiction and the claim needs no new grounds of jurisdiction to support it; (2) a short and plain statement of the claim showing that the pleader is entitled to relief; and (3) a demand for judgment for the relief to which the plaintiff deems himself or herself entitled. Relief in alternative forms may be demanded." A complaint must identify the parties; allege the basis for the court's jurisdiction; state the date and place of the transaction or occurrence; describe the nature of the *legal* wrong allegedly perpetrated by the defendant; describe the nature and extent of the losses/injuries sustained by the plaintiff; and, finally, identify the type and amount of relief or compensation demanded by the plaintiff. The Rules do not require the allegations to be stated in a particular, legalistic manner; nevertheless, the elements of a cause of action must be set forth or else the complaint is subject to dismissal, and the lawsuit is terminated.

COMPLAINT FOR BREACH OF CONTRACT

For his cause of action against defendant, plaintiff alleges:

1. That plaintiff is a resident of the state of New York, and defendant is a resident of the state of New Jersey; the amount in controversy exceeds ten thousand dollars ($10,000), not including costs and interest.

2. That on May 10, 1989, plaintiff and defendant entered into a written contract in which plaintiff agreed to purchase from defendant and defendant agreed to sell a certain XYZ electronic computer bearing the manufacturer's serial no. 54321 and then located at defendant's plant at 33 Hart Street, Newark, New Jersey.

3. That the agreed purchase price for the computer to be delivered at defendant's said plant was thirty thousand dollars ($30,000).

4. That a copy of said contract is attached hereto as Exhibit A and incorporated herein by reference.

5. That defendant promised to deliver said computer to plaintiff at defendant's plant in Newark, New Jersey, on June 15, 1989.

6. That defendant failed to deliver said computer to plaintiff at said time and place, although plaintiff has made demand upon defendant to do so.

7. That plaintiff tendered to defendant the agreed purchase price of thirty thousand dollars ($30,000), and all other conditions precedent have occurred or have been performed by plaintiff.

8. That by reason of defendant's breach of contract, plaintiff has been required to purchase another electronic computer, similar in type, at a cost of fifty thousand dollars ($50,000); therefore, defendant's breach of contract has caused plaintiff to sustain a loss in the amount of twenty thousand dollars ($20,000), plus interest thereon at the legal rate of 8 percent per annum.

Wherefore, plaintiff prays for judgment against defendant in the sum of twenty thousand dollars ($20,000), together with interest thereon at the legal rate of 8 percent per annum from the date of defendant's breach, together with plaintiff's costs and disbursements herein.

Plaintiff demands trial by jury.

    (date)

_____

                         Attorney for Plaintiff

The complaint has identified the contract, the place of its performance, the time and place of the breach, the nature of the breach, and the nature and extent of the loss claimed. The contract document has been fully identified by attaching a photocopy to the complaint. Photocopying exhibits reduces the possibility of error in critical wording. Clearly, the defendant has been provided with enough information to decide whether to deny the claim or admit liability.

Whether the basis for the claim is a transaction or an occurrence, the time and place must be specified in the complaint. Time factors are important not only to identify the occurrence but also to determine whether the statute of limitations has run against the claim and whether the parties have complied with notice requirements. The place of the occurrence may determine which court has jurisdiction. The place of the occurrence may determine which state's laws are to be applied in determining the parties' substantive rights.

The complaint must describe the legal wrong committed by the defendant, such as assault, battery, negligence, trespass, slander, etc. The complaint must describe, in general terms, the type and extent of the loss or injury the plaintiff sustained. The loss may take various forms such as a loss of profits, expenses, damage to property, total loss of property, physical pain, mental anguish, disfigurement, embarrassment, disability, loss of good reputation, loss of use of money, loss of support. The loss may relate to the past and/or the future. The complaint may specify a certain amount of money damages claimed for each item of loss.

Fundamental to all tort litigation is the requirement that the alleged wrongful act or omission be a direct (proximate) cause of the loss sustained by the plaintiff. If there is a lack of causation, if the wrongful conduct of the defendant did not actually cause the plaintiff's loss, the plaintiff is not entitled to compensation from the defendant. Therefore, the complaint must specifically allege that the tort committed by the defendant was the proximate or direct cause of the plaintiff's loss.

Finally, the complaint must contain an *ad damnum* clause—the "Wherefore" clause—in which the plaintiff specifies the relief or recovery desired from the defendant. The ad damnum clause puts the defendant on notice of the amount of money damages the plaintiff is claiming. Nothing but a sense of professional responsibility prevents the plaintiff's counsel from asking for an excessively large amount of money. The news media is unduly impressed by large demands stated in complaints. Consequently, a few jurisdictions have enacted laws or rules that provide that the complaint shall state an amount up to fifty thousand dollars. If the claim is for more than fifty thousand dollars, the complaint simply states that the amount demanded is in excess of fifty thousand dollars.

The amount stated in the ad damnum is particularly important in those courts where jurisdiction is affected by the amount in controversy. If the amount is too much, a county or municipal court does not have jurisdiction over the case. Courts such as a United States district court may not have jurisdiction in certain types of cases unless the plaintiff, in good faith, is able to demand judgment for an amount in excess of $10,000, exclusive of costs and interest. [50,000]

If the defendant fails to serve an answer to the complaint within the time specified, he or she is considered to be in default. The plaintiff is able to obtain a default judgment against the defendant by application to the court (Rule 55). The plaintiff's recovery is limited to the amount of the ad damnum even though he or she is able to show more damages when "proving up" the default judgment. It can happen that, by duly appearing and defending against the claim, the defendant's obligation may be determined to be more than the amount demanded in the complaint. Whereas, if the defendant defaults, the plaintiff's recovery is limited to the amount stated in the ad damnum clause.

Occasionally, a case seems to be minor when sued but develops into a very serious one commanding a much higher award than originally presumed. The plaintiff's counsel may move the court for an order allowing an increase in the ad damnum as soon as the real value becomes known. The motion must be supported by one or more affidavits setting forth the change in circumstances. The plaintiff must show the court that the amendment will not prejudice the defendant's preparation for trial. For example, if a defendant has let his or her liability insurance company defend the claim but the amendment permits a recovery of money damages in excess of the insurance policy limits, sufficient time must be given to the defendant to consult with his or her own personal lawyer about the personal exposure. And the insured's personal lawyer should have enough time to become acquainted with the case.

Ordinarily, the plaintiff is not allowed to increase the ad damnum clause to an amount in excess of the defendant's liability insurance policy limits once the case reaches trial. When the ad damnum exceeds the coverage provided by the defendant's insurance policy, a substantial conflict may develop between the defendant and his or her liability insurance company. The defendant may need the advice and services of a lawyer whom the defendant must retain at his or her own expense. One problem they must address is whether the insurance company should pay the full amount of its policy to settle the case if there is an opportunity to do so, given the possibility of a recovery against the insured defendant for an amount in excess of the insurance policy limits. If there is time for everyone to further evaluate the case and prepare for trial, the plaintiff is usually allowed to increase the ad damnum, assuming he or she is able to convince the court that there is good cause for the increase.

Service of Process

A civil action is commenced in federal district court when the plaintiff files the complaint with the clerk of court (Rule 3). Most state courts have the same rule. On the other hand, there are a few states in which the plaintiff does not have to file the complaint with the clerk of court before serving the summons and complaint on the defendant. In those states the plaintiff's lawyer prepares both the summons and the complaint. The action is commenced when the summons and complaint are served upon the defendant. Determination of the exact time an action is commenced may be critical to maintenance of the lawsuit. For example, a question may arise whether the action was commenced before the statute of limitations ran against the cause of action. Some contracts, especially insurance policies, provide that an action on the contract must be brought within a specified period of time after the occurrence in question. Failure to comply constitutes a breach of a condition, which bars an action on the contract. A single day's delay can and has made the difference.

Due process requires that the procedure for commencing an action effectively notify the defendant that he or she has been sued. The procedure must give the defendant the opportunity to appear in the case and defend. Service of process pursuant to Rule 4 fulfills this requirement. The clerk of court for federal district courts prepares the summons. Then the clerk delivers the summons and complaint to the United States marshal. The marshal must serve the summons and complaint upon the defendant. The court may appoint some person, other than the marshal, to serve the summons and complaint. A person appointed must be at least eighteen years of age (Rule 4(c)(2)(A)). A party to the action is forbidden to serve the summons and complaint. The possibility of violence and fraud is greatly reduced by having a marshal or some other independent person serve the papers.

The summons notifies a defendant that he or she has twenty days after the date of service in which to "appear and defend." The defendant does not have to actually appear in court. All the defendant has to do is appear in the case within the twenty days by serving an answer to the complaint or filing a Rule 12 motion or by obtaining an extension of time in which to do these things. The court may order an extension of the twenty-day period, or the plaintiff may grant an extension. Note that the twenty-day period does not necessarily begin to run on the same day that the action is "commenced."

Personal service is the most sure and usually the simplest method for effectuating service of the summons and complaint. Personal service is made when the process server hands a copy of the summons and complaint to the defendant. If a copy of the summons and complaint are not served upon the defendant within 120 days after the complaint is filed with the clerk of court, the action is subject to dismissal without prejudice.

Personal service of the summons and complaint does not require that the process server actually hand the summons and complaint to the defendant. If the defendant decides to be uncooperative and "turns his or her back" on the process server, the process server may simply leave the summons and complaint in the defendant's presence. There is no need to touch the defendant as if playing a game of tag. The marshal makes a record of the service of process in a document called the "Marshal's Return," which he or she files with the clerk of court before the time for answering expires. If for some reason a person other than a United States marshal is appointed by the court to serve the summons and complaint, he or she must use an affidavit (sworn statement) establishing the fact of service. The Marshal's Return or process server's affidavit of service must show the date, time, manner, and place of service; they must also identify the person upon whom service was made. (Almost without exception, documents filed with the clerk of court in civil litigation are public documents which anyone may examine.)

The law does not require that service of process be made at any particular time of the day; but, service must be made at a reasonable hour considering the circumstances. Service may be in the dead of the night if the defendant ordinarily works nights and sleeps days. There is no prohibition against service on Sundays or legal holidays.

There are several other ways in which the summons and complaint may be served upon the defendant. The methods are simple, fairly inexpensive, and reasonably effective for putting the defendant on notice of the suit. Service of the summons and complaint may be accomplished by leaving them at the defendant's usual place of abode with a person *who resides therein* and who is of suitable age and discretion. The Rule purposely does not require that the papers be left with an adult. Historically, anyone fourteen years of age or older is presumed to meet the age requirements. A younger person may qualify, but if any question should later arise as to whether service was valid, the burden is upon the plaintiff to show that the person with whom the summons and complaint were left was of "suitable age and discretion." Almost any member of the defendant's family or other resident may be a proper person to receive service of process for the defendant.

Suppose the defendant's adult sister is staying at the defendant's home for only a few days. Could the summons and complaint be effectively served upon the defendant by leaving the papers with her? No, she is not a resident of the household.

Some companies are frequently involved in litigation, so it is convenient for them to appoint a particular person or agent to receive service of process for them. Service may be made upon the company by delivering the summons and complaint to the appointed agent. An agent may be appointed by law to receive service of process for certain defendants. Most, if not all, states provide for service of process on the secretary of state as an agent for domestic and foreign corporations. By state statute, the commissioner of highways or secretary of state is appointed to be an agent to receive service of process for nonresident motorists who have had motor vehicle accidents within the state. The commissioner of insurance is appointed by statute to receive service of process on behalf of any insurance company doing business within the state where the insured lives or does business. A copy of the summons and complaint are actually delivered to the official's office. The official stamps the original summons and complaint, thereby acknowledging receipt and admitting service of them.

The summons and complaint may be served upon an adult defendant by mailing a copy of the summons and complaint to the defendant along with two copies of a notice and acknowledgment of service. The defendant may elect to accept service by mail, in this manner, by signing and returning to the sender one copy of the notice and acknowledgment. It is customary for the sender to provide a self-addressed envelope with postage prepaid. The notice informs the defendant to return the acknowledgment within twenty days; otherwise, the service by mail is without effect. The consequence is that the plaintiff will have to use the services of the United States marshal or a process server to effectuate service of the summons and complaint. The cost of service may be taxed to the defendant if the defendant loses the case. When service is made by mail, as described, the date of service is the date of the acknowledgment signed by the defendant.

The notice states that once the defendant acknowledges service, the defendant must appear by serving an answer or motion within twenty days; otherwise, the plaintiff may take a default judgment against the defendant. If service upon a corporation or partnership is made by mail, the officer of the defendant who accepts service must state his or her authority to accept service of process for the corporation or partnership.

The prescribed form of notice and acknowledgment uses language that mandates that the defendant sign and return the acknowledgment. A defendant may not appreciate, from the wording, that the only adverse consequence of not accepting service by mail is that the defendant may have to pay for the cost of having the summons and complaint served by a process server, and that should be well under a hundred dollars.

In some state courts the action is not commenced until the summons and complaint are served upon the defendant. In those states, if the plaintiff chooses to serve the summons and complaint by mail, the statute of limitations is not tolled while the defendant decides whether or not to "acknowledge" service. Therefore, it could happen that the defendant's delay could cause the plaintiff's cause of action to become "time barred." If time is running short and there is a possibility that the statute of limitations could run out, the plaintiff should not attempt service by mail but instead should use personal service. Of course, in federal court, the action is commenced by filing the complaint with the clerk of court, so there is no danger of running into a statute of limitations problem. But remember, if the action is not perfected by service within 120 days after filing the complaint, the action is subject to dismissal.

The law requires the plaintiff to provide the agent with at least one additional copy, which the agent sends to the defendant's last known address or registered address. In addition, the plaintiff may be required to mail a copy of the summons and complaint to the defendant's last known address. Ordinary mail will suffice, unless registered mail is specified by state law. The plaintiff or plaintiff's lawyer must file an *affidavit of compliance*, showing compliance with the mailing requirements. The affidavit is prima facie evidence of compliance and must be filed with the clerk of court. There is nothing preventing an individual from appointing another person such as a lawyer to act as his or her personal agent to receive service of process. Believe it or not, this is a convenience for some entrepreneurs.

If the defendant is a minor, service must be made upon him or her in the manner prescribed by the laws of the state in which the defendant minor resides. Usually, service must be made upon one of the minor's parents or other legal guardian. The plaintiff may cause a guardian to be appointed for the child if he or she doesn't have one. A guardian who is appointed for the sole purpose of the lawsuit is called a "guardian ad litem." Some states authorize service directly upon a minor at least fourteen years of age. A guardian ad litem may be appointed later.

Age is only one type of legal disability that may affect service of process. If a defendant has been adjudged mentally incompetent to handle his or her own legal matters, the plaintiff must serve a copy of the summons and complaint on the guardian. The guardian must act to protect his or her ward's legal interests. Of course, the guardian will not actually conduct the litigation. The guardian's responsibility is to select and hire a lawyer to represent the ward and make decisions that are ordinarily reserved to the party, such as whether or not to settle the claim. Some states require that a guardian be bonded so as to guaranty faithful performance on behalf of the ward.

Service on a corporation may be made by delivering the summons and complaint to a managing agent or office (Rule 4(d)(3)). The corporation cannot restrict the method of service by limiting its officers' authority. But a corporation may appoint a nonofficer, or even a nonemployee, to receive the papers.

Service on the United States government requires at least two steps. The summons and complaint must be served upon the United States district attorney or assistant district attorney for the particular district in which the action is commenced. Also, copies must be sent to the United States attorney general in Washington, D.C., by registered mail or certified mail. Copies must be mailed to all United States offices or agencies affected by the litigation. Again, registered or certified mail must be used. Service is not complete (effective) until all the requirements are met. Nevertheless, the action is effectively *commenced* by filing the complaint with the clerk of court. The local United States district attorney may designate a nonlawyer to accept service at his or her office. When that is done, a letter or notice must be filed with the clerk of court naming the administrative employee who has been so designated. A plaintiff cannot sue the United States government per se but only its agencies as authorized by law. The various statutes creating the agencies designate the manner for service of process and specify the proper person for receiving service within the agency.

When a municipality is a defendant, service can be made upon the chief executive officer or in any other manner established by local law.

The summons and complaint may be served by the United States marshal anywhere within the state of his or her jurisdiction, but not outside the state. If the defendant has left the state to evade service of process or is in the state but is hiding to avoid service, another method of service must be available to the plaintiff. In such cases, service may be made by publishing the summons in a newspaper with substantial circulation in the area. The methods prescribed are intended to give the defendant actual notice, especially if he or she is more or less expecting to be sued. Most state laws require the summons to be published for a period of three weeks. As part of the publication procedure, the complaint must be filed with the clerk of court and be available for inspection. The plaintiff is still required to mail a copy of the summons and complaint to the defendant's last known address. The name of the plaintiff's lawyer, the publisher's affidavit proving publication, and copies of the published notice are included for filing. If the defendant can be found in another state so that a copy of the summons and complaint can be delivered to him personally, that may constitute service by publication and give the court jurisdiction. In divorce actions, where the defendant is not a resident of the state, service of process may be accomplished by publication. As noted elsewhere in this book, federal courts do not handle divorce actions or other domestic relations cases.

On occasion, the subject of litigation is land or a tangible object within the state. In such cases, the local court has jurisdiction over the subject matter, and anyone claiming an interest in the property, even nonresidents, can be compelled to submit to the court's jurisdiction or forfeit their interests in the property. A lawsuit against the property is called an *action in rem*. Service of a summons and complaint must be made on each person known to claim an interest in the subject matter. Furthermore, the "world" must be given notice through publication of a notice of the action. In these cases, no person is designated as a defendant. Nonetheless, anyone who claims an interest in the property must assert his or her claim by filing an answer or the interest will be forfeited.

The defendant has twenty days in which to appear and defend (Rule 4(b)). The defendant may appear in the action, within the meaning of the rules, by serving and filing an answer or motion contesting the sufficiency of the complaint or contesting sufficiency of the service of process (Rule 12).

Once a party is represented by a lawyer, all pleadings, orders, motions, etc. must be served directly upon the lawyer. This is the most convenient arrangement for the parties and the lawyers. Service of the answer, motions, orders, etc. is made by simply mailing the documents to the lawyers at their last known address (Rule 5(h)). Service by mail is complete when the document is deposited at a post office or put in a United States postal mailbox. The date of mailing is the date of service. Whenever a pleading, motion, notice, etc. is served by mail, the addressee is given an extra three days in which to respond, that is, three extra days from the date of mailing (Rule 6(e)).

On occasion it is desirable, even necessary, to serve motions, interrogatories, demand for documents, orders, and other documents by personal service upon the opposing lawyer. Personal service is complete when the papers are delivered to the lawyer. If the lawyer cannot be found, personal service can, nevertheless, be made upon the lawyer by handing the papers to the lawyer's clerk or secretary or a person who is in charge of the lawyer's office. Otherwise, the papers may simply be left in a conspicuous place at the lawyer's office during regular business hours. Personal service may be accomplished by leaving the papers at the lawyer's home with a resident, therein, who is of suitable age and discretion (Rule 5(b)). The person to whom the papers are given must be old enough to realize the importance of the matter and not be inclined to forget to bring the papers to the lawyer's attention. Personal service on the lawyer may be ordered by the court whenever time is critical and short. The process server must make an affidavit describing the manner of service and stating the time and place of service.

If neither the opposing party nor his or her lawyer can be found so that service can be made by mail or personally, service may be made by leaving the documents with the clerk of court. An affidavit must be prepared stating that the party and his or her lawyer could not be found. The affidavit should contain a brief description of the efforts made to locate them (Rule 5(b)). When service is by mail, the lawyer making service or his or her secretary must make an affidavit of service by mail. The affidavit does not have to include the title of the case. For example:

AFFIDAVIT OF SERVICE BY MAIL

STATE OF _____

COUNTY OF _____

_____, being first duly sworn, deposes and says:
That on the _____ day of _____, 19___, she served the attached
_____, upon _____, the attorney representing the _____ , by depositing a true and correct copy thereof in the United States mail in the city of _____, state of _____ , with postage prepaid, in an envelope directed and addressed to said attorney at _____.

_____.

                       /s/ _____

Subscribed and sworn to
before me this _____
day of _____, 1990.

The original copy of the affidavit must be attached to the original document, which is then filed with the court. It is highly desirable, if not essential, to attach a copy of the affidavit of mailing to the file copy for future reference. The preferred method of service depends upon the amount of time available and expense.

Once the complaint has been served upon the defendant, a time schedule automatically goes into effect to insure a steady progression of the case toward trial and ultimate disposition. The summons informs the defendant that he or she has twenty days in which to answer the complaint. If the defendant does not obtain an extension of time from the plaintiff or by order of the court and fails to serve an answer within the twenty days, the defendant is in default. This means that judgment may be taken against him or her as demanded in the complaint. The rules do not specifically provide for stipulation by the parties extending the period of time for answering the complaint; regardless of the Rule's silence, the practice is very common. It is well recognized that the twenty-day period authorized by the Rules is a relatively short period of time. Consequently, courts are quite willing to grant reasonable extensions of time. The plaintiff's lawyer knows that the defendant can probably obtain an extension from the court and so actually retains a little more control over the situation by accommodating the defendant by stipulating to an extension of time.

There are many circumstances which justify granting the defendant additional time in which to answer the complaint. For example, once a defendant's lawyer receives a complaint, he or she may need a few extra days to meet with the defendant, digest the factual information, and analyze the case so that the answer will adequately state the issues. An informal extension of time for answering helps everyone.

If the defendant has liability insurance, he or she should deliver the complaint to the insurance agent promptly. Unfortunately, sometimes defendants delay contacting their agents. The insurance company may have difficulty determining whether the claim is covered by the insurance policy and whether to accept defense of the case. The insurer may need extra time in which to make that corporate decision. More often than not, the plaintiff's lawyer informally agrees to grant additional time for answering. Both sides should try to avoid any unnecessary expenditure of time and money on procedural motions. An attitude of goodwill and cooperation benefits all parties and the court. Actually, it is amazing to many laypersons just how much and how often "adverse" lawyers accommodate each other.

Demand for Jury Trial

If the plaintiff wants a jury trial, he or she may demand it by "endorsing" the demand on the complaint (see example, page 91, supra). This simply means that the plaintiff may state on the complaint, in some conspicuous place, that "plaintiff demands trial by jury." If the plaintiff fails to make the demand in the complaint, he or she may still make the demand anytime within ten days after service of the last pleading directed to the issues to be tried. The defendant may make a demand for a jury trial during the same ten-day period. For example, the plaintiff's demand may be made ten days after the defendant serves the answer. The demand may be made in a separate document, but the time requirements must be met. Of course, if the defendant demands a jury trial in his or her answer, there is no need for the plaintiff to make a separate or additional demand. A third-party defendant may demand a jury trial by endorsing the demand on his or her third-party answer or in a separate document served within ten days after the third-party answer was served. Failure to demand a jury trial in the manner prescribed by Rule 38(b) results in a waiver of the right to a jury trial, and all the issues shall be tried to a judge without a jury (Rule 38(b)).

State Court Note of Issue

In federal court, a case is automatically placed on the trial calendar when the summons and complaint are filed. But in many courts, a case is not put on the trial calendar until one of the parties serves and files a note of issue. The note of issue informs the clerk of court that the case is ready for trial; at least the party who files is ready. A note of issue identifies all of the parties and their respective lawyers, so the clerk is able to send notices to the lawyers. The party who serves and files the note of issue may demand "trial by jury" or "trial by court." Trial by court precludes having a jury.

If the first party to serve a note of issue demands a jury trial, there is no need for any other party to file a note of issue. A demand for a jury trial takes priority over the opposing party's preference for a trial by judge without a jury. If the first note of issue demands "trial by court," any other party who wants a jury trial must serve a *counternote of issue*, usually within ten days after the first note of issue, specifically demanding "trial by jury."

If the state court has terms of court, the state rules of procedure usually require service of the note of issue at least thirty days before the opening of the term, or the case will have to wait until the next term. This is not a consideration in those courts that have a continuous general term, that is, where jury cases are tried year round. If a party fails to demand a jury trial in the proper manner, it is still possible to move the court for an order setting the case for trial by jury. However, the right to a jury trial is lost. The motion is addressed to the court's discretion. The adverse parties may oppose the motion. The trial court may deny a motion for a jury trial even if the parties reach an agreement that they want the case to be tried by a jury. This illustration points up the importance of making a seasonable demand for a trial by jury.

NOTE OF ISSUE

(Title of Cause)

To Defendant Sally Smith and _____, her attorney,

Please take notice that the above entitled action will be placed upon the trial calendar for the next general term of court for trial by ___Jury___ at the district courthouse in and for said county in the city of _____ , (state) beginning on the _____ day of _____ , 19___

_____
Attorney for Plaintiff

There are times when a case simply cannot be ready for trial at the time scheduled. Personal injury actions involving serious injuries or the probability of permanent disability usually cannot be evaluated until twelve to eighteen months after the injury was sustained. It may take that long before the attending physician can make a reasonably accurate prognosis. A trial at an earlier date might result in an unjust verdict for either side because of the difficulty in evaluating the medical evidence. The defendant may not want to obtain a Rule 35 independent medical examination until the plaintiff's injuries have stabilized and a prognosis can be made. If a delay ("continuance") of the trial is necessary, the parties may stipulate to a continuance or show the court good cause why it should order a continuance. Time may be a natural healer, but the passage of time can only detract from a good cause of action or a good defense.

Motions

Parties to an action may apply to the court for assistance or guidance concerning almost any aspect of the case. The application for an order is called a motion. Rule 7(b) states:

1. An application to the court for an order shall be by motion which, unless made during a hearing or trial, shall be made in writing, shall state with particularity the grounds therefor, and shall set forth the relief or order sought. The requirement of writing is fulfilled if the motion is stated in written notice of the hearing of the motion.

2. The rules applicable to captions and other matters of form of pleadings apply to all motions and other papers provided for by these rules.

3. All motions shall be signed in accordance with Rule 11.

Motions made during the course of a trial are usually made orally and "on the record." Motions made before or after the trial are usually made in writing. A written motion must be served at least five days before the motion is to be heard (Rule 6(d)).

A **notice of motion** must be served with the motion. The notice informs the nonmoving party or parties when and where the motion will be heard. A motion may be scheduled as provided by the local court's rules or by special arrangements made directly with the judge or judge's clerk.

A written motion ordinarily has several parts, although the parts may not be separated into numbered paragraphs as is customary with pleadings. The first part of the motion is the application, which tells the court what assistance and what order the moving party wants. The second part of the motion should identify the authority by which the motion is made, such as one of the Rules of Civil Procedure. The third part of a motion should state the grounds for the motion. The grounds are the underlying factors that cause the moving party to need the court's assistance or direction and the court's authority to provide that assistance. Fourth, the motion should specify any documents, records, affidavits, exhibits, etc. upon which the moving party is relying to support the motion.

The following is an example of the structure of a properly drawn motion.

MOTION

Pursuant to Rule 12 of the Federal Rules of Civil Procedure, defendant hereby moves the court for an order dismissing plaintiff's complaint on the grounds that the complaint fails to state a claim upon which relief can be granted. The complaint fails to allege the claim of fraud with particularity as required by Rule 9(b).

This motion is based upon the allegations of plaintiff's complaint, which is on file with the court, the allegations and denials set forth in defendant's answer, which is on file with the court, a copy of the parties' contract upon which plaintiff's claim is based, and the affidavit of _____ , which is attached hereto.

Rule 12

Any document that the moving party relies upon, to support the motion, must be served with the motion, unless previously served and filed. If previously served and filed, it is sufficient to merely identify the documents in the motion. If the nonmoving party wants to bring additional documents to the court's attention to oppose the motion, the additional documents must be served and filed no later than one day before the motion is heard (Rule 6(d)).

Since a motion is the means by which a party asks the court for an order or guidance or permission to do something, there really is no limit to the kinds of motions which can be made. Nevertheless, there are a few motions which deserve special mention and consideration.

Motion for Judgment on the Pleadings—Rule 12(c)

If a complaint, answer, or other pleading is insufficient to state a claim or defense, the opposing party may move the court to strike the pleading. For example, an answer that merely alleges that the parties' contract is unfair does not allege a defense. The plaintiff could move the court to strike the answer. If the answer is stricken as insufficient, the defendant would be left in default.

Motion for More Definite Statement

The rules for pleading allow the pleadings to be quite general. Sometimes the pleadings are too general, and that leads to ambiguities and uncertainties. The parties have a right to know what is being claimed against them. One way of forcing the opponent to be specific and descriptive is to move the court for an order compelling a more definite statement. For example, a complaint that attempts to allege a cause of action for defamation and that merely alleges that the defendant made various false statements about the plaintiff over a specified period of time is not, technically, adequate. The time and place of each defamatory publication should be stated in the complaint (Rule 9(f)). The defendant could properly move the court for an order directing the plaintiff to specify each defamatory statement: what was said, when it was said, where it was said, and to whom the defamatory statement was communicated. Each publication is a separate tort. The court should order a more definite statement of the tort if asked to do so. The court should not leave the defendant to obtain the information in answers to interrogatories, because the missing information is fundamental to the cause of action.

Motion to Strike—Rule 12(f)

It does not happen very often, but on occasion, a lawyer or party pro se may use a pleading to make a derogatory, impertinent, or scandalous remark about the opposing party. If a pleading contains such allegations, they are subject to being stricken upon motion. The mere fact that such allegations are subject to being stricken helps to keep pleadings from being abused in that manner.

Ex Parte Motions

Making a motion is part of the adversary process. Consequently, most motions must be served upon all other parties in the case. The few motions which may be made to a court without notice to other parties are called **ex parte motions.** The most common ex parte motion is a motion to obtain an extension of time in which to comply with a court rule or court order. If the time allowed has *not* already expired, a motion may be made ex parte to secure additional time. The motion must be in writing and conform generally with the four-part format discussed previously. The grounds for an ex parte motion to extend the time for complying with a rule or court order include excuse and justification for being unable to comply, an expectation of compliance within a reasonable period of time, and the absence of prejudice to the opposing party.

The following ex parte motion is illustrative.

EX PARTE MOTION

Pursuant to Rule 6(b), plaintiff hereby moves the court for an order extending the time in which plaintiff may answer defendant's interrogatories which were served upon plaintiff on (date). The grounds for this motion are that plaintiff has been out of the country on business from _____ to _____ and has not been able to gather the evidence requested by defendant's interrogatories. Plaintiff believes that an additional ten days in which to answer the interrogatories will provide sufficient time to plaintiff to prepare the necessary answers. The case is currently one year away from trial. Therefore, defendant will not be prejudiced by a ten-day extension.

This motion is supported by plaintiff's affidavit, which is attached hereto explaining that plaintiff was unable to attend to the preparation of answers to interrogatories while on his business trip.

A proposed order extending the period of time for answering is attached hereto.

(date)   _____
                                                    Attorney for Plaintiff

---

A copy of the ex parte motion could be sent to the opposing party as a courtesy.

An ex parte motion is addressed to the judge's sound discretion. The motion may be granted subject to terms and conditions which the judge believes are appropriate.

Paralegals may assist in the preparation of motions and supporting documentation. Rule 11 requires that a lawyer read, approve, and sign every motion, but that does not mean that a lawyer has to prepare the motion. There must be a good basis for a motion. A motion must not be made for an improper, ulterior purpose.

Subpoenas

The Federal Rules of Civil Procedure provide for issuance of subpoenas in civil actions to compel any witness or party to appear at a specified time and place to testify. "Subpoena" means that the command to appear is subject to the penalties provided by law. A subpoena may be used to compel deposition testimony or testimony at trial. A subpoena may be used to compel a witness to produce records, books, papers, documents, or tangible things, as specified in the subpoena, to be used at the trial or deposition (Rules 45(b) and 45(d)(1)). A subpoena must state the time and place for the witness to appear and testify.

The clerk of court issues the subpoena upon request of a party. If the subpoena is to be used to compel a witness or party to appear for a deposition, it is necessary to provide the clerk of court with a copy of the notice of taking deposition along with proof of service of the notice (Rule 45(d)(1)). It usually is not necessary to subpoena a party, because parties are already under the jurisdiction and authority of the court.

The United States marshal or any person eighteen years of age or older and who is not a party may serve a subpoena. A subpoena is served by delivering a copy of the subpoena to the person who must be named in the subpoena. The witness must be paid one day's witness fee and mileage. The amount is established by statute and changes from time to time. A subpoena may be served anywhere within the territorial jurisdiction of the court. In addition, a subpoena may be served upon a witness outside the judicial district to testify at trial, provided that the witness is not required to travel more than one hundred miles from the place where he or she resides, works, or was actually served with the subpoena (Rule 45(e)). A subpoena that is used for the purpose of compelling a witness to give deposition testimony cannot be served outside the jurisdictional limits of the court which issues the subpoena. Furthermore, a witness cannot be compelled to travel more than one hundred miles from his or her home, place of employment, or where he or she was actually served with the subpoena.

A couple of examples should help to illustrate the application and limitations of Rule 45. Suppose that the plaintiff needs to have witness Smith testify *at trial* in New York City, but Smith resides in Newark, New Jersey. Since Newark is less than one hundred miles from the federal district court in New York City, the New York federal court could issue a subpoena to be served in Newark. However, the New York federal court could not issue a subpoena to require Smith to travel from Newark to New York City for a deposition. The party who wants to depose Smith would have to travel to New Jersey to take the deposition, and if a subpoena were necessary, the party would have to obtain the subpoena from the Federal District Court for the state of New Jersey.

A subpoena could be used to require a witness to travel from Rochester, New York, to New York City to testify at a trial. However, a witness could not be compelled to travel that distance for a deposition, even though the Federal District Court for the District of New York has jurisdiction covering the entire state of New York. Depositions are supposed to be taken at a place that is reasonably convenient for the witness, not the litigants. But if the resident of Rochester is found in New York City while on a shopping trip and served with a subpoena to appear in New York City for a deposition, the service would be valid and effective.

7 Pleadings

A civil action is commenced by filing a complaint with the clerk of district court. The complaint must describe the plaintiff's claim by stating a cause of action against the defendant. The defendant is allowed twenty days in which to serve an answer to the complaint. The defendant's answer must admit the allegations of the complaint that are true, deny the rest, and allege all the affirmative defenses he or she has. Thus, the complaint and answer establish the legal issues between the plaintiff and defendant. The legal issues determine what facts are relevant to the case. Civil litigation procedures center upon the use of pleadings. Each party's lawyer prepares the necessary pleadings to set forth the client's allegations and responses. By filing or serving a pleading, a party appears in the case. ("Appears" as used in civil litigation means that a person comes into the case as a party or comes before the court as a litigant. When a party appears in a case, he or she submits to the court's jurisdiction unless the party specifically challenges jurisdiction at the outset.) Paralegals may prepare pleadings, but the lawyer handling the case must review and approve the pleading and certify that it is proper by signing it (Rule 11).

Complaint

The complaint has several important functions. Its caption identifies the court chosen by the plaintiff's lawyer. The clerk of court assigns to the case a file number, which is part of the caption. The complaint's title identifies the intended plaintiff(s) and defendant(s). However, a person does not become a defendant until he or she is actually served with a summons and copy of the complaint. Under certain circumstances, service may be by publication (Rule 4(e)). The complaint must contain allegations showing that the named court has jurisdiction over the subject matter and over the named defendant. The plaintiff automatically submits to the court's jurisdiction by filing the lawsuit.

A lawyer must have the substantive law in mind as he or she draws a complaint, making sure that the allegations establish a cause of action. Not every wrong or controversy gives rise to a claim that can be litigated. A man may say his neighbor is "stupid" or a "jerk." As unflattering as these remarks are, they do not give rise to a cause of action for defamation. A salesman may spend many hours helping a customer with the selection of a house, car, or appliance and then lose the sale to another salesman who spent only a few minutes with the customer. The first salesman may feel that he has been wronged and his time and help abused, but he does not have a cause of action for breach of contract. A complaint must state a cause of action, that is, a claim upon which a court can grant relief; otherwise, it is subject to being stricken on motion (Rule 12(b)).

Before the Federal Rules of Civil Procedure were adopted, a complaint had to set forth, in detail, all the facts constituting the plaintiff's cause of action. For example, in a trespass action, the plaintiff had to set forth in detail all the facts that proved he or she occupied the particular parcel of land as owner or lessee; that the defendant entered upon the land on a particular date in a particular manner; that the entry was without the plaintiff's consent; that the defendant lacked authority to enter the land at the specified time and place; and that the entry resulted in specified damage to the land. From these allegations, the defendant's lawyer knew that the plaintiff was claiming the defendant had committed a trespass. Those were the facts that the plaintiff would have to prove at trial. The plaintiff could not attempt to prove different or additional facts. Also, the defendant had no right to take the plaintiff's deposition. The defendant's only source of information about the plaintiff's claim came from the complaint. If the complaint failed to state sufficient facts to constitute a cause of action, it was subject to dismissal on motion by the defendant. The motion was called a demurrer.

The defendant had only one means of discovery available. (Discovery refers to any procedure authorized by law that enables one party to obtain information from another party about the claims and defenses and facts in the case.) This means of discovery was to ask for a **bill of particulars,** which is a request for a more detailed statement of the plaintiff's claim. A bill of particulars was not available as a matter of right. Each party secured information and evidence concerning the claims and defenses by conducting his or her own investigation. There was no right to impose upon the other party to provide information in addition to the complaint or answer.

Though still central and fundamental to civil litigation procedures, pleadings have lost the informative function that they once had. Now the complaint may omit many of the factual details of the alleged wrong, but the complaint still must specify the legal wrong, that is, the cause of action. The complaint merely puts the defendant on notice of the cause of action claimed and specifies the transaction or occurrence to which the cause of action relates by identifying its time and place and particulars of the transaction or occurrence (Rule 9(f)).

The complaint must identify the nature and extent of the loss that the plaintiff claims the defendant caused. The complaint ordinarily concludes by specifying the remedy and relief that the plaintiff wants the court to award. When two or more plaintiffs have claims against a defendant arising out of the same transaction or occurrence, they may join as coplaintiffs in a single action (Rule 20).

The various allegations constituting the cause of action are separately stated in short paragraphs, usually arranged in chronological order. Each paragraph should be limited to a single set of circumstances or a single idea (Rule 8(a)). If more than one transaction or occurrence is involved, each should be set forth in a separate count. If a document such as a contract or promissory note is the subject of the claim, a copy of the document may be attached to the complaint. The complaint gives a fairly good picture of the claims against the defendant so that he or she is able to admit the legal obligation or begin preparation of defenses against the claims. The complaint, then, establishes the scope of the plaintiff's claims. Items of special damages must be specifically stated (Rule 9(g)). Special damages are the "out-of-pocket" expenses that the plaintiff has incurred because of the defendant's wrongful conduct. In a personal injury action, the plaintiff's medical expenses, loss of past income, and property damage are items of special damages and must be listed. A monetary value need not be given for each item—though that is frequently done. In a breach of contract action, the amount of the lost profits and consequential expenses should be stated. This information is really necessary for the defendant to know at the outset. The other pertinent facts can be obtained by the defendant through discovery procedures.

If the complaint is vague or ambiguous so that the defendant's lawyer feels uncertain about the nature or scope of the claim being made, he or she may move the court for an order compelling the plaintiff to state the allegations with more particularity, more specifically, or more definitely (Rule 12(e)).

The complaint must be filed for the purpose of making a claim and not for some ulterior or collateral purpose. All pleadings filed with the court are public records. Obviously, they are subject to engendering publicity—publicity that could be very harmful. Therefore, a pleading must be signed by a lawyer or by the party who acts as his or her own lawyer. The signature is a certification that the person who signs has read the pleading; that he or she believes there are good grounds to support the allegations in the pleading; and that the pleading has not been filed for the purpose of delaying a claim or for some other collateral purpose. (Note that a lawyer does not have to draft the complaint. Paralegals may be asked to prepare pleadings.) Any allegation that is scandalous, impertinent, or immaterial to the cause of action may be stricken by order of the court. Parties must not use a pleading as a vehicle with which to malign another party (Rules 11 and 12(f)). Any allegation that is redundant, incompetent, or insufficient to state a claim or defense is subject to being stricken by court order (Rule 12(f)).

The date the complaint is filed establishes the date on which the action is commenced. The clerk prepares a summons, which is attached to the complaint, and directs a United States marshal to serve the summons and complaint upon the named defendant(s). The plaintiff's lawyer must advise the clerk or marshal of the defendant's last known addresses. It is helpful to give to the marshal the defendant's employment address, too. The summons is not a pleading.

The rules of civil procedure for some state courts provide that the plaintiff's lawyer shall prepare and sign the summons. The lawyer also arranges for service of the summons and complaint on the defendants before filing the summons and complaint with the court. In those states, the cause of action is commenced either (1) when the summons and complaint are delivered to the proper public officer, such as a sheriff, for service or (2) when the summons and complaint are actually served upon the defendant. If the latter procedure is followed, the action may be commenced against multiple defendants on different days.

The summons directs each defendant to serve an answer to the complaint within twenty days after the date on which the summons and complaint were served. The twenty-day period begins to run on the next day after service. If the summons and complaint were served on Tuesday, the twenty-day period begins to run on Wednesday. The answer may be prepared by the defendant, his or her lawyer, or someone on the lawyer's staff. However, it must be signed by the defendant or the lawyer—no one else. The answer uses the same title as the complaint, even if the defendant's name is misspelled or there is some other technical problem with the title. Later on, the title may be amended by court order. The correct spelling of the parties' names may be set forth as a separate allegation in the answer, but the original title as set forth in the complaint is used until it is amended by court order. If there are two or more plaintiffs or two or more defendants, the answer and all subsequent pleadings may omit all names except the name of the first plaintiff and the name of the first defendant. The abbreviation "et al." is used to indicate that there are additional parties who have not been specifically named, but the summons and complaint must list all the parties.

The clerk of court assigns a file number to the action when the complaint is filed. The number may be similar to: "89 Civ. 532." The "89" means that the case was filed during the year 1989. "Civ." means it is a civil action. The last number indicates its chronology. All subsequent pleadings, motions, orders, affidavits, and depositions must use that file number.

Amended Complaint

The plaintiff may amend his or her complaint as a matter of right, and without leave of the court, if done within twenty days after service of the original complaint or before the defendant serves his or her answer (Rule 15(a)). Otherwise, the plaintiff must secure leave of the court to serve and file an amended complaint. Of course, the defendant may agree (stipulate) to accept service of an amended complaint. Usually this is done by admitting service on the original copy of the amended complaint. For example:

Due and proper service of the amended complaint is admitted this _____day of _____, 1989.

_____

Attorney for Defendant

An amended pleading is usually identified as "amended."

There are a number of reasons why a party might agree to accept an amended pleading without forcing the opponent to make a motion to the court. The amendment may simply correct a technical defect or clerical error that does not affect the parties' substantive rights. Or, the amendment may contain corrections or allegations that the adverse party considers beneficial or, at least, true. Generally, courts are very liberal in permitting pleadings to be amended unless the opposing party is able to show actual prejudice resulting from a late amendment (Rule 15). With that fact in mind, lawyers know that opposition to a proposed amendment would probably be a waste of time and money. Ordinarily, the party seeking to amend volunteers to permit his or her opponent to conduct whatever additional discovery procedures are necessary to prepare on the new issues raised by the amendment.

The defendant has at least ten days in which to answer an amended complaint. But if the amended complaint was served within just a few days after the original complaint was served, the defendant must answer within the same period of time as established by service of the original complaint. In other words, the defendant's answer to the amended complaint is due at the same time as it would be to the original complaint, or within ten days after service of the amended complaint, whichever time period is longer.

Amendments relate back to the date of the original pleading. For example, suppose that the plaintiff brings an action to recover compensation for damage to real estate, that the original complaint alleged only a cause of action in negligence, and after the suit was started the statute of limitations ran on all tort claims. If the plaintiff is allowed to amend the complaint to allege a cause of action in trespass too, the amendment is deemed to relate back to the date on which the action was originally commenced. By amending the original complaint the plaintiff has successfully avoided having the statute of limitations bar the claim.

If, for some cogent reason, a party needs additional time to prepare and serve any pleading and the opposition will not agree to an extension of time, the party may apply to the court for an order granting an extension. Such an application (motion) may be made with or without notice to the opposing party if it is made before the prescribed time period expires. The moving party must show the court that he or she has good reason (grounds) for making the request. The reasons ordinarily are set forth in an affidavit, which must be filed with the motion.

If the time allowed by the rules has already expired, the party seeking an extension to correct a default must make a motion to the court with notice duly served upon the opposing lawyer. He or she must not only show the court good cause for extending the period of time but must also show that the failure to act was the result of a justified mistake or excusable neglect. Just what circumstances may constitute excusable neglect is a matter left to the discretion of the court. The rules do not attempt to detail circumstances that provide valid excuses. Judges consider not only a party's explanation or excuse but also the possibility of prejudice to the opposing party. A court may grant a motion extending the period of time, thereby avoiding a default, but the grant of additional time may be made subject to a payment of costs incurred by the opposing party as a consequence of the delay. The costs that may be awarded may include reasonable attorney fees. A few time periods cannot be extended (Rule 6(b)).

Supplemental Complaint

The plaintiff has a right to serve and file a supplemental complaint to state a cause of action against the defendant where a new cause of action has accrued in favor of the plaintiff since the original complaint was served. The supplemental complaint uses the same title and court number, assuming the plaintiff wants to have the new action heard with the first action.

Answer

The defendant defends against the allegations made in the complaint by serving and filing an answer to the complaint. The defendant must serve the answer twenty days after service of the complaint. If more time is required, the defendant may request that the plaintiff extend the time in which to answer. Customarily, the defendant's lawyer simply telephones the plaintiff's lawyer and requests an additional few days in which to serve the answer. If an informal extension of time for answering is obtained, it should be confirmed by letter stating the date on which the answer is due. A formal stipulation is not essential but certainly could be used. If the plaintiff will not or cannot voluntarily accommodate the defendant, the defendant may move the court for an order extending the time for answering (Rule 6(b)).

The defendant determines the date the answer is due by counting twenty days beginning with the next day after the summons and complaint were served. All of the time periods prescribed by the rules exclude the day of the act or event. So it makes no difference to the defendant whether he or she was served at 10:00 A.M. or 8:00 P.M.; the twenty-day period begins to run the next day. The answer is due on the twentieth day, not after twenty days. If the twentieth day falls on a Saturday, Sunday, or legal holiday, the time period is automatically extended to the next day that is not a Saturday, Sunday, or legal holiday.

The defendant's failure to answer the complaint within the time allowed by law or allowed by stipulation permits the plaintiff to secure a judgment by default (Rule 4(b)). On the other hand, the defendant may appear in the case by serving a motion challenging jurisdiction, by moving the court for an order striking the complaint, by moving for judgment on the pleadings, or by moving for an order compelling a more definite statement of the allegations in the complaint (Rule 12(a)). There is no need to serve an answer while a Rule 12 motion is pending. After the court rules on the motion, an answer is due within ten days of the ruling—unless the court dismisses the complaint or sets a different time for answering (Rule 12(a)).

The defendant's answer must admit the truth of those allegations in the complaint that are known to be true. Formal admissions in the answer establish conclusively that the specified facts and allegations are not in controversy; that is, they are not at issue and the plaintiff will not have to prove the admitted facts. The jury will be informed about the admissions. Obviously, it is to the plaintiff's advantage to draft the complaint in such a way as to encourage the defendant to admit as many facts as possible. The answer must specifically deny the allegations that are not true. Any allegation in the complaint that is not denied is presumed to be admitted (Rule 8(d)).

Consequently, an answer usually begins with a general denial such as: "Defendant denies each and every allegation, statement, matter, and thing in the complaint, except as hereinafter expressly admitted or alleged." If the defendant does not have sufficient knowledge upon which to form a belief concerning an allegation in the complaint, he or she may so state. The statement has the effect of a denial. A general denial, standing alone, is insufficient and contrary to the spirit of the Rules of Civil Procedure, unless the defendant disputes that he or she was even involved in the transaction or occurrence in question. The language typically used is: "Alleges that defendant does not have sufficient knowledge or information upon which to form a belief concerning plaintiff's claims of injuries and damages and, therefore, puts plaintiff to his strict proof of same."

The answer uses numbered paragraphs, just like the complaint, to separate each set of circumstances and each affirmative defense. It is common practice to use one paragraph to set forth admissions. For example:

> **2.** Admits the allegations of paragraphs 1, 2, and 3 of the complaint and further admits that the motor vehicle accident occurred about the time and place specified in the complaint.

An admission that the accident occurred is not an admission of negligence or legal responsibility. Nevertheless, some lawyers seem constrained to add a statement such as, "Specifically denies that the defendant was negligent," after admitting the occurrence. Again, the plaintiff's lawyer should draft the complaint in a manner that enables the defendant to admit full paragraphs. But if the defendant's lawyer determines that he or she is able to admit only a portion of a paragraph, the admission should be made, clearly indicating the scope of the admission.

The admissions and denials in the answer do not have to be consistent with one another. For example, the answer may deny that the plaintiff and the defendant entered into a contract so that the plaintiff cannot maintain an action on the contract for breach of contract. In addition, the answer may allege that the plaintiff's claim is barred by affirmative defenses such as accord and satisfaction, release, fraud, or waiver, which are defenses that assume the contract was made (Rule 8(e)). See Rules Appendix Forms 20 and 21 for examples of answers.

The answer must allege all the affirmative defenses that the defendant has (Rule 8(c)). Any affirmative defense not asserted in the answer is waived. Any affirmative defense is a fact or set of circumstances which defeats the plaintiff's claim even though the plaintiff is able to prove his or her cause of action. A partial list of affirmative defenses appears in Rule 8(c). The defendant has the burden of proving his or her affirmative defenses. The plaintiff is not obligated to serve and file a responsive pleading to the answer for the purpose of admitting or denying the defendant's affirmative defenses. The affirmative defenses are presumed to be denied. Each affirmative defense should be set forth in a separate, numbered paragraph for convenience of the parties and court. (See Rules Appendix Form No. 20.)

An answer concludes with a "Wherefore" clause in which the defendant states his or her request for relief. The following is a typical concluding paragraph in an answer:

> Wherefore, defendant prays that plaintiff take nothing by reason of his alleged cause of action, and that defendant have judgment for his costs and disbursements herein.

The defendant must obtain permission from the courts to amend the answer to allege any additional defense unless the plaintiff stipulates to an amendment (Rule 15(a)). However, the answer may be amended, as a matter of right, without a court order if the amended answer is served within twenty days after the original answer was served (Rule 15(a)).

Most courts liberally permit amendments to pleadings, additional pleadings, and supplemental pleadings in the absence of prejudice to the party to be served. A party is prejudiced only if the delay adversely affects his or her ability to present a claim or defense on the merits (Rule 15(b)). The merits of the case refers to the substance of the claim, that is, the underlying facts. A determination on the merits means that the case is not decided on the basis of a procedural technicality.

Counterclaim

If a defendant has a claim against the plaintiff that he or she wants to pursue, the defendant may assert the claim in a counterclaim, which must be served with defendant's answer. The claim may arise out of the same transaction or occurrence as the plaintiff's claim. In that event, the counterclaim is *compulsory*, which means that the counterclaim must be asserted with the defendant's answer or it is waived (Rule 13(a)). If the claim arises out of another transaction or occurrence, the defendant may elect whether or not to pursue it as a counterclaim. The counterclaim is considered to be *permissive* (Rule 13(b)).

The counterclaim is, in effect, the defendant's complaint against the plaintiff. The requirements applicable to preparation of complaints apply to counterclaims. Many of the essential allegations are already set forth in the complaint and answer. Those allegations may be incorporated into the counterclaim by reference. It is quite common for a counterclaim to contain a paragraph similar to the following:

> Defendant hereby incorporates the allegations of paragraph 1 of the complaint and all of the allegations of defendant's answer as though fully set forth herein.

Of course, the counterclaim must concern a matter over which the court has jurisdiction. But the mere fact that the relief sought is more than the amount claimed in the complaint or different in kind is not a basis for the plaintiff to avoid the counterclaim in federal court (Rule 13(c)). These factors may affect jurisdiction in state courts, which have limited jurisdiction.

Obviously, it would be unfair to require the defendant to assert a cause of action in a counterclaim if it is already the subject of a pending suit, whether in the same court or another court; therefore, it is not required (Rule 13(a)). For example, suppose that four motorists were involved in a single accident consisting of multiple "rear-end collisions," and motorist A sued motorist B for damages, and motorist C sued motorist A in a separate action. If motorist A decided to make a claim against motorist C, A could join C in the first action as a direct defendant or counterclaim in the action brought by C. If the cases were all in the same court, they probably would be consolidated for trial anyway (Rule 42). But if the two cases were in different courts, motorist A could have some difficulty deciding which procedure to follow.

A counterclaim based upon a cause of action that accrues after the answer was served may be made through a supplemental counterclaim (Rule 13(e)). Supplemental pleadings are permitted only by order of the court upon a showing that the cause of action accrued after service of the original pleading (Rule 15(d)). The court order allowing the supplemental pleading should specify whether or not a responsive pleading is necessary, that is, an answer, answer to cross-claim, or reply to counterclaim.

If a counterclaim requires the presence of a third person who is not subject to the court's jurisdiction, the counterclaim need not be asserted; it is not then compulsory. For example, a plaintiff sues a defendant for breach of contract. The defendant claims that the plaintiff and the plaintiff's partner caused the defendant to be defrauded in the same transaction and that the partner is not subject to this court's jurisdiction. The defendant may assert his or her claim for fraud against both persons in another action in a court that does have jurisdiction over both persons.

The form of a counterclaim is similar to a complaint. If the counterclaim is added to the answer, the combined documents are usually identified as "Answer and Counterclaim." The counterclaim may be separately stated but, nevertheless, served with the answer. If the defendant inadvertently fails to serve a counterclaim with the answer, he or she may move the court for an order allowing the counterclaim. The grounds for the motion include oversight, inadvertence, and excusable neglect (Rule 13(f)). A defendant must obtain permission to serve a counterclaim if not served with the answer since failure to assert the counterclaim in a timely manner may cause a delay in the normal progression of the case toward trial. Since it probably raises new issues, the parties may need additional time to investigate and conduct additional discovery procedures. Generally, the courts allow late pleadings and/ or amendments to pleadings so as to avoid prejudicing a meritorious claim or defense. But courts often place a burden on the delinquent party to expedite the necessary discovery procedures and all other trial preparation. Costs and sanctions may be imposed as a condition precedent to allowing a late counterclaim. If the court refuses to allow the late counterclaim, the defendant is precluded from asserting the claim at a later date if the proposed counterclaim arose out of the same occurrence or transaction as the plaintiff's claim (Rule 13(a)). Some lawyers are of the opinion that a counterclaim may be served anytime within twenty days of service of the answer because the answer may be amended without a court order during the first twenty days (Rule 15(a)).

Most courts liberally permit amendments to pleadings, additional pleadings, and supplemental pleadings in the absence of prejudice to the party to be served. A party is prejudiced only if the delay adversely affects his or her ability to present a claim or defense on the merits (Rule 15(b)).

A counterclaim has obvious application in a case where the defendant in an automobile accident case sues for his or her own injury and/or property damage—claiming the plaintiff is liable. A counterclaim may also be used by the defendant to make a claim against one plaintiff for contribution to the claim of another plaintiff. For example, suppose the two plaintiffs are husband and wife. They sustained injuries when their automobile was struck by the defendant's truck. If the plaintiff husband was driving and he was partially at fault, the defendant could counterclaim against the plaintiff husband for contribution to the wife's claim. (The right to contribution in this example assumes that the lawsuit is brought in a state that does not recognize interspousal immunity.)

As a general rule, the courts favor consolidating claims to be determined in a single trial. Consolidation usually leads to a speedier, more economical determination by avoiding duplicated effort, but if trial of the counterclaim with the "main action" would unduly complicate the trial, the court may order a severance of the claims for purpose of trial (Rules 13(i) and 42(b)).

Reply to Counterclaim

Since a counterclaim is for the purpose of stating a claim against the plaintiff, the plaintiff must be given the opportunity to deny the allegations made and to plead affirmative defenses. The plaintiff responds to the counterclaim by serving and filing a reply to counterclaim (Rule 7(a)). The reply is tantamount to an answer, so the preceding discussion relevant to the defendant's answer applies to the requirements of a reply to counterclaim. A reply must be served within twenty days after service of the counterclaim. Since the counterclaim is usually served by mail, three days are added to the time period (Rules 12(a) and 6(e)).

Cross-claim and Answer to Cross-claim

Two or more persons who are liable to the plaintiff for injury or property damage may be joined as codefendants (Rule 20). The codefendants may have claims to make against each other. The claims may be for injuries or losses that they sustained or for contribution to the plaintiff's claim. A defendant may make a claim against a codefendant by serving and filing a cross-claim. A cross-claim is, in effect, a complaint that states one or more causes of action against a codefendant. The rules and guidelines for drafting complaints apply to cross-claims.

The following is typical of allegations found in cross-claims.

Comes now defendant and for his cross-claim against defendant C, alleges:

1. That plaintiff has commenced the above entitled action against each defendant above named and alleges that defendants are jointly and severally liable to plaintiff; for money damages, as more fully set forth in the complaint, a copy of which has been duly served upon each defendant.

2. That defendant B has denied liability to plaintiff as set forth more fully in his answer, which has been served on all parties and filed with the court (attached hereto as Exhibit A).

3. That defendant C's negligence was the proximate cause of the accident described in the complaint.

4. That if defendant B is determined to be liable to plaintiff as alleged in the complaint, or otherwise, defendant B is entitled to contribution from defendant C on the grounds that C's negligence was a proximate cause of the accident and concurred with defendant B's alleged negligence to cause plaintiff's alleged loss.

Wherefore, defendant B prays for judgment of contribution from defendant C to any sums awarded in favor of plaintiff against defendant B, together with his costs and disbursements herein.

A cross-claim is usually served as a separate document. If a defendant has appeared in the case by serving an answer or Rule 12 motion, the cross-claim may be served by mail upon his or her lawyer (Rule 5(b)). Usually, the cross-claim cannot be served with the answer because the identity of the codefendant's lawyer is not yet know. If a named codefendant has not yet been served with summons and complaint, a cross-claim must be served in the manner provided by Rule 4 like an original summons and complaint.

The rules do not express a time limit for serving and filing cross-claims. Nevertheless, there is an inherent principle that service of a cross-claim shall not be so late as to unduly delay the trial of the main action, that is, the plaintiff's case. A defendant who is served with a cross-claim must respond by serving and filing an answer to the cross-claim (Rule 12(a)). If the cross-claim was served by mail, add three days to the date of service. The answer to the cross-claim serves the same function as an answer, and the same general rules apply.

The identity of the lawyer representing a codefendant is easily obtainable through the plaintiff's lawyer. The note of issue, which is used in most state courts to place an action on the active trial calendar, must identify all of the parties and lawyers who have appeared in the case. The note of issue must give the lawyers' addresses and must be served upon all of the lawyers to be effective. Consequently, a note of issue is a convenient vehicle for informing each lawyer about the identity of all other lawyers who have appeared in the case.

The use of cross-claims establishes technical adversity between the defendants. This may be important at trial in determining whether there is a right to cross-examination and whether the defendants have to share preemptory challenges in the jury selection.

Third-party Practice

The same facts which give rise to the plaintiff's cause of action against the defendant may also create rights in favor of the defendant against some third person who has not been sued. For example, if a plaintiff consumer was injured due to a defect in a product he purchased, the consumer has a cause of action against the retailer and against the manufacturer. If the plaintiff chooses to sue only the retailer, the retailer may commence a third-party action against the manufacturer for contribution and/or indemnity. Frequently, the manufacturer has the ultimate responsibility for the injury. If the retailer succeeds in showing that the manufacturer was responsible for the defect and injury, the retailer may obtain full reimbursement from the manufacturer for any money damages the retailer is obligated to pay to the plaintiff consumer. Another example: When an employee acts within the scope of her employment to carry out her employer's business purposes, the employer is vicariously liable to any person injured by reason of the negligent acts of the employee. This is true whether the employer is an individual or a corporation. If an injured party brings an action against the employer, the employer may have a cause of action against the employee or agent for indemnity. So if the employer is held liable to the plaintiff, the employer may be able to recover the same amount of money damages from the negligent employee, together

with the employer's costs incurred in defending against the plaintiff's action. The employer may bring a third-party action against the employee for indemnity if the employee was not sued directly by the plaintiff.

Joint tortfeasors are entitled to contribution between them. For example, if two negligent motorists collide causing injury to a passenger and the passenger sues only one driver, that defendant driver may sue the other driver for contribution through a third-party action. This situation frequently arises when a wife is injured in an accident while her husband is driving. She may elect to sue only the other driver. The defendant driver may bring a third-party action against the husband for contribution—assuming that the husband was negligent and assuming there is no family immunity in the state where the accident occurred.

The defendant commences a third-party action by serving a summons and complaint upon the third-party defendant. The defendant is thereafter identified as "defendant" or "defendant and third-party plaintiff" or "third-party plaintiff." Service is made in the same manner as service of an original summons and complaint (Rule 4). The defendant has a right to commence a third-party action anytime within ten days after serving the answer to the complaint (Rule 14(a)). Otherwise, the defendant must apply to the court for leave to commence the third-party action. Of course, the reason for limiting the time in which the third-party action may be started is that the defendant must not cause the plaintiff's case to be unduly delayed, and the act of bringing in an additional party certainly has the potential for causing some delay. A substantial delay may seriously prejudice the plaintiff's right to a speedy trial. The Rule tends to discourage any delay. A third-party action unavoidably complicates the litigation. But that fact does not preclude the right to a third-party action.

The third-party complaint should be drafted with the same considerations in mind that apply to the original complaint and to cross-claims. The third-party complaint typically alleges that the plaintiff commenced the action by service of a summons and complaint on the defendant, and a copy of the complaint is attached to the third-party complaint. It alleges the gist of the plaintiff's claim and that the defendant denies liability; that the defendant duly interposed an answer on (date); that a copy of the answer is attached; that the plaintiff is liable for the transaction or occurrence (the third-party complaint must state a cause of action against the third-party defendant); and that the third-party plaintiff is entitled to indemnity or contribution, as the case may be, from the third-party defendant for any sums that may be awarded to the plaintiff against the defendant. The third-party complaint uses an ad damnum clause to specify the relief sought.

to the damages→
statement of TT's $
loss, or damages
which TT claims

The ten-day period for starting a third-party action begins to run the day after service of the defendant's answer. The defendant may move the court for an extension of time. If the motion for an extension of time is made within the ten-day period, notice of the motion need not be given to the plaintiff (Rule 6(b)). That is to say, the motion may be made "ex parte." But if the ten-day period has expired, the defendant must make the motion by giving due notice to the plaintiff (Rule 6(d)). A motion made after expiration of the ten-day period should show there was excusable neglect for failing to act within the ten-day period prescribed by Rule 14; that the plaintiff will not be unduly prejudiced by the joinder; and that there is reason to believe that the proposed third-party defendant is liable to the defendant for indemnity or contribution. Frequently, such motions are accompanied by a proposed third-party complaint that states the cause of action for indemnity or contribution. If the plaintiff does not oppose a defendant's motion for an order extending the time for commencement of the third-party action, the court usually grants the motion as a matter of course.

The third-party defendant has twenty days in which to serve an answer. The third-party answer must be served upon the plaintiff and upon the defendant and third-party plaintiff. In turn, the third-party defendant may commence a fourth-party action for indemnity or contribution against anyone who is liable to him or her because of the transaction or occurrence in question. The third-party defendant then has the additional title of fourth-party plaintiff. Theoretically, there is no limit to the number of parties who may be joined in a lawsuit in this manner.

Third-party actions are not compulsory, as are most counterclaims. Any party may move the court to sever the third-party action from the main action. There are numerous reasons and grounds for obtaining a severance (Rule 42). However, consolidations are generally favored. If the defendant is unsuccessful in the belated effort to obtain leave to commence a third-party action, he or she may, nevertheless, start a separate lawsuit against the would-be third-party defendant for the same purpose of obtaining contribution or indemnity. But by starting a separate lawsuit, the defendant runs a risk that he or she will be found liable to the plaintiff and yet be unsuccessful in proving a right to indemnity or contribution in the second action. The facts established in the first lawsuit may not be established by the evidence in the second lawsuit. Furthermore, the losing defendant has the burden of proving the plaintiff's damages when seeking indemnity or contribution in a subsequent trial when seeking indemnity or contribution. Of course, a second trial also increases the expense of the litigation.

A third-party defendant may serve a claim against the plaintiff if that claim arises out of the same transaction or occurrence. The plaintiff may also serve a claim upon the third-party defendant. When that is done, the third-party defendant is then treated as a direct defendant. The two or more defendants are referred to as codefendants.

If there is more than one third-party defendant, each may serve a cross-claim against the other, just as codefendants may do (Rules 13(g) and 14(a)). A third-party cross-claim requires an answer to the cross-claim.

The third-party defendant's answer must assert whatever defenses the third-party defendant has to the third-party plaintiff's claim. In addition, the third-party defendant may allege defenses which the third-party plaintiff has against the plaintiff's claim. For example, if the defendant has a defense to the plaintiff's claim, such as contributory negligence, assumption of risk, release, immunity, or statute of limitations, the third-party defendant may raise that defense in the answer. This is important because the third-party action is, by its nature, predicated entirely upon the defendant's liability to the plaintiff. If the defendant is not liable to the plaintiff, the third-party defendant cannot have any liability to the third-party plaintiff for indemnity or contribution. In other words, if the third-party defendant succeeds in keeping the plaintiff from recovering against the defendant, the third-party action automatically fails.

Defaults

If a defendant defaults by failing to serve an answer or a Rule 12 motion within the twenty days allowed, the plaintiff may obtain judgment by default (Rule 55). The procedure is relatively simple and inexpensive. The first step is for the plaintiff's lawyer to prepare an affidavit showing that the defendant is in default. The fact of service of the summons and complaint is established through the United States marshal's *return* or the process server's affidavit of service. The plaintiff lawyer's affidavit avers that an answer was not duly served within the time allowed and that he or she has not granted an extension of time or that any extensions granted have expired. The affidavit of default is filed with the clerk.

If the claim involves a sum certain, the clerk of court is authorized to enter judgment without the necessity of a court order. The plaintiff only needs to show the clerk, by affidavit and appropriate documentation, what amount is due and owing. For example, the amount due on a promissory note can be calculated and established as a sum certain. Many contract actions involve a sum certain, such as a claim for rent. The clerk of court enters the judgment forthwith.

Whenever the amount of the recovery is dependent upon a resolution of facts, even though not disputed by the defendant in default, the court must pass on the validity of the claim. Default matters are usually heard by a magistrate or by the judge at a special term. The plaintiff must be prepared to present evidence that proves the transaction or occurrence, the wrongful conduct of the defendant that makes him or her liable, and the nature and extent of the damage sustained by the plaintiff. The court is not concerned with the form of the evidence at default hearings. If testimony is taken, the lawyer usually asks leading questions going to the very heart of the matter. Hearsay evidence is readily received and considered by the court. The plaintiff needs only to prove a prima facie case—not a persuasive case. The judge has no reason to doubt plaintiff's claim or right to judgment. The presentation may take only a few minutes. If personal injuries are involved, the medical evidence may be submitted through medical reports that are filed with the court.

A default judgment cannot be taken against a minor or a person who is under a legal guardianship (ward) without some additional steps. If the minor does not have a guardian, the plaintiff must have one appointed. The legal guardian of a minor or incompetent must be served with a written notice of the plaintiff's application for a default judgment. Service upon the guardian may be made as provided in Rule 4. The notice of application for a default judgment must be served at least three days before the hearing (Rule 55(b)(2)). The rule preserves the right to a jury trial, but the plaintiff almost never elects to present his or her default cause to a jury. Whether right or wrong, trial judges are inclined to be very liberal in their allowance of damages in default proceedings. Nevertheless, the amount of the recovery cannot exceed the amount demanded in the complaint as originally served upon the defendant. The complaint ad damnum cannot be increased by amendment without serving an amended complaint on the defendant. Of course, that would give the defendant in default another opportunity to appear and defend against the claim.

A judgment obtained by default may be set aside for good cause shown (Rule 55(c)). The various grounds establishing good cause are listed in Rule 60(b):

1. Mistake, inadvertence, surprise, or excusable neglect.
2. Newly discovered evidence which by due diligence could not have been discovered in time to move for a new trial under Rule 59(b).
3. Fraud (whether heretofore denominated intrinsic or extrinsic), misrepresentation, or other misconduct of an adverse party.
4. Judgment is void.
5. Judgment has been satisfied, released, or discharged, or a prior judgment upon which it is based has been reversed or otherwise vacated, or it is no longer equitable that the judgment should have prospective application.
6. Any other reason justifying relief from the operation of the judgment.

The motion shall be made within a reasonable time and for (1), (2), and (3) not more than one year after the judgment, order, or proceeding was entered or taken.

A judgment obtained by fraud can always be set aside. A judgment rendered by a court that does not have jurisdiction is always subject to attack. If a defendant seeks to have a default judgment set aside claiming "excusable neglect," the court may require him or her to show a valid defense and a reasonable expectation of prevailing. Also, as a condition to being allowed to serve and file an answer after being in default, the court may require the defendant to pay certain costs to the plaintiff.

Supplemental Pleadings

Upon motion, the court may allow any party to serve a supplemental pleading. Supplemental pleadings pertain to new matters occurring since the original pleadings were served. No party has a right to serve a supplemental pleading; leave of the court must be obtained. The alternative, of course, is for the complaining party to institute a new lawsuit, which may or may not be consolidated with the pending action. For example, suppose a plaintiff commenced an action against the defendant for damming a stream, thereby depriving the plaintiff of water rights. But subsequently, the plaintiff suffered a loss of crops because of the unavailability of water. The original wrong resulted in two separate losses, separated in time. A supplemental complaint could be used to state the additional claim.

Adversity between Parties

The pleadings determine whether or not there is adversity between the parties. Obviously, there is adversity between the plaintiff and defendant. But the presence of adversity is not as clear between codefendants and between the plaintiff and third-party defendants. As a general rule, there is no adversity unless one of them formally creates the adversity by serving a pleading that raises issues between them. Codefendants may do this by serving cross-claims. A third-party defendant may do this by serving an answer to the original complaint. The plaintiff may establish adversity by amending the complaint to include a third-party defendant as a direct defendant. Some courts authorize a document called *notice of direct claim*, which the plaintiff may serve upon the third-party defendant's lawyer.

There are some very important consequences that depend upon adversity between parties. Statements of an adverse party may be treated as admissions. The ultimate judgment or decree of the court may not be binding between codefendants in the absence of adversity between them, because, at least by inference, they have chosen not to litigate the matter as between them.

Filing Pleadings

All pleadings and other papers served in a lawsuit must be filed with the clerk of court within a reasonable period of time and before any hearing involving the pleading. Of course, all documents must be filed with the clerk of court before the trial begins. In federal court, only the plaintiff has to pay a filing fee, and that is paid upon commencement of the action when the complaint is filed. So the parties have no reason to delay filing their papers. Failure to file in good season may result in a delay of the proceedings and even result in sanctions imposed by the court against the delinquent party.

Jury Demand

The plaintiff may demand trial by jury by stating on the complaint: **"Plaintiff demands trial by jury."** The demand is usually stated at the end of the pleading. The defendant may make demand for "trial by jury" on the answer or in a separate document, which must be served within ten days after the answer was served. If the plaintiff elects to file a separate document demanding a jury trial, the demand must be served and filed within ten days after service of the last pleading directed to the issues for which a jury is sought. That may be the defendant's answer or a cross-claim or even a counterclaim. If a jury trial is not demanded within the prescribed time, the parties waive their right to a jury trial (Rule 38(d)).

See chapter 6 for a discussion of *Note of Issues*, which are used in many state courts.

8 Joinder of Claims and Parties

One of the objectives of the Rules of Civil Procedure is to make civil litigation relatively inexpensive (Rule 1). The consolidation of claims and the joinder of parties can significantly decrease the overall cost of litigation; nevertheless, other factors may mitigate against consolidation, such as delay and confusion. Therefore, trial courts have been given broad discretion in determining whether or not to join claims and parties into one case and one trial. The possible variations on consolidations and joinder are nearly endless. The ramifications of consolidation and joinder are many. Not every party always benefits. Courts must be careful not to prejudice the parties in the name of economy.

Consolidation of Claims

A plaintiff may include in one lawsuit all of the claims he or she has against the defendant, even if some of the claims arose out of unrelated transactions or unrelated occurrences. Each separate claim should be stated in the complaint as a separate count. Rule 18(a) provides that

> A party asserting a claim to relief as an original claim, counterclaim, cross-claim, or third-party claim may join, either as independent or as alternate claims, as many claims, legal equitable, or maritime, as he has against an opposing party.

The possibility of one party having several claims against the defendant may seem remote, but it is not. For example, suppose that the plaintiff company has been purchasing bolts of cloth from the defendant company for many years, but for the last three years the defendant's deliveries have been late, frequently causing the plaintiff to experience "downtime"; the bolts of cloth are increasingly defective; and orders are being misplaced. Finally, the defendant company makes a major error that causes the plaintiff to suffer a large loss. Their business relationship is at an end. Once the plaintiff company has decided to sue, it might as well sue for all of the breaches of contract and warranties that occurred over the past several years. Of course, the statute of limitations will act as a bar to the older claims. This example involves a series of transactions between two parties. All of the claims could be joined into one lawsuit. Each claim should be stated in a separate **count** in the complaint.

A series of occurrences that gives rise to multiple claims in favor of a plaintiff is a little more difficult to envision. But it can happen. Suppose that the defendant is a large contractor who has overall responsibility for construction of a large interstate freeway interchange next to a large shopping center owned by the plaintiff. The highway construction work may cause damage to the plaintiff's property at various times by use of explosives, pile driving, and trespasses by large machinery. The contractor may have blocked access to the shopping center causing a loss of business. Dust and noise from the project might have created a legal nuisance. Each of these untoward events is subject to creating a cause of action against the unfortunate contractor. Again, each claim and/or each cause of action should be stated in the complaint in a separate count. The time and place of each event is material to the cause of action (Rule 9).

Suppose that the plaintiff and defendant are neighbors and on one occasion the defendant damaged the plaintiff's tree and on another occasion the defendant damaged the plaintiff's automobile. The claims could be asserted in one complaint and brought to trial together. Theoretically, the plaintiff could consolidate into one lawsuit a claim that arose out of an occurrence with a claim that arose out of a transaction.

Claims and cases are easily consolidated when the causes of action all accrue in the same jurisdiction and venue. But consolidation is impermissible when a party's venue rights are impaired or the court lacks jurisdiction over one or more of the claims.

The defendant also has the right to join two or more claims into one lawsuit. The defendant may assert multiple claims in the counterclaim (Rule 18(a)). Or, the defendant could start a separate lawsuit, as plaintiff, against the original plaintiff, and then the defendant could seek a court order consolidating that action with the one brought by the original plaintiff.

Severance of Claims

Even though the plaintiff may elect to consolidate into one lawsuit all claims against the defendant, the court may order that certain claims be tried separately (Rule 42(b)). The severance may be requested by the defendant by making a motion for severance, or, the court may order a severance on its own motion (Rule 42). A severance of claims is desirable when consolidated claims make a trial too complicated, too long, or too cumbersome. Consolidation might even make the proceedings more expensive for one or both of the parties. Even the plaintiff may decide, when the case reaches trial, that a trial of both claims before the same jury would be inconvenient or more expensive. If a resolution of one of the claims may lead to a settlement, or other summary disposition of the other claims, a severance benefits everyone.

Rule 42 allows the court to order a *severance of issues* as well as a severance of claims. For example, a negligence action in which the plaintiff seeks money damages for a personal injury involves at least three major issues: (1) negligence, (2) proximate cause, and (3) damages. Pursuant to Rule 42 a trial court could order that the issues of negligence and causation be tried together and that the damages issue be tried in another proceeding. Obviously the damages issue is material only if the plaintiff prevails on the negligence and causation issues. By severing the issues there is the opportunity for saving a good deal of time and expense for everyone.

We will just note in passing, that lawyers representing plaintiffs in personal injury cases usually want the injury (damages) issue presented at the same time as the liability issues because there is a generally held belief that the sympathy engendered by the plaintiff's injuries helps to carry the liability portion of the case.

Consolidation of Cases

Federal district courts have authority to consolidate cases for trial whenever cases involve common questions of law or common questions of fact (Rule 42(a)). This is true even though the cases involve different parties. Cases are never consolidated for trial merely because they coincidentally involve common questions of fact or law. For example, the fact that two automobile accident cases happen to involve stop-sign violations is no reason to consolidate those cases. Even if the two automobile accidents involved the same intersection and the same stop sign, a trial judge would not be inclined to consolidate the cases. There must be some underlying unifying factor that makes a consolidation convenient for the court without unduly complicating or prolonging the trial for the parties.

A few examples may be helpful to show when cases are likely to be consolidated on the basis that they involve common questions of fact or law. Suppose that five people sustain injuries in the crash of a small airplane. Each injured person decides to sue the pilot, manufacturer, and the airplane maintenance company. Suppose that legal responsibility is very unclear. The court may elect to consolidate the five cases for purposes of trial, at least for the purpose of determining the liability issues. The five cases may take twice as long as proving one case but only two-fifths as long as trying each case separately. If the plaintiffs are able to establish liability, there is the possibility that some of the plaintiffs can settle the damages issue. The defendants gain by having to defend only once rather than five times. The basis for consolidation is the common question of facts, that is, the facts surrounding the accident.

Another example of cases involving common questions of fact is where the plaintiff has been injured in two separate accidents and has two separate claims. Of course, each defendant is likely to contend that the plaintiff's injuries occurred in "the other" accident. The parties may determine that they would prefer to consolidate both cases because they involve a common question of fact, that is, what injuries were sustained in which accident? Consolidation is possible only when the one court has jurisdiction over both actions.

Consolidation is useful in business transaction cases as well as accident cases. Suppose that a corporation is engaged in the business of selling franchises for fast-food stores. Suppose that a problem develops with ten of the franchisees. Their contracts with the franchisor are all the same. The parties may want to have the cases consolidated for one trial. Everyone saves time and expense.

Many cases involve common questions of law but a consolidation would not be convenient or helpful. For example, assume that during the course of three months, five pedestrians fell on city sidewalks at separate locations, sustained injuries, and sued the city. All of those cases involve common questions of law. Could they be consolidated? Perhaps. Should they be consolidated? No. The questions of law are not the major consideration. The points of law in issue are pretty well settled. A consolidation of those cases for trial would be of no value if there is no genuine dispute about the application of legal principles common to the several cases. But, using the same example, suppose that in each of the five cases a legal question exists whether the plaintiffs gave due notice of claim to the defendant city within thirty days of the accident. The notice of claim is a condition precedent to maintenance of actions against municipalities in some states. Suppose further that the plaintiffs each challenge the constitutionality of the statute or ordinance requiring the plaintiffs to file a notice of claim within thirty days of the accident. The legal issue is important and common to all. The cases may be consolidated for the purposes of determining the issue. If the legal issue were resolved in the plaintiff's favor, the cases subsequently would be separated (severed) for individual jury trials.

Another example may be helpful. In a recent case, property owners near an airport sued the airport commission, claiming that the noise from airplanes landing and taking off constituted an involuntary partial condemnation, or taking of their property, for which they should be compensated. The legal theory was novel. Consolidation of those cases permitted the property owners to participate in a trial of the legal issue, that is, whether there was a cause of action. The property owners were able to minimize their expenses by hiring one lawyer for all cases. If the legal issue were resolved in favor of the plaintiffs, clearing the way for an award of money damages to each property owner, each plaintiff could prove his or her damage in a separate hearing (Rule 42).

Intervention

In the preceding examples, we discussed reasons for consolidating pending cases. Another procedure called intervention permits a person to join in a pending lawsuit by applying to the court for leave to become a party (Rule 24). He or she may apply to be a defendant or plaintiff. The criteria is the same as that for consolidating cases pursuant to Rule 42, that is, common questions of law or fact. The intervenor must show the court that he or she has an interest in the outcome of the case. The original parties have a right to object to the motion to intervene. Intervention could be opposed on the grounds that the intervenor does not have an actual interest in the outcome of the case or the intervention would unduly delay or complicate the case.

A motion for leave to intervene must show the court that the applicant's claim or defense does involve an important common question of law or fact and that his or her intervention in the case will conserve the court's time, save the parties' expense and cause prejudice to no one. Some statutes expressly encourage consolidation and direct the courts to order consolidations. Certain federal civil rights actions are typical of those encouraging consolidation and intervention. In those instances, a party may intervene as a matter of right (Rule 24(a)). This means the party has an absolute right to intervene and does not have to convince the court of the desirability of the intervention. The motion for leave to intervene is not addressed to the court's discretion.

A person may intervene as a matter of right if his or her interests in the subject matter may be affected by the outcome of the litigation (Rule 24(a)). For example, suppose the defendant caused damage to real estate by creating a nuisance. The real estate is owned by three joint tenants, and two of the joint tenants sue for damages. The third joint tenant would be allowed to intervene in the case as a matter of right (Rule 24(a)). If a trustee sues or is sued, the beneficiary may elect to intervene to protect his or her interest in the trust res. ("Res" is a Latin word meaning "thing" or "matter." A trust res is the subject of the trust.) If an agent is sued for a wrongful act committed in the course and scope of the agency, the principal, who is vicariously liable for the agent's acts, may intervene to make sure the defense is adequately presented (Rule 24). The right to intervene is granted whenever a person could properly be joined as a party or his or her claim or defense would properly be consolidated as involving common questions of law or fact.

The procedure for intervening is clearly described in Rule 24(c). A motion must be served upon all parties, which states the grounds for the consolidation, that is, the moving party's interest in the subject matter. Or, the moving party must show relationship to the parties to the action. Or, the motion must show the common questions of law or fact which permit the intervener's matter to be joined with the pending action. A copy of the proposed pleading, with the proposed new title, must be attached to the motion. The pleading must fully set forth the claim or defense (Rule 24(c)). The motion must give the parties at least five days notice of the hearing (Rule 5). The original parties may appear in opposition to the motion.

Class Actions

The most ambitious consolidation of claims, defenses, and parties is the use of class actions as authorized by Rule 23. The subject of class actions is beyond the scope of this book. The subject is complex and presents problems that paralegals seldom are required to handle. It is enough for our purposes to understand that, on occasion, an entire class or group of persons may be the plaintiffs or defendants in an action in which the class or group is represented by one or just a few litigants. Class actions are not generally favored because the procedure limits the parties' actual participation. The courts have to exercise close supervision over the representatives of the class to make sure the class is adequately represented. The prerequisites for a class action are difficult to meet.

An example should be helpful to illustrate the use and prerequisites of class actions. Suppose that a large commercial bank contracted to pay interest on money it collects from mortgagors to hold in escrow to pay real estate taxes as the taxes come due. Suppose further that a dispute arises as to whether the bank has calculated the interest properly or has made questionable charges against the escrow accounts. The number of mortgagors may be several thousand, but they can be easily identified. If an action is brought by one or several mortgagors to recover their alleged losses due to overcharges by the bank, it would be best for the class (all mortgagors) and the bank to have a resolution of the problem in one lawsuit and one trial. The active participation of each and every mortgagor should not be necessary if the class is adequately represented. If liability exists, the damages for each mortgagor should be easy to calculate. The bank avoids the expense of multiple suits. The amount to be recovered may be small for each member of the class, so having a large number of claimants may be important to justify the cost of the litigation. The total recovery could be very substantial.

If the case were not certified as a class action, the bank's successful defense against the initial plaintiff could not be binding upon other plaintiff mortgagors. The decision would be binding only upon the parties to the action. As to them, the decision is res judicata. The decision in the first case would have some value as precedent, but that does not make the decision binding. Theoretically, if the prerequisites of Rule 23 are met so that a class action is permissible, everyone tends to benefit.

It should be apparent that a defendant may benefit by keeping the court from certifying the case as a class action. If the potential recovery by each of the plaintiffs in the proposed class would be quite small, they, as individuals, might have no interest in pursuing the claim. Indeed, there are situations in which the proposed members of the class have no interest in being involved. Their cooperation is solicited, usually by the proposed class representative, as a duty owed to others similarly situated. They have a wrong that must be corrected. The class representative then seeks compensation for his or her services to the class. Class actions are potentially very lucrative for the lawyers who handle them.

If a party wants to move the court for an order certifying a class action, he or she must show the court that all the following factors are present:

1. The class is so large it is not practical for them to sue or defend as individual parties in a consolidation of cases or joinder of parties in a single action.
2. There are common questions of law or fact affecting the right or obligations of all members of the class in the same way.
3. The party or parties applying for class certification are truly representative of the proposed class.
4. Separate suits by or against individual members of the proposed class might result in varying or inconsistent determinations for the members.
5. A class action can effectively dispose of all the legal and fact issues that exist between members of the proposed class and the adverse party.
6. The individual members of the proposed class do not have a superior interest in controlling how the litigation is handled.
7. There is no other pending litigation that would be adversely affected by certifying the class action.
8. Commencement of a class action would not unduly burden the court or cause prejudice to persons who might choose to have their case presented in another forum.

If a class action is allowed, the court exercises control over the case to make sure that the class members receive notice of the case and their rights and obligations in connection with the action. The class action cannot be compromised or dismissed without court approval (Rule 23(e)).

One type of class action has been given special treatment: a shareholders' derivative action to enforce rights of their corporation against a party when the board of directors wrongfully refuse or neglect to do so (Rule 23). Since the board of directors (not shareholders) is charged with the responsibility for running the business, the shareholders may institute actions only in extreme circumstances. The shareholders must show the court that an effort has been made to have the directors take the appropriate action and that they have refused. The shareholder who seeks to institute a derivative action must show that he or she was a shareholder at the time the transaction or occurrence in question took place and that he or she adequately represents the other shareholders. As in other class actions, a shareholder's derivative action cannot be compromised or dismissed without court approval.

Substitution of Parties

If a party dies while a lawsuit is pending, a representative party may be substituted, assuming that the cause of action did not die with the party. Any party may move the court for an order directing the substitution. If a representative has been appointed in a probate proceeding, that representative may move the court for an order substituting himself or herself for the decedent. If a party makes the motion for a substitution, and there is already a representative appointed by a probate court to handle the estate, that representative must be served with the motion and notice of hearing. The motion must be served in the manner provided in Rule 4 for service of a summons. The motion must not be served by mail upon a nonparty.

Once the parties and court are given formal notice of a party's death, which is served like an ordinary motion, the remaining parties have just ninety days in which to act to obtain a substitution party. Otherwise, the action against the decedent will be dismissed (Rule 25(a)). The rule implies that the court shall order the dismissal upon its own motion.

If a party becomes legally incompetent to handle his or her business, a representative party must be appointed and substituted. For example, if a party becomes senile, a guardian should be appointed by a probate court having jurisdiction. The guardian must replace the senile party in the manner discussed previously.

If an action is brought by joint tenants to realty and one dies before a determination is reached, the action will continue in the name of the survivor. One of the characteristics of ownership of property as joint tenants is that title inures to the survivor. The title of the action may be amended by order of the court showing that the surviving joint tenant plaintiff is the only plaintiff (Rule 25(c)).

The cost of the litigation, the convenience of the court, the convenience of the witness, and trial strategy are the primary considerations concerning the consolidation of actions and joinder of parties.

9 Gathering the Evidence

Each party to a civil lawsuit has responsibility for gathering and presenting the evidence necessary to establish claims and defenses. A lawyer assumes that responsibility for the client. This means finding the evidence, identifying the evidence, and preserving it. Before the evidence can be effectively used at trial it must be sorted, organized, analyzed, and evaluated. The entire process may be very simple when dealing with a small, routine case. Conversely, it may be very complex in a major case. The evidence is gathered through investigation and through discovery procedures authorized by Rules 26 through 37. Paralegals must have a good understanding of the procedures and methods for locating, obtaining, and preserving evidence. The facts which give rise to the parties' dispute can be proved only through the parties' admissions, the parties' stipulations, and evidence. Our primary concern is with the evidence, but the admissions and stipulations have a definite impact on gathering and using the evidence.

A party's own investigation is the most basic and economical means of obtaining information and evidence. Anyone may conduct an investigation. No license or certification is required. There are some important considerations and useful guidelines for conducting an effective investigation. Some of these will be discussed in chapter 10.

The Rules of Civil Procedures include several very effective procedures for obtaining and preserving evidence. Rule 33 authorizes the use of interrogatories (written questions) which may be propounded to another party. The party who answers the interrogatories (deponent) must answer the interrogatories under oath. Rule 30 authorizes oral depositions of parties and witnesses. The deponent must answer the questions orally under oath. Rule 34 authorizes a procedure for inspecting real estate, personal property, and documents which are in the custody of another party. Rule 35 provides the means for obtaining an independent medical examination of a party who makes a claim for personal injury. Rule 36 creates a means of compelling another party to admit the truth of facts and genuineness of documents. Rule 37 provides means for enforcing compliance with the discovery procedures. Though each discovery procedure is interdependent, the procedures should complement each other. Each procedure has its own special use and capability and is subject to limitations. The discovery procedures should complement the investigation.

The Objectives of Investigation and Discovery

The objectives of investigation and discovery are to obtain as much knowledge as possible about the facts that gave rise to the dispute and to prepare a persuasive presentation of the evidence for trial. The evidence has no value unless it can be effectively and persuasively presented in trial. Therefore, before trial, lawyers and paralegals must conduct an analysis of the available evidence, which includes the evidence known to be available to the other parties in the case. The purpose of the analysis is to determine what the evidence proves and what it does not prove.

Ordinarily, the parties and lawyers begin the process of gathering evidence by investigating the occurrence or transaction that gave rise to the suit. The investigation does not require the cooperation of the other party or the assistance of the court. Lawyers prefer to conduct the investigation as soon as possible and with as little involvement of the other side as possible. There are two profound jurisprudentia principles that guide lawyers in the investigation: (1) "the early bird catches the worm" and (2) "what your opponent doesn't know won't hurt you." The party who starts the investigation first is usually able to obtain the most evidence and the better evidence. Clearly, the more information and facts a party can obtain, the better the party can evaluate the case and prepare for trial.

By the time a case reaches trial, some evidence that seemed very important in the early stages of the investigation may be less significant in light of information obtained through discovery, and vice versa. Trial preparation begins by obtaining an overview of the case. The first step is to review the legal issues. Since the pleadings establish the legal issues and should contain the basic facts, this is a good place to begin trial preparation. The legal issues determine what facts are material to the case. The fact issues determine what evidence is needed to prove the client's claims or defenses and what evidence is needed to disprove the opponent's claims or defenses. Many lawyers obtain an overview of the fact issues by preparing their final arguments. The process helps them to determine what they want to be able to tell the jury about the facts in light of the applicable law. Trial preparation involves organizing and preparing the evidence to make it authoritative, appealing, and interesting. The client and witnesses must be prepared by a lawyer or paralegal to testify. Exhibits, often referred to as *demonstrative evidence*, must be prepared for presentation in court.

The pleadings frame the legal issues and fact issues through the allegations, admissions, and denials. The facts that have been admitted in the pleadings need not be proved at trial. Therefore, there is no need to present evidence on those "established" facts. Facts established by the pleadings are conclusively established for all purposes of the case. Admissions made in response to Rule 35 requests for admissions need not be proved by evidence at trial. Those admissions are similar to admissions made in the pleadings. At the proper time the jury is told about the judicial admissions and the conclusiveness of those admissions.

The facts which have been established by judicial admission set a framework for all other facts. In other words, a party must be sure that his or her evidence is not going to be in conflict with facts which are judicially recognized as admitted. For example, if the pleadings establish that an automobile accident occurred on December 22 at 9:30 P.M. standard time, it would be anomalous to offer testimony from an eyewitness who claims that it was daylight at the time of the accident, that he could see the collision clearly, and that the client's automobile did not have its headlights turned on. Either the judicial admission concerning time should not have been made, or the witness is badly mistaken. The witness's testimony is discredited before it is offered.

The facts which a party intends to present must be reconciled. If the preceding judicial admission was made on the basis of an inaccurate police accident report (the officer recorded 9:30 P.M. when he should have recorded 9:30 A.M.) a motion must be made for leave to withdraw the admission. If the admitted time of 9:30 P.M. is correct, the witness's version is in error. The reasons for the error must be determined, and they will determine whether the witness can be used at trial, and if used, how the witness can be rehabilitated, assuming the erroneous version has been preserved by a statement or deposition.

Evidence from Witnesses

A lawyer must not conceal evidence, suppress evidence, tamper with evidence, or procure false testimony. If lawyers disregarded these proscriptions, the judicial system, as we know it, would collapse. Lawyers must look upon the truth as sacred. In light of these restrictions, how does a lawyer deal with a witness who has a mistaken version of the facts either because of a defect in memory or perception?

It is proper to point out to a witness that he or she may be mistaken on a particular point and the apparent reason for the witness's mistake. There is nothing improper about a lawyer telling a witness that the witness's version of the facts is inconsistent with physical facts or with the observations made by other witnesses who had a similar or better view. It is proper to ask a witness to conduct a detailed review or study of the facts and circumstances of the transaction or occurrence in light of other evidence of which the witness was unaware. The witness may or may not appreciate such help. The witness's response will depend, in part, on how he or she is approached about the problem. If the witness feels that improper pressure is being applied, the witness should be resistant and upset.

Usually, the best approach is to inform the witness that there is a problem and then explain the problem. Show a desire to help the witness obtain an understanding of the big picture so that the witness can see how and why the evidence is inconsistent. Be prepared to offer suggestions for dealing with the problem. For example, using the hypothetical situation already presented, tell the witness that the police report states the time to be 9:30 P.M. and the dispatcher's records corroborate the time. The United States Weather Bureau records show that sunset was at 5:00 P.M., and by 9:30 P.M. the accident scene would have been dark. Headlights would have been necessary. Your client is adamant that his lights were on. The witness's perspective may have caused him or her to misinterpret the natural lighting conditions, because the witness may have been standing under a very bright street light and other artificial lighting may have added to make the scene seem as "bright as daylight." If the reasons for the witness's error in perception or recollection can be determined, explanation for the mistake can be made. The error is then justifiable. Of course, this approach is of little or no value where the witness was simply lying.

We have been discussing the effect of facts that have been established by judicial admissions. The parties are "locked into" those facts. The rest of the case and evidence should be consistent with those admitted facts. Similarly, a lawyer's trial preparation must make certain that the client's version of the transaction or occurrence is not inconsistent with *manifest* physical facts. The physical facts may include time, place, size, measurements, color, etc. In automobile accident cases the physical facts include point of impact on the roadway, point of impact on each vehicle, the amount of damage caused by the impact, gyrations of the vehicles after impact, lighting conditions, road surface, weather, etc. If photographs show that both cars were red, a lawyer does not want a client and witnesses describing cars as brown and gray. The witness should be shown the photographs. They should be confronted with the physical facts. The client should know important distance factors by making measurements and examining plats and diagrams.

Trial preparation is necessary to help witnesses, especially the client, to fully understand what they observed, to refresh their recollections, and to appreciate all of the facts relevant to their observations. Lawyers and paralegals must not tell witnesses what to say. A witness's testimony must be based upon what the witness knows from personal observations and knowledge, not from what the witness has heard from others. But sometimes the witness's observations must be put into perspective. For example, a witness may have a valid estimate of the width of an intersection by reason of the witness's own observations. It is not wrong to inform the witness of the exact measurement to assure the witness that the estimate is reasonable. If the witness's estimate is not reasonable, the witness ought to examine the intersection again and revise the estimate, or the witness could actually measure the distance in question, assuming it has not changed since the time of the accident. It is perfectly proper to help a witness to be accurate with estimates and recollections.

Lawyers and paralegals must always have in mind that the communications they have with a witness may be brought out by the other side at trial or in the witness's deposition. Therefore, assurance must be given to the witness that it is proper to meet and prepare to testify; acknowledge the preparation if asked about it. If handled properly, preparation should cause no embarrassment and should add to the witness's authority. Careful preparation should help a witness be more comfortable about testifying. It is common for a lawyer to ask an adverse witness whether the witness was told what to say when testifying. The stock answer to such questions is: "I was told to tell the truth." It should never be otherwise!

Documentary evidence, such as business records, should comport with the judicial admissions, physical facts, and anticipated testimony. If they do not, a reason must be found so that evidence can be reconciled or a proper explanation made. Finally, the anticipated testimony of the witnesses, including parties, must be compared, reconciled where possible, and corrected as needed.

The Process of Gathering Evidence

The process of gathering evidence may be divided into two phases: investigation and discovery. The investigation phase is any search for evidence that a party can conduct without involvement of the court or the other party. The discovery process includes various procedures (authorized by court rules) which always require notification and sometimes, cooperation of the other parties. Discovery procedures include the use of interrogatories (written questions propounded by one party to another); oral depositions (interrogation of another party or witness under oath); inspections of documents, real property, personal property, and "things" which are owned or in the custody of an adverse party; and independent medical examinations of a party conducted by a physician selected by the adverse party.

The scope of discovery is quite broad. Discovery procedures may be used to discover information and evidence. Inquiry through discovery procedures is limited to information and evidence which are relevant to the case. Evidence is considered relevant, for purposes of discovery, if it would be admissible at trial to prove a fact or if the inquiry is calculated to lead to discovery of evidence that would be admissible at trial. Therefore, it is important to note and be aware that the term *relevancy* is broader when used in discovery procedures to locate evidence than when used at trial concerning the use of evidence.

The discovery procedures are available to the parties as soon as the action has been commenced, and in some situations they may be utilized even before an action has been started (Rule 27(a)). The Rules governing discovery provide sufficient direction and guidance to the parties to conduct discovery in most cases without any involvement of the court. However, for various reasons the court or a party may want to establish a plan for discovery. Upon motion or by an order **sua sponte** the court may order a discovery conference for the purpose of establishing a discovery plan. If a party moves the court for an order setting a discovery conference, the moving party must state that the parties have tried and failed to establish their own discovery plan. In that event, the party seeking a discovery plan must have prepared and submitted a proposed plan to the other parties.

A discovery plan must identify the legal and fact issues to which discovery shall be directed and, perhaps, limited. The plan should establish a timetable or schedule for completing discovery or phases of discovery. The plan may establish limitations on discovery such as the number of interrogatories which may be served, the number of a party's employees who may be deposed, the number of inspections which may be conducted, or the terms for deposing each other's expert witnesses. A discovery plan may provide for the allocation of expenses, such as expert witness fees. Of course, a discovery plan, whether prepared by the parties or by the court, may be modified from time to time as circumstances require, but, once established, the plan should be religiously followed as a commitment made by the parties to the court.

A party's investigation is not limited by a discovery plan. Nevertheless, since lawyers should use both approaches in gathering evidence, so that each complements the other, the discovery plan does affect the parties' investigation indirectly.

Although the discovery procedures are well defined and well understood, there are occasions when the procedures must be modified for the purpose of protecting a party against untoward consequences of disclosure of information. Therefore, Rule 26(c) provides that a party against whom discovery is sought may apply to the court for a protective order. A protective order may be issued to avoid unnecessary "annoyance, embarrassment, oppression, or expense." For example, a plaintiff who has a personal injury claim may be asked about her general medical history. Her history may include an elective abortion, which is not relevant to the case. The plaintiff could seek an order excluding evidence about the abortion and relevant records from further discovery or impose limits on the use to which the medical information could be put. The burden rests upon the party from whom discovery is being sought to move the court for a protective order.

If a party fails to comply with discovery demands, the party seeking discovery may move the court for an order to compel the opposing party to comply with the demands (Rule 37). If the court orders a party to answer questions put to him or her in interrogatories or an oral deposition, the court may order the culpable party to pay the moving party's costs incurred to obtain the order compelling discovery (Rule 37(a)(4)). On the other hand, if the court determines that the deponent was correct in refusing to respond to discovery demands, the court may require the moving party to pay the costs the deponent incurred in defending against the motion. Rule 37 motions to compel discovery do not always result in an award of costs. The court may determine that both parties had reasonable grounds for their respective positions and acted in good faith. On that basis the court could decide to let each party bear his or her own costs.

If a party fails to comply with an order compelling discovery, the next step for the party seeking discovery is to move the court for sanctions (Rule 37(b)). The court is given a broad range of sanctions it may impose upon remiss parties. The court may strike all or part of the remiss party's pleading. For example, suppose that the plaintiff in a personal injury action refuses to name her past and present employers. The refusal to permit discovery would significantly interfere with the defendant's ability to evaluate and meet the plaintiff's claim for loss of income. The court could strike the plaintiff's complaint or strike that portion which seeks damages for loss of income and loss of earning capacity.

Where a party refuses to disclose evidence on a particular subject, the court may order that the determinative facts are resolved against the remiss party (Rule 37(b)(A)). A case in point would be where the plaintiff claims damage to personal property but will not permit the defendant to examine the property. The court could issue an order that provides that, for purposes of the pending action, the property was not damaged.

A court may issue an order that precludes the disobedient party from asserting a claim or defense or offering evidence of a particular nature or on a particular subject (Rule 37(b)(B)). The court may hold a party to be in contempt of court for failing to comply with a discovery order (Rule 37(b)(D)). The right to discovery includes the right to an independent medical examination of a party who has put his or her physical, mental, or blood condition in issue; however, a party who refuses to submit to an independent medical examination cannot be held in contempt of court even though ordered to submit. Some other sanction must be utilized. Probably the most severe penalty that a court may impose is to enter judgment against the disobedient party (Rule 37(b)(C)).

If a party wrongfully refuses to make admissions pursuant to Rule 36, the only penalty the court may impose against that party is an award of costs in favor of the proponent of the request for admissions. The costs recoverable are the costs which the proponent incurred to prove the facts which should have been admitted by the respondent. On the other hand, a court may disallow the costs of proving facts where it appears that the respondent had reasonable grounds to believe that the request for admission was not true or justifiable (Rule 37(c)).

10 Investigation

Material Facts and Relevant Evidence

The parties' pleadings establish and define the legal issues. The legal issues determine what facts are **material** to the case. Evidence is material if it relates to the legal issues raised by the pleadings. In addition to being material, evidence must be **relevant** to the issues. Evidence is relevant if it tends to prove or disprove a fact that is in dispute. Logic and reason determine what facts have probative value and, therefore, are relevant to the case. Evidence must be material and relevant to be admissible in court. The Federal Rules of Evidence establish additional requirements for the admissibility of evidence and certain limitations on its use.

The trial of a civil action focuses upon disputed facts. The parties try to prove their respective versions of the facts by presenting evidence. Of course, parties also offer evidence to disprove the opposing party's version of the facts. The effectiveness of a lawyer's presentation is directly dependent upon the quality of the client's evidence. Everything builds on the investigation, and it is usually the backbone of a lawyer's trial preparation. Lawyers act on the premise that the party who does the best job of collecting, preserving, and presenting evidence will prevail. The premise is not inconsistent with society's larger purpose of obtaining a disposition of private controversies on the basis of the truth and according to law.

Since evidence is subject to various limitations when presented at trial, an investigator who understands the potential uses and limitations can be more effective in collecting and preserving evidence. With experience, an investigator can eliminate the irrelevant more quickly and avoid being sidetracked by false evidence. But experience does not enable an investigator to sit in the office and determine the facts. An investigator must actually *get out* and contact the witnesses, locate the documents, look for clues, seek information, and find sources of information. Experience does not give an investigator a right to assume anything. An investigator must pay strict attention to details.

Information must be recorded accurately. An investigator needs to be objective and have a good deal of common sense.

The client ordinarily has a substantial amount of information concerning the transaction or occurrence. The investigation is usually predicated upon the information initially supplied by the client. The investigation often continues into and during the trial of the case. The client should be able to identify witnesses who should be contacted and direct the investigator to potential sources of evidence. Too often the client fails to appreciate the value of some of the evidence he or she has. Consequently, it is usually necessary to interrogate the client about possible information and sources of information which the client has not volunteered.

The nature of the occurrence, the type of claim, and the possible defenses tend to dictate the scope of the investigation. There is no set formula for conducting an investigation. Of course, the investigator should start the quest for evidence as soon as possible, because, like vapor, evidence tends to vanish with the passage of time. Physical evidence gets lost. Witnesses quickly forget the facts they observed. They lose their notes and records get misplaced. The transaction or occurrence quickly loses its importance to the witnesses, but not to the case. Some witnesses try to forget. Some witnesses try not to be found. An investigator must make an effort to be at the right place at the right time to collect evidence and to see witnesses. A *timely* investigation does not just happen. The investigator must make it happen.

Conducting an Investigation

An investigation should be pursued with a plan, so that time and effort are not wasted by unnecessary duplication. The plan should allow the investigation to build naturally as information and evidence are obtained. The plan for investigation should (1) identify the pertinent facts; (2) establish a logical sequence for locating evidence and sources of evidence; (3) provide for collecting and preserving the evidence; (4) provide for organizing the evidence to make it usable at trial; and (5) coordinate the investigation with discovery procedures, which will be discussed in the next chapter. The investigation plan should determine the order in which the witnesses should be interviewed, the type of information which may be expected from each witness, and which witnesses should be asked to give statements. For each witness, it should be determined what kind of a statement should be obtained. The investigation is not complete until the investigator knows what happened, has the means of proving to others what happened, and can refute any claims to the contrary.

The usual starting point is to obtain the client's version of the transaction or occurrence, preserve it, and proceed from there. The optimum arrangement, in accident cases, is to meet the client, get acquainted, and proceed to the location of the accident or the accident scene (for our purposes, we will refer to the site of the accident as the **accident scene** when the circumstances relevant to the accident are still the same). The client can demonstrate what happened. The client can explain the accident much more meaningfully at the scene. For example, in an automobile accident case, the client can drive through the occurrence again—noting relevant speeds, times, and distance.

In an accident case involving a fall the client can show the investigator what he or she was doing and how the accident happened.

If the client is the defendant and did not actually see the accident, it is still useful to visit the location of the accident. The client's impressions about what probably happened should be obtained. Impressions are not admissible as evidence, but the investigation is not locked into admissible evidence. After conducting an on-site inspection, an investigator will be able to communicate with the client and witnesses more effectively. This is true even if conditions have changed since the accident occurred.

The character of the site of an accident may have a good deal to do with how and why the accident happened. The perspective which an investigator obtains by an on-site inspection is an invaluable aid to understanding and appreciating the circumstances of an occurrence. As soon as possible, then, the site of an accident should be inspected, photographed, and perhaps diagrammed. Diagrams are useful even if they are not exactly to scale. Diagrams help to reinforce the investigator's memory and provide a convenient method of recording pertinent measurements. An on-site inspection enables an investigator to identify the important physical features and obtain an accurate perspective of the physical conditions. In the typical automobile accident case, the investigator should observe and record the widths of the roadways, the location of traffic controls, signs and markings, and the presence of any obstructions to view.

Even if photographs of the actual accident scene are available, such as photographs made by police at the scene, there is no substitute for an on-site inspection. After seeing the place of the accident, photographs will be more meaningful, and the investigator can be more authoritative when speaking with witnesses. The investigator is also better equipped to ask the right questions, secure relevant details, and avoid being misled by witnesses who have biases, wrong perspectives, or imperfect memories.

Photographs should be obtained not only for the purpose of showing the subject matter but also as aids to interviewing witnesses. Photographs may help witnesses to remember important details and to be more specific in their descriptions. Remember the adage: one picture is worth more than a thousand words.

Photographs which depict the very objects and conditions which are the subject of the dispute may, in themselves, constitute evidence. If a photograph shows a "fact," such as a skid mark, a rotted wooden step, or a body wound, the photograph is, in itself, evidence of the fact. To be evidence of the fact, the photograph must accurately show the subject matter in the condition it was in at a particular, relevant time. A photograph is readily received into evidence as proof of what it shows if a witness can verify that it is a reasonably accurate representation of the subject matter. For example, a photograph of an accident scene which shows conditions as they were at the time of the accident is evidence of those conditions. On the other hand, photographs which do not show exactly the same conditions and circumstances as existed at the time of the accident may still have value. They may be used at trial to help witnesses explain what they observed. Those photographs may be received into evidence as **illustrative** photographs. Illustrative exhibits help witnesses to explain their testimony. The evidence is the testimony, not the photographs. A jury may not be allowed to examine illustrative exhibits during their deliberations, but they do have the chance to see the illustrative exhibits while listening to the witnesses who use them.

Preserving Evidence

If physical evidence is in the custody of a nonparty, the custodian should be apprised of the importance of the evidence and of preserving it for purposes of litigation. The custodian should be offered assistance with storing it, and if some expense is involved, suitable arrangements must be made to cover that expense. The custodian should be informed that the case might not be resolved for a couple of years, or more, and that the evidence must be retained until notified that it is no longer needed. There may be official records and reports which bear on the issues. Copies should be obtained, again, as soon as possible. Such documents often provide the names and addresses of additional witnesses.

Seldom is an investigator fortunate enough to be on the scene soon enough to preserve all the relevant evidence; however, it is surprising how long the remnants of some accidents remain. Even if the skid marks and debris at an automobile accident scene are already gone, good photographs of the place where the accident occurred may be used to *illustrate* the conditions as they were at the time of the accident. For example, a witness may be able to draw on photographs to show the location of skid marks as they were at the accident scene. A witness may be permitted to mark on the photograph the exact location where he or she was standing at the time the collision occurred or show where the car was when he or she first saw it. As mentioned, photographs may be used effectively in the investigation as well as at trial. This points out the value of having more than one set of photographs, plats, etc.

If photographs are used in the course of the investigation or to prepare witnesses to testify at trial, any marking on the photographs might disqualify them from being used at trial. For example, if witness A were to draw skid marks on a photograph and witness B attempts to use the photograph at trial with A's illustration of skid marks showing, A's markings could be considered as "leading" witness B. It is safer to work from copies. Make marks only on expendable copies!

Records

Many records cannot be obtained without signed authorizations, such as tax returns, hospital records, medical records, police reports, employment records, school records, and official death records. Each law office has its own forms for this purpose. The record custodian may have a preferred form, and this preference should be honored. The client should sign the necessary authorizations at the first meeting. It is usually a good idea to leave the authorizations undated. In the event there is some delay before the authorizations are used, dates can be supplied at the time they are used. In that way, they will be current. In at least one state, the hospital association arbitrarily decided not to honor authorizations which are more than six months old. This rule is easily circumvented by not dating the authorizations until they are to be used. It is not always convenient or desirable to use authorizations right away. For example, the defendant may have an authorization to obtain a copy of the plaintiff's employment records, but it may be preferable to wait until the injured plaintiff returns to work before obtaining the employment records and personnel file. This decision is influenced by whether or not the defendant's lawyer will be able to obtain another authorization at a later date.

Witnesses

The investigation plan should take into consideration the most effective method of coping with the witnesses. Of course, the manner in which an investigator approaches a witness greatly depends upon the investigator's own personality, the witness's relationship to the parties, the witness's age, and numerous other factors. If a witness is known to be friendly to the client, the interview should be relatively easy; on the other hand, if the witness is aligned with the opposing party, some difficulties should be anticipated. The witness may be evasive, contrary, or even belligerent. Witnesses should always be approached in a manner calculated to gain their confidence and to develop their interest in the case, if not the client's problem. An investigator should identify himself or herself to the witness and explain the purpose of the interview. The witness should be assured that there is nothing improper in meeting and discussing the transaction or occurrence.

The interview should begin with an explanation to the witness of the purpose and importance of the meeting. The witness should be made to feel that his or her role is important. The feeling of importance may come from the witness's ability to help either or both of the parties from being part of the system and doing one's duty. Some witnesses do not want to be involved merely because they do not understand the procedures. Consequently, they tend to be evasive and reluctant to give statements. If the situation is explained in an understandable and considerate manner with an emphasis on the importance of the witness's role in the case, there is a good chance that such witnesses can be induced to cooperate. Of course, if the witness's reluctance to become involved has some other basis, it may be more difficult to solicit cooperation. For example, witnesses who have criminal records often shy away from interviews and refuse to give statements. Witnesses who have been involved in litigation of their own that did not go well for them are often reluctant to cooperate in someone else's case.

Consideration should be given to determining the best time and place to interview each witness. Should the witness be contacted at home or at work? Would the witness consider meeting at the scene of the accident? Will it be necessary to compensate the witness for the time? Should the client attend the interview? If the witness is particularly friendly to the client, it may be very useful to have the client attend the interview. If the witness is "neutral" or somewhat hostile, it might be counterproductive to have the client attend the interview. On occasion, a preliminary interview may persuade the investigator that no statement is needed or that a statement would be detrimental to the client's interests.

Sometimes an investigator can set the stage for a productive interview by informing the witness about the evidence already obtained. The information enables the witness to understand how the testimony fits into the case. Briefing the witness in this manner sometimes helps to catch the witness's interest and cooperation. If the witness believes the investigator is being candid and concludes that the information the investigator has supplied is probably correct, the witness will be reluctant to say anything that contradicts the investigator's statements and descriptions. A preview also helps the witness to recall additional facts which the witness might otherwise forget or feel to be unimportant and not mention.

It is useful to know something about the witness's background and position in the community to evaluate his or her evidence. Therefore, the information to be obtained from a witness usually includes age, address, employment, education, relevant experience (for example, if the case arises out of an industrial accident, it would be useful to know what experience the witness has had with the particular equipment involved. In automobile cases, it is useful to know whether the witness is a licensed driver and has been directly involved in any motor vehicle accidents), experience testifying, relationship to the parties, and contacts with the other parties. An investigator should find out whether the witness has been interviewed by anyone else and given a statement. Details are important to a good statement. Accurate details make a witness's statement more authoritative. The details help to establish and test credibility. Details help a lawyer to present a sharper, clearer picture of the transaction or occurrence at trial. This is true, even though lawyers usually avoid *unnecessary* detail when presenting the evidence to a jury. When a lawyer has a good understanding of the details, he or she is able to effectively cross-examine witnesses about them. Being able to work with the factual details may make the difference between winning and losing a case.

There are several different kinds of witness statements. Probably the most common is the written statement, which the witness signs. The procedure is very simple. It requires only one person to make the statement. The investigator has quite a bit of control over what does and does not go into the statement. Electronically recorded interviews are becoming more popular as tape recorders become smaller and more reliable. Tape-recorded interviews relieve the investigator of the chore of writing while interviewing, and they are inexpensive to make. Tape recorders can be used unobtrusively. They permit the investigator and witness to enter into a natural dialogue. A tape-recorded interview takes much less time than making a written, signed witness statement. The investigator should keep in mind that some witnesses develop stage fright when they see a tape recorder. The investigator has little control over exactly what goes into the recorded statement. A written statement can be "edited" as it is made, but a tape-recorded statement can almost never be edited.

Some statements are stenographically recorded. The investigator must retain the services of a stenographer. In civil litigation, the stenographers are often referred to as "court reporters," even though they do not necessarily work in a courtroom or for a judge. The procedure involves interviewing the witness in the presence of a stenographer, who makes a verbatim record and transcript of the questions and answers. Ordinarily, these statements are not made under oath, but they may be. The stenographer may make notes in shorthand or by using a stenographic machine. The stenographer uses the notes to prepare a transcript, which usually resembles an oral deposition transcript. The transcript has several uses. Of course, it provides a record of what the witness said, and it may be used to help prepare for trial. If the witness reads the transcript and adopts it by signing it, it may be used as a written/signed statement at trial. If the witness does not sign the transcript, the court reporter can, nevertheless, testify from his or her notes concerning the witness's prior statements. The stenographer testifies to what he or she heard during the interview and may use the stenographic notes to refresh and confirm his or her memory. The stenographer's transcript is not used for impeachment. The transcript which is prepared from the stenographic notes is not usually received into evidence as a signed statement would be, unless the witness signs it.

Stenographically recorded statements are particularly valuable where the witness's willingness to cooperate is doubtful. The stenographer is an independent witness to the interview, and that may be some protection if the witness should later claim undue pressure was applied by the investigator to obtain the statement. The reporter provides the investigator with a typed booklet containing a verbatim transcript of the interview. If the witness tries to deny the statement, the stenographer can testify about the meeting.

Some witness interviews are conducted by telephone. A telephone interview can be recorded and a transcript made. The witness must be told that the conversation is being recorded. The advantages of telephone interviews are that they are inexpensive. Usually the witness can be contacted very quickly. Very little time and effort are needed to set up and conduct the interview. A telephone interview causes the witness the least amount of inconvenience. On the other hand, telephone interviews are difficult for an investigator to do well. The witness can easily avoid or terminate the interview, and the investigator cannot evaluate the witness's appearance. Too often, portions of telephone recordings are garbled. Tapes of telephone conversations are difficult to present and use at trial if the transcripts of the recordings are challenged.

Each method of recording witness statements has its own advantages and disadvantages. Therefore, careful consideration should be given to selecting the type of statement to be obtained from each witness. The manner in which the witness is approached depends, in part, on whether a statement will be obtained and how that statement will be recorded. The reverse is true also. For example, if there is reason to believe that a particular witness is not going to be cooperative, it may be desirable to employ a stenographer to observe and record the interview, because the witness is not likely to sign a written statement and may object to a tape recorder. An experienced stenographer can be quite unobtrusive during the interview. Also, a stenographer may be a very effective witness for the investigator if the *interviewee* challenges the statement or complains about the conduct of the investigator.

If a statement is to be obtained, it is well to preview the subject with the witness before recording the interview. The preview gives the investigator an opportunity to determine exactly what the witness knows and is willing to say. The investigator can do a better job of framing questions and can avoid matters which are sensitive or counterproductive. After obtaining a good overview of the witness's knowledge, the interviewer may simply state to the witness that he or she would like to cover this same material in a recorded statement. The recorder should be ready to be turned on. The interviewer should state his or her name, the name of the witness, the date and the time of the interview. Then the witness should be asked to state his or her name (and spell it) and address. Generally speaking, it is perfectly all right for the interviewer to ask *leading* questions. Witnesses do not mind, and leading questions do not impair the usual uses of recorded witness statements.

The investigator almost always prepares the written statements for the witness to sign, because most witnesses simply would not make the effort to write a statement. The interviewer may tell the witness that he or she will prepare a statement to be signed. Or, the interviewer may simply ask the witness a series of questions and write down the answers in a statement format, which at the end of the interview the witness is asked to read and sign. The investigator's notes become the witness's statement. The witness's own words should be used insofar as possible. A statement ought to be single spaced to reduce the possibility of interpolation. When the interview is completed, the statement is done. If the witness agrees that the statement is accurate, the witness should be encouraged to sign it. It is very important to have the statement signed. Indeed, the witness should be asked to sign all pages of the statement. A lawyer cannot safely rely upon an unsigned statement. The witness cannot be cross-examined from the statement unless the witness has adopted the statement by signing it. Nor can a witness be impeached with the statement unless it is signed. The witness statement ought to conclude with an acknowledgment showing that the witness has read it and received a copy. It is easy to make a carbon copy for the witness to keep.

A witness can be encouraged to sign the statement by the investigator's offering to provide a copy to the witness for his or her future reference. The witness's own signature will be assurance that the statement is accurate. It is fair to point out to the witness that in one or two years the witness's memory will not be as clear as it is currently, so by signing the statement, the witness will be assured that it was true and correct when made. In other words, signing the statement is for the witness's own benefit and protection. If the signed statement is totally beneficial to the investigator's client, the investigator may suggest that by signing this statement and obtaining a copy, the witness can use the statement with other investigators. In some states the law requires that the witnesses be given a copy of any signed statement. Rule 26(b)(3) requires parties to give witnesses copies of their statements upon request. Another consideration is that many courts require parties to provide copies of witness statements to the opposing parties if duly requested. Those states do not recognize the preparation of witness statements to be part of a *party's work product* or an *attorney's work product*.

In those states where parties must give exchange witness statements on demand, lawyers are reluctant to obtain statements except for very specific and compelling reasons, because they do not want to share their efforts with the opposition. A practice has evolved in those states of making *memoranda of interview* which contain the witness information but are not directly adopted by the witness by signing it. On occasion, the lawyer may supply the memorandum of interview to the witness, so that the witness can refer to it. But the memorandum is not considered to be a statement, because it is not a verbatim recording and has not been signed by the witness.

An investigator must use common sense in determining what should go into the written statement and what, if anything, should be omitted. It might be beneficial to keep certain things out of the statement and out of evidence.

If a statement is used at trial for any purpose, the whole statement might be received into evidence. There is no law or rule which provides that a statement must be complete in every detail, but a witness has the right to object to giving or signing a statement which omits facts the witness considers to be important. The witness's sense of propriety must be respected. Of course, a statement must accurately reflect the witness's version of the facts.

A good statement, whether written and signed or a stenographer's transcript, should commit the witness to his or her version of the occurrence or transaction. It should clearly set forth the facts known by the witness and establish the basis and sources of this knowledge. For example, it is not enough to record the fact that the witness saw a vehicle traveling at a stated speed in miles per hour. The statement should show when and where the witness first observed the vehicle, how long it was observed, and the direction of its travel. The statement should record the location of the witness when making the observations and the fact that he or she has adequate eyesight and is sufficiently experienced to make valid observations concerning speed. A good statement should also record the witness's lack of knowledge of important facts. For example, a statement could properly note that the witness did not look for skid marks; does not know of any other witness; did not talk to any of the parties; is not acquainted with any of the parties; observed that a horn did not sound before the collision *or* did not hear a horn sound before the accident; did not see the traffic light, etc. Some signed statements are purely "negative" statements, which are good insurance against having problems from the witnesses later. A good negative statement neutralizes a witness from being a problem or threat to the client's case. If a witness is reluctant to give a statement indicating that he or she does not have certain information, that is a "red flag" that the witness may be hiding information or cooperating with the other side.

Preparing Witness Statements

As mentioned, an investigator should not rush into writing out a statement for the witness. It is better simply to talk with the witness for a while to find out what the witness knows and what the witness's attitude is about the accident or transaction. After developing the basic facts, the investigator should start writing out a statement for the witness to sign. The witness may or may not be told at the beginning of the interview that he or she will be asked to sign the statement. Written statements often begin with the date and place at the top:

(Date)

(Place)

Statement of John E. Doe

I live at _____ . I am _____ years of age and employed at _____ . My parents are _____ , and they live at

_____ . They usually know where I am
if I have to travel out of the state. On (date), I was a witness to an
accident at

* * *

I have read the above statement consisting of three pages. <u>Yes</u>
The statement is true and correct. <u>Yes</u>
I have received a copy of this statement. <u>Yes</u>

(Witness Signature)

A signature on each page makes the statement more authoritative and more
readily usable, and it helps to protect the witness, investigator, and party
who is relying upon the statement. The investigator may say that he or she
is really helping the witness by preparing this "record" for the witness's use.
The witness can be made to appreciate that, for better or worse, the witness
is involved in the case. It will be easier for everyone if the witness cooperates.
The witness really needs a record of his or her observations, and the proposed
statement will be that record.

It is not uncommon for investigators to make minor errors in the preparation
of written statements—sometimes on purpose. When errors are made, the
investigator should identify the errors and ask the witness to initial the corrections. The initials in the body of a written statement are evidence that the
witness has read and corrected the statement; therefore, the inference is that
the final product is true and correct and specifically approved by the witness.

Witnesses will be more cooperative and responsive if they feel the investigator is being candid, sensitive to their concerns, and fair. If the witness is
less than cooperative, the witness may be told that he or she is already
involved, and a lack of cooperation will not help avoid involvement. The
witness can be told that the alternative to an informal statement is a deposition, which will require a response to a subpoena and testimony under oath.

A signed statement from a witness tells the lawyer where he or she stands
with that witness and, thus, is better able to evaluate the client's claims or
defenses. Signed statements are relatively easy to obtain and inexpensive to
make. Unlike taking depositions, procurement of statements does not expose
the witness to the opposing side (but see Rule 26(b)(3)). The witness can
require the lawyer to provide a copy of the statement and then share the
statement with the other party.

Some law firms have "witness statement forms," which they mail to witnesses with a request that the form be completed by the witness and mailed
back. Such forms must be short and very specific. Consequently, they have
limited value. It is not known what percentage of witnesses actually respond
to the form questionnaires. Perhaps the primary value of such forms is to
help a paralegal decide whether or not to interview certain witnesses. The
forms may be particularly useful where many witnesses cannot be contacted

quickly in any other manner. A sample of one of these witness forms is found in Appendix V.

Ethical Considerations

Suppose that immediately before trial the client confesses that the information supplied in a written signed statement is false. Suppose further that the lawyer and paralegal have been relying upon the information in preparing the case for trial, but the statement has not been disclosed to anyone else. What course of action should be taken? Of course, the client cannot be allowed to use fraud or deceit against the adverse party. As officers of the court, lawyers have a duty to prevent clients and witnesses from testifying falsely. In this situation, the false information has not yet been communicated to the other parties, their lawyers, or the court. Therefore, there is no need to disclose the fact that the client has lied; however, if false information has been supplied to the opposing side, through answers to interrogatories or in some other manner, the opposing party would have to be told of the error. There is no inherent need to explain how the error occurred. If the client is unwilling to allow the corrections to be made to answer to interrogatories, a dilemma is created for the lawyer. A lawyer must not disclose privileged communications. However, a lawyer must not permit the client to perpetrate a fraud upon the court. The dilemma is resolved in favor of disclosing the privileged information to the court. The lawyer would also have to withdraw from the case if the client persists with the lie.

INVESTIGATION SUMMARY

The claimant's causes of action, the defendant's affirmative defenses, and the applicable measure of damages determine what facts are material to an action at law. Therefore, the material facts should be ascertainable from the pleadings.

Facts are the conditions, circumstances, and relationships which gave rise to the dispute.

The purpose of an investigation is to learn as much as possible about the facts and to obtain evidence with which to prove the facts.

A fact may be established for purposes of a case by the court taking judicial notice of the fact or by a party's judicial admission made in the pleadings or Rule 36 admissions, by the parties' stipulation which is accepted by the court, or by evidence which is received at trial.

Evidence consists of sworn testimony and exhibits which the court considers for the purpose of determining the facts which gave rise to the parties' controversy. By way of illustration, the speed of a party's vehicle is a fact; a witness's testimony about the speed is evidence of the fact. A party's loss of income is a fact; tax returns and employment records are evidence of the fact of loss or the fact that there was no loss.

Evidence is relevant if it has a tendency to prove a fact that is material to the dispute.

A party who has the burden of proving a fact must present evidence which establishes that the fact is more likely true than not true. There are a few types of cases in which a fact must be proved by clear and convincing evidence.

There is no one formula for conducting all investigations.

INVESTIGATION OUTLINE

I. Purpose.
   A. Discover the facts.
   B. Obtain evidence with which to prove the facts.
   C. Preserve evidence.
   D. Prepare and organize evidence for use at trial.

II. Guidelines.
   A. Identify the purposes for the investigation.
   B. Obtain client's version of the transaction or occurrence.
      1. Pay attention to details.
      2. Test claims and assumptions against physical facts.
   C. Begin the investigation as soon as possible.
   D. Establish an investigation plan with priorities.
   E. Build on the evidence as evidence is acquired.
   F. Preserve the evidence.
      1. Witness information.
         a) Depositions before suit.
         b) Statements.
            (1) Signed.
            (2) Recorded.
         Memorandum of interview.
         d) Letter to witness regarding gist of witness's information.
      2. Scene: measurements, diagrams, photographs, models.
      3. Documents—always record sources.
      4. Considerations.
         a) Making or keeping evidence to be admissible in court.
         b) Making evidence authoritative.
   G. Evaluate evidence for the following:
      1. Completeness—check on records and other documents volunteered by opposing party; there should be no need to verify records supplied pursuant to discovery rules by a lawyer.
      2. Accuracy—even determinations made in official investigations may need to be verified.
      3. Availability—now and in the future.
      4. Authenticity, for example, unsigned copies of affidavits, statements, and documents.
   H. Keep the "big picture" in mind while collecting and evaluating evidence.
   I. Be concerned about "negative evidence" and the absence of evidence. For example:
      1. Absence of skid marks.
      2. Absence of physical complaints, symptoms, findings.
      3. Absence of property damage.
   J. Do not let appearances mislead or cause you to make false assumptions.

    K. Evidence which at first may not seem relevant may become critical as the investigation continues; do not be too quick to discard available evidence.

    L. Evidence which at first seems detrimental may turn out to be very helpful; therefore, collect the evidence and sort it out later.

III. Beginning the investigation.

    A. Obtain client's version.

    B. Visit scene of occurrence.

    C. Collect all documents relevant to transaction.

    D. Locate and interview eyewitnesses.

    E. Interview friendly witnesses.

    F. Interview neutral witnesses.

    G. Interview potential adverse party if not represented by a lawyer.

    H. Obtain official records and documents concerning the transaction or occurrence.

    I. Locate photographs and make photographs.

        1. Photographs which show facts are evidence.

        2. Photographs which are illustrative help witnesses testify to the facts.

    J. Interview hostile witnesses last.

IV. Witnesses.

    A. Determine best circumstances for conducting interviews: scene, work, office, home, telephone, restaurant.

    B. Should the client participate in the interview to help the witness and to promote relations with the witness?

    C. Determine whether a statement should be obtained from the witness.

    D. Determine the purpose for which a statement will be used if one is to be obtained: preservation of information, impeachment, to negate the witness's role, to justify intended settlement or other disposition.

    E. Determine how much of what the witness has to say should be included in the statement.

    F. Will witness be available and accessible in the future?

V. What information should be included in a statement?

    A. General rule: the client's statement should be complete and as detailed as possible. Preserve the client's privilege by protecting against disclosure of the statement!

    B. Independent witness statements should be accurate but need not include everything.

    C. Adverse parties' statements should be accurate and all-inclusive; do not omit anything, whether good or bad.

    D. Statements should be as factual as possible but opinions should be used when that is the only manner in which the witness can express his or her information.

E. Telephone recorded statements should be conducted to advance the client's version of the accident; use leading questions.

F. If the client tells you that he was traveling only twenty-five miles per hour at the time of the accident and you believe him, then say to the witness: "Wouldn't you agree that Mr. Jones was driving at not more than twenty-five miles per hour?" Do not ask: "Was Jones traveling more than twenty-five miles per hour or in excess of the speed limit?"

G. If a telephone recorded statement can be taken on the second contact, an investigator can be better prepared to ask the right questions and avoid the wrong questions.

H. Should the witness be given a copy of the statement?

VI. Coping with witnesses.
  A. Extend yourself to establish rapport.
  B. Cultivate cooperation.
    1. Make witness feel appreciated.
    2. Stress civic duty.
    3. Show witness why information is important.
    4. Establish a line of communication with witness.
    5. Determine whether witness will be available when needed.
  C. Determine how to find witness if he or she were to move.
  D. Make witness appreciate that you are being fair.

VII. Photographs.
  A. Selection of camera: 50mm lens does not distort.
  B. Objects should be photographed from several angles to obtain several perspectives.
  C. Photographs should be taken in sequence from a distance leading to the particular subject so viewer can see the scene and objects in context.
  D. Must not "touch up" accident *scene* before taking pictures.
  E. Should clean up accident *location* (pictures of location do not purport to show conditions as they were at the time of the accident; no one should ever tamper with the appearance of the accident scene). Distorted or prejudicial photographs should not be received into evidence.
  F. Foundation for use at trial.
    1. Photographer: date, time, camera, lens, direction, distances, subject matter.
    2. Reasonably accurate portrayal of subject matter.
    3. Picture as evidence, such as the accident scene.
    4. Picture as illustrative evidence helps witness to explain what the witness saw.
  G. It is better to take too many pictures than not enough. Take pictures of entire scene or location even though relevance may not yet be evident.

VIII. Evidence from witnesses should always be weighed against physical fact.

IX. The evidence should make a pattern or a picture. If part of the "picture" is missing, there is something wrong with the evidence.

X. Be objective about the evidence.
   A. Good witness: good ability to know, remember, and relate the facts; articulate.
   B. Poor witness: no opportunity to know the facts, inaccurate memory, easily confused, difficulty in expressing self; easily led by interrogator.

XI. Use experts to help conduct the investigation.
   A. Very useful for identifying problems; helpful for preserving information and evidence.
   B. Often able to suggest additional areas of inquiry and use of scientific literature.
   C. Engineers are particularly useful in dealing with claims involving machines, structures, real estate, and products.

11 Interrogatories

Interrogatories are the most basic and economical discovery procedure used in civil litigation. A written interrogatory is merely a written question propounded by one party to another party. They may be served only upon parties to the lawsuit. Even though interrogatories are inherently "questions," an interrogatory may be stated as either a question or as an imperative. For example, an interrogatory may be phrased: "State your date of birth." For convenience, we shall refer to the author of interrogatories as the **proponent** and the party who receives the interrogatories and must answer them as the **deponent.**

Interrogatory Format

Each interrogatory should be directed to a single subject. It should be short, specific, and to the point. Carefully drawn interrogatories encourage responsive answers that provide specific information. It is a common practice to divide an interrogatory into subdivisions, and there is no reason to avoid that form if it fits the needs. For example:

1. For each witness statement obtained by the defendant, state the following:
   a. The name and address of the person who interviewed the witness.
   b. The date on which the statement was obtained.
   c. The means by which the statement was recorded.
   d. The name and address of each person who was present when the statement was obtained.
   e. Whether the witness has been given a copy of his or her statement.

Each subdivision counts as a separate interrogatory in those jurisdictions which limit a party to fifty interrogatories.

Each interrogatory is usually numbered for convenient reference. Interrogatories are usually served in sets. A set of interrogatories is made up of all the interrogatories which the proponent has or intends to serve at that particular time. Sets of interrogatories are not based upon subject matter. For example, when the defendant serves initial interrogatories upon the plaintiff, the defendant does *not* serve one set relevant to liability and another set relevant to damages. When more than one set is served, the better practice is to continue with the same numbering system, so that the numbers and system established by the first set is continued into the second set. By way of illustration, if the first set ends with interrogatory number 20, the second set should begin with number 21. The Rules do not limit the number of interrogatories which may be propounded by a party. Nevertheless, some state courts and the special rules of some federal district courts limit to fifty the number of interrogatories which may be served upon another party. Of course, if there are two defendants, the plaintiff may serve up to fifty interrogatories on each defendant.

Purpose

Interrogatories may be used to obtain information about facts known to the other party or available to the other party. They may be used to obtain information about the other party's evidence and legal theories. Rule 26(b) establishes the scope of inquiry permitted through interrogatories. The principal limitation on the scope of interrogatories, as in other discovery procedures, is that they must be relevant to the case in which they are used. For purposes of discovery in civil litigation, an inquiry is relevant if it is calculated to lead to discovery of evidence which will be admissible at trial. Note, that does not mean that the specific subject of inquiry must be admissible. It means that the inquiry must have a reasonable possibility of leading to discovery of a matter which is admissible into evidence. Questions which are relevant to a divorce action may not be relevant to a tort action or to a contract action.

Some interrogatories are relevant to almost every civil action, such as interrogatories concerning the identity of witnesses, the existence of documents, and the existence and identity of tangible things. By requiring that interrogatories be relevant, the Rules help to limit the use and number of interrogatories on a reasonable basis.

Interrogatories are particularly useful for obtaining basic background information about the opposing party, such as the party's address, date of birth, marital status, employment history, accident history, medical history, litigation history, criminal convictions, educational background, use of other names, and social security number. Interrogatories are used to force the deponent to disclose sources of information such as the existence of witness statements, photographs, records, and conversations. The information obtained through the deponent's answers to interrogatories provides a basis for conducting additional investigation and for pursuing more detailed discovery.

One of the primary functions of initial interrogatories is to discover the identity of witnesses known to other parties. A proponent is entitled to disclosure of all witnesses by their named addresses and whether statements have been obtained from them. Interrogatories may not be used to find out what the witnesses know about the transaction or occurrence. Nor may interrogatories be used to find out what witnesses the deponent intends to have testify at trial. Most courts permit interrogatories which require the deponent to identify witnesses by categories, such as witnesses to the accident, witnesses who arrived after the accident, or witnesses who have information concerning damages. The categorization of witnesses does not require disclosure of their actual knowledge. Interrogatories which require a party to disclose to another party the knowledge of witnesses would require the deponent to disclose the "attorney's work product." Such interrogatories are objectionable and should not be answered.

Initial interrogatories commonly ask for the deponent's version of the transaction or occurrence. For example, in an automobile accident case, the defendant may ask an interrogatory such as: "Describe fully how you claim the accident occurred." The question does not contemplate that the deponent must set forth the entire claim, such as describing all the details of who did what and who observed what. Otherwise, the interrogatory would be improper as calling for disclosure of attorney's work product. The interrogatory *does* contemplate that the deponent will state the basic facts concerning the claim of negligence, breach of warranty, or other cause of action. A proper response by the plaintiff could be: "Defendant entered the intersection in violation of the traffic signal (red light) and struck the right side of the automobile in which plaintiff was riding as a passenger; defendant was negligent for violating the traffic light, failing to keep a proper lookout, and traveling at an excessive rate of speed." This answer gives the defendant a fairly good picture of the plaintiff's version of the accident and helps the defendant to focus the rest of the investigation and discovery. Interrogatories do not provide any opportunity for cross-examination of the deponent.

Interrogatories are used primarily to obtain information, but they have other uses as well. The answers may establish that the opponent lacks certain evidence. For example, when the defendant serves interrogatories requiring the plaintiff to disclose the identity of witnesses to the accident, the plaintiff's disclosure that he or she does not know of any witnesses assures the defendant that the plaintiff will not have any eyewitnesses at trial to testify about the accident. The answer assures the defendant that the plaintiff has not found a witness unknown to the defendant. The disclosure may allow the defendant to stop spending time and effort to locate witnesses who do not exist. The interrogatory has eliminated a potential problem.

If the deponent should try to produce a surprise witness at trial, after stating that he or she has no witnesses, the court, on motion, should preclude the witness from testifying, or the court may order a postponement of the trial, allowing the defendant additional time in which to prepare. The court may order that the deponent, who failed to disclose information about a witness, arrange for the witness to appear for a deposition so that the opposing party can find out everything about the witness and the anticipated testimony. The delinquent party may be required to pay all costs of the oral deposition. This procedure gives the "surprised party" an opportunity to determine whether he or she really needs more time to prepare for trial and how much time is needed. A deponent's disclosure that he or she is not aware of any relevant documents, photographs, or other tangible evidence gives the proponent grounds for excluding from evidence any nondisclosed items or, in the alternative, obtain a postponement of the trial.

Limitations

Interrogatories may not be used to obtain information about the opposing party's attorney's mental impressions, conclusions, opinions, or legal theories about the case (Rule 26(b)(3)). This limitation on discovery is commonly referred to as the "attorney's work product" rule. The proscription against discovery applies to discovery of the "work product" of a party's employees, agents, and other representatives such as insurance representatives.

There are several practical limitations on the usefulness of interrogatories. The answers lack spontaneity. They are the answers of the deponent's lawyer or they are the deponent's answers as edited by the lawyer. And, the format used by interrogatories does not allow for cross-examination of the deponent. Notwithstanding these minor limitations, interrogatories play a very important role in civil litigation.

Preparation

Preparation of interrogatories is an important responsibility. Paralegals should strive to develop a high degree of skill in preparing and answering interrogatories. Well-drafted interrogatories are clear and concise. Each question should be precisely stated to elicit specific, relevant information. Interrogatories should not be propounded to another party without a specific purpose in mind. Poorly drafted interrogatories are a curse on the profession. They irritate the opponent. They lead to misunderstandings and sometimes to retaliation. The task should be approached intelligently and conscientiously. It is all too easy for the proponent to serve a myriad of questions which require the opponent to spend days collecting information. The fact that it is so easy to prepare interrogatories places a responsibility on every party to be careful not to abuse the right. If interrogatories are served just to make the file look substantial or to satisfy the client's curiosity or to harass the deponent, the proponent has abused their use. Of course, the deponent has the right to object to improper interrogatories or the misuse of interrogatories (Rule 37); however, the parties should rarely have to ask the court for protection from harassment. Paralegals and lawyers must act responsibly, with restraint and for proper purposes.

Interrogatories should not be unreasonably burdensome in their number or their demand for information. The relevancy and importance of the questions should be weighed against the burden and inconvenience to the deponent. Form interrogatories are acceptable and frequently used, but they must be directly applicable to the case. It is poor usage to serve interrogatories which were drafted for another case and do not really fit the issues in the present case. Great care should be used to make interrogatories clear and understandable. Some lawyers try to insure specificity and clarity in their interrogatories by using a list of definitions at the beginning of their sets of interrogatories. The format seems to work reasonably well, but sometimes it does seem a little pedantic.

One fault commonly found in poorly drafted interrogatories is that two interrogatories are used where one will do. For example, (1) "Do you know of any witnesses to the accident?" (2) "If your answer to the preceding interrogatory is yes, state the name and address of each witness." The question would have been simpler and better as an imperative: (1) "State the names and addresses of all witnesses to the accident."

Each interrogatory should be drafted to make it easy to answer. For example, if it is possible to obtain the needed information by having the deponent answer yes or no, that is the best approach. It is easy for the deponent to answer. The deponent will be less likely to put off answering. The answer cannot be misinterpreted. If any dispute develops over the adequacy of the deponent's answer to an interrogatory, the deponent will probably blame the answer's alleged inadequacy on ambiguities in the question. Lawyers and judges lose respect for law offices which serve poorly drafted interrogatories.

Scope

It is proper to use interrogatories to discover facts, evidence, and information which is "calculated" to lead to the discovery of evidence which is admissible at trial. The proponent must have some intent and expectation of discovering usable evidence. Otherwise, the inquiry is nothing more than the proverbial "fishing expedition." Mere "fishing" is impermissible.

The defendant's initial interrogatories usually ask specific questions about the plaintiff's alleged loss and claim for damages. The defendant needs to know how the loss was determined, how the damages were calculated, and what evidence the plaintiff has to support the claim for damages. It is useful for the defendant to ask what amount of money is claimed for each item of loss. Many factors must be considered in determining the amount of damages which may be recovered by the plaintiff. Each of those factors is a proper subject for an interrogatory. Among the factors to be considered are the measure of damages, the nature of the loss, the extent of the injury, the original cost of damaged property, the age of damaged property, the cost of repairs, the cost of replacement, the availability of cost estimates, the costs actually incurred, the method of calculating damages, and the supporting documentation such as repair bills, invoices, and receipts. Interrogatories may be used to obtain the identity of witnesses who have information about the alleged damages.

The defendant is also entitled to know whether the plaintiff's loss is covered by the plaintiff's own direct-loss insurance. The information is relevant because the defendant is entitled to know who else has any interest in the subject matter and outcome of the case. The insurer may be another source of evidence which would be admissible at trial. For example, the insurer may have photographs relevant to the damages, repair estimates, repair bills, and statements.

Interrogatories may require the deponent to disclose facts, evidence, opinions, and even legal conclusions. Interrogatories may be used to find out how the opponent contends the law applies to facts in the case. Rule 33(b) states the following:

> An interrogatory otherwise proper is not necessarily objectionable merely because the answer to the interrogatory involves an opinion or contention that relates to fact or the application of law to fact, but the court may order that such an interrogatory need not be answered until after designated discovery has been completed or until a pre-trial conference or other later time.

For example, in an automobile accident case, the defendant may require the plaintiff to specify all acts and omissions which the plaintiff attributes to the defendant and which the plaintiff claims were negligent. The plaintiff and his or her lawyer must answer the interrogatory with specific allegations such as unlawful speed, failure to yield right-of-way, driving on the wrong side of highway, failure to signal a turn, or failure to keep a proper lookout. In a products liability case, the plaintiff would have to disclose those factors which the plaintiff contends make the product defective in its design, fabrication, warnings, or instructions. The plaintiff's answers to such interrogatories enable the defendant to focus the rest of the investigation and discovery procedures on the particular acts or omissions related by the plaintiff.

If at trial, the plaintiff were to attempt to prove that the defendant was negligent in some other unidentified respect or that the product was defective in some other unidentified respect, the defendant may be able to exclude the plaintiff's evidence bearing on that issue or be entitled to a postponement of the trial, so that he or she can prepare on the "new" issue. For example, if the plaintiff's answer to interrogatory only specifies the defendant's excessive speed as a cause of the automobile accident, and at trial, the plaintiff attempts to prove that the defendant's brakes were negligently maintained, the defendant may be able to exclude any such evidence about the condition of the brakes or, in the alternative, obtain a continuance of the trial so that the defendant can adequately prepare on the issue. Of course, the plaintiff may pose the same type of interrogatory to the defendant concerning affirmative defenses asserted in the answer. In this way, interrogatories enable the parties to concentrate on specific fact issues and to fully prepare on the legal issues. Interrogatories may be used to obtain information about any claim or defense whether in contract, tort, or based upon statutes.

The explanation in the preceding paragraphs is *not* in conflict with the rule against disclosure of the attorney's work product. The interrogatories referred to do not require disclosure of what the deponent or deponent's lawyer has done to develop or substantiate the legal theories or legal conclusions. Remember, the plaintiff's complaint and the defendant's answer are sufficient to state a cause of action or an affirmative defense by merely alleging "negligence" on the part of the opposing party. There must be a way of obtaining a more specific description of the negligence allegation without, in each case, making a motion to the court for an order compelling a more specific description of the negligent acts or omission upon which the opposing party relies and will try to prove at trial.

Interrogatories may be used to obtain information about facts, expert opinions, and even legal conclusions of the adverse party's lawyer. Rule 33(b) provides: "An interrogatory otherwise proper is not necessarily objectionable merely because an answer to the interrogatory involves an opinion or contention that relates to the fact or the application of law to fact." The purpose of the rules is to give parties the means to obtain more specific, detailed information about another party's claims or defenses. For example, the complaint may assert a cause of action against the defendant by simply alleging that the defendant was negligent in the operation of the automobile so as to cause the automobile accident.

Interrogatories are frequently used to obtain information from and about the contents of business records which belong to an opposing party. Rule 33(c) gives the deponent the option to extrapolate the requested information or to produce the records for inspection and copying by the proponent. Obviously, the primary consideration in deciding how to proceed is the time, expense, and inconvenience involved.

Interrogatories are useful to obtain information about conversations between parties and between parties and other persons. Interrogatories concerning conversations should request disclosure of the exact words, but, in the alternative, request disclosure of the substance of what was said by each participant if the deponent avers that he or she cannot recall the exact words. It is also important to discover who else was present and may have heard the conversation. Is there a record or memorandum concerning the conversation? Who made it? Who has custody of it?

Both the plaintiff and defendant are entitled to know whether the opposing party has insurance coverage applicable to the losses in question. Therefore, the rules expressly allow discovery of insurance information. The amount and availability of insurance may significantly affect the parties' evaluations and attitudes toward settlement. Technically, the availability of liability insurance is irrelevant to most civil lawsuits. On occasion, a direct-loss insurer who has made payments to the insured plaintiff may have subrogation rights. The insurer may even be the real party in interest. The defendant is entitled to know all the circumstances affecting an insurer's interest in the case, and such information is most conveniently obtained through interrogatories.

If the defendant's liability insurance policy is the only asset with which to pay any judgment the plaintiff may obtain, the amount and availability of that insurance may be very significant to the plaintiff's evaluation of the claim and directly affect the plaintiff's willingness to settle. On occasion, a difficult situation develops between the defendant and his or her liability insurer because one may be anxious to settle and the other opposed to any settlement. Dealing with such problems is outside the scope of this book.

A proponent may use interrogatories to discover whether the deponent has any liability insurance which can be used to pay any of the judgment which the proponent might obtain against the deponent. If there is insurance, the proponent is entitled to discover the name of the insurer, the identity of the particular insurance policy, the amount of the available coverage, and whether there is any dispute over the coverage (Rule 26(b)(2)). Technically, the availability of liability insurance is not relevant to accident cases because insurance does not affect issues of liability or damages. Discovery of insurance is allowed, however, because it may have a significant effect on the parties' willingness or ability to settle their dispute.

As a general proposition, the scope of inquiry through interrogatories is the same as in other discovery procedures. But there is one very important exception. The use of interrogatories is the only means for obtaining information about expert witnesses retained by another party (Rule 26(b)(4)). A proponent may serve interrogatories to obtain information about the identity of the deponent's experts, the subject matter to which the expert will testify, and the grounds for the expert's opinions. If the proponent can show exceptional circumstances to the effect that the proponent cannot obtain facts or opinions on the same subject, then, upon motion and court order, the proponent may be allowed to take the deposition of the deponent's expert. Note, the rules do not require disclosure of the identity of experts with whom the deponent or deponent's lawyer has consulted but does not intend to have testify. Consultation with an expert who is not selected to testify is considered part of the "attorney's work product" and not discoverable.

A court would order a party to permit his or her expert to be deposed if the expert conducted tests on an item that is no longer available to be tested. The opposing party has a right to know about the details of the test, and the only fair way to obtain all of the necessary information is to cross-examine the expert in a deposition. Another situation in which a court may order a party to have the party's expert submit to an oral deposition is where the expert was disclosed just before trial or after discovery was ordered closed. The oral deposition may be the alternative to a complete bar against the witness testifying when not disclosed in a timely manner.

As useful as interrogatories are, they have some significant limitations. The deponent has the opportunity to ponder the questions, so the answers are not spontaneous. The answers end up being the product of the deponent's lawyer.

ANSWERS TO INTERROGATORIES

Form and Procedure

Each interrogatory must be answered in writing. Each answer must be stated separately for each respective interrogatory. The answers must be complete and fully stated (Rule 33(a)). The answers to interrogatories should begin by restating the interrogatory being answered. Although the Federal Rules of Civil Procedure do not require a reiteration of the interrogatory, it makes the answers much more understandable and convenient to use. Many state court rules of procedure require a restatement of the interrogatory before each answer.

An answer should follow the same wording and form as the interrogatory. For example, if an interrogatory has used subdivisions, the answer should refer to those subdivisions. Short, declarative sentences are best; however, an answer may be just a word or a phrase. There is no requirement that full sentences be used. Answers may be made upon "information and belief" as well as upon knowledge. If an answer is *not* made upon actual knowledge, that fact should be stated.

If an interrogatory is improper for any reason, the respondent may state an objection in lieu of an answer. Or, the respondent may answer the interrogatory *subject to* an objection. For example, an answer might give the respondent's addresses for the past ten years and state an objection that earlier addresses are irrelevant and not calculated to lead to discovery of evidence admissible at trial. If the respondent objects to an interrogatory, the proponent has the right to move the court for an order compelling the respondent to answer. There is no time period within which the objection must be noticed for hearing. On the other hand, if a discovery plan is in effect, that plan may provide time periods for having objections heard. Or, if no effort is made to compel discovery until the case reaches trial, a judge is not likely to be sympathetic to the motion. In the absence of a motion to compel an answer, there is a presumption that the proponent of the interrogatory concurs in the respondent's objection.

Interrogatories are not subject to objection on the grounds that they call for the respondent to state an opinion or contention relevant to the respondent's claims or defenses. An interrogatory may properly ask for another party's explanation concerning the application of law to certain facts. If such a question were put to the deponent in the course of an oral deposition, the question would be objectionable, because the answer requires a legal analysis. But since a lawyer prepares the deponent's answers to interrogatories, such interrogatories are permissible (Rule 33(b)).

The answers to interrogatories are customarily drafted by a lawyer or paralegal for the client's signature. The answers to interrogatories must be based upon the collective information available to the party, the party's lawyer, the party's employees, and the party's agents. In other words, the answers to interrogatories must be accurate and complete in light of all of the information that is available to the party. Parties are expected to make full and candid disclosures. A deponent's answers must be complete in light of the information that is *available* to the deponent, not just what the deponent actually knows. In other words, the deponent has a duty to make reasonable inquiry to obtain the information called for by the interrogatories. If the information is unknown to the deponent and is *equally* available to the proponent, there is no duty upon the deponent to do the proponent's work.

Answers to interrogatories must be put into final form, signed, notarized, and served within thirty days after the interrogatories were served. Objections to interrogatories must be served within the same time period. Often they are served together. The following example should be helpful to understand the applicable time periods. If the defendant serves interrogatories upon the plaintiff by placing them in a United States mailbox on June 1, the thirty-day period begins to run on June 2. June 2 is the first day of the thirty-day period. Then add another three days because service was by mail (Rule 6(e)). Therefore, the answers to interrogatories must be served on July 5. By adding three days for mailing, the time period actually ends on July 4, but that is Independence Day, a legal holiday, so another day must be added. If the legal holiday were not the last day of the time period, it would not extend the time for answering (Rule 6(a)). Parties frequently accommodate each other by voluntarily granting reasonable extensions of time. Parties may stipulate to modify the discovery rules in almost any manner that is convenient for them. There is an important exception: the time limitations prescribed by Rule 33 may be extended only by court order (Rule 29). The parties are generally encouraged to accommodate each other and avoid imposing upon the courts' time by making motions.

The deponent may be asked questions concerning the contents of business records. The amount of time and effort necessary to examine the records to obtain the information could be very great, even to the point of being unreasonably burdensome. Rule 33(c) authorizes the deponent to answer the interrogatories by simply agreeing to produce the records for the proponent to examine. The Rule specifies that "the specification [answer] shall be in sufficient detail to permit the interrogating party to locate and identify . . . the records from which the answer [information] may be ascertained." The deponent must allow the proponent reasonable access to the records and permit copying. If the proponent could not understand the records or it would be unreasonably expensive for the proponent to examine the records, a court could require the deponent to answer the interrogatory by preparing a compilation, abstract, or summary and charge the proponent with the reasonable cost for its preparation.

Uses of Interrogatories

A party's answers to interrogatories may be used at trial "to the extent permitted by the rules of evidence" (Rule 33(b)). However, a party cannot introduce into evidence his or her own answers to interrogatories even if the party had personal knowledge of the facts and the facts are relevant, etc. Under the circumstances, the answers to interrogatories are considered not to be self-serving hearsay and not the best evidence. There is a possible exception. The answers to interrogatories might be admissible at trial on behalf of the deponent if the deponent dies before trial (see Rule 804(b)(5)). The most common basis for receiving into evidence a party's answers to interrogatories is that the answers constitute admissions against interest. For example, if a defendant in an automobile case admits in his answer to interrogatories that he did not stop for the stop sign, the answer is admissible in evidence to prove the stop sign violation. Answers to interrogatories may be used for impeachment purposes, that is, to contradict a party's testimony at trial. For example, if the deponent's answer to interrogatories stated that the deponent was traveling forty miles per hour as she entered the intersection but, at trial, the deponent testified to a speed of only thirty miles per hour, the inconsistency may be shown for its impeachment effect. Also, the admission of forty miles per hour constitutes substantive evidence as an admission of a party. (Substantive evidence is any evidence that supports a verdict. Not all impeachment evidence is substantive evidence. Some impeachment evidence is heard by the jury only for the purpose of discrediting a witness but cannot be considered by the jury as proof of any facts in dispute between the parties.)

Would the proponent always try to impeach the deponent with inconsistent answers to interrogatories? Not necessarily. Suppose that, in the preceding example, the deponent stated, in the answers to interrogatories, that her speed was twenty miles per hour as she entered the intersection; but, at trial, she admitted to a speed of forty miles per hour. Should the proponent show the jury that the deponent's prior answer is inconsistent and impeaching? Perhaps. Like so many things about trial strategy, it depends upon how the evidence fits into the big picture and the overall strategy. It is a judgment call that the proponent's lawyer will have to make, and he or she may not have much time to consider all of the ramifications. You ask, What is there to lose by not showing the inconsistency? Perhaps the witness will decide that her deposition testimony was correct and that she was driving only 20 miles per hour. She might retract her courtroom admission that she was traveling 40 miles per hour. The jury may conclude that she was only traveling 20 miles per hour. The inconsistency was demonstrated, and the witness was impeached. However, the net effect helped the opponent's case.

Suppose that interrogatories served upon the plaintiff ask the plaintiff to describe her personal injuries, and she describes only head and neck injuries in her answers. Then, at trial, she testifies that she has had lots of low back pain ever since the accident. Her failure to refer to the low back pain in her answers to interrogatories may be used for impeachment and be substantive evidence tending to show that she did not have any back injury. Answers to interrogatories are not considered to be judicial admissions, that is, the answers do not conclusively establish the admitted facts. This is one of the important differences between Rule 33 answers to interrogatories and Rule 36 responses to requests for admissions. Her answers to interrogatories merely affect the weight which the jury may or should give to the deponent's testimony.

The deponent must sign his or her answers to interrogatories. The signature is made under oath. The lawyer may sign objections to interrogatories. A corporate officer or authorized agent may sign for a corporation. If specifically authorized by the corporate party, the lawyer handling the case may sign on behalf of the corporation. If the answers, or some of them, are not made upon personal knowledge, it is appropriate to state in the notary clause that the answers are "made upon information and belief."

ABUSES AND SANCTIONS

If the deponent wrongfully withholds or conceals information by giving incomplete or misleading answers, the deponent is subject to sanctions (Rule 37).

If the deponent believes that the proponent's interrogatories are excessively burdensome or constitute harassment, he or she may move the court for a protective order limiting the interrogatories in number or in scope (Rule 26(c)). The special rules of some federal district courts and the rules of practice in some state courts limit the number of interrogatories to fifty, including subdivisions to questions. If a set of interrogatories exceeds the specified number, the responding party may refuse to answer any of them or choose the fifty interrogatories which he or she prefers to answer. Of course, the courts which limit the number of interrogatories also provide a means for obtaining a court order authorizing more interrogatories when more are necessary. The limitation helps to reduce the use of nuisance interrogatories.

12 Expert Witnesses

Civil litigation is becoming more complex and increasingly dependent upon experts. Experts provide assistance in a variety of ways in addition to testifying at trial. An expert may be retained to review the client's claim or defense for the purpose of determining how to go about gathering evidence to develop and support the client's position. Experts are familiar with sources of information, such as the identity of other experts who can provide advice and testimony. They are familiar with relevant literature and how to obtain it. Experts can help start the investigation on the right path by postulating how and why the problem arose. As facts and evidence are obtained, experts can assess the strengths and weaknesses of the client's case and the opponent's case. Even though the ordinary juror has a good education, jurors often need experts to help them understand the significance of certain evidence and to explain how the evidence applies to the facts. Lawyers are constantly finding new ways of using expert witnesses to develop parties' claims and defenses.

Civil litigation is conducted on the premise that the jury should decide the case on the basis of the facts and not on the basis of witnesses' opinions, conclusions, or suppositions. The reasons for the premise are valid. A verdict based upon the facts is a fair verdict. The prejudicial effect of witnesses' opinions and conclusions ordinarily outweighs their probative value. The limitations on opinion evidence promote objectivity and fairness. Nevertheless, there are quite a few exceptions to the rule against opinion evidence, and the use of expert witness testimony is one of the most important exceptions.

Opinions and Conclusions

Experts are allowed to use their education, training, and experience to form *expert opinions*, which they may express to the jury to help them understand disputed facts or the application of the evidence to the disputed facts. Rule 702 states the following:

> If scientific, technical, or other specialized knowledge will assist the trier of fact to understand the evidence or to determine a fact in issue, a witness qualified as an

expert by knowledge, skill, experience, training or education may testify thereto in the form of an opinion or otherwise.

Although expert witness opinions are admissible in evidence, conclusions by witnesses, whether or not they are experts, are not admissible. The Rules of Procedure and the Rules of Evidence do not undertake to define "opinions" or "conclusions," probably because the subject is too esoteric and any definition which could be devised would be riddled with exceptions.

Notwithstanding the absence of an official definition or even explanation for these terms, the following explanations are offered. A conclusion is merely a product of deductive reasoning from given facts. Any person with normal intelligence can reason to the conclusion. Performing a mathematical calculation is a good example of reasoning to a conclusion. On the other hand, an opinion is a personal judgment derived from facts. The opinion is the product of application of the witness's education, training, and experience. The facts upon which the opinion is based may have been observed by the witness or merely communicated to the witness. The witness must use his or her education, training, and experience to evaluate the facts. The witness's special abilities make it possible for the witness to have an understanding and appreciation which nonexperts could not have. An expert witness's belief about a particular matter or subject is not an opinion if it is nothing more than speculation or a mere guess. An opinion must be based upon **reasonable certainty** or, in some jurisdictions, at least a **probability** of correctness. That degree of certainty means the expert, being intellectually honest, must firmly believe that the opinion is more likely true than not true.

Let's take a look at an example of an expert opinion which would be admissible in evidence. Suppose a patient seeks treatment for a rather sudden onset of nausea with abdominal pain, indications that the pain is beginning to localize in the right lower quadrant of the abdomen, and a low-grade fever. A physician will probably make a differential diagnosis which includes the possibility of appendicitis. The physician will probably elect to check the patient's abdominal reflexes, order a white blood count, and observe the patient for a while. If the patient's condition worsens and the white blood count is greatly elevated, the physician may form an *opinion* that the patient *probably* has appendicitis. Until the physician is able to form an opinion that the diagnosis is probable, the physician will elect not to operate. In other words, the opinion must have a degree of certainty about it before the physician will act upon it. Of course, the diagnosis or opinion cannot be confirmed until the operation is actually performed and the physician can actually see the inflamed appendix. Until then, the opinion has the possibility of being mistaken even though it is very reasonable and well supported. Certainly the patient would not want the physician to wait until he or she knows for sure that the appendix is inflamed before operating, because then it may be too late. On the other hand, the patient certainly does not want the physician to operate on the basis of a mere guess that the appendix is inflamed and might need to be removed.

An opinion differs from a conclusion in that a conclusion is merely a process of reasoning from the established or presented facts without any element of expertise added to form a judgment about the matter. In the preceding example, the physician had a number of facts to consider: nausea, pain, location of pain, type of pain, elevated temperature, elevated white blood count, change in abdominal reflexes, etc. The physician could actually observe some of these facts, such as the elevated temperature. Some of the facts were merely reported to the physician, such as the pain. Some of the facts were observed by others, such as the elevated white blood count, which was determined by a laboratory technician. Some of these facts might cause a layperson to suspect appendicitis, but without the expertise of a physician, the layperson's suspicion or belief is nothing more than conjecture.

The law uses experts' opinions almost the same way as the physician used the diagnosis in the preceding example. The expert may take into consideration the facts, which are ordinarily important to professionals in forming opinions. But the law will not permit the jury to rely and act upon an opinion until the opinion has a reasonable degree of certainty to it. The physician's education and experience are essential factors to the formation of an expert opinion. The jury does not have the necessary experience to know the significance of the history, symptoms, and findings which were necessary to the preoperative diagnosis. Therefore, if the question of fact before the jury is whether the patient has appendicitis, the physician's opinion would be helpful to the jury in trying to make that determination. Keep in mind, that another expert might have made a different diagnosis based upon reasonable probability. Because experts do not always agree and there is room for honest disagreement, patients often choose to obtain second opinions before submitting to treatment. The law recognizes that the jury is entitled to hear experts who disagree and chose from among their opinions.

A layperson with an average education and ordinary intelligence can make conclusions by reasoning from the facts, usually just as well as an expert. The jury should conduct its own analysis of the facts to arrive at its own conclusions about the facts. The lawyers will suggest conclusions in their final arguments. There is no good reason for having experts also argue for conclusions. Therefore, mere conclusions are not received into evidence, but expert opinions are.

Let's look at another example. Suppose two salespersons have rented an automobile for a business trip. One is driving and the other is a passenger. The driver misses a turn in the road causing the automobile to go into the ditch and roll over and both salespersons are thrown out. Both die instantly. A question arises as to which person was driving the automobile and, presumably, responsible for the accident. A thorough, careful investigation of the accident scene shows the position of the bodies, their belongings, the path of the automobile, the types of injuries sustained, and the fingerprints within the automobile. Suppose further that salesperson A had a fractured skull, and the windshield in front of the passenger's seat is shattered by the occupant's head having struck it. Suppose that salesperson B's fingerprints are all over the steering wheel, and only one indistinct print might be that made by salesperson A. An accident reconstruction expert could take all of these facts and *conclude* that salesperson B was driving. But a jury using its own experience and common sense could reasonably arrive at the same conclusion without the input from the reconstructionist. The reconstructionist's education, training, and experience with similar cases really adds very little to the analysis or determination of the facts. Therefore, the reconstructionist's conclusions should not be deemed useful to help the jury to understand the evidence or to determine a fact in issue (Rule 702).

Expert Witness Qualifications

A witness must qualify as an expert before the court will allow the witness to express any expert opinions. The foundation is laid through preliminary testimony in which the witness shows that he or she has special education, training, or experience in the subject matter. Lawyers place great importance on the witness's credentials: the extent of the witness's education, training, and experience. Of course, the better the expert's qualifications, the more persuasive the testimony is likely to be. Usually, the witness testifies to his or her own qualifications. Just how much education or experience an expert is required to have is a matter left to the **sound discretion** of the trial judge. This means that the trial judge has a great deal of latitude in such matters. The witness qualifies if the judge concludes that the witness's opinions would probably be helpful to the jury to understand other evidence in the case (Rule 702). The tendency seems to be for trial judges to resolve any doubt on the side of allowing the testimony, rather than excluding it.

As mentioned above, a person qualifies to be an expert witness by showing that he or she has had special education, training or experience in a subject which is relevant to the case. Of course, a highly trained surgeon qualifies to be an expert about medical procedures. The surgeon's expertise comes from the surgeon's education, training, and experience. However, expertise does not always depend upon having higher education. A mechanic with less than a high school education may qualify to be an expert witness concerning matters with which the mechanic is familiar through on-the-job training and experience. A machine operator may qualify as an expert solely by reason of the operator's job experience. On the basis of experience a truck driver may qualify as an expert concerning the proper methods of loading and operating a particular type of truck.

Use of Expert Opinion Evidence

Certain types of litigation, such as professional malpractice cases, usually require expert testimony to establish a prima facie case of liability. For example, suppose that a bridge collapses and a malpractice action is brought against the structural engineer who designed the bridge. The fact of the collapse does not, in itself, establish that the engineer failed to use due care in preparing the bridge's design or specifications. To prove malpractice, the plaintiff must prove that the engineer failed to comply with the standards, practices, or procedures applicable to structural engineers. The plaintiff must also prove that the engineer's deviation from applicable standards was a direct cause of the bridge's failure. A jury could not know or determine, from the jurors' collective experience, what the professional standards are, so they could not determine whether the engineer violated the standards. It takes testimony from someone who is familiar with the standards of the profession, usually a member of the profession, to describe the applicable standards for the jury.

Most medical malpractice cases require expert testimony to establish the standards applicable to the defendant physician. Without such testimony, the evidence is insufficient to prove a case of negligence (malpractice) against the physician. Similarly, just because a lawyer loses a case, that does not mean that the lawyer has been negligent in preparing for the trial or negligent in the presentation of the case. An action for malpractice against a lawyer requires evidence that the lawyer neglected professional standards relevant to the preparation or presentation of the case.

Some cases do not require expert witness testimony, but expert testimony is allowed because such evidence is helpful to the jury to better understand the evidence and the application of the evidence to the disputed facts. For example, if two automobiles have a "head-on" collision on a two-way highway and there are no survivors or witnesses, expert witnesses may be able to reconstruct how the accident occurred by studying the skid marks, location of debris, points of impact on the vehicles, point of impact on the roadway, consequential damage, gyrations of the cars after impact, etc. The jurors could use their own knowledge and experience and probably do a pretty good job of determining, from the same evidence, what happened. Nevertheless, the experts' observations and opinions may be helpful to the jurors; therefore, courts are prone to allowing experts to reconstruct the accident where there are no witnesses. Some courts would hold that if there are eyewitnesses who can testify to what happened, no experts should be allowed to reconstruct the accident for the jury. The apparent need for expert testimony is diminished where there is an eyewitness to the occurrence.

The use of expert testimony does not always make the jury's job easier, because, more often than not, each party is able to find an expert who will contradict the opinions of the opposing expert. The jury is then confronted with having to choose between two or more experts and their opinions. The net effect may be that the jury hears the experts "argue" the case from the witness stand, in addition to hearing the lawyers' final arguments. Jurors have some difficulty with the idea that honest experts can really differ in their opinions.

There seems to be an increasing tendency to use expert witnesses to prove matters that really do not require expert testimony. Accident reconstruction experts are leading this trend. They examine the accident scene, talk to witnesses, read the parties' depositions, examine the vehicles involved in the accident, review their scientific data and tables, and then undertake to explain *how* and *why* the accident occurred. This seems to be a very logical approach, but it is common for equally qualified experts to come to diametrically opposed conclusions. In automobile accident cases, the accident reconstruction experts may be allowed to express conclusions concerning the point of impact, angle of collision, speeds of the vehicles at impact, and speeds of the vehicles when the brakes were applied, etc. Having seen a number of such experts testify, the author holds an "expert opinion" that many of these professional expert witnesses engage in a good deal of sophistry. The trend is not healthy for the legal system. Jurors should decide cases on the facts.

Discovery of Experts' Opinions

Good trial preparation requires each side to find out as quickly as possible about the other side's expert witnesses, their opinions, and the grounds for their opinions. It usually takes quite a bit of time to fully analyze the expert's reasoning processes, check the expert's data, and check on the expert's background. In addition, it usually takes time to locate opposing expert witnesses who are knowledgeable, authoritative, and persuasive. The need for such information must be weighed against the adversary nature of civil litigation.

If courts were to allow unbridled access to the adverse party's hired experts, the very heart of the adversary system would be threatened. If the parties' experts could be interviewed or deposed like ordinary witnesses, opposing parties could discover much of each other's **work product** through the expert witnesses. This is true because experts obtain most of their information, at least initially, from the lawyer. They discuss most of the facts and even the legal theories. In other words, the hired expert is usually given the entire plan for trying the case. This is the information which would be sought when interviewing or deposing the experts.

Sometime after the lawyer and expert have consulted, the expert may decide, for one reason or another, that he or she cannot help or does not want to help. Or, the lawyer might decide against using that particular expert even if he or she is willing to help. If their communications were subject to discovery, the disclosures could be devastating. The theories advanced and rejected in the course of their frank discussions might be used against a party. Statements of facts and assumptions about the facts made only tentatively might be used against the party in an effort to suggest a lack of certainty or apparent inconsistency.

The Federal Rules of Civil Procedure have, with some difficulty, steered a course calculated to preserve the adversary nature of civil litigation and, yet, make available to each party essential information about the opposing party's experts and their opinions. To begin with, the Rules distinguish between those experts with whom a party or party's lawyer has merely consulted and those experts who have been selected to testify at trial. A party does not have to disclose the identity of the experts who have provided advice or information for the case but who will not be called upon to testify at the trial. Absent very unusual circumstances, they are of no consequence to the trial.

The experts who will testify at trial are subject to disclosure. A party may require any other party to disclose experts who have been selected to testify at trial. In addition, those experts' opinions and the grounds for their opinions are subject to discovery through written interrogatories directed to the party who has retained the experts.

Interrogatories

Information about experts who have been selected to testify at trial is obtainable only through written interrogatories unless, for good cause shown, a court orders that some other means of discovery, such as an oral deposition, be used.

Unless otherwise stipulated by the parties, the only means of discovering information about the opponent's experts is through interrogatories directed to the party who retained the expert. Rule 26(b)(4) specifies how and to what extent interrogatories may be used to discover expert opinions. Volumes have been written concerning the Rule's application.

Interrogatories may be used to obtain the expert's *identity*, a description of the *subject matter* about which the witness will testify, a statement of the *facts* relied upon by the expert for the opinion, and the *grounds* for the expert's opinion.

The following is a typical set of interrogatories used to obtain the information made discoverable by Rule 26(b)(4).

If you intend to call upon any expert witnesses, including medical experts, to testify at the trial:

1. state the name, age, address, and employment of each such expert;

2. describe in detail the qualifications of each expert with particular reference to the subject matter on which each expert may testify at trial;

3. state fully the opinions to which each expert is expected to testify;

4. describe in detail the facts upon which each expert relies for the expert's opinion, respectively;

5. state a summary of the grounds for each opinion to which each expert is expected to testify;

6. identify by author, title, publication date, and publisher all writings which may be used at trial by your experts as "learned treatises;"

7. identify separately any document that you intend to call to the attention of any expert witness upon cross-examination.

Let's examine the type of information which each of these interrogatories demands. The first interrogatory should be easy to understand. The answer to the second interrogatory should describe fully the expert's education, training, and experience. Interrogatory 3 asks for each expert's opinion. Using the preceding example of a physician who is attending a patient who presents symptoms suggestive of appendicitis, the opinions to which he or she would testify are that the patient has appendicitis and is in need of surgery to treat the problem.

Interrogatory 4 asks about the facts relied upon by the witnesses as a basis for the experts' opinions. The facts are the patient's history of nausea, localized abdominal pain, low-grade fever, elevated white blood count, and worsening symptoms during observation. Interrogatory 5 asks for the grounds of the expert's opinion. In our example, the grounds for the expert's opinion are that the syndrome of symptoms and findings presented by the patient is most commonly associated with appendicitis; these symptoms are all consistent with appendicitis; the syndrome tends to rule out most other maladies, such as food poisoning, which could cause some of the symptoms; and the onset of the symptoms and the progression of the symptoms are consistent with appendicitis. The witness has treated other patients with similar symptoms and they had appendicitis.

Interrogatories 6 and 7 require disclosure of publications upon which the plaintiff's experts rely as authorities to support their opinions. It is very common for experts to justify their opinions by looking to textbooks and professional journals for authorities who seem to agree with their opinions. Since the Rules of Evidence allow experts to use learned treatises to "bootstrap" their opinions, it is a good idea to find out, in advance, what publications the experts may use (Rule 803(18)). Apparent support from one or more publications may be additional grounds for the expert's opinions.

There are some significant limitations to the effectiveness of discovery of expert opinions through interrogatories. The answers to interrogatories do not give an adverse party the opportunity to evaluate the expert's personal appearance. Is the expert able to express himself or herself orally? Does the expert appear authoritative? Does the expert recognize, for example, that other formulas or methods of calculating the strength of the metal are accepted in the industry and give different results? Can the expert rule out the possibility that the alleged fissures developed at some time after the ladder was sold to the plaintiff? Have comparisons been made with other ladders? Can the expert rule out consumer misuse? How? What are the weaknesses in the theory about which he or she is aware? What tests did the expert conduct which do *not* support the opinions expressed in the answers to the interrogatories? With whom has the expert consulted for advice and guidance in forming the expressed opinions? Who has already expressed disagreement with the stated opinions?

Experts' Reports

It is customary to obtain written reports from experts. Written reports are desirable because they reduce the opportunity for misunderstanding. A lawyer needs to know exactly what his or her experts are saying and what their testimony will be. Rule 26 precludes discovery of experts' reports, except in rare circumstances. A lawyer's consultation with experts for advice and guidance is treated as the lawyer's work product. The experts' reports are similarly treated as the lawyer's work product. The protection afforded to experts' reports, as provided by Rule 26(4), permits and encourages open, candid discussions between lawyers and their experts. The court rules recognize that, in almost every field, experts may have bona fide disagreements and hold different opinions. There is no reason why a party should be limited to the opinions of the first expert that the party happens to consult. It is perfectly reasonable and proper for a lawyer to consult with a number of experts before deciding on the one to testify. The consultation with experts not selected to testify is considered attorney's work product and not discoverable by other parties. For this reason, as a general rule, discovery concerning experts who have been consulted but not retained to testify is very limited.

Notwithstanding the limitations on discovery of the opponent's experts, their opinions, and reports, it is common for parties to provide the opposing party with a copy of the expert's report. There are several reasons for doing so. The report may be very persuasive and offered in the hope of getting the case settled. The parties may agree to exchange reports so there is, in effect, an even trade. Or, by producing an expert's report, a lawyer may seek to avoid the inconvenience of answering interrogatories concerning the expert's opinion.

A party should not take too much comfort in obtaining the opposing party's experts' reports. The reports may not contain or provide as much information as proper answers to interrogatories would. The report may not contain all of the information available through the expert. The report may be selective and especially prepared for the purpose of supplying it to the opposition. One must always be on guard for diversionary tactics. Of course, it would be unethical to supply a false report. Use of a false report should subject the lawyer to disbarment, or worse.

On rare occasion, a party may be entitled to discover the opinions of another party's expert who will not be called to testify as a witness at a trial. It requires a showing to the court that "exceptional circumstances" exist making it impracticable to obtain facts or opinions on the same subject matter by other means. An example may be helpful to understanding this limited but important exception. Suppose that a woman buys a bottle of a soda pop, consumes about half of it, and becomes ill about an hour later. She assumes that the soft drink caused her illness. Her husband has the remaining soda pop analyzed by a local chemist. The chemist finds nothing unusual in the sample. Two months later the husband takes the remainder of the soda pop to another chemist, who purports to find a toxin in the remaining portion. Assume further that the foreign substance is something not ordinarily found at the bottling plant but is common to households. An action is commenced months later. None of the soda pop is left for the defendant vendor to have analyzed. For obvious reasons, the plaintiffs may elect not to ask the first chemist to testify. Would it be fair to deny the defendant vendor the right to have the information which is available through the first chemist? Of course not! The example is extreme for the purpose of showing the kind of situation which makes exceptions to the rule necessary.

Suppose that some of the soft drink is still available for an independent analysis by a chemist to be chosen by the defendant. Should the defendant, nevertheless, be entitled to the first expert's opinion, analysis, factual data, and records? Probably yes. The soft drink may have been contaminated after the first chemist completed his or her analysis. Therefore, the very *same* subject matter is not necessarily available for analysis. The exception can work in favor of plaintiffs just as well.

If an expert is uncooperative after the court has authorized a deposition to be taken, the expert may be compelled to appear for a deposition and testify by serving a subpoena upon the expert. An expert may be compelled by subpoena to produce his or her records for inspection at the deposition. Violation of a subpoena subjects the expert to a contempt of court order. A party is presumed to be able to control his or her hired expert, so ordinarily subpoenas are not used. If a party cannot control an expert witness and obtain reasonable cooperation, he or she should notify the other side, so that the witness can be placed under subpoena.

When a party seeks to use or benefit from the efforts of an expert originally hired by another party, he or she may be required to pay a "fair portion" of the expert's fee and expenses already incurred by the party who first hired the expert. Ordinarily, the parties or the court determines how the expense should be assessed before the discovery is conducted (Rule 26(b)(4)(C)).

In the ordinary case, answers to interrogatories provide sufficient information about the opponent's experts to make additional means of discovery unnecessary. Not infrequently, lawyers agree to exchange experts' reports, like exchanging medical reports pursuant to Rule 35, as an alternative to answering interrogatories. Parties should use the most expeditious methods of discovery available to keep down the cost of litigation. Of course, the determining factor must be the adequacy of the procedure to obtain the information which is or should be available.

How should interrogatories be used in the typical case? Suppose that the plaintiff suffered an injury when a five-year-old metal extension ladder collapsed while he was on it; that he was carrying a heavy object and was near the top when the ladder's tread and side rail bent and gave way; and that the ladder and the plaintiff fell to the ground. The plaintiff claims that the ladder was defective and that the manufacturer is strictly liable in tort because of the alleged defect. The complaint may or may not specify the type of defects claimed. There are countless possible defects, including defective materials, a defect in the metal creating a localized weakness, a defect in design such as making the treads too narrow or too thin or using inadequate fasteners, or failing to warn the user about foreseeable dangers such as the need to use the ladder at only certain angles or the danger of overextending or overloading it. The plaintiff discloses that he has an expert who will testify that the ladder is "defective." What information can be obtained through written interrogatories directed to the plaintiff?

The defendant can secure the expert's identity, including name, address, curriculum vitae, relationship to the plaintiff, and a description of his or her areas of expertise. Next, the defendant may inquire about the subject matter to which the expert may testify. The answers to the defendant's interrogatories should specify the defect or defects claimed. For example, the interrogatory answer may state that the ladder was defective because the metal in the side rail had fissures in it making the ladder too weak to support ordinary loads. The defendant is entitled to obtain a summary of the grounds for the plaintiff's expert's opinion. The grounds are the expert's calculations and the apparent application of standards of the industry. The interrogatories should demand disclosure of all tests conducted by the expert such as analysis of cross-sections of the side rail at the point where the side rail collapsed and any microscopic examinations and X-ray studies conducted to show the presence of fissures. The expert presumably determined the load strength by testing and making calculations. The expert will have to disclose the tests of the ladder's load strength and the methods by which the determination was obtained. Obviously, a lot of information can be obtained through interrogatories which are carefully drawn and properly answered.

It should be obvious that the involvement of an expert witness adds another dimension to the case. If one party elects to hire an expert to testify, it almost becomes mandatory for the other parties to obtain experts to counteract the testimony of the first expert. In all probability, if one looks hard enough, he or she can find a professional expert to conjure up a theory helpful to the case. The use of experts substantially adds to the cost of preparing and trying cases.

Party as an Expert

The collapse of a roof on a large, new building is almost certain to engender litigation. Even if no one is injured, there is still the likelihood of a very large property damage claim. The owner will look for someone to compensate for the loss. If the owner's loss is covered by insurance, the insurer will probably have subrogation rights against whomever is liable for the collapse by reason of negligence, strict liability, breach of warranty, or even breach of contract. It is not at all unusual for the building's owner or insurer to bring a negligence action against the architect, general contractor, and selected subcontractors in these kinds of cases. The defendants usually serve cross-claims making everyone adverse parties. Each party in such litigation usually has its own "in-house" experts on the business payroll. More often than not, however, the parties hire independent (outside) experts to assist and advise concerning the litigation. A party who happens to be an expert is not protected by Rule

26(b)(4) from having his or her deposition taken and opinions discovered. The rules do not protect expert employees from having their depositions taken concerning their expert opinions relevant to the claim. The adverse party may inquire into the expert's background, education, training, experience, relationship to the project, and opinions about the adequacy of the structure and cause of its collapse. The work product limitation applies only to experts who are hired for the purpose of assisting with the particular litigation.

What if the plaintiff's lawyer notices the depositions of the defendant's employees who are experts but who had nothing to do with the particular project? May the plaintiff's lawyer ask them questions about the building's structure and for opinions about the adequacy of design, materials, fabrication methods, etc.? Rule 26 does not seem to cover this situation. Most likely, a court would quash the notice for taking their depositions if the defendant showed by affidavit that they had no connection with the project. If they were deposed, they could probably elect to have no opinions concerning the subject matter. They should be compensated for their time by the party taking their depositions. Otherwise, courts would be encouraging "fishing" for expert opinions, trying to secure expert opinions through "admissions."

If a patient sues a physician for medical malpractice, the defendant physician will probably hire another physician to review the medical case for the purpose of determining whether he or she has committed malpractice. The same hired physician may conduct a Rule 35 independent medical examination of the plaintiff. It should be apparent that the one expert has *two* quite distinct roles. Each roll must be handled separately. If the plaintiff asks for a report on the independent medical examination, Rule 35 requires the physician who conducted the independent medical examination to provide a complete report. The report is available through the party who requested the examination—not directly from the independent medical examiner. The Rule 35 report should discuss the patient's medical history, the findings, diagnosis, etc.; however, the report should not discuss the malpractice issues. The expert witness should prepare a separate report concerning the malpractice allegations. The examining physician should make a separate report concerning his or her evaluation of the defendant's alleged malpractice. That phase of the case and evidence falls under Rule 26(b)(4) and is protected as part of the defendant attorney's work product.

Cross-examination of Expert Witnesses

The most fruitful areas for cross-examining experts are their background, the sources of their information, the assumptions they have made as a basis for their opinions, and the reasons (given or not given) for their opinions.

Costs

Expert witnesses are expensive. They require payment for the time spent analyzing the problem, rendering their opinions, and participating in legal proceedings. The rules provide guidelines for determining who shall pay an expert for time spent in discovery proceedings. When an expert's opinion is sought through interrogatories, the party who hired the expert must pay the expert's fees for the time spent helping to answer the interrogatories. If an oral deposition is ordered, the party who takes the deposition must pay a reasonable fee for the time the expert spends testifying. An expert cannot extort an excessive fee from the opposing side. If the parties and expert cannot agree on what amount is reasonable, the issue may be submitted to the judge for determination. If the judge awards a smaller fee than is acceptable to the expert, the expert's remedy is to obtain the balance from the party who retained him or her. The party who takes the deposition should not have to pay for time spent by the expert preparing for the deposition. The party who retained the expert should pay for any preparation time. The preparation time is not at the request of the party who requested the deposition, nor is it for that party's benefit.

Sanctions

If a party fails to disclose an expert as a potential witness, the expert will not be allowed to testify at trial. Obviously, it is preferable to err on the side of disclosure.

13 Oral Depositions

The word "depose" means to testify under oath. "Deposition" means sworn testimony. Rule 30 authorizes a party to require other parties and even non-party witnesses to give *oral* testimony relevant to the case. The procedure is commonly referred to as a "deposition." Usually depositions are conducted in the office of one of the lawyers. But depositions may be held almost anywhere, such as a courthouse, hospital, hotel, airport meeting room, or private home. One party may require another party to appear at a reasonably convenient, designated time and place for his or her deposition merely by serving a notice for taking deposition. A nonparty witness may be required to appear for a deposition by serving a subpoena upon the witness.

The **deponent** is required to answer questions propounded by the lawyers. The deponent is entitled to have his or her own lawyer present to advise even if the deponent is not a party to the suit. Interrogation of the deponent proceeds in a manner similar to the interrogation of a witness in court. A stenographer makes a verbatim record of the entire proceeding. The transcript contains each question, answer, statement, and stipulation made during the course of the oral deposition.

Purposes

Discovery procedures are designed to provide parties with the means for obtaining and preserving testimony of any witness who has information about the case. The oral deposition procedure is probably the most important discovery tool and most valuable means of preserving evidence. An oral deposition allows a lawyer to have direct contact with adverse parties and with noncooperative witnesses. The procedure is relatively simple and very effective. It is moderately expensive but usually well worth the cost. There is no other way of obtaining as much detailed information directly from the deponents.

There are two basic purposes for taking depositions: the preservation of testimony for use at trial and the discovery of information available through the deponent. A deposition transcript may be of various incidental uses and values. Once the deposition has been taken, regardless of the original purpose for which it was taken, the transcript may be used at trial in lieu of the witness's live testimony if he or she is unavailable for trial. Or, it may be used to contradict and impeach the deponent at trial. Deposition transcripts are regularly used to refresh the deponent's memory in preparation for trial. What is more, under certain circumstances, a deposition taken in one case may be used in another case (Rule 804(b)(1)).

A paralegal is not permitted to take a witness's deposition; nevertheless, a paralegal's work often revolves around oral depositions, including scheduling, noticing, preparing, observing, reviewing, correcting, digesting, consolidating, indexing, and utilizing the transcript for trial preparation. One of the more important roles may be for a paralegal to prepare a client or nonparty witness for deposition. A paralegal's ability to competently prepare a person for a deposition depends upon a good understanding of the entire process. Therefore, a paralegal must have a good understanding of the oral deposition purposes, uses, and procedures.

Notice of Deposition and Scheduling

The procedures for scheduling and taking oral depositions are intended to protect the parties from abuse and to insure the integrity of the proceedings. When a deposition is scheduled, *all* parties must be given notice (Rules 5(a), 30(b)(1)). If a party is not served with notice *and* his or her lawyer does not appear at the deposition, the deponent's deposition may not be used against that party for any purpose. As to that party, it is as though the deposition had never been taken. On the other hand, he or she is entitled to buy a copy of the deposition transcript and use it at trial for any proper purpose (Rule 32). The party who did not receive notice of the deposition may take the deponent's deposition at another time. If the deposition is scheduled at a time that is very inconvenient for a party or his or her lawyer, whether or not the party is the deponent, he or she has the right to move the court for an order setting a different time. Rule 30(b)(3). Lawyers are usually able to agree on a mutually satisfactory time, so motions are seldom necessary.

Scheduling a deposition is very simple. The party who wants to take someone's deposition prepares a *Notice of Deposition* and serves the notice upon all other parties. The notice must be in writing and signed by a lawyer. Service is usually by mail. The notice states that the deposition of a person, who is named or otherwise identified, will be taken at a specified time and place before a person who is authorized to administer oaths. The notice must give everyone a *reasonable period of time* in which to prepare. The Rules do not specify any certain number of days for giving the notice.

The notice may require a party deponent to produce specified documents which are under his or her control (Rule 30(b)(1)). If the deponent is not a party, a demand that the deponent produce documents for use in the deposition shall be made in the subpoena, which must be served upon the deponent. If the identity of the person to be deposed is not known, he or she may be described by position or relationship to the parties.

A notice of deposition is, in itself, a mandate to a party to appear at the time and place scheduled. If the time or place is inconvenient for the party whose oral deposition has been noticed, he or she has the responsibility for obtaining a cancellation or a new time or a different place. Lawyers seldom have difficulty agreeing on a mutually convenient time and place. Occasionally, a deposition has to be rescheduled several times due to conflicts. Professional courtesy requires lawyers to cooperate and accommodate each other.

The plaintiff is *not* permitted to take the defendant's deposition during the first thirty days following service of the summons and complaint. The rules recognize that the defendant and his or her lawyer would have difficulty preparing for it. Furthermore, the issues have not been established until the defendant serves an answer to the complaint. But if the defendant elects to take the plaintiff's deposition within the thirty-day period, the plaintiff may obtain the defendant's deposition as well (Rule 30(a)).

The plaintiff may be able to obtain a deposition within thirty days by moving the court for an order authorizing it, but the plaintiff must show good cause, that is, special need, for an accelerated deposition date. Rule 30(b)(2) specifies three situations (exceptions) which automatically give the plaintiff the right to take anyone's deposition during the first thirty days: (1) the deponent is about to leave the judicial district and will be at least one hundred miles from the place where the trial is to be held; (2) the deponent is about to leave the United States; or (3) the deponent is about to leave on a sea voyage. No court order is necessary if any of these reasons are stated in the notice along with a brief explanation of the facts. Progressive illness, impending death, or a call to military service are additional examples of situations in which a court would probably order an accelerated date for a deposition. Rule 30(a) appears to provide that any discovery procedure instituted by the defendant permits the plaintiff to schedule the defendant's deposition within the first thirty days after service of the summons and complaint. Taken literally, it means that as soon as the defendant serves an interrogatory upon the plaintiff, the plaintiff may schedule the defendant's deposition at a reasonable time.

A nonparty may be subpoenaed for a deposition at a designated time and place. The subpoena may require the witness to bring specified documents which are in his or her custody. The notice of deposition must also list the documents (Rule 30(b)(1)). If the witness is willing to appear without being subpoenaed, the expense and inconvenience of the subpoena can be avoided. If the nonparty witness fails to appear at the scheduled time and place for his or her deposition, however, the party who scheduled it may be required to reimburse the other parties for their time and the expenses, including attorneys' fees, incurred by reason of the aborted deposition. If a nonparty witness had been served with a subpoena and failed to comply with it, the party who scheduled the deposition cannot be blamed for the nonappearance, and costs cannot be assessed against the party (Rule 30(g)(2)). The witness would be subject to a contempt of court citation. If the party who serves the notice fails to appear to take the deposition, he or she may be required to pay the costs incurred by all parties who did appear (Rule 30(g)(1)).

A deposition should be conducted at a *convenient* place. The lawyer who schedules a deposition has the responsibility to arrange for the place and for a court reporter to record the testimony. Of course, convenience is relative. If a nonparty is to be deposed, the deposition should be taken in his or her hometown or the town where he or she works. Otherwise, the deposition may be taken at the county seat of the county in which the deponent lives. If the deponent is a party, the primary consideration is the convenience of all the parties and their lawyers. If they all live in the same town, that is where the deposition should be taken, regardless of the fact the court is located in another city or county. If the parties and lawyers are located at various places around the state (federal district), the most convenient place is usually the city in which the court is located. If the parties cannot agree on a convenient place, the judge may select it for them.

On occasion, it is necessary for a party to obtain a deposition of an officer or employee of a corporation, partnership, or government agency, but the party does not know the name of the person who should testify or even the deponent's position within the organization. The Rule 30(b)(6) authorizes a lawyer to specify in the notice of deposition the subject matter for which the witness's testimony is needed. The organization's managers are required to determine, if possible, who within the organization should appear in response to the subpoena and/or notice of deposition. The subject matter must be specified with reasonable particularity. If a nonparty corporation is subpoenaed, the subpoena must clearly inform the corporation of its duty to respond by designating someone to appear at the deposition on its behalf. The person who does appear must be able to speak for the organization concerning the subject matter. The subpoena may cite and quote the rule.

If the organization is a party, there is no need to use a subpoena, and it is not necessary to inform the organization of its duty to designate someone to appear on its behalf. The organization's lawyer presumably knows the rule. In the event the organization selects the proper person to appear but he or she refuses, the organization should notify the lawyer who noticed the deposition. He or she can then subpoena the individual to appear. An organization is expected to act in good faith and exercise its influence to facilitate the judicial process.

If a deposition is taken within thirty days after service of the summons and complaint due to circumstances specified in Rule 30(b)(2) but a party was unable to obtain a lawyer to represent him or her at the deposition, the deponent's testimony may not be used against that party (Rule 30(b)(2)). The Rule requires due diligence on the part of each party to obtain a lawyer, and the burden of persuading the court is on a party to show diligence. An illustration may be helpful. Suppose that the plaintiff sued three defendants but the summons and complaints were served at two-week intervals so that the last defendant was served four weeks after the first defendant. Suppose that within five days after the last complaint was served, the plaintiff notices the deposition of a nonparty witness to be taken in the plaintiff lawyer's office in just seven days because the deponent is intending to move out of state permanently. The reason for taking the deposition early must be stated in the notice (Rule 30(b)(2)). Assume that the first defendant served appeared in the case by service of an answer. The notice for deposition may be served upon him or her by mail, but personal service upon the lawyer would be preferable because of the shortness of time (Rule 5(b)). Suppose that the second defendant has retained a lawyer but the lawyer has not yet interposed an answer. If the plaintiff's lawyer can, nevertheless, find out who is representing the second defendant, service of the notice of deposition should be made upon that lawyer (Rule 5(b)). Otherwise, service of the notice must be made upon that defendant by delivering it to him or her personally or by mail (Rule 5(b)). Again, personal service is preferable because of the shortness of time. The third defendant has had the summons and complaint for only five days. Suppose this defendant promptly delivered them and the notice of deposition to his or her liability insurance agent who, in turn, delivered them to the liability insurance company's claim department in another town for processing. There is a probability that the third defendant will not have a lawyer by the time the deposition is taken, notwithstanding due diligence on his or her part. Under the circumstances, the deposition could not be used *against* him or her at trial. But suppose through some miracle the liability insurer was able to provide a lawyer in time. Then the lawyer's appearance at the deposition would result in a waiver of any defect in the notice and service of the notice (Rule 32(a)).

Procedure

Everyone should make a genuine effort to be on time for the deposition. It is helpful to have an extra copy of the notice of deposition for the court reporter. The notice of taking deposition provides the reporter with most of the information that he or she must have, including the title of the action, court file number, correct spelling of the deponent's name, the names of the lawyers who are appearing, and the identity of their respective clients.

Usually the first questions concern the witness's identity and background: name, address, age, marital status, birth date, birthplace, employment, social security number, and criminal record. The other areas of questioning concern liability and damages. Each question should be singular and clearly stated. Double negatives should be avoided by the lawyers and deponent. Careful attention should be given to the use of words and their meanings. For example, consider the question: "Did you make a left-hand turn?" Answer: "Right." Does *right* mean a "right turn" or "correct"? It is the lawyer's responsibility to make sure that the questions are clearly stated and the answers are meaningful, that is, definitive and responsive. A deponent does not have the right to "go off the record." Only if the lawyers agree to an intermission may the court reporter stop recording the dialogue. No lawyer has a right to ask the "last question." A lawyer may ask leading questions and, otherwise, cross-examine the deponent if he or she is an *adverse party* or a *hostile witness* (Rule 611(b)(c)).

A lawyer does not necessarily object to every question that is "objectionable." That is true whether the testimony is given in a deposition or at trial. Rule 32(d)(3)(B) provides that the right to object at trial to questions or answers which are improper only because of the form of the question is waived unless the objections are made. For example, questions that are multiple in form or leading or argumentative are improper because of the form of the question. In the absence of any objection to such questions during the deposition, no objection may be made to those questions when the transcript is used at trial. But Rule 32(d)(3)(A) preserves the right to make objections for the first time at trial if the objections concern the competency of the witness (Rule 601). (Competency of the testimony, Rules 602, 701–703; relevancy of the testimony, Rules 401–411.)

The court reporter notes the lawyers' appearances, the presence of each party to the action, and the time at which the deposition begins. On occasion, one of the lawyers may have a preliminary statement to make for the record.

The deponent is placed under oath by the court reporter or other person authorized by law to administer oaths. Then the lawyer who noticed the deposition proceeds to question the deponent. The lawyer continues questioning the deponent until the facts with which he or she is concerned are covered. Then, in turn, the other lawyers have the opportunity to ask questions. Seldom is there any argument or problem among the lawyers about the order in which the lawyers may ask questions. The deponent's own lawyer is always the last to ask questions. His or her decision whether or not to ask questions usually depends upon the purpose for which the deposition is being taken. If it is being taken by another party to obtain information (discovery), the deponent's own lawyer probably will not ask any questions except, perhaps, for the purpose of clarifying answers previously given. If, on the other hand, the deposition is taken for the purpose of preserving the deponent's testimony or there is a probability the deposition will be used in lieu of the witness's personal appearance in court, the examination proceeds the same as it would at trial. The rules specifically authorize a party to schedule his or her own deposition so that the party's testimony can be preserved.

All lawyers who have appeared in the case have a right to be present throughout each deposition. A lawyer may interpose objections to questions and object to any irregularity in the proceedings. The objections are recorded for subsequent ruling by a judge if necessary. A party may obtain a ruling on an objection by making a motion at some convenient time after the deposition is concluded, or the party may elect to wait until the deposition is used at trial and then renew the objection. When an objection is made to evidence, whether to a question or an answer or an exhibit, the customary practice is to receive the evidence *subject* to the objection (Rule 30(c)). If the testimony were not taken and recorded and subsequently the court were to determine that the objection was not valid, the witness's deposition would have to be taken again concerning the matters omitted. By receiving the evidence, subject to the objection, the evidence is available. If the evidence is not admissible at trial, the court may order it stricken from the deposition transcript when offered at trial. The jury will never hear it. Also, there is the possibility that the lawyer who made the objection may find that the answer is actually helpful to his or her theory and may decide to withdraw the objection. Or, he or she may decide that the answer is innocuous and not worth fighting about.

On occasion, an objectionable item of evidence may be so damaging to the deponent if disclosed that his or her lawyer determines the deponent should not answer certain questions even if the answers were given "subject to objection." Questions related to privileged communications, to records, and to the attorney's work product often fall into those categories. Two alternatives are open to the parties and their lawyers. They may elect to terminate the deposition at that point and schedule a motion to obtain an order compelling the deponent to answer the contested questions. Or, the lawyer may elect to proceed with other questions and finish the deposition concerning all other matters. Thereafter, the party seeking discovery may make the motion to compel answer to the questions to which objections had been made. If the court sustains the objections, there is no need to resume the deposition. If the objections are overruled, the deponent may be allowed to respond to the particular questions by answering written interrogatories. That is more convenient and more economical than resuming the deposition. The court is authorized to award costs and attorney's fees in favor of the party whose position is determined to be correct (Rules 30(d) and 37(a)(4)). However, the award of costs is discretionary with the court.

The deposition testimony is recorded by stenographic means (shorthand or stenotype) unless the parties stipulate to another means or unless the court orders that another method be used (Rules 29 and 30(b)(4)). What other means are available? The deposition could be tape–recorded, providing an audio record. If the deposition is to be used at trial, the tape would have to be played back for the jury. Another means of recording a deposition is the use of video equipment. Video has the advantage of permitting the jury to see and hear the witness. The disadvantages are that video–recording tends to be expensive and somewhat cumbersome. It is necessary to have a technician to operate the equipment when the videotape is made and when it is played. A video recording is inconvenient to edit. Also, a video recording seems to magnify the problems witnesses have articulating their answers. Witnesses tend to be even more nervous when appearing before a camera. The pauses between questions seem eternal. Discussions between the lawyers may seem more argumentative. On the other hand, a witness who is authoritative and who makes a good physical appearance will be a good witness by video presentation. Many plaintiff's lawyers prefer to present some of the medical expert testimony on videotape because of the difficulty in scheduling doctors to appear in court. By presenting some of the medical evidence on videotape they are assured of having the testimony. Sometimes it is less expensive to present expert medical testimony at trial on videotape than in person.

A videotaped deposition requires experience and good planning to make it work well. If a law firm has its own video equipment, the firm may want its paralegals to operate the equipment. It should be noted that any party has a right to have a stenographic record and transcription made of the deposition even if some other means has been agreed upon or ordered by the court. The party who wants the stenographic record must pay for it (Rule 30(b)(4)). A typed transcript is clearly the most convenient form of record to work with when preparing for trial and to use at trial.

A party's lawyer may elect to appear at an oral deposition by submitting written questions through the party or lawyer who scheduled the deposition. The written questions and the deponent's answers are incorporated into the reporter's stenographic notes and the deposition transcript. This is a little-used but potentially valuable procedure. For example, suppose that a third-party plaintiff schedules the deposition of a witness to be taken halfway across the country, but the testimony will be relevant only to the third-party claim against the third-party defendant. The plaintiff's lawyer may avoid a substantial expense by not traveling to the deposition. He or she may be able to cover the few matters of concern by submitting a few simple questions. Written questions must be served upon the lawyer who noticed the deposition and the person who will be taking it. The written questions must be placed in a sealed envelope which is not opened until the deposition begins. The lawyer gives the written questions to the deposition officer (court reporter) who then presents the questions to the witness. The procedure obviously lacks flexibility and there is no opportunity for follow-up questions which might be useful for clarification or to develop a point that suddenly appears to be more important than previously believed.

Who may be excluded from the deposition? The media does not have a right to be present. On the other hand, in the absence of objection, anyone may observe the deposition proceedings. The parties may agree to exclude certain persons from observing or they may agree to allow observers (Rule 29). For example, a representative from the defendant's liability insurance company might want to observe the deposition of the plaintiff for the purpose of evaluating the claim; however, one or more parties (lawyers) may object to the presence of certain persons. The reasons may be tactical or just because the room is crowded. If an objection is raised to the presence of certain persons, the party wishing to exclude persons from the deposition may move the court for an order sequestering witnesses pursuant to Rule 26(c)(5) and Rule 615. A party cannot be sequestered. Otherwise, the taking of a deposition must be treated like a trial because, in fact, the deposition eventually may become part of the trial.

If a public or private corporation is the party, it is entitled to have a designated representative attend all proceedings, along with its lawyer. The most common reason for a party to exclude persons from a deposition or trial is to keep a witness from hearing what other witnesses have to say. There is always the possibility that the testimony of one witness may cause another witness to change his or her testimony in some way. For example, suppose two bartenders were witnesses to a fight in the bar. The likelihood of developing inconsistencies in their versions of the fight is better if neither hears the testimony of the other. If witnesses are trying to be honest and helpful to the court, however, it is probably better for everyone that all witnesses do have the opportunity to hear each other. Consequently, sequestration of witnesses is the exception.

Each party's lawyer has the right to put questions to the deponent. The deponent's lawyer may ask questions even if the deponent is not a party. It is unusual for a nonparty deponent to be represented by a lawyer. There is no set limit on the number of questions which may be asked. Nor is there any time limit. A lawyer may ask additional questions following the interrogation by other lawyers. The questions must not become repetitious or irrelevant. The deposition ends when the lawyers have run out of questions to ask or a court orders the deposition terminated.

Verification by Deponent

The deponent has a right to read the deposition transcript to make corrections or changes before it is filed with the court and before it is used for any purpose. The court reporter is required to submit the transcript to the deponent as soon as it has been prepared. The deponent must review the transcript and make his or her corrections within thirty days from the date it is received. The deponent may correct any errors in his or her testimony whether the errors are of *substance* or *form*. The deponent must make a written statement giving reasons or an explanation for each change made in the transcript. The usual procedure for making changes is for the deponent and deponent's lawyer to review the transcript—not necessarily together. Each notes the appropriate corrections and changes. Then the lawyer prepares an addendum or errata sheet, which the deponent must sign under oath. The addendum is then sent to the court reporter who may or may not retype it for incorporation into the transcript. The deponent must sign a certification sheet verifying that he or she has read the deposition and that, as changed, it is correct. A paralegal should be able to provide considerable help in making sure that the client's transcript is correct.

A deponent may waive the right to make changes in the transcript if the parties agree (Rule 30(e)). The deponent waives the right to make changes and corrections by stating at the conclusion of the deposition that he or she elects to waive the right to read and sign the transcript. The oral waiver is noted by the court reporter in the transcript. If the deponent waives the right to review the transcript, he or she necessarily relies upon the accuracy of the stenographer (court reporter). In many cases, lawyers advise their clients to waive the right because, usually, there is no need to make substantive changes. The changes concerning form (such as spellings) are obvious and do not really affect anyone's legal rights. It is easier to simply rely upon the accuracy of the reporter. Most court reporters are very skillful, conscientious, and reliable.

A deponent automatically waives the right to review and correct the transcript if he or she delays signing it for more than thirty days after it is submitted by the reporter. Day one of the thirty-day period begins on the day after the deponent or deponent's lawyer receives the transcript (Rule 6(a)). If the deponent does not sign the transcript, the court reporter is supposed to make a statement in the transcript explaining why the deponent was unable or unwilling to sign it. The transcript may then be used as though it has been signed by the deponent.

A party may move the court for an order suppressing the use of the deposition, or any part of it, if there is some irregularity. But the burden rests upon the moving party to persuade the court that the deposition is invalid or that its uses would cause prejudice outweighing its value to the court and jury. The motion to suppress must be made promptly after the error or irregularity in the proceedings is discovered (Rule 32(d)(4)).

If any party orders a transcript, the court reporter is obligated to promptly file the original copy of the deposition transcript with the clerk of court. The reporter must place it in a sealed envelope showing the title of the action, the name of the deponent, and the date of the deposition. If the reporter cannot deliver the transcript to the clerk for filing, he or she must send it by registered mail for filing (Rule 30(f)).

The party who noticed the deposition does not have to order a transcript for the court, for himself or herself, or for anyone else. The court reporter may sell copies of the transcript to anyone who wants them—whether or not a party to the action. On occasion lawyers search for copies of depositions given by an adverse party in other cases. The lawyer may be able to find out about a party's other litigation by examining the litigation indexes kept by the clerk of court. The court files are available for public inspection. The clerk also keeps a list of all documents filed in connection with each case, so it is relatively easy to determine whether a person gave a deposition in the case. As part of the discovery procedure, it is proper to inquire whether a party has given a deposition in any other case and in what cases.

The original copy of a deposition transcript must be filed in a sealed envelope. The envelope may not be unsealed without a court order. Upon motion to the court, for good cause shown, it may be possible to review the original. But an easier way to gain access to the deposition transcript is to contact one of the lawyers who was involved in the other case and review his or her copy of the transcript. Today, it is an easy matter to photocopy transcripts. If for some reason it is not desirable to contact one of the lawyers in the other case, the court reporter who took the deposition may be contacted. There is no legal proscription against discussing depositions with the court reporters. It is unlikely that he or she will have a copy of the deposition, but the reporter should still have the stenographic notes. A new copy can be made from the notes. Obviously, it is cheaper and more convenient to try to find an existing copy.

Depositions are usually taken near the court where the action is pending, that is, within the same city or within one hundred miles. But the Rules contemplate that depositions may be taken out of the home district. If problems arise during a deposition away from the home district, the parties may apply for help or relief in the federal district court where the deposition is being taken. For example, if it appears to one or more of the parties that the deposition is being taken in a manner which unnecessarily embarrasses or oppresses the deponent, any party may stop the deposition and move the court in that district for an order terminating the deposition or for an order limiting the scope of the deposition, or directing the manner of taking the deposition (Rule 26(c)). It would be inconvenient for everyone to return to the home district court, obtain a ruling, and then journey back to the place where the deposition was being taken. Rule 30(c) appears to reserve to the home district court the obligation of ruling on the admissibility of the evidence at trial. If the deposition is terminated by order of a court other than the home district, the deposition cannot be resumed until ordered by the home district court, that is, an order of the court in which the action is pending. The deponent or party has an absolute right to demand that the deposition be suspended until the court rules on the objection. The party or lawyer at fault may be required to pay expenses of the motion and deposition (Rules 30(d) and 37(a)(4)).

Subpoenaing the Deponent

If the deponent must be subpoenaed, the procedure is to prepare, serve, and file a notice for taking the deposition. When the clerk of court receives the notice of deposition for filing, the clerk, on request, will issue a subpoena, which requires the deponent to appear at the time and place scheduled. The subpoena may direct the deponent to produce specified documents and/or materials for inspection and/or copying (Rule 45(b)(d)). If the deponent finds the demand for documents or things too burdensome, he or she may serve and file an *objection to inspection*. Of course, the grounds for the objection must be stated. The objection must be delivered before the deposition is taken. If more than ten days notice was given for taking the deposition, the objection must be served within ten days. If an objection is made, the party serving the subpoena has the right to move the court for an order compelling production (Rule 45(d)). Otherwise, by electing to proceed with the deposition, the party who noticed the deposition must assume the documents will not be available for the deposition.

A subpoena may be served by the United States marshal or by anyone at least eighteen years of age and not a party to the suit. The subpoena must be *delivered* to the deponent along with a witness fee for one day's attendance (currently twenty dollars) and a mileage fee (currently twenty cents per mile) (Rule 45(c)). Ordinarily, subpoenas are not used unless the deponent is a nonparty. So when a motion is noticed for the purpose of compelling the nonparty deponent to produce documents or things for inspection, a copy of the notice and motion must be served upon the deponent. He or she has a right to appear in opposition to the motion (Rule 45(d)).

A deponent cannot be required to travel great distances to attend a deposition simply by serving a subpoena upon him or her. The rule is quite protective of people who are subpoenaed. If the deponent is a resident of the district (state), the deponent may be required to travel to any place within the county in which he or she resides or is regularly employed. A third alternative is a little more esoteric in its application; a deponent may be subpoenaed to appear for a deposition in the county in which he or she transacts business in person (Rule 45(d)). By implication, he or she must regularly transact business in the county selected. If the deponent is not a resident of the district where the deposition is to be taken, the subpoena may direct him to appear for a deposition in the county in which the subpoena was served or within a one-hundred-mile radius of the place of service. If those two alternatives are not satisfactory, the party noticing the deposition has to obtain a court order setting another reasonably convenient place (Rule 45(d)(2)). If a person fails to comply with a subpoena, he or she may be held in contempt of court and is subject to various penalties (Rule 45(f)). The rules for subpoenaing a deponent for his or her deposition are not necessarily the same as those for subpoenaing a witness to testify at trial.

Almost no one wants to be subpoenaed for a deposition or a trial. Subpoenas tend to scare most people. A subpoena makes a person feel as though the whole weight of the court is upon his or her shoulders. Consequently, a lawyer runs a significant risk of alienating a witness by "dropping" a subpoena on him or her. It is a very good idea to explain personally to the witness before the subpoena is served why the subpoena is being used. If a better reason cannot be found, tell him or her that the Federal Rules of Civil Procedure require it. A witness may be more comfortable about receiving the subpoena if told that, in case of an emergency, he or she can be released from the subpoena. To obtain a release, the witness should contact the lawyer who caused the subpoena to be served. The lawyer's name and address are on the subpoena. If the witness has a cogent reason for being unable to appear, he or she may be released and other arrangements made. It is never a good idea, however, to permit the person subpoenaed to believe that if he or she avoids the deposition this time, it will never be taken. The witness should be counseled against trying to put off the inevitable. Of course, there are times when certain witnesses will purposely make themselves unavailable to be served with a subpoena if they have any advanced warning. Therefore, no advance warning should be given to them.

When the court reporter files the original copy of the deposition transcript with the clerk of court, he or she must so advise the lawyer who took the deposition—specifying the date of filing. In turn, the lawyer who noticed and took the deposition has the responsibility for notifying all other parties that the original transcript has been filed (Rule 31(c)). This is done by serving a *notice of filing of deposition.* If this procedure is not followed, there is a very real danger that the original transcript may not be on file when the case is reached for trial. Nevertheless, a custom has developed among lawyers in many jurisdictions to stipulate on the record that they "waive notice of filing." If notice of filing is waived, the lawyer who took the deposition should still make sure that the original transcript is duly filed. Lawyers frequently waive notice of filing simply to lessen the amount of paperwork.

Other witnesses may review the deponent's transcript to ascertain how their own testimony compares with the deponent's testimony. Lawyers study deposition transcriptions to prepare their examinations of the deponents and their examinations of other witnesses who will be testifying on the same subject matter. A lawyer's decision whether or not to ask questions of the deponent and what questions not to ask depends upon how he or she expects the deposition to be used. For example, where a party takes the deposition of an adverse party for the purpose of discovering evidence, the deponent's lawyer seldom asks any questions. Obviously, the purpose of the deposition is to obtain information. There is no reason for the deponent's lawyer to ask the deponent additional questions and further educate the other parties. If there is reason to believe that the deponent is not going to be available for the trial, his or her lawyer should conduct a complete examination in the deposition.

Why should a party incur the expense and inconvenience of obtaining an oral deposition from another party or witness? There are a number of good reasons. An oral deposition is the only means a lawyer has for compelling another party to appear and testify before the trial. The direct contact permits a lawyer to evaluate the deponent's "witness appeal." It is a fact of life that some people are more attractive witnesses than others. Appearance is only one factor, but it is an important one affecting persuasiveness. Factors affecting appearance and persuasiveness are discussed in greater detail in chapter 15. It should be noted here, however, that a good appearance depends, to a large degree, on adequate preparation. The hallmarks of a good witness are authority and sincerity.

An oral deposition allows a lawyer to obtain the witness's own statements, descriptions, and explanations, for he or she can put the questions directly to the deponent without going through the deponent's lawyers. The deponent must phrase his or her own answers. The strengths and weaknesses of the testimony may become visible by the deponent's manner of answering. Or, the manner of answering may indicate dishonesty. A positive, strong attitude may be indicated toward the subject matter or other persons involved in the case.

A lawyer may interpose objections to improper questions of other lawyers, just as would be done at trial. There is no judge to rule on the objections. Therefore, the prescribed method for proceeding is for the witness to answer the questions, "subject to the objections." This means that the question, objection, and answer are recorded, and when it comes time to use the deposition, whether in a motion or at trial, the presiding judge will have to rule on the objection and admissibility of the testimony. If the proponent has any doubt about the propriety of the question, it is a good idea to rephrase the question to assure that the question is proper. On occasion, however, the deponent's lawyer may instruct the deponent not to answer questions because the questions call for privileged communications or are abusive, etc. The procedure for handling such objections is not entirely clear. Nevertheless, most lawyers do not hesitate to instruct their client-deponents not to answer improper questions when the deponent needs to be protected or the information being sought is privileged.

The mere fact that the testimony is recorded is no assurance that the testimony will be admissible in evidence and, therefore, usable at trial. Rule 30(c) states, in part, the following:

> All objections made at the time of the examination to the qualification, of the officer taking the deposition, or to the manner of taking it, or to the evidence presented, or to the conduct of any party, and any other objection to the proceedings, shall be noted by the officer upon the deposition. Evidence objected to shall be taken subject to the objection.

The general rule is that objections concerning the form of the questions must be made during the course of the deposition; otherwise, the objections are waived. The rationale is that if the objections had been made during the deposition, the defect could have been corrected. As part of the adversarial nature of civil litigation, it is incumbent upon the objecting party to flag evidence problems by making appropriate, timely objections. Leading questions and argumentative questions are prime examples of the kind of questions which are objectionable due to form rather than substance. On the other hand, questions and answers which are fundamentally inadmissible in evidence may not be used at trial even though objections were not made during the deposition. Rule 32(d)(3)(A) states the following:

> Objections to the competency of a witness or to the competency, relevancy or materiality of testimony are not waived by failure to make them before or during the taking of the deposition, unless the ground of the objection is one which might have been obviated or removed if presented at that time.

At trial the parties can try to persuade the judge whether the grounds for an objection made for the first time at trial could have been obviated had the objection been made during the deposition while the witness was available to provide the missing information.

Perhaps the largest worry a lawyer has when taking an expert's deposition for use at trial is that he or she may fail to show that the expert's testimony is competent. The court will not rule on the admissibility of the evidence until the trial. The deponent's testimony must be competent to be admissible in evidence at trial. In this regard, an expert witness's opinion evidence is not competent if the opinion lacks sufficient *foundation*. The foundation is laid by presenting evidence which shows that the expert has special training and experience in the field and that the expert has sufficient knowledge and information about the subject matter of the case to have an opinion that will assist the jury in understanding the case. If the necessary foundation is not laid during the deposition, the expert's opinions cannot be used.

Nonexpert witnesses are seldom permitted to give opinion testimony. But when allowed, there must be a showing that the witness had an opportunity to observe, understand, and recall the events about which they are to testify. Failure to make the necessary showing makes the evidence subject to objection on the grounds of lack of foundation. Again, presenting such testimony by deposition is worrisome and risky because of the danger that sufficient foundation will not be laid in the deposition. The lawyer taking the deposition does not have a final ruling on the admissibility of the evidence until trial, and a deficiency in foundation cannot be supplied then. For example, suppose that a nonexpert witness is asked for her opinion about the speed of a vehicle that she observed. Suppose that she observed the automobile for two seconds or five seconds or fifteen seconds. Was the length of time sufficient to make a valid observation? The value judgment falls within the discretion of the trial judge. The fact is that fair-minded judges may differ on the ruling—hence, the lawyer's concern about the adequacy of foundation. In all probability, two seconds is not enough time to form a valid opinion about a vehicle's speed. Five seconds may or may not be a sufficient period of time, depending upon the witness's age and experience. Ten seconds certainly is ample time for a qualified witness to make a valid observation of a vehicle's speed.

Suppose the deponent is ten years old. Would the deponent qualify to form an opinion about a vehicle's speed? Suppose the deponent is fourteen years old. Is the deponent now competent to form an opinion about speed? The decision will ultimately be made by the trial judge. The judge has a great deal of latitude in such matters, and properly so.

Hypothetical Questions

Hypothetical questions are not common in depositions. Many lawyers contend that hypothetical questions are not calculated to discover admissible evidence. They are not useful as a means of discovering facts. However, they may be used to obtain an adverse party's expert opinions, especially in malpractice actions. A determination of whether or not hypothetical questions are proper in discovery proceedings is not a subject for this book. It is enough, for our purposes, to appreciate that this is an area of controversy. Also, a client should be prepared to cope with hypothetical questions.

Hypothetical questions are primarily used as a means of obtaining opinion evidence from a witness who does not have sufficient *personal knowledge* of the facts to give an opinion. If the facts can be proved through other witnesses, an expert is permitted to assume the truth of those facts and, relying upon them, give an opinion concerning their effect. But when hypothetical questions are used in depositions, the most common purpose is to try to get the witness to establish a legal duty owed by one party to another. This is especially true in tort actions involving professional malpractice, construction accident cases, and products liability cases.

For example, suppose a question exists whether a general contractor on a construction project is responsible for erecting restraints around the floors of a multilevel building. One of the iron workers fell from the second structural level while the steel beams, columns, and flooring were being installed. He was an employee of the steel erection company which had a subcontract for the work. No other subcontractors were on the job. No one but iron workers were allowed on the steel framework while it was being erected. A lawyer might ask the general contractor's superintendent whether he would take action to prevent an iron worker from engaging in an unsafe act. If so, what action would be taken? What is his authority to act? More specifically, if the superintendent saw an iron worker on the second floor who was repeatedly throwing down objects in a pedestrian area, would the superintendent speak directly with the iron worker to stop him? Could he cause the iron worker to be taken off the job? Does his authority to act come through the contract, the subcontractor union contract, or customs and practice? The probable answer is none. But if the general contractor's superintendent were to answer that he could stop the iron worker's misconduct, that answer in the deposition may be used to establish a legal duty to protect the iron workers from themselves. The deposition would be used at trial to try to establish that the general contractor has a legal duty to put up perimeter restraints for the steel workers.

The vice of conducting discovery through the use of hypothetical questions is that if the superintendent denies any responsibility for supervising the iron workers, the opposing lawyer will contend that the superintendent's *opinions* lack foundation. But if the superintendent recognizes some authority or responsibility, the superintendent's statement will be used against the general contractor as an admission at trial. So the hypothetical question is frequently a "heads I win, tails you lose" effort to get admissions from another party. Hardly ever is a hypothetical question used to actually discover facts or evidence.

The deponent's lawyer may try to avoid the problem by preparing the deponent to cope with hypothetical questions by explaining the interrogator's objectives and going through some examples. The deponent's lawyer may try to object to the use of hypothetical questions unless and until the examiner establishes that the witness has authority to give opinions and he or she accepts the witness's authority. Only then do his or her opinions have relevancy. The interrogator may then create a problem for himself or herself. A paralegal should discuss the subject thoroughly with the supervising lawyer to determine how he or she handles such matters. A paralegal may be assigned the task of preparing some hypothetical questions to be used in a deposition or at trial. Beware, it is not an easy assignment. Many lawyers have considerable difficulty preparing intelligible, useful, and relevant hypothetical questions.

Deposition Summaries

Lawyers often need deposition summaries as convenient sources of information. Sometimes summaries are needed as an aid to trial preparation. Sometimes the client or other interested person needs a summary to aid in the evaluation of the case. Lawyers in private practice who represent corporations are usually required to provide detailed reports to management or the corporation's legal department, including summaries of important depositions.

There is no one format for making deposition summaries. Indeed, the format of choice depends upon the purpose for which the summary will be used. Some of the possible formats include an ordinary paragraphed letter without any references to the transcript. This is the kind of summary which is usually made by a person who attends the deposition and reports on the testimony before the transcript is available. The letter form is useful as a general future reference for insurance company purposes or for the information of another lawyer who is overseeing the case. If the summary is going to be used for trial preparation, citations to the transcript are indispensable. Such a summary paraphrases the testimony, but critical statements may be quoted verbatim. In the later format, it is useful to leave a wide margin for editorializing. The summary may be chronological so as to cover facts as they occurred in time, or the summary may parallel the transcript, or the summary may categorize the testimony by subject matter.

A paralegal must have some understanding of the case to be able to prepare a good, useful summary. The problem is to include all the important information and omit the unimportant. To know what to include and what can safely be left out of the summary, a paralegal needs to know and understand the legal issues, the fact issues, and the parties' theories of the case. Needless to say, experience is very helpful. The preparation of summaries should be thoroughly discussed with the employer so that the employer's expectations and needs are met.

Scope

The scope of permissible inquiry in depositions is much broader than in court. A lawyer may examine the deponent about any matter that is relevant to the issues as framed by the pleadings. Evidence is considered to be relevant if it has a tendency to prove or disprove a fact in issue. But since a major purpose for taking depositions is to *discover* facts and evidence, the examination of the deponent is considered proper if the questions are reasonably calculated to lead to discovery of evidence admissible at trial. Therefore, the standard adopted by courts and applied by lawyers is to permit examination as long as it is not excessively burdensome or abusive. For example, in a personal injury accident case the defendant's background, including such things as employment, education, past residences, and criminal convictions, is considered acceptable examination. A court should not preclude such inquiry even though the inquiry has very little to do with the facts of the accident. On the other hand, a court would not condone a line of questioning which is calculated to harass or embarrass. It would be unfair, thus not permissible, to question the deponent about the details of his or her divorce or other personal matters. Sometimes the line between relevancy and abuse is difficult to discern.

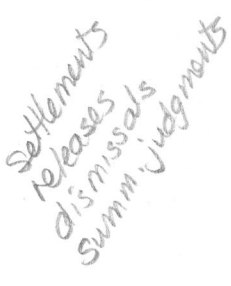

Settlements
releases
dismissals
Summ. Judgments

14 Use of Oral Depositions at Trial

Depositions may be used at trial to present a person's testimony if he or she is unavailable for the trial. The deponent is considered unavailable for trial if he or she is (1) deceased, (2) more than one hundred miles from the place of trial, (3) ill, (4) in prison, or (5) has not responded to a subpoena. Other reasons may be accepted by the court as establishing the witness's unavailability (Rule 32(a)(3)).

Any portion of a *party's deposition* may be presented by the adverse party as in the nature of admissions by the deponent (Rule 32(a)(2)). A party's admissions in a deposition constitute substantive evidence as well as impeachment evidence when used against the party. The deposition of a non-party witness who is available for trial may be used only for the purpose of impeachment (Rule 32(a)(1)). If the deposition is used at trial, that means that a relevant portion or all of it may be read to the court and jury. The transcript is never made available to the jury to read. If the jury were given a copy of the transcript to read, there is a danger that more or less weight would be given to that particular evidence.

A deposition transcript may be used at trial to present testimony regardless of the purpose for which the deposition was originally taken. Therefore, if a lawyer elects not to ask a witness any questions in a deposition taken for purposes of discovery, he or she is gambling on the witness's availability for the trial. Frequently, it is a gamble or a risk worth taking.

Presentation at Trial

The deposition may be presented to the jury in various ways. The manner chosen depends upon the amount of testimony to be presented from the deposition, the lawyer's personal preference, and economics. The simplest and most economical method is for the lawyer to read the pertinent parts of the deposition to the jury. Depending upon the rules of the particular court, the lawyer may stand in front of the jury or sit in the witness stand and read the transcript. An introductory statement may be made explaining why the deposition is being read in lieu of the witness's personal appearance. The introductory statement may explain that the witness testified under oath, subject to cross-examination, when and where the deposition was taken, and who was present. Then the lawyer may state for the court record which pages and lines are being read. While the lawyer reads the questions and answers, the other lawyers watch their copies of the transcript to make sure that it is read accurately. When the lawyer finishes reading those portions of the deposition which he or she feels are important to the case, the other lawyers may read any other portion which they feel is relevant. Of course, the deposition testimony is admissible only if it otherwise comports with the rules of evidence.

This method of presenting deposition testimony is satisfactory if the reading is short; it is not very satisfactory if all or a substantial portion of the deposition is to be read. It is too monotonous for the jury to listen to one person read more than just a few pages of a deposition. It tends to be boring and somewhat difficult for the jury to follow. These problems are compounded if the deposition is read rapidly. A deposition should be read very slowly, with pauses between sentences. Otherwise, the jury has difficulty concentrating and assimilating the evidence. Jurors are supposed to look for conflicts in the evidence. They must have a moment to reflect on what they are hearing. There are natural pauses when a witness testifies in person which, too often, are omitted in reading the testimony. The reader must make a conscious effort to inject appropriate pauses. Also, it is easier to observe a dialogue between two people than listen to a monologue, because the exchange tends to stimulate the listeners' interest.

Another method of presenting deposition testimony is for someone, such as a paralegal, to sit in the witness stand, in place of the deponent, and read the deponent's testimony while a lawyer reads the questions. Each lawyer reads his or her own part. This method helps to establish a dialogue, which is much easier for the jury to follow and to appreciate. The procedure is less boring. An effective reader can make himself or herself appear to be the deponent. Some readers make better appearances than the deponent would have made. Generally speaking, this procedure is much more desirable than having one person read all parts.

The deposition may be presented to a jury with a videotape which allows the jury to see and hear the witness. If the witness makes a particularly good appearance or the use of exhibits is particularly important to the testimony, a video presentation has obvious advantages over other methods. There are, however, some significant disadvantages and problems associated with the use of video. Video is expensive. In addition to the cost of the typed transcript, there is the cost of the videotape, video operator, and the equipment for taking and presenting the testimony. Taking a video deposition is cumbersome. The room must be large enough to accommodate the lights, camera, and other paraphernalia. The replay equipment has to be set up in the courtroom for presentation of the evidence and arranged so that the judge, jury, and lawyers are able to see the video picture. If an objection is made, the whole production must be stopped until the court can rule on the objection. Usually a video picture shows only the deponent and the exhibits. After awhile, a video picture of one person tends to become tedious. The witness may become uncomfortable being on camera for a long time. Notwithstanding these problems, the trend is toward more and more use of video deposition testimony.

Impeaching a Witness

A deposition may be used to impeach a witness, whether or not the witness is a party. A witness is impeached by showing that, on some previous occasion, the witness made statements which are inconsistent with the witness's testimony at trial. The inconsistency is shown merely by reading that portion of the deposition which appears to be inconsistent with what the witness says in court. The jury is instructed, at the end of the trial, to consider any impeachment when evaluating a witness's credibility. Impeachment merely affects the weight or credibility of the testimony, not its admissibility; however, impeaching statements made by a party may be used as substantive evidence against that party. Substantive evidence is any evidence which can be used to support a verdict. The out-of-court statements by a nonparty cannot be considered as substantive evidence because these statements are not always under oath or subject to cross-examination, and the jury was not able to hear and observe the person who made the alleged inconsistent statement. The jury's verdict should be based on the sworn testimony which they hear in court. Naturally, there are some exceptions to these rules, but we need not examine them here. Impeachment does not cause the witness to be disqualified from testifying or even subject to penalties. Of course, if a witness is guilty of perjury, that would be a basis for finding the witness in contempt of court and criminal charges could be brought against him or her.

It is relatively easy for lawyers to use depositions, which are on file with the court, to show inconsistencies between the deposition testimony and testimony at trial. For example, suppose that in a personal injury action, the plaintiff testified at trial that her various aches and pains began immediately after the accident, and such testimony appears to be at variance with her deposition testimony in which she admitted that her low back discomfort did not begin until two months after the accident in question. Of course, a delay in the onset of pain by two months suggests that the accident did not cause the problem. The impeachment could be accomplished in the following manner on cross-examination:

Q. You will recall, Mrs. Johnson, that on May 10, 1989, you appeared, with your attorney, at my office for your deposition?

A. Yes.

Q. At that time, you testified concerning your accident and the injuries you sustained?

A. Yes.

Q. Before testifying, you took an oath to tell the truth, the whole truth, just as you did before testifying here in court?

A. Yes.

Q. Mrs. Johnson, you will recall that during your deposition I asked you the following questions, and you gave the following answers.

A. Well, I don't know!

Q. Please listen. Beginning at page 24, line 10, you testified as follows: Right after the collision occurred and the cars came to rest, how did you feel?

A. Shook up; kind of sick.

Q. Well, did you have any specific aches or pain?

A. Yes. My neck began hurting and I had a headache.

Q. Where was your headache located?

A. In the back of my head.

Q. When did the headache begin?

A. Right away.

Q. Did you have any other pains while at the accident scene?

A. No.

Q. Are you claiming any other injuries to your person besides your head and neck?

A. Yes.

Q. What?

A. My back hurts.

Q. Where does your back hurt?

A. In the lower part, here (indicating).

Q. When did that begin to bother you?

A. It came on kind of gradual.

Q. Well, when did you first become aware of the problem? What were you doing?

A. I'm not too sure.

Q. So you can't say whether it was two months, six months, or any particular time after the accident?

A. I know it wasn't six months—maybe two months.

Q. That's your best recollection?

A. Yes.

Q. Do you remember what you were doing when you first noticed that your low back was uncomfortable?

A. No.

Q. Now, just where in the low back do you have this pain?

A. Here (indicating).

Q. Let the record show that the witness has pointed to an area just below the waistline, directly over the spine. Have I accurately described the location to which you were pointing?

A. Yes.

(End of Deposition)

Q. Now, that was your testimony when your deposition was taken, wasn't it?

A. Yes.

Q. And that was the truth—your testimony under oath?

A. Yes, but after the deposition I talked with my husband about it; and he said I complained about my back hurting the same day of the accident.

Attorney: Your honor, I move that the witness's last answer be stricken as not responsive and on the grounds that it is hearsay.

Court: The last answer is stricken and the jury is instructed to disregard it.

Q. Certainly your memory about the accident and related events would have been better when your deposition was taken than now.

A. I don't know.

Q. You do not have any current recollection now as to when your back started hurting, do you? That is, of your own memory.

A. Well, we talked about it and I'm just trying to remember—it's been so long, and I've seen so many doctors.

Attorney: I move that the last answer be stricken as not responsive.

Court: The last answer is stricken and the jury is instructed to disregard it.

(End of Trial Testimony)

It is hard to believe that the witness lied, that is, committed perjury in either her deposition or her court testimony; nevertheless, she was inconsistent. Both answers could not be correct. She was quite satisfied to yield her recollection to that of her husband. But she cannot testify as to his recollection, because that is hearsay testimony. Perhaps her husband will be allowed to testify concerning his observations of her condition and such testimony would help to rehabilitate the witness. The jury will be instructed that impeachment of a witness or impeachment of the witness's testimony is a factor which they may and should consider when weighing the believability of the testimony.

It should be noted that the deposition testimony concerning the onset of the plaintiff's back pain is substantive evidence, because it is the prior statement of a party. Based upon the deposition testimony the jury could decide that the plaintiff's back pain did not begin until two months after the accident.

A witness may be impeached in other ways too. Anytime a witness's testimony at trial is shown to be inconsistent, in some material respect, with the witness's prior statements or conduct, the inconsistency constitutes impeachment. If, for example, a witness testifies that he saw that the traffic light was green for the plaintiff, another witness would be allowed to testify that she heard the first witness state that he was not looking at the traffic light at the time of the collision. The impeaching witness must come to court and testify under oath to what the witness heard. Whereas, a witness can be impeached by his or her deposition by simply reading the pertinent portions from the transcript. The safeguards against abuse are in the court reporter's certification that the transcript is accurate and the witness's right to read and verify the transcript before it is used. As part of trial preparation, a lawyer or paralegal should make sure that all depositions which will be used at trial have been properly filed.

A witness may be impeached by the witness's recorded statement if the contents of the statement differ from the witness's testimony in court. The necessary foundation for using a recorded statement to impeach a witness is more difficult than using a deposition transcript (see Rule 613). If the statement is in writing and signed by the witness, the cross-examination may be conducted as follows:

Q. Do you recall that on (date) you were interviewed by a Ms. Jones [paralegal] about this accident?

A. No. Well, maybe. I'm not sure. I've talked to so many people and it has been a long time. (Counsel has statement marked as defendant's Exhibit 1 for identification.)

Q. I am now showing you a document marked as defendant's Exhibit 1. Can you identify it?

A. No.

Q. I am showing you the bottom of the second page, is that your signature?

A. It appears to be.

Q. Do you now recall that on the date shown here (date) you were interviewed at your home concerning this accident?

A. Could be.

Q. At that time, you were asked about your version of the accident as you saw it.

A. Perhaps.

Q. Please take the Exhibit now and read it to yourself.

A. Yes, I seem to recall it.

Q. This is your signature?

A. Yes.

Counsel: I offer defendant's Exhibit 1 into evidence.

Court: For what purpose, counsel? I don't see the connection yet.

Counsel: The Exhibit is being offered for impeachment purposes.

> [At this point, plaintiff's counsel would probably demand
> to see the statement as provided in Rule 613.]

Court to witness: Is that your signature and your statement?

A. Yes.

Court to plaintiff's counsel: Is there any objection?

Counsel: Yes, there has been no foundation for the Exhibit, and it is not impeaching.

Court: Objections overruled. Exhibit received.

> [Note that the contents of the document cannot be referred
> to until after the Exhibit is received into evidence.]

Q. You stated at the time you gave this statement that you did not see the traffic light before the collision.

A. I don't specifically remember saying that.

Q. Please read with me. Now referring to defendant's Exhibit 1: "I was standing at the southwest corner waiting for a bus which would be coming from the west. I was looking westerly when I heard the collision behind me. I turned around right away. The southbound car (white convertible) was stopped in the middle of the intersection. The eastbound car (Ford) slid sideways and came to rest at the southwest corner of the intersection. It was turned almost 180 degrees around. I could see the driver of the Ford was slouched over. As soon as I was sure that no other cars were coming, I ran over to the Ford."

Q. Now, that is what your signed statement said, isn't it?

A. That's what it says.

Q. And when you gave that statement you were trying to be truthful—to give a truthful account of what you observed?

A. Yes.

Q. And you did not intend to claim that you saw things that you didn't see?

A. But the statement doesn't say everything I saw. . . .

Q. When you signed it you considered it to be accurate, didn't you?

A. Yes.

Q. If an important point had been left out of the statement, you would have brought that to the attention of Ms. Jones (paralegal) when she took the statement, wouldn't you?

A. Well, I didn't know what she thought was important.

Q. We're talking about what you think is important.

A. (No response)

Q. No further questions.

Redirect Examination

Q. Is this written statement, defendant's Exhibit 1, in your handwriting?

A. No.

Q. But the signature is yours?

A. Yes.

Q. Did you choose the wording used in this statement?

A. No.

Q. Did you choose the things to be said or included in the statement?

A. No.

Q. Were you told when this statement was being written down that you would be asked to sign it?

A. No.

Q. Were you given a copy of the statement?

A. No.

Q. Did you read it before signing it?

A. Well, I just sort of glanced over it, and it looked O.K., so I signed it. I think she told me I had to.

Q. Did you, in fact, look at the traffic light?

A. Yes, I did.

Q. What color was it?

Counsel: Objection. The question is objected to for lack of foundation— there is now showing of just when the observation was made; and the witness had disqualified himself.

Court: Perhaps a little more foundation should be laid.

Counsel: Yes, I was just about to do that, your honor.

Q. You say you did take notice of the traffic signal light?

A. Yes, sir.

Q. Just when did you make this observation of the light?

A. Soon as I heard the crash and turned around—when I looked to see if any other cars were coming; that's when I saw that the light was green for east-westbound traffic.

Q. No further questions. Thank you.

Re–cross-examination

Q. Let's see now. On direct examination this morning, you said that you saw the light before the crash, but now you say you saw it after the crash. Is that right?

A. I guess the statement refreshed my memory.

Q. Are you familiar with the intersection? Do you catch a bus there every day?

A. No. I go that way to see my sister sometimes.

Q. Where is the traffic light located—the one you observed after the collision?

A. There is only one. It sort of hangs on a wire over the center. I saw the light that faces west, and it was definitely green.

Q. But you said that you saw the Ford sliding sideways and turning around and coming to rest at the northwest corner.

A. Yes.

Q. You saw all that, and then you saw the driver of the Ford slump over?

A. Yes.

Q. And you felt that you should get over to help him?

A. Yes.

Q. You realized that there might be an emergency right there in front of you?

A. I don't know if I . . . Well, yea, sort of.

Q. As soon as you could see that no cars were coming, you dashed right over to the Ford?

A. Yes.

Q. Isn't it true that you could not see the color of the light by looking from the place where you were standing, the bus stop?

A. I don't know. I saw the light and it was green.

Q. But after hearing the crash, seeing the Ford slide to a stop, and looking for other traffic in the area—about five or six seconds lapsed before you could have looked at the light?

A. I didn't time it. You don't have a stopwatch.

Q. It would have been at least five seconds, wouldn't it?

A. Four, maybe five. I suppose, something like that.

Q. You didn't tell Ms. Jones (paralegal) when she interviewed you on (date) when this statement was given, that you saw the light, now did you?

A. No.

Q. Why not?

A. She didn't ask.

Q. And you didn't think she was interested or needed that information from you?

A. If she'd asked, I would have told her. I talked to a lot of people. And I was getting kind of tired of it all.

Q. You didn't tell the investigating police, either, that you saw the light, did you?

Counsel: Objection. That's irrelevant and calls for hearsay.

Court: Overruled.

Q. You may answer. Did you tell the police that you saw the light?

A. They were too busy. I gave them my name.

Q. I have no further questions of this witness.

Re–cross–examination

Q. There is no doubt in your mind about it, is there? You did see the light?

Counsel: The question is objected to on the ground that it is repetitious, leading, and suggestive.

Court: Sustained.

Q. Thank you, Mr. (witness). That will be all for now. You are excused.

The signed statement has almost the same value and effect for impeachment purposes as a deposition. But the statement is more cumbersome to use, because the statement must be identified and the witness must acknowledge that it is his or her statement. If, in the preceding example, the witness continued to deny that the signature was his, the person who took the statement would have to be called as a witness to identify the statement and relate the circumstances under which the statement was given by the witness. Then it becomes the paralegal's word against the word of the witness. If the statement had been secured by the attorney who was examining the witness, a further problem would be introduced, because an attorney is forbidden by ethics to testify in a case which he or she is trying. It would be very difficult for the lawyer to put the statement into evidence if the witness remained adamant that he did not sign the statement.

15 Preparation of Client for Deposition

Paralegals can play a significant role in preparing clients for their oral depositions. While a lawyer must assume ultimate responsibility for the client's preparation, much of the actual work can be done by a paralegal who understands the purposes of depositions, deposition procedures, and the case at issue. A paralegal should not be disappointed at not being assigned responsibility for deposition preparation until gaining experience with deposition procedures through observation and training by lawyers. A client's deposition is an extremely important aspect of any case. The opposing lawyer will evaluate the client's testimony by what the client says and how he or she says it.

The testimony given in the deposition must be consistent with what the client says at trial. If there is any variance, the discrepancies may be shown for purpose of *impeaching* the client's testimony at trial. Furthermore, any misstatements made during the deposition are subject to being used against the client as **admissions** against interest. These things should be carefully explained to the client so that the client appreciates the importance of the deposition and of adequate preparation. This is a time when a client appreciates the value of good competent advice and guidance by people who are sincerely interested in his or her welfare.

Though the client must be impressed with the importance of the deposition, every effort should be made to avoid increasing the client's anxiety. Therefore, a paralegal should try to appear relaxed and confident about the deposition. The prospect of testifying in a deposition should be presented as a positive and useful experience which is going to make the client feel more confident about the case and the trial. The deposition transcript will be useful to the client in preparing for the trial. The interrogator's questions tend to reveal what information the other side does and does not have. The questions also tend to suggest what facts the other side considers important. The deposition gives the client an opportunity to have the experience of testifying, and that is beneficial. The client comes to realize that he or she can handle it.

Methods of Preparation

There is no one method or formula for preparing a client for a deposition. The various steps in the preparation may be changed in their order and some omitted entirely, depending upon the particular case. However, the witness guidelines, discussed in the following pages are always applicable, regardless of whether the client is a plaintiff or defendant and regardless of the type of case involved. There can be no doubt about the fact that the very best preparation for a deposition is to actually take the client through a question and answer session. The same questions should be asked that the opposing lawyer is expected to ask and in the same manner.

Clients are usually apprehensive about the prospect of being cross-examined by the opposing lawyer. But a deposition does not have to be a difficult or unhappy experience. Through careful preparation a client can avoid pitfalls and gain confidence about the case. Paralegals can prepare the client for the deposition by instructing the client how to handle the questions which will be posed by the opposing lawyer. If the client becomes comfortable with the deposition procedure and provides a good deposition, the paralegal will win the undying gratitude of a pleased client. The key to success is adequate preparation, which usually includes a mock cross-examination. There is no reason why an experienced paralegal should not be involved in the examination.

The client should be told that the discovery deposition is for the benefit of the party who schedules and takes the deposition. The client is not volunteering for it. The client is appearing because the law and court rules mandate that the client submit to the examination. The primary purpose of an oral deposition is to enable the opposing party to find out what the deponent knows and does not know about the case. The more a lawyer can find out about the adverse party and the adverse party's evidence, the better the lawyer can prepare the case for trial. As a general rule, the client should not volunteer information or give explanations, unless specifically called for by proper questions. The best answer is the client's shortest answer. The client should be assured that, with the help and experience gained in the deposition, he or she will be fully prepared and ready to testify. The procedure must be fully explained to the client, including the physical arrangements, personnel involved, and the role each person plays.

A lawyer or paralegal generally begins the preparation by providing the client with an overview of the case. The client should be told about the legal theories and fact issues so that he or she can understand how the testimony fits into the case as a whole. The legal issues should be described in terms which a layperson can understand. Particular care must be used to identify the facts which are disputed and those facts which are not contested. Explain the opponent's theory of the facts. That kind of an overview enables the client to understand the interrogator's questions and the effect of the answers. The big picture gives the client a frame of reference which should help the client to appreciate the importance of the questions. Clients are much more comfortable during their depositions if they know what is happening and why. For most of us, the unknown is the principal cause of fear and nervousness. The more apprehensive or nervous the client is, the more likely he or she is to make mistakes.

Deposition Procedures

The deposition will probably be taken at the office of the lawyer who scheduled it. However, it could be taken almost anywhere. The primary consideration is the convenience of a majority of the people involved. Each party has a right to be present and hear any witness testify. More often than not, the parties themselves elect not to attend other parties' depositions. Notwithstanding the customary practice, there can be considerable value in having the client attend other parties' depositions. The experience may help the client to prepare for his or her own deposition. The client can obtain a better appreciation for the problems in the case and may be able to suggest additional questions to put to the opposing party. One not so obvious benefit is that a party's presence seems to have a sobering effect on the deponent. Deponents may not exaggerate or minimize quite as much. Members of the public and news media do not have a right to attend discovery depositions.

The deponent's testimony is under oath, subject to the penalties of perjury. The deponent's lawyer is present throughout the deposition to provide guidance and assistance. Everything that is said is recorded, verbatim, by a stenographer. The client does not have a right to make statements "off the record"; but, if it is necessary to interrupt the deposition, usually the lawyers can work out suitable arrangements. The length of the deposition depends upon the type of case and the extent of the deponent's involvement. In a typical accident case the plaintiff's deposition lasts about two hours. If more than one lawyer interrogates the plaintiff, the deposition will last longer. The defendant's deposition typically lasts about one and a half hours. But it is possible for a deposition to last as long as several days. There is no prescribed time limit, unless the "discovery plan" or a court order imposes a limit.

The client should be told that lawyers have the right to ask questions about almost anything relevant to the case. Each lawyer asks all the questions he or she has to ask, and then the next lawyer begins to interrogate the witness. Each lawyer has an opportunity for re-cross-examination. The deponent's lawyer has a right to ask questions, but in the typical *discovery* deposition, the lawyer usually chooses to ask few if any questions. The deponent's lawyer may object to improper questions. If an objection is made, the lawyer who asked the question may elect to rephrase the question, abandon it, or insist upon an answer. If the interrogator insists on an answer, the deponent's lawyer has to decide whether or not to let the deponent answer. By making the objection, the lawyer has protected the record in the sense that if the deposition is used at trial, a judge will have to rule on the objection before the deponent's answer can be read to the jury. That is some protection. It means that the objectionable question gets answered and the interrogator obtains information to which the interrogator may not be entitled.

The deponent's lawyer may elect to instruct the deponent not to answer the question. In that event, the interrogator has a right to adjourn the deposition and seek a court order compelling the deponent to answer. In the alternative, the interrogator may elect to complete the deposition on other matters and then seek a court order requiring the witness to answer the questions which the witness was instructed not to answer. If the deponent's lawyer objects to a question, that should be a signal to the deponent that the question may present some problem, and the deponent should try to be certain that he or she understands the question.

One approach is to tell the client that if an objection is interposed, the client should remain silent and wait for further instructions. The lawyer who asked the question may rephrase the question or go on to another question. If the interrogator insists on an answer, the lawyer who objected will have to decide whether or not to let the deponent answer notwithstanding the objection. If the lawyer allows the client to answer the question *subject to the objection*, the deponent should have the question read back by the court reporter so that the deponent can make sure he or she understands the question. The lawyer's objection may contain a clue as to what the problem is with the question, so the deponent should listen carefully to the objections that are made. In other words, sometimes the objections are made for the deponent's edification. For example:

(Questions put to a landlord in an action brought by tenant)

Q. How long had the stairway light been burned out, before the plaintiff fell on the stairway?

Objection: The question is objected to on the grounds that it assumes facts not in evidence and is argumentative in form. Defendant does not know that the plaintiff fell on the stairway.

Q. You don't deny that the plaintiff fell on the stairway, do you?

A. I have no knowledge of his alleged fall.

Q. Well, how long was the light out?

A. I don't know that it was burned out. I heard from the plaintiff's wife that she changed the bulb in the stairway after the plaintiff went to the hospital. I understood that she put in a brighter light bulb.

This witness was adequately prepared on the points in issue. The objection helped the witness to focus on the problem.

The other lawyer's probable objectives should be carefully explained to the client. Usually there are just a few key points. The client should be told that one of the objectives of a deposition is to find out what the deponent does not know. There may be a lot of questions which the client cannot answer. The client should not be afraid to admit he or she does not know the answers. A deposition is not like a test in school where the person being tested loses points for not being able to answer questions. On the other hand, a client should be cautioned against saying he or she does not know the answer merely because it is an easy way to avoid controversy.

The use of exhibits should be explained to the client, including the procedure for identifying and marking exhibits. The witness may be asked to make sketches relevant to the occurrence or things in issue. It would be good to practice before the deposition if that is likely to be required. Some lawyers take the position that a witness does not have to *create* evidence in a deposition, so they do not permit the client to make drawings or sketches. Other lawyers prepare by making sketches in advance of the deposition. They produce the prepared sketches if and when the client is asked to make one.

The client should be told about the right to read and sign the deposition transcript. The right to read the transcript and correct errors gives the deponent a last opportunity to avoid inconsistencies and mistakes; however, paralegals should be aware that courts differ on the effect of the corrections. Rule 30 clearly allows the deponent to correct the transcript. The corrections may relate to mistakes by the court reporter or the deponent may correct mistakes in testimony. The corrections may relate to matters of form, such as spelling or use of proper names. Or, the changes may relate to the substance of the deponent's testimony. For example, the deponent may have testified in the deposition that he saw the traffic light was red and change the testimony to say that the light was green. The deponent must give a reason for each change. Some courts would allow the opposing party to show that originally the deponent said the light was red. In effect, the court is allowing the deponent to be impeached by the inconsistent statement even though Rule 30(e) expressly preserves the right to make changes. The point is that care should be exercised to avoid making any mistakes during the deposition.

An introduction in this manner enables a client to understand where his or her testimony fits, why certain questions will be asked, and the probable effect of the answers on the outcome of the case. The explanations should come in the form of a dialogue with the client, not as a lecture. The client's understanding and retention will be much better if he or she *actively* participates in the preparation.

If a lawyer is going to ask the client any questions in the deposition, those questions and the answers should be discussed and rehearsed. More often than not, the deponent's lawyer elects not to ask any questions in a discovery deposition. After all, why help the opposition? The plaintiff in a personal injury action usually wants the defendant's lawyer to know all about the plaintiff's injuries. Presumably the information will increase the defense's evaluation of the case for settlement purposes. This is one area where the deponent may want to volunteer information. On occasion, clarifying questions may be useful or even necessary to protect the deponent. A witness may think he or she said one thing, but it came out quite differently. The mistake should be corrected and explained before the deposition is concluded; leading questions may be necessary. If the lawyer is not quite sure how the client will respond to the attempt to correct the mistake, the better practice is to correct the mistake as provided by Rule 30(e).

A lawyer must not tell the client what to say, other than to tell the truth; but a lawyer can be very helpful by advising a client *how* to testify. There are certain guidelines to testifying in a deposition which are useful for the deponent to know. The guidelines help deponents to avoid mistakes; they facilitate the proceedings. The guidelines help the deponent to be more authoritative and persuasive. The guidelines are mostly common sense but also take into consideration some of the peculiarities of the rules of evidence and court procedures. The guidelines are not necessarily applicable to testifying in trial before a jury.

A minimum of two hours should be allowed for the client's deposition preparation. A paralegal should be fully prepared on the file before meeting the client. After the witness has been instructed in the guidelines for testifying, the next step is to interrogate the client just as though the deposition were being taken. This gives the witness an opportunity to use the guidelines and practice phrasing answers. As questions or problems arise, either the paralegal or the witness should be permitted to stop the mock interrogation to discuss them.

Guidelines

TELL THE TRUTH. Testimony is given under oath. A witness who testifies falsely is subject to the criminal penalties of perjury—a felony. Jurors are instructed that if they conclude that a witness has testified falsely, they may disregard everything the witness said. There is no surer way to lose a case than for a party to be caught in a lie. Telling the truth means testifying accurately—without exaggerating or minimizing. A witness must not fabricate or twist the facts. Opinions must comport with what he or she actually believes.

Lawyers are obligated to prevent clients from perpetrating frauds upon the courts. A lawyer must not allow the client to testify falsely. Lawyers must not present evidence which they have reason to believe is false. As officers of the court, they are subject to severe penalties for allowing clients to abuse the procedures or rules. The adversary system is effective at finding the truth. If a party tries to win a case on the basis of false testimony, that party is fighting against heavy odds and faces severe penalties.

A witness who takes the stand intending to lie looks anxious, uneasy, and tends to overcompensate in various ways. The witness may actually believe that he or she can deceive everyone, but when the witness takes the stand and faces the jury, he or she is not so sure. If the witness took the stand in good faith but suddenly has lied, there is a sudden change in demeanor. It is human nature. This is one of the reasons why the adversary system for examining witnesses has proven to be effective for getting at the truth.

The nature of the adversary system assumes that each party will give himself or herself the benefit of any actual, honest doubt concerning a disputed matter. For example, if a motorist honestly believes he was not exceeding a thirty-mile-per-hour speed limit, but did not look at the speedometer to determine actual speed, he should testify to what he believes his speed was. The deponent should be prepared to deny driving any faster than what he believes he was doing. He must candidly admit that his opinion of speed is based upon experience and is merely an estimate. He did not look at the speedometer. But he should *refuse* to *speculate* that it is possible he was going faster than what he truly believes the speed was. A client may indicate that he or she wants to be told what to say. The witness must be firmly told that he or she is to tell the truth and only the truth.

LISTEN CAREFULLY TO EACH QUESTION. A witness should feel certain that he or she understands the question before answering. The burden is on the lawyer to make each question clear and understandable. If the witness does not understand a question, it is not the witness's fault or problem. The lawyer must repeat or rephrase the question if asked to do so. When the witness realizes that the onus is on the lawyer to make the witness understand, the witness feels much more comfortable and confident. The witness is less reluctant to admit that he or she did not hear or understand a question.

The witness should be encouraged to reflect on each question for a moment and silently phrase the answer before responding aloud. This procedure helps the witness to avoid interrupting the lawyers' questions. All too often witnesses are prone to answer before the question is completed. Not only are they in danger of making mistakes, but they cause the court reporter a lot of frustration and unnecessary stress. It is difficult enough for the stenographer to record one person's remarks but nearly impossible to record statements by two people speaking at the same time. The usual consequence is that the court reporter has to stop everyone, and the question has to be repeated. Obviously, the answer which is made "too quickly" serves only to complicate and delay the proceedings.

If a witness takes a moment to reflect on the question and to think through the answer, that gives the witness's lawyer an opportunity to interpose objections to improper questions. If the deponent answers too quickly, he or she loses that protection. The witness should even be cautioned against permitting the opposing lawyers to hurry him or her by showing impatience or irritation. Lawyers know that a thoughtful witness is less likely to be tripped up than one who rushes the answers.

A witness can hardly be too thoughtful or deliberate when testifying in a deposition. Testimony at trial presents a little different situation. There, excessive hesitancy or delay may be interpreted, rightly or wrongly, as uncertainty, a lack of authority, or even a lack of candor. The pauses and little delays do not show up in a deposition transcript, unless a video system is used.

ANSWER JUST THE QUESTION. The purpose of a discovery deposition is to find out what the deponent knows and does not know. The more information the interrogator obtains, the better the interrogator can prepare for trial. With that explanation, it is obvious that the client should not help the interrogator by volunteering information or by providing explanations which are not specifically called for by the questions. A witness should strive to make answers responsive, direct, and specific. The deponent's best answer is the shortest answer, provided the answer is truthful. Short answers help to make the witness appear polite, authoritative, and nonargumentative. In other words, short answers usually keep the testimony brief and provide the least help to the opponent. A deponent may be inclined to volunteer information when the deponent does not understand the questions or wants to explain his or her knowledge or simply wants to emphasize his or her importance. A talkative deponent tends to gravitate to the problems in the case which are most bothersome to the deponent. A verbose deponent opens new subjects and areas for questioning. The more the deponent talks, the greater is the opportunity for inconsistencies.

The deponent should feel as though he or she is a "well" of information, and the interrogator has to dip into the well with each question. If the deponent feels the information is being "pulled" out, then the deponent is handling a discovery deposition correctly. The deponent should not feel like a fountain that gushes forth with information. This advice does not mean that the deponent should be uncommunicative, stubborn, or difficult.

Each deposition question should be singular. The deponent's lawyer can help the deponent to avoid volunteering and to keep answers short by insisting that the interrogator avoid multiple questions. The deponent should be watching for vague and multiple questions too. The deponent should be aware that if it appears a question is multiple or vague, the deponent may ask to have the question narrowed or made more specific. The deponent does not have to wait for an objection from his or her lawyer.

These observations and advice should be helpful in preparing the client for a *discovery* deposition. Please note that these guidelines do not necessarily apply to a client's testimony at trial. Short answers may appear to be evasive. Short answers keep the client from presenting his or her version of the facts. Indeed, full narrative answers are the rule at trial, because the purpose of testifying is to fully inform and persuade the jury. Short answers do not do that! Additionally, most lawyers who handle a plaintiff's personal injury case feel that the plaintiff's deposition testimony should give full descriptive answers to all questions relative to injuries and losses.

DO NOT GUESS. A witness should candidly admit to not knowing the answer to a question rather than guess at the answer. Generally speaking, a wrong guess can do more harm than a lucky guess can help. It is usually evident when a witness is merely guessing. If jurors determine that a witness is prone to guessing, they are inclined to discount the witness's testimony as a whole. A witness's authority is severely diminished by guessing. What is worse, a wrong guess may be interpreted as false testimony.

A witness does not create any difficulty by admitting that he or she does not know the answer to a question. Indeed, the witness has a duty to admit a lack of knowledge or information. The rule against guessing does not mean that a witness should refrain from giving estimates or judgments, opinions, or best recollections. By way of example, a witness may not know the exact width of the roadway but may be able to make a reasonably accurate estimate. A reasonably reliable estimate is not a mere guess. The law usually does not require exactitude. Nor does the law require perfect recall. The law does require the witness to *believe* that his or her memory and judgment are reasonably accurate. To express some degree of uncertainty without guessing, witnesses often use expressions such as, "to the best of my memory," "as best as I recall," "I believe," or "I'm not certain, but. . . ." Whenever a witness is constrained to qualify an answer in this manner, he or she loses some authority and persuasiveness. These expressions should be avoided in depositions and at trial.

A client should be advised that he or she must believe the testimony given is true; however, there is no need to emphasize the belief. There is no need to qualify the answers. For example, when the client is asked for a time, distance, or location, the client may respond with the answer that he or she believes is true. Just state the time, distance, etc. If the interrogator asks whether the time was "clocked" or the distance measured, the answer is a simple no. If asked whether the testimony is merely an estimate, the answer is yes. Again, the best answer is the shortest answer. Otherwise, a witness is inclined to say something like: "I don't know what it is, but I'd guess that it's about fifteen feet." This answer would tend to disqualify the witness from having and giving a reasonable estimate of the distance in question. But if the witness has never made an estimate of the time or distance, the only proper answer is, "I don't know."

Once a witness realizes that he or she does not have to guess and, consequently, does not have to answer every question, he or she may tend to believe that "not knowing" is an easy way out. This is especially true of nonparty witnesses. Deponents should be cautioned against evasion of their responsibility to the parties, court, and community by claiming an imperfect memory. They should do the very best they can to remember and to be accurate. If a party testifies that he or she does not know the answer to a particular question, that may give the other side evidence on the subject that may go unchallenged. For example, if the plaintiff testifies in his deposition that he cannot recall whether he talked with the defendant at the scene of the accident, he is in a difficult position at trial to refute the defendant's testimony that the plaintiff admitted at the scene that the accident was his fault.

The client should be made aware that if he or she cannot remember a certain fact at the time of the deposition, but believes the fact or information can be obtained, the client should so indicate. Perhaps the information is available in records or a diary or is subject to recall later. A statement to that effect keeps the door open to supply the information after the deposition is completed. The subsequent production of the evidence will not be looked upon with suspicion. By agreeing to try to obtain the requested information, the client keeps from being discredited by producing the information at a later date.

DO NOT BE SUSPICIOUS OR DEFENSIVE. A deponent should be respectful and polite, but reticent. A deponent should exhibit a positive attitude about testifying when in a deposition and at trial. A deponent should not assume an attitude of hostility. The deponent should not presume that the adverse lawyers will be abusive or ask tricky questions. Any apparent hostility tends to mitigate the deponent's objectivity and, therefore, work against his or her effectiveness. If the opposing lawyers do appear to be overbearing and abusive, the deponent should make a conscious effort to remain polite but reserved.

ANSWER OUT LOUD. We frequently communicate by signs and gestures, such as a nod of the head or a shrug of the shoulders. But the court reporter may not see gestures and is not required to record them. So, each answer must be stated orally and loud enough for everyone in the room to hear. Deponents should use the word "correct" rather than the word "right." Use "yes" or "no" rather than "ah-huh" or "huh-ha."

BE SINCERE. Sincerity is one of the hallmarks of an effective witness. Second to sincerity is authority. A lawsuit is a serious matter for all concerned. Seldom, if ever, is there occasion for wisecracks or jokes. If there is an opportunity for the witness to poke fun at another person, the temptation should be resisted—even if this is seen as a means of "putting a lawyer in his place." As often as not, someone will be offended. The joke may well boomerang. If a duel of sharp-tongued wit develops, the forum favors the lawyer, because only he or she is authorized to initiate questions. Of course, a witness may ask questions for clarification.

DO NOT SHOW ANGER OR IMPATIENCE. A witness must consciously strive to avoid losing his or her temper. A display of temper usually reflects adversely on the witness though the anger may be perfectly justified. The deponent may even feel like the "star of the show" because of self-righteous indignation. A display of temper creates a risk of being offensive and the possibility of becoming confused. The risk of damage is too great. A witness who loses his or her temper tends to lose perspective and forgets the big picture. He or she is much more subject to making avoidable errors. A show of anger is likely to cause the deponent to forget the other guidelines for testifying. Once a feeling of anger takes over, it is likely to grow. It usually does not go away spontaneously or quickly. When in trial, a lawyer usually tries to obtain a court recess when the opposing lawyer has the client angry and not thinking clearly. But it is not easy to obtain a recess for the benefit of a party who is undergoing a cross-examination. A witness should try to respond to each lawyer the same way, in a polite, courteous, reserved manner.

OPINION EVIDENCE MUST BE REASONABLE. As a general rule, lay witnesses are not permitted to give opinions about facts—just the facts. There are many conditions, situations, and "facts," which, in ordinary human experience, can only be described in the form of opinions. Courts recognize this. Some examples may be helpful. Witnesses seldom determine the speed of a motor vehicle in an accident by seeing the speedometer, obtaining a radar reading, or clocking the vehicles. A witness who is reasonably familiar with motor vehicles and who observed a vehicle long enough to form an opinion of its speed in miles per hour is allowed to state an opinion or estimate of the automobile's speed. The witness gives an opinion concerning the facts. A witness is not permitted to state an opinion that the automobile was going "fast" or "slow." A witness is allowed to give an opinion of a distance in some unit of measurement: feet, yards, miles, etc. Again, he or she may not state an opinion that the subject was "close" or "far."

When a witness describes a street as "slippery," a room as "fairly dark," rainfall as "heavy," the streetlight as "dim," an embankment as "steep," or elevator doors as "fast," he or she is giving an opinion. But how else can an ordinary person describe such conditions? There is no other practical way. Therefore, courts allow laypersons to give such opinions. It may be the best evidence available concerning the facts.

If opinion evidence is admissible, the witness should be sure that the opinion is reasonable in light of his or her own experience and in the experience of most people. The opinion should be tested against physical facts. The most common area of opinion evidence involves time and distance estimates. Remember, a witness must not guess. A witness may have the opportunity to revisit the accident scene to make comparison observations to help make an accurate estimate about a speed or distance. If a moving object is involved, the correlation between time and distance should be considered.

Estimating Speed

Miles per hour	equals	Feet per second
5		7
10		15
20		29
30		44
40		59
50		73
60		88

When a witness is questioned about a speed, distance, or time factor, the witness should first determine whether or not he or she has a valid estimate or judgment. If so, then he or she must decide whether or not to express an opinion in terms of a range or a precise measurement. For example, a witness could estimate skid marks to be forty to fifty feet in length, or forty-five feet in length. Either approach is legitimate and reasonable. Tactics or strategy may determine, however, that one approach is preferable to the other in the particular case.

A witness must be prepared to stay with the estimate if challenged. The challenge usually begins by forcing the witness to "admit" that the figure given is only an estimate—not a measured quantity. Next, the lawyer may ask the witness to admit that it is *possible* that the estimate could be off by one, two, or three miles per hour and later suggest it could be off by even five miles per hour (slower or faster). Again, the cross-examiner will resort to the phrase: "Isn't it possible?" If the estimate could vary by five miles per hour more or less, that creates a spread of ten miles per hour. Pretty soon, it appears that the estimate is of no value at all. Not only is the estimate likely to be rejected as unreliable, but the witness's authority—if not credibility—has been impaired. The solution is for the witness to refuse to speculate about the *possibility* that the estimate could be slightly off. When asked if it is possible that he or she was traveling one mile per hour slower or faster than estimated, the witness should respond that the best estimate is as previously stated and he or she will not speculate about mere possibilities. Even if the questioner persists, the witness should continue to refuse to go beyond the original estimate. The witness thereby avoids weakening the testimony. The same principle applies to almost any type of estimate involving measurements.

MEMORY AND OBSERVATIONS MUST COMPORT WITH PHYSICAL LAWS. Estimates and memory should be tested against natural laws and physical or scientific facts. For example, if a witness has the impression that a motor vehicle collision occurred at thirty miles per hour, but the property damage is slight, the witness's observation or memory is in error. When preparing the witness to testify, the lawyer or paralegal must gently show the witness that his or her present recollection or estimate is not possible. Then they must try to determine what the facts are. If, however, the witness's recollection cannot be refreshed, and if, in fact, he or she has no valid estimate or recollection, the witness must not try to fabricate evidence.

DO NOT OVEREMPHASIZE HONESTY. A witness should avoid using expressions such as "to be honest with you," "to tell you the truth," "if I remember correctly," "to the best of my recollection," or "it seems to me." These expressions weaken the witness's authority and credibility. Testimony should be given without equivocation and without qualification unless absolutely necessary.

AVOID HYPOTHETICAL QUESTIONS. Hypothetical questions relate to fact situations that are merely assumed to be true for the purpose of having the witness render an opinion or otherwise comment on the assumed facts. The facts used in hypothetical questions must be supplied by other testimony or exhibits. Hypothetical questions have a legitimate and important role in trials. Nevertheless, it is questionable whether hypothetical questions may properly be used in discovery depositions when the witness is not an expert. Of course, clients must answer questions about the facts of the case. They must tell what was done and what was not done. They must tell what they know. They must admit a lack of knowledge when they really do not know. But a client should not speculate about what he or she would do or not do in hypothetical situations. The basic reason for this is that it is nearly impossible to prepare adequately for all conceivable hypothetical situations. Secondly, many hypothetical questions that are used to *test* a witness's knowledge, judgment, or expertise are irrelevant to the case at hand. On occasion, a question is phrased as a hypothetical question but is actually based upon the facts of the present case. In any event, the witness must be prepared to answer.

A paralegal should not have to worry about helping and protecting the client from hypothetical questions in the deposition. That is the lawyer's job. But it is important to be aware of the problem and recognize the dangers. Unless the opposing attorney objects to such inquiry, this type of questioning can at times be very productive in a discovery deposition.

FOLLOW INSTRUCTIONS. If an objection is made, the witness should remain silent until the interrogator asks a new question or rephrases the question or until the witness's lawyer tells him or her that the question may be answered notwithstanding the objection. Whenever a difference of opinion occurs between the lawyers about the propriety of a question, they must decide what to do. The witness has no responsibility to do anything until his or her lawyer provides specific directions.

The deponent's lawyer might object to a question but immediately follow up with a direction to the witness that the question may be answered "if he or she understands it." The usual purpose of such an objection and instruction is to warn the witness that the question is dangerous and possibly confusing. He or she should be particularly careful of this question.

A deponent may elect to read the deposition transcript to make corrections in form and in substance. Quite often deponents are advised that they may waive the right to review and sign the transcript. If either the deponent *or* the lawyer thinks that the transcript should be reviewed, the right to review should not be waived. The witness should be told during the preparation about the right to read the transcript before it is certified and filed. If the lawyer decides at the end of the deposition that it is all right to waive the right to read and sign, he or she will ask the deponent whether he or she wishes to waive the right. That is a signal to the witness that the lawyer believes a waiver is acceptable. The witness may still indicate that he or she prefers to review it. If the lawyer wants the witness to review the transcript, he or she will simply tell the reporter to make the transcript available for review.

Testimony at Trial

When a witness testifies at trial, whether to a judge or a jury, appearance is very important. The following suggestions apply more to a trial than a deposition. Nevertheless, it is useful to take them into consideration whenever preparing to give testimony.

SIT ERECT AND LEAN FORWARD. A witness's physical posture may affect the believability of his or her testimony and will certainly affect appearance. Obviously, the witness looks best if sitting erect, but leaning forward a little helps the witness to appear interested and unafraid. It also adds to his or her appearance of authority. This posture helps the witness to pay attention to the proceedings. The witness should try to look at the lawyer who is asking the questions. At trial, a witness should look at the lawyer while the questions are being asked and at the jury at least half of the time while answering the questions. A conscious effort should be made to avoid looking at the floor or ceiling or out the window. A witness should approach the witness stand with the attitude that the jury is empathetic and will understand and appreciate his or her version of the matter. By assuming this attitude, the witness can help to avoid appearing defensive, which always detracts.

FULL EXPLANATIONS. Whereas the best answer in a discovery deposition is usually the shortest answer, in trial a witness should not limit testimony. After all, the purpose is to educate and persuade the court and jury. The witness should seize upon each question, whether asked by the witness's own lawyer or the opposing lawyer, to advance the witness's version of the facts. The witness cannot do that with short answers. Trial preparation, which is discussed in chapter 22, explains some of these important differences.

16 Medical Examinations and Records

Introduction

The parties' legal rights may turn upon one of the parties' physical, mental, or blood condition. The typical personal injury claim, which arises out of an accident, is a classic example. But there are many other types of cases which involve a party's medical condition, including actions concerning an employee's ability to perform the work required in a particular job; a party's right to insurance benefits; actions to determine paternity; and actions to determine mental competency. These cases present a unique problem in that the subject matter (mental, physical, or blood condition) is peculiarly under the one party's control. The subject matter may be very personal. In addition, a party's medical records and communications kept by the treating physicians are privileged. The privilege further limits the opposing party's access to necessary evidence about the medical condition.

A personal injury claim usually involves a number of separate but related medical questions. In accident cases, what injuries were caused by the accident? What pain and suffering were caused by the injuries and for how long? What other symptoms and complaints are attributable to the injuries? What impairments or disabilities were caused by the injuries? How long will they last? Are they permanent? How does an impairment affect the party's daily living activities and employment? What medical treatment was reasonably necessary for the injuries and for how long? Did the plaintiff use reasonable care to obtain proper medical treatment? To answer these questions, it is necessary to know something about the plaintiff's pre–accident condition and medical history, the plaintiff's version of the effect of the accident, the plaintiff's description of his or her symptoms and ability to function, the results of medical treatment, etc. The plaintiff's communications with his or her own physicians are privileged. So are the medical and hospital records. So how is the defendant to evaluate the claim and prepare to defend against it?

Parties' Right to Medical Examinations

As part of the checks and balances in the adversary system for civil litigation, Rule 35 gives the defendant a right to obtain one or more independent medical examinations of the plaintiff. The defendant's lawyer ordinarily chooses the doctors who will examine the plaintiff. Rule 35 steers a course which seeks to protect a party's medical privilege and privacy. When a party puts in issue his or her physical, mental, or blood condition, that party may be compelled to submit to an independent medical examination concerning the condition. The party who submits to an independent medical examination is entitled to request a copy of the examiner's report about the medical examination. By requesting a copy of the examination report, the party waives his or her medical privilege concerning records and reports prepared by his or her own physicians.

The Rules of Civil Procedure do not prescribe any limits on the length, scope, or nature of the independent medical examination. There is no expressed limit on the number of examinations. There is no specification for what information must be contained in the independent examiner's report. Rule 35 clearly states that nonparties cannot be required to submit to medical examinations. A party may be required to submit to a medical examination only if that party puts his or her medical condition in issue. If a party refuses to submit to a medical examination, the court has several options. The court may dismiss the party's claim. The court may resolve the medical facts against the party. If the party is a defendant, his or her answer may be stricken and the defendant held in default. A court may *not* hold a party in contempt of court for refusing to submit to an independent medical examination.

Limitations on Medical Examinations

Courts are very pragmatic in dealing with parties' disputes over the scope of independent medical examinations. Courts do not require parties to submit to medical tests which subject a person to a risk of harm. For example, courts do not require plaintiffs to undergo angiograms, which involve the injection of a dye into the patient's's circulatory system. The test involves a risk of stroke and death. Courts do not require parties to submit to invasive testing, such as a laparoscopy or arthroscopy. Even so, courts routinely require parties to submit to electromyograms, to test nerve function, and electroencephalograms, to test electrical activity of the brain. Both of these medical tests involve the insertion of small needles into the patient's skin. The tests are uncomfortable. They are not dangerous. They are useful. Consequently, they are required when relevant to the physical condition in issue.

If the plaintiff sustained multiple injuries as a result of one accident and has been treated by several specialists, courts recognize that the defendant may need to have two or more specialists examine the plaintiff. If the case takes a long time to reach trial, the defendant may need, and be entitled to, a repeat medical examination of the plaintiff. The number of examinations and the scope of each examination depend upon the circumstances. If disputed, the trial court has broad discretion in determining what is appropriate.

The Rules of Civil Procedure for most states provide that if the plaintiff commences an action to recover money damages for personal injuries, the plaintiff thereby waives medical privilege. The extent of the waiver may vary from a total waiver to only a waiver of the privileged status of medical reports and/or records. The federal courts apply state law concerning medical privilege and its waiver. Therefore, the application of Rule 35 and its procedure may vary depending upon state law.

A physician who provides medical care to an injury victim needs to have the patient's complete confidence. The physician is not part of the adversary system. Presumably, information is obtained from the patient for the purpose of providing appropriate treatment. A physician may be aware of the possibilities of litigation but is not charged with any responsibility for establishing the patient's claim. Indeed, the Rules of Evidence presume that the patient is candid with his or her physician and goes for medical treatment—not for the purpose of fabricating a claim. The physician is not expected to cross-examine the patient concerning accident and medical histories or symptoms. A physician is expected only to obtain sufficient information to make an accurate diagnosis and to prescribe the proper treatment.

Reasons for Requesting a Medical Examination

There are a number of reasons why the defendant's lawyer may feel that the treating physician's evaluation of the patient is inadequate or even in error. The medical or accident history may be erroneous or incomplete. The findings may be inconsistent with the symptoms. Sometimes the defendant's lawyer has more detailed information about the plaintiff's history and symptoms than the treating physician. The symptoms may vary from time to time in an inexplicable way, which creates doubt about their validity. Or, the treating physician may not have sufficient expertise in the various areas which must be considered. On rare occasion, collaboration may be suspected.

An extreme, but true, case may serve as an example of how an independent medical examination works. The plaintiff was a forty-eight-year-old homemaker who stopped her automobile in response to a traffic light. The defendant's semitruck bumped the rear of her car. She told her treating physician that her car was struck forcefully by a big truck and that she was thrown about. She felt dazed and soon her neck, left arm, and shoulder began to hurt. The physician's diagnosis was that she suffered a strain of the muscles and ligaments in her neck and shoulders. He began to treat her with medications and physical therapy. The treatment continued for several years. At one point, the treating physician called in a psychiatrist for consultation, who determined that the plaintiff was neurotic and a hypochondriac. These psychiatric problems were deep-seated and had existed long before the automobile accident.

The defendant arranged for a Rule 35 independent medical examination by an orthopedic surgeon. The surgeon concluded that there was no objective evidence of injury or disability, but based upon the accident and medical history, as related by the plaintiff, and the continued symptoms of pain in the neck and left shoulder, she had a musculoligamentous strain without any apparent disability of the shoulder or neck. The surgeon had to assume the correctness of her subjective symptoms and medical history. After the defendant's physician testified in accordance with this report, the defendant's lawyer asked the physician to assume, as true, certain additional facts contained in the testimony of the defendant truck driver. Namely, he was called to assume that the defendant was almost stopped at the moment of contact; that the contact merely resulted in a scratch to a chrome strip on the right corner of rear bumper of the plaintiff's automobile as shown by photographs; that the vehicles remained in contact after the "collision"; that the plaintiff's automobile was not moved by the contact; and that the plaintiff stepped out of her automobile immediately after the accident; and that she did not appear injured and did not complain of injury while at the accident scene.

The independent physician testified that if the additional accident history were true, he would have to conclude that the plaintiff was not physically injured in the accident, because to cause overstretching of her musculature there would have to have been some movement of the plaintiff's automobile to move her inside the car. In the absence of some significant movement, she could not have been injured. Her subjective complaints could not be attributed to any physical injury. Of course, the psychiatrist's diagnosis then provided the logical explanation for the plaintiff's overreaction to the accident and continued symptoms. The jury determined that she was not injured at all. The accident provided her with an opportunity to secure "secondary gains," including help with her household duties, sympathy, and the opportunity to visit the doctors regularly. The possible recovery of money damages seemed to be of lesser importance in this case. The result would have been quite different if the defendant had not been able to have an independent medical evaluation and opinion.

Compelling a Medical Examination

Rule 35 authorizes the defendant to obtain a court order requiring the plaintiff to submit to an independent medical examination at a reasonable time and place. The defendant must show good cause (need) for the examination. The defendant does this merely by showing that the plaintiff's physical, mental, or blood condition was put in controversy by the plaintiff. The plaintiff cannot be compelled to submit to an independent medical examination. On the other hand, if he or she refuses to submit, the case may be dismissed (Rule 35).

A paralegal should be able to prepare the motion and supporting documents necessary for compelling an independent medical examination. A paralegal should also be equally able to prepare affidavits and memoranda to oppose such motions. (See Appendix V for suggested forms.)

More often than not, the plaintiff's lawyer recognizes that the defendant is entitled to have an independent medical examination, so the lawyers schedule the examination without the necessity of a motion and court order. In fact, a court order is seldom sought except when a dispute arises about the number of examinations or the examination's length, scope, or time and place. On rare occasion, the plaintiff may object to the defendant's selection of a physician to conduct the examination. As a general rule, the defendant has a right to an examination by a person in whom the defendant has confidence, just as the plaintiff is entitled to be treated by a physician in whom the plaintiff has confidence.

Whether the examination has been ordered or agreed to, the method of scheduling is the same. The lawyer must find a physician who is willing and able to conduct the examination. A date and time is selected—usually through the physician's secretary. A letter is then sent to the plaintiff's lawyer confirming the arrangements. It is a good idea to request that the plaintiff's lawyer contact the plaintiff immediately to insure availability. If the plaintiff fails to keep the appointment, he or she may be responsible for the physician's charges—assuming the charge is reasonable for the amount of time reserved by the physician for the examination.

Scheduling a Medical Examination

The lawyer who schedules the independent medical examination should send a letter to the physician confirming the arrangements for the examination. The lawyer should fully inform the examiner about relevant details of the accident, the nature of all the plaintiff's complaints, the type of treatment received, and the treating physician's diagnoses and prognosis. Copies of the treating physician's reports and records should be included with the letter with instructions that the enclosures may be used to direct the examination and history taking; however, the doctor's report should be based upon the history obtained from the plaintiff and his or her own examination and findings. It is not appropriate for the independent examiner to comment to the patient on findings, evaluation, or the treatment which has been administered by other physicians. Nor should the physician suggest treatment to the patient. If he or she thinks additional or different treatment should be tried, this may be indicated in the report to the lawyer who arranged for the examination.

Medical Reports

A good medical report has separate sections for the medical history, patient's symptoms and complaints listed in order of importance to the patient, examination, findings, diagnoses, evaluation, and the prognosis, including whether or not future treatment is necessary. These sections may be broken into appropriate subparagraphs. For example, the history section should contain paragraphs discussing the plaintiff's personal history, pre–accident condition, the accident, and post–accident condition.

The independent medical report is the property and work product of the defendant's lawyer, that is, the lawyer who requested the examination. The plaintiff's lawyer does not have a right to be present during the examination. He or she does not have a right to interview the physician but does have a right to a copy of the report(s) which the examiner issues to the defendant's lawyer. The report(s) may be obtained only through the defendant's lawyer. When the plaintiff demands a copy, under federal rules, he or she becomes obligated to provide the defendant's lawyer with copies of all reports obtained from the treating physicians. Failure to comply would preclude the plaintiff from having the physician testify. In most jurisdictions, however, the plaintiff's medical records become available to the defendants as soon as the plaintiff commences the action.

The independent medical examination report provides the lawyers with information for evaluating the case and preparing for trial. The plaintiff's lawyer ordinarily supplies the treating physicians with copies. The report serves another invaluable function. When the case reaches trial and the independent examiner testifies, his or her testimony is ordinarily based upon the report. The examiner may not even remember the plaintiff and the examination by that time. It is quite common for the physician to read the report almost verbatim. A skilled defense lawyer knows how to establish a dialogue with the physician even though the physician is primarily reading from the report.

What are the defendant's lawyer and the independent medical examiner looking for? They want to know to what extent the claims of injury and disability are corroborated by objective medical findings. Objective findings are distinguished from subjective complaints and subjective symptoms in that the examiner can observe them by sight, touch, or sound. A condition is subjective when a determination of its existence depends solely upon the patient's response. A scar on the face is objective. An atrophied limb is objective. A headache is subjective. A limited range of motion in the body may be objective or subjective. When the claim is based exclusively or primarily on subjective complaints, the defendant's lawyer and independent examiner are interested in knowing whether the plaintiff has been consistent with his or her complaints. A lack of consistency suggests that they are fabricated. Do the complaints comport with the type of injury diagnosed? If the symptoms come and go (recur), what causes them to relent and what causes them to begin? When do they recur? Is there a pattern? Is there evidence of normal progressive healing? If the diagnosis is based solely upon the patient's history and subjective complaints, there is no actual medical corroboration of the injury or disability.

Medical Tests

There are numerous medical tests regularly used for the purpose of diagnosing injury. Some of the tests available include X rays, computerized tomography, electromyograms, electroencephalograms, myelograms, angiograms, psychometric tests, discograms, and others. When the treating physician obtains such tests, the results ordinarily are available to the parties as part of the patient's medical-hospital records. The tests results are quite objective and seldom need to be repeated. Even if the physicians differ in their interpretations of the tests, the raw data is usually available to both sides for review and evaluation. The one significant exception is the interpretation of an electromyogram. (Electromyography is the study of the electrical activity of nerves and muscle activity. The electrical activity is measured and evaluated by sound and reading an oscilloscope. No record is made during the testing. The examiner simply records his or her interpretations.)

If the plaintiff's own physician has not obtained the appropriate tests, the independent examiner may want to put the plaintiff through the tests; however, there is a potential problem. Some of the tests are painful and some subject the patient to a significant medical risk. If the patient will not voluntarily submit to painful or risky tests, a court will not order him or her to submit. (Electromyograms and electroencephalograms are not considered too painful or too risky.) The potential evidence is not available to either side. The defendant may not be permitted to cross-examine the plaintiff about his or her refusal to submit to the tests. On the other hand, the defendant's lawyer should be permitted to cross-examine the treating physicians about the availability of the tests to help make a definitive diagnosis. They will have to justify not obtaining the tests.

The Legal Assistant's Role

A paralegal should be able to help prepare the client for an independent medical examination. The client must be assured that the examination is routine for the type of case and perfectly proper. The client should be urged to be on time. He or she should not fear the examining physician but should be relaxed and treat the physician with respect and cooperation throughout the examination.

The client should be prepared to accurately relate his or her medical history. On occasion, a plaintiff takes a diary or notes to help in answering the questions. There is no law against it, but juries usually react negatively to the need for notes.

The client should be advised that he or she is not required to tell the examiner about conversations with his or her lawyer. Symptoms or other problems caused by the injuries should not be minimized but neither should they be exaggerated. A lack of candor may seriously affect the case. The client should realize that the examination really begins from the moment he or she enters the physician's office. From the very outset, the physician will observe how the client walks, sits, and uses his or her extremities. Some of the tests may be repeated during the examination to determine whether responses are consistent. The client must not let the physician or the tests upset him or her. Submission to unusually painful testing or embarrassing procedures is not required. The client should be told to refuse to submit to requests by the examiner that are clearly unnecessary. For example, if the plaintiff's only complaint is neck pain, a rectal examination is not necessary. But a physician may need to perform a rectal examination if the patient has lower back pain.

On occasion, a party may receive treatment from a physician who does not want to take the time to prepare a report summarizing his or her findings and conclusion. This creates a problem for both sides. The physician is not a party to the action and cannot be punished by the court. Under the circumstances, either party may be able to secure the physician's deposition. The physician can be required to attend the deposition by serving a subpoena upon him or her.

Many physicians insist upon being paid for their reports even before the report is prepared. The court has authority to require either party to pay the physician's bill for the report. If the plaintiff does not want the treating physician's report and does not intend to call that physician as his or her own witness at trial, the court may require the defendant to pay for the cost of preparing the report. Another problem is presented if the physician refuses to render a report until the bill for providing medical treatment has been paid. Occasionally, a plaintiff is unable to pay for medical expenses until the litigation is concluded. If the reluctant physician is "required" to sit through a deposition in lieu of providing a report, he or she may be able to find a way of accommodating the parties.

Since a physician is considered to be an expert witness, the party presenting him or her can be compelled under Rule 26 to disclose the substance of the expert's testimony. Rules 26 and 35 are not exclusive of each other. It should be noted that for the convenience of the parties, they may agree to some other method of discovery of the medical reports, hospital records, and medical opinions. In most cases, the procedures outlined by the rules work well and are followed by litigants without difficulty.

The federal rules provide that the adverse examination may be obtained whenever there is a controversy about a party's condition. Some state court Rules of Civil Procedure provide that a Rule 35 medical examination may be obtained only if the medical condition was voluntarily put in issue by the party to be examined. Of course, when a plaintiff seeks compensation for injuries sustained in an accident, his or her physical condition has been put into issue. But suppose that the defendant wants to have the plaintiff's eyes examined because the defendant contends that the plaintiff's vision is defective and that is what caused the accident. Clearly, the eye condition is a physical condition which is in controversy, and the best way of determining whether there is a visual defect is to have a medical examination. It cannot be said that the plaintiff has placed his or her eye condition in issue, however, and under those state rules, a Rule 35 medical examination could not be obtained.

Letter Scheduling a Medical Examination

The following letter to a physician and physician's report on an independent neurological medical examination are illustrative of the use of Rule 35. The letter and report also illustrate the value and importance of an independent medical examination. Notice that the writers have carefully developed *relevant* details.

May 23, 1990

John A. Smith, M.D.
Room 527 Medical Arts Building
1000 5th Street
Dallas, Texas

Re: Diersen V. Machacek
   Our File: 37610

Dear Dr. Smith:

This letter will confirm the arrangements we have made for an independent neurological examination of Elizabeth Diersen to be conducted by you at your Medical Arts Office at 9:00 A.M. on July 14, 1990. Mrs. Diersen is represented by Attorney Thomas Tiger. His telephone number is 292-1555. The arrangements for this examination have been made through his office.

Mrs. Elizabeth Diersen is claiming neck and back injuries which she attributes to a rear-end type automobile accident. She is also claiming a problem with headaches, dizziness, and pain in her right thigh.

Mrs. Diersen was born on January 21, 1967. She is now twenty-three years of age. She is married to Paul Diersen, who is twenty-six years of age. They have one child. Mrs. Diersen completed high school. Her past gainful employments have been light assembly work. She worked with hand tools and circuit boards. She states that she has not been involved in any other motor vehicle accidents. She broke a couple of ribs many years ago when she fell in a school parking lot. Otherwise, she has enjoyed good health.

The automobile accident in question occurred on Monday, March 6, 1988, about 7:00 A.M. on State Highway 5 in Eden, Texas. Mrs. Diersen stopped her Ford Mustang for a traffic light. She was in a line of traffic that was backed up from the light. Without any warning, she suddenly felt her car pushed ahead an undetermined distance. She did not strike the car in front of her. She did not hear any contact at the rear of her car. Her car seats had high backs. Her head struck the back of the seat. She did not strike anything else within the car. She did not sustain any cuts, bumps, swelling, or bruises.

What apparently happened was that my client, Mr. Robert Machacek, bumped the rear of an automobile driven by Mr. Bellman and Mr. Bellman's car was pushed against the rear of Mrs. Diersen's automobile. Photographs show very minor damage to the back of the Diersen car. All three cars were capable of being driven. Neither Mr. Bellman nor Mr. Machacek was injured. Mrs. Diersen did not feel injured at the accident scene. She continued on to work, called her husband, found herself feeling very upset about the accident, and she started crying. Her husband was off work that day. He came to the plant, examined the car, and drove it home. Mrs. Diersen left work early and drove their camper vehicle home. Upon her husband's suggestion, she saw Dr. F. P. Ekrem that same afternoon. He is a general practitioner at the Spencer Clinic. Her complaints, at that time, included a headache and slight thigh tenderness. On examination, he found that the reflexes in the upper and lower extremities were normal and she had an excellent range of motion in her neck with minimal tenderness at extremes. She had slight occipital tenderness at the left, minimal vertebral tenderness in the neck, and no muscle spasm. No X rays were taken. Tylenol and Valium were prescribed.

She returned on March 17 complaining of neck discomfort. He records:

> While working she has her head in one position looking downward, causing some neck strain. She also has to cut wire and there is associated bending. She has constant pain with bending down, then straightening up.

He found a good range of motion in her neck with tenderness at the extremes of motion. His diagnosis was neck and low back strain and sprain. He felt she could return to work, gave her a booklet on back care and prescribed outpatient physical therapy. She returned April 12, complaining of more back pain, especially while doing household activities and picking up her child. She was having pain in her thigh and calf on the left side. These symptoms worsened toward evening. Dr. Ekrem found a full range of motion of the neck with no muscle spasm. The straight leg raising test was negative. Her back pain was identified as being at the insertion of the paraspinal muscles at the iliac crest posteriorly. He notes that *she* felt she could not go back to work. He last saw her on August 15, 1988, but in the meantime, she started seeing chiropractor John Zimmerman. His first examination was April 28, 1988. When she saw Dr. Ekrem in August, she complained of dizziness and continued pain, the location of which is not specified. He felt she might benefit from physiotherapy. He suspected that the dizziness was due to postural hypotension.

Chiropractor Zimmerman treated Mrs. Diersen's neck and low back with chiropractic manipulation. Sometimes the adjustments were painful. He explained to her that her spine was out of alignment and that was causing her symptoms. He referred her to Chiropractor James Brandt for a consultation. He last saw Mrs. Diersen in July of 1988. His services were discontinued because Mrs. Diersen was unable to pay his bill and because the Diersens moved from Eden to Crystal, Texas.

On July 28, 1988, Mrs. Diersen started treatment with Chiropractor Donald Wahlen. He felt she had myocytis of the cervical, dorsal, and lumbar spine. She was treated with chiropractic adjustments, ultrasound, etc.

It appears that Chiropractor Wahlen referred Mrs. Diersen to D. L. Anderson and Dr. Allan Schut for evaluation. She was examined by one of them on September 6, 1988, at which time she was complaining of dizzy spells, neck pain, and low back pain. He records that the low back pain did not begin until about a week after the accident. According to her history, the physical therapy she had received at Methodist Hospital per Dr. Ekrem had not provided any help. The problem with dizziness began while she was under Chiropractor Zimmerman's care. The neurological examination was essentially normal. Specifically, testing of muscle strength and reflexes in the extremities was normal. Sensation was normal throughout the body. No Hoffman nor Babinski signs were present. Gait and leg swinging were negative. Romberg test was negative; however, she demonstrated some limitation in the range of motion of her neck. In this regard Dr. Anderson states:

> However, the patient has a long thin angular neck probably capable of more range of motion than is elicited at this time. She has palpable muscle spasms

in the cervical muscles bilaterally as well as the upper trapezius muscles, particularly on the left side.

He found the motion in the dorsal and lumbar spin to be within normal limits. Nevertheless, again, he describes "palpable muscle spasms bilaterally over the lumbosacral spine." Straight leg raising test was negative at 90 degrees. The cause of her dizziness was not determined.

Dr. Anderson eventually had Mrs. Diersen admitted to the Eden Health Center for testing. She was also evaluated by Dr. Allan Schut. An electromyogram dated September 20, 1989, was negative for both lower extremities. Mr. Steven Rush, psychologist, conducted an evaluation. A Minnesota Multiphasic Personality Inventory test [psychological test] showed Mrs. Diersen to be significantly neurotic. In addition, he felt she sought secondary gain by obtaining financial benefits from her insurance coverage and other benefits which exceeded her wage loss. He also felt that she wanted to remain at home with her child rather than work. Though she states her home and family life is good and satisfying, the indications are to the contrary.

During the September 1989 hospitalization, a myelogram was performed and interpreted by radiologist L. O. Campbell. His conclusion is as follows:

> Congenital partial sacralization of L5. Bilateral small extra dural defects at L4-5 suggesting central bulging disc at this level.

Dr. David Olson, who was called in for consultation by Dr. D. L. Anderson, concluded that surgery was not appropriate at the time, but he does not rule it out for the future.

More recently, Mrs. Diersen has come under the care of a psychologist named Stanley Baker at Clifton Court in Dallas. He is putting her through various physical stress activities that cause her to shake. The purpose is to release her tensions. He massages her neck. They talk. So far she has gone through seven such sessions at fifty dollars per session. She thinks that Mr. Baker is helping her a lot. She intends to continue seeing him.

Mrs. Diersen's medical expenses now exceed eleven thousand dollars. She continues to remain off work. She is apparently seeking Social Security disability benefits. She appears highly motivated to cling to her symptoms.

Please provide me with a narrative report on your examination and findings. Certainly psychiatric and psychological evaluations are necessary. Thank you for your very able assistance in this matter.

Very truly yours,

R. D. Blanchard

Report on Medical Examination

RE: Diersen, Elizabeth
7001 Lombardy Lane
Crystal, Texas
Your file #37610

Dear Mr. Blanchard:

On July 14 of 1990 I examined this twenty-three-year-old female whom you so kindly referred for a neurologic and psychiatric evaluation.

FAMILY HISTORY
The patient's mother is fifty-three and well. Her father is fifty-eight years of age and well. She has two brothers and one sister. Her husband is twenty-six years of age and presently is unemployed. She has one boy age three. The patient graduated from Eden High School in 1985.

PERSONAL HISTORY
This patient denies any serious illnesses. She had a tonsillectomy at the age of five. Her appendix was removed in 1983. In December of 1989 the patient had a pyelonephritis and some bladder polyps removed by Dr. Walonick at the Eden Hospital.

PRESENT ILLNESS
The patient was involved in an automobile accident on March 6, 1988. It occurred about 7:00 in the morning at Highway 5 and Mitchell Road. She was driving her car and was struck from the rear. At the time of the impact, she said that her head hit the back of the seat, but that nothing happened to her. She was not knocked unconscious and, actually, did not feel very much. The police came and information was exchanged. She went on to work. She said she rested in the ladies room and after an hour went home.

At about 2:00 in the afternoon she saw her family physician Dr. Ekrem. He examined her, but did not take any X rays. He gave her some Valium and told her to go home, rest, and take a couple of days off work. At that time she said her left leg was aching.

The patient rested at home, and, according to the patient, her neck started to bother her later in the day. Two days later she attempted to go back to work and a few days after this she developed some soreness in her back. She went back to Dr. Ekrem who sent her for some physiotherapy on an outpatient basis at the Methodist Hospital. She went there two or three times a week for about five weeks and kept working off and on. Finally on March 21, 1988, she was put on medical leave. According to the patient, the physiotherapy did not help.

The patient then went to John Zimmerman, a chiropractor in Eden, who took X rays and adjusted her neck and back. He also gave her a neck and back brace. He sent her to a Dr. Brandt, a chiropractor, for a consultation sometime in June of 1988. Later she moved to Crystal, Texas, where she went to Dr. Donald Wahlen, a chiropractor. She took adjustments from him which started out three times each week and now she sees him as necessary.

The patient was having some dizzy spells so she went to a Dr. Malmoud, who apparently is a partner of Dr. Ekrem. He felt that she was possibly having hypotension, but when he examined her, her blood pressure was normal.

The patient was referred to Dr. Allan Schut and Dr. D. L. Anderson. They examined her and gave her physiotherapy in their office, and on two occasions, she has been hospitalized. The first time was in April of 1989, where she was given in-hospital physiotherapy for two weeks and rehabilitation for her neck and back. This was at the Eden Hospital. In September of 1989, Dr. Anderson put her back in the Eden Hospital where a myelogram was done. Dr. David Olson, who looked at the myelogram, said that she might possibly have a low midline ruptured disc. She was put on an exercise program and given a better back brace, but this did not cure her.

The patient has also been seen by Dr. Hammond for an insurance examination. She went to a doctor in Kellogg Square about a year ago who examined her, but she cannot remember his name. She had a Social Security examination at the University but does not know the doctor's name. In addition, she has been to Dr. Walonick for her kidney problems at the request of Dr. Anderson. She is still seeing Dr. Anderson about once a month.

The patient was sent to a psychologist, Mr. Stanley Baker, on Clifton Avenue. His wife, Sandy Baker, helps him. They talk with her and, according to the patient, they discuss the lawsuit, the attorneys involved, and the letters that are coming to her. They try to get her to relax. They give her neck massage and put her in unusual positions. According to the patient, she will stand, bent over, for a long period of time or they may have her stand against the wall or even on her head. She has seen him about ten or twelve times and she thinks he might be helping her. According to the patient, they are giving her advice about what to do about the examinations.

The patient has been seen by the people from rehabilitation. Two names are Betty Johnson and Maddy Boll. They have told her how to fill out the application blanks for rehabilitation benefits. They have told her that she will continue to be paid as long as she earns less money than she earned in the job she had when she was injured. They got her a job at the Spa Petite in Eden, which she has been on for three days. She said she shows the members how to use the equipment and she is on a running and exercise program with the members of the club. The patient volunteered to me that she will continue to be paid by rehabilitation as long as her compensation from Spa Petite is less than she had when she was working for EMT Electronics.

The patient presently takes only Ampicillin for a strep throat, which was prescribed by Dr. Ekrem. If her headaches become too bad, she takes Excedrin or Tylenol 3.

Prior to her employment with EMT Electronics, she worked for Ross Shadow doing electronic soldering. After this, she had a child and at one time worked for Kentucky Fried Chicken preparing food and waiting on tables. According to the patient, she has had a cortisone shot in her left hip at one time for bursitis. When she was in the hospital, as well as having a myelogram, she had an electromyogram of her left leg. According to the patient, she does not think she is getting much better. She said that all the therapy she has taken has really not helped very much as far as her neck, leg, and back are concerned. She said that the doctors might think she is better, but she really is not.

PRESENT COMPLAINTS

1. Daily headaches. This bioccipital and bifrontal. They last a couple of hours and are relieved by Excedrin. The headaches are not associated with any nausea or vomiting and generally come on about noon.
2. Dizzy spells. She gets them approximately once a day. It is a light-headedness rather than a vertigo.
3. Some stiffness and discomfort in her neck and shoulders (primarily left). It is brought on by anything and any type of paperwork or keeping her neck in one position bothers her.
4. Pain in the low back. This is a stiffness and soreness and is always present. She wears a brace from time to time, particularly when driving or if she is going to sit for a long time.
5. Aching in her left leg which is primarily in the thigh or hip region. It is worse in the evening. It is bothered by cold. Coughing and sneezing do not produce pain.

At this point, the patient has no blurred vision or double vision. She does not have any complaints as far as her chest and abdomen are concerned. She has had no syncope or convulsions. She is sleeping better on a water bed. The patient's appetite is good. She does a lot of exercises but does not play tennis, golf, or any sports. She does a fair amount of walking.

PHYSICAL EXAMINATION
The patient is 5'5" tall and weighs 123 pounds. She is well developed and well nourished. Blood pressure 100/70, pulse 66, respirations 18. Teeth and gums are normal. Eardrums are normal. Throat is negative.

The chest is clear to auscultation and percussion and there are no cardiac irregularities or murmurs. The abdomen reveals no scars, masses, or tenderness.

NEUROLOGICAL EXAMINATION

Cranial Nerves: The patient can smell test odors. The visual acuity is 20/20-2 bilaterally without correction. The visual fields were normal. The ophthalmoscopic examination did not reveal any evidence of any increased intracranial pressure, hemorrhages, or exudates. No optic atrophy. Good pulsation of the veins. The third, fourth, and sixth cranial nerves were normal. The pupils were equal and react to light. No nystagmus. No facial asymmetry. No hypesthesia of the face or cornea. Hearing revealed to be normal.

Sensory Functions: The examination of the body to cotton, pin prick pain as well as vibration and position sense was normal.

Motor Functions: The patient has a good grip bilaterally and there is no atrophy, hypertrophy, twitching, or tremor of the muscalature.

Measurements	Right	Left
Biceps	9¾"	9½"
Forearm	7½"	7¼"
Wrist	5¾"	5¾"
Hand	7"	7"
Thigh	14½"	14½"
Calf	12½"	12½"

Movements: The patient's neck goes through a full range of motion in all directions without any complaint of pain or evidence of spasm. The patient bends over to 90 degrees and comes about 1 inch from her toes. Straight leg raising tests go to 90 degrees. She is able to walk on her heels and toes and do a deep knee bend.

The patient has some tenderness over the left intertrocanteric bursa indicating a bursitis in this area.

Coordination: The patient's gait is normal. The finger to finger, finger to nose, and heal to knee tests were done normally.

Reflexes: All of the reflexes were present and equal. The toe signs were negative. She does not have any bowel or bladder dysfunction and speech is normal.

X RAYS

Roentgenograms were made of the cervical spine in the anteroposterior, lateral, and both oblique directions.

Diagnosis: Negative for evidence of old or recent fracture or other bone or joint abnormality. A normal curvature is seen in flexion and extension.

Conclusion: Negative cervical spine study.

Roentgenograms were made of old or recent fracture. There are no productive or destructive changes and the disc spaces are maintained. The fifth lumbar vertebra is transitional. The sacroiliac joints and hips appear normal.

A few droplets of contrast material are seen in the spinal canal as the result of a previous myelogram.

An IUD is identified and appears to be normal in location.

ELECTROENCEPHALOGRAM

Basic alpha rhythm ten per second. This is an awake record with some eye-blink artifact, movement, and tension artifact. Some low voltage and low voltage fast activity. No evidence of any localized or diffuse spiking, slow waves, or delta activity. No amplitude asymmetry. No seizure discharges of any sort. Photic stimulation did not produce any driving response. Hyperventilation did not produce any buildup or slowing.

Impression: Within normal limits.

ELECTROMYOGRAM

An electromyogram was done by Jane E. Wilson, M.D., on July 14, 1990. She found the entire left leg to be normal. A copy of her entire report is included with this letter.

ECHOENCEPHALOGRAM

This enchoencephalogram demonstrates a normal position for the midline echo complex.

MINNESOTA MULTIPHASIC PERSONALITY TEST

This was a valid test. There was a marked elevation on hysteria or conversion reaction. Some mild depression and hypochondriasis was noted. This profile indicated the patient had tension within herself that was being converted to psychosomatic or psychophysiological symptoms. The symptoms undoubtedly have a secondary gain.

PSYCHOLOGICAL EXAMINATION

This patient was evaluated by Patrick Noble, Ph.D., Licensed Consulting Psychologist, on July 14, 1990. A copy of his entire report is included with this letter. His summary is as follows:

> The testing reveals an immature, dependent woman who has a basic personality that is in keeping with an individual who could easily convert her psychological conflicts into physiological manifestations. This type of personality develops over the years and is closely related to the fact that she apparently lived in a situation where she felt she was being controlled by a rather overpowering mother figure. Thus, her only out is to develop symptomatology to blame her psychological difficulties onto some medical problem.

CONCLUSIONS

If one considers the mechanism of the accident, it is very difficult to imagine that the patient was seriously injured. She had no symptoms at the time of the accident and the back pain did not come on for several days. It is possible she could have had a very minimal strain of her neck, but one would expect that this would have disappeared with time. She has been overexamined, overtreated, and has had a tremendous number of chiropractic appointments. She has been going from doctor to doctor in an attempt to be cured, and this is not possible because 95 percent of her symptoms are psychological in nature. She has recently returned to work as a demonstrator at the Spa Petite. The patient's complaints are of headaches, light-headedness, pain in the neck and both shoulders, low back pain, and aching in her left leg.

The physical examination is entirely normal for any abnormality as a result of this accident.

A complete neurological examination is negative. She does have bursitis in the left intertrochanteric bursa and this is probably producing discomfort in the left leg. This is a degenerative affair and not related to the accident. She has had an injection of hydrocortisone in this area in the past.

X rays of the cervical spine were normal. An X ray of the lumbosacral spine was negative. A few droplets of contrast material were seen in the spinal canal, which was the result of a previous myelogram.

The electroencephalogram is normal.

The echoencephalogram is normal.

And electromyogram of the left leg is entirely normal.

The Minnesota Multiphasic Personality Test shows definite evidence of a conversion reaction with secondary gain. These secondary gains are obviously that the patient does not have to go to work but can stay home and receive more compensation than she would get if she were working. In this respect there is a compensation neurosis present.

The psychological testing showed, "an immature, dependent woman who has a basic personality that is in keeping with an individual who could easily siphon off her psychological conflicts into physiological manifestations. This type of personality develops over the years and is closely related to the fact that she apparently lived in a situation where she felt she was being controlled by an overpowering mother figure. Thus, her only out is to develop symptomatology to blame her psychological difficulties onto some medical problem."

A great deal of the patient's symptoms are very close to consciousness. She has been told that a lot of her symptoms are based on tension and that they are not organic in character. A lot of this is very close to being a conscious mechanism, particularly with her desire not to return to work and enjoy life at home as long as she can obtain financial rewards. The financial reward is paramount in her mind. This mechanism is so close to consciousness that it is really not far from malingering. These mechanisms have been investigated by psychologists who have treated her and have been documented but seemingly disregarded by her physicians and chiropractors. I find no evidence from a clinical standpoint of a herniated lumbar intervertebral disc. There is no weakness, reflex disturbance, or atrophy, and movements are excellent. The pain, I believe, is a result of the bursitis, which is not attributable to the accident.

Sincerely yours,

John A. Smith, M.D.

ELECTROMYOGRAPHY REPORT

PATIENT: Mrs. Elizabeth Diersen
DATE: July 14, 1990

NERVE CONDUCTION STUDIES

Nerve	Motor conduction velocity	Distal motor latency	Motor response amplitude
Left peroneal	46.5 meters/ second	5.0 milli- seconds	5.0 millivolts

LEFT LOWER EXTREMITY
NEEDLE ELECTRODE STUDIES

Muscle	Insertional activity	Motor unit activity
Iliopsoas	normal	normal
Rectus femoris	normal	normal
Vastus lateralis	normal	normal
Vastus medialis	normal	normal
Tibialis anterior	normal	normal
Extensor digitorum longus	normal	normal
Peroneus	normal	normal
Medial gastrocnemius	normal	normal for strength of contraction
Soleus	normal	normal
Gluteus maximus	normal	normal
Lumbar paraspinal	normal	normal

SUMMARY
The motor conduction velocity, distal motor latency, and action potential are normal in the left peroneal nerve.

The needle electrode examinations reveal no significant variation from normal.

IMPRESSION
The above electromyographic studies are within normal limits.

Jane E. Wilson, M.D.

PSYCHOLOGICAL EVALUATION

RE: Elizabeth Diersen
TESTS
ADMINISTERED: HILLSIDE SHORT FORM OF THE WESCHLER
               BELLEVIEW EXAMINATION
               RORSCHACH
               KAHN TEST OF SYMBOL ARRANGEMENT
               SENTENCE COMPLETION

This lady indicates that she was in an accident 3-6-88. She states she was not unconscious and was not hospitalized and her only symptom is headache. At the present time she states her symptoms are "headaches and dizziness, left leg aches, neck and lower backaches." Currently she is on no medication except Tylenol 3 for headaches. In the past, she apparently has had various medications. She states she does not smoke, drinks occasionally, and denies the use of drugs. She indicates that she started a job last week where she is working at a health club. In terms of social activity, she states they do not do much because it is too expensive and they tend to sit around home and watch television, although they do some camping.

The patient states that she comes from a family of four children where she is the oldest. Her father is a truck driver and her mother is a waitress. She has been married four years and her husband currently is unemployed. He has worked for the Milwaukee Railroad in the past and has been laid off for about eight or nine weeks. There is one child of this marriage, a boy age three. The patient states she completed high school. She indicates that she has had no serious illnesses except for an appendectomy. She has no history of any other serious accidents.

The patient is a rather stoic-faced individual who has very little expression on her face. Speech is coherent, relevant, under good control, and shows no loose associations. Affective responses are felt to be somewhat flat at this time and one gets the impression that she may have some feelings of depression. There are no evidences of psychotic ideation, the patient is considered to be of average intelligence and is oriented in contact, and she shows good comprehension, good attention span, and no loss of recent or remote memory.

This patient has been tested previously and the evaluation done in March of 1989 indicated that she was a person who was immature and had some self-esteem problems, with a diagnosis as immature woman in stress with self-esteem issue, unexpressed anger, and some sadness in relationship to her heterosexual life.

Testing at this time reveals a woman of average intelligence with a prorated IQ of 109. She continues to show the same type of immaturity and dependency that she apparently showed when she was tested previously. It would appear that she has been unsuccessful in separating from parental figures in the past and has more or less been living in a situation where the mother figure assumed a very domineering and controlling role. As a result of this, the patient has developed a very passive, dependent, and somewhat negativistic approach in dealing with her interpersonal life. She has problems also in attaining an adult heterosexual relationship and apparently would have some marital problems if this is not cleared up in the near future. The unresolved hostile feelings are still seen although it may very well relate to her resentments over how she has been treated in the past. The testing also indicates that she is a person who more than likely tends to siphon off her emotional problems into this accident as a way of attempting to resolve her psychological problems. It may also very well be, even at the present time, that because of the financial conditions, this intensified her symptomatology for she knows no other way of coping with the current changes except to maintain her symptomatology.

In summary, the testing continues to reveal an immature, dependent person who has a basic personality that is in keeping with an individual who could easily siphon off her psychological conflicts into physiological manifestations. This type of personality develops over the years and is closely related to the fact that she apparently lived in a situation where she felt she was being controlled by a rather overpowering mother figure. Thus, her only out is to develop symptomatology to blame her psychological difficulties onto some medical problem.

Patrick Noble, Ph.D.

Licensed Consulting Psychologist

These reports illustrate the types of medical inquiries and considerations involved in independent medical examinations. They also indicate why parties can develop differences of opinion concerning the medical aspects of personal injury cases. Though these reports have been modified, they are based upon an actual case. The physician who prepared the report appreciated the importance of thoroughness and detail. Those qualities lend authority to the physician's opinions.

Careful consideration should be given to the timing of an independent medical examination. The timing may significantly affect the examination's usefulness. If the plaintiff is claiming injuries due to an accident and the preliminary indications are that the injuries are quite minor, good strategy may dictate that the defendant obtain an independent medical examination right away. An *early* examination can establish an early date for the plaintiff's medical recovery. The examiner may be able to state that the plaintiff is ready to return to work or should be able to return to work within a week or two. An early examination is usually sought where an insurance company is attempting to terminate benefits to an insured or a claimant.

If the plaintiff has clearly sustained serious, long term injuries, the defendant may want to wait awhile before obtaining an independent medical examination, because the purpose of the examination is to evaluate the plaintiff's recovery, not the nature or extent of the injuries. If the examination is performed too soon after the injury, another examination may be required for the purpose of evaluating the claim.

17 Inspection of Things and Copying of Documents

Interrogatories and oral depositions are very useful for discovering what other people know or do not know about the facts of a case. But where the case centers upon a tangible item such as a machine or instrumentality, a document, or real estate or improvements to real estate, it is usually necessary for the parties or their representatives to inspect, measure, photograph, and test the tangible property. Where documents are involved, it may be necessary to obtain copies of the documents or even conduct tests on the originals.

A party who has custody of tangible property that is the subject of the litigation may be reluctant or even opposed to allowing other parties to have access to the property. The party who has custody may have a legitimate fear that an opponent might tamper with the property. Or, the reluctance to allow access may be motivated merely by a desire to keep other parties from having equal access to the facts. The parties' legitimate concerns for their property rights versus the parties' need to have "equal" access to the evidence imposes a difficult burden upon the courts to balance these rights, concerns, and needs.

Rule 34 establishes a procedure by which any party may demand that any other party produce, for inspection and copying, any tangible property in that party's custody which is relevant to the case. Relevancy is determined by Rule 26(b), as in other discovery procedures. The general rule is that the inquiry (inspection) is relevant if it concerns a matter which is admissible in evidence to prove a fact in issue or if the inspection is calculated to lead to the discovery of evidence which is admissible at trial.

Demand for Inspection

The procedure for obtaining access to relevant tangible property in the custody of another party is quite simple and fairly inexpensive. The procedure is initiated by preparing and serving a **demand for inspection.** The demand must be served upon all parties even though it is directed to just the party who has custody of the items in question. The demand does not have to be in any particular form, but see Form 24 in the Rules' Appendix of Forms for a suggested style. A mere letter which sets forth the request in sufficient detail is adequate and commonly used in many states. The demand must identify the tangible property with "reasonable particularity." A demand for inspection should not be so broad and vague as to be a mere "fishing expedition." If there is a serious question concerning the existence or identity of things to be inspected, the proper procedure is to obtain such information through interrogatories and depositions.

A demand for inspection may be made only upon parties to the action. A subpoena duces tecum is used for the purpose of requiring nonparties to produce tangible items for inspection at trial or at depositions. Actually, a subpoena duces tecum may be served upon parties, too. There may be occasion when a lawyer might prefer that method to force production of personal property. But a subpoena duces tecum is not usable to gain entrance to real estate.

Rule 34 allows the respondent at least thirty days in which to respond to a demand for inspection. Forty-five days is allowed if the demand is served upon the defendant with the summons and complaint. Therefore, the defendant has at least fifteen days after the answer is due in which to comply with the demand. Of course, the demand may grant more than thirty days for the production. If it is necessary to have the inspection earlier than is provided for in Rule 34, the party seeking the inspection may move the court for an order setting a shorter period of time. In fact, what usually happens is that a party who is in need of an inspection serves a demand which arbitrarily designates a time and place for the inspection. The respondent then notifies the proponent that the designated time is not convenient, and he or she may suggest a different time and place for the inspection. The lawyers try to agree upon a mutually convenient time and place for the inspection. It is generally recognized that other discovery efforts may be delayed until the inspection can be accomplished. Therefore, the arrangements should be made as soon as convenience will permit.

If the parties cannot agree upon a mutually convenient time and place for the inspection or cannot agree upon the conditions and reasonable limitations on the scope and extent of the inspection, the parties will have to obtain an order which specifies when and how the inspection is to be conducted.

Response to a Demand for Inspection

The initial response to a demand for inspection may be a written statement indicating that the respondent will comply; or the respondent may seek to impose some conditions or limitations on the inspection (Rule 34(b)). The respondent may serve formal objections to the requests. Objections must specify the respondent's reasons for objecting to the demand. If the objection is only to a portion of the request, that should be clearly indicated. Respondents are encouraged to use a narrative explanation rather than technical legal objections. Objection to a request for inspection must be served within the thirty days allowed by Rule 34. This is true even if the original demand for inspection allows more than thirty days before the inspection. Of course, if the demand for inspection is served with the summons and complaint, the defendant has forty-five days in which to serve objections.

The respondent should determine, as soon as possible, what position he or she will take concerning the demand for inspection and advise the proponent so that the proponent does not waste time, effort, and money preparing for an inspection that will not take place. For example, if the plaintiff has demanded an inspection to take place in forty days, the defendant may cause the plaintiff a great deal of inconvenience by waiting until the thirtieth day to serve objections. This is an area where the parties should extend themselves to provide cooperation. One of the things courts always look at when considering parties' discovery motions is whether a party has been diligent. Diligent parties who act in good faith are seldom penalized and seldom have to pay costs in connection with discovery motions.

In the vast majority of cases the parties are able to agree upon mutually satisfactory arrangements for inspections. Sometimes the parties find it more comfortable to reduce their agreements to written stipulations which will control the scope of the inspection.

The following is a Response to Demand for Inspection:

Defendant hereby responds to plaintiff's demand for inspection pursuant to Rule 34 of the Federal Rules of Civil Procedure:

1. Plaintiff's lawyer and the experts designated in the Demand for Inspection may enter defendant's plant at Des Moines, Iowa, for the purpose of inspecting the specified conveyor system on Thursday, January 5, 1989, between the hours of 2:00 and 5:00 P.M.

2. Plaintiff's representatives may take still pictures and motion pictures of the conveyor system in question.

3. Plaintiff's experts may take measurements of the conveyor system and appurtenances.

4. Defendant objects to plaintiff's proposal to take sample swatches of the conveyor belt because that would seriously damage the integrity of the belt and conveyor system. Furthermore, the B. F. Goodrich Company presumably has samples of the type of belt in question.

5. Defendant does not have any plans or specifications for the installation of the conveyor system. Therefore, defendant will not produce any plans or specifications at the scheduled inspection.

6. The only report of the accident in question was made for defendant's liability insurer. The report was not made in the ordinary course of defendant's business. It was made for the insurer in anticipation of litigation. The report is privileged and work product. It is not subject to discovery.

_____
Attorney for Defendant

The objections should be clearly stated and specific. The objections should be accompanied by a reasonable explanation with suggestions for alternatives when that is possible. Of course, the parties may agree to different terms and conditions than those stated in either the demand or the response.

Inspection Procedures

Document inspections usually take place at the office of one of the lawyers. On the other hand, if the inspection involves a large quantity of business documents, it is customary to conduct the inspection at the place of business where the documents are used. Business records are to be produced in the same form and condition as they are ordinarily kept and used in the business. The respondent has the obligation to identify the documents and even categorize them, when appropriate, to facilitate the inspection and copying.

As an alternative to a formal document inspection, the parties may agree that the respondent may simply make photocopies of the specified documents and deliver the copies to the proponent's lawyer. The proponent may receive more documents than he or she would have selected at a formal inspection, but the savings in time may be worth the cost of a few extra document copies. This approach is particularly helpful when the documents are all on microfilm, which is very tiring to review in quantity. Customarily the proponent of the inspection agrees to pay a reasonable cost for copies. The parties should be sure that they have a clear understanding concerning the quantity and costs before the copying is begun.

Copies of photographs can be made from negatives or from the photographs themselves. But it is cheaper to work from the negatives. Usually, the party who has custody of the negatives arranges to have copies made by a reliable processor. It is desirable to impress upon the processor that the photographs are evidence to be used in court and extra care must be taken to protect them against loss or damages. The party who requests the copies must pay the reasonable cost of having copies made. It has become quite common for parties to examine the original photographs and request *photocopies* of the photographs. Photocopies are cheap. They can be made in the office. They provide a convenient reference. If the originals are needed, presumably they are available for comparison. Photocopies are never as clear as duplicate photographs. They would not be used at trial; nevertheless, they may suffice for trial preparation.

A party may need to inspect land or enter a building which is under the control of another party. The reason may be to inspect and photograph features of the property, conditions of the property, activities on the property, or the property's relationship to other property. It may be necessary to obtain samples by taking soil borings, concrete borings, or samples of steel from metal structures. Rule 34 gives all parties the right to such inspections if relevant to the pending litigation. The inspections should be timed so as not to interfere with the occupant's normal use of the premises. For example, inspections of business or industrial property should be conducted after working hours, unless the purpose is to observe the customary business activity.

A more difficult problem is presented when the demand for inspection of personal property involves plans to conduct destructive tests on the property. For example, suppose that the controversy centers upon the flammability of an article of clothing and only a few small pieces remain. The necessary tests will destroy the remaining fragments. What can the parties do? In all probability, all parties need the same tests. The usual and best solution is to have the parties' experts agree on a testing procedure in which everyone participates. A video recording can be made to show the tests and the results. If the parties cannot agree on how the tests are to be done, it may be possible for the court to appoint an expert to do the testing for the parties. In such cases, the judge usually tries to get the parties to agree on the selection of an expert, but if the parties cannot agree, the court has the power to make the decision without their input or agreement (see Rule 706).

18 Requests for Admissions

Lawyers should strive to identify areas of agreement as well as areas of disagreement concerning the facts and the application of law to the relevant facts. After identifying areas of agreement, steps may be taken to establish that there is no controversy concerning the particular facts. This approach to litigation promotes economy because the parties can avoid wasting time and money on unnecessary investigation and discovery procedures. Also, if a matter is taken out of controversy, the lawyers have taken a major step toward reducing surprises at trial.

Of course, the pleadings (complaint and answer) are supposed to establish the legal issues through the allegations, admissions, and denials made in them. But modern day pleadings are so generalized that they do not do a good job of particularizing the material facts or fact issues. And, when the action is commenced, the defendant usually is not in a position to admit much of anything. The defendant's lawyer needs time to gather information and assimilate the facts.

At some point before trial, usually after discovery is completed, the lawyers are able to make an objective determination about which facts are controverted and which facts are undisputed. It is then that the party who has the burden of proving facts relevant to the cause of action or to the affirmative defense should consider establishing those facts by using *requests for admissions*. Through requests for admissions, a party may demand that another admit the truth of specified facts, the genuineness of specified documents, the validity of specified opinions, and the correct application of law to particular facts. This is done by serving a set of written requests for admissions upon the party's lawyer just like serving interrogatories.

A request for admissions may be directed to any matter within the scope of discovery as set forth in Rule 26(b). If the admission is to be used at trial, it must comport with the rules of evidence. Requests for admissions may be served only on parties to the suit. A request for admissions is not a means of discovery, because the party who propounds a request should *know* the facts he or she wants another party to admit and should be sure that he or she wants the facts established. The effect of admitting a request is to take the particular matter out of issue. The matter becomes uncontrovertible for purposes of the case. In other words, a party cannot change the admission at trial and is bound by the admission unless he or she secures a court order, for good cause shown, allowing an amendment or revocation of the admission.

Service of a request for admissions may be made with the summons and complaint or thereafter. The response may be signed by the responding party or by his or her lawyer. The response is due in thirty days after service of the request or within forty-five days of the service of the summons and complaint. Failure to serve a response to the request for admissions, within the allotted time, operates as an admission. If more time is needed, the proponent of the request may give an extension. Otherwise, a court order is necessary. Though not provided for in the Rules, when a party fails to respond to a request for admissions, it is customary for the lawyer who served the request to prepare and serve an **affidavit of no response,** which includes a statement that the admissions requested are deemed admitted for purposes of the pending action.

If an admission pertains to the application of law to facts, the court takes judicial notice of the admission. The admission becomes part of the law of the case. If the matter admitted is one of fact, the court informs the jury of the admitted facts at the appropriate time. A fact may be "admitted" in answers to interrogatories or in a deposition and, subsequently, denied or qualified at trial. The change may result in impeachment of the deponent's testimony. It is then up to the jury to determine the truth. But an admission of fact, made in response to requests for admissions, is conclusive and absolute. The admission may be withdrawn only by permission of the other parties or by leave of the court.

A party responding to requests for admissions has several alternatives: (1) deny the request, (2) admit the request, (3) assert an inability to admit or deny and explain the reasons, (4) make a qualified denial, or (5) object to the request. An objection has the effect of a denial. Any denial must be carefully considered and truthful. As stated in Rule 36: "A denial shall fairly meet the substance of the requested admission, and when good faith requires that a party qualify his answer or deny only a part of the matter of which an admission is requested, he shall so specify so much of it as is true and qualify or deny the remainder."

The more specific and clearly a request is drafted, the more difficult it is for the responding party to avoid making the admissions. Each request should be singular. But even then, a response may be to admit only a portion of the request. For example, a request to a defendant that he occupied certain real estate during the year 1989 may draw a response that he occupied the premises only during the month of January 1989. But if he occupied the premises only in 1987, he could simply deny the request without any explanation. As mentioned, requests for admissions should be made upon information *known* to the proponent for the purpose of taking a potentially disputed fact or opinion out of the case, not for the purpose of discovery.

The burden is upon the proponent of the request to be accurate and specific. Otherwise, the purposes of Rule 36 are not served. A misuse of requests for admissions increases the cost of litigation and creates friction between the parties. A request that is admitted is binding upon the proponent *and* responding party. Though not specifically stated in the Rules, an admission is not binding upon a party who did not propound the request or was not required to respond to the request for admissions. Therefore, if a request for admissions is served by the plaintiff on one defendant and admitted by that defendant, the admission does not affect any other defendant.

The use of requests for admissions should facilitate trial preparation and the trial itself by establishing the truth. Is there a duty to correct a response which was true when given but subsequently became incorrect? What if the response was believed to be correct when given but later is found to be incorrect? What if a party erroneously makes an admission? Does it make any difference if the error was technical or inadvertent or now clearly demonstrable or always subject to some doubt? An admission duly made is not irrevocable. The party who mistakenly made the admission should first request the opponent for permission to withdraw or correct the admission. If the parties can resolve the problem by agreement, usually reduced to a formal stipulation, that is the quickest and easiest method of handling it. Otherwise, admission may be withdrawn or modified only by permission of the court pursuant to a timely motion.

A motion to rescind a Rule 36 admission must (1) specifically request permission to withdraw or amend the admission, (2) state precisely how the proposed amended admission would read, (3) explain the reason for the amendment or withdrawal, and (4) explain why the other parties will not be prejudiced by the correction. The motion should be supported by affidavits to establish facts relevant to the motion. Of course, withdrawal of an admission may adversely affect another party's claim or defense in a significant manner. That, however, does not mean the party has been prejudiced. The truth does not prejudice a party! On the other hand, if a party's ability to prove the truth has been prevented or hindered, as where a witness has died or other evidence lost, that party has been prejudiced. Also, a party is prejudiced if he or she is deprived of time in which to investigate or conduct discovery to gather evidence which was available. A motion to withdraw or amend an admission ought to anticipate these *time* and *availability of evidence* problems.

A request for admissions may relate to specific facts. The following illustrative examples relate to specific facts of various kinds.

Please admit the following:

1. Defendant entered the intersection in question without stopping for the stop sign.
(This request might be prompted by a notation in a police accident report that the party admitted a stop sign violation. Perhaps a follow-up request should be used as in number 2 following.)

2. Defendant stated to officer Burt Jones that defendant did not stop for the stop sign in question.
(This request involves the same subject matter but a different fact, that is, the fact of a conversation. An admission that the conversation took place is not an admission that the stop sign violation occurred.)

3. Defendant was owner of the motor vehicle that struck the plaintiff pedestrian at the time and place specified in the complaint.

(Ownership of a vehicle is often critical to a claim and a disputed fact. The matter of ownership may also be a mixed question of law and fact.)

4. Defendant <u>delivered</u> <u>four (4) tons</u> of <u>wheat</u> <u>to plaintiff</u> on <u>September 5,</u> 1989.

(Though the request is a single simple sentence, it contains a request for admission of five separate facts. Each fact is underlined. If the controversy centers only around the *value* of the wheat delivered, the plaintiff may be able to admit all five of the facts without any difficulty. But if there is a dispute over how many tons were delivered, all the facts but the quantity should be admitted by the plaintiff. This same request could be directed by the plaintiff to the defendant to establish that the defendant delivered *less* wheat than he or she contracted to deliver.)

5. Plaintiff was not wearing his eye glasses at the time of the accident referred to in the complaint.

6. The accident referred to in the complaint occurred at 6:04 P.M.

7. The signature that appears on the attached promissory note (copy) was made by defendant.

8. Plaintiff was familiar with the stairway on which she fell. Or, plaintiff used the stairway on ten (10) or more occasions before the accident in question.

9. On (date) defendant received written notice of a defect in the pipe in question.

10. The sidewalk on which plaintiff fell was:

   a. four feet wide;

   b. made of cement;

   c. dry;

   d. used by plaintiff at least three (3) times a month for one year before plaintiff's alleged accident.

Requests for admissions may relate to opinions; the following illustrative examples relate to various kinds of opinions. Theoretically, any opinion that a layperson or expert may testify to is a proper subject for a request for admissions.

Please admit the following:

1. That when you observed defendant at the scene of the accident in question, you observed that defendant was not intoxicated.

(Of course, the request could be phrased to establish the defendant was intoxicated. Either way, the matter of sobriety is an opinion.)

2. That while you were at the accident scene you did not form an opinion whether or not the plaintiff was intoxicated.

(Sometimes it is just as important to establish the absence of an opinion as the existence of an opinion.)

3. That the sidewalk on which the plaintiff fell was slippery due to ice at the time she fell.

("Slippery" is an opinion. The presence of ice is a simple fact.)

4. That Dr. Stanley Smith's charges in the amount of five hundred dollars for services to the plaintiff were unreasonable.

(This type of request is used frequently by plaintiffs in personal injury actions, especially if the lawyer does not intend to have the physician or hospital administrator appear at trial to testify. But in most cases, the plaintiff will not permit the defendant's lawyer to *talk* with the plaintiff's treating physicians;

consequently, it is doubtful that the defendant has the information that is necessary to confirm the truth of the request. The monetary value of the physicians' services depends upon many factors, including the physicians' experience, time spent, and skill. Such information usually is not available in the records. Therefore, unless the plaintiff will permit the defendant to interview the attending physicians, the defendant may properly deny the request on the basis that he or she lacks sufficient information upon which to make the admission.)

5. That the lumber delivered by the defendant to the plaintiff per the contract in question complied with the specified grades and qualities.

6. That the fair market value of the plaintiff's automobile before the accident was four thousand dollars.

7. That the ignition point for natural gas is 3,300 degrees.

8. That rust caused the steel bar joists to fail.

All of the foregoing requests involve opinions which would be relevant and admissible at trial.

Requests for admissions may relate to *mixed questions of law and fact*, or, otherwise stated, to the application of law to facts. The following illustrative examples involve the application of law to facts.

Please admit the following:

1. That at the time the contract was signed by Joseph Smith, he was acting within the course and scope of his agency for the plaintiff.

(The existence of an "agency" and the "scope" of the agency depend upon the existence of a legal relationship, which may be created in various ways.)

2. That defendant was negligent in the operation of his airplane.

(The admission may be directed to the **ultimate question of fact,** which requires the application of law to a collage of facts. If the admission is made and negligence is thereby established, there are still the issues of causation and damages to be established.)

3. That on October 1, 1989, plaintiff was an employee of defendant who is entitled to benefits under the terms of defendant's contract with the teacher's union dated August 1, 1989.

4. That at the time plaintiff was discharged from her employment by defendant, she was a "tenured" teacher within the meaning of the contract referred to in the complaint.

(If certain factors must be proved to establish "tenure," the admission may save considerable time and effort proving those factors.)

5. That defendant's failure to stop for the stop sign was a proximate cause of the automobile accident in question.

(Proximate cause is probably the most subject legal conclusion in tort law. Appellate courts are reluctant to hold, as a matter of law, that any set of facts establishes that an alleged cause is a proximate cause of an accident.)

Requests for admissions may relate to the genuineness of documents. The usual procedure, as recommended by the rule, is to attach a good photocopy of the document to the request, although that is not necessary. A request to admit the genuineness of a document may be made concerning documents that are in the possession of the party to whom the request is directed, or, if the documents are "furnished or made available for inspection," the request may simply identify the documents. A strict reading of Rule 36 places a burden on the *requestor* to provide the original or a suitable copy to the *respondent*. If a responding party admits that a document is *genuine,* he or she merely admits that it is what it purports to be. Neither Rule 36 or Rule 37 define "genuineness". There is some concern and controversy over its precise meaning. Nevertheless, the lack of a clear definition does not seem to impair use of the request for admission procedure.

The wording of each request for admission should make clear the scope of the request. Suppose that the lawsuit centers around a counterfeit document; that both parties know that the document is counterfeit; but a dispute exists over who prepared the document and who signed it. The preceding definition of "genuineness" would be difficult to use in this situation. Neither party would ask the other to admit that the document is what it purports to be. But a party may request the other to admit that *this* is a true copy of the counterfeit document; that the document is a counterfeit; that the opponent has possession of the original counterfeit; and that the opponent knows or does not know who actually signed the counterfeit document. Of course, there is even less difficulty using a request that a document is genuine when the document is known to be valid. Then requests for admissions may be sought concerning the date of execution, identity of signatories, place of execution, and the consideration for it.

If a party admits that a certain document is genuine, he or she does not, thereby, admit that it is also admissible in evidence. For example, a defendant may admit that a certain photograph of the plaintiff's decedent at the accident scene is genuine—as being that of the decedent and accurately showing his mutilated body. Nevertheless, the photograph is still subject to the objection that it is inflammatory, and therefore, its prejudicial effect outweighs its probative value. Or, a document that is admittedly genuine may, nevertheless, be excluded from evidence because it contains statements that are mere hearsay.

Requests for admissions may be used to help insure that a certain document will be received into evidence or, at least, the necessary foundation for the document exists. For example, the following requests may be directed to the plaintiff in a tort action where the defendant is claiming the plaintiff previously executed a release:

Please admit

1. That the attached "Release of All Claims" is genuine.
2. That plaintiff signed the attached release on the date specified therein.
3. That plaintiff received the money described in the release as the consideration.
4. That the monies plaintiff received in exchange for the release have not been tendered or returned to defendant.

Affirmative responses to these requests should greatly facilitate the defendant's trial preparation.

A response to a request for admissions is due in thirty days after service. If service was by mail, add three days. If service was made with the summons and complaint, responses are not due until forty-five days after service. If the responses cannot be prepared within the time provided by the rules, the respondent has the burden of securing an extension of time. If the proponent will not accommodate him or her, the respondent must obtain an extension by moving the court for an order granting more time. But the motion must be served before the time for answering expires (Rule 6(b)).

If a party refuses to make admissions to requests for admissions duly made, the proponent of the requests must prove the facts or opinions or documents in the usual manner—with evidence—at trial. If the proponent succeeds in establishing the truth of a matter covered in a request, there is an inference that the request should have been admitted. Having successfully proven the matter denied, the proponent may move the court (apply) for an order requiring the opponent to pay reasonable expenses necessarily incurred to establish the matter (Rule 37(c)). Note, the proponent of the request for admissions does not have to be the prevailing party to take advantage of the Rule.

In most cases, it is difficult to know whether a specific fact or opinion was accepted by the jury as unqualifiedly true. The trial judge may submit interrogatories to a jury for answers to specific questions about the case (Rule 49(b)). Otherwise, it is nearly impossible to know what the jury found. For example, suppose that the plaintiff, in a personal injury action, was treated by three physicians and the defendant is asked to admit that the treatment by each physician was necessary and the charges by each physician were reasonable. The requests for admissions are denied. The jury returns a verdict in the amount of seven thousand dollars. The verdict neither says nor implies anything about the necessity or value of the medical treatment by each physician. The only permissible inference is that the plaintiff did sustain *an* injury and probably required *some* medical treatment. Of course, if the case is tried by a judge, he or she knows which facts in the determination were established.

Proving the truth of the matters requested is only the first step and requisite to recovering the costs of proving the matter. In addition, the proponent of the request for admissions must convince the court that the requests were proper in form and substance. Recovery of costs may still be disallowed if the court determines that the requests were "of no substantial importance" or that the respondent had good reason to believe that he or she would prevail on the matter. Obviously, these criteria are very subjective and give the trial judge a great deal of latitude. The wording implies that the judge should lean toward disallowance of costs unless the respondent acted in bad faith. Nevertheless, bad faith is *not* the test or standard.

The following is a sample of a negative response to requests for admissions.

Response to Request for Admissions

TO: Plaintiff and _____, her attorney,

Come now defendants Dwight G. Hall and Willard Rosen and for their response to plaintiff's request for admissions, state:

REQUEST No. 1. That the reasonable value of the medical expenses incurred by plaintiff as a result of the injuries received by plaintiff in the accident of September 20, 1989, are as follows:

Dr. Jerome Cowan	9-15-89 thru 9-22-89	$ 92.00
Dr. Maynard Berwin	9-22-89 thru 2-5-90	308.00
Dr. Richard Copes	10-15-89 thru 10-31-89	125.00

Midwest Medical Ctr.	9-21-89 thru 9-27-89	1,082.60
Metro. Medical Assoc.	1-19-89 thru 5-18-89	31.00
Drs. Peters and Elmer	3-5-90	75.00
Prescriptions	10-3-89 thru 7-15-90	21.00
TOTAL		$1,734.60

RESPONSE: DENIED

Defendants Hall and Rosen object to the request for admissions for failing to provide adequate documentation and information concerning these requests for admissions seeking to impose upon defendants the burden of securing copies of records at defendants' expense and reviewing those records at defendants' expense. Defendants have been unable to make reasonable inquiry of the various physicians due to plaintiff's failure and/or refusal to provide authorizations permitting defendants' counsel to interview them. Therefore, the information known to defendants or information readily obtainable by the defendants is insufficient to enable them to admit the request for admissions.

As of this time, plaintiff has not authorized defendants' counsel to interview the attending physician and hospital personnel. Therefore, defendants cannot verify the matters set forth in the various bills attached to plaintiff's request for admissions. Nor are the defendants able to determine the qualifications, experience, or expertise of the various providers of health care to determine whether or not their charges for medical services are reasonable. If plaintiff would specify the amount of time spent by each provider of health care for each service rendered, defendants would be in a better position to evaluate the truth of the requests. Also, plaintiff should supply a copy of all hospital and medical records which are the bases for making the charges reflected in the bills attached to the request for admissions.

REQUEST No. 2. That if the proper parties were called to testify, they would testify that each of the aforementioned expenses for medical care and attention referred to in request for admission number 1 was reasonable.

RESPONSE: DENIED. Please refer to response 1.

REQUEST No. 3. That in the event you deny either request for admission number 1 or request for admission number 2, supra, state the name, address, age, occupation, and employer of every person whom you will call to testify to dispute the reasonableness of such medical expenses.

RESPONSE: DENIED. Please refer to response 1.

Dated: November 10, 1990.

_____

Attorney for Defendants

Requests for admissions should not be used as a substitute for a trial concerning fact issues over which there is a bona fide dispute.

19 Summary Judgments

Application

The purpose of a trial is to resolve disputed fact issues. For example, in an automobile accident case where each party claims the benefit of a green traffic light, the fact finder must decide from the evidence which driver had the green light. But where the parties are in agreement on the material facts, there is no need for a civil trial. The judge may decide the case as a matter of law. Once the facts are determined or established, the judge can apply the law to those facts and determine the parties' legal rights and obligations. The summary judgment procedure enables the parties to avoid the time, expense, and inconvenience of a trial. Additionally, motions for summary judgment can be heard and decided with very little delay, whereas it may take more than a year to have a case brought up for trial.

Any party may serve and file a motion for an order granting summary judgment any time after twenty days following the commencement of the action. Motions for summary judgment usually should not be made until after the parties have completed their discovery procedures. The summary judgment procedure can be initiated only by motion. The party who seeks a summary judgment must *document* the material facts so that those facts are before the court in written form, including pleadings, affidavits, deposition transcripts, records, etc. A motion for summary judgment cannot be supported with oral testimony during the hearing of the motion. A court will entertain a motion for summary judgment only if it clearly appears that there is no dispute on the material facts. Therefore, it is common for the moving party to prepare a stipulation of facts for the court to show the absence of any dispute.

Motions for summary judgment have two principal values or applications. They are useful for submitting issues of law to the court for determination where there is no real dispute on the governing facts. And they are useful for determining how the law is to be applied to a given set of facts. Though motions for summary judgment are usually thought of as a defense tactic, they may be used effectively by plaintiffs to eliminate nonmeritorious affirmative defenses (Rule 56(a)).

Summary judgments allow courts to decide disputed questions of law and how the law is to apply to particular fact situations. One common situation in which the summary judgment procedure is useful is when the parties agree that they have a written contract, but they disagree on the meaning of the words of the contract. The court can construe the contract and, thereby, resolve the dispute. Another example which illustrates the use of summary judgments concerns the application of a municipal ordinance or state statute. Suppose an ordinance provides that all property line fences must have a two-foot setback, but the plaintiff's fence is on the property line shared with a neighbor and was in existence long before the ordinance was adopted. The plaintiff could use the summary judgment procedure to obtain a court declaration that the ordinance does not apply to the plaintiff's fence. There is no dispute on the facts. The issue concerns how the law is to apply to uncontested facts.

In these two examples it is assumed that the parties specifically agreed to all of the underlying facts; however, total agreement is not always necessary. Nor is it necessary that both parties want to have the case decided by way of a summary judgment. If one party can show the court that there is no dispute on the *material* facts so that the case can be decided as a matter of law, a motion for summary judgment is appropriate. For example, in the typical automobile accident case the cause of action accrues, and the statute of limitations begins to run when the accident occurs. Let us suppose that the applicable statute of limitations is two years. The date on which the action was commenced is easily determined from the clerk of court's records. If the indisputable facts show that the action was commenced more than two years after the accident occurred, the plaintiff's claim is subject to dismissal as a matter of law. It does not matter that there is a dispute concerning liability and damages, because the statute of limitations defense is controlling and dispositive of the entire case. Therefore, for purposes of the summary judgment motion, the only *material* facts are the facts relevant to the statute of limitations defense, that is, the date of the accident and the date on which the action was commenced. The plaintiff's complaint must state the date and place of the accident (Rule 9(f)). Consequently, the material facts are easily established in this example. The defendant is entitled to an order granting summary judgment of dismissal of the action.

Material Fact Issues

If there is any dispute over a material fact, summary judgment cannot be granted. For example, suppose that the plaintiff has brought a negligence action against her physician for medical malpractice. Suppose that the defendant physician alleges that the plaintiff's claim is barred by a two-year statute of limitations. The general rule in medical malpractice actions is that the statute of limitations does *not* begin to run when the malpractice occurs. The statute of limitations begins to run when the defendant physician ceases to treat the patient for the condition out of which the claim arose. (In some states the statute of limitations does not begin to run until the patient acquires information which would cause a reasonable person to know that the physician committed malpractice. The rationale for this approach is that the patient's reliance upon the physician makes it tantamount to a fraud for the physician not to tell the patient "what went wrong" and about the probable consequences.) So the question arises: When did the defendant physician stop treating the plaintiff for the particular condition in question? Suppose that the physician's office records show the dates of the patient's office visits, all hospital visits made by the physician, and all significant telephone calls. Suppose further that according to the physician's office records, two years have elapsed since he had any contact with plaintiff. The physician could move the court for summary judgment of dismissal on the grounds that the statute of limitations has run against the cause of action. The motion could be supported by the physician's office records, the physician's affidavit, and affidavits by personnel in the physician's office. If the physician's deposition had been taken, the relevant testimony from the deposition could be used in support of the motion. It is a simple matter for the court to apply the law to the facts when the facts are not controverted. But if the plaintiff submitted an affidavit claiming that she had a telephone conference about her condition during that two-year period, the affidavit would be sufficient to raise a *fact issue* which would preclude the court from granting summary judgment. It does not matter that the great weight of the evidence favors the motion for summary judgment.

Another example may be helpful to illustrate the use and limitations of summary judgment motions. Suppose that the plaintiff brought suit on a written contract in which the plaintiff claims the defendant agreed to sell a certain parcel of land to the plaintiff. Suppose further that a dispute exists concerning one of the terms of the contract. If the parties agree that the contract is binding and that the only issue concerns the proper interpretation of the contract, the matter can be determined by summary judgment. If the court determines that the contract is ambiguous and that evidence outside the written document is necessary for a proper construction of the contract, there is an issue of fact which precludes the court from granting summary judgment.

Partial Summary Judgments

In the preceding examples, the order for summary judgment is dispositive of the actions. But a summary judgment may be granted which is only partial. The summary judgment may dispose of one or two issues without disposing of the case as a whole. For example, suppose that plaintiff brought an action against the defendant for injuries caused by a product sold by the defendant. Suppose further that the plaintiff's action is based upon breach of warranty and negligence. Assume that breach of warranty claims are subject to a four-year statute of limitations and the negligence claims are subject to a six-year statute of limitations. If the plaintiff commenced the action five years after the causes of action accrued, the defendant would be entitled to a partial summary judgment dismissing the warranty claim only. The order grants a partial summary judgment.

These examples involve summary judgments against the plaintiff; however, orders for summary judgments may have application to eliminate the defendant's affirmative defenses as well. For example, suppose a property owner brought an action in trespass against the defendant for entering upon the plaintiff's property and removing trees, and the defendant alleges in the answer that he had the plaintiff's consent to cut down and remove the trees. The plaintiff could move for dismissal on the basis of his affidavit, which states that he did not consent to the defendant's entry upon the land or the removal of the trees. If the defendant were unable to refute the plaintiff's affidavit in good faith, the plaintiff would be entitled to an order striking the affirmative defense of consent. The defendant cannot avoid a summary judgment merely by a general claim that he believed he had consent. A general denial does not meet the thrust of a summary judgment motion. The respondent must allege specific facts (Rule 56(e)). That may lead to the conclusion that the defendant is absolutely liable for the plaintiff's damages, leaving only the amount of damages to be litigated (Rule 56(c)).

Summary judgment procedures create somewhat of an anomaly in civil litigation. For it is the general rule that the plaintiff most prove his or her claim. It is not encumbered upon the defendant to disprove the plaintiff's claim. Nevertheless, Rule 56(e) states, in part, the following:

> When a motion for summary judgment is made and supported as provided in this rule, an adverse party may not rest upon the mere allegations or denials of his pleading, but his response, by affidavits or as otherwise provided in this rule, must set forth specific facts showing that there is a genuine issue for trial. If he does not so respond, summary judgment, if appropriate, shall be entered against him.

This clause cannot be applied literally to all cases. For example, if the plaintiff is a business invitee upon the defendant's premises and claims that she fell due to a small accumulation of water in the hallway of the defendant's building, and the defendant has no knowledge of the water or the alleged accident, how can the defendant present "specific facts showing there is a genuine issue for trial?" The answer is that the defendant's affidavits would have to show that no one else reported any slippery condition or accumulation of water on the premises at the time of the accident and the plaintiff did not give the defendant notice of the alleged accident until days later. These are merely general denials, not specific facts which mitigate against the plaintiff's accident. Nevertheless, the allegations should be sufficient to preclude a summary judgment in the plaintiff's favor. The jury would have to decide whether there was a puddle of water; whether it existed for such a period of time that the defendant should have discovered it and removed it; whether the plaintiff actually fell on the premises; and whether the puddle caused the plaintiff to fall.

Affidavits made in support of and in opposition to motions for summary judgment must be made upon personal knowledge. The facts stated must be admissible into evidence. The affidavits must show that the affiant is competent to testify concerning the facts set forth in the affidavits. Where the court is confronted with conflicting affidavits and the court believes that they have been made in good faith, the court must deny the summary judgment motion and let the case proceed to trial. There is no occasion for the judge to weigh the credibility of the affidavits or the quantity of evidence offered by the respective parties. The conflict concerning a material fact necessarily precludes summary judgment. Even though the court denies a summary judgment motion, the court may determine, and provide in its order, that certain facts are conceded and, therefore, for purposes of the trial, established (Rule 56(d)). The effect is like a Rule 36 admission.

Procedure

A motion for summary judgment is a serious step. It requires careful consideration by both parties. Rule 56(c) requires the moving party to give at least ten days notice before the hearing of the motion. Of course, three more days must be added if the motion is served by mail. All supporting affidavits and documents must be served with the motion. The respondent must serve and file any opposing affidavits at least one day before the hearing (Rule 56(c)). Though not clearly stated, the rule contemplates that the moving party will *receive* the opposing affidavits at least one day before the hearing.

In the event that the respondent needs more time to prepare to oppose the motion, the respondent can request the moving party to extend the time or move the court for an order extending the time for hearing. The respondent may file affidavits in support of the motion to extend the time. The respondent's lawyer may use an affidavit to explain why more time is needed, what further evidence is needed, and how he or she intends to obtain the evidence.

The affidavits must be made in good faith. If a nonparty's affidavit is used, the party who relies upon the affidavit must believe that it is true. If the court determines that affidavits filed by a party were made in bad faith or for the purpose of falsely causing an "apparent" issue of fact for the purpose of delaying a summary judgment, the court may order that party to pay to the other party the latter's expenses incurred by reason of the deficient affidavits. A party who misuses affidavits is subject to being held in contempt of court (Rule 56(g)). Furthermore, the affiant who gives a false affidavit is subject to criminal prosecution for perjury.

Suppose a plaintiff moves the court for an order granting summary judgment, which the defendant wrongfully opposes using affidavits that are misleading and interposed not in good faith. Suppose, further, that the plaintiff spends five thousand dollars for attorney's fees and other costs preparing for trial. The plaintiff would be entitled to recover those costs because of the improper affidavits. The costs could be added to the plaintiff's judgment or made the subject of a separate order.

Paralegals may assist with the preparation of motions for summary judgment. The following is a sample of a summary judgment motion.

MOTION

Pursuant to Rule 56 of the Federal Rules of Civil Procedure plaintiff hereby moves the Court for an order determining that defendant is liable to plaintiff for money damages, in an amount to be determined by trial, for defendant's wrongful trespass upon plaintiff's property and destruction of plaintiff's trees.

This motion for partial summary judgment is made upon the grounds that defendant's answer admits that defendant entered plaintiff's property by mistake and mistakenly cut down plaintiff's trees and denies only the amount of plaintiff's loss.

> There is no dispute concerning any material fact which would prevent the court from holding defendant liable in trespass as a matter of law.
>
> This motion is made upon plaintiff's complaint, defendant's answer, and plaintiff's affidavit which identifies the trees, their location upon plaintiff's property, and plaintiff's ownership.
>
> (date)
>
> _____
>
> Attorney for Plaintiff

A party runs a risk in making a motion for summary judgment. The risk is that the court will agree that there is no fact issue but award summary judgment in favor of the nonmoving party, that is, the respondent. The court has authority to do so, and it has happened. Consequently, the moving party ought to be sure about the law and that he or she wants to take the position that the material facts are not in dispute.

The ten days allowed by Rule 56 may not be sufficient to enable a party to obtain all the information needed to oppose a motion for summary judgment. In that event, the party may obtain a continuance of the motion by filing one or more affidavits showing that certain facts are not presently available by affidavits or otherwise. The court may order a continuance of the motion and that depositions be taken or other steps implemented to complete the preparation for the summary judgment hearing (Rule 56(f)). Though the rule refers to affidavits of the parties, usually lawyers make their own affidavits to show why the needed evidence is not currently available.

20 Evidence

Evidence is the testimony, exhibits, and factual stipulations which the judge allows a jury to consider for the purpose of deciding disputed fact issues. Fundamentally, all evidence is sworn testimony. If a document or item is received in evidence, it is because a witness has been able to show that it is genuine and contains reasonably reliable information. Very few documents are self-authenticating. Much of a lawyer's trial preparation is concerned with gathering and organizing the evidence for presentation at trial. The investigation and discovery are the means for obtaining evidence. A plaintiff may have a valid claim, but unless the plaintiff can present evidence which will *prove* the claim, the claim must fail. The defendant may have a valid affirmative defense, but without competent evidence to *prove* the defense, it fails. As a lawyer marshals the evidence to be used at trial, the lawyer must consider, first, the admissibility of the evidence and, second, the evidence's persuasiveness.

Many factors affect a lawyer's decisions about what evidence to offer at trial and how that evidence should be presented. A lawyer must determine what evidence is essential to the case, that is, necessary to prove a prima facie case or defense. There is a temptation to present more evidence than is needed, because many lawyers have a justifiable fear that the omission of some item of evidence could cause the case to be lost. They feel that it is better to err by presenting too much evidence than not enough. For most lawyers, it is easier to decide what evidence to present than what evidence to omit. A lawyer must decide how much time and money should be spent in the presentation of the evidence. For example, should the client have the benefit of one expert witness or three? Should the operation of a machine be explained by using an operator, an engineer, photographs, a model, or all of these? Should a matter be illustrated by simply using a blackboard, or should a drawing be prepared, or should a working model be made or should the "thing in question" be brought into the courtroom? The amount of time and expense may vary significantly.

In addition to these technical considerations, a lawyer must be concerned with the affect that the presentation will have on a jury. Will the jury be bored by too much evidence? Will they feel that the evidence is trustworthy? What is the best order for presenting the evidence? Can a weak witness be "sandwiched" between two strong witnesses? Needless to say, a lawyer has many judgments to make concerning the quality of the evidence and the means for presenting it.

Juries are instructed to consider the evidence as a whole in determining the truth, regardless of who presented it. The jurors may draw inferences from established facts, but they are not allowed to speculate about facts not proved by the evidence. The jury must not supply missing evidence by speculation and conjecture. The jurors may not, through their own independent knowledge, supply any apparent missing facts. For example, if the witnesses to an accident cannot remember whether the roadway in question had a painted center line, jurors who are familiar with the roadway are not allowed to use their independent knowledge of the roadway to make that determination. Jurors are not witnesses. They are not subject to cross-examination. It is for this reason that jurors who profess familiarity with the accident in question or with some of the facts about the accident in the voir dire examination usually are stricken from the panel. On the other hand, jurors may use their knowledge for the purpose of evaluating the evidence which they have heard and seen at trial. For example, if one physician testifies that the plaintiff's broken arm will cause some permanent disability and another physician testifies that the injury should not result in permanent disability, the jurors may use their own experience in life to decide which physician is the more believable.

Most cases involve a dispute on critical facts. The parties' legal rights and obligations cannot be determined until the fact issues are resolved. A trial gives parties the opportunity to present evidence for the purpose of proving their respective versions of the facts. The evidence is the predicate for the factual determinations. The factual determination is a predicate for a court's judgment. Obviously, the reliability and, ultimately, the acceptability of courts' judgments are directly dependent upon the quality of the evidence which courts allow. Courts must have a rational basis for allowing and disallowing evidence. Some kinds of evidence, such as repetitious and cumulative evidence, are objectionable because the evidence is disruptive to the proceedings. Some evidence, which parties would like to present, is fundamentally unsound, such as unsworn statements and hearsay evidence. But courts must be practical about what evidence is reasonably available to parties. It would be unfair to the parties to allow only the very "best" evidence. The procedures for proving facts and the rules of evidence must promote the truth, be founded in fairness, and be practical.

The common law developed a battery of *exclusionary rules of evidence* which were formulated to promote justice between the parties. The *Federal Rules of Evidence* were promulgated by Congress on July 1, 1975. They are a codification of the common law exclusionary rules. The Federal Rules of Evidence apply to all judicial proceedings in our federal courts. Many states have adopted similar codifications of rules of evidence following the federal rules. One important reason why many states have followed the lead of the federal courts is that there is a real desire to keep laws and procedures uniform throughout the nation.

The exclusionary rules operate on the premise that any sworn testimony is competent to prove a fact unless the evidence violates one of the exclusionary rules. The presumption is in favor of the admissibility of evidence. The burden rests upon the party desiring to exclude evidence to show that it should not be considered because one or more of the exclusionary rules applies. An objection to evidence must be made in a timely manner. If no objection is interposed or the objection is untimely, the trial judge usually receives proffered evidence. For example, if a party introduces evidence which is hearsay and, therefore, subject to exclusion, the evidence will, nevertheless, be received in the absence of a timely objection. Any evidence which the judge allows may be considered and used by the jury to determine the facts.

Broadly speaking, the exclusionary rules preclude evidence in the following instances:

1. The witness is *incompetent* or disqualified from testifying because he or she
   a. has not taken the oath;
   b. is not mentally competent;
   c. lacks knowledge about the matter;
   d. cannot qualify as an expert.
2. The testimony lacks probative value and is, therefore, *irrelevant* because
   a. it is logically too weak;
   b. it is too remote in time;
   c. it is too remote in location;
   d. it concerns a collateral matter which could cause more confusion than assistance.
3. The testimony is not based upon what the witness observed but upon what someone else told the witness. The testimony is objectionable as *hearsay*. Documents containing unsworn statements which are not subject to cross-examination contain hearsay evidence and are objectionable on that ground.
4. The testimony would contradict or change a legally enforceable, fully integrated, written agreement. The evidence is objectionable as *parol evidence*. Parol evidence is objectionable because it impairs the validity of written agreements which were intended to embody the full agreement.
5. The testimony would require the disclosure of *privileged* communications or records. The privilege must be duly asserted or it is waived. The exclusion applies to oral and written communications and to documents. Matters which are subject to a privilege include the following
   a. communications between lawyer and client and related documents;
   b. conversations between husband and wife during marriage;
   c. conversations between a physician and patient about the patient's medical condition, and the physician's treatment records;
   d. conversations between a person and that person's priest or minister for spiritual guidance;
   e. statements which require a witness to incriminate himself or herself.
6. The testimony lacks *foundation*. Before a witness may testify about a fact, it must be shown that the witness is competent to make observations and did make observations concerning the matters to which he or she is to testify.

If the witness is to testify as an expert, it must be shown that he or she has adequate training and experience to render expert opinions concerning the subject matter.

7. Testimony is subject to objection and exclusion because a statute forbids the court to allow the evidence. A legislature or other rule-making body may establish a public policy against use of certain evidence.

This brief description of the exclusionary rules is not all-inclusive. This explanation indicates the areas of concern and some of the considerations which lead to the exclusionary rules of evidence.

After determining the facts and making appropriate inferences, the jury must resolve the *ultimate questions of fact.* In a negligence action, the *ultimate* facts are the answers to questions such as the following: (1) Was the defendant negligent? (2) Was the defendant's negligence a proximate cause of the accident? (3) Was the plaintiff negligent? (4) Was the plaintiff's negligence a proximate cause of the accident? If both were casually negligent, what are their percentages of causal negligence? (5) What sum of money would provide full and adequate compensation? In a contract case, the ultimate questions of fact are the answers to questions such as: (1) Did the parties have a valid contract? (2) Did the defendant breach the contract? (3) Did the plaintiff breach the contract? (4) What sum of money would fairly compensate the plaintiff?

CATEGORIES OF EVIDENCE

Evidence takes various forms and can be categorized in various ways. The law does not prefer one form of evidence over another. Application of the exclusionary rules of evidence does not turn or depend upon categories of evidence. Categorizing evidence is useful only for the purpose of gaining an understanding of the uses and interrelationship of evidence.

Testimony

Testimony is given under oath and subject to the right of cross-examination. The oath or affirmation required of witnesses emphasizes the court's commitment to the truth and the witness's duty to tell the whole truth. Also, the oath subjects a witness to criminal prosecution if the witness testifies falsely. A witness may testify to almost anything that the witness observed. It must be shown, usually through the witness himself or herself, that the witness was able to perceive and comprehend the matters he or she claims to have observed. Even a child of tender years may qualify as a witness if the court is satisfied that the witness appreciates the duty to tell the truth.

A witness must be mentally competent to testify. He or she must not be under the influence of intoxicants or drugs when in court. But a witness who was intoxicated at the time of an occurrence may, nevertheless, be permitted to testify concerning observations about the occurrence or transaction. The witness's state of intoxication goes to the witness's credibility but not to the admissibility of the witness's testimony. A lawyer is prohibited by legal ethics from testifying at a trial in which he or she appears as counsel.

Testimony is introduced into evidence through a process of examination conducted by the lawyers. In other words, a lawyer asks the witness a question and the witness answers the question. The process is repeated until the witness has covered all of the matters which that lawyer wants covered by that witness. The lawyer directs the testimony through the selection of questions to help keep the witness from interjecting matters that are irrelevant or otherwise inadmissible. The witness is not given the responsibility to know what to talk about. The process of examining witnesses really benefits everyone involved.

The examination of witnesses takes two forms: direct examination and cross-examination. The rules of evidence apply somewhat differently to each method of examination. The direct examination is the questioning or interrogation conducted by the lawyer for the party on whose behalf the witness is called. A cross-examination is conducted by the lawyer for the party against whom the witness has testified. Cross-examination is also allowed against any witness who is *aligned* with an adverse party.

Testimony is supposed to come from the witness, not from the lawyer who is questioning the witness. For that reason, leading questions are generally disfavored. Any question that suggests the answer that is desired by the questioner is considered to be a leading question. There is a strong tendency for witnesses to simply agree with the answer suggested by the lawyer. Consequently, leading questions on direct examination are subject to objection. Nonetheless, for the purpose of saving time, leading questions are regularly used, even during the direct examination, when the examiner is obtaining background information from witnesses and covering matters that are not disputed. Leading questions help to expedite the noncontroversial portions of the testimony.

Leading questions may be put to any witness at any time. In the absence of an objection by one of the parties, the answer to a leading question will be received into evidence. If a party fails to object to a leading question, the objection is waived. The fact that a question is subject to objection as leading does not make the answer incompetent. Experienced trial lawyers know, however, that leading questions used in the direct examination of a friendly witness tend to reduce the witness's authority and effectiveness. If a lawyer leads his or her own witnesses, the presentation lacks authority and persuasiveness. Most students of trial strategy believe that the juries want to hear the witnesses, not the lawyers.

Leading questions are not only proper but necessary on cross-examination. There is a presumption that an adverse witness or adverse party will not permit himself or herself to be led by the opposing lawyer. By asking carefully phrased leading questions a lawyer can effectively limit a hostile witness's responses during a cross-examination. There is general agreement that the limitation is a good one. It keeps the proceedings from becoming a shouting match or a debate. On redirect examination, the witness has an opportunity to make any explanations that are really necessary in light of the cross-examination.

Demonstrative and Illustrative Evidence

Demonstrative evidence tends to demonstrate facts, as opposed to verbalizing facts. Any tangible evidence is considered by most lawyers to be demonstrative evidence. Demonstrative evidence may involve the very heart of the controversy such as an allegedly defective product. For example, an allegedly defective tire may be the subject of the lawsuit. The tire in question, if received into evidence, is demonstrative evidence. It will be used to *show* what is allegedly wrong with the tire, what happened to the tire, and how it happened. Pictures and models are common types of demonstrative evidence.

Tangible evidence which is directly related to the case is ordinarily received into evidence as exhibits. Exhibits are evidence which may be used to determine fact issues. The jury may take most exhibits with them into their deliberations. They have the opportunity to examine the exhibits without the lawyers present to point out things or offer explanations. In the preceding example, the tire would be an exhibit which the jury could examine during their deliberations.

Not all tangible evidence is allowed to go to the jury. Some exhibits are received into evidence and used during the trial solely for *illustrative* purposes. This means that the exhibit, by itself, does not tend to prove any fact relevant to the case; however, the exhibit is helpful to one or more witnesses to explain testimony. The following is a list of commonly used exhibits which are used for illustrative purposes: photographs which were taken after the scene of the accident has changed; products which are similar to the one in question but which have some differences; or a freehand drawing that is not made to scale. A physician may use a model of the human spine to illustrate an injury to a vertebra or intervertebral disc or a model to show how a nerve injury occurred. The illustrative exhibits need not be examined by the jury during their deliberations, because the exhibit is not evidence of anything. Indeed, it might actually mislead jurors to think of it as evidence of some fact. It should be noted that in some cases, some judges allow illustrative exhibits to be used by the jury in their deliberations. It should also be noted that photographs taken well after the scene of the accident has changed may, for some purposes, be received as exhibits which are not merely for illustrative purposes. For example, a photograph may show a particular feature of the scene which is relevant to the case, but other matters shown in the photograph may not pertain to the accident. The photograph would be received and not limited to the illustrative purpose role; however, the jury would be cautioned about its limited application.

Suppose that a large machine has been made the subject of a lawsuit. It is much too large to bring into the courtroom. Suppose further that the plaintiff claims that the machine is defective in design because it is top heavy and dangerously unstable. Photographs which fairly depict the machine are evidence of what the machine looks like. A motion picture or videotape could be used to show its operation. A model of the machine may be useful to show physical characteristics, including the alleged inherent instability. All of these exhibits could be received into evidence as exhibits which the jury could examine during their deliberations. Demonstrative evidence has the obvious value of psychological impact. Jurors are more likely to understand and remember the facts and a party's theory of the facts when demonstrative evidence is used. Lawyers are always looking for new and better ways of using demonstrative evidence. Paralegals who have a good appreciation for the role of evidence and understand the client's case can be very helpful in locating and preparing demonstrative evidence.

Photographs may be used to show the facts in issue such as photographs of an accident scene which depict the vehicles in their at-rest positions, skid marks, and vehicle damage. A film of an airplane crash would be the most graphic kind of evidence of an event giving rise to a lawsuit. However, unless the motion picture tends to establish controverted facts, there is a danger that such a pictorial presentation would merely cause passion and prejudice on the part of the jury. In such cases, the judge must decide whether the photographs' prejudicial effects outweigh their probative value. There is a similar problem with the use of photographs taken to show the plaintiff's injuries in their acute state or photographs of the plaintiff while undergoing surgery. If the prejudicial effects of the photographs outweigh their probative value, they should be excluded from the jury's view and consideration.

Engineers' scale drawings may be very helpful at trial to show sizes, relationships, and even functions. Often, the drawings are used by several different witnesses to illustrate each witness's observations. The jury could not possibly absorb and remember all of the detail shown in the drawing. Consequently, such drawings often become evidence that does go to the jury for consideration during their deliberations.

Other forms of demonstrative evidence that are encouraged by courts as time-savers are summaries, charts, and graphs, which reduce voluminous documents down to the essentials (Rule 1006). The preparation of such summaries requires a thorough knowledge of the subject and the purpose of the evidence. Legal assistants may assume a primary role in the preparation of such exhibits.

Facts and Opinions

Generally, courts require evidence to be factual rather than someone's opinion or belief about the facts. Consequently, witnesses are precluded from testifying as to what they think about the facts which they observed. It is the jury's responsibility to draw conclusions from the facts observed by the witnesses; however, there are some very important exceptions.

In everyday situations, people act and react more on the basis of their opinions and conclusions than they do on the basis of established facts. For example, when a motorist decides to pass another automobile the decision is made on the basis that the oncoming vehicles are far enough away to permit the pass to be made safely. The motorist has made a judgment and acts on the basis of his or her conclusions about speeds and distances. No measurements or calculations are made to reduce the situation to a mathematical fact. The motorist would describe the situation in ordinary conversation as having sufficient time or room in which to pass safely. This is a mere conclusion on the part of the motorist. But can a motorist really be expected to know the relevant distances in terms of feet or yards or even car lengths? When an experienced driver observes that the automobile ahead of her has stopped, she knows she must stop before she gets there. She does not need to know the number of feet involved. She only needs to know whether or not she is too close or whether she was following at a safe distance. Again, these are conclusions. Most drivers are able to bring an automobile to a smooth, complete stop at a reasonable distance behind a stopped or stopping vehicle without *knowing* the measured distance or the measured braking force. A driver stopped in an intersection to make a left-hand turn knows he must yield to oncoming traffic that is close enough to constitute a hazard if he were to proceed to make his turn. The left-turning motorist must make a judgment concerning an oncoming vehicle's distance and speed. These judgments are usually quite reliable even though a motorist might not be able to state the number of feet or yards involved.

How does a person measure, factually, the slipperiness of a floor or the condition of lighting at a certain place at dusk? How can an eyewitness ever know, factually, the speed of a passing vehicle? At best, he or she can have an opinion about the facts. The law is established to enable people to deal with human situations and human problems. It must, therefore, deal with these human problems on human terms. When a condition or situation is one which can best be described in the form of a meaningful opinion, opinion evidence is generally permitted. So, ordinarily, a witness who has personal knowledge about the condition of a floor or sidewalk or street is permitted to express an opinion that it was or was not slippery. In addition, the witness would have to be able to describe the conditions or factors which caused the slipperiness. A lay witness who admits to some "worldliness" usually qualifies to express an opinion whether a person he or she observed was or was not intoxicated. Lighting conditions may be described in commonly used terms such as "pitch black" or "fairly dark" or "easily visible" or "bright." These terms are probably more meaningful to a jury than scientific measurements.

EYEWITNESS VIEWS

Fact	Opinion
miles per hour	fast
one mile	far or close
ten thousand candle power	bright
specific color	dark or light
without variations	smooth
many variations	rough
inches, feet, yards, meters	"block" or "car length" as unit of measurement
inches, feet, yards, meters	wide or narrow
inches, feet, yards, meters	high
one hundred decibels	loud or soft
crying	sad, depressed, unhappy, hurting
grimaced, muscle spasm	painful
weight lifted or moved	weak or strong
sixty-watt bulb	dim or bright
disfigured	ugly
in compliance	sufficient, adequate, correct
out of compliance	wrong, mistake

Of course, a witness cannot have a valid opinion unless he or she had an adequate opportunity to observe the occurrence, condition, or person in question. Only after the witness has shown that he or she is capable of observing, did observe, and is able to recall the observations may he or she go on to render an opinion about what was observed. In other words, the opinion evidence requires a foundation. A witness would not qualify to give an opinion that a sidewalk was slippery due to ice if he or she merely observed it at a distance or had not used it for over a week. A witness would not qualify to give an opinion that another person was intoxicated unless he or she observed signs of intoxication such as slurred speech, unsteady gait, loud inappropriate conduct, loss of inhibitions, flushed appearance, odor of alcohol, or red eyes. A witness may express an opinion about the speed of a passing vehicle only if he or she observed it long enough and has sufficient experience to form a valid opinion about speed in miles per hour. In automobile accident cases, witnesses are *not* allowed to express opinions of speed in relative terms such as "fast," "slow," or "normal." But, if a party *admits* to going "too fast," the admission would be received into evidence against him or her.

The following typical jury instructions contain guidelines for the jury for evaluating testimony.

> You are the sole judges of whether a witness is to be believed and of the weight to be given to his or her testimony. There are no hard and fast rules to guide you in this respect. In determining believability and weight to be given to the testimony given by each witness, you should take into consideration the following:
>
> 1. interest or lack of interest in the outcome of the case,
> 2. relationship to the parties,
> 3. ability and opportunity to know, remember, and relate the facts,
> 4. manner and appearance,
> 5. age and experience,
> 6. frankness and sincerity, or lack thereof,
> 7. the reasonableness or unreasonableness of his or her testimony in light of all the other evidence in the case,
> 8. any impeachment of his or her testimony,
> 9. any other factors that bear on believability and weight.
>
> You should, in the last analysis, rely upon your own experience, good judgment, and common sense.

Expert Witnesses

A person who has special education, training, knowledge, and experience in a particular subject or field *may* qualify to give expert opinion testimony about the subject. A physician's diagnosis of an injury may be the determination of a fact or an opinion based upon apparent facts. The physician's determination of the cause of an injury or disability is almost always a matter of opinion. The preferred method of treatment is frequently a matter of opinion. A partial list of experts includes scientists, accountants, farmers, carpenters, electricians, engineers, architects, physicians, mechanics, and machine operators. The author was helped by a professional baseball manager, Billy Martin, and a professional baseball player, who explained to a jury that even when a batter uses due care in gripping the bat, it might inadvertently fly out of the batter's hands. The expert testimony was sufficient to overcome the permissible inference of a *res ipsa loquitur* case presented by the plaintiff. The claim was that the bat slipped out of the defendant's hands, so the jury should infer that the batter was negligent in controlling the bat. So the types of cases in which expert witnesses may be used is practically without limit. There are many kinds of experts. Again, the opinion evidence requires a foundation to establish that the witness has the necessary background and is sufficiently knowledgeable about the subject in question to have a reasonably reliable opinion.

The judge must decide, in each case, whether the foundation is adequate. It is not uncommon for competent expert witnesses to reach different conclusions. The fact that the experts' opinions differ is not a concern to the judge. If there is sufficient foundation for the opinion, the jury must consider and weigh the opinion along with the other evidence. Even though the jurors are not experts, they may have to evaluate the experts' opinions and choose between experts. Jurors may conclude that none of the expert witnesses are believable. That has happened.

Cases involving claims of professional malpractice (whether or not medical) usually depend upon expert testimony in at least three or four areas. First, experts must determine the underlying facts concerning the *nature* of the injury, loss, or failure. Second, experts must determine what *caused* the injury, loss, or failure. Third, was the cause of the injury, loss, or failure due to *negligence* on the part of the professional? The expert witness must be familiar with the customs and standards of the defendant's profession. Negligence is synonymous with malpractice in such cases. A professional person is liable for the harm proximately caused by his or her negligence.

In many cases, it is necessary to go another step with the proof and show that a deviation from the applicable professional standards cannot be justified on the basis of professional judgment. When an expert gives such testimony, he or she is actually giving an opinion on the ultimate question of fact— telling the jury how he or she would decide the case based upon the information available to or assumed by him or her. Historically, a witness was not permitted to invade the province of the jury by testifying to the ultimate question of fact; however, the law has changed. Rule 704 expressly authorizes such opinion testimony—even by laypersons. Perhaps a lay witness is now permitted to testify not only that the sidewalk was "slippery" but that it was "too slippery to walk upon." The courts have not yet established the parameters of this relatively new and somewhat controversial rule.

The following is a typical jury instruction which contains guidelines for the jury on how to evaluate an expert witness and his or her testimony.

> A witness who has special training, education, or experience in a particular science, profession, or calling is an expert and, in addition to giving testimony as to facts, may be allowed to express an expert opinion. In determining the believability and the weight to be given such opinion evidence, you may consider, among other things, the following:
>
> 1. the education, training, experience, knowledge, and ability of the expert;
> 2. the reasons given for his or her opinion;
> 3. the sources of information;
> 4. factors already given for evaluating the testimony of a witness.

Direct and Circumstantial Evidence

A fact may be proved by either direct evidence or circumstantial evidence or both. The law does not prefer one form over the other. Direct evidence is the testimony from witnesses who observed the facts to which they testify. Direct evidence also includes the exhibits, which, in themselves, establish facts. The testimony of a witness that he or she saw certain automobile skid marks is direct evidence proving the existence of the skid marks. A photograph showing skid marks is direct evidence proving the existence of the skid marks.

Circumstantial evidence is *indirect* proof that depends upon principles of logic and common experience to prove a fact. The process depends upon deductive reasoning. Where one or more facts are established through direct evidence, it is *permissible* to infer, from those established facts, the existence of other facts. For example, by proving the existence of skid marks by direct evidence, a party may prove, by circumstantial evidence, the location of the vehicles before impact and at impact. The skid marks also permit an inference that the driver applied her brakes at a certain point and, further, that the driver observed the danger at some point before applying her brakes. Or, suppose that a construction worker spent two weeks working in close proximity to an electric power line but then sustained an electrical burn by contacting the wire. The circumstantial evidence permits an inference that he knew the wire was there and considered it to be dangerous, since he successfully avoided it for two weeks. The inference is permissible and valid, even though the construction worker denies that he was aware of the power line. Circumstantial evidence is really a matter of common sense.

Substantive and Impeachment Evidence

Substantive evidence is *any* evidence the jury is allowed to consider that is capable of supporting a verdict. The form of the evidence makes no difference.

Impeachment evidence is considered for the purpose of testing the credibility of a witness. It is evidence that the witness has said something or written something or conducted himself or herself in a manner inconsistent with what was testified to in court. For example, if a witness testified that he observed the defendant enter the intersection without stopping for the red light, he would be impeached by the testimony of another witness who heard the first witness say that he did not notice the color of the traffic lights at the time of the accident, or who heard the first witness say, at the accident scene, that the *plaintiff* went through the red light. The reason that the second witness's testimony is not substantive evidence (but merely impeachment) is that the first witness's out-of-court statement is not sworn testimony subject to cross-examination. The second witness's testimony about what he heard the first witness say at the accident scene is sworn testimony subject to cross-examination but not testimony as to the truth of the first witness's observations—only about what the first witness said. If the jury chose to believe the sworn testimony of the first witness, they could determine that the defendant did violate the traffic light. But if the jury believed the second witness, who heard the first witness say that the plaintiff went through the red light, the jury would be left with no substantive evidence from these two witnesses about the color of the traffic light. More specifically, only the first witness claimed to see the color of the light, and he cannot be believed, so there is no evidence on the point through these two witnesses.

If impeachment evidence applies to a party, the impeachment evidence may also be substantive evidence. For example, if a witness heard the plaintiff admit that he went through the stop sign but the plaintiff testifies at trial that he stopped, the *party admission* would be received as impeachment and as substantive evidence that the plaintiff did go through the stop sign.

Hypothetical Questions

An expert witness must base an opinion on facts that he or she has observed or upon facts which have been proved through other witnesses and exhibits. "Proved," in this sense, does not mean that the jury necessarily accepted those facts; it means that the facts have been received into evidence and the jury is allowed to consider them. Since an expert witness usually does not have personal knowledge about the occurrence and many other important facts, the question arises: How can he or she qualify to render an opinion based upon those facts? The answer is: Through the device of the hypothetical question.

A hypothetical question permits the expert to *assume* that facts contained in the hypothetical question are true, just as though he or she had personally observed those facts. Sometimes, the hypothetical questions are very long, involving many paragraphs. The longer the hypothetical question, the greater the risk that it might fail, either because it is technically defective or because it lacks persuasiveness. The jury is instructed, at the end of the trial, that the expert's opinion assumes and depends upon the truth of *all* the facts contained in the hypothetical questions. If the jury should determine that any one or more of the assumed facts is not true or not established, the expert's opinion based upon the hypothetical questions should be rejected. The cross-examination of an expert who has answered a hypothetical question is often directed at showing that the hypothetical question is *incomplete,* and that with the addition of other facts, the answer would be different. Sometimes, the cross-examiner is able to show that the hypothetical question contains facts that are contrary to the expert's own records or inconsistent with calculations or observations that the expert has made. To some extent, the cross-examiner is also permitted to test the expert with additional hypothetical questions.

Hypothetical questions are almost always reduced to writing and previewed with the expert before he or she takes the stand. An experienced paralegal could help with preparation of the hypothetical questions. Each lawyer develops his or her own form and approach. As a general rule, the shorter the hypothetical situation, the more reliable and effective it is.

Exhibits

Any tangible item that a party offers into evidence for the jury to consider must, first, become an exhibit and part of the record. It becomes an exhibit only after one or more witnesses have identified it and have shown that it is relevant to the case. Once it has been given an exhibit identification mark, the lawyers refer to it by the marking, usually a number or a letter.

The following dialogue is representative of the necessary foundation establishing identity, authenticity, and relevancy of an exhibit. In the following scenario the lawyer is questioning a personnel manager of a company to lay foundation for admissibility of personnel records. The lawyer has had the exhibit marked by the court reporter for identification.

Q. I am now showing you what has been marked as plaintiff's Exhibit A. Can you identify that for us?

A. Yes, that is Mr. John Smith's personnel file with the XYZ Corporation.

Q. Who has custody of these records?

A. As personnel manager of the XYZ Corporation, I have custody of these records.

Q. How long have you been the personnel manager?

A. For the past ten years.

Q. Did you bring these records with you to court pursuant to a subpoena served upon you yesterday?

A. Yes.

Q. Have you brought with you all of Mr. Smith's personnel records that are kept in your custody and control?

A. Yes.

Q. Are these records kept in the ordinary course of the business of the XYZ Corporation?

A. They are.

Counsel to the court: Plaintiff offers plaintiff's Exhibit A into evidence.
Court to defendant's counsel: Is there any objection to the Exhibit?

If the relevancy of the records is not apparent, relevancy must be shown by indicating how the documents tend to prove controverted facts. When a party offers a record into evidence, he or she must have the entire record available so that any portions omitted from the offer can be examined, and perhaps offered, by the cross-examiner. Otherwise, there is danger that facts might be taken out of context.

Once the original records are made available for examination, it is common for the parties to stipulate that photocopies may be received into evidence in lieu of the originals. The originals are then returned to their custodian. In the following scenario the plaintiff's lawyer is questioning the plaintiff to lay foundation for a photograph that the plaintiff took of his automobile after the accident.

Q. I am now showing you a photograph marked as plaintiff's Exhibit A. Can you identify it for us?

A. Yes, it is a photograph that I took of my automobile.

Q. When was the photograph taken?

A. On June 7, 1989.

Q. Where was it taken?

A. At the Anderson Chevrolet garage.

Q. What portion of your vehicle is depicted in the photograph?

A. The rear portion of my automobile.

Q. Does the picture fairly show the condition of your automobile as it appeared after the accident?

A. Yes.

Q. Is the damage that appears in the photograph entirely a result of the automobile accident on June 4, 1989?

A. No.

Q. What damage is shown in the photograph that, to your knowledge, did not occur in the accident?

A. The photograph shows the rear bumper pulled back on the right side. That happened at the garage—maybe when the car was towed in.

Q. Otherwise, does the photograph fairly show and represent the damage that the rear portion of the car sustained in the accident?

A. Yes.

Counsel to the court: Plaintiff offers plaintiff's Exhibit A into evidence.
Court to defendant's counsel: Is there any objection?

At this point, the defendant's lawyer is allowed to ask questions only about foundation for the exhibit, that is, questions concerning admissibility of the exhibit. Any questions he or she has about its probative value will have to wait until the plaintiff's lawyer has finished his or her direct examination.

When a photograph is offered into evidence, it is desirable to have the photographer available to explain the method of making the photograph as well as its subject matter. It is well known that the type of lens used in a camera can significantly change the subject matter's appearance, especially its depth and apparent width. Distances between two points can be made to look quite different depending upon the type of lens used. It is often sufficient for purposes of laying foundation, however, to have a witness or party to the suit who is acquainted with the subject matter testify that the photograph accurately portrays the subject. Note that the photograph does not establish itself. It is just an extension of the testimony of the witness. The extent of the foundation that is required depends upon the purposes for which the photograph is offered and whether there is any actual dispute over it. As often as not, both sides want the photograph in evidence.

Judicial Notice

A trial judge may take judicial notice of certain facts and those facts are binding upon the parties and the jury. Rule 201(b) states the following:

> A judicially noticed fact must be one not subject to reasonable dispute in that it is either (1) generally known within the territorial jurisdiction of the trial court or (2) capable of accurate and ready determination by resorting to sources whose accuracy cannot reasonably be questioned.

For example, a judge may determine that December 25, 1989, fell on a Sunday, or that there are 5,280 feet in a mile. When the judge takes judicial notice of a fact, the parties do not have to present evidence to establish the fact. The judge simply tells the jury that it is an established fact which they must accept as true.

Suppose a plaintiff brought a negligence action for damage to certain property and that it becomes material to the case whether the accident occurred within the corporate limits of a municipality. If there was no controversy over the precise location of the accident, the trial judge could take judicial notice of the fact that the conduct occurred in or outside of the corporate limits. Any controversy over the location of the accident, however, would have to be resolved by the jury from the evidence.

A court may take judicial notice of scientific, mathematical, and geographic facts. For example: an object traveling at sixty miles per hour moves eighty-eight feet per second; December 25, 1990, fell on a Tuesday; water boils at 212 degrees Fahrenheit; zero degrees centigrade equals thirty-two degrees Fahrenheit; Los Angeles is in the Pacific time zone. By statute, in some states, a trial judge is authorized to take judicial notice of a person's normal life expectancy as established by approved actuarial tables. That fact may be very important in determining future damages in personal injury cases.

According to Rule 201, the court may take judicial notice of such facts whether or not requested to do so by the parties. In civil litigation, which is our concern, judicially noticed facts are to be accepted by the jury as conclusive. The judge may conduct a hearing in the absence of the jury to determine whether or not the fact in question is true and whether he or she should take judicial notice of it.

Summaries

Occasionally, litigation involves thousands of records and documents, the contents of which are essential to proving a claim or defense. More often than not, the parties do not have any real dispute about the contents of the documents but they do differ on the effect of the documents or conclusions to be drawn from them. The discovery rules provide a means for reviewing and copying the documents in advance of trial. Rule 1006 authorizes a party to prepare a summary of the records or charts that may be received into evidence in lieu of the original documents. The rule encourages the parties to conduct a thorough review of all the relevant documentation *before* the trial and, thereby, reduce the amount of time needed for presentation of the essential evidence from the documents. The rule authorizes the following:

> The contents of voluminous writings, recordings, or photographs which cannot conveniently be examined in court may be presented in the form of a chart, summary, or calculation. The originals, or duplicates, shall be made available for examination or copying, or both, by other parties at a reasonable time and place. The court may order that they be produced in court.

Summaries which are prepared for use as provided in Rule 1006 are not part of a lawyer's work product. They are discoverable and should be seasonably disclosed to all other parties to avoid unnecessary delay at trial. The original documents must be available for inspection and comparison.

Presumptions

Some facts may be established at trial by presumptions in law. The presumptions, unlike judicially noticed facts, are not binding upon the parties and jury. A jury may find for or against a presumed fact.

Suppose the plaintiff has the burden of proving that a certain written notice was delivered to the defendant. The plaintiff may prove it by showing that the notice was sent to the defendant by United States mail in an envelope that was properly addressed, had the proper postage, and was deposited in a United States mailbox or delivered to a post office. By proving these facts and that the envelope was not returned, a presumption in law arises that the letter was delivered to the defendant addressee. This is true even though the defendant denies receiving the letter. The underlying facts concerning addressing and mailing the notice must be established by a witness who has personal knowledge or through business records. A post office receipt is not necessary but helpful. The jury must decide whether or not the presumption of delivery is more convincing or less convincing than the defendant's sworn denial. The presumption exists because of the necessity of such proof and the probability that it is true.

As described by Rule 301:

> In all civil actions and proceedings not otherwise provided for by statute or by these rules, a presumption imposes on the party against whom it is directed the burden of going forward with evidence to rebut or meet the presumption, but does not shift to such party the burden of proof in the sense of the risk of nonpersuasion, which remains throughout the trial upon the party on whom it was originally cast.

In cases involving death, there is a presumption that the decedent did not commit suicide. In cases where the plaintiff delivers personal property to the defendant's custody and it is returned in a damaged condition, there is a presumption that the damage was caused by negligence on the part of the defendant. If the defendant fails to present any evidence explaining how the damage occurred, so as to negate any negligence on his or her part, the plaintiff is entitled to a verdict against the defendant. If the defendant does offer an explanation, however, it must be weighed by the jury against the presumption in law that the loss was caused by the defendant's negligence.

There are many other presumptions in law. Some have been created by the courts as part of the common law. Other presumptions have been created by statute. Their use and limitations are important in litigation. A comprehensive listing of presumptions and their applications is beyond the scope of this book.

Res Ipsa Loquitur

The plaintiff in a "negligence action" has the burden of proving that the defendant was negligent and that the defendant's negligence was a proximate cause of an accident and the plaintiff's injury or other loss. Ordinarily, the burden of proof is met by showing how the accident occurred and that the defendant violated some statute, contractual duty, custom, practice, or other standard establishing a duty of reasonable care. But once in a while, there is no evidence available to the plaintiff to show how or why the accident occurred, because the instrumentality was solely under the control of the defendant at the time of the accident. The problems that the plaintiff has in such cases have been given special treatment by the courts.

Where the accident is of the type that, in itself, speaks of negligence on the part of the defendant, the plaintiff is given the benefit of the res ipsa loquitur doctrine, which creates a permissible inference of negligence on the part of the defendant. Res ipsa loquitur means that the thing (accident) *speaks for itself* of negligence. The defendant has the opportunity to try to explain why he or she denies the negligence. The doctrine has its origin and justification in the probability that the accident was due solely to the defendant's negligence and the evidence concerning the occurrence is more readily available to the defendant, so he or she should come forward with an explanation. In most states, the doctrine does not shift the burden of proof. The permissible inference, however, is sufficient in itself to carry the burden of proof even if the defendant has an explanation that exonerates him or her from any fault.

The following jury instruction on res ipsa loquitur is typical:

> When an accident is such that ordinarily it would not have happened unless someone had been negligent, and if the instrumentality which caused the injury is shown to have been under the exclusive control of the defendant, you are permitted to infer from the accident itself and the circumstances surrounding it, that the defendant was negligent.
>
> Before you are permitted to make this inference, you must find all of the following:
>
> **1.** The accident is of the type that does not ordinarily occur in the absence of negligence.
> **2.** The defendant was in *exclusive* control of the instrumentality which caused the injury (or property damage) claimed.
> **3.** The accident did not result from any voluntary act or negligence on the part of the plaintiff or some third person for whom the defendant would not be responsible.

The doctrine has applicability in the following types of cases: a restaurant customer is injured by a foreign object in his or her food; an airplane passenger is injured or killed due to an unexplained crash; a passenger on a railroad train is injured when the train derails or crashes into another train operated by the same railroad; a patient undergoes surgery and sustains injury to another part of his or her body during the operation; a passenger is injured when an automobile leaves the highway and crashes for some unknown reason; an elevator falls; city gas escapes from utility pipes; electricity escapes from an appliance under the defendant's control; a dentist's drill slips and causes injury to the patient's mouth; a surgeon leaves a surgical instrument or sponge in the patient; or a baseball player lets the bat fly out of his hands causing the bat to strike another player. In the example involving the physician, a jury would be allowed to infer that the physician was negligent for leaving the surgical sponge in the patient even though no physician testified on behalf of the plaintiff that a professional medical standard was violated. Most courts have concluded that laypersons are capable of making that decision without the necessity of expert testimony.

There are numerous other situations in which the doctrine may have applicability. In all cases, it must be shown that the defendant was in exclusive control of the instrumentality at the time the alleged negligence occurred. For example, if the defendant's building collapsed, damaging the plaintiff's property and the defendant could show that the collapsed building was occupied by trespassing vandals at the time, the plaintiff would fail to establish the requisite of exclusive control by the defendant and, therefore, would not have the benefit of the doctrine. The doctrine may work in favor of the defendant against the plaintiff where the plaintiff has exclusive control of the instrumentality.

THE FEDERAL RULES OF EVIDENCE

The ultimate objective of the Federal Rules of Civil Procedure is the determination of each case on a just basis. Justice is accomplished when the truth is ascertained and the law is correctly applied to those facts (Rule 102).

Most of the exclusionary rules of evidence are merely common-sense rules which help to insure that the jury's verdict is based on evidence that is factual, probative, the best available, and not fabricated for purposes of the lawsuit. The exclusionary rules are premised in logic, practicability, human experience, and human nature. Trial judges have a great deal of latitude or discretion in determining whether or not evidence should be excluded. When a judge has acted within his or her discretion, the judge will not be reversed. The trial judge may be reversed only for a clear abuse of discretion. The exclusionary rules cannot be applied with mathematical precision or certainty. The tendency is to rule in favor of admissibility, letting the jury decide what weight to give to the evidence.

If a party fails to object or neglects to move the court to strike evidence improperly received, he or she waives the right to complain. The party is not permitted to use the error as a basis for seeking a new trial or reversal upon appeal. As always, there is an exception to the general rule. If the error was so manifest and so likely to have brought about an unjust result, the trial court or appellate court may take notice of "plain error" and grant relief in the form of a new trial, directed verdict, or reversal (Rule 103(d)).

If a lawyer believes that the court has erroneously excluded evidence which would be helpful to a client, he or she has a right to make an *offer of proof* outside the hearing of the jury. The offer of proof is nothing more than a statement by the lawyer or testimony of a witness showing the facts which would have been established if the evidence had been allowed. The lawyer's statement or witness's testimony is made part of the trial record and, therefore, may be considered by the appellate court in the event there is a subsequent appeal (Rule 102(a)(2)).

Objections to evidence should be stated in a concise technical form without argument. For example, a lawyer may state: "The question is objected to on the grounds of hearsay." A lawyer is subject to criticism by the court and possibly receives a counterobjection if he or she argues: "The question is objected to because this witness does not have any personal knowledge about the subject matter and is only relying upon some highly questionable statement she heard or read." Lawyers are not supposed to argue the value, weight, or effect of the evidence until the final arguments (Rule 103(c)). The lawyers may seek leave of the court to argue their positions on the evidence outside of the hearing of the jury.

Materiality

Probably the most fundamental requirement of evidence is that it be material. Evidence is material if it has a bearing on the issues in the lawsuit. If one party attempts to inject facts into the case which do not relate to the issues as raised by the pleadings, the opposing lawyer should object on the grounds that the facts are immaterial. If there is no objection to evidence which is immaterial, that evidence may have the effect of amending the pleadings by implication. The pleadings are then construed to conform to the evidence, rather than vice versa (Rule 15(b)). A judge may exclude immaterial evidence on his or her own motion to keep the parties from digressing and to avoid abuses of the court's time.

There is an unfortunate trend toward the use of the word "relevancy" instead of "materiality." The distinction should be maintained. They involve different concepts.

Relevancy

To be admissible, evidence must be relevant. This means the evidence must be material *and* have probative value. Rule 401 defines relevancy as "evidence having any tendency to make the existence of any fact that is of consequence to the determination of the action more probable or less probable than it would be without the evidence." If the evidence does not logically tend to prove or disprove a controverted fact, the evidence is subject to exclusion on the grounds that it is irrelevant.

Relevancy may be determined by such factors as time and distance. For example, if a witness observed a motor vehicle traveling at a high rate of speed when it was ten miles away from the point where it was subsequently involved in an accident, the question arises whether the evidence of speed so distant would logically tend to prove excessive speed at the time of the accident or how the accident occurred. The answer is not always easy. If the observation was made on a freeway and there was no occasion for the driver to change speeds during the ten miles, maybe the evidence would be relevant. But if the driver had traffic and traffic controls to deal with while traveling the ten miles, as in a typical urban area, the prior excessive speed ten miles away is probably irrelevant.

There is a presumption that parties involved in an accident were sober. A claim of intoxication must be proved. Evidence which proves that the defendant motorist is an alcoholic and that he was intoxicated during the day *preceding* the accident in question would not tend to prove that the defendant was drunk at the time of the accident. The evidence is too remote in time. The prejudicial effect of the evidence would outweigh its probative value. If there were other competent evidence to prove that the defendant was intoxicated at the time of the accident and the defendant controverted that evidence, however, perhaps the defendant's habit of drinking and recent intoxication would be relevant (Rule 406—Habit; Routine Practice).

Evidence that the defendant had been involved in a similar accident at the same place three years earlier does not tend to prove how or why the second accident occurred. However, where the alleged cause of the accident, such as a defective step, has caused other accidents, proof of the prior accidents is relevant to prove that the conditions were dangerous, known to the defendant, and have the capacity to cause an accident of the type in question. The courts usually distinguish between animate and inanimate causes of accidents when determining relevancy.

The absence of prior accidents may be relevant. For example, suppose that a visitor in an apartment building falls on a common stairway and contends that the accident was due to inadequate lighting. The landlord would be allowed to present evidence that the stairway was frequently used; the lights which were in use at the time of the accident had been in use for ten years; and no one else had ever reported a fall due to insufficient lighting. Of course, this example assumes that all of the lights for the stairway were working at the time of the accident.

Proof that the defendant was found liable on other contracts, which he contested, does not prove he is liable on the one in question. Evidence which shows that the defendant had a small quantity of alcohol (one beer) before the accident should be excluded unless it can be shown that the party's conduct was actually affected by the alcohol. Irrelevant evidence tends to cloud and confuse the issues. Too often, it has a prejudicial effect because it raises innuendos of wrongdoing without any factual basis. If the evidence does not adversely affect the opposing party, it probably should not even be offered; it is probably immaterial. So courts must balance the probative value against the prejudicial effect of evidence when determining relevancy.

Best Evidence

Courts require the parties to present the best evidence reasonably available. This means that a copy of a document should not be used if the *original document* is reasonably available (Rule 1002—Requirement of Original). Otherwise, copies of documents are subject to the objection that they are "not the best evidence." If the absence of the original can be explained, then a copy is the best evidence and may be used. For example, if it can be shown that the opponent was last to have custody of the original, or that the original is needed elsewhere, a copy may be used. Of course, parties may stipulate to the use of copies and that is often done in cases involving hospital and business records.

Hearsay

Hearsay evidence is any out-of-court statement, oral or written, which is offered to prove the truth of matters referred to in the statement. The rule excluding hearsay is logical and goes to the very heart of the adversary system. Facts should be established through witnesses who have firsthand knowledge of them. It is a witness's powers of observation, memory, and truthfulness which the jury should assess and not that of another person who heard the observer's description of the facts. Hearsay evidence deprives the parties of the *right* of cross-examination. The basic rule against hearsay and its application are fairly easy to understand. The numerous important exceptions to the hearsay rule are what create difficulties for lawyers and the courts. The exceptions are based upon the usual reliability of some kinds of hearsay evidence and the convenience of using it.

Historically, any statement made by an adverse party could be received into evidence against him or her as an "admission." Admissions by a party were received into evidence as an exception to the hearsay rule. Rule 108(d)((2) provides that such admissions shall be received into evidence on the basis that they are not hearsay. An admission may be made by the party or by the party's agent, who had authority to make such statements. The admission by an agent, of course, must be made during the agency relationship. Rule 801(d)(1) also provides that prior out-of-court statements made by a witness may be received into evidence as substantive evidence, not merely impeachment, if the prior statement was under oath and subject to cross-examination. Such prior statements would have to be part of a deposition or testimony at a hearing or a trial. Again, the rule declares such statements not to be hearsay.

Parol Evidence

When the parties enter into a written contract which purports to contain the entire agreement, it would be unfair to have either party attempt, at trial, to change the terms of that agreement by oral testimony. Consequently, an exclusionary rule of evidence has evolved, known as the parol evidence rule, which precludes any evidence that attempts to vary or contradict the clear language of a writing that the parties have used to formalize their agreement. The rule applies to contracts, promissory notes, mortgages, deeds, wills, etc.

As is true of most rules, there are exceptions to the parol evidence rule. Parol evidence may be received to clarify ambiguities in the writing. But a judge must first determine that the writing is ambiguous, that is, reasonably subject to more than one meaning. Also, parol evidence may be used to prove that the written document was induced or procured by fraud by the other party. A contract may be set aside (rescinded) where there is a mutual mistake by the parties, if the mutual mistake goes to the very heart of the contract. Fraud or mutual mistake may be proved by parol evidence. Proof of a mutual mistake must be established by *clear and convincing evidence*—not by a mere preponderance of the evidence. Parol evidence may be received to establish a subsequent change in the contract mutually agreed to by the parties; but, most formal written agreements or undertakings expressly provide that any modification must be in writing and signed by all parties.

Dead Man Statute

Some states have the so-called dead man statute, which provides that a party to a lawsuit may not testify concerning any oral statements he or she heard another person make if, at the time of trial, the person who made the utterance is deceased. The statute is intended to reduce the possibility that parties may fabricate evidence. If a party fails to object to such testimony when presented, the evidence will be received, and a verdict may be based upon it. In other words, the exclusionary rule created by the statute must be asserted in a timely manner at trial or the statutory prohibition is waived. Note that the exclusionary rule applies only to prevent *parties* from testifying. It does not prevent independent witnesses from testifying about oral statements made by persons who died before trial. The dead man's statute has no application to writings; it applies only to oral statements.

The Federal Code of Evidence does not recognize the dead man statute.

Settlement Negotiations

Some evidence is excluded because it would be contrary to public policy to allow its use at trial. A primary example is the rule which precludes parties from putting in evidence another party's statements made in the course of settlement negotiations (Rule 408—Compromise and Offers to Compromise).

The courts want parties to discuss their differences and to settle their controversies without having to go through a trial, if possible. In other words, settlement negotiations are favored in the law. If parties had to labor under the fear that their efforts to compromise would be used against them, negotiations would be sharply curtailed, if not impossible. Therefore, a jury is never told about the parties' negotiations. The danger is much too great that a jury would be unduly influenced by such knowledge.

Rule 409 goes on to provide that a party's offer to pay another's medical expenses may not be used against the offeror as an admission of liability for the accident. A typical situation is where a person falls down on a premises where he or she is visiting. The owner of the premises may suggest, even urge, the guest to have a medical checkup, which the owner will pay for. The suggestion cannot be used against the offeror as an admission of fault. The offer may be proved, however, for the purpose of holding the offeror to his or her promise.

Remedial Measures

In a personal injury action involving a dangerous condition of a building, such as a stairway, the plaintiff would undoubtedly benefit from evidence showing that, immediately after the accident, the defendant remedied the condition by repairing it. Such evidence would help to show that the defendant considers the condition to be dangerous. The inference is that a reasonable person would have repaired the condition *before* the accident. Otherwise, there would be no need to make any repairs. The evidence would help the plaintiff meet the burden of proving that the condition was unreasonably dangerous.

On the other hand, if the courts were to allow evidence of *remedial measures*, defendants would be discouraged from making changes which may provide greater safety in the future. Furthermore, it is human nature to be extra careful about conditions once there has been an accident. Remedial measures are often taken, not because they are really necessary, but because the repairs or changes are some kind of insurance against the accident happening again. Furthermore, a party's standard of care should not be judged on the basis of hindsight. Public policy considerations have led the courts to exclude evidence of *most* remedial measures (Rule 407—Subsequent Remedial Measures).

Where changes have been made after an accident, the defendant's lawyer usually brings that fact to the attention of the court at the very beginning of the trial and requests the court to order the plaintiff and the plaintiff's witnesses to avoid any reference to the change. Evidence of the changes could be so prejudicial as to require a **mistrial**. Proof that the condition was dangerous will have to come from some other source or be accomplished in some other manner.

In cases where a dispute develops as to whether a product is unreasonably dangerous, one of the considerations may be the cost of making changes to make the product safe. If the cost is prohibitive, the manufacturer may be excused for not eliminating the hazard. Evidence of subsequent improvements in product liability cases is allowed where the defendant claims that the changes, which would have prevented the plaintiff's accident, would have been too expensive to be justifiable. The fact that the defendant made changes after the accident is very persuasive evidence that the expense was not prohibitive. The "remedial measures" evidence is received, in those cases, to impeach the defendant's claim that the cost was prohibitive. Note, the exception to the remedial measures exclusionary rule does not come into effect unless invoked by the defendant. The defendant can avoid any evidence of the changes in the product simply by not claiming that the cost of the changes would have been prohibitive before the accident.

Evidence of remedial measures is permissible whenever the defendant contends that it was *not feasible* to make the product or premises safe. For example, if the manufacturer of a drill press claims, by way of defense, that it was not feasible to install the type of guard which the plaintiff's expert says was needed, and without which the drill press was a defective product. The plaintiff could offer into evidence proof that the defendant modified the product after the accident by installing the type of guard which the plaintiff contends should have been in place before the accident. Again, the evidence of remedial measures is received on the basis that it impeaches the defendant's claim that the guard was not feasible.

Evidence that the defendant made subsequent changes to the property involved in a plaintiff's accident may be admissible to prove that the defendant was an owner of the property. The evidence is admissible to prove ownership only if the defendant, who made the repairs or changes after the accident, denies that he or she was the owner of the property (Rule 407).

Evidence of Conduct

Admissions may be made by conduct or silence. These are sometimes called verbal acts. For example, immediately following an automobile accident, one driver might accuse the other of failing to signal or failing to stop for a stop sign. If the person accused of wrongdoing fails to respond by denying the accusation, his or her silence, under some circumstances, may be considered to be an admission that the accusation was true. The test is whether, under the circumstances, one would ordinarily expect a denial if the accusation were false. Perhaps the party was hard of hearing or incapacitated due to injuries— then silence could not be considered to be an admission of fault.

If a party's "admission" is offered into evidence against him or her and the admission came out of a written statement, deposition, oral conversation, etc., the party who made the admission has a right to introduce into evidence the entire conversation or entire statement insofar as it relates to the "admission" in dispute. The Rules of Evidence do not allow parties to take alleged "admissions" out of context.

Rules 803 and 804 undertake to codify many of the exceptions to the hearsay rule. A detailed discussion of the exceptions goes beyond the scope of this book. They are quoted here for convenient reference.

RULE 801 *Definitions*

The following definitions apply under this article:
   (a) **Statement.** A "statement" is (1) an oral or written assertion or (2) nonverbal conduct of a person, if it is intended by him as an assertion.
   (b) **Declarant.** A "declarant" is a person who makes a statement.

(c) **Hearsay.** "Hearsay" is a statement, other than one made by the declarant while testifying at the trial or hearing, offered into evidence to prove the truth of the matter asserted.

(d) **Statements which are not hearsay.** A statement is not hearsay if:

(1) **Prior statement by witness.** The declarant testifies at the trial or hearing and is subject to cross-examination concerning the statement, and the statement is (A) inconsistent with his testimony, and was given under oath subject to the penalty of perjury at a trial, hearing, or other proceeding, or in a deposition, or (B) consistent with his testimony and is offered to rebut an express or implied charge against him of recent fabrication or improper influence or motive, or

(2) **Admission by party-witness.** The statement is offered against a party and is (A) his own statement, in either his individual or a representative capacity or, (B) a statement of which he has manifested his adoption or belief in its truth, or (C) a statement by a person authorized by him to make a statement concerning the subject, or (D) a statement by his agent or servant concerning a matter within the scope of his agency or employment, made during the existence of the relationship, or (E) a statement by a co-conspirator of a party during the course and in furtherance of the conspiracy.

RULE 802 *Hearsay Rule*

Hearsay is not admissible except as provided by these rules or by other rules prescribed by the Supreme Court pursuant to statutory authority or by Act of Congress.

RULE 803 *Hearsay Exceptions; Availability of Declarant Immaterial*

The following are not excluded by the hearsay rule, even though the declarant is available as a witness:

(1) **Present sense impression.** A statement describing or explaining an event or condition made while the declarant was perceiving the event or condition, or immediately thereafter.

(2) **Excited utterance.** A statement relating to a startling event or condition made while the declarant was under the stress of excitement caused by the event or condition.

(3) **Then existing mental, emotional, or physical condition.** A statement of the declarant's then existing state of mind, emotion, sensation, or physical condition (such as intent, plan, motive, design, mental feeling, pain, and bodily health), but not including a statement of memory or belief to prove the fact remembered or believed unless it relates to the execution, revocation, identification, or terms of declarant's will.

(4) **Statements for purposes of medical diagnosis or treatment.** Statements made for purposes of medical diagnosis or treatment and describing medical history, or past or present symptoms, pain, or sensations, or the inception or general character of the cause or external source thereof insofar as reasonably pertinent to diagnosis or treatment.

(5) **Recorded recollection.** A memorandum or record concerning a matter about which a witness once had knowledge but now has insufficient rec-

ollection to enable him to testify full and accurately, shown to have been made or adopted by the witness when the matter was fresh in his or her memory and to reflect that knowledge correctly. If admitted, the memorandum or record may be read into evidence but may not itself be received as an exhibit unless offered by an adverse party.

(6) **Records of regularly conducted activity.** A memorandum, report, record, or data compilation, in any form, of acts, events, conditions, opinions, or diagnoses, made at or near the time by, or from information transmitted by, a person with knowledge, if kept in the course of a regularly conducted business activity, and if it was the regular practice of that business activity to make the memorandum, report, record, or data compilation, all as shown by the testimony of the custodian or other qualified witness, unless the source of information or the method or circumstances of preparation indicate lack of trustworthiness. The term "business" as used in this paragraph includes business, institution, association, profession, occupation, and calling of every kind, whether or not conducted for profit.

(7) **Absence of entry in records kept in accordance with the provisions of paragraph (6).** Evidence that a matter is not included in the memoranda, reports, records, or data compilations, in any form, kept in accordance with the provisions of paragraph (6), to prove the nonoccurrence or nonexistence of the matter, if the matter was of a kind of which a memorandum, report, record, or data compilation was regularly made and preserved, unless the sources of information or other circumstances indicate lack of trustworthiness.

(8) **Public records and reports.** Records, reports, statements, or data compilations, in any form, of public offices or agencies, setting forth (A) the activities of the office or agency, or (B) matters observed pursuant to duty imposed by law as to which matters there was a duty to report, excluding, however, in criminal cases matters observed by police officers and other law enforcement personnel, or (C) in civil actions and proceedings and against the government in criminal cases, factual findings resulting from an investigation made pursuant to authority granted by law, unless the sources of information or other circumstances indicate lack of trustworthiness.

(9) **Records of vital statistics.** Records or date compilations, in any form, of births, fetal deaths, deaths, or marriages, if the report thereof was made to a public officer pursuant to requirements of law.

(10) **Absence of public record or entry.** To prove the absence of a record, report, statement, or data compilation, in any form, or the nonoccurrence or nonexistence of a matter of which a record, report, statement, or data compilation, in any form, was regularly made and preserved by a public office or agency, evidence in the form of a certification in accordance with Rule 902, or testimony that diligent search failed to disclose the record, report, statement, or data compilation, or entry.

(11) **Records of religious organizations.** Statements of births, marriages, divorces, deaths, legitimacy, ancestry, relationship by blood or marriage, or other similar facts of personal or family history, contained in a regularly kept record of a religious organization.

(12) **Marriage, baptismal, and similar certificates.** Statements of fact contained in a certificate that the maker performed a marriage or other ceremony or administered a sacrament, made by a clergyman, public official,

or other person authorized by the rules or practices of a religious organization or by law to perform the act certified, and purporting to have been issued at the time of the act or within a reasonable time thereafter.

(13) **Family records.** Statements of fact concerning personal or family history contained in family Bibles, genealogies, charts engravings on rings, inscriptions on family portraits, engravings on urns, crypts, or tombstones, or the like.

(14) **Records of documents affecting an interest in property.** The record of a document purporting to establish or affect an interest in property, as proof of the content of the original recorded document and its execution and delivery by each person by whom it purports to have been executed, if the record is a record of a public office and an applicable statute authorizes the recording of documents of that kind in that office.

(15) **Statements in documents affecting an interest in property.** A statement contained in a document purporting to establish or affect an interest in property if the matter stated was relevant to the purpose of the document, unless dealings with the property since the document was made have been inconsistent with the truth of the statement or the purport of the document.

(16) **Statements in ancient documents.** Statements in a document in existence twenty years or more the authenticity of which is established.

(17) **Market reports, commercial publications.** Market quotations, tabulations, lists, directories, or other published compilations, generally used and relied upon by the public or by persons in particular occupations.

(18) **Learned treatises.** To the extent called to the attention of an expert witness upon cross-examination or relied upon by him in direct examination, statements contained in published treatises, periodicals, or pamphlets on a subject of history, medicine, or other science or art, established as a reliable authority by the testimony or admission of the witness or by other expert testimony or by judicial notice. If admitted, the statements may be read into evidence but may not be received as exhibits.

(19) **Reputation concerning personal or family history.** Reputation among members of his family by blood, adoption, or marriage, or among his associates, or in the community, concerning a person's birth, adoption, marriage, divorce, death, legitimacy, relationship by blood, adoption, or marriage ancestry, or other similar fact of his personal or family history.

(20) **Reputation concerning boundaries or general history.** Reputation in a community, arising before the controversy, as to boundaries of or customs affecting lands in the community, and reputation as to events of general history important to the community or state or nation in which located.

(21) **Reputation as to character.** Reputation of a person's character among his associates or in the community.

(22) **Judgment of previous conviction.** Evidence of a final judgment, entered after a trial or upon a plea of guilty (but not upon a plea of nolo contendere), adjudging a person guilty of a crime punishable by death or imprisonment in excess of one year, to prove any fact essential to sustain the judgment, but not including, when offered by the government in a criminal prosecution for purposes other than impeachment, judgments against persons other than the accused. The pendency of an appeal may be shown but does not affect admissibility.

(23) Judgment as to personal family or general history, or boundaries. Judgments as proof of matters of personal, family or general history, or boundaries, essential to the judgment, if the same would be provable by evidence of reputation.

(24) Other exceptions. A statement not specifically covered by any of the foregoing exceptions but having equivalent circumstantial guarantees of trustworthiness, if the court determines that: (A) the statement is offered as evidence of a material fact; (B) the statement is more probative on the point for which it is offered than any other evidence which the proponent can procure through reasonable efforts; and (C) the general purposes of these rules and the interests of justice will best be served by admission of the statement into evidence. However, a statement may not be admitted under this exception unless the proponent of it makes known to the adverse party sufficiently in advance of the trial or hearing to provide the adverse party with a fair opportunity to prepare to meet it, his intention to offer the statement and the particulars of it, including the name and address of the declarant.

RULE 804 *Hearsay Exceptions: Declarant Unavailable*

(a) Definition of unavailability. "Unavailability" as a witness" includes situations in which the declarant:

(1) is exempted by ruling of the court on the ground of privilege from testifying concerning the subject matter of his statement; or

(2) persists in refusing to testify concerning the subject matter of his statement despite an order of the court to do so; or

(3) testifies to a lack of memory of the subject matter of his statement; or

(4) is unable to be present or to testify at the hearing because of death or then existing physical or mental illness or infirmity; or

(5) is absent from the hearing and the proponent of his statement has been unable to procure his attendance (or in the case of a hearsay exception under subdivision (b) (2), (3), or (4), his attendance or testimony) by process or other reasonable means.

A declarant is not unavailable as a witness if his exemption, refusal, claim of lack of memory, inability, or absence is due to the procurement or wrongdoing of the proponent of his statement for the purpose of preventing the witness from attending or testifying.

(b) Hearsay exceptions. The following are not excluded by the hearsay rule if the declarant is unavailable as a witness:

(1) **Former testimony.** Testimony given as a witness at another hearing of the same or a different proceeding, or in a deposition taken in compliance with law in the course of the same or another proceeding, if the party against whom the testimony is now offered, or, in a civil action or proceeding, a predecessor in interest, had an opportunity and similar motive to develop the testimony by direct, cross, or redirect examination.

(2) **Statement under belief of impending death.** In a prosecution for homicide or in a civil action or proceeding, a statement made by a declarant while believing that his death was imminent, concerning the cause or circumstances of what he believed to be his impending death.

(3) **Statement against interest.** A statement which was at the time of its making so far contrary to the declarant's pecuniary or proprietary interest, or so far tended to subject him or her to civil or criminal liability, or to render invalid a claim by him or her against another, that a reasonable man in his position would not have made the statement unless he believed it to be true. A statement tending to expose the declarant to criminal liability and offered to exculpate the accused is not admissible unless corroborating circumstances clearly indicate the trustworthiness of the statement.

(4) **Statement of personal or family history.** (A) A statement concerning the declarant's own birth, adoption, marriage, divorce, legitimacy, relationship by blood, adoption, or marriage, ancestry, or other similar fact of personal or family history, even though declarant had no means of acquiring personal knowledge of the matter stated; or (B) a statement concerning the foregoing matters, and death also, of another person, if the declarant was related to the other by blood, adoption, or marriage or was so intimately associated with the other's family as to be likely to have accurate information concerning the matter declared.

(5) **Other exceptions.** A statement not specifically covered by any of the foregoing exceptions but having equivalent circumstantial guarantees of trustworthiness, if the court determines that (A) the statement is offered as evidence of a material fact; (B) the statement is more probative on the point for which it is offered than any other evidence which the proponent can procure through reasonable efforts; (C) the general purposes of these rules and the interests of justice will best be served by admission of the statement into evidence. However, a statement may not be admitted under this exception unless the proponent of it makes known to the adverse party sufficiently in advance of the trial or hearing to provide the adverse party with a fair opportunity to prepare to meet it, his intention to offer the statement and the particulars of it, including the name and address of the declarant.

RULE 805 *Hearsay Within Hearsay*

Hearsay included within hearsay is not excluded under the hearsay rule if each part of the combined statements conforms with an exception to the hearsay rule provided in these rules.

21 Fact Brief

A fact brief is used to conduct a formal analysis of a case and to teach analysis of fact issues. Lawyers seldom take the time to prepare a fact brief; however, they must go through the same mental processes to determine the state of his or her preparation and the soundness of the evidence. A fact brief begins with a dissection of the pleadings and a determination of the remaining fact issues. The brief then itemizes and categorizes the fact issues. Finally, the brief discusses how each contested fact will be proved or disproved.

A fact brief is to be distinguished from a *trial brief* which is prepared for the information of the trial judge concerning matters of law. A trial brief ordinarily discusses facts but is not concerned with how those facts will be proved. A fact brief is for the benefit of the lawyer or paralegal who prepared it. Indeed, it is like a game plan which should be kept out of the hands of the opposition.

The sample fact brief in this chapter is concerned with an action to enforce a decedent's contract to make a will. The plaintiffs claim they had a contract with the testator-decedent by which he was going to bequeath his house to the plaintiffs if they would take care of him for the rest of his life. Unfortunately for the plaintiffs, the decedent's will left the house to the defendant. This fact brief is one prepared by the defendant's lawyer to guide his trial preparation. He wants to help the court sustain the will, thereby giving his client the house and defeating the plaintiffs' claim of a contract. The reader should note that the fact issues have been sharply delineated. The purpose of the brief is to compile, correlate, and analyze the evidence according to the legal issues.

ABSTRACT OF PLEADINGS

Complaint	Answer	Reply or no required
On June 7, 1980, plaintiffs and decedent entered into an agreement whereby plaintiffs agreed to give up their home and to move into decedent's house, and to take care of decedent and his house until his death.	Denied—that the plaintiff agreed to care for the decedent.	Responsive pleading
In consideration of the agreement, decedent promised to convey his house and lot at 74 Golf Terrace, Edison, Minnesota, to the plaintiffs.	Denied	
Plaintiffs gave up their home, moved in with William Brown, and fully performed their part of said agreement.	Denied—that plaintiffs performed their part of the agreement.	
Decedent devised his house to Edward Bordon in his will dated July 20, 1987, instead of devising his real property to the plaintiff as required by the agreement.	Denied—the existence of the agreement to devise decedent's property to the plaintiffs.	
Plaintiffs performed personal services valued at $30,000.	Denied—the performance of the services. No cause of action exists. Agreement is unenforceable because it is within the statute of frauds. Plaintiffs have been fully compensated by the salary of $100 per month, free rent and utilities, and the $2,0000 bequest in the decedent's will.	

ISSUES

1. There was no agreement between the decedent and the plaintiffs whereby the decedent agreed to devise his real property at 74 Golf Terrace, Edison, to the plaintiffs in return for their services.

2. The services were not satisfactorily performed by the plaintiffs, and therefore, they breached the contract, if there was one.

DEFENDANT'S CASE-IN-CHIEF

1. There was no agreement made between the plaintiffs and the decedent whereby the decedent promised to convey his real property at 74 Golf Terrace, Edison, Minnesota, in return for the performance of services by the plaintiffs, for the facts are as follows:

a. The complaint states that there was only one arrangement made between the plaintiffs and the decedent.

b. This arrangement was initiated and consummated on June 7, 1980, during a dinner party at the decedent's home, given in honor of Dr. Olson.

c. Negotiations and statements concerning the arrangement were made during a card game in the presence of Dr. Carl Olson, William Mitchell, John Hughes, and William Brown, the decedent.

d. The terms of the alleged arrangements were substantially these: The Hugheses agreed to move into the upstairs apartment of the decedent's home, and to take care of the yard and walks and perform other external maintenance on the house; in return the decedent agreed to pay the Hugheses $100 per month, and to provide the apartment and utilities at no cost.

e. At no time during the negotiations or the ensuing arrangement was any reference to or mention made concerning the decedent's house, or any agreement to devise said house to the plaintiffs at decedent's death.

f. This proposal was made by the decedent to John Hughes, and after a short discussion with Mrs. Hughes, the plaintiffs accepted these terms.

g. No mention was made by either party that the plaintiffs would be personally caring for the decedent.

The law is as follows:

> Whether a contract was made is primarily a question of fact to be determined by the trial court. The burden is upon the plaintiff to prove the fact of the contract and its terms. The terms of the contract must be definite and certain, and the contract must be established by clear and convincing evidence. The oral contract is within the statute of frauds and may be enforced only through an action in equity.

2. The plaintiffs failed to satisfactorily care for the decedent's house and yard as provided by the contract.

a. The plaintiffs failed to rake the leaves as a result of which the yard usually appeared unkept in the fall and spring and aroused ill will among several of the neighbors.

b. The plaintiffs failed to mow the grass at reasonable intervals, causing large portions of the lawn to become infested with crabgrass and other noxious weeds.

c. The plaintiffs were normally several months late in changing the storm windows and screens and failed entirely to change the storm windows in 1986.

d. The plaintiffs never shoveled the snow from the sidewalks.

e. The plaintiffs failed to remove an accumulation of ice from the front sidewalk, the accumulation having occurred from the runoff of an eaves spout. As a result, a passing neighbor fell and broke his ankle, and under threat of an action at law, decedent paid $750 to the claimant as a settlement.

f. The reason for the lack of care given to the maintenance of the yard and house, besides irresponsibility, can be attributed to the fact that the plaintiff was gainfully employed as a paintbrush salesman, and in carrying on his business, had little time to devote to the property.

g. The decedent did some of the outside work himself, when it became apparent that it would not otherwise be done.

h. The plaintiffs sporadically helped the decedent clean the lower floor of the house, and the decedent normally did his cleaning himself.

i. The decedent did his own cooking, laundry, and other personal duties.

j. The plaintiffs, although friendly with the decedent, remained a part from the decedent both in their everyday life and social activities. Mrs. Hughes was often out with her friends and entertained often in the apartment.

k. Robert Burger, decedent's attorney, acted as decedent's financial advisor and kept all of his accounts.

l. As compensation for the arrangement, the plaintiffs received $100 per month, free rent, and utilities. They also received a bequest of $2,000 in the decedent's will.

m. Decedent was at all times in good physical condition and capable of caring for himself.

The law is as follows:

When an oral agreement is made unenforceable by the statute of frauds and does not merit specific performance, the plaintiff may recover only damages for services rendered under the agreement under the theory of quasi contract, and the measure of such recovery will be the value of the services rendered less the benefits the plaintiffs received under the contract. Nor can the plaintiff recover damages for breach of the oral contract. The value of the property to be devised is not a measure of recovery.

To recover specific performance, the terms of the contract must be definite and certain. The services must be performed under the terms of the contract. To merit specific performance, the services must be of a peculiar and personal nature. If the part performance of the contract is as beneficial to the plaintiff as to the deceased, specific performance will not be allowed.

ANTICIPATED CASE OF PLAINTIFF

1. There was an oral contract in which the decedent promised to devise his house and lot to the plaintiffs: "If you come live with me and care for me and my house until I die, I will devise you my house." Mr. Hughes, "I accept."

Meet this by disputing the terms of the alleged contract, and by contending that these terms do not specify that the plaintiffs were to assume a peculiar domestic relationship with the decedent.

2. That the plaintiffs are entitled to recover $30,000 for the value of the services that they performed.

Meet this by showing the services were not fully and adequately performed. Show what the proper measure of recovery is, and show that the plaintiffs have been fully compensated. Show the plaintiffs' failure to present their claim in probate court. Also show the actual value of the services that the plaintiffs allegedly performed.

3. That decedent has made statements to neighbors to the effect that the plaintiffs were to receive the property when the decedent died.

Meet this by showing that the witness is a friend of the plaintiffs and is biased. Show that plaintiffs never objected to the will. Also show that the plaintiffs made statements adverse to their pecuniary interest.

4. Plaintiffs will testify as to their close relationship with the decedent.

Meet this by showing that the decedent addressed the plaintiffs by their last names and did not appear well acquainted with them at the party on June 7, 1980. Show that decedent was interested in activities with his own friends, that he was independent and capable, and that the relation was merely friendly. Show that Mr. Hughes worked a large number of hours per week, and that Mrs. Hughes was absorbed with her friends and community interests.

5. Plaintiffs will testify that they gave up a lease at a loss of $100, a $5,000 per year job, and friends in moving from Anoka.

Meet this by showing that plaintiffs moved into a nice apartment, had many new friends, and that the plaintiff appeared to be fully employed.

MEMO OF TESTIMONY-IN-CHIEF FOR DEFENDANT

1. William Mitchell, witness
  a. *As to relationship with decedent—*
   Long time friend.
   Did work for same railroad. Now retired.
   Lives at 72 Golf Terrace.
   Hunting and fishing companion of decedent.
   Conversation with decedent about getting someone to help him.
   Suggested calling minister.
   Decedent told him of the minister's suggestion.
  b. *As to the oral agreement—*
   Was invited to the dinner party of the decedent on June 7, 1980.
   Purpose of the party.
   Was with decedent when Olson asked if he could bring plaintiff.
   Was a member of the card game and heard negotiations.

Heard the terms: $100 per month, apartment and utilities for services.
Was with decedent at all times during evening and helped straighten up.

c. *As to the will—*

Was present when drawn up.
Made on July 20, 1981, in evening.
Presence of the plaintiffs.

d. *Quality of the work performed—*

Always had seasonal work done much before plaintiffs.
William Brown did some of the yard work.
Plaintiffs repainted porch, but it had to be repainted.
Specific items of disrepair and unperformed or misperformed services.
Decedent did own cooking, and enjoyed it.
Decedent did his own housecleaning, and laundry professionally.

e. *As to decedent's health—*

Decedent's health was excellent for his age.
Accompanied decedent on hunting and fishing trips.
Decedent's illness of 1981 a mild heart attack.
Recovery in one and one-half months—two-week confinement to house.
Subsequent to illness, sound as before—fishing, officer in church.

f. *As to plaintiff's living quarters—*

Complete apartment in second floor of decedent's house.
Originally furnished for Paul Smith and wife while going to university.
Outside entrance.

2. Robert Burger, witness

a. *As to the will of decedent—*

Called to hospital on July 20, 1981, to draw up will.
Reads the will to court after identifying signature.
That plaintiffs were present when will was made.
All persons in position to hear provisions—read provisions to decedent.
Plaintiffs did not object to provisions and have not to date.
Decedent specific and clear on provisions he desired.

b. *As to decedent's financial matters—*

Decedent a client for ten years.
Took care of all monthly expenses as decedent did not wish to be bothered.
Paid taxes, utilities, and other monthly bills.
Paid the plaintiffs $100 per month by check.
Canceled checks sent to decedent—does not know of their whereabouts.
Paid threatened claim in amount of $750 as a settlement.
Thought claim valid because unnatural condition.
Took over decedent's investments in 1982.
Told by decedent that plaintiff incompetent to invest and lost money.
Finally back into stable securities.

c. *As to the upstairs apartment in decedent's house—*
Knew of the previous occupancy by Smith and wife.
Had advised what kitchen equipment to buy.
Has gone through it—five rooms and bath—all necessary facilities.
Expert in real estate—sells—buys—has made many leases.
Familiar with decedent's neighborhood and price of apartments.
Rental value $100 plus utilities.

d. *As to decedent's health—*
Saw him every month or two during the six years.
As alert and active after the illness as before.

3. Allen Anderson, witness

a. *As to the quality of work done by the plaintiffs—*
Went by decedent's house everyday on way to the bus.
Grass never cut on time—crab grass and noxious weed set in.
Storms and screens never changed on time.
Storms never removed in 1986.
Sidewalks never shoveled, except for a few times when decedent did it.
Leaves never raked unless decedent did it—heard neighbor complain.
Saw plaintiff painting porch, later saw another painter doing it.
Fell on sidewalk and fractured left ankle.
Off work for three weeks.
Told attorney to start action, but settled with decedent for $750.
Fall occurred from hump of ice which had accumulated from eaves spout.

b. *As to plaintiff's hours away from home—*
Many times saw plaintiff leaving house at 8:00 A.M.
Often noticed him driving into the yard at about 5:00 P.M.
Was given a ride to work by plaintiff several times.
Plaintiff told him business good and working long hours.
Business rushing during spring, summer, and fall according to plaintiff.

c. *As to plaintiff's statements adverse to his interest—*
During one ride, plaintiff said hated to leave house when old man died.
During another ride, said too bad the old man had relatives.
State that witness had nothing against plaintiff; thought him O.K.

MEMO OF ANTICIPATED TESTIMONY FOR PLAINTIFF

1. Raymond Quin, friend of decedent's, will probably be called to testify to the terms of the oral agreement.
   a. See that he testifies only to facts within his own knowledge.
   b. Determine his relation with the plaintiffs. Impeach by use of friendly witness by showing intimacy with the plaintiffs.
   c. Test his certainty of the agreement.
   d. Have him corroborate the purpose of the party.

2. John Hughes, plaintiff, will probably be called to testify to the extent of his services and also to the oral agreement.

 a. See that he testifies only to facts within his own knowledge.

 b. See that he does not testify to any part of the oral agreement.

 c. Bring out the fact that he is an interested party.

 d. Impeach on investments and personal services by friendly witnesses.

3. George Robb, friend of decedent's, will probably be called to testify to the quality of services performed by the plaintiffs, and subsequent statements of decedent indicating his obligation to plaintiffs.

 a. See that he testifies only to facts within his own knowledge.

 b. Determine how he observed the performance of the services.

 c. Counter subsequent admissions by plaintiffs' statements to Anderson.

Lawyers ordinarily do not sit down and diagram issues or write fact briefs. Some cases are so simple or routine that a written fact brief would be of no value; however, every lawyer goes through the procedure in his or her mind when preparing a case for trial. Each lawyer must prepare a case in the manner which is most effective for him or her. For example, there are some lawyers who believe that putting together a good final argument is the place to begin. They feel that the argument will determine what evidence they need to develop and the manner in which the evidence should be presented.

A legal assistant may be asked to prepare an analysis of the facts in light of legal issues stated by the lawyer who is preparing the case. The analysis method could be similar to the above. It is almost as important, in these exercises, to anticipate the opponent's case as to define and develop the client's case.

22 Trial Preparation

Court Calendars

Most courts have periodic calendar calls for the purpose of scheduling cases for trial. The judge selects a group of cases, usually on the basis of age from the date of filing, to be placed on the calendar. The cases are listed chronologically. In some jurisdictions the calendar may have fifty or more cases. The lawyers must appear at court for the call of the calendar. At that time the judge inquires whether the cases are ready for trial and whether there are any scheduling problems that need to be considered. Usually cases are not placed on the calendar for trial unless the parties are ready for trial. If there is a good reason why a case cannot be tried during the current term of court, the case may be stricken from the "ready calendar." The remaining cases are scheduled for hearing. The order in which the cases are set is determined by the age of the case and availability of the lawyers, parties, and witnesses. The court establishes an order of priority for the cases as a result of the information obtained and decisions made at the calendar call. Usually the clerk of court prepares a new list of the cases showing the order in which the cases will be tried during that term of court.

The parties are notified concerning their relative positions on the calendar. Each lawyer tries to determine when his or her particular case will be reached for trial by keeping in contact with the lawyers on the preceding cases. The clerk of court can also help in that regard, but the clerk's estimates concerning the probable length of the preceding trial is usually not as good as the lawyers' estimates. Sometimes some cases are given *day certain* settings. This means that those cases are given a high priority and will be started on a specified date. The court clears its calendar of all other matters so that the case can begin at the designated time. Day certain settings are reserved for cases which involve numerous parties or many witnesses, especially if they have to travel long distances to attend the trial.

Sometimes courts are unable to dispose of all the cases which had been set for trial during the term. Those cases which are not reached are usually given a priority setting at the next calendar call to insure that they will not be passed over again. A court's inability to try the cases as scheduled may cause the parties considerable expense and frustration. Nevertheless, no one has been able to devise a system that completely solves this problem. The parties' convenience is weighed against the need to keep the courts active. If courts did not schedule "too many" cases, it is probable that they would run out of work before the end of the term. Considering the current delay that parties are experiencing in getting their cases concluded, it is probably better for the courts to schedule too many cases for hearing during a term, rather than run the risk of running out of work.

When a lawyer receives a trial date, he or she must notify the client and all of the witnesses so that they can arrange their schedules to be available. Subpoenas may be used to require witnesses and even parties to attend court at a specified time. The word "subpoena" means that the person served is subject to penalties provided by law if that person disregards the court's command. The only means that a lawyer has for compelling a reluctant witness to come to court is to serve a subpoena upon the witness. Parties are already under the court's jurisdiction so they can be ordered to attend the trial and testify and produce evidence. Without a subpoena or court order, however, a witness could elect not to attend. Lawyers are responsible for having their witnesses in court at the time they are needed. By serving a subpoena upon a witness or party the onus shifts from the lawyer to the person subpoenaed to be at court at the designated time. If the subpoenaed witness does not show up, the lawyer who needs the testimony or other evidence which is in the witness's possession is in a good position to obtain a continuance of the trial or even an order for a mistrial because of the unavailability of the evidence. A party who has taken the precaution of subpoenaing a reluctant or forgetful witness cannot be blamed for the witness's failure to come to court at the designated time. A party's inability to proceed is justifiable.

Usually the parties have at least one week's time between the calendar call and the commencement of the trial. Once the series of trials begins, a party may have no more than a half day's notice. When the clerk of court calls during the morning hours to tell the lawyer that his or her case will begin at 1:30 P.M., a paralegal can provide invaluable help by getting everything ready to go. Obviously, the parties cannot wait until the calendar call to begin their trial preparation.

Continuances

If a case has been placed on the calendar for trial but the parties agree that it really is not ready, the court will usually accept the parties' stipulation to have the case stricken. If a case is stricken under such circumstances, it may be reinstated by stipulation, which leads to the appropriate court order, or the case may be reinstated by motion made by one or both of the parties. If a party is not ready to go to trial because he or she has been dilatory, however, the court has authority to order the case to trial regardless of the difficulty, or even disastrous consequences, that an immediate trial may have for the dilatory party. A party's neglect or dilatory conduct should not work to the prejudice or disadvantage of any other party. Otherwise, a dilatory party could obstruct justice. Justice should not be delayed. A good case, whether for the plaintiff or defendant, tends to deteriorate with the passage of time. Consequently, a poor case tends to improve with the passage of time.

Pretrial Conferences

Many trial courts use pretrial conferences to facilitate trial preparation and the disposition of cases (Rule 16). A pretrial conference is a meeting between the judge to whom the case has been assigned and the lawyers for the purpose of facilitating trial preparation and the trial. Another important function is to stimulate settlement negotiations. A pretrial conference may be ordered on the court's own initiative or upon request by one of the parties. The lawyers are required to attend. The parties may be required to attend. If an insurance company is interested in the case, although not a named party, the insurance company's representative is often invited to attend the conference. There is a question whether the court can order the insurance representative to attend. If the insurer is controlling settlement negotiations, it is particularly important for the insurer to be represented at the conference.

Rule 16 lists the following objectives for having pretrial conferences:

1. simplification of the fact issues and the legal issues;
2. determining the necessity of amending the pleadings and establishing time limitations for doing it;
3. consider the possibility of obtaining parties' admissions to uncontroverted facts;
4. consider limiting the number of expert witnesses;
5. consider referring the matter to arbitration or mediation or a referee;
6. consider any other matters which may aid the court in facilitating a disposition of the case.

Simplification of the issues means that the parties, with the judge's help, should try to eliminate claims and defenses which no longer have any validity. It is common for parties to allege claims and defenses in their pleadings that they expect to be able to prove, which subsequent investigation shows to have no basis in fact. The court tries to persuade the lawyers to voluntarily dismiss such claims and defenses. For example, if at the time the defendant interposed the answer he believed that the plaintiff's claim would be barred by the statute of limitations, but new information shows that the statute of limitations is not applicable, the defendant should withdraw that defense. A party who fails to withdraw a claim or defense which does not have merit is subject to sanctions (see Rule 11).

If a party is unwilling to admit facts which he or she knows are true, any claim or defense based upon those facts is considered to be "frivolous." Any party who prosecutes a frivolous defense or claim is subject to sanctions and possibly to disciplinary action. The sanctions may include the assessment of costs, an order striking the party's pleadings, or even an award of judgment in favor of the opposing party. A lawyer and/or party could even be held in contempt of court.

The pretrial conference is a time to correct or amend pleadings as needed. The need for amendments may arise from new information which the party obtained after the pleading was served. Of course, Rule 15 provides the means for amending pleadings by motion. But the pretrial conference presents the ideal time to take care of such "housekeeping" matters and may present the last opportunity to do so. The plenary power of the court enables the court to order amendments at the pretrial conference even though no notice of motion was served by the party who wants the amendment.

The pretrial conference gives the judge and lawyers the opportunity to discuss the anticipated evidence. If the parties can reach an agreement on relevant facts, the court's pretrial order will specify the agreement. The effect is similar to a signed stipulation or Rule 36 admission. Much time and expense can be saved if the parties can agree to the receipt in evidence of documents without requiring witnesses to lay the foundation by which the documents are identified. For example, it is very common for the parties to agree to foundation for use of the plaintiff's hospital records without requiring someone from the hospital to come to court to identify the records. It is also common for the parties to stipulate that copies of records may be used at trial in place of the originals. Agreements of this type, which are reached at the pretrial conference, are reiterated in the court's subsequent pretrial order.

The court may determine that the case raises a particularly difficult legal issue concerning the evidence, jury instructions, constitutional issues, or other legal problems. The court may order the lawyers to file memoranda of law concerning the particular issue or issues. The memoranda may be due at the time of trial or before. Or, the court may schedule another pretrial conference for the purpose of dealing with the issues.

Usually courts hold pretrial conferences a few weeks before trial. A pretrial conference gives the court another opportunity to determine whether the case is ready for trial and, if not, what more needs to be done. Pretrial conferences may be held before or after the calendar call.

District courts are authorized to issue scheduling orders for the purpose of insuring active case management. A scheduling order may place time limits for joining other parties to the case, for amending the pleadings to include new issues, for making motions, and for completing discovery. The schedules are subject to modification upon a showing that more time is needed, but a lack of diligence is not good cause for obtaining more time. A scheduling order usually contemplates a subsequent pretrial conference.

Trial Strategy

There is no one moment when the discovery and investigation phases of a case end and the trial preparation phase begins. But, for purposes of this chapter we shall assume that the parties have obtained all of the information they need to evaluate the case. The evidence has been collected and preserved. The witnesses have been located and interviewed. Each witness has been committed to a version of the facts either by way of a deposition or signed statement. Admissions have been made pursuant to Rule 36. The parties resolved some disputes through written stipulations filed with the court. Nevertheless, the parties have not been able to settle the case. And now the parties must prepare for trial.

Trial strategy dictates that legal theories be considered in light of the available evidence. If one theory has a good deal of support in the evidence, that is the theory to emphasize and build upon. Also, legal theories must be considered in light of the impact that one legal theory may have on the other. For example, assume that the facts of the case are such that the plaintiff may be entitled to recover punitive damages from the defendant as well as compensatory damages. It seems logical to pursue both claims; however, there are some ramifications to be considered. Suppose that the defendant has no assets out of which to pay the punitive damages, and his liability insurance policy does not cover punitive damages. In that event there is considerable likelihood that the plaintiff would never be able to collect on an award for punitive damages. That fact must be considered in conjunction with the common belief that juries tend to award less compensatory damages when they have awarded punitive damages. By pursuing a punitive damages claim the net effect might well be to reduce the client's net recovery of damages. Therefore, the better strategy may be to give up a potential claim for punitive damages. All of this points out the importance of looking at the case as a whole—the big picture. It also emphasizes that a paralegal must be aware of the case strategy in order to appreciate what work needs to be done and how it should be done.

Each party usually acquires a mass of information and evidence which must be organized and evaluated. The evidence must be prepared so that it can be used at court and be presented most effectively. The witnesses must be prepared to testify. They cannot be told *what* to say, but they can be helped with *how* to testify. All of these activities and concerns come under the general heading of trial preparation. Trial preparation has the additional value of helping the parties to further evaluate the case for purposes of settlement.

Each party needs to develop a plan for presenting his or her case-in-chief and a plan for meeting the opponent's case-in-chief. In some respects, preparing a trial plan and strategy is like a game of chess. There must be an overall plan with a grand strategy. But the players must remain flexible so they can deal with changing circumstances. There are moves and counter-moves. The strategy includes the use of various means for dealing with the opponent's moves. For example, the opponent is known to have a very strong witness concerning a crucial fact. The trial strategy must take into consideration the best method of proving the fact and either block the adverse witness's anticipated testimony or reduce its effectiveness. The witness may be countered or even neutralized in various ways. He may be contradicted by two witnesses who are totally unbiased, or there may be a way of impeaching the witness by his own prior statements, or a rule of evidence may be used to keep his testimony from being heard by the jury, or there may be circumstantial evidence available which effectively contradicts the witness. The point is that trial strategy must deal with many variables. Lawyers may strongly disagree over the best strategy to use. Furthermore, the strategy that works for one lawyer may not work for another lawyer.

Organizing the Evidence

The case must be evaluated as a whole. What evidence is available? What does it tend to prove? The analysis may begin with a hypothesis which supports the client's version of the transaction or occurrence. The weight of the evidence should appear to support the hypothesis. Usually there are some or many conflicts in the evidence. The next step is to determine whether the conflicts are real or merely apparent. Apparent conflicts may arise out of a misunderstanding of the evidence or false assumptions about the facts. The evidence must be examined objectively.

Organizing the evidence involves determining what evidence is now available, what needs to be obtained, and what needs to be prepared. Presumably the answers to interrogatories, deposition transcripts, witness statements, photographs, and documents are readily available. If expert testimony will be presented, there are probably reports in the file. The important information must be extracted. It must be determined just how the evidence can and should be presented. For example, foundation for the admissibility of hospital records could be established by the hospital administrator or by stipulation or maybe through a treating physician who made entries in the records and is otherwise familiar with how they are kept. Each method of introducing the records has its own benefits and disadvantages. For example, a representative from the hospital may be more impressive but also more time consuming and expensive. It must be determined whether the tangible evidence is in the best form for presentation. Should documents and photographs be enlarged? Should illustrative exhibits be created? These are exhibits which help a witness to explain his or her testimony. For example, it may be apparent that the client will have great difficulty explaining how the automobile collision occurred; however, if he has a scale drawing of the intersection, he could do a much better job. Then a scale drawing should be obtained. Again, it is important to keep in mind that each item of evidence presented by a party should complement all of the other evidence.

In the organization and pretrial analysis of the evidence lawyers contemplate using the evidence in such a way that the evidence builds from one fact to another and each item of evidence supports the other items of evidence. A good example of using items of evidence for mutual support is in medical malpractice cases where the defendant physician has medical and hospital records made contemporaneously with the treatment in question. Entries are made by the physician and by other personnel. The physician's testimony should find support in the records, so that the records and testimony complement each other. If there is a significant inconsistency, even a suspicious omission, the physician's case is in trouble.

One of the best ways of avoiding traps created by false assumptions is to become personally acquainted with the subject matter of the case. If the case involves an occurrence, examine the site of the occurrence—not just the photographs. An inspection of an accident site may show why one witness could make an observation that another witness at another location could not make. If the case involves a transaction, such as a contract to build a structure, examine the structure—not just the written contract. Seeing the structure will give the lawyer and legal assistant a better feel for the case. Personal knowledge provides an invaluable basis upon which to conduct an analysis of the evidence. Personal knowledge is often crucial to an effective cross-examination.

A detailed analysis must be made of all the facts and the evidence by which those facts are to be proved. Details are very important, because details give credibility and persuasiveness to the client's case. If the details are carefully developed and kept consistent, the rest of the case takes care of itself.

Alternative approaches to presenting the evidence must be considered. Yet, one must never lose sight of the big picture. A party must not become beguiled by his or her own case. Lawyers must consciously strive to be objective about the evidence, the facts, law, and application of the law. If the lawyer does not see any problem in his or her case, the lawyer needs to look again and look harder. If you have the impression that conscientious trial preparation is a complicated, difficult process, you are correct. On the other hand, it does become easier with experience. There is logic and reason to what must be done.

Preparation

The amount of time that a lawyer has available to prepare for trial varies from case to case and from court to court. As a general rule, the sooner the preparation is begun, the better. But some phases of the preparation are ephemeral and the value of the efforts fades with passage of time. Some facets of the preparation are less affected by the passage of time than others. In particular, the organization and analysis of documents comes within this category. On the other hand, the preparation of individual witnesses to testify must be done shortly before each witness is to take the stand. Usually, the trial preparation continues even into the trial phase. In spite of diligent effort in the discovery phase of the case, all too often new evidence comes to light during the trial. A legal assistant who is familiar with the case can provide invaluable help in dealing with such evidence. As a legal assistant gains experience he or she should be able to assume increased responsibility for initiating and conducting trial preparation.

There is no established formula to guide trial preparation. Deciding when to begin each phase of the preparation is a matter of judgment. Nevertheless, there are some fundamental considerations which are applicable to most cases. A review of them should be helpful in understanding the process.

The preparation should begin with an analysis of the client's claim (causes of action) or legal defenses. Is the client's legal position sound? Should the case be forced to trial? Does the case have jury appeal? What is the best that the client can hope to gain from a trial? Is the anticipated expense of a trial justified? Could a trial have an adverse impact or consequences for the client, the client's family, or the client's business? Can the client's case or defense be proved through the available evidence? Is the evidence admissible? Is the evidence credible? Is the evidence persuasive? The same questions should be asked about the opponent's claims or defenses. Each item of evidence must be examined and evaluated in light of common sense and experience.

Pragmatic trial preparation requires a review of the legal issues and then the fact issues. It must be determined what evidence is necessary to prove a prima facie case and to prove the alleged affirmative defenses. After determining that there is sufficient evidence, which is admissible at trial, to establish the client's claim or defense, the next step is to determine how best to present the evidence for its maximum effect. This means conducting a thorough analysis of all the available evidence. Remember, that even though the court may order a termination of discovery procedures well before trial, the right to investigate never ends. The parties may keep looking for more evidence even during the trial. Of course, new witnesses and new documents, etc. must be disclosed on a timely basis.

The facts which have been established by the pleadings and admissions made in response to Rule 36 requests for admissions do not required evidence to be proved at trial. They are conclusively established. The jury will be told that those facts are established and the jury is to accept those facts as un-controvertible. Therefore, as part of the overall trial strategy each party ought to make a conscious effort not to present evidence which is in conflict with those established facts, because the evidence is impeached by the judicial admissions.

A party should be careful not to present evidence which is inconsistent with incontrovertible physical facts. Such evidence is not believable. Conse-quently, the presentation of such evidence reflects adversely against the party who offers it. For example, if the defendant's answer admits that defendant's automobile struck the plaintiff's automobile, it is self-defeating to try to offer any testimony that is contrary to the admission. If the admission is in error, the admission should be corrected, assuming that is possible. Similarly, if the plaintiff has good photographs showing that the defendant's automobile left skid marks twenty feet in length leading to the point of collision, it would be counterproductive to offer "eyewitness" testimony that the defendant did not try to stop before the collision. On occasion the plaintiff's lawyer is faced with the problem that his or her client may want to testify that the defendant's car was traveling thirty miles per hour, or more, when it struck the plaintiff's car; however, photographs show that the contact caused only a slight dent in a fender and the repair bill is consistent with only minor damage. If the plaintiff were to *mistakenly* testify to a thirty-mile-per-hour collision, the tes-timony would adversely reflect upon the plaintiff's credibility. The plaintiff's testimony is in conflict with common experience and the physical facts. The trial strategy and preparation must deal with this kind of problem.

The process of organizing and evaluating the evidence usually begins with a review of the investigation materials, interrogatory answers, experts reports, and oral deposition transcripts. Some of the evidence which seemed very important in the early stages of the case may be less significant at this stage because of stipulations or admissions made pursuant to Rule 36. On the other hand, some evidence which, at first, seemed minor may have become critical in the case because it bears on an apparent conflict in the anticipated testi-mony. Some lawyers like to begin the organization of the evidence after composing their final arguments. They decide what they want to be able to tell the jury. Then, insofar as possible, they try to make sure that the evidence will support the proposed argument.

A legal assistant may take a major role in preparing a client for trial. As part of the trial preparation, it is useful to explain to the client the legal claims, the legal defenses, the evidence which is available to both sides, the process of getting ready for trial, and the trial procedures. This information will help the client feel more comfortable about the upcoming trial and confident that he or she is being well represented.

Preparing the Client to Testify

The client needs to establish rapport with the jury. Unless the client has been schooled in public relations work, he or she will need a lot of help. The client must be helped to look and feel comfortable, not only while testifying, but throughout the trial. The hallmarks of a good witness are *sincerity* and *au-thority*. The appearance of sincerity comes from the testimony, the manner of testifying, posture, demeanor, manner of dress, grooming, etc. The appearance of authority comes from an ability to remember and relate the facts, concern for the details, consistency with the physical facts, and an attitude of confidence without being arrogant or overbearing.

The client was probably told, in preparation for his or her deposition, to answer the question with a short answer, not to explain the answer, and not to volunteer information. That was good advice for handling the discovery deposition; however, it is not the correct advice for testifying at trial to a judge and jury. The deposition was an information-gathering process. The presentation at court is for the purpose of proving and persuading. A witness who merely answers each question with a short, defensive statement is not going to be persuasive. The short answers would probably make the witness look evasive and defensive. Instead, the client must be coached to tell his or her version in an open narrative manner. The client should seize upon every question as an opportunity to tell the jury what the jury needs to know about the case; however, it takes a lot of preparation to make that kind of a presentation without appearing egotistical. The first step is to get the client to testify using full sentences, not just single words and short phrases.

If the client's deposition was taken, the client should be given a copy of the transcript to *study*. The client should review the transcript before preparing for the direct examination and cross-examination to be conducted at trial. The significant points in the deposition may be highlighted. The client should be encouraged to write down questions as they occur. The questions can be answered during the next meeting. If the client does not write down the questions and suggestions, it is likely that he or she will forget some of them before the next meeting. Then the client tends to worry that he or she has overlooked something. This is a source of anxiety which can be avoided.

The best preparation is an actual direct examination and cross-examination. This will uncover the problems and weaknesses in the client's testimony. The client should be asked a few "trick" questions which assume facts that are favorable to the opposition. Help the client to deal with such questions to the point that there really is little need to object to improper questions because the client has "all the answers." The client should write down the important facts and figures. This will help the client's recall. But it must be made clear to the client that he or she will not be taking any notes to the witness stand. The client may take a copy of the deposition transcript and other tangibles which will be exhibits, but nothing else.

Is there a danger that the client can know his or her "story" so well it appears fabricated? Not really. That certainly could happen if the client undertakes to memorize prepared testimony. It is important to know the facts and have them committed to memory. But that is quite different from memorizing a line of testimony. If the client briefly reflects on each question before answering, then answers in a deliberate manner while looking into the jurors' eyes and occasionally looking at the lawyer who is asking the questions, the client should appear very credible.

The following recommendations for testifying in court before a judge and jury should be helpful:

1. Develop a positive attitude about the trial and about the jury. Look upon the trial as an opportunity to obtain deserved justice.

2. Be polite in and out of the courtroom. Do not overreact to the evidence or anything else that happens in the course of the trial. Never lose your temper. Do not make jokes. Regardless of what happens, be calm and deliberate. Be relaxed as much as possible. If you become irritated, tired, confused, or physically uncomfortable, ask for a short recess or just a drink of water.

3. Try to keep the "big picture" in mind. It provides a frame of reference. Become acquainted with what the other witnesses will probably say when they testify. If the testimony of other witnesses conflicts with yours in some significant respect, be sure you know why the conflict exists and know how you are going to deal with the fact of the conflict when on the witness stand.

4. Avoid discussing confidential matters in the presence of strangers, other witnesses, or jurors. The privilege status of attorney-client communications is lost if another person is permitted to hear or see the communication.

5. Make written notes about important developments during the trial so they can be discussed later.

6. Act interested and sincere on the stand or anywhere you might be observed by members of the jury.

7. When a lawyer asks a question, whether on direct examination or cross-examination, look at the lawyer. When answering the questions look at the jury about two-thirds of the time and the lawyer who asked the question about one-third of the time. Avoid looking at the ceiling, out the window, or at the floor. Do not steal furtive glances at "your" lawyer as if to say: "I really made a good point!" or "Please help me!"

8. Explain your answer when it seems appropriate. A witness has the right to answer fully. This right cannot be abridged or defeated by the lawyers. If the lawyer objects that the answer is not responsive or went beyond the question, you should not feel as though you did anything wrong, as long as you felt that your answer was relevant to the question.

9. If you realize that you have given an incorrect answer, correct the mistake as soon as you realize it. You can simply tell the judge that you want to correct something you said earlier and the judge will tell you that you may speak now or that it can be taken care of when your lawyer has the opportunity to ask questions. Your request will be a signal to your lawyer that you have something more to say about a matter already covered.

10. Avoid expressions such as: "To tell you the truth" or "To be honest with you" or "To the best of my knowledge." If you believe that the testimony is true, there is no need or reason to qualify it. These phrases weaken the testimony and take away from the witness's authority. If you are dealing with an *estimate* or *judgment* use those words. Remember that a mere *guess* will not be received into evidence.

11. Avoid exaggerating and minimizing.

12. Visit the accident location and study it. Compare the site with photographs of the scene and diagrams which may be used as exhibits.

13. Do not argue, fence, or joke with the lawyers while you are on the witness stand. Statements of disagreement should not be made in a disagreeable manner.

14. If a lawyer tries to put you on the defensive by starting a question with "Do you admit that . . ." it may be appropriate to tell him or her that you do not know what is meant by "admit," but you do *agree* with the statement or suggestion.

15. Do not deny that you prepared yourself to take the stand by reading your deposition transcript, viewing the accident scene, examining the exhibits, and conferring with your lawyer. But do not let the opposing lawyer suggest that you do not have an independent recollection of the facts to which you have testified. You cannot testify to something that someone else has written or based upon what you heard from someone else. Your testimony must be based upon what you observed and know of your own knowledge. You may testify from something that you wrote when the information was fresh in your mind. But then the writing becomes the best evidence, and the entire writing may come into evidence whether you want it to or not.

16. Do not refer to insurance unless specifically advised by your lawyer, before taking the witness stand, that "insurance" is a proper subject in the case. The judge, lawyers, and other witnesses will carefully avoid mentioning insurance, because there is the belief that jurors might be too generous if they thought they were awarding insurance benefits. An improper reference to insurance could cause a mistrial.

The client should be informed about the procedures which will be followed at trial so that the client understands what is happening as it happens. The client will be more comfortable knowing that the case is proceeding as it should. The client should be told that the lawyers will meet with the judge in his or her chambers for a few minutes to discuss questions of law, scheduling of witnesses, preliminary motions, and the possibility of settlement. The jury will be selected. The client will be asked for his or her input as to which veniremen should be stricken. Therefore, the client should pay close attention to the selection process. The client should listen carefully to the opening statements. The client can catch any misstatements which his or her lawyer might make and tell the lawyer about them. That gives the lawyer a chance to correct the problem, if any, later on in the trial. The client should listen carefully to the opposing lawyer's opening statement, because the lawyer usually explains exactly how he or she is going to prove the case. This is a good preview of what the opposition has to offer.

The client should be forewarned that, as a party, he or she may be called for cross-examination by the opponent during the opponent's case-in-chief (Rule 43(b)). The more familiar the client is with the procedures, the more comfortable the client will be. If the client is comfortable, the client can make a better presentation. Remember, the hallmarks of a good witness are sincerity and authority.

Preparation of Witnesses

The file should contain the witness's home address, business address, telephone numbers, and the names and telephone numbers of other persons who know how to contact the witness, such as relatives, co-workers, etc. Locate witnesses before they are actually needed. Do not take chances on a witness's availability. The sooner a "witness problem" is discovered the easier it is to obtain help, or at least consideration, from the court. Make sure necessary witnesses are available to attend the trial as scheduled. Make sure that the witness can be contacted on short notice. Each witness must be prepared to testify. Some witnesses require a great deal more preparation than others. For example, an experienced police officer who testifies in court regularly may not be interested in help learning to testify. Nevertheless, some preparation would be useful so that the officer can be told what the issues are. The better the officer understands the issues, the better he or she can focus on the problem. The officer probably has a wealth of information which he or she could present, but much of what the officer could say may be unimportant because it may not be relevant to *contested* facts. Every case is unique, so even experienced witnesses can benefit from a little preparation. Of course, preparation of the witness results in preparation of the lawyer. It is a two-way process.

Common sense dictates that witnesses should be approached in a friendly, open, respectful manner. An effort should be made to solicit the witness's interest in the case and its outcome. He or she should be made to feel important because the witness *is* important. There is always the danger that an independent witness may misinterpret contacts as an illegal effort to tamper with the evidence. The witness must be assured that the contact is appropriate and even necessary.

Lawyers must not tamper with evidence or produce false testimony. And they must not let their clients or associates do this either. As officers of the court, lawyers are subject to strict supervision. But it is proper for a lawyer to tell a witness that the witness's version of the facts is clearly contrary to the established physical facts or inconsistent with observations made by other witnesses who had just as good a view. The reasons for the apparent mistake or inconsistency in the evidence must be determined. It is proper to ask a witness to conduct a review of the transaction or occurrence for the purpose of determining whether he or she might be mistaken on a particular point. If the case involves an accident, it would be appropriate to go to the location of the accident with the witness to try to visualize what happened and how it happened.

A witness may nor may not appreciate receiving such help. The witness's attitude or response to these efforts will depend, in part, on how the witness is approached about the problem. Usually the best approach is to identify the apparent inconsistency in such a way that the witness does not feel challenged. He or she should *not* be given an opportunity to reiterate the erroneous "opinion" until the inconsistency has been identified. If the witness's version conflicts with photographs of the accident scene, show the witness the photographs. If the witness's version conflicts with another witness's deposition testimony, show him the deposition transcript. Otherwise, if the witness does reiterate the mistaken version before the problem is outlined, the witness tends to stand by his or her position even though clearly wrong. He or she will insist that the photograph or other witnesses are wrong. This is human nature. But once the witness has had an opportunity to see the "big picture," that is, what the other witnesses have to say, what the other evidence shows, and how his or her testimony fits, most witnesses are willing to correct their honest mistakes. Witnesses usually appreciate being helped to avoid embarrassment and unnecessary complications with the legal system. It might even be helpful to let the witness know that you can appreciate how he or she could have misinterpreted the particular fact or incorrectly remembered the fact. *Lawyers and legal assistants must use great care not to lead any witness into error.* The penalty could be severe.

Consider the following hypothetical situation. A police accident report shows that an accident occurred at 9:30 P.M. during hours of darkness. The United States Weather Bureau's records show that the sun set at 8:45 P.M. and the weather was overcast. Nevertheless, a witness, who has essential and reliable testimony to offer about the collision, has the mistaken idea that the accident happened during hours of daylight. By taking the witness to the accident location under similar conditions it may be possible to show the witness that the artificial lighting from the street lights and stores made the area seem to be as "bright as day." There should be no concern that this extra effort will hurt the client's case in any way. No undue influence was applied. The effort should manifest to the jury that a sincere, diligent effort has gone into the trial preparation to establish the truth. Once the reason for the witness's error in perception or recollection is ascertained, the explanation for the witness's mistake can be explained and thereby justified. Of course, this approach is of help where the witness has simply been lying. A lawyer must not knowingly present false testimony.

Witnesses who are uncooperative but who are needed for the client's case should be placed under subpoena right away. A person who fails to comply with a subpoena may be held in contempt of court. The penalty could be incarceration, a fine, or merely a stern lecture. Sometimes it is prudent to subpoena even the cooperative witnesses, because if a witness were to become unavailable, the fact that the witness is under subpoena will help to justify a court-ordered continuance of the trial. It is wise to check on the availability of the opponent's witnesses as well. There is nothing unethical about contacting witnesses who are aligned with the opposition as long as no privileged relationship is violated. For example, it would not be unethical for the defendant's lawyer to telephone the plaintiff's treating doctor's office to find out whether the doctor will be in town during the week that the case has been set for trial. If the doctor is scheduled to be out of town for a convention, such information could be helpful in evaluating the case.

There are times when some witnesses prefer to be subpoenaed so that their appearance in court is not considered to be entirely voluntary. They feel that the subpoena protects them from appearing to be aligned with one side. As an example, public officials and police officers often ask to be subpoenaed for that reason. Another example is the plaintiff's treating physician, whose testimony really favors the defendant's position. The physician may recognize that he or she has a duty to testify but is reluctant to come to court "against" his or her patient. The physician may be more comfortable about testifying if under subpoena.

A subpoena must designate the time and place that the witness is to appear for the purpose of testifying. But the lawyer who subpoenas the witness may not know precisely when the witness will be needed. The problem may be resolved by designating in the subpoena the earliest probable time that the witness will be needed and then telling the witness that if he or she will cooperate by staying near a telephone, so that the witness can be reached on very short notice, he or she may wait at home or work until contacted. The alternative is for the witness to sit in the courtroom and wait. The wait could be hours or even days. A lawyer takes a bit of a risk by accommodating a witness in this manner. But a larger risk is taken by not subpoenaing a witness whose reliability is questionable.

Federal court subpoenas are usually served by United States marshals, but any person eighteen years of age or older, who is not a party to the suit, may serve subpoenas in civil cases (Rule 45(c)). The process server must pay to the witness the established witness fee. Also the witness must be paid a mileage fee based upon the mileage from his or her home to the courthouse. If there is any doubt about the mileage, the process server should be sure to tender adequate payment. Failure to tender adequate payment could cause service to be defective. The process server's affidavit of service must state the time, place, manner of service, and amount of fees paid. The affidavit of service may be filed with the court.

Courts may order the parties to have all their exhibits "marked for identification" before a magistrate a few days before trial. The parties may be encouraged to stipulate to the foundation for use of all marked exhibits. Any exhibit which is not disclosed and marked as ordered is subject to exclusion for failure to comply with the court's order. The federal rules do not establish any particular system for identifying exhibits; however, local court rules may establish a mandatory method to obtain some uniformity. The trend is to use number identification rather than letters. Letters may then be used to supplement identification numbers. For example, if Exhibit 1 contains three pages and each page contains important information, the pages may be marked 1-A, 1-B, and 1-C.

The exhibits must be carefully examined to make sure that they do not contain any inappropriate marks, notations, or statements. Once in a while a photograph gets marked up by a witness or removable labels are applied when organizing the exhibits. They must be removed. Underlining, notations in the margins, or Xs used on photographs to pinpoint locations or provide other information might cause the exhibit to be inadmissible or reduce its authority. For example, while preparing a witness for deposition the witness might have carelessly penciled in the point of impact on a photograph. A new photograph should be made from the negative so that an "undamaged" one can be used at trial. Markings made on an exhibit before the witness uses the document in court are considered to be similar to hearsay evidence (out-of-court unsworn statement) or leading questions (the lawyer's question suggests the answer he or she wants). If the marking cannot be explained, there may be a lack of foundation for the document, making it inadmissible.

If an exhibit will be put into evidence through a particular witness, the procedure should be explained to the witness and, if there is any uncertainty exhibited by the witness, the procedure should be rehearsed.

It is often desirable to make photocopies of the documents that will be used as exhibits at trial, because once the documents have been received into evidence, the owner may not have convenient access to the exhibit. Copies may be useful in preparing witnesses to testify, for preparing the final argument, or for preparing posttrial motions. Even photographs may be photocopied, and that may be adequate for the exhibit reference file.

Witnesses do not have any legal duty to cooperate with the parties and their lawyers outside of court. Witnesses can be required to come to court by serving subpoenas on them, and, once in court, they can be compelled to answer questions under oath. But they do not have to come to the lawyer's office to discuss the case. If they talk to the lawyer and legal assistant, they are doing the latter a favor. But in the long run, they are helping themselves too. By cooperating in trial preparation the witnesses have the opportunity to learn what questions will be put to them at trial and how to answer them. They have the opportunity to see the exhibits that will be used, police reports, weather reports, and the like.

It is common for witnesses to an accident to immediately take sides. They feel that they know who was right and who was wrong. And they may well be correct. Consequently, the witness may not want to talk with a representative of the party he or she considers to be at fault. But if the witness knew what the real problem is, he or she would cooperate. For example, a witness to an automobile intersection collision may "know" that the accident was the defendant's fault. If he realized that the defendant acknowledges that the accident was his fault and the only reason he is defending is that the plaintiff's claim for damages is excessive, the witness might be more cooperative with the defendant's representatives.

In dealing with uncooperative witnesses, consider using exhibits, especially photographs, as "bait" to catch their interest. Even hostile witnesses are usually interested in seeing exhibits pertinent to what they have to say at trial. Initially, the emphasis should be placed upon those points where there is no real disagreement. Show the hostile witness that there are areas or points of agreement. Then, step by step, show the witness how his or her testimony fits into the "big picture." Once the witness senses that the interviewer is a sincere and pleasant person who appreciates cooperation, the witness will most likely become receptive. It is hoped that a witness who harbors erroneous beliefs will abandon them when the case is put in a proper perspective. Even if the witness will not abandon erroneous ideas about the case, he or she may be less adamant about them at trial.

Sometimes it is desirable to have a meeting with two or more witnesses at the same time so that they can help each other recall pertinent details and avoid unnecessary inconsistencies. As a general rule, each witness should be given an overview of the case, the legal issues, and the fact issues so that the witness can appreciate how his or her testimony fits in with the other evidence. This part of the preparation gives the witness assurance that he or she is not carrying the whole case and is not going to be asked questions about matters outside the witness's knowledge. The witnesses should be assured that it is perfectly proper for them to talk about the case. The witnesses should be coached to admit that they were interviewed in preparation for trial.

If a witness will be compensated for testifying at trial, the witness should be assured that it is proper to be reimbursed for time missed from work, mileage, parking, and meals. The witness should be coached to acknowledge the fact that he or she has been promised reimbursement and the basis for the payment. Usually the exact amount cannot be determined until after the witness has completed his or her part of the trial, and that is the best answer to any cross-examination questions about the amount.

A somewhat different situation is presented by expert witnesses who fully expect to be paid for their services. The amount of the fee is subject to disclosure. Indeed, the expert witness may be asked about past payments for testifying. If the payment is extraordinarily high, the jury may derive the impression that the witness is selling testimony; that he or she would say whatever is necessary if the price is right. As part of witness preparation it is necessary to make sure that fees are appropriate. If it were disclosed that an expert witness charges a contingent fee, so that he or she is paid only if the party who retained him or her wins, the credibility of the witness would be destroyed. Even if the expert is reluctant to discuss the amount of fees, that will reflect adversely against the witness and the party who presented the witness.

Jury Instructions

Another important step in a lawyer's preparation for trial is the preparation of written proposed jury instructions. Each lawyer not only has the right but perhaps the duty to submit proposed jury instructions on his or her theory of the case. Some courts' local rules require each party to file proposed jury instructions for every case. If a party submits proper requested instructions which for some reason the court does not give, the court's failure to give the instructions may be grounds for appeal. For the routine type of accident case many lawyers have prepared instructions which can be submitted merely by changing the caption on the papers. Most judges have their own "boiler plate" instructions with which they are comfortable and which they will give regardless of the lawyers' requests. Nevertheless, it is always a good practice to submit requested jury instructions.

Summary

Trial preparation begins with an overview of the case, including the legal theories and fact issues. The facts which have been established by judicial admission set a framework for all of the other facts. Parties should be careful to work within the confines of incontrovertible physical facts surrounding the transaction or occurrence. All of the evidence which was gathered during the investigation and discovery procedures must be examined and organized. The objectives are to establish a prima facie case of defense and to make a persuasive presentation. The evidence must be viewed objectively. The trial strategy must be subject to adjustment as problems arise. The evidence should be consistent and mutually supportive. The witnesses should be prepared for testifying by explaining to them the trial procedures, the "big picture," and how their testimony fits into the case as a whole. The witnesses should be coached so that their presentations appear sincere and authoritative. The witnesses cannot be told what to say. They can be helped to avoid mistakes. They can be helped by explaining to them how to testify so that the jury will understand them.

23 Juries

The parties to a civil action have a constitutional right to a trial by jury. The Seventeenth Amendment to the United States Constitution states the following:

> In Suits at common law, where the value in controversy shall exceed twenty dollars, the right of trial by jury shall be preserved, and no fact tried by a jury shall be otherwise re-examined in any Court of the United States than according to the rules of the common law.

The right to a jury trial is preserved and implemented by Rule 38. The jury's sole function is to determine the *facts* so that the law, as determined by the judge, can be applied to the facts. A jury verdict results from the jury's conclusion about the facts and the jury's application of the rules of law to those facts.

If a party does not assert the right to a jury trial, he or she automatically waives it. Then the trial judge is the fact finder. A *demand for a jury* may be made by the plaintiff by noting the demand on his or her complaint. The defendant may make the demand on his or her answer. Or, either party may serve a *jury demand* in writing. But the written demand must be served within ten days after service of the last pleading. The demand for a jury trial may specify the fact issues to be tried by the jury leaving all nonspecified fact issues to be determined by the trial judge. An unlimited general demand for trial by jury, however, has the effect of making all disputed facts issues subject to determination by the jury. If a party receives a demand for a jury that is limited to a specific issue, he or she has ten days in which to serve a counterdemand for a jury specifying additional fact issues or making a general demand which is all-inclusive. Usually a party makes a general demand because he or she can always waive the right to a jury at any time—assuming the other parties do not object (Rule 38(d)).

If a demand for a jury was not made by either party as required by the rules, the judge may, nevertheless, order a jury trial if he or she thinks that one is preferable. The order may be made pursuant to a motion by one or more of the parties or upon the court's own initiative. Why would a judge encourage a jury trial? The role of a fact finder is usually difficult, stressful, and time consuming. A judge may have to spend a considerable amount of time reviewing and weighing the evidence to decide disputed issues of fact. After a judge determines all of the issues in the case, the judge must prepare and file a document called **Findings of Fact, Conclusions of Law, and Order for Judgment.** It is common for the judge to attach a memorandum of law to the order explaining his or her rationale for the decision. This is a time-consuming process. The clerk must serve the findings and related documents upon the parties. The clerk of court enters judgment in accordance with the Order for Judgment. Litigants obtain earlier decisions from juries than they do from judges, at least on the average that is true. Juries certainly help to expedite litigation and the court's business by relieving judges of a very taxing function.

Even though the parties may not have a right to have their case decided by a jury, a judge may elect to have an *advisory jury* hear the case and render an *advisory verdict.* The advisory verdict may relate to the whole case or to only one or more fact issues in the case. For example, the parties to an action for reformation of a written contract do not have a right to a trial by jury since the remedy is provided by equity rather than law. A judge may nevertheless, have a jury decide whether the evidence establishes grounds for reformation of the instrument. In other words, a jury may be asked to determine whether the written contract is the product of the parties' mutual mistake or the product of fraud perpetrated by one party upon the other. Based upon the jury's findings, which the judge may or may not accept, the judge makes findings of fact, conclusions of law and issues an order for judgment.

No determination made by an advisory jury is binding upon the judge. Indeed, a judge who decides to use an advisory jury must make his or her own findings notwithstanding the jury's "advisory" verdict. The value of an advisory jury's verdict is primarily in the assistance it gives the judge to evaluate the credibility of witnesses.

There is an important exception to the rule which allows judges to impanel advisory juries. A judge may not use an advisory jury in an action brought against the United States when the statute under which the action is brought does not authorize a jury trial. See Rule 3(c).

Jury Selection

Jurors are selected at random from voter registration lists in the district or division in which the court sits. Some courts use a combination of voter lists and driver license lists in an effort to obtain a broader cross-section. Each potential juror must fill out a juror qualification form. A person must meet certain minimum requirements to qualify for jury service in the federal courts. A juror must be a citizen of the United States, at least eighteen years of age, able to read and write, able to understand English, physically capable of participating, and mentally competent to serve. A person *may* be disqualified from service if he or she has been convicted of a crime punishable by imprisonment for one year or more or has criminal charges pending against him or her for such a crime. A term of service does not exceed thirty days unless more time is needed to finish a trial already begun within the thirty-day period. Jurors are not called for service more than once during any two-year period.

When a jury panel is needed, the court directs the clerk to issue subpoenas to qualified jurors. The subpoenas are served by registered mail or by the marshal. The subpoena states that failure to appear as directed subjects the venireman to a fine of one hundred dollars or three days imprisonment or both. A person may be excused from jury service only if he or she can show an "undue hardship" or "extreme inconvenience." If so, his or her term of service is only postponed. Jurors may be called upon to hear and decide either criminal cases or civil cases during a single term of service.

When the parties and lawyers arrive at the courtroom, ready to begin trial, they usually spend some time with the judge discussing the case, procedures, scheduling problems, and settlement. When it appears that the case is ready, the judge directs a deputy clerk or bailiff to bring a jury panel to the courtroom. The size of the panel depends upon the number of jurors needed to try the case. Historically, a civil action required twelve jurors plus one or more alternates if the case promised to be a long one.

Most civil actions are now tried by a jury of six persons. The six jurors are selected from a panel of twelve or more jurors. The panel of twelve are commonly referred to as veniremen. From the twelve veniremen a jury of six is selected by the lawyers through a procedure called the **voir dire** examination. The voir dire examination may be conducted by the lawyers or by the judge or both. If court rules specify that the judge is to ask all voir dire questions, the lawyers have a right to submit written questions to the judge for him or her to ask. The judge has broad discretion in deciding what questions may be asked. Each party is entitled to three **peremptory** challenges. So when the peremptory challenges are all used, a jury of six is left. The peremptory challenges may be exercised on any basis. No reason has to be given, and usually none is given. The parties have an unlimited number of *challenges for cause*. Jurors are subject to being stricken for cause if they know the parties or the lawyers or about the case or declare that they would have difficulty being impartial because of the type of case. When veniremen are stricken from the panel "for cause" additional veniremen are added to the panel.

The apparent trend toward having judges, rather than lawyers, conduct the voir dire examination is primarily grounded in the belief that trials are significantly shortened if lawyers do not have a discussion with each juror. A few judges feel that lawyers tend to take too long; however, a possible solution to the problem, if there is one, is for the judges to exercise their authority and control the proceedings by ordering counsel to avoid repetitive and irrelevant questions. The trial judge does not need to wait for the opposing counsel to object. Legal assistants often prepare the proposed voir dire questions for those cases in which judges ask all of the voir dire questions.

The judge begins the voir dire examination by telling the jury panel why they have been assembled and the purpose of the voir dire examination. He or she briefly explains the nature of the case, identifies the parties, introduces the lawyers, and defines the issues. The names and addresses of probable witnesses are read to the jury for the purpose of determining whether the jurors are acquainted with any persons who may testify. If it turns out that a juror does know a party, lawyer, or witness, the nature of the relationship must be disclosed.

The judge's introductory remarks may be similar to the following:

> Members of the jury panel: You have been summoned to this courtroom so that of your number six may be selected to hear, try, and determine this case. It may be that you would be an excellent juror in 99 out of 100 cases; however, because of the fact that you may be acquainted with one or more of the parties, the lawyers, or the witnesses, or because you have a present leaning one way or another about *this* case or this type of case, you may be considered to be biased or prejudiced. What we need are six persons from varying walks of life who will diligently seek the truth; who will fairly and impartially and without fear or favor try the issues of fact; and who will decide this case upon the evidence adduced here in the courtroom and upon the law that will be given to you by me.
>
> In order that we may ascertain if you are a proper or qualified person to sit as a juror in this case, I first, then counsel, will ask you questions about your qualifications. In so doing, it is not the lawyers' intention to pry into your private life, but it is their duty to select a jury of the quality and character indicated. Please be open, frank, and responsive to the questions put to you so that justice may be done between the parties.
>
> So that you may intelligently respond to questions put to you testing your qualifications, I shall briefly state: the identity of the parties; the nature of the case as reflected by the pleadings; the identity of the lawyers; the names of possible witnesses; and certain fundamental rules of law applicable to this and all cases of like character.

The judge and lawyers may ask questions of the veniremen concerning their

1. family;
2. education;
3. past and present occupations;
4. prior jury experience;
5. experience with similar occurrences or transactions;
6. experience with litigation as a party or witness;
7. attitude toward the judicial system or type of lawsuit in question;
8. attitude toward the parties or witnesses;
9. willingness to follow and apply the law.

This list is by no means exclusive.

The questions may be put to veniremen in the order they were seated. Or, questions may be put to the panel as a whole, and each juror responds with a raised hand if a question applies to him or her. This, of course, is the faster method and tends to avoid unnecessary repetition. Nonetheless, it is also the least satisfactory, for it fails to develop sufficient thought, discussion, and commitment to the process on the part of the veniremen.

The defendant's lawyer questions the panel first. He or she usually concludes a voir dire examination by requesting that the jurors set aside their natural feelings of sympathy, to keep an open mind about what the evidence proves until they have heard *all* the evidence, and to follow the court's instructions on the law even if the jurors feel that the law should be different. The plaintiff's lawyer usually concludes his or her examination with a request that the jurors listen carefully to the evidence and that they give the case the same thoughtful consideration that they would want for their own important matters. There is a general prohibition against asking jurors to put themselves in the position of either of the parties. For example, it would be impermissible to ask a juror: "How would you feel about this injury if it had happened to you?" The techniques employed by lawyers differ greatly, but always the primary objective is to weed out undesirable jurors from the panel without causing annoyance or embarrassment to anyone. The process works well.

A peremptory challenge permits a lawyer to excuse (strike) a potential juror without giving a reason. A juror who is excused "for cause" is stricken because there is, at least, the appearance of actual or implied bias. Actual bias exists when a juror acknowledges that he or she cannot be totally fair. His or her bias may be against or for a party. Or, a juror may be biased because of the type of case. A venireman may hate dogs—all dogs. Such a person should not sit on a case where the plaintiff alleges injuries caused by the defendant's dog. Or, a potential juror may have a religious belief that it is wrong for anyone to sue another person to collect money damages. Such a person should not sit as a juror in a personal injury case. If a venireman is related to one of the parties or to one of the lawyers or works for a party, there is implied bias, and he or she will be excused by the court even if the person claims he or she can be fair.

In a typical case, the plaintiff and defendant are each allowed three peremptory challenges. But if there is more than one defendant, they have to share the peremptory challenges unless adversity exists between them. Ordinarily, the parties are considered adverse to each other only if the pleadings raise issues between them. For example, cross-claims make codefendants adverse. The same factors determine whether or not coplaintiffs must share the three peremptory challenges. The judge must try to keep veniremen from claiming bias for the purpose of evading jury service.

The most common procedure for conducting the voir dire examination in civil cases is for the defendant's lawyer to question the entire panel first. Then the plaintiff's lawyer conducts his or her examination. Veniremen who have actual or implied bias are stricken for cause before the examinations are concluded. After the questioning is concluded, the defendant's lawyer is required to strike one venireman from the jury list. Then the plaintiff's lawyer must strike one juror. The process continues until each side has exercised three peremptory challenges, and only six jurors are left plus any alternate jurors that are needed. The last venireman to enter the jury box and to survive the challenges is the alternate.

Some courts use a different voir dire procedure whereby each lawyer interrogates each venireman in the order seated. The venireman is challenged or accepted before the next venireman is questioned. The procedure is more cumbersome and does not give the lawyers an opportunity to compare all the veniremen before exercising their precious pre-emptive challenges. The procedure may cause a little more embarrassment because the peremptory challenges have to be exercised before going on to the next juror rather than striking all extra jurors from the jury list at the end of all the questioning. In the system first discussed, the jurors know that six of their number must be eliminated even though all of them may be perfectly acceptable; in the latter procedure, each juror is accepted or rejected personally by the parties before the lawyers have the opportunity to interview the remaining jurors.

Instructions to Jurors

Upon selection of the twelve or six jurors who will try the case, the jurors take an oath to follow the court's orders and instructions. The following is typical of the juror's oath:

> You each do swear that you will impartially try the issues in this case and a true verdict give according to the law and the evidence given you in court; your own counsel and that of your fellows you will duly keep, you will say nothing concerning the case, nor suffer anyone to speak to you about it, and you will keep your verdict secret until you deliver it in court. So help you God.

The jurors are usually reminded at this point that they must act upon reason and good judgment, not feelings or emotion or speculation. Some preliminary instructions are usually given by the judge as follows:

> As to the law of this case, it will be given to you by me at the appropriate time. However, you are instructed that you must take the law exactly and precisely as I shall give it to you, that you apply such law to the facts as you find them to be from the evidence, and that you render your verdict accordingly, regardless of where the "chips may fall." The court (trial judge) does not make the law but merely declares it in a given case. The law comes from federal and state constitutions, from federal and state statutes, and from declarations contained in judicial decisions stating the public standards of rights and duties in matters not covered by the constitutions and statutes. In this connection, you are instructed that if judges and juries were not bound by these tangible statements of the law, if in each lawsuit the judge or the jury could set up private and personal standards of rights and duties as a basis for deciding the case, one would never know in advance of a decision how he or she should have acted in a particular situation and no one would be safe.
>
> Cases arising out of similar relationships or circumstances must be decided on settled principles of law and not on the notions of the trial judge or of a jury. Accordingly, it must be readily apparent to you that even though you may have an opinion as to what the law is or should be, you must set that aside; you must accept and apply the law exactly and precisely as I shall give it to you. I cannot at this time instruct you as to all rules of law applicable to this case because I have not, as yet, heard the evidence.
>
> I have some general instructions which I think will be of assistance. Our hours are generally 9:30 A.M. to 12:00 P.M., 2:00 P.M. to 5:00 P.M. Those hours may be modified or extended depending upon circumstances. For example, should a witness's testimony be near completion at the customary recess time, we would tend to continue so that the witness would not need to come back for the next session.
>
> Promptness, of course, is extremely important, and I am sure I need say no more about that.
>
> During the morning session, about midway, and the afternoon session, about midway, we will take a fifteen-minute recess. On those occasions, as well as during the noon hour and after hours, you will be among the public. Do not discuss this case or the subject matter of the case with anyone. Once the case is over and you have rendered your verdict and you have been discharged from the case, then you can speak as fully and freely as you wish. On the other hand, if anyone should inquire, it is up to you. You can say, "I have done my best; I would rather not discuss it."
>
> You know where the accident occurred. Please do not go out and view the premises. You are not investigators. You are to determine the facts from the evidence submitted here in the courtroom—so keep that in mind.

You must try to keep an open mind until all of the evidence has been presented and until you have been instructed, by me, concerning the applicable rules of law. The plaintiff will proceed with his or her case first, followed by the case-in-chief of each of the defendants. If new material is submitted, the plaintiff will have the right of rebuttal. If on rebuttal new material is submitted, then each of the defendants will have a right of rebuttal. In that way, all of the evidence that is proper and competent will be submitted to you without repetition. After all of the evidence has been presented, and the parties have rested their cases, you will have the opportunity to hear the attorneys' summations. The attorneys will review the evidence and draw conclusions from it. They will also discuss the rules of law as they apply to the evidence. Prior to those summations, I will have discussed with counsel the law which I have determined applies to the case and which I will give to you. The summations may be—and usually are—of assistance to you, but the responsibility of decision is yours—not that of the attorneys. When you enter the jury room, you will have all of the tools with which to determine the facts of the case and to apply the law in an appropriate manner. In the meantime, do not jump to conclusions as each witness takes the stand. You must keep an open and objective mind while the case is being presented. You should maintain that same objectivity when you commence your deliberations.

You may take notes if you wish. However, those notes are *your* own personal notes for refreshing *your* own memory. If your memory has then been refreshed so that you can say, "Now of my own knowledge, I know this was said," or whatever the case may be, then, of course, you can say that to your fellow jurors. But your fellow jurors *should not* use your notes to refresh their memories. Such notes are no more authoritative than another juror's memory. There is a danger that when writing notes, other important evidence will not be heard.

There may be, from time to time, conferences here at the bench. Those conferences with counsel are intended to be out of your hearing. They involve questions of law or procedure, not questions of fact. Do not attempt to overhear our conversation. Under no circumstances should you guess the subject of our conversations and permit that to bear upon your determination of facts or the ultimate issues of the case. If you were to do so, your decision or determination would not be on solid facts and the law but would be based upon speculation and conjecture—which is repugnant to good judicial administration.

If at any time during the course of the trial something of a personal nature bothers you, you come to me about it. I am sure I can handle it so that it will not be detrimental to any party. But do not ask me what the evidence is, because that is solely within your province. That is your responsibility. As I indicated before, you should not consider or even know what I think of the evidence.

Sometimes, after the jury commences deliberations, there is a disagreement as to what a witness may have said—and it seems simple to call the court and say, "May we come back and have the court reporter read a witness's testimony?" I do not permit that, except under unusual circumstances. In all probability, I will have started another trial. Counsel have perhaps gone their respective ways and may be trying another lawsuit—even in another county. In order to have you come back in and have portions of the testimony read to you, I would have to contact counsel, get them back, and recess my case. And then, after I have permitted the reading of that one witness's testimony, the attorneys may be constrained to point out that, in fairness, the testimony of other witnesses who touched upon that subject ought to be read; otherwise, there may be an overemphasis of one facet of the case. By the time I comply, we would be trying the case all over again.

If you fail to hear a question of an attorney or an answer of a witness, speak up, raise your hand, then I will make sure that it is read back at that time in its proper continuity and without any fear of possible overemphasis.

The Jury's Function

The jury performs its ultimate function by returning a verdict. The verdict which it uses will be of a type and form selected by the trial judge. The most common verdict form is a "general verdict." It is very short. The jury simply states that it finds for the plaintiff in $X.00 or it finds "for the defendant," which means the plaintiff recovers no money damages. If the defendant prevails on his or her counterclaim, the amount is noted. In federal courts, the verdict must be unanimous, and it is signed only by the foreman or forewoman. In civil actions in some states, courts allow the jury to return a *five-sixths verdict* after six hours of deliberation. In other words, a verdict must be unanimous if rendered during the first six hours of deliberation. Thereafter, five of six or ten of twelve jurors may agree on the verdict. Each concurring juror must sign the verdict form. The foreman does not sign it unless he is a concurring juror. The concurring jurors must agree to all parts of the verdict. The United States Supreme Court has held that five-sixths verdicts in criminal cases deny the defendant due process of law and, therefore, are unconstitutional.

A case may be submitted to the jury on a special verdict which consists of specific questions pertaining to the facts in controversy. The jury must answer each question thereby resolving the basic issues of fact. The court then applies the law to the facts as determined by the jury and issues an order for judgment accordingly. The jury's answer to each question may be short; usually yes or no. For example:

1. Did the defendant sign the promissory note (plaintiff's Exhibit A)? Yes or No: _____
2. Was the defendant negligent? Yes or No: _____
3. If your answer to question 2 is yes, was the defendant's negligence a direct cause of the accident? Yes or No: _____

When a case is submitted to the jury for its determination, it usually takes several hours for them to review the evidence and reach a verdict. Four to six hours seems to be an average length of time for deliberations in a typical civil case. While the jury is considering the case, the trial judge may begin trying another case. Or, he or she may conduct other essential business of the court. When the trial judge acts as the fact finder, he or she must conduct a similar careful review of the evidence, just as the jury does, and then prepare written Findings of Fact, Conclusions of Law, and Order for Judgment. The length of time required by the judge to go through this procedure justifies the expense of the jury system. Just as important, it often takes the trial judge a long time to make his or her decision—sometimes months. During that period of time, it is said that the judge has the case "under advisement." The delay may cause the parties a great deal of anxiety as well as inconvenience. Yet, lawyers are very reluctant to pressure the judge for an early decision.

Jurors must not discuss the case with anyone while the case is being tried; they should not even discuss the case among themselves. Such discussion might cause them to reach a conclusion prematurely. There is also danger that a juror might express an unfortunate conclusion or opinion that he or she may be reluctant to forego. For the same reason, jurors are often urged to avoid making strong, unretractable statements at the beginning of their deliberations.

After the verdict is received by the judge in open court, the lawyers may ask to have the jury polled for the purpose of confirming that it is the true verdict of each juror. Usually, the right to poll the jury is waived. Often lawyers elect not to be present when the verdict is returned. This is because they do not want to spend time waiting at the courtroom. The judge or clerk will notify them of the verdict by telephone within minutes after it is received.

Occasionally, jurors determine that they need clarification on some point of law or procedure before rendering their special verdict (see glossary regarding special verdicts), so they notify the judge, through the bailiff, that they need additional instructions. In that event, the judge summons the lawyers to the courtroom, so they can hear the jury's question or problem and try to assist the judge in resolving it. The responsibility, of course, belongs to the judge. Usually the problem can be solved merely by rereading the instructions already given. Sometimes the jury wants to know the effect of their special verdict before signing it. The ordinary answer is that they are not supposed to concern themselves with the consequences of the verdict— just the truth; however, some state laws permit the judge and lawyers to inform the jury about the effect of the jurors' answers to the special verdict questions.

Jurors do not have to talk to anyone about their verdict, deliberations, or any other aspect of the trial after the case is concluded. On the other hand, there is no law against a juror talking to the parties, lawyers, reporters, or anyone else about the case. If it should appear that the jury or any of its members was guilty of misconduct in the course of the trial, that could be a basis for setting aside the verdict. If either party learns of or suspects that there has been misconduct by the jury, he or she must inform the trial judge of the suspicion or information. The court, not the parties, must conduct an investigation of the alleged jury misconduct. Interviewing jurors after the verdict should not be used as a subterfuge for finding error and obtaining a new trial. Contact with jurors after the trial by the parties or their lawyers may result in a waiver of any right to complain of jury misconduct.

There is a dynamic quality to the jury system. Most litigants seem to prefer to have their cases decided by a jury rather than by a judge, although the judge *may* be more intelligent and better educated. Litigants tend to be suspicious of decisions made by one person regardless of that person's qualifications. Litigants seem to be more concerned about being treated impartially than wisely. "Impartiality," in this sense, is *not* synonymous with "fairness," which suggests extrajudicial considerations and judgments as to what is the better result. The jury system, it is said, is for the losing litigant, because a jury verdict is usually more palatable to the loser than is a judge's decision. The prevailing party is probably going to be satisfied with whatever system is used.

When jurors complete their term of service, they have been enriched by the experience of serving their government and community in a very important role. They have a better understanding and appreciation for the judicial system. Within a few days jurors are usually able to set aside the worries and anxieties inherent in making a conscientious effort to find the truth and apply the law.

24 Civil Trials

If the parties cannot resolve their dispute, they have the right to have the matter resolved through a trial in a court of law. By resorting to a trial the parties give up the right to use their own standards, values, and procedures for resolving their dispute. Instead, their dispute will be decided according to law which applies to such transactions or occurrences. A trial is conducted pursuant to fairly strict rules. The rules exist to insure that the parties are treated fairly, to give the parties the opportunity to prove the facts upon which they rely, and to enable the court to apply the law to the facts established in the trial.

A judge presides over all aspects of the trial. The judge determines what substantive law applies to the facts as established by the evidence. The judge determines what procedural rules apply and controls the conduct of all participants. Lawyers help the judge to preside over the trial by helping the judge to understand the legal issues, evidence which is to be presented and directing the judge to relevant legal authorities such as cases, statutes and rules. Lawyers help facilitate the trial procedures by making motions and offering advice to resolve problems as they occur. Lawyers are expected to control their clients and, to some extent, the witnesses that they bring to the courtroom.

Conference between the Judge and Counsel

When the parties and lawyers report to the courthouse to begin trial, the judge usually has a conference with the lawyers. The conference may cover a broad range of subjects relevant to the impending trial. Usually the judge wants to know about the status of settlement negotiations. Some judges want to know what amount has been demanded by the plaintiff and what amount has been offered by the defendant. Other judges do not want to be told about the actual amounts, but need merely an indication of whether there is a possibility of settlement and whether the parties want time to discuss settlement. Most judges will give the parties a few minutes to pursue settlement negotiations if there is any reason to think that such negotiations would be fruitful. On the other hand, some judges take the attitude that the parties will have to negotiate on their own time, not on the court's time. Obviously, a lawyer has some benefits, if not advantages, by knowing the particular judge's attitudes and procedures.

The conference gives the judge an opportunity to become better acquainted with the case. Usually the judge has reviewed the pleadings and other documents filed with the clerk. Some courts have special rules which require each party to serve and file a **statement of case** which contains a current summary of the facts, list of witnesses and identification of the legal issues and disclosure of insurance information. These documents give the judge an overview of the case. However, in order to conduct the jury voir dire examination and otherwise preside over the trial, the judge really needs more information than is ordinarily contained in the file.

The lawyers are expected to tell the judge about their legal theories and the problems which they anticipate will arise during the course of the trial. The judge and lawyers try to establish a tentative schedule for the presentation of evidence. There is almost always a problem with scheduling witnesses, but the problem is eased somewhat if the parties cooperate to establish a schedule. Some judges require the lawyers to submit their proposed jury instructions before the trial begins.

The meeting in chambers provides counsel with an opportunity to make *motions in limine.* These are so called "threshold motions," made in anticipation of problems affecting evidence or procedure. Motions for orders made at the very beginning of the trial can set the stage for the entire trial. However, the principal purpose for motions in limine is to prevent foreseeable problems from complicating or interfering with the trial. Motions in limine may be made orally upon the record. However, sometimes they are made in writing and filed with the court even before the case is called for trial. Usually the written motions are supported by memoranda of law.

A good example of a motion in limine is a party's motion to suppress any evidence of that party's consumption of alcohol preceding the accident in question. The motion is made on the grounds that there is no evidence that the party was intoxicated or that the consumption of alcohol contributed to the cause of the accident. The court should grant the motion if the opposing party does not have any evidence of intoxication or a causal connection between the use of alcohol and the accident. Under these circumstances, the grounds for suppressing the evidence concerning use of alcohol is that the prejudicial effect of the evidence outweighs its probative value.

Another example of a motion in limine is a defendant's motion to suppress use of certain photographs of plaintiff's injuries on the grounds that the prejudicial effect outweighs their probative value. Courts are inclined to limit the number of photographs of a particular subject to avoid repetition and the cumulative effect of evidence. Repetition wastes time and tends to give an undue emphasis to the matters repeated.

Jury Selection

Most parties and most trial lawyers prefer to try their cases to jurors rather than to a judge. Lawyers have a concern that judges tend to be influenced by the many cases they have observed in the past. By contrast, the inexperience of jurors permits them to approach the case with a fresh perspective and they will probably have considerable interest in the proceedings. Also, trial lawyers seem to have a preference for decisions by the consensus of a group rather than a decision by one person—regardless of the judge's competency. It is said that juries are for "losers." Somehow, it is more satisfying for the losing party to know that six or more people heard the case and agreed on the verdict, rather than being forced to accept the decision of one person, even if that person is a learned judge.

Potential jurors are drawn from voter registration lists and driver's license rolls. A new jury panel is selected periodically. In state district courts a new jury panel is chosen every two weeks. The prospective jurors go through an indoctrination session which usually includes a lecture and a motion picture. They are also given a booklet which explains their role and duties.

Most civil trials require the services of six jurors. When a case is called for trial, between fifteen and twenty potential jurors are brought to the courtroom. Out of that group ten or twelve are selected at random to sit in the jury box. The veniremen are placed under oath. They are advised that the judge and lawyers will ask them questions about their background and experience for the purpose of determining whether there is any reason why they should not be jurors in the particular case.

The Federal Constitution and state constitutions guarantee the right to trial by jury whenever the claim is for money damages. However, the constitutions do not specify how many individuals are to be included in a jury. Historically, the number was twelve. That number has been maintained in criminal cases. The number has been reduced to six in civil cases for purposes of economy. The government has fewer people to pay, and the trials may be slightly shorter. However, most lawyers and judges who remember working with twelve person juries believe that their verdicts were less likely to go to extremes. They were more predictable and, therefore, preferable.

When the parties anticipate that the case may last more than a week, it is common to add one or two alternate jurors to the panel. Alternate jurors, usually the last persons called to the jury box, participate in the trial in the same way as other jurors during the trial. In fact, the alternate jurors might not even know that they are alternates. Some judges are concerned that if jurors are told that they are alternate jurors, they might assume that they will not have to decide the case. Consequently, they may not pay close attention to the evidence. The alternate jurors participate in the trial until the very end. They hear the final arguments. They listen to the judge's instructions on the law. They are excused from further service when the jurors are sent to the jury room to conduct their deliberations. On occasion, the parties may stipulate that the alternate jurors may participate in the deliberations and vote.

In most Federal District Courts the judge conducts the *voir dire* examination. In other words, the judge asks *all* of the questions put to the jury panel. If the lawyers want certain questions asked, they may be required to submit those questions to the judge in writing before the trial begins. In most state courts, the lawyers have an opportunity to conduct the voir dire examination, or at least participate to a substantial degree. This means asking the jurors about their background and qualifications to sit on the particular case. The voir dire examination provides the only opportunity that the lawyers have to converse directly with the jurors. The lawyers try to determine whether there is anything in the jurors' backgrounds which would adversely affect the juror's ability to be fair to his or her client. Of course, it is only natural that the lawyers also try to determine whether any of the potential jurors might have attitudes, experiences or relationships which might make the jurors tend to *favor* the client or *disfavor* the opposing party.

The jurors need some background information about the parties and the transaction or occurrence so they can appreciate the significance of the voir dire questions and make their answers responsive. The voir dire examination usually begins with the judge giving the jury a very brief description of the case, including some of the basic facts such as time and place. The lawyers may supplement the judges' statements, but they may not turn the voir dire examination into an opening statement.

Of course, the jurors' answers to the lawyers' questions during the voir dire examination are very important to the lawyers in deciding which jurors to keep. However, most lawyers are almost as concerned with *how* the jurors respond to the questions as they are to the substance of what the jurors say. The manner of their response indicates whether they have any difficulty hearing or understanding the questions. If they do, they will probably have the same difficulty during the trial. Does a juror show a dominant or submissive personality? Is the juror really interested and willing to be conscientious about deciding the case? Does the juror's position in the community indicate that the juror would follow the law even if the juror disagrees with the consequences of following the law?

The lawyers carefully watch the jurors as the jurors walk from the back of the courtroom to their seats in the jury box. At this time they notice whether the jurors manifest any physical impairments or disabilities, how they are dressed, how they carry themselves and what they have brought with them to pass the time, such as reading material. These outward indicators may suggest questions that should be put to the juror. For example, in a personal injury case, the defense lawyer ought to be very concerned about the potential juror who manifests a limp as the juror walks to the jury box. The juror who has brought a supply of comic books to read may not be an attentive juror. An obviously shy person may not contribute to the jury's deliberations and may be unduly influenced by the opinions of others. Perhaps, in the particular case and in light of the other choices, the shy juror may be the preferred juror. The lawyers' observations during the voir dire examination are considered to be just as important as the jurors' responses to the lawyers' questions.

The rules absolutely forbid any lawyer to ask questions in such a way as to create prejudice in the minds of the jury. Potential jurors must *not* be asked to put themselves in the place of either party. The lawyers must not ask questions that suggest that the parties have liability insurance or are not insured for all or part of the loss. However, in some cases the judge asks the jurors whether they are employed by the insurance companies that might have an interest in the outcome of the case. The judge does not point out the interest, or identify who is insured, but merely asks about any connection they might have with the insurance companies.

In civil actions, lawyers often ask some of the voir dire questions to the panel as a whole. For example, the lawyer may ask the panel whether any of the members have: (1) had previous jury experience, (2) ever been a party to a lawsuit, (3) ever been involved in a similar accident. The jurors respond by raising their hands when the question applies to them, and then the lawyer may ask those jurors follow-up questions. The practice is to ask questions of individual jurors in the order in which the jurors were seated. Those questions are usually of a more specific or personal nature.

If at any time during the voir dire examination it appears that a potential juror should be stricken for "cause," the proceedings are turned over to the judge to conduct further inquiry or to rule on a party's motion to have a particular juror stricken. Jurors may be stricken for cause if they are related to a lawyer involved in the case, related to the parties, or have other close connections with the case. A juror may be stricken for cause simply because the juror says that he or she could not be fair considering the circumstances of the particular case. When a lawyer seeks to have a juror stricken for cause, the motion to strike is usually made out of the jurors' hearing, because if the motion is denied, the lawyer does not want his or her remarks heard by the juror in question and cause that juror to be even more prejudiced toward the client. The jury selection procedures allow the parties an unlimited number of challenges for cause.

When the defendant's lawyer completes his or her portion of the voir dire examination, the plaintiff's lawyer repeats the process from the plaintiff's perspective. When both sides have concluded their voir dire examination they are required to exercise their pre-emptory challenges to reduce the jury panel from ten or more, to six jurors plus alternate jurors. Usually each adverse party is given two pre-emptory strikes.

The parties exercise their pre-emptory challenges by noting on the clerk's jury list which ones are to be stricken. The defendant's lawyer must exercise the first pre-emptory strike. Now the plaintiff strikes one juror from the panel. Then the defendant strikes a third juror from the panel, and plaintiff strikes the fourth juror. Since the lawyers know which jurors will be alternates they avoid "wasting" their pre-emptory strikes on the alternate jurors, because ninety percent of the time the alternate jurors do not participate in the verdict.

As soon as the jury is empaneled, the judge instructs them concerning their responsibilities and how they are to conduct themselves during the trial. There is a trend in the courts for judges to give the jury some preliminary instructions concerning the probable applicable law even before any evidence is received. These preliminary instructions are usually repeated at the end of the trial. The preliminary instructions may cover guidelines for evaluating evidence and some of the substantive law such as definitions of negligence and proximate cause. These preliminary instructions should help the jury to follow the evidence and appreciate the significance of the evidence.

Jurors are allowed to take notes in most courts. However, the jurors are generally cautioned that their notes are not to be imposed upon other jurors. Notes are not necessarily more reliable or authoritative than another juror's memory. One reason for this is that a juror may be so busy writing that the juror may not be listening. The juror's notebooks are collected and kept by the clerk during evening recesses to prevent anyone from tampering with them and to keep them from being lost.

The jurors are cautioned against discussing the case with anyone until after they have been instructed in the law at the end of the case and authorized to begin their deliberations. This means that the jurors are not even to discuss the case between themselves until they are sent to deliberate. The reason for this rule is that if jurors were to discuss the evidence with each other, the discussion might result in jurors taking a position which would tend to become fixed or hardened as the trial progressed. In other words, the discussions might lead jurors to become advocates for a particular position or result before they have heard all of the evidence.

In federal court, the jury verdict must be unanimous. In many state courts, the jury may return a 5/6 verdict after deliberating at least six hours. If the verdict is arrived at during the first six hours, the verdict must be unanimous. When the deliberations take more than six hours, five jurors may decide the case if they agree to all of the answers on all questions contained in the verdict. Therefore, one dissenting juror cannot prevent a verdict from becoming final. The five concurring jurors sign the verdict. The dissenting juror does not sign the verdict. If the verdict is unanimous, only the foreperson need sign the verdict. Obviously, the five-sixths rule results in fewer hung juries and fewer new trials.

Opening Statements

After the jury has been selected, the plaintiff's lawyer has the opportunity to make the first opening statement. The party who has the burden of proof has the right and obligation to present evidence first. That party is usually the plaintiff. The party who will present evidence first has a right to make the first opening statement. The defendant's lawyer may make his or her opening statement immediately following the plaintiff's opening statement or wait until the plaintiff's case-in-chief is concluded. Usually, the defendants' lawyers prefer to make their opening statements at the beginning of the trial, immediately after the plaintiff's opening statements. They feel that it is important to show that there are two sides to the case. They want the jury to know, at the outset, about the problems in the plaintiff's case. The defendants' lawyers also want the jury to withhold any judgments about what the evidence proves until they have heard all of the evidence. By making an opening statement directly after the plaintiff's opening statement, the defendant's lawyer is more likely to persuade the jury to keep an open mind about the case until they have heard all of the evidence.

The lawyers' opening statements give the jury an overview of the evidence which will be presented. The most common format for an opening statement is a chronological summary of the material facts. Hearing a chronology at the outset helps the jury to follow the evidence as it is presented. This is particularly useful because evidence is not always presented as a chronology. The opening statements are useful to give the jury a frame of reference in which to consider the evidence. A good opening statement enables the jury to see how the pieces of evidence fit together. Consequently, the jurors can better understand and appreciate the evidence as the evidence is presented. A good opening statement is like having a road map to follow.

A lawyer must not make any statement about the evidence which he or she knows is not supportable. The opening statement is not supposed to be an argument. Indeed, if the statement becomes argumentative, it is subject to objection. When the news media refer to the attorneys' opening "arguments" they manifest a fundamental misunderstanding about judicial procedures.

A lawyer is expected to identify and describe the evidence which he or she intends to present. It is proper to state what happened or what did not happen. It is improper to characterize the conduct or to argue the effect or consequences of the conduct or to justify or condemn the conduct of the other party. While making the opening statement, some lawyers frequently use the expression, "The evidence will show that . . . ." This preface helps the lawyers to focus on the evidence to be offered, rather than argue the case.

The opening statement not only educates the jury but it also educates the opposing party and his or her lawyer. Consequently, probably no one listens more carefully to a lawyer's opening statement than the opposing lawyer. If a lawyer makes claims in the opening statement which are not borne out by the evidence, that can become the theme of the opposing lawyer's final argument. The opposing lawyer can legitimately ask the question, "Where is the evidence that was promised?"

The parties must listen carefully to the opening statements because the statements tell them exactly what the opponent thinks is important and what the opponent is likely to ask during the cross-examination. A party should listen to his or her own lawyer's opening statement to see if the lawyer makes any misstatements. The client can help the lawyer to clarify or correct any apparent misstatements.

Only rarely does a court permit the lawyers to refer to or use exhibits during the opening statements. Judges generally seem to feel that opening statements should be short and general in nature. On the other hand, experienced trial lawyers feel that the opening statements should be as long as necessary to give the jury a clear understanding of what the case is about. The opening statements provide counsel with an opportunity to explain technical procedures, terms, definitions and procedures, as well as to prepare the jury to listen to expert witnesses. A lawyer may use the opening statement to explain concepts, relationships and potential problems.

A great deal of thoughtful consideration goes into the preparation of a good opening statement. A lawyer must not overstate his or her case, but he or she must tell the jury enough to make the jury appreciate that the client has a strong and just position. The statement will be tested by the evidence. The opponent is sure to capitalize on any flaws in the statement. The jury must be left with the feeling that the statement was authoritative and candid.

Plaintiff's Case-in-Chief

A party's case-in-chief is the initial presentation of evidence to support that party's claims or defenses. The plaintiff's case-in-chief is concerned with establishing all of the elements to the causes of action which the plaintiff alleged against the defendant. The first concern must be to establish the legal duty which the defendant owed to the plaintiff and which the defendant allegedly breached. The plaintiff must prove that the legal duty was breached and that the defendant's wrongful conduct caused injury, property damage or some other harm to plaintiff. The plaintiff's evidence may anticipate the affirmative defenses raised by the defendant's answer. However, the plaintiff is given the opportunity to present rebuttal testimony after the defendant's case-in-chief, and the rebuttal evidence is usually concerned with defendant's affirmative defenses.

The party who has the burden of proof has the duty to present his or her evidence first. Since the plaintiff almost always has the burden of proof concerning the principal issue(s) in the case, the plaintiff almost always presents his or her evidence first. However, if the defendant were to have the burden of proof, the defendant would have to go forward with the evidence first. For example, if the plaintiff entrusted her fur coat to the defendant for storage during the summer season and the coat was lost or damaged while in the storage company's possession, the defendant storage company would have the burden of proving that the loss occurred without any negligence on its part. Therefore, the defendant would have the right and duty to present evidence first. In the absence of any evidence as to how the loss occurred, the legal presumption of negligence on the part of the storage company (bailee for hire) would control.

Another common example of the defendant bearing the burden of proof on the principal issue is when an insurance company has denied coverage solely on the basis of an *exclusion* in the insurance policy, and the plaintiff insured brings a lawsuit to recover benefits under the policy. The defendant insurer has the burden of proving facts which bring the claim within the exclusion. Therefore, the defendant insurer has the first opening statement and proceeds first with the evidence. However, if the insurance company denied coverage on the basis that the policy was not in force at the time of the insured's loss, the plaintiff insured would have the burden of proving that the policy was in force and that the loss is of the type covered by the policy. Then the plaintiff insured would have the first opening statement and be the first to present evidence.

The rules of procedure authorize a party to call any adverse party to the witness stand for cross-examination. The plaintiff often calls the defendant to be plaintiff's first witness. There are many good reasons for this strategy. The defendant is probably most nervous about the case during the first hours of the trial and that may detract from the defendant's appearance before the jury. The plaintiff's lawyer may elect to cross-examine the defendant on just a few matters essential to the plaintiff's case or cover only a few matters where the defendant's credibility is particularly weak. This approach is often good strategy because it may make the plaintiff's case appear strong at the beginning. Furthermore, the defendant doesn't have an opportunity to hear the other witnesses before testifying. It is usually an advantage to testify after hearing the other witnesses, because the testimony by the other witnesses may help to refresh the party's memory.

If the defendant is put on the stand by the plaintiff's lawyer for cross-examination as part of the plaintiff's case-in-chief, the defendant's lawyer may elect to conduct a direct examination of the defendant immediately after the cross-examination or reserve the direct examination until after the plaintiff's case is concluded. However, most trial judges permit the defendant's lawyer to ask the defendant a *few* questions to clarify one or two points developed during the cross-examination which might be confusing or misleading if not promptly explained without requiring the defendant to go forward with all of the defendant's testimony during the plaintiff's case-in-chief.

Facts may be proved by *direct evidence, circumstantial evidence* or a combination of the two. Most facts are proved through the testimony of witnesses who obtained knowledge about the facts through their observations. A witness's testimony about facts which the witness observed is direct evidence. If a witness testifies that he or she saw the defendant strike the plaintiff with a closed fist, the witness has presented direct evidence of the fact. Proof of a fact through circumstantial evidence is indirect proof. Circumstantial evidence is not any less trustworthy or credible than direct evidence. Therefore, the law does not prefer direct evidence over circumstantial evidence.

Circumstantial evidence requires use of the powers of reasoning. When using circumstantial evidence, the principal fact is inferred from other facts which were proved by direct evidence. In other words, circumstantial evidence is indirect proof by which the existence of one or more facts may reasonably be drawn from other facts that are established by direct evidence. Using the above example, if a witness testified that he saw the plaintiff's black eye on the day following the alleged battery, the black eye would be circumstantial evidence of the attack. Using another example, a witness who testifies to the length of skid marks provides direct evidence concerning those skid marks. From that direct evidence a jury may also infer that the driver was near the point where the skid marks began when the driver saw the danger; the driver sensed the need to stop; the driver applied the brakes; and the driver was or was not keeping a proper lookout. Matters of intent, motive and understanding often have to be proved through circumstantial evidence.

There is a growing tendency among the courts to look to expert opinion evidence, rather than circumstantial evidence, to prove how accidents happened. There are experts who "reconstruct" how accidents of all kinds occurred, including construction site accidents, automobile accidents, and airplane accidents. The rules of evidence authorize the use of expert witnesses when their opinions are useful to help the jury understand other evidence material to the case. Expert witnesses may be used to testify about almost any subject. Witnesses qualify to be experts on the basis of their education, training and experience concerning a particular subject. No law requires that an expert be a college graduate or otherwise have a strong academic background. Welders, mechanics, and plumbers may be expert witnesses. The court must be satisfied that the expert witness' background does, in fact, qualify him or her to be an expert. The weight and credibility to be given to an expert's testimony is a matter for the jury to decide. As a general rule, the expert's persuasiveness usually depends upon the reasons given by the expert for his or her opinions as well as the expert's credentials and background.

In litigation today, much of a lawyer's preparation for a trial is concerned with how to deal with the opposing party's expert witnesses. Each party is entitled to use interrogatories to discover the expert's opinions, the grounds for those opinions and the sources of the expert's information. These items will be important in preparing the cross-examination. The cross-examination is usually concerned with the expert's ability to analyze the problem and the reasons given for the expert opinion. The cross-examination of an opponent's expert may lay groundwork for presenting opinions of other expert witnesses who will testify later.

A party runs a very real risk of losing credibility by using too many expert witnesses. Two experts may be one expert too many. Experts don't always agree with each other even if they are testifying for the same party. They might arrive at the same basic conclusion but their assumptions, analyses and reasons may differ. These differences may weaken their overall authority.

The use of expert witnesses adds considerably to the cost of preparing the trial and presenting the evidence. Scholars of jurisprudence have expressed a good deal of concern that courts should become sensitive to the overuse of experts and place additional restraints on their use. Courts are beginning to discourage the use of experts when the expert testimony is not really needed to establish material facts. Expert witnesses should not be the trial advocates. Of course, experts should be allowed to explain technical evidence and facts which the jury could not understand without the guidance of experts.

Defendant's-Case-in-Chief

The defendant's case-in-chief is developed and presented much like the plaintiff's case-in-chief. Of course, the defendant's lawyer seeks to present the defendant's evidence and develop his or her contentions even during the plaintiff's case, but he or she does not have any control over the flow of the evidence during that phase of the trial. After the plaintiff has rested, the defendant's lawyer takes charge of the proceedings. The defendant's lawyer must have three objectives in mind. The defendant must meet and disprove the plaintiff's evidence and theories. The defendant must offer evidence which will prove the defendant's theory about the transaction or occurrence. Finally, the defense lawyer must develop the applicable affirmative defenses. Experienced lawyers know that it is not enough for the defendant's lawyer to "poke holes" in plaintiff's evidence. The defendant must have a theory which the lawyer must start developing as soon as possible. The trial is not compartmentalized for pursuing these objectives.

Witnesses

As soon as the court announces the date on which the case will begin trial a lawyer must contact the client and all witnesses whom he or she intends to have testify. It is usually desirable to contact the witnesses, first by telephone and then follow up with a letter which states the date, time and place of the trial. Additional information is helpful, such as the title of the action, the judge's name, the court room number, name of the other lawyer, probable length of the trial, the date on which the particular witness will probably be needed to testify, and the amount of time that the witness should set aside for the trial. If there is an agreement on compensation to be paid the witness, the terms may be stated in the letter. Of course, the letter is not privileged, and anything that is contained in the letter might be brought out during the witness's testimony. Therefore, some discretion should be used in deciding just what to put in the witness letter.

The above procedure works well when dealing with friendly witnesses. Different arrangements may be needed, however, when dealing with an unfriendly witness. The approach to be taken with unfriendly witnesses greatly depends upon the degree of hostility. As soon as the trial date is set, the unfriendly witness should be subpoenaed so that the witness cannot avoid service of the subpoena. A person who does not want to be called as a witness can find ways of making himself difficult to find so that a subpoena cannot be served upon him.

Sometimes it is desirable to subpoena friendly witnesses. For example, suppose that the lawsuit arises out of an accident that occurred as part of a church activity parties. The parties and witnesses are members of the same church. Some witnesses who have helpful information, who are willing to testify, may worry that the other party will look upon the witness's participation in the trial as a breach of friendship. That concern may be overcome by serving a subpoena upon the witness, so that the witness can readily explain to the other party that he or she had no choice in the matter. The witness had to testify because he or she was subpoenaed to testify.

There is another good reason for, on occasion, subpoenaing friendly witnesses. If there is a chance that the witness may have a serious problem in coming to court at the time needed, a subpoena may be useful in facilitating the witness's availability. For example, many people have difficulty getting off work, but a subpoena provides the witness with an absolute excuse or authorization for missing work. If a witness is ill so that the witness cannot come to court, a party can "excuse" his failure to have the witness in court by serving a subpoena upon the witness. The witness then has the burden of explaining his or her situation to the court, and that may require an affidavit or letter from an attending physician. The unavailability of a crucial witness may be grounds for obtaining a mistrial, but not if the witness hasn't been subpoenaed.

It is not unlawful or improper to reimburse a witness for the witness's time spent at court testifying. The fee should be based upon the value of the witness's time, not the value of the testimony to the case. Therefore, witness fees are ordinarily based upon the amount of money which the witness regularly earns in his or her occupation. In addition, it is perfectly proper to reimburse witnesses for expenses they incur when they come to court. This is true whether the expense is merely for bus fare or two hours of parking in a parking ramp or the expense is for traveling across the country by airplane. Whatever agreement is made concerning the payment of fees and expenses, it is subject to disclosure during the cross-examination of the witness. The reason for this is that the agreement to pay anything to the witness could affect the witness's credibility. Therefore, it is important to make sure that the agreement is one which a jury would find to be fair and appropriate. The worst type of agreement to have with a witness is that the witness will be paid only if the client prevails. The jury would properly see such an agreement as one which makes the witness an advocate and adversely affects the witness's credibility.

It is perfectly proper for a lawyer or legal assistant to talk with the opposing party's witnesses at any time, unless the witness is represented by another lawyer. Of course, there is no basis for forcing a hostile or unfriendly witness to discuss the case, except by taking the witness's deposition. If a witness, who appears to be aligned with the opposing side, does decline to speak about the case, the witness's refusal may be brought out on cross-examination to emphasize the bias of the witness. A manifest bias works against the witness's credibility.

Again, the hallmarks of a good witness are sincerity and authority. All witnesses should be committed to telling the truth. The preparation of a witness to testify at trial is, essentially, the same as the preparation for a deposition. However, there is one major exception. A witness who testifies in a discovery deposition should just answer the question; the witness should not volunteer or explain his or her answers, unless an explanation is specifically called for by the question. However, a witness at trial is there to educate and persuade the jury. Short answers are not educational and certainly not persuasive. Therefore, a witness's answers at court should be complete and as long as necessary to tell the jury what they need to know. Witnesses should testify only to what they know. For additional guidelines, see pages 208–215 in this text. Witnesses should be told, before they come to court, that they are not to try to communicate with the jury when they are off the witness stand, and they have no obligation to talk to the other lawyer, except when on the witness stand.

The order in which witnesses are called to testify depends primarily upon each witness's availability. Unfortunately, the importance of a logical development of the evidence too often must take a second place to witnesses' schedules and convenience. Of course, a witness's convenience or problems may be disregarded and the witness subpoenaed to come to court. But there is a very real danger that a disgruntled witness may be less helpful than the witness would have been if the witness's situation had been accommodated. In personal injury cases, the lawyers on both sides find that it is very important to accommodate the doctors' schedules.

A witness should be cautioned that anything the witness takes to the witness stand is subject to being examined by the lawyers. Consequently, most witnesses take nothing to the stand, except their deposition transcripts. Of course, medical doctors and expert witnesses take their "business" files with them to the witness stand. The business files are directly relevant to the case. The experts could hardly testify without their files in front of them.

A lawyer who puts a witness on the stand should know all about the witness, including such things as the witness's criminal background. If the witness is presented as an "important" witness and, during the testimony is shown to be a bad person with an unsavory reputation or background, the negative effect of such information may adversely affect the entire case.

Objections

If a party offers evidence which is contrary to the Rules of Evidence or contrary to law, the evidence is subject to objection, and if the objection is sustained, the evidence will not be received. If the evidence is not received, it may not be considered by the court or jury in deciding the case.

In deciding whether to object, a lawyer must first consider whether he or she has grounds for the objection. If there are grounds, then the lawyer must consider the value of making the objection by determining how the matter fits into the theory of the case, the overall trial strategy, and the importance of preserving the record for purposes of appeal.

Nothing highlights the adversarial nature of civil litigation more than the parties exercising their right to present evidence and object to improper evidence. As a general rule, the trier of fact (jury) may consider and rely upon any evidence which is presented without objection from the opposing side. For example, hearsay evidence may be sufficient to prove a claim or defense if it is received without objection from the opposing party. Nevertheless, if an objection is made, the jury may consider the evidence if the objection is overruled. In that event, the objection *may* only serve to highlight the evidence in the eyes of the jury.

Trial lawyers are constantly deciding whether or not to object to evidence. When an objection is made, the jury may feel that the objecting lawyer is trying to hide something. Too many objections, even if justified, may look bad to a jury. There is always the problem that an objection may not be sustained even when properly made. The judge may be wrong in overruling an objection, but the jury will not be aware that the judge is wrong. These factors are considered by a lawyer before he or she interposes an objection.

An objection duly made and *erroneously overruled* establishes error in the record which may entitle the objecting party to a new trial. However, an error justifies a new trial only if the error is prejudicial. Many errors may occur during the course of a trial which cannot be considered prejudicial. So before deciding to object, a lawyer needs to consider the ramifications of the objection. He or she must consider the probable impact of the anticipated answer. If the answer is sure to be innocuous, it may be better not to object. If the opposing lawyer may properly get the evidence before the jury in another way, for instance, by asking a different question or by asking the same question in a different manner, it may be better not to object. There is also the possibility that an improper question opens opportunities for cross-examination which otherwise might not be available. Does the jury understand the question? Is the probable answer easily explained? Does the question reflect adversely on the opposing lawyer? What is the likelihood that an objection will be sustained? The list of considerations for objecting or not objecting is almost without limit. Making an objection should never be a mere reflex reaction!

When the judge overrules or sustains an objection, the lawyer against whom the ruling is made may ask permission to approach the bench to discuss the ruling. The judge has discretion in deciding whether to allow additional discussion. The discussion must take place out of the hearing of the jury. On occasion, the judge might find the issue to be so difficult that he or she calls a recess to discuss the issue with the lawyers in the judge's chambers. The discussion in chambers may be on the record or, if everyone agrees, the discussion may be off the record.

If an objection is sustained so as to preclude a lawyer from presenting evidence, the lawyer has a right to make an **offer of proof,** out of the hearing of the jury, to show what the evidence would prove. The judge cannot prevent a party from making an offer of proof. The offer of proof helps appellate courts to appreciate the significance of the excluded evidence. The offer also gives the trial judge an opportunity to reconsider the ruling.

Use of Depositions

Depositions may be used at trial in various ways, whether taken for the purpose of discovery or to preserve testimony. The most common use is to impeach a witness whose testimony at trial varies from what the witness previously said in his or her deposition. If the inconsistency is significant, it may reflect adversely upon the witness's credibility. The jury must decide whether the deposition testimony is true or whether the court testimony is true.

At the end of the trial, the jury is instructed to consider impeachment in evaluating the witnesses' testimony. The fact that a witness has been inconsistent does not necessarily mean that the witness has lied. The witness is not necessarily subject to charges of perjury. Nor is the witness disqualified from testifying.

If a deposition is used to impeach a witness who is not a party, the impeachment testimony may be considered by the jury only for the purpose of testing the witness's credibility. Ordinarily, out of court statements are not evidence which will support a verdict. Such statements are hearsay; furthermore, the witness has retracted the prior out of court statement. Technically, the out of court testimony is not competent to establish any fact in the case. If the court testimony is believed, even though the witness was impeached, the testimony given at court will support a verdict.

If a party has made a statement in his deposition that is contrary to his testimony at trial, the adverse party may offer the prior deposition statement into evidence as a *party's admission*. The party's admission, even though it was made out of court, is considered to be substantive evidence which will support a verdict. A party's inconsistent prior testimony may also be offered and used to discredit the party.

Some examples may be helpful to illustrate these points. If a witness testifies in this deposition that he saw the defendant driving at 50 miles per hour in a 30 miles per hour zone, and at trial testifies that the defendant's speed was 25 miles per hour, the witness's testimony is competent only to prove a speed of 25 miles per hour. The deposition testimony of a higher speed casts doubt on the witness credibility, but the jury could not use the out of court testimony as a basis for determining, as a fact, that the defendant traveled 50 miles per hour. On the other hand, if the defendant testified in his deposition that he was driving 50 miles per hour at the time of the accident but at trial testified to a speed of 25 miles per hour, the jury could accept the "admission" in his deposition as substantive evidence and find, as a fact, that his speed was 50 miles per hour.

Depositions may be used as the "best evidence" when a witness is not available to testify in court. Unavailability may be the result of death, illness, absence from the jurisdiction or other circumstances. Using the examples in the previous paragraph, if the witness is not available to testify at trial, his deposition testimony that defendant was traveling 50 miles per hour will be received as substantive evidence because he has not retracted his sworn testimony.

A party may offer into evidence any portion of an adverse party's deposition. The testimony may be read to the jury. The deponent may subsequently read to the jury other portions of the deposition to explain, clarify or put the testimony into proper context. Witness statements may be used in a similar manner for purposes of impeachment and proof of facts.

Final Argument

The party who has the burden of proof has the right to make the last final argument. As discussed above, usually the plaintiff is the party who has the burden of proof. A few jurisdictions require the plaintiff to argue first but those courts give the plaintiff the opportunity to make a short rebuttal argument after the defendant's final argument. The rebuttal argument is supposed to be limited to answering the defendant's argument. It is not supposed to raise any new points. It may be subject to a time limit such as five minutes.

The purpose of a final argument is to persuade the jury that the client's claim or defense is correct. The jury must be persuaded that the client's version of the facts is true. A lawyer must analyze the evidence for the purpose of persuading the jury that the evidence proves the facts claimed by the client. The next step is to persuade the jury concerning the proper application of the law to those facts. Lawyers may comment on the applicable law and relate the law to the evidence. The judge's instructions at the end of the trial, however, will point out that the jury is to follow the law as the judge gives it. If the lawyers say anything about the law that is different than the judge's instructions, the jury is to disregard the lawyer's remarks. The lawyers may argue to the jury what facts the evidence have established and how those facts work in the client's favor. Lawyers may suggest to the jury how to answer the questions in the special verdict.

The lawyers have a right to know exactly what the judge intends to tell the jury about the law before they make their arguments. Lawyers often use charts in their final arguments to illustrate points, compute money damages, list items of damages, list critical items of evidence, etc. Each lawyer has a right to know about any "charts" the opposing counsel intends to use in their argument, unless the charts have been received in evidence as exhibits. The lawyers may refer to or use any of the exhibits that were received in evidence. They may read from documents received in evidence, but not from documents not received in evidence. For example, a lawyer may read from hospital records received in evidence. But a lawyer could not read from a textbook which was not received in evidence.

Lawyers are given a great deal of latitude in making arguments. However, they must not misstate the facts or law. They must not ask jurors to put themselves in a party's position. They must not make reference to God or call upon religious faith. Lawyers cannot engage the jurors in conversation. Jurors are not allowed to ask questions. The argument is supposed to educate the jury about the evidence and the applicable law.

If a lawyer makes any improper remarks in his or her argument, the opponent may object. If the argument is misleading, the opponent may be entitled to a corrective jury instruction. Lawyers usually try to keep their arguments under an hour in length. However, the length and complexity of the case will determine the scope and length of the argument.

Jury Instructions

The final phase of the trial is for the judge to instruct the jury on the law and the procedures that the jurors must follow in conducting their deliberations. The instructions are always read by the judge to minimize the opportunity for error. The instructions tell the jury how to evaluate witnesses and evidence. The jury is given the rules of law which govern the parties' substantive rights. It is becoming increasingly common for the judge to give the jury a copy of the written instructions to take with them into their deliberations.

The jurors may ask the judge for additional instructions or have the instructions reread if they have difficulty understanding or remembering what they were told. If additional instructions are given, the lawyers have a right to know about it and make any objections they deem appropriate. If the judge merely rereads the instructions previously given, the lawyers may not even return to the courtroom to participate. The verdict form is read and explained. The jury is encouraged to enter into a full discussion about the case as they deliberate. They cannot communicate with anyone, except the marshal or the bailiff who is charged with sequestering them.

If the jury has any questions about the law or procedures, they may present those questions to the judge in writing by giving the question to the marshal to deliver to the judge. When the jury asks for additional instructions, the judge contacts the lawyers. The judge explains to the lawyers the jury's question and how he or she intends to answer the question, or otherwise deal with the question. The judge may ask the lawyers for suggestions or for the lawyers to agree (stipulate) upon an answer to the jury's question. Regardless of the course of action taken, a record is made concerning the jury's question and its resolution.

Ordinarily, jurors are allowed to go to their own homes during the evening hours. However, if they want to continue with their deliberations, as is often the case, they are allowed to work into the night. In federal court the verdict must be unanimous. In most state courts all six jurors must agree if they return a verdict during the first six hours of their deliberations. After six hours, five of the six may return a verdict. However, all five must agree to all parts of the verdict. In other words, the same five must agree on all liability questions *and* all damages questions.

When the jury returns its verdict, the parties have a right to poll the jury to insure that all jurors really do concur. More often than not, the parties waive the right to poll the jury. The verdict is then filed with the clerk of court. If the court used a special verdict, which determines only questions of fact, the judge must use the verdict to prepare his or her own findings of fact, conclusions of law and order for judgment. If the jury returns a general verdict, they simply find for the plaintiff for a specified sum of money or for the defendant. The clerk enters judgment on a general verdict. This procedure does not involve the judge.

Taxation of Costs

The prevailing party is entitled to recover certain costs and disbursements incurred in the prosecution of the case. The recoverable costs are specified by statute or rule of the court. The prevailing party must prepare a bill of costs and disbursements which itemizes the various costs claimed. The losing party is given an opportunity to object to the items listed and the amounts claim. If objections are made, there must be a hearing on the objections. Otherwise, the clerk of court automatically enters the claimed costs as part of the judgment. If the defendant is the prevailing party, the defendant obtains a money judgment against the plaintiff for taxable costs. Before any judgment may be filed, the prevailing party must file an affidavit of identification which fully describes the judgment debtor. Each court has a form or recommended form for this.

25 Posttrial Motions

It is hoped that the jury's verdict or the judge's order for judgment will resolve and conclude the parties' controversy. But, unfortunately, not every trial proceeds without error. If an error does occur and if the error significantly affects the outcome of the case, the losing party may seek to have the error corrected by making a posttrial motion. There are numerous posttrial motions which may be used, depending upon the type of error and the relief which the moving party wants. Posttrial motions may be made for the purpose of having the award set aside, of having a new trial, or to obtain a change in the award of damages. Mere disappointment in a judge's decision or a jury's verdict is not grounds for obtaining a new trial or for appealing the case to a higher court. If the trial was conducted without any *prejudicial* error, there is no basis for changing the result. Error is considered prejudicial only if it appears that the error significantly affected the outcome of the case. The first step to obtaining posttrial relief is to make a posttrial motion to have the error corrected.

Motion for a New Trial

The most frequently made posttrial motion is a *motion for new trial*. The motion must be served upon all parties within ten days after the entry of judgment. If the judgment was entered on Monday, the ten-day period begins to run on Tuesday. The motion must specify the alleged errors. There are many possibilities for error in the course of a trial. Errors may concern substantive points of law or matters of procedure. Where error is shown, the court can order a new trial on the issue of liability or on the issue of damages or both.

Some of the more common grounds for a new trial are as follows:

Misconduct on the part of one or more jurors.   If a juror were to conduct an investigation of the case outside of the courtroom, that would constitute misconduct, which could require a new trial. A juror's contact with one of the parties or witnesses before or during the trial could give the appearance of favoritism or worse. A juror's false statement in the voir dire examination could be the basis for a new trial.

Misconduct on the part of the prevailing party. If the prevailing party concealed evidence, concealed witnesses, suborned perjury, presented false testimony, made an improper remark during final argument, etc., the trial court would be obligated to order a new trial in favor of the losing party. The misconduct must be substantial, prejudicial, and not corrected during the trial.

Discovery of new evidence. If the losing party can show that there is new, additional evidence which could change the outcome of the case *and* that the evidence could not have been discovered or obtained by the exercise of due diligence before the trial was completed, a new trial may be ordered. Parties are required to be diligent in gathering their evidence in preparation for the trial. If a party finds that more time is needed to secure important evidence, the party who needs more time may move the court for an order postponing trial. The moving party must be able to show the court that he or she has not been dilatory, and that the delay will not cause substantial prejudice to other parties.

It would be unfair for a party to neglect gathering or presenting evidence and then use the omission to obtain a new trial. For that reason, the losing party must be able to convince the court that the newly discovered evidence was unavailable or could not have been discovered before the trial concluded. This rule probably illustrates the adversarial nature of civil litigation as well as any. It manifests the duty each party has to be self-reliant in obtaining and presenting evidence. It also illustrates that the decision is final, even if wrong, where the parties have had a full, fair opportunity to present their claims and defenses.

Inappropriate award of damages. The amount of compensation to be awarded is peculiarly a question of fact for the jury. Nevertheless, courts have developed a sense of proportion about the adequacy or inadequacy of money damages for most types of cases. If the award is one which does not shock the judge's conscience as being either too much or too little, the award is allowed to stand. But an award which is manifestly unfair will be set aside and a new trial ordered. A new trial is appropriate whether the award is too much or too little. The new trial may be limited to the issue of damages only. A motion for a new trial on the issue of damages is usually a blended motion in which the moving party asks for an *additur* to the verdict (assuming the award is too little) or a *remittitur* to the verdict (assuming the award is too much). The trial judge may determine that a certain amount of money added to or taken away from the verdict will do substantial justice, and by ordering a change in the award, the expense of a new trial may be avoided. He or she may issue an order providing that if the plaintiff will accept a remittitur, in a stated amount, he or she will deny the defendant's motion for a new trial due to the excessiveness of the verdict. On the other hand, he or she may issue an order granting an additur for the plaintiff and, unless the defendant agrees to pay the additional specified sum over and above the verdict, the court will grant the plaintiff's motion for a new trial on the issue of damages.

The order for an additur or remittitur does not have to be tied to an order for a new trial.

Occasionally, a case is presented where an injured plaintiff claims to have spent many thousands of dollars for medical treatment for injuries allegedly sustained in an accident, but the defendant is able to present persuasive evidence establishing that the medical expenses were not due to the accident in question. A very small award may result. Weighing the evidence and equities of such a situation can be a very difficult responsibility for the trial judge and an appellate court.

Unrectified Errors of Law at Trial

Throughout a trial, the presiding judge is confronted with questions of law. The judge has to rule on the admissibility of controverted evidence. He or she must rule on requested jury instructions and often prepares his or her own jury instructions. If any of the rulings are erroneous and the error was duly brought to his or her attention, the losing party is entitled to a new trial if he or she can show that the error probably adversely affected the outcome of the case (Rule 103). Technical errors of little substance are never the basis for securing a new trial.

A lawyer's objection to evidence is sufficient notice to the judge that the admission of the evidence is in error. There is no need for a lawyer to argue each evidentiary ruling or to make a specific exception to the judge's rulings. There may be a problem, however, where a lawyer objects to certain improper evidence but inadvertently states the wrong grounds for his or her objection.

If a lawyer believes that the court has misstated the law in the jury instructions, he or she is required to bring that error to the judge's attention before the jury commences its deliberations. Ordinarily, as soon as the judge is finished with the instructions, he or she returns to the lawyers and asks whether there have been any errors or omissions in the instructions. The lawyers must speak then if they have concerns. It is unnecessary to discuss errors in the instruction if those errors were discussed on the record in chambers, before the judge undertook to instruct the jury. A lawyer may protect his or her record by filing written requested instructions which state his or her understanding of the applicable law.

Many procedural problems and issues of law are discussed by the lawyers and judge in the judge's chambers. This happens throughout the trial. Usually the judge and lawyers are able to reach a consensus about how the problem or issue is to be handled. However, when the lawyers can't agree and the judge has to make a decision (order), the lawyer who is adversely affected by the decision should have the record reflect his or her objection. The court reporter does not need to record everything that is said in chambers. It is enough for the lawyers and judge to summarize their discussions on the record and the decision that the court has made.

Verdict Not Supported by the Evidence

If the losing party feels that he or she was entitled to a directed verdict on an issue because there was no evidence to support the particular claim or defense, and the motion for directed verdict was denied, he or she may make a motion for a new trial on that ground. Usually, it is very difficult to obtain a new trial on this ground because almost any believable evidence on the issue is enough to carry the issue to the jury. The trial court, in effect, has a duty to try to sustain the verdict if that is reasonably possible. Every reasonable doubt is resolved in favor of the verdict. This motion is always accompanied by another motion called motion for judgment notwithstanding the verdict.

A motion for a new trial must state precisely the grounds for the motion. Proof of the error may be shown to the trial court by having a partial transcript of the proceedings prepared by the official court reporter. The motion may be supported by affidavits of persons who have knowledge of the claimed errors. Additionally, the motion is almost always based on the facts as recorded in the judge's minutes made during the trial.

The rules provide that a trial judge may order a new trial within ten days after the entry of judgment even though neither party has made a motion for a new trial. The same power permits the trial judge to order a new trial on grounds which were not raised by the losing party's motion for a new trial. The order for a new trial must state the reasons or grounds for granting a new trial; however, an order denying the motion for a new trial needs no explanation.

A motion for a new trial is considered the first step to an appeal. In some state courts, a motion for a new trial is practically a prerequisite to an appeal. It gives the trial judge an opportunity to consider and correct an alleged error. It also gives the judge an opportunity to explain the reasons for his or her decision. In federal court, however, the losing party may simply appeal from the judgment. The *scope* of review in certain appellate courts is broader if the appeal is from an order denying a new trial rather than an appeal from the judgment.

Motion for Judgment Notwithstanding the Verdict

The grounds for making a motion for judgment notwithstanding the verdict (j.n.o.v.) are that the determinative issue or issues must be decided as a matter of law, or the evidence is insufficient to establish the opponent's cause of action or the opponent's affirmative defense, even though the jury has found in favor of the opponent. The standard for challenging the sufficiency of the evidence has been variously stated. The verdict must be set aside if: (1) the verdict is contrary to the entire evidence; or (2) reasonable minds would have to agree that the outcome is wrong; or (3) there is no competent evidence which reasonably tends to support the verdict. The grounds for granting judgment n.o.v. are the same as the grounds for granting a directed verdict.

The necessity for the motion may come about because the trial judge may have believed that the jury would not find as they did and the judge wanted the parties to have their case decided by the jury. Since the jury made the unexpected decision, the judge must now correct the error. Another situation which may give rise to the motion is when the judge does not have time to fully consider the requirements of the applicable law and, rather than make the jury wait for the court and lawyers to fully consider the law, the judge may decide to submit the case in line with the prevailing party's theory of the law. However, after further consideration, the judge may conclude that the legal theory was incorrect or unsupported by the evidence. To correct the problem the judge may grant judgment notwithstanding the verdict. This motion is usually combined with a motion for a new trial. See Rule 50.

26 Judgments

A judgment is the court's final expression of the parties' legal rights and obligations. A judgment is entered in the court file and judgment docket after a full trial on the merits. Or it may be entered as the result of a party's default as shown by the court records. Most courts also allow judgments to be filed on the basis of a party's **confession of judgment.** The terms **judgment** and **decree** are frequently used interchangeably. Historically, a decree was the ultimate determination by a court in **equity.** The court decreed what the parties were or were not to do. Whereas, a judgment was rendered by a court of law and usually awarded a sum of money or disallowed the claim for a sum of money.

The judgment document is usually prepared by the clerk of court. If the case is decided upon a general verdict and results in an award of money or a determination that no recovery should be had by the plaintiff, the clerk of court is required to forthwith enter judgment according to the verdict (Rule 58). If the jury returns a special verdict or a general verdict with answers to interrogatories, however, the trial judge must prepare an **Order for Judgment.** The order directs the clerk of court how to prepare and state the terms of the judgment. The judge must approve the form of the judgment before it is officially filed. Approval is indicated by his or her signature.

A court's order for judgment may be similar to the following:

The above-entitled action came on for trial before the court and a jury, the Honorable Russell A. Smith, United States District Judge, presiding, and the issues have been duly tried, and the jury having duly rendered its verdict,

It is Ordered and Adjudged that plaintiff, Robert I. Miller, recover from the defendant, Thomas Jones, the sum of twenty-five thousand dollars and his taxable costs.

Dated at Chicago, Illinois, this _____ day of October, 1990.

/s/ Raymond A. Johnson
Clerk of Court

The clerk of court notes on the *judgment docket* or *judgment roll* the fact that the judgment was entered on a particular date and in a particular amount. The judgment may conclude that the plaintiff is entitled to recover specific property or that he or she is the owner of certain property. As discussed in the section on remedies, there are various forms of relief which may be ordered by a court. Whatever the form of relief, it is stated in the judgment.

Courts are reluctant to allow the prevailing party to enforce a judgment before the losing party exhausts or waives his or her posttrial remedies. Therefore, it is common for judges to attach to an Order for Judgment a thirty-day stay against entry of judgment or a ten-day stay against execution on the judgment (Rule 62). If an appeal is taken and the proper bond is posted by the appellant, he or she is entitled to a court order staying any proceedings by which the judgment creditor may attempt to enforce the judgment.

Judgment Creditors and Debtors

A judgment is, in itself, a valuable property right for a judgment creditor. When the judgment is filed, it becomes a lien against the judgment debtor's property, at least, that property which is not exempt from seizure through a writ of execution or writ of attachment. A judgment for money may be assigned or transferred to another person. Of course, such transfers should be in writing and filed with the clerk of court. State law determines the length of time during which a judgment is enforceable. The federal courts follow and apply state law in this regard. A typical period of time for a judgment to remain effective is ten years. The judgment creditor may, however, renew the judgment before expiration by applying for a renewal and paying a nominal fee. Once the judgment expires, it becomes a nullity. It is no longer a lien or encumbrance against the judgment debtor's property. It cannot be enforced against him or her.

Under the laws of most states, a judgment creditor is entitled to interest on the amount of the judgment. Interest begins to accumulate on the date the judgment is entered. It should be noted that in many jurisdictions, interest accrues on the jury's verdict from the day the verdict is rendered. Where interest is allowed on the verdict, that amount should be incorporated into the amount of the judgment.

If a judgment states that property owned by the judgment debtor should be transferred to the judgment creditor, the court may order the judgment debtor to execute (sign) a quit claim deed running in favor of the judgment creditor. If the judgment debtor refuses to do so, the court may appoint a trustee to do the act for the judgment debtor. In some jurisdictions, the court is empowered to declare: that which the judgment debtor should have done, is done. In other words, the court order, which declares that the judgment creditor is entitled to have the property transferred to the creditor, has the effect of an actual deed. A judgment creditor ordinarily prefers to have an actual deed, rather than a court order; therefore, a creditor resorts to a court order for transferring title only when the judgment debtor refuses to comply with the court's order to execute a deed. The judgment becomes a public record transfer of title and is accepted for filing by the local Register of Deeds.

If the judgment is for a sum of money and the debtor cannot or will not pay it, the court may issue a *writ of execution*, which directs the executive branch of the government, usually a sheriff, to locate the defendant's property, seize it, and sell it in the manner prescribed by law. The usual procedure is to sell the property at a public auction with due notice given to the public and to those persons who have special interests in the property. Usually, the property is held for a designated period of time during which the judgment debtor has an opportunity to redeem the property by meeting his or her obligation. A judgment creditor may be required to post a bond protecting the judgment debtor against any errors or improprieties which might occur when the property is seized and sold. The sheriff probably does not know the exact location of the judgment debtor's property. Therefore, it behooves the judgment creditor to provide the sheriff with whatever information he or she can about the identity and location of nonexempt property to be seized. The sheriff charges the creditor for his or her time and expenses, but these expenses ultimately become the responsibility of the judgment debtor.

Occasionally, the judgment creditor and sheriff cannot locate any of the debtor's properties or monies. In that event, the judgment creditor is allowed to conduct *supplementary proceedings* for the purpose of trying to locate the debtor's monies and properties. Upon motion, the court will issue an order requiring the judgment debtor to appear at a specified time and place for a deposition in which the debtor may be questioned about his or her earnings, properties, past transfers of property, and any expectancy of future acquisitions. The debtor may be asked about his or her current and recent employment, salary, mode of payment, checking accounts, savings accounts, accounts receivable, etc. The debtor's testimony is under oath, so he or she is subject to the penalties of perjury. If the debtor refuses to answer questions about the nature and extent of properties and financial condition, he or she is subject to a contempt of court order. Armed with the new information obtained in the supplementary proceedings, the judgment creditor is able to secure a new writ of execution directed to the sheriff, who can try once more to locate, seize, and sell the debtor's monies and properties. If the sheriff is able to find cash, the money itself may be turned over to the judgment creditor. Again, the sheriff deducts his or her fees and expenses before the judgment creditor is paid. Nevertheless, the judgment creditor's total recovery is not necessarily reduced by the amount of the sheriff's fees. If enough money or property is found, the judgment debtor ends up paying the additional costs incurred.

A judgment debtor should not be subject to harassment by supplementary proceedings. Therefore, judgment creditors are allowed to have only a certain number of depositions during a year. A court order is required for each deposition. The proceedings are governed by state law.

If a third person is indebted to the judgment debtor or holds monies or properties of the debtor, the judgment creditor may claim and recover such monies and properties through a garnishment proceeding. He or she does this by obtaining a *garnishment summons,* which must be served on the third person who is designated as the *garnishee.* The summons advises the garnishee of the fact of the indebtedness and the amount of it. It directs the garnishee to disclose to the judgment creditor the amount of monies, if any, that is being held by the garnishee. The garnishee does this by serving and filing a *garnishment disclosure.* Garnishment procedures are frequently used to tie up bank accounts and wages earned. In most states, if not all, wages are given a partially exempt status so that only a fraction of the debtor's take-home pay may be seized.

Transfer of Judgments

A judgment of one court may be transferred to a court in another jurisdiction for enforcement. The procedure is relatively simple. An authenticated, sometimes called "exemplified," copy of the original judgment must be filed with the second court. The judgment establishes the nature and extent of the debtor's obligation. As provided in the United States Constitution, the states are required to give full faith and credit to each other's judgments. The defendant—judgment debtor—may contest the judgment on the grounds that the original court lacked jurisdiction or that he or she has paid the judgment. Either of these defenses requires a trial to establish the truth. A defect in jurisdiction may occur because the trial court failed to obtain jurisdiction over the person of the defendant or over the subject matter of the litigation. The trial court may lack jurisdiction because it went beyond its power in granting a particular remedy or it acted beyond its geographical limitations. The judgment debtor has the burden of showing that jurisdiction was lacking. The judgment is presumed to be valid, and the judgment debtor has the burden of proving facts in avoidance of the judgment.

When a judgment creditor transfers the judgment to another jurisdiction and brings an action on that judgment to enforce it against the debtor, the judgment debtor cannot attempt to relitigate any of the issues which were decided in the first trial or issues which should have been determined in the first trial. He or she may not challenge the sufficiency of the evidence. He or she cannot even attempt to show that errors occurred in the first trial which caused the loss.

27 Appeals

On occasion, trial courts misapply the substantive law; and sometimes they make procedural errors. These errors may be very minor or they may go to the very heart of the controversy. The trial judge ordinarily has an opportunity to correct errors which are brought to the judge's attention during the trial and by posttrial motions. However, if the trial judge determines that the contested rulings or conduct were not erroneous, the party who is adversely affected by the judge's rulings has the right to an independent review by an appellate court. In the federal judicial system, there are thirteen circuit courts of appeals to handle appeals from the federal district courts including the District of Columbia Circuit and the U.S. Court of Appeals for the Federal Circuit. A party who prosecutes an appeal is commonly referred to as the *appellant*. The party against whom an appeal is brought is referred to as the *appellee*. Many state courts identify the party against whom an appeal is taken as the *respondent*.

An appeal is taken against the prevailing party, not against the presiding judge. There are rare occasions when a party may ask an appellate court for an order (writ of mandamus) which requires the trial judge to do a particular act; or a party may seek an appellate order (writ of prohibition) which prohibits the trial judge from doing a particular act. These appellate writs are obtained during prosecution of the case, usually before the trial, not after the case has been tried. For example, the parties might have a disagreement over the scope of discovery in a party's deposition. The deponent may believe that the questions require disclosure of privileged information that would cause serious damage to the deponent. The deponent might be able to challenge the judge's order, which requires disclosure, by seeking a writ of prohibition from an appellate court which prevents the judge from enforcing the order.

There are two appellate levels in the federal judicial system. Under some circumstances, a party may appeal to the United States Supreme Court from a decision of a court of appeals. The United States Supreme Court is the highest appellate court. In most instances, an appeal from the trial court's judgment may be taken to the appropriate circuit court of appeals as a matter of right. Subject to a few exceptions, parties do not have a right to appeal to the United States Supreme Court. An appeal to the Supreme Court is permitted only when the Supreme Court is persuaded that the case is particularly important. For example, the Supreme Court is likely to grant review if two circuit courts have reached opposite conclusions on the law, and a decision by the Supreme Court is needed to harmonize the law.

A federal district court judgment may be appealed only to the circuit court of appeals which serves the circuit in which the particular district court is located. Remember, each state is a separate judicial district. There are thirteen federal circuit courts of appeals. See page 501 for a map of the thirteen circuits.

Appellate Procedure

An appeal to a circuit court of appeals is governed by the *Rules of Appellate Procedure.* Few cases can be appealed to the United States Supreme Court from a circuit court of appeals.

The appellant must be able to demonstrate to the appellate court that one or more errors occurred and that the error adversely affected the outcome of the trial. Appealable errors may arise out of the application of the substantive law or through the application of procedural law or both. In either event, the appellant has the burden of persuading the appellate court that the alleged error was prejudicial. This means that the appellant must show that if the law had been correctly applied, there is good reason to believe that the trial court's verdict or decision would have been different. The news media give the impression that parties appeal from the trial court's judgments merely on the basis that they feel the verdict or decision is unfair; however, much more is required.

A relatively small percentage of cases are appealed. The system tends to favor the party who prevailed at trial. There are several factors which mitigate against the successful prosecution of an appeal. First of all, appeals are expensive. The amount in controversy may not justify the cost and effort that necessarily goes into an appeal. An appeal may be more expensive than the trial. A large majority of the cases appealed are affirmed.

An appellant initiates an appeal by serving and filing a *notice of appeal.* In federal court, the notice of appeal must be filed within thirty days of the date on which the judgment was entered. A notice of appeal may be similar to the following:

(Title of Cause)   NOTICE OF APPEAL

To: Plaintiff John Smith and Joe Brown, his attorney:

Notice is hereby given that (name), defendant above named, hereby appeals to the United States Court of Appeals for the _____ Circuit from the final judgment entered in this action on the _____ day of _____, 1990, in the above entitled action on (date of judgment).

                                    _____
                                    Attorney for Defendant
                                    Address

When the notice of appeal is filed with the clerk of district court, the appellant must pay a filing fee. The district court may require the appellant to file a cost bond or give other security to guaranty that, if the appellant loses the appeal, the appellee's costs will be covered. If there is a judgment for a sum of money against the appellant, some state courts require the appellant to file a supersedeas bond, which protects the prevailing party for the amount of the judgment. In the event the appeal is denied, the bond guarantees that the prevailing party can collect the amount of the judgment docketed in the trial court as well as taxable costs. It is not uncommon for the parties to enter into a stipulation waiving the appeal bonds. The respondent benefits by the waiver because if he or she loses the appeal, the cost of the bond is taxable against the respondent in most cases.

The appellant must order a transcript of the proceedings from the official court reporter within ten days after filing the notice of appeal. The appellant must make arrangements with the court reporter to pay the reporter's fees for transcribing the testimony. The trial transcript, exhibits, and district court file—which make up the record on appeal—must be sent to the clerk of the court of appeals. The record on appeal is composed of all the pleadings and all other documents filed with the clerk, plus all of the exhibits and an original copy of the transcript of the trial. The transcript usually includes all of the testimony, motions at trial, and jury instructions. In addition, the lawyers may stipulate that certain parts of the record may be omitted. Frequently, the opening statements and closing arguments are omitted. If the appeal is concerned only with a liability issue, the testimony concerning damages may be omitted. The original transcript must be filed with the clerk of court by the reporter. The appellant must supply at least one copy of the transcript to each party.

The appellant must prepare a brief on the law and the "appendix to appellant's brief." The brief and appendix ordinarily are printed—not merely typewritten. Printed briefs help to insure ease of reading and care in preparation. Consequently, federal court rules require printing of the briefs and appendices. The appendix consists of the pleadings and other documents filed with the district court in connection with the case. It also contains pertinent portions of the transcript relating to the issues to be submitted to the appellate court. The appellant is supposed to notify the respondent of those portions of the transcript which he or she intends to include in the appendix. The respondent may request that other portions be included, and if the appellant refuses to include those additional portions, the respondent may arrange for a supplemental printing of them.

The appellant has only forty days in which to prepare the appendix and appellant's brief after the original record has been transmitted to the clerk of the appellate court. The Rules of Appellate Procedure allow the appellee only thirty days in which to reply to the appellant's brief. If more time is needed for preparing a brief and appendix, the appellant must make his or her request before the forty-day period expires. The request is made to the district court—not to the appellate court.

The appellant's brief is divided into several sections and should be as concise as possible. It must contain a statement outlining the nature of the case and a chronological review of the case listing the date on which the action was commenced and each important procedural date thereafter. It must contain a concise, nonargumentative statement of the facts which were established through the pleadings and the evidence at trial. Preparation of the statement of facts is considered by most lawyers to be the most difficult part of good brief writing. Each important fact necessary to the appeal must be stated, along with a page reference showing where the fact may be found in the record.

The appellant must formulate and state the legal issues to be decided by the appellate court. If the appellee disagrees with the legal issues as propounded by the appellant, the appellee may submit a statement of the issues in his or her brief. It is hoped that the parties will agree, at least, on the issues to be argued. But stating a legal issue precisely is not always an easy task.

The body of the brief is an argument on the law. The appellant's lawyer attempts to convince the appellate court that errors occurred in the district court and that the errors prejudiced the outcome of the case. The argument may be concerned with how the appellant was prevented from proving the facts or how the trial court misapplied the law. Although a verdict may be set aside where it is manifestly contrary to the weight of the evidence, the appellant is not permitted to argue that the jury merely reached the wrong verdict. The appellate court assumes that the verdict is consistent with the evidence which favored the appellee. Any evidence favoring the appellant, which is inconsistent with the verdict, is presumed to have been rejected by the jury. Of course, the jury cannot reject admissions and stipulations.

The fact that more witnesses and exhibits supported the appellant's theory of the evidence is of no importance on appeal. For example, suppose that the plaintiff claims to have sustained brain damage in an accident; that the evidence showed he was attended by six physicians; that one of the six was of the opinion that the accident caused the plaintiff's alleged brain damage; that one physician had no opinion on the issue; that four were emphatic that the accident could not have caused any brain damage; and that one independent medical examiner, chosen by the defendant, testified that, to a reasonable medical certainty, the accident did not cause any injury. If the appellate court determined that the *one* physician, who supported the plaintiff's claim of brain damage, was competent to render such an opinion and that there was adequate foundation for his opinion, the verdict would stand even though the greater number of witnesses testified to the contrary. The appellate court is not supposed to act as a super jury. Its function is to make sure that the law was correctly stated and applied, and that the trial procedures were properly followed.

The legal authorities used in the appellate briefs may include published decisions of the appellate court in which the case is pending and decisions of other courts that have considered the issue. Decisions made in cases rendered by the appellate court in which the appeal is pending, are, of course, the most persuasive for determining the issues on appeal. Indeed, if the decisions are directly in point, they should be determinative. A court should always follow the precedent of its own decisions. Such decisions are considered binding upon the court and are followed unless the appellate court chooses to *overrule* its prior decisions. The holdings by other appellate courts on the issues raised are helpful because of the rationale of the opinions; courts ordinarily strive for uniformity concerning rules of law.

The last section of a legal brief is the conclusion. Customarily, the conclusion is used to state the legal issues in a positive way, indicating how the court should rule. The conclusion also specifies the type of relief requested by the appellant, that is, a new trial or judgment notwithstanding the verdict or a new trial on a single issue, such as damages. A good conclusion is concisely stated and is not a reargument of the case.

Occasionally, an appellate matter raises an issue of law that may have a substantial impact on persons or companies who are not parties to the suit, and they may want to participate in the appeal. Such persons may apply to the court for leave to file an *amicus curiae brief*—a brief by a "friend of the court." No one has an absolute right to file an amicus brief. The court considers the nature of the applicant's interest in determining whether or not to permit the appearance. Obviously, the parties have an interest in who will participate and to what extent. But the parties have no veto power over a motion for leave to file an amicus brief.

The appellee has thirty days from the date the appellant's brief is received to prepare and file a responsive brief. The appellee argues in support of the trial court's rulings and that any errors which did occur were not prejudicial. The format of the appellee's brief is similar to the appellant's brief. In some appellate courts, the appellant may file a reply brief, which merely gives the appellant a chance to make a rebuttal to the appellee's brief.

Appellate Decisions

The circuit court of appeals clerk schedules the appeals for oral argument before three or more appellate judges. The parties usually have at least thirty days notice of the hearing date. An appellate court ordinarily hears three or four arguments during the course of a morning's session. Each case is allotted one hour or less. Therefore, each lawyer has only thirty minutes or less in which to present his or her oral argument. The appellant may be allowed to save some of the allotted time for replying to the appellee's argument. During the arguments, the judges ask such questions as they deem necessary. The appellate judges almost never state what their decision will be. A lawyer is often able to make an educated guess about the probable outcome, however, by the nature of the judges' questions and by their apparent attitude toward the issues. The appellate court's decision is usually rendered within three or four months after the argument, sometimes sooner. Of course, the length of time for the court's decision depends upon many factors, and a decision could take even longer.

Upon receiving the appellate court decision, the losing party may determine that some point has been neglected or overlooked by the appellate court. The remedy is to file a motion for a rehearing in which he or she sets forth the reasons why a rehearing is necessary. If the court is convinced by the written motion that a rehearing is justified, a rehearing is ordered. More often than not, however, motions for rehearing are denied without explanation.

Only a small percentage of the cases which go to the circuit courts of appeal are carried to the United States Supreme Court. There are very few types of cases in which the parties have an absolute right to appeal to the Supreme Court. Most cases are appealed to the Supreme Court pursuant to a writ of certiorari, which is an order from the Supreme Court to a circuit court of appeals directing that a certified record of its proceedings in the particular case be sent up for review. A party applies to the Supreme Court for issuance of the writ. If it appears to the Supreme Court that there is a split of authority among the circuit courts of appeal concerning the particular issues and that an important issue is involved, the justices are likely to allow the appeal, so that the conflict can be resolved. If an appeal raises significant constitutional questions or questions of general importance to the nation, the appeal may be accepted. The amount of money or property in question is not a major factor in determining whether the Supreme Court will elect to hear the case.

Appellate courts have inherent power to overrule their prior decisions and to propound new rules of law. To a large extent, however, the stability of our legal system depends upon the reluctance of appellate courts to change rules of law once decided. The principle is referred to as stare decisis. Most changes in the law should come through the legislatures. The appellate courts cannot change laws enacted by the legislature. The courts can change their "interpretations" of statutes, and that has almost the same effect. An appellate court may determine that a legislative law is invalid because the statute violates the Constitution or there was some defect in the procedures by which the statute was enacted. A statute may be too vague to be enforceable, thus violating due process requirements. Of course there are times when an appellate court recognizes that it erred in propounding a rule of law. The court may overrule its prior decision by declaring a new rule of law.

When an appellate court determines that the trial court did commit a prejudicial error, it may reverse the decision of a trial court and order entry of judgment in favor of the appellant. In that event, the litigation is put to an end. Or, the appellate court may determine that an error was committed, but the appellant is not entitled to judgment on the present state of the record. The appellate court may *remand* the case to the trial court for a new trial. A new trial may be ordered on all issues or on certain specified issues. For example, a court may determine that the error in question did not affect the jury's determination of liability in favor of the plaintiff against the defendant; however, the error did affect the jury's determination of the amount of damages awarded to the plaintiff. Under those circumstances, the court could direct the trial court to have a new trial on only the issue of damages. In that event, the first trial was of some value to the parties. In light of the appellate court's decision, the parties may be able to settle their dispute without actually going through another trial.

The appellate courts have broad discretion in determining what costs if any, are allowed and to whom the costs are awarded. Costs are not always awarded to the prevailing party.

Each circuit court of appeals has eight or more judges; however, each case is assigned to just three judges for consideration and decision. Only three judges will listen to the oral arguments. After the argument they confer and determine how the case should be decided. One of the three judges writes the opinion for the court, and he or she signs the opinion. If a case has unique importance, all of the judges in the circuit may hear the arguments and participate in the decision making.

If one or more of the judges disagrees with the majority opinion, he or she may write a *dissenting opinion*, which is published along with the majority opinion. On occasion, a judge may agree with the result reached by the majority but disagree with the reasons given for the majority decision. The judge may file a *concurring opinion* in which he or she states the reasons why he or she reached the decision. Of course, a unanimous decision is usually considered to be more forceful authority for use as a precedent. If a court is closely divided in reaching a decision, it is quite possible that the decision will be overruled the next time it comes before the court. On occasion the judges on an appellate court are evenly divided on how the case should be decided. The consequence is that the trial court's decision breaks the tie. The trial court's judgment is affirmed.

A paralegal may be asked to outline portions of the trial transcript much in the same way that depositions are outlined and summarized. Paralegals may help to assemble the appendix to an appellant's brief. Paralegals may also help proofread the brief and verify citations. Some paralegals have been allowed to assist in writing nontechnical portions of briefs.

28 Settlements, Releases, and Dismissals

When the parties to a dispute cannot resolve the dispute, the civil litigation system is available to provide a resolution which will permanently end the controversy. Unfortunately, the civil justice system cannot guarantee a remedy or resolution that will satisfy all of the parties. Indeed, a court mandated solution may not satisfy any of the parties. Furthermore, there is seldom any way of knowing what the court's decision will be before the verdict is rendered or the appeal is concluded. The goal of the civil justice system is to provide a resolution which comports with society's standards of what is fair and reasonable, not necessarily a remedy which satisfies the parties.

The civil courts can promise, however, that the controversy will be permanently concluded. For better or for worse, the controversy is put to an end, and the government will act to protect the rights established through the litigation process and enforce the obligations. It is important that the dispute be brought to a conclusion, permanently, so as to discourage the parties from resorting to violence and revenge. The ability to provide a termination of controversies is one of the most important objectives of the civil justice system. As long as the controversy lasts, it tends to fester. The above factors make private settlements a very attractive alternative to pursuing a lawsuit to a conclusion.

A vast majority of claims are resolved by settlements rather than bringing the claims to trial. When the parties are able to agree upon a satisfactory resolution of their controversy without a court determination, they avoid uncertainty, gain economies, and obtain a disposition which they know they can tolerate, if not embrace. When the parties are able to agree upon a resolution, they may enter into a settlement agreement for the purpose of permanently concluding their dispute. A settlement agreement is a contract. Since the effect of the settlement agreement is to release causes of action, the written settlement agreement is customarily referred to as a "release." A written release is the embodiment of the parties' negotiated settlement. A release is enforceable like any contract. Or, the contract can be the basis for a judgment which establishes the parties' rights and obligations between them.

Offer of Judgment

In almost every case that goes to trial the parties have conducted some settlement negotiations, but the negotiations proved to be unfruitful. Therefore, the parties are forced to incur the expense of a trial. The prevailing party will be allowed to tax costs against the losing party. The defendant who is clearly liable to the plaintiff, but cannot reach a settlement with the plaintiff because of the plaintiff's demands are excessive, is at a real disadvantage. However, Rule 68 provides some help. The Rule allows the defendant to make a formal offer in writing to let judgment be taken against him or her for a specified amount. The offer must include an agreement to pay the plaintiff's taxable costs which have accrued to the date of the offer. An offer of judgment may be served by mail in accordance with Rule 5. The plaintiff has ten days in which to accept the offer of judgment. If service was by mail, the plaintiff has an additional three days in which to accept. If the offer of judgment is not accepted within the authorized period of time, it is considered rejected.

There is no limit on the number of offers of judgment which the defendant may make. However, to be effective, an offer must be made at least ten days before trial. The effect of making an offer of judgment is that the plaintiff must obtain a verdict for more than the offer; otherwise, the plaintiff cannot tax costs against the defendant, and the defendant may tax his or her costs against the plaintiff. An offer of judgment is not an offer to make an immediate payment of money. Therefore, even if the defendant does not have enough money to pay the judgment, he or she may still make the offer of judgment. As with settlement negotiations in general, neither the plaintiff or defendant may inform the jury about the offer of judgment.

If the plaintiff elects to accept the offer of judgment, either party may file the offer and acceptance with the clerk of court along with the proofs of service. The clerk is authorized to enter judgment as provided by the offer and acceptance. The lawsuit is concluded by the judgment. An offer of judgment cannot be made unless a civil action has already been commenced and is pending.

Confession of Judgment

If the person against whom a claim is made recognizes the obligation but has no money or other means by which to satisfy the obligation, the laws of all states provide a method by which that person may *confess judgment*. There is no need for a lawsuit or other legal proceeding. The obligor simply executes the necessary affidavits and forms which authorize the clerk of court to enter a judgment pursuant to the parties' agreement. Of course, a confession of judgment is binding only upon the parties to the agreement. It would not be binding upon the confessor's partners, spouse, heirs, assigns or the confessor's liability insurance company. The judgment remains a legally enforceable obligation for ten years, more or less, depending upon the laws of the particular state.

Settlements

A large majority of claims and civil actions are concluded through compromise settlements. When the parties settle their dispute they may establish their own criteria, terms, and conditions for concluding the dispute. They avoid expending time and money on litigation procedures. The reasons for their settlement may be contingent upon their ability or inability to prosecute a cause of action or prove an affirmative defense. Another reason for settlement may be based upon relative financial conditions. The reasons for a settlement may be totally unrelated to legal considerations relevant to a lawsuit. For example, parties may settle their dispute on a handshake because they are friends and their friendship is worth more to them than winning money damages in a lawsuit. Friendship or even past friendship is not a consideration in determining or proving legal rights and obligations in court.

A "settlement agreement" is a contract between the parties which terminates their civil dispute. The parties' agreement is commonly referred to as a **settlement**. A party who pays money to settle a disputed claim is said to have "bought his peace." Settlement agreements are used to resolve contract disputes and claims which arise out of alleged torts.

An **accord and satisfaction** is a type of settlement agreement used in disputes arising out of transactions. Instead of paying a sum of money "to buy peace" and sever their relationship, the parties agree to substitute a new agreement (accord) for the old agreement. The performance of the new agreement (satisfaction) fully discharges the controverted obligation. In other words the execution of the new contract is called the "satisfaction." As noted in Chapter 4, an accord and satisfaction is an affirmative defense which must be pled and proved by the defendant if the plaintiff brings an action on the original contract.

Settlement agreements and accords and satisfactions are governed by the law of contracts. To be enforceable as contracts, these agreements must be made by parties who are legally competent to enter into contracts. If a party is a minor, that party must have a guardian appointed who can advise the minor and make the decision for the minor. Furthermore, a settlement is not binding upon the minor unless the guardian obtains court approval of the settlement agreement. Consequently, any party who must deal with a minor ordinarily insists upon negotiating through a guardian and having court approval of their agreement to settle. If one of the parties is a business organization, the other party must determine the business's legal status. A business's legal status is defined as a corporation, partnership or a sole proprietorship. The business's ability to execute a contract depends upon its status as a legal entity.

The parties to a settlement agreement must have a meeting of the minds concerning the terms and conditions of their agreement. A meeting of the minds comes about through a process of offers, counteroffers and an acceptance. The process is commonly referred to as the settlement negotiations. The importance of a meeting of the minds is highlighted by the personal injury cases in which the claimant settles his or her claim for a relatively modest amount but subsequently discovers that he or she had injuries which were not known at the time of the settlement. Or, the claimant may subsequently discover new consequences of known injuries. Either way, the claimant did not consider these problems when he or she executed a full and final release. Was there a meeting of the minds? For example, suppose that the claimant's leg is broken in an automobile accident; the leg heals straight, strong and without any loss of motion. However, two years after the accident it is discovered that the injury damaged the bone so that it cannot grow anymore. Consequently, when the claimant obtains his full growth his injured leg is two inches shorter than the other leg.

Because of the very real possibility that the claimant has injuries which he and his doctors don't know about or because there may be unanticipated consequences of known injuries, all "full and final releases" used in personal injury cases provide that the claimant release his or her claims for all injuries, whether known or unknown. On that basis there is a meeting of the minds as to what is being released. Of course, the parties may agree to settle their dispute on the basis that the claimant is releasing only known injuries. Then neither party really gambles. However, there are many reasons why the defendant or defendant's liability insurer may refuse to settle unless the claimant gives a full and final release. Suppose that the case used in the above example had gone to trial rather than settled. The plaintiff's evidence would not have disclosed the fact that the bone's ability to grow had been damaged, so the plaintiff would not have received any compensation for that problem. The problem of unknown injuries and unknown consequences of known injuries points out the importance of not settling personal injury cases too quickly.

The agreement must be voluntary and not the result of duress or undue influence. A threat of personal injury or property damage is an example of duress which would vitiate the settlement agreement. On the other hand, a party's desperate need for money or compelling desire to end the dispute, do not constitute duress which would give grounds to avoid a settlement agreement.

The terms of a settlement agreement must provide for an exchange of consideration. The most common consideration used in settlement agreements is the payment of money. The second most common form of consideration is a promise to do something or to refrain from certain conduct. The promise, and performance of the promise, is valid consideration which will support a settlement contract, provided the promisor is not already under a legal compulsion to do what he or she has promised. In that event, the promisor has really given nothing of value for the settlement. Accords and satisfactions are ordinarily predicted upon mutual promises, rather than a payment of money.

The consideration given for a release is usually a sum of money paid by the defendant or his insurance company in exchange for the claimant's agreement to drop his claim against the alledged wrongdoer. Additionally, payment to an individual other than the claimant may constitute consideration. The exchange of consideration does not have to be the payment of money. For example, an agreement by the wrongdoer to waive all claims that he or she may have against the claimant is a valid form of consideration. However, the waiver of claims does not constitute a legal consideration if the claim is specious.

The consideration given for a release must be clearly stated. The consideration must actually be paid or exchanged for the contract to be effective. A mere recital of payment is not effective. The consideration must have actual value to have legal effect. If it is discovered that the consideration has no value, the release is unenforceable for lack of consideration.

Settlement agreements do not have to be in writing. However, as a practical matter, they should be reduced to a writing so that there is no subsequent disagreement over the scope and effect of the settlement. There is one significant exception. The statute of frauds requires that all contracts which, by their terms, are not to be performed within one year from the date on which it is made, must be in written form and signed by the parties. *Structured settlements*, discussed later in this chapter, often fall into that category, so they should be reduced to a writing and signed.

The law favors voluntary settlements. Everyone benefits from an early, reasonable settlement. The parties avoid the expense, delay and inconvenience of litigation. The government and community avoid the cost of providing a court for the trial. The parties have the opportunity to make a commitment with which they can live. Whereas, if they go to trial, the plaintiff may obtain a large verdict which the defendant is unable to pay or the plaintiff may recover nothing, leaving the plaintiff in a desperate financial condition. A large verdict in favor of the plaintiff might force the defendant to go into bankruptcy, so neither party benefits. A wise settlement is a better resolution, even if neither party is particularly happy with the terms of the settlement. Indeed, it is often said that if neither party is happy with the settlement, it is probably a good settlement.

Because the law favors settlements, the parties are encouraged to conduct settlement negotiations. Nothing they say in the course of their negotiations may be used against them at trial. The parties cannot tell the jury about the offers and counteroffers made during negotiations. On the other hand, statements made during settlement negotiations are not absolutely privileged. Therefore, some discretion must be used during the course of settlement negotiations. For example, if the defendant stated during the settlement negotiations that he went through the stop sign, then at trial the plaintiff could seek to prove the fact of the violation and that the defendant admitted he went through a stop sign. On the other hand, suppose the defendant were to say, "For purposes of settlement, let us assume that I went through the stop sign, still your demand is too high." In that context, the statement made in negotiations could not be brought out at trial.

A release should identify the parties, the transaction or occurrence which gave rise to the claim, the type of injury or damage claimed, the consideration given for the release and any special conditions or limitations which are part of the agreement. If the claim is for money, the money is ordinarily paid at the time the release is signed by the claimant. There is no need for the released party to sign the release. However, if the agreement provides for a mutual release, then both parties must sign it. It is customary to have the claimant's signature witnessed and notarized even though there is no rule or law that requires those formalities.

The writing which sets forth the parties' entire agreement and which is signed by the parties becomes the embodiment of the contract. If any dispute arises over the terms and conditions of the settlement agreement, a court would look to the writing to determine the terms, scope, and conditions of the agreement. The writing is also *evidence* of the parties' agreement. This means that if a dispute does arise concerning the terms of the settlement agreement, the written release is proof of the terms. But if the written release is determined by the court to be ambiguous, the court may hear additional evidence for the purpose of determining the parties' intent at the time they made the contract.

Historically, the common law looked upon a release as having a single purpose and effect: to release the claimant's claim. Therefore, the *ancient common law* gave a broad and decisive effect to releases. A release was effective to bar all claims arising out of the specified transaction or occurrence. It also released all persons who might have been liable to the claimant. The law now permits releases to be as broad as the parties want them to be, or releases may be customized to have a very narrow, specific, and limited effect.

Many different release forms have been devised to apply to various settlement situations. The following discussion provides an overview of some of the releases which are used. Of course, a claim may be concluded by paying the claim in full. In that case, nothing more than a receipt should be necessary to prove satisfaction of the obligation. However, in most cases the parties find a basis to compromise their claims. Ordinarily, any money obtained by a claimant out of a tort action, whether by verdict or settlement, is not subject to state or federal income tax.

General Releases

A very broad release is customarily called a "general release." The term "full and final release" is also used. In a general release the claimant may agree to release, not only all claims arising out of a particular transaction or occurrence, but also agree to release any and all claims that the claimant *might* then have against the persons released. A broad type release may release not only the person who pays the consideration for the release, but everyone else in the world who might be liable for the harm sustained by the claimant as a result of the particular transaction or occurrence. There are good reasons why a party may insist upon such a broad release. For example, the dispute between the parties may have arisen out of a long time business relationship which is now at an end, and the parties may want to ensure that they have settled *all* matters between them—even problems they are currently unaware of which might arise out of their past dealings.

By executing a general release, the claimant releases all claims arising out of the transaction or occurrence in question and releases all persons who *might* be liable to the claimant's injury or loss. The release must identify the transaction or occurrence by type, time and place. A general release is intended to put an end to all claims the plaintiff may have as a result of the transaction or occurrence in question. If an action is pending, the plaintiff is required to stipulate to a dismissal of the action.

The full and final release protects the settling tortfeasor from any further claims by the claimant. It may provide the settling defendant with another benefit. Any tortfeasor who did not pay his or her fair share for the release is liable for contribution to the party who bought the release. The settling defendant may bring an action against those persons to obtain contribution from them, so that they pay their fair share. The general release is a predicate for the settling defendant's action to obtain contribution. It is customary to attach the general release to the complaint as an exhibit to show that the settling defendant is the proper person to bring the contribution action. The release shows that the nonsettling tortfeasors are fully protected against any future claims by the claimant. The purchaser of a release must be able to prove that he or she settled the claim under a legal compulsion (not as a volunteer) and that he or she paid more than his or her share. When the released party contemplates bringing an action against a third person for contribution, it is customary to add the word "assignment" to the title of the release: "Release and Assignment." However, technically, it is not an assignment of a cause of action.

A settling tortfeasor may insist on obtaining a release of all persons who might be alleged to be responsible for the claimant's loss, because by obtaining a release of *everyone* the settling party prevents the claimant from making a claim against others who, in turn, might bring a claim against the settling party for contribution. The general release provides a defense to everyone against any claim by the plaintiff arising out of the transaction or occurrence identified in the release. The all inclusive release is calculated to put an end to the matter or the release may be used to seek contribution from nonsettling tortfeasors who are jointly liable if the settling party chooses.

Partial Releases

The general release was consistent with the historic common law concept that a release must put an end to the controversy. Partial releases were considered to be an anathema to the law. It was felt that partial releases lead to uncertainty and didn't actually terminate litigation, so they were not allowed. Over the last four or five decades the courts have come to readily accept and enforce partial settlements in tort actions. Partial releases are seldom, if ever, used in disputes arising out of the contracts. Partial releases are frequently used in claims based upon tort. Many tort claims would not be settled if partial settlements and partial releases were not possible. Furthermore, experience has shown that when one facet of a dispute is settled the rest of the case is more likely to be settled. Having a portion of a dispute settled is better than not having any settlement. However, experience has also shown that creative partial settlements frequently lead to uncertainties concerning their scope and effect. Nevertheless, the modern view is that partial settlements are valid, provided there is no secrecy surrounding the settlement and the partial settlement does not act to prejudice the rights of persons who do not participate in the settlement agreements.

One of the considerations that the parties must give to their partial release is the effect which the release will have upon the settling party's joint liability with joint tortfeasors and/or concurrent tortfeasors. Joint and concurrent tortfeasors are jointly liable for all of the claimant's injuries. Joint liability means the claimant may sue one or more of the wrongdoers separately for all of the claimant's damages, or the claimant may sue all of them in one action, with each tortfeasor being fully responsible for the entire loss. When a claimant releases one settling tortfeasor from all liability and agrees to indemnify the wrongdoer against any contribution claims made by the nonsettling parties, the joint obligation or joint liability between the settling tortfeasor and the nonsettling tortfeasors is destroyed. In short, the claimant must look solely to the resources of the nonsettling tortfeasor(s) for any additional recovery.

Therefore, if a claim involves two wrongdoers, only one of whom is financially able to pay a judgment, it may not be wise for the claimant to enter into a partial release.

When the case goes to trial against the nonsettling tortfeasors, the jury is told at the outset about the partial settlement, but the jury is not told about the amount of the settlement. In comparative fault states, the jury is instructed at the end of the trial that they must determine whether the settling alleged tortfeasor was negligent and what percentage of causal negligence to attribute to the settling alleged tortfeasor along with the percentage of causal negligence to be attributed to each nonsettling defendant.

A partial release which releases one of several tortfeasors, in effect, releases a percentage or fraction of causal fault. A partial release cannot be used to discharge one of two defendants when one of the defendants is only vicariously liable. A full and final release of an agent's liability necessarily releases the principal if the principal did not commit any separate wrongful act. For example, if the plaintiff brings an action against a driver and the owner of an automobile, and the plaintiff settles with the driver, there can be no residual liability against the owner. The claim against the owner is extinguished by a full and final settlement with the driver. There is no separate causal negligence on the part of the owner, at least in most cases. The example assumes that there is no claim that the vehicle was negligently maintained or defective so as to contribute to the accident. Similarly, if the plaintiff brings an action against the defendant and defendant's employer, a settlement with the employee would automatically release the employer.

Partial Settlements Involving Comparative Fault

Where the claimant has a claim against two or more persons as a result of a single occurrence, the law now permits the claimant to make a separate settlement with each alleged wrongdoer. If the law of comparative fault applies, each settlement is for the percentage of causal negligence attributable to the settling tortfeasor. If the law of comparative fault does not apply, a partial settlement discharges the fraction of the recovery which could be made against that tortfeasor. For example, a settlement with defendant A discharges the percentage of causal negligence attributable to him. When the case goes to trial against the nonsettling defendant the jury must determine the amount of plaintiff's total money damages and the percentage of causal negligence attributable to *both* defendants. Suppose the verdict is in the amount of twenty thousand dollars. Suppose further that defendant A is found to be ten percent negligent and defendant B found to be ninety percent negligent, defendant B receives credit for ten percent of the verdict. Defendant B owes eighteen thousand dollars to the plaintiff.

The basic elements of this kind of release are:

1. The claimant releases a settling wrongdoer from the cause of action and discharges that part of the action which the wrongdoer was responsible for;
2. the claimant does not release his cause of action against the non-settling wrongdoers; and
3. the claimant agrees to pay for (indemnifies) any claims that are brought against the settling party by the nonsettling parties who are asking the settling party for a contribution.

In addition, the claimant agrees to satisfy any judgment obtained from the nonsettling party to the extent of the liability or fault of the settling party.

There are some interesting ramifications to these partial settlements in comparative fault states. Suppose, in the above example, defendant A paid ten thousand dollars to obtain his release from the plaintiff. In the light of the jury's verdict, which apportioned only ten percent of the causal negligence to him, he paid eight thousand dollars too much. He is not entitled to reimbursement of his overpayment. The plaintiff recovers ten thousand dollars from defendant A and eighteen thousand dollars from defendant B for a total of twenty–eight thousand dollars. That amount is eight thousand dollars more than plaintiff's actual damages. The result may seem anomalous and unfair. However, the rationale for allowing the result is that defendant A bought his peace by voluntarily paying the ten thousand dollars.

A settlement is somewhat of a gamble. The verdict might have been the reverse of what it was; in that event, defendant A would have paid too little and the plaintiff would have been bound by the settlement. The important consideration is that their settlement agreement was voluntary and did not adversely affect defendant B's rights or obligations. Defendant B will not have to pay any more in damages than what he or she would have had to pay had there not been a settlement. Furthermore, defendant B should not obtain a windfall as a result of the voluntary settlement agreement negotiated between plaintiff and defendant A.

In the event the jury were to find that the plaintiff was solely responsible for the accident and consequential injuries, the plaintiff would end up receiving only the ten thousand dollars paid by defendant A. We should note in passing, that because defendant A settled plaintiff's claim, defendant A does not have to participate in the trial as a party. As a practical matter, the burden falls upon the nonsettling defendant to try to show that the settling defendant was solely or primarily responsible for the accident.

Partial Settlements Not Involving Comparative Fault

In states that do not have comparative fault, juries are not asked to determine percentages of causal negligence. Each defendant who is found liable is liable equally with the other defendants. If there are two alleged tortfeasors, settlement with one alleged tortfeasor discharges one-half of the recoverable damages—assuming that the jury determines the settling tortfeasor is partially liable. If there are three alleged tortfeasors, settlement with two of them discharges two-thirds of the recoverable damages. The claimant may give a partial release if the release expressly states that it is not to release anyone but the settling party. It is even a good idea to specifically identify the known tortfeasors who are not released by the settlement agreement. If the jury determines that the settling tortfeasor was solely responsible for the accident and injuries, the plaintiff will not obtain any compensation over and above the settlement.

High-Low Releases

A high-low release is an agreement in which the settling wrongdoer guarantees a minimum amount to be paid to the plaintiff, and also puts an upper limit on his or her potential liability. In a multi-party situation, the agreement provides that if the verdict is against the plaintiff, the settling defendant will pay the guaranteed amount. If the plaintiff wins, but receives a verdict for less than the guaranteed amount, the settling defendant will pay to the plaintiff an additional amount to make the recovery equal the guarantee. Also, the claimant agrees that if there is a verdict against the nonsettling tortfeasors that equals or exceeds the guaranteed amount, the plaintiff will pursue collection remedies only against the nonsettling defendants, and no payment will be required from the settling defendant.

A simplified version of a high-low release agreement can be used in cases not involving multiple tortfeasors. In a case where there is only one tortfeasor, the high-low agreement may provide that the claimant will receive a minimum guaranteed amount even if he or she loses the suit, and a maximum guaranteed amount if he or she wins on liability.

A high-low release agreement differs from an agreement that releases a percentage of causal fault because no money is paid to the claimant at the time the settlement agreement is made. In addition, the settling party remains in the case throughout the trial. A high-low release can be advantageous in situations when the claimant has a weak case, but the settling defendant risks a huge damage award if the claimant wins. Consequently, this type of settlement agreement helps to move cases along in a speedy fashion, reduces the likelihood of appeals, and permits the settling parties to avoid the risk of a disastrous outcome. On the other hand, a high-low release may serve to misalign the parties when there are multiple defendants and distort the eventual outcome.

Covenant Not to Sue

In a covenant not to sue, the claimant dismisses all pending actions against the settling tortfeasor in exchange for a payment of money. The covenant not to sue has the effect of releasing the settling tortfeasor, but does not protect the settling party from claims for contribution from nonsettling parties. In other words, if the plaintiff brings a lawsuit against a joint tortfeasor or concurrent tortfeasor, the tortfeasor could bring a third-party action against the settling tortfeasor for contribution.

Loan Receipt Agreements

In a loan receipt agreement, a settling defendant agrees to "loan" the plaintiff a specified sum of money for the plaintiff's agreement to dismiss the action against the defendant and pursue the claim against another person. (To this extent, a loan receipt resembles a covenant not to sue.) However, in addition, the plaintiff agrees to repay all or part of the "loan" out of the recovery, if any, that the plaintiff may obtain from the other alleged tortfeasor. If no recovery is obtained, the loan is cancelled.

A loan receipt agreement may be used by a defendant's liability insurer who makes an interest free "loan" to its insured who, in turn, pays the money to the plaintiff for a full and final release. As part of the agreement, the insured agrees to prosecute an action for contribution against another alleged tortfeasor. The insurer agrees to pay all of the expenses incurred in the prosecution of the action for contribution. The "loan" is to be repaid out of any proceeds the insured might obtain in the contribution action. The reason for the "loan" is to keep the liability insurer from becoming the *real party in interest* for prosecuting the contribution action. In other words, the action for contribution can be pursued in the name of the individual, rather than the insurer, when the loan receipt device is used.

Loan receipt agreements can take many different forms and may be used in conjunction with other release agreements such as a release of a percentage of causal negligence. A loan receipt agreement is advantageous in situations where the claimant and settling tortfeasor are able to agree on the value of the claimant's claim, but feel a second tortfeasor is substantially responsible for the damage. It is important to note that if a loan receipt agreement is used alone, and not in conjunction with another release agreement, the lendor is not protected against claims brought by other tortfeasors for contribution.

Mary Carter Agreements

A Mary Carter agreement is similar to the high-low and loan receipt agreements. However, there are important differences between them. The Mary Carter agreement is a secret or semi-secret agreement between the claimant and one or more of the tortfeasors. However, not all of the tortfeasors can be involved in the arrangement. A Mary Carter agreement provides that the settling party must remain in the lawsuit. In addition, the settling party can benefit from a verdict or judgment which is favorable to the claimant.

A Mary Carter release is made up of three elements:

1. A guarantee clause which provides that the claimant will receive a guaranteed sum of money from the settling party even if the claimant loses or receives a recovery less than the guaranteed settlement amount. The claimant agrees to collect the amount of any verdict from a nonsettling tortfeasor. (In this situation, the settling party hopes a verdict will be larger than the amount he has guaranteed to pay.)
2. The settling party agrees to remain in the lawsuit until a judgment is reached or the claimant consents to its dismissal.
3. Finally, the settling party agrees to keep his or her agreement secret. In essence, the terms of the agreement are hidden from the knowledge of the court, jury and the nonsettling parties.

The third element of secrecy is the most complained about aspect of Mary Carter agreements. Many people believe such secrecy permits the claimant and the settling party to work together to the harm of the nonsettling parties. Furthermore, the fact that the settling parties remain in the lawsuit is a matter of concern to many commentators. It is felt that such arrangements pervert the adversarial system and amount to a fraud on the court.

In light of the secrecy attached to Mary Carter agreements, some state courts have held that they are illegal. However, it is usually permissible for settling parties to remain in the lawsuit as long the arrangements are not kept secret and the settlement agreement does not pervert the adversarial system.

Partial Releases In Workers' Compensation Cases

Most employees who are injured in the course and scope of their employment receive workers' compensation benefits which include payment of medical expenses, wage loss and disability benefits. Even though the employee's injuries occurred while he or she was working, the injuries may have been caused by someone other than the employer. In that event, the injured employee has a right to receive workers' compensation payments and to pursue a common law action tort action against the tortfeasor. The most common causes of action are product liability actions and negligence actions. The employer who pays workers' compensation benefits is entitled, by law, to be reimbursed from any monetary recovery that the employee makes against the tortfeasor. If the employee neglects or refuses to pursue a claim against the tortfeasor, the employer may bring a subrogation action against the tortfeasor. Therefore, when an employee is injured, the injury may give the employee rights against the tortfeasor and create rights in favor of the employer against the tortfeasor. On occasion, the tortfeasor finds that he or she can settle with one but not the other.

A special type of partial release is used in these cases so that the tortfeasor may make a partial settlement. A special workers' compensation release allows the employee who has received workers' compensation benefits to enter into a full and final settlement with the tortfeasor without affecting the employer's subrogation rights. No monies are paid to the employer. The employer is left to pursue its own subrogation rights. The subrogation claim may be settled separately or go through a trial. The partial settlement is valid, but the settlement must not prejudice the employer's subrogation interests.

Reverse Special Workers' Compensation Release

The tortfeasor may negotiate a full and final settlement of the employer's workers' compensation subrogation claim and leave open the plaintiff employee's claim. The form of the partial release is similar to that used to settle the employee's claim.

Consent Judgment against Liability Insurer

A stipulated consent judgment is a unique settlement agreement which a tortfeasor may use to escape personal liability when his or her insurer has denied coverage for the particular claim. The settlement agreement provides that the defendant–insured agrees to permit judgment to be entered against him or her. The judgment establishes the defendant's liability to the claimant/ plaintiff and, perhaps, the amount of the plaintiff's damages. However, the judgment may be collected only from the proceeds of the insured's liability insurance policy. The insured tortfeasor is able to escape any personal financial responsibility to the plaintiff by stipulating to the consent judgment.

There are times when a stipulated consent judgment becomes a very practical means of proceeding for both the plaintiff and the defendant–insured. Suppose that the defendant's personal liability insurer has denied coverage because it contends that the "business exclusion" in the insurance policy precludes coverage. Suppose further that the plaintiff's lawyer believes the facts of the accident do not invoke the business exclusion. Assume that the defendant does not have any means of paying a judgment except through the liability insurance policy. Under such circumstances, the stipulated consent judgment eliminates the necessity of a trial to establish the defendant's liability. With a judgment on the books against the defendant, the plaintiff may institute a garnishment action against the defendant's insurer. The defendant is then referred to as a judgment debtor. The insurer has a right to challenge the reasonableness of the settlement and to maintain its position that the insurance policy does not apply.

One benefit to the insurer is that a stipulation to a consent judgment precludes the insured from prosecuting a *bad faith* against the insurer for the insurer's failure to settle the claim, because the insured has been fully exonerated from any further liability to the plaintiff. Another benefit that the insurer derives is: if the plaintiff prevails on the insurance coverage issue, then the insurer has avoided the expense of defending the insured in the tort action and the cost of the insured's attorney's fees for a declaratory judgment action to determine coverage.[1]

A consent judgment has some negative consequences for the insured even though, technically, it is not enforceable against the insured. Some title insurance companies and mortgage companies don't appreciate the niceties of consent judgments. They see the consent judgment as a cloud against the insured's title to any real estate the insured may own. Consequently, the insured should take steps to have the judgment roll show the judgment to be "satisfied" as soon as the coverage issue is determined. Indeed, the terms of the agreement leading to the consent judgment should specify who will take the necessary action to obtain a satisfaction or cancellation of the consent judgment.

Unless the insurer has denied coverage, an insured violates the liability insurance policy's cooperation clause by entering into a stipulated judgment. A violation of the cooperation clause gives the insurer another coverage defense.

Structured Settlements

Structured settlements are relatively new. They evolved out of the need to provide periodic payments over a long period of time to individuals who might not be able to manage and/or conserve a large settlement. Structured settlements allow the tortfeasor to pay a lump sum of money to a bank or insurance company which can issue a customized annuity to the claimant which will provide scheduled benefits to the claimant over a period of years or over the claimant's lifetime. Because the company that issues the annuity has the right to use or invest the money over the same period of time, the company can add significantly to the initial payment from the tortfeasor. Consequently, a settlement funded in the amount of fifty thousand dollars may result in payments over the claimant's lifetime of several hundred thousand dollars. In addition, the money which the claimant receives is free of any income tax.

The structured settlement annuity must be purchased by the defendant and the claimant must not be able to control the trustee's handling or investment of the funds; otherwise, the settlement would lose its tax advan-

---

[1]In most states, a liability insurance company that brings an action to determine whether the insurance policy provides coverage for the claim brought against its insured is required to pay the costs and attorneys' fees its insured incurs if the court determines that the insurance policy does provide coverage.

tages. That situation would be the same as if the claimant obtained an award and proceeded to invest the money. The interest earned on *his* or *her* monies is taxable as ordinary income. Customarily, a structured settlement is accompanied by the payment of additional monies used to cover past medical expenses, past lost wages, attorney's fees and litigation expenses. Despite the many benefits of structured settlements, a majority of personal injury claims are still settled with a single lump sum payment.

Settlements of Wrongful Death Actions

A wrongful death action is prosecuted by a trustee or administrator who represents the decedent's heirs and next of kin. The trustee or administrator must apply for the office. When appointed, the representative must provide a bond guaranteeing performance of his or her responsibilities. The representative must act to represent the best interests of all persons who have an interest in the claim. If the representative is able to negotiate a settlement which he or she believes to be in everyone's best interests, the proposed settlement must be submitted to the court for approval. The court will then order how the money damages are to be allocated to the survivors. The court will discharge the representative only after a distribution of the settlement proceeds has been made.

Minors' Settlements

All states have laws which authorize parents and guardians to prosecute claims on behalf of their minor children. But the parents are not permitted to settle a child's claim without court approval. The statute provides that "no settlement or compromise of the action is valid unless it is approved by a judge of the court in which the action is pending." Most district courts have specific procedures for obtaining court approval of settlements on behalf of minors. If the procedures established by statute and court rules are followed, a release executed by a guardian on behalf of a minor is fully binding and enforceable against the minor. Though a minor cannot be bound by a release which he or she signed, the release may become valid and binding if the release is ratified once he or she gains legal capacity.

Recision or Cancellation of Releases

A release is merely a contract which settles the dispute between parties. A release may be broken if it was induced by fraud or if there was a mutual mistake concerning a significant term or condition of the release. Proof of the mutual mistake requires challenging the language contained in the written release. Therefore, in order to avoid the release or to obtain reformation of the release the claimant must present proof which is clear and convincing. On the other hand, fraud in the inducement of the release is predicated upon conduct and statements which precede execution of the release and have nothing to do with the terms and conditions as set forth in the written document. Therefore, fraud in the inducement can be proved by a mere preponderance of the evidence. The elements necessary to prove fraud are the same elements which apply to a cause of action in fraud.

With regard to a claim of mutual mistake, there are several factors which courts consider in determining whether a release should be avoided. They are:

1. The length of the time between the injury and the settlement. (It is more likely that the parties didn't really understand or appreciate the extent of the loss and the significance of the release if the settlement was made quickly.)
2. The amount of time that elapsed between the settlement and the attempt to avoid the settlement. (The longer the delay, the less sympathetic the courts are to the claim of mistake.)
3. The presence or absence of independent medical advice of plaintiff's own choice before and at the time of settlement. (If the plaintiff did not have competent medical advice concerning the nature, extent, and effect of his or her injuries, the claim of mistake is probably well founded.)
4. The presence or absence of legal counsel of plaintiff's own choice before and at the time of settlement. (If the plaintiff has the advice of a lawyer concerning the terms of the release and the recommendations of a lawyer concerning settlement value, it is very difficult to claim a mistake.)
5. The language of the release itself.
6. The adequacy of the consideration paid for the release in light of the nature and extent of the injuries or other loss, and the chances of the settling party being found liable for the accident.
7. The general competence of the releasor. The plaintiff's education and experience may be considered by the court.
8. Whether the injury claimed by the releasor was a known injury at the time the release was signed or a consequence flowing from unknown injury.

Generally, only mistakes of fact permit avoidance. However, where a claimant is not represented by an attorney, and the tortfeasor's liability insurer undertakes to advise the claimant of his or her rights, a "fiduciary" type relationship may be established. Such a relationship could convert a mistake of law into a mistake of fact. Hence, the settlement between the parties may be voidable.

While a release may also be avoided because of fraud, such situations present difficult problems of proof for the claimant. Basically, the claimant must show that the person who procured the release made a material misrepresentation with the intent that the claimant act upon that representation. Additionally, the claimant must show that he or she did act in reliance upon the representation and, consequently, suffered damages.

DISMISSALS

A lawsuit may be concluded by entry of judgment or by a dismissal. If the parties' rights and obligations have been adjudicated by the court, those rights and obligations are prepounded by the court's judgment. The judgment is prepared by the clerk of court pursuant to an order of the court. The judgment is made part of the clerk's permanent records. Judgments are discussed in greater detail in Chapter 26.

A lawsuit may be terminated before a judgment is entered. Such a termination is called a dismissal. There are three basic types of dismissals: court ordered involuntary dismissal, voluntary unilateral dismissal, and stipulated dismissal. As a general rule, the plaintiff cannot unilaterally terminate the lawsuit once it has been commenced. The plaintiff must obtain either the court's permission or the defendant's permission to dismiss. The Rules expressly protect the defendant from having his or her counterclaim dismissed through the plaintiff's efforts to dismiss plaintiff's claim.

Court Ordered Dismissals

If there is a fatal defect in the plaintiff's case, the court must order the case dismissed. For example, if the defendant were to prevail on any of the motions authorized by Rule 12, the court would enter an order dismissing the plaintiff's case. The court may also order a dismissal as a sanction where the plaintiff fails to comply with a valid court order, such as an order to permit discovery pursuant to Rule 37. A court may dismiss the plaintiff's case if the plaintiff has been dilatory in prosecuting the action. A court may order an involuntary dismissal if the plaintiff's evidence fails to prove a prima facie case of liability against the defendant. There are many other bases for courts to order involuntary dismissals. The point is that not every court determination necessarily leads to a judgment.

The effect of an order for dismissal is that the case is put to an end. Ordinarily, the dismissal does not result in entry of a judgment. However, if the plaintiff decides to appeal the court's decision to dismiss, the losing party would probably arrange to have judgment entered against himself so that he or she could appeal from the judgment.

Voluntary Dismissal on Notice

The plaintiff may voluntarily dismiss his or her claim. Rule 41 provides that:

> . . . an action may be dismissed by the plaintiff without order of the court (i) by filing a notice of dismissal at any time before service by the adverse party of an answer or of a motion for summary judgment, whichever first occurs. . . . * * * Unless otherwise stated in the notice of dismissal, . . . the dismissal is without prejudice, except that a notice of dismissal operates as an adjudication upon the merits when filed by a plaintiff who has once dismissed in any court of the United States or of any state an action based on or including the same claim.

Though not expressly stated in the Rule, the plaintiff should serve a copy of the dismissal upon the defendant. Many state courts allow the plaintiff to voluntarily dismiss upon notice at any time before the case is alerted for trial.

A dismissal *without prejudice* means that the plaintiff can bring the lawsuit at another time in any court that has jurisdiction. If a case is dismissed *without prejudice*, that means that the dismissal acts as an adjudication which precludes the plaintiff from ever again asserting the claim against the same defendant(s). Unless the court order specifies that the dismissal is with prejudice, the presumption is that the dismissal is without prejudice.

Stipulated Dismissal

Parties are able to stipulate to a dismissal at any time on any terms. A stipulated dismissal may be with prejudice or without prejudice. The stipulated dismissal may be the result of a settlement agreement and release, but not necessarily. A stipulated dismissal usually provides that all parties waive the right to recover costs from each other. Of course, the stipulation for dismissal should be very specific as to whether it is with or without prejudice.

Rule 41 provides in part:

> . . . an action may be dismissed by the plaintiff without order of court by filing a stipulation of dismissal signed by all parties who have appeared in the action. Unless otherwise stated . . . in the stipulation, the dismissal is without prejudice.

If the parties fail to be specific, the rule presumes that the stipulation is without prejudice. Even though the Rule specifies that the stipulation is to be signed by the parties, the Rule is understood to authorize the parties' lawyers to sign the stipulation on behalf of the parties.

The terms and conditions of the stipulated dismissal may be whatever the parties agree upon. If the parties have negotiated a settlement of their controversy and they stipulate to dismiss the case, the terms and conditions of the settlement need not be stated in the dismissal.

A Personal Note

As you prepare to assume responsibilities which, historically, were reserved for lawyers, you should give some consideration to the attitude with which you will approach those responsibilities. A few suggestions may help you to avoid mistakes, embarrassment, and disappointment.

A paraprofessional career in law should be interesting, fulfilling, and, on occasion, exciting. You should be proud of your association with the legal profession and judicial system. Conduct yourself as a professional. Dress appropriately. Be courteous to all persons with whom you come into contact, especially when dealing with an adverse party or an opposing lawyer. Be on time and keep appointments. Use a calendar to schedule your appointments and deadlines. Avoid creating time conflicts. Operate on the premise that by being timely, you will do the best job possible. Strive to develop a reputation for reliability and candor.

Recognize that each of your tasks is important to someone, even though the work may seem routine. When you handle an assignment for a client, demonstrate the same interest and concern that you would want for your own important matters. Some matters which you will handle are very personal in nature. All matters, whether of a business nature or otherwise, should be treated as confidential. Avoid the temptation to make "innocent" disclosures about the cases you are handling. Equally important, guard against making accidental disclosures.

You must not violate court rules, court orders, or professional ethics. There is no question that, on occasion, some advantage may be gained by disregarding professional responsibilities. Do not let anyone mislead you into a violation. There is no case, no client, and no employer important enough to sacrifice your integrity and professional standing for his or her convenience. Remember that litigation is an adversarial process. The system works well because each party has the opportunity and responsibility for presenting his or her own case. The process would collapse if it were not conducted by professionals in accordance with rules and standards that establish fair play. Do not do anything to upset that delicate balance.

Continue your education by attending seminars and reading professional articles relative to your work. Ask questions about assignments. Find out why you have been given assignments. Learn from your mistakes, and do not become defensive because of past mistakes. Accept responsibility for what you have done and for what you should have done but did not. Accept advice, corrections, and suggestions graciously. Usually, there is more than one way to perform a task. Accept the fact that the lawyers you work with might prefer a different method than you learned or prefer.

Try to make helpful suggestions for accomplishing work. Be thoughtful and innovative. But be careful not to exceed your authority. Look for ways of working more effectively and more efficiently. Keep copies of the documents (even letters) you prepare. When working on similar assignments they will help you do the job better and faster than the first time. One of the surest ways to gain satisfaction, if not enjoyment, from your work is to strive to perform each task perfectly. There is always satisfaction in doing a job well— whether or not anyone else notices. Even a tedious task can be made interesting by approaching it with the intent of doing it perfectly.

Lawyers and all who serve the judicial system depend upon effective communications, both oral and written. Strive to express yourself concisely. Try to be precise in your statements and questions. Develop a concern for using words correctly. Use the language of the profession. Legal jargon will help you to be more precise in your thinking and effective in your communications. Be alert to the meaning of words you use in your correspondence and reports. Organize your thoughts before you write your letters, reports, and memorandums. Make your reports while the information is still fresh and clear in your mind. Learn to use short, specific questions when you make inquiries of witnesses and clients.

As you work on assignments, try to keep the whole picture and the ultimate objective in mind. Try to be objective in analyzing the facts and the case as a whole. It is all too easy to become oversold on a client's claim or defense. We tend to delude ourselves in an effort to help our clients. But a client is better served by objective advisors than by fervent "yes-persons." Do not compromise your integrity for any case or any person.

Appendixes

Appendix I

Time Table for Civil Cases

This Time Table revised to September 1, 1989, indicates the time for each of the steps of a civil action as provided by the Federal Rules of Civil Procedure, the Federal Rules of Appellate Procedure, the 1970 Revised Rules of the Supreme Court and Title 28 of the United States Code Annotated. Most time periods may be enlarged by the court. Civil Rule 6(b) and Appellate Rule 26(b) state when, and under what conditions, an enlargement of the time period may be allowed.

Service by mail is complete upon mailing. Civil Rule 5(b) and Appellate Rule 25(c). Whenever a period of time is computed from the service of a notice or other paper, and the service is made by mail, 3 days are added to the prescribed period of time. Civil Rule 6(e) and Appellate Rule 26(c). Variations which make impossible the application of any rigid limitation of time to all steps of the action are indicated in the Time Table. Citations are to supporting rules and are in the form "Civ.R. ___" for the Rules of Civil Procedure and "App.R. ___" for the Rules of Appellate Procedure. Citations to the 1970 Revised Rules of the Supreme Court are not abbreviated.

ADMISSIONS

Requests for admissions, service of	On plaintiff after commencement of action and on any other party with or after service of summons and complaint on him. Civ.R. 36(a).
Response to requested admissions	Answers or objections must be served within 30 days after service of the request, or such shorter or longer time as court may allow, but unless court shortens time, defendant need not serve before expiration of 45 days after service of the summons and complaint upon him. Civ.R. 36(a).

ANSWER
   To complaint

See also, "Responsive Pleadings," this table. Service within 20 days after service of summons and complaint unless otherwise ordered by the court or provided by an applicable state statute or rule when substituted service is made under Rule 4(e) upon a party not an inhabitant of or found within the state. Civ.R. 12(a).

Service within 60 days after service upon the United States Attorney, in action against the United States or an officer or agency thereof. Civ.R. 12(a).

The time for responsive pleading is altered by service of Civ.R. 12 motions. See "Responsive Pleadings," this table.

   To cross-claim

Service within 20 days after service of pleading stating cross-claim. Civ.R. 12(a).

Sixty days for United States. Civ.R. 12(a).

The time for responsive pleading is altered by service of Civ.R. 12(a) motions, see "Responsive Pleadings," this table.

   To third-party complaint

Same as answer to complaint. Civ.R. 14(a).

   To notice of condemnation

Service within 20 days after service of notice. Civ.R. 71A(e).

   Removed actions

Twenty days after receipt of pleading, or within 20 days after service of summons, or within 5 days after filing of removal petition, whichever is longest. Civ.R. 81(c).

   Proceedings to cancel certificates of citizenship under 8 U.S.C.A. § 1451

Sixty days after service of petition. Civ.R. 81(a) (6).

ANSWERS (or objections) to interrogatories to party

Service within 30 days after the service of the interrogatories, except that a defendant may serve answers or objections within 45 days after service of the summons and complaint upon him. Court may allow a shorter or longer time. Civ.R. 33(a).

CLASS actions

As soon as practicable after commencement court is to determine by order whether action is to be so maintained. Civ.R. 23(c) (1).

CLERICAL mistakes in judgments, orders, or record	May be corrected at any time; but during pendency of appeal, may be corrected before appeal is docketed in the appellate court, and thereafter while appeal pending may be corrected with leave of appellate court. Civ.R. 60(a).
COMPLAINT	Filing commences action—must be served with summons. Civ.R. 3.
COMPUTATION of time	Exclude day from which period runs and include last day of period unless a Saturday, Sunday, or holiday, in which case period runs to the end of next day which is not a Saturday, Sunday, or holiday. Civ.R. 6(a); App.R. 26(a).
	Intermediate Saturdays, Sundays, and holidays are included except where the period is less than 7 days, in which case they are excluded. Civ.R. 6(a); App.R. 26(a).
	Service by mail is complete upon mailing. Civ.R. 5(b); App.R. 25(c).
	Service by mail adds three days to a period of time which is computed from such service. Civ.R. 6(e); App.R. 26(c).
	Legal holidays are defined by Civ.R. 6(a) and App.R. 26(a).
COSTS	Taxation on 1 day's notice. Motion to review taxation of costs 5 days after taxation. Civ.R. 54(d).
DEFAULT	
Entry by clerk	No time stated. Civ.R. 55(b).
Entry by court	If party against whom default is sought has appeared, he shall be served with written notice of application for default judgment at least 3 days prior to hearing on such application. Civ.R. 55(b).
DEFENSES and objections, presentation of	
By pleading	See "Answer," this table.
By motion	Motion shall be made before pleading if further pleading is permitted. Civ.R. 12(b).

At trial	Adverse party may answer at trial any defense in law or fact to claim for relief to which such party is not required to serve responsive pleading. Civ.R. 12(b).
Motion affects time for responsive pleading	Service of motion under Civ.R. 12 alters times for responsive pleading. See "Responsive Pleadings," this table.
DEPOSITIONS	See, also, "Interrogatories," and "Depositions on written questions," this table.
Notice of filing	Promptly. Civ.R. 30(f) (1), (3) and Civ.R. 31(b), (c).
Notice of taking	By either party after commencement of action except that plaintiff must obtain leave if he seeks to take a deposition prior to the expiration of 30 days after service of the summons and complaint upon any defendant or service made under Civ.R. 4(e), except that leave is not required (1) if defendant has served a notice of taking deposition or otherwise sought discovery, or (2) if the special notice provided by Civ.R. 30(b) (2) has been given. Civ.R. 30(a).
	Reasonable notice to every party. Civ.R. 30 (b).
Objections	As to admissibility, objection may be made at trial or hearing, but subject to Civ.R. 28(b) and 32(d) (3). Civ.R. 32(b).
	As to errors or irregularities in the notice, service promptly. Civ.R. 32(d) (1).
	As to disqualification of officer, objection made before deposition begins or as soon thereafter as disqualification becomes known or could be discovered. Civ.R. 32(d) (2).
	As to competency of witness or competency, relevancy, or materiality of testimony—not waived by failure to make such objection before or during deposition unless the ground might have been obviated or removed if presented at that time. Civ.R. 32(d) (3) (A).
	As to errors and irregularities at oral examination in manner of taking deposition, in the form of questions or answers, in the oath or affirmation, or in conduct of parties, and errors which might be obviated, removed, or cured if promptly

presented—seasonable objection made at taking of deposition. Civ.R. 32(d) (3) (B).

As to form of written questions submitted under Civ.R. 31—service within time allowed for serving succeeding cross or other questions and within 5 days after service of last questions authorized. Civ.R. 32(d) (3) (C).

As to completion and return (transaction, signing, certification, sealing, etc.)—motion to suppress made with reasonable promptness after defect is or might have been ascertained. Civ.R. 32(d) (4).

Orders of protection	No time stated. Civ.R. 26 (c).
Motion to terminate or limit examination	Any time during the taking of the deposition. Civ.R. 30(d).
Perpetuate testimony pending appeal	Motion in district court upon same notice and service thereof as if action was pending in district court. Civ.R. 27(b).
Perpetuate testimony before action	Service of notice and petition 20 days before date of hearing. Civ.R. 27(a) (2).
Taking	Time specified in the notice of taking unless enlarged or shortened by the Court. Civ.R. 30(b) (1), (3).
DEPOSITIONS on written questions	See also "Depositions," this table.
When taken	After commencement of action. Civ.R. 31(a).
Cross questions	Service within 30 days after service of the notice and questions. Civ.R. 31(a).
Redirect questions	Service within 10 days after being served with cross questions. Civ.R. 31(a).
Recross questions	Service within 10 days after service of redirect questions.
Notice of filing of deposition	Promptly. Civ.R. 31(c).
Objections to form	Service within the time allowed for serving the succeeding cross or other questions and within

	5 days after service of last questions authorized. Civ.R. 32(d) (3) (C).
DISCOVERY	Orders for physical or mental examination of persons—
	Time stated in order. Civ.R. 35(a).
	See also, "Admissions," "Depositions," "Depositions on written questions," "Interrogatories," "Production of Documents," this table.
DISMISSAL for want of subject-matter jurisdiction	Any time. Civ.R. 12(h) (3).
DISMISSAL by plaintiff voluntarily without court order	Any time before service of answer or motion for summary judgment. Civ.R. 41(a) (1).
DISMISSAL of counterclaim, cross-claim or third-party claim, voluntary	Before service of responsive pleading, or if none, before introduction of evidence at trial or hearing. Civ.R. 41(c).
DOCUMENTS, Production of	See "Production of Documents," this table.
ENLARGEMENT of time generally	
Act required or allowed at or within specified time by Civil Rule, notice thereunder, or court order	Court for cause shown may (1) with or without motion or notice order period enlarged if request therefor is made before expiration of period originally prescribed or as extended by previous order, or (2) upon motion made after expiration of the specified period permit act to be done where failure to act was result of excusable neglect; but court may not extend time for taking any action under Civ.R. 50(b), 52(b), 59(b), (d) and (c), and 60(b), except to extent and under conditions stated in them. Civ.R. 6(b).
On appeal	Court for good cause shown may upon motion enlarge time prescribed by App.Rules or by its order for doing any act or may permit act to be done after expiration of such time; but court may not enlarge time for filing notice of appeal, petition for allowance, or petition for permission to appeal; nor may the court enlarge time prescribed by law for filing petition to enjoin, set aside, suspend, modify, enforce or otherwise

review, or a notice of appeal form, an order for an administrative agency, board, commission or officer of the United States, except as specifically authorized by law. App.R. 26(b).

Affidavits in opposition, service	Time may be extended by court. Civ.R. 6(d).
Taking deposition on oral examination	Court for cause may enlarge or shorten time. Civ.R. 30(b) (3).
Hearing of motions and defenses	May be deferred until trial. Civ.R. 12(d).
Mail, service by	Adds three days to a period that is computed from time of service. Civ.R. 6(e); App.R. 26(c).
Injunction— temporary restraining order	May be extended 10 days by order of court or for a longer period by consent of party against whom order is directed. Civ.R. 65(b).
Response to request for admissions	Time may be enlarged or shortened by court. Civ.R. 36(a).

EXECUTION

Stay	Automatically: No execution to issue, nor proceedings for enforcement to be taken, until expiration of 10 days after entry of judgment; exceptions—injunctions, receiverships, and patent accountings. Civ.R. 62(a).
	Stay according to state law. Civ.R. 62(f).
	Motion for new trial or for judgment. Civ.R. 62(b).
	Stay in favor of government. Civ.R. 62(e).
	Supersedeas on appeal. Civ.R. 62(d).
	Stay of judgment as to multiple claims or multiple parties. Civ.R. 62(h).

FILING papers

Complaint must be filed at commencement of action. Civ.R. 3.

All papers required to be filed must be filed with clerk unless the judge permits them to be filed with him. Civ.R. 5(e).

All papers after the complaint required to be served must be filed either before service or within reasonable time thereafter. Civ.R. 5(d).

FINDINGS
    Motion to amend

Ten days after entry of judgment. Civ.R. 52(b). Exception from general rule relating to enlargement. Civ.R. 6(b).

FOREIGN law

Reasonable written notice required of party intending to raise an issue concerning the law of a foreign country. Civ.R. 44.1.

HEARING of motions

Unless local conditions make it impracticable, district court shall establish regular times and places for hearing and disposition of motions requiring notice and hearing; but judge may make orders for the advancement, conduct, and hearing of actions. Civ.R. 78.

Service of notice 5 days before time specified for hearing unless otherwise provided by these rules or order of court. Civ.R. 6(d).

Hearing of certain motions and defenses before trial on application of any party unless court orders deferral until trial. Civ.R. 12(d).

HOLIDAYS

New Year's Day, Washington's Birthday, Memorial Day, Independence Day, Labor Day, Columbus Day, Veterans Day, Thanksgiving Day, Christmas Day, and any other day appointed as a holiday by the President or the Congress of the United States or by the state in which the district court is held. Civ.R. 6(a); App.R. 26(a).

INJUNCTION
    (Temporary restraining order granted without notice)

Order shall be indorsed with date and hour of issuance, filed forthwith in clerk's office, and entered of record. Civ.R. 65(b).

Expiration within such time, not to exceed 10 days, as court fixes, unless within time so fixed the order is extended for like period or, with consent of party against whom order is directed, for longer period. Civ.R. 65(b).

Motion for preliminary injunction shall be set down for hearing at earliest possible time—takes precedence of all matters except older ones of same character. Civ.R. 65(b).

Motion for dissolution or modification on 2 days' notice or such shorter notice as court may prescribe; hear and determine motion as expeditiously as ends of justice require. Civ.R. 65(b).

INSTRUCTIONS

Requests	At close of evidence or such earlier time as court directs. Civ.R. 51.
Objections	Before jury retires to consider verdict. Civ.R. 51.

INTERROGATORIES to parties

	Service on plaintiff any time after action is commenced. Service on any other party with or after service on him of summons and complaint. Civ.R. 33(a).
Answers or objections	Service within 30 days after the service of the interrogatories, except that a defendant may serve answers or objections within 45 days after service of the summons and complaint upon him. Civ.R. 33(a).

INTERVENTION

Upon timely application. Civ.R. 24(a), (b).

Person desiring to intervene shall serve a motion to intervene upon the parties as provided in Civ.R. 5. Civ.R. 24(c).

JUDGMENT or order

Alter or amend judgment, motion to	Shall be served not later than 10 days after entry of judgment. Civ.R. 59(e). Exception to general rule relating to enlargement. Civ.R. 6(b).
Clerical mistakes	May be corrected any time; but during pendency of appeal, may be corrected before appeal is docketed in the appellate court, and thereafter while appeal pending may be corrected with leave of appellate court. Civ.R. 60(a).
Default	See "Default," this table.
Directed verdict— motion for judgment in accord with motion for directed verdict	Within 10 days after entry of judgment or after jury has been discharged without verdict. Civ.R. 50(b). Exception from general rule relating to enlargement. Civ.R. 6(b).
Effectiveness	Judgment effective only when set forth on a separate document and when entered as provided in Civ.R. 79(a). Civ.R. 58.
Entry of judgment	Upon general verdict of jury or upon court decision that a party shall recover only a sum certain or costs or that all relief shall be denied, entry forthwith and without awaiting any di-

	rection by court (unless court otherwise orders). Upon court decision granting other relief or upon special verdict or general verdict accompanied by answers to interrogatories, entry upon prompt court approval of form. Entry shall not be delayed for taxing of costs. Civ.R. 58.
Entry, notice of	Immediately upon entry clerk shall serve notice thereof by mail in manner provided in Civ.R. 5 and make note in docket of the mailing. Such mailing is sufficient notice for all purposes for which notice of entry of order is required by these rules; but any party may in addition serve a notice of such entry in manner provided in Civ.R. 5 for service of papers. Civ.R. 77(d).
	Lack of notice of entry by clerk does not affect time to appeal or relieve or authorize court to relieve party for failure to appeal within time allowed, except as permitted by App.R. 4(a). Civ.R. 77(d).
Offer of judgment	Service more than 10 days before trial begins. Civ.R. 68.
	Acceptance, written notice of—service within 10 days after service of offer. Civ.R. 68.
On pleadings, motion for judgment	After pleadings are closed but within such time as not to delay the trial. Civ.R. 12(c).
Relief from, on grounds stated in Rule 60(b)	Motion within a reasonable time and not more than 1 year after judgment, order, or proceeding entered or taken, for following grounds: (1) mistake, inadvertence, surprise, or excusable neglect; (2) newly discovered evidence; (3) fraud, misrepresentation, or other misconduct. Civ.R. 60(b). Exception from general rule relating to enlargement. Civ.R. 60(b).
	Motion within a reasonable time, for following grounds: (1) judgment void, (2) judgment satisfied, released, or discharged, (3) prior underlying judgment reversed or otherwise vacated, (4) no longer equitable that judgment have prospective application, (5) any other reason justifying relief. Civ.R. 60(b). Exception from general rule relating to enlargement. Civ.R. 6(b).
Stay	See "Execution," this table.
Summary judgment	See "Summary Judgment," this table.

JURORS	Alternate jurors (in order in which called) replace jurors who, prior to jury's retiring to consider verdict, are found unable or disqualified to perform duties; alternates not replacing regular jurors shall be discharged after jury so retires. Civ.R. 47(b).
JURY trial	
Demand	Service any time after commencement of action and not later than 10 days after service of last pleading directed to the triable issue. Civ.R. 38(b).
	Adverse party may serve demand for jury trial within 10 days after service of first demand or such lesser time as court fixes. Civ.R. 38(c).
Removed actions	If at the time of removal all necessary pleadings have been served, demand for jury trial may be served:
	By petitioner, 10 days after the petition for removal is filed;
	By any other party, within 10 days after service on him of the notice of filing the petition. Civ.R. 81(c).
	Demand after removal not necessary in either of two instances: (1) prior to removal, party has made express demand in accordance with state law; (2) state law does not require express demands and court does not direct otherwise. Civ.R. 81(c).
LEGAL HOLIDAY	See "Holidays," this table.
MAIL	Service by mail adds 3 days to period computed from time of service. Civ.R. 6(e); App.R. 26(c).
MORE DEFINITE STATEMENT	
Furnished	Must be furnished within 10 days after notice of order or other time fixed by court or court may strike pleading. Civ.R. 12(e).
Motion for	Must be made before responsive pleading is interposed. Civ.R. 12(e).
MOTIONS, notices, and affidavits	See, also, specific headings, this table.
In general	A written motion, supporting affidavits, and notice of hearing thereof—service not later than 5

days before time specified for hearing unless a different time is fixed by rule or by order of court. Civ.R. 6(d).

Opposing affidavits may be served not later than one day before hearing, unless court permits otherwise. Civ.R. 6(d).

NEW TRIAL	
Motion and affidavits	Motion shall be served not later than 10 days after entry of judgment. Civ.R. 59(b). Exception from general rule relating to enlargement. Civ.R. 6(b). If motion based on affidavits, they shall be served with motion. Civ.R. 59(c).
Opposing affidavits	Shall be served within 10 days of service of motion for new trial; period may be extended for additional period not exceeding 20 days either by court for good cause shown or by parties by written stipulation. Civ.R. 59(c).
Initiative of court	Not later than 10 days after entry of judgment, court may order new trial for any reason for which it might have granted new trial or motion. Civ.R. 59(d). Exception to general rule relating to enlargement. Civ.R. 6(b).
	After giving parties notice and opportunity to be heard, court may grant motion for new trial, timely served, for reason not stated in the motion. Civ.R. 59(d). Exception to general rule relating to enlargement. Civ.R. 6(b).
Judgment notwithstanding verdict, verdicts set aside on motion for	Party whose motion has been set aside may serve motion for new trial pursuant to Civ.R. 59 not later than 10 days after entry of such judgment. Civ.R. 50(c).
OBJECTIONS to orders or rulings of court	At time ruling or order of court is made or sought; if party has no opportunity to object to ruling or order at time it is made, absence of objection does not thereafter prejudice him. Civ.R. 46.
OFFER of judgment	Must be served more than 10 days before trial. Civ.R. 68.
	Acceptance must be served within 10 days after service of offer. Civ.R. 69.
ORDERS	See "Judgment or order," this table.
PARTICULARS, Bill of	Abolished. Civ.R. 12(e), as amended in 1948. See, however, "More Definite Statement," this table.

PLEADINGS

Amendment of

Once as matter of course before responsive pleading served or within 20 days if no response is permitted and action has not been placed on trial calendar. Civ.R. 15(a).

By leave of court or written consent of adverse parties, at any time. Civ.R. 15(a).

During trial or after judgment to conform to evidence or to raise issues not raised in pleadings but tried by express or implied consent of parties. Civ.R. 15(b).

Supplemental

Upon motion of party—court may upon reasonable notice permit service of supplemental pleading setting forth transactions, etc., since date of pleading to be supplemented. Civ.R. 15(d).

Adverse party pleading to supplemental pleading—if court deems advisable, it shall so order, specifying time therefor. Civ.R. 15(d).

Averments of time

Such averments are material and shall be considered like all other averments of material matter. Civ.R. 9(f).

Judgment on, motion for

After pleadings are closed but within such time as not to delay the trial. Civ.R. 12(c).

Striking of matter from

Motion made before responding to a pleading or, if no responsive pleading permitted, within 20 days after service of pleading. Civ.R. 12(f).

On court's own initiative at any time. Civ.R. 12(f).

PROCESS

Amendment

At any time, unless it clearly appears that material prejudice would result to substantial rights of party against whom process issued. Civ.R. 4(h).

Return

Person serving process shall make proof of service thereof to court promptly and in any event within time for response to process. Civ.R. 4(g).

PRODUCTION of documents

Request for, service of

On plaintiff any time after commencement of action. On any other party with or after service of summons and complaint upon him. Civ.R. 34(b).

	May accompany notice of taking deposition. Civ.R. 30(b) (5).
Response to request	Within 30 days after service of the request except that a defendant may serve response within 45 days after service of the summons and complaint upon him. Court may allow longer or shorter time. Civ.R. 34(b).
Time of inspection	The request shall specify a reasonable time. Civ.R. 34(b).
Subpoena	See "Subpoena," this table.

REFERENCES AND
Referees

Order of reference	When reference is made, clerk shall forthwith furnish master with copy of order. Civ.R. 53(d) (1).
Hearings before master	Time for beginning and closing the hearings, as fixed by order of reference. Civ.R. 53(c).
Meetings	First meeting of parties or attorneys to be held within 20 days after date of order of reference. Vic.R. 53(d) (1). Upon receipt of the order of reference, unless order otherwise provides, master shall forthwith set time and place for such meeting and notify parties or their attorneys. Civ.R. 53(d) (1).
	Speed—either party, on notice to parties and master, may apply to court for order requiring master to speed the proceedings and make his report. Civ.R. 53(d) (1).
	Failure of party to appear at appointed time and place—master may proceed ex parte or adjourn to future day, giving notice to absent party of adjournment. Civ.R. 53(d) (1).
Report of master	Filing of, time as fixed in order of reference. Civ.R. 53(c). Clerk shall forthwith mail notice of filing to all parties. Civ.R. 53(e) (1).
	Objections (in non-jury actions) may be served within 10 days after being served with notice of filing of report. Civ.R. 53(e) (2).
	Court action on report and objections thereto—application (in non-jury actions) for such action shall be by motion and upon notice as prescribed in Civ.R. 6(d). Civ.R. 53(e) (2).

Speed—either party, on notice to parties and master, may apply to court for order requiring master to speed the proceedings and make his report. Civ.R. 53(d) (1).

REMOVED actions

Answers and defenses

Within 20 days after the receipt through service or otherwise of a copy of the initial pleading setting forth the claim for relief upon which the action or proceeding is based, or within 20 days after the service of summons upon such initial pleading, then filed, or within 5 days after filing of the petition for removal, whichever period is longest. Civ.R. 81(c).

Demand for jury trial

Demand after removal not necessary in either of two instances: (1) prior to removal, party has made express demand in accordance with state law; (2) state law does not require express demands and court does not direct otherwise. Civ.R. 81(c).

Petition for removal

Within 30 days after receipt through service or otherwise of a copy of the initial pleading setting forth the claim for relief upon which the action or proceeding is based, or within 30 days after service of summons if such initial pleading has then been filed in court and is not required to be served on defendant, whichever period is shorter. 28 U.S.C.A. § 1446(b).

If the case stated by the initial pleading is not removable, a petition for removal may be filed within 30 days after receipt by the defendant, through service or otherwise, of a copy of an amended pleading, motion, order or other paper from which it may first be ascertained that the case is one which is or has become removable. 28 U.S.C.A. § 1446(b).

REPLY

See, also, "Responsive pleadings," this table.

To answer or third-party answer

Only if ordered by court. Civ.R. 7(a). Service within 20 days after service of order, unless order otherwise directs. Civ.R. 12(a).

To counterclaim

Service within 20 days after service of answer. Civ.R. 12(a).

United States or agency or officer thereof shall serve reply within 60 days after service upon U.S. attorney. Civ.R. 12(a).

Alteration of time by service of Civ.R. 12 motion	See "Responsive pleadings," this table.
RESPONSIVE PLEADINGS	See, also "Answer," and "Reply," this table.
To amended pleading	Within 10 days after service of amended pleading or within time remaining for response to original pleading, whichever is longer, unless court otherwise orders. Civ.R. 15(a).
To supplemental pleading	As ordered by court. Civ.R. 15(d).
Alteration of time by service of Civ.R. 12 motion	Service of motion permitted under Civ.R. 12 alters times for responsive pleadings as follows unless different time fixed by court (see Civ.R. 12(a)): (1) if court denies motion, service of responsive pleading within 10 days after notice of denial; (2) if court postpones disposition until trial on merits, service of responsive pleading within 10 days after notice of postponement; (3) if court grants motion for more definite statement, service of responsive pleading within 10 days after service of the more definite statement.
RESTRAINING order, temporary, without notice	See "Injunction," this table.
RETURN	Amendment of process or proof of service at any time unless it clearly appears that material prejudice would result to substantial rights of party against whom process is issued. Civ.R. 4(h). Prompt proof of service required not later than time fixed for response. Civ.R. 4(g).
SUBPOENA Discovery rule, production of books etc., under	Objection (written)—service (by person to whom subpoena directed) within 10 days after service of subpoena or on or before time specified in subpoena for compliance if such time is less than 10 days after service. Civ.R. 45(d) (1).

If objection made, party serving subpoena may move upon notice to deponent for order at any time before or during deposition. Civ.R. 45(d) (1).

Documentary evidence, generally

Motion to quash—made promptly and in any event at or before time specified in subpoena for compliance. Civ.R. 45(b).

Witness

Subpoena specifies time for attendance and giving of testimony. Civ.R. 45(a).

SUBSTITUTION of parties

In cases of death, incompetency, or transfer of interest—motion for substitution, together with notice of hearing, served on parties as provided in Civ.R. 5 and upon persons not parties in manner provided in Civ.R. 4 for service of a summons. Civ.R. 25(a), (b), (c).

Dismissal as to deceased party unless motion for substitution is made not later than 90 days after death is suggested upon the record. Civ.R. 25(a).

Successor of public officer substituted automatically. Order of substitution may be entered at any time. Civ.R. 25(d).

SUMMARY JUDGMENT, motion for
Claimant

May move at any time after expiration of 20 days from commencement of action or after service of motion for summary judgment by adverse party. Civ.R. 56(a).

Defending party

May move at any time. Civ.R. 56(b).

Service

Service of motion at least 10 days before time fixed for hearing. Civ.R. 56(c).

Service of opposing affidavits prior to day of hearing. Civ.R. 56(c).

SUMMONS

Issues forthwith. Civ.R. 4(a). No time prescribed for service but undue delay may permit statute of limitations to run or warrant dismissal for want of prosecution. Civ.R. 3.

Proof of service—person serving process shall make proof of service thereof to court promptly and in any event within time for response to process. Civ.R. 4(g).

SUPPLEMENTAL pleadings	See "Pleadings," this table.
SUPERSEDEAS or stay	See "Execution," this table.
TERM	The district courts deemed always open. Civ.R. 77(a).
	Terms of court have been abolished. 28 U.S.C.A. §§ 138-141, as amended by Pub.L. 88-139, Oct. 16, 1963, 77 Stat. 248.
THIRD-PARTY practice	Third-party plaintiff need not obtain leave if he files third-party complaint not later than 10 days after he serves his original answer. Otherwise, must obtain leave on motion upon notice to all parties to the action. Civ.R. 14(a).
VERDICT	
Judgment in accordance with prior motion for directed verdict	Party who has moved for directed verdict: (1) not later than 10 days after entry of judgment may move to have verdict and any judgment entered thereon set aside and to have judgment entered in accordance with his motion for directed verdict, or (2) if verdict was not returned, such party within 10 days after jury has been discharged may move for judgment in accordance with his motion for directed verdict. Civ.R. 50(b).
	Exception from general rule relating to enlargement.
New trial after verdict set aside	Party whose verdict set aside on motion for judgment notwithstanding verdict may serve motion for new trial pursuant to Civ.R. 59 not later than 10 days after entry of judgment notwithstanding verdict. Civ.R. 50(c) (2).

Appendix II

Sample Pleadings Used in Federal District Court in Products/Negligence Action

UNITED STATES DISTRICT COURT

DISTRICT OF (STATE)

_____ DIVISION

Wayne Brown,

Plaintiff,

vs.

Lamb Motoren, a foreign corporation; Johnson Power, Inc., a Wisconsin corporation; and Eldon Motors, a division of Tri-State Industries, a California corporation,

Defendants.

COMPLAINT

Plaintiff, for his Complaint and cause of action against the above-named defendants, and each of them, states and alleges as follows:

1. At all times material herein plaintiff was and is a citizen of the State of Minnesota, and a resident of the County of Hennepin.

2. At all times material herein, defendant Lamb Motoren, was and is a corporation organized under the laws of West Germany and was and is a citizen of West Germany, having its principal place of business in the United States of America in a state other than the State of Minnesota.

3. At all times herein mentioned defendant Johnson Power, Inc. was and is a corporation organized under the laws of the State of Wisconsin, and was and is a citizen of said state and has its principal place of business in a state other than the State of Minnesota.

4. At all times herein mentioned defendant Eldon Motors, a division of Tri-State Industries, Inc., was and is a corporation organized under the laws of the State of California, and was and still is a citizen of said state and has its principal place of business in a state other than the State of Minnesota.

5. The amount in controversy between the parties exceeds the amount of Ten Thousand and no/100 Dollars ($10,000.00), exclusive of costs and interest.

6. At all times herein mentioned defendant Lamb Motoren was engaged in the manufacture, distribution and sale of gasoline motors and engines, and prior to the date of the accident hereinafter mentioned, manufactured the gasoline engine involved herein, and caused the same to be distributed and sold in the State of Minnesota.

7. At all times herein mentioned defendant Eldon Motors, a division of Tri-State Industries, Inc. was a corporation engaged in the handling, sale and distribution of gasoline motors and engines manufactured by the defendant Lamb Motoren and sold such gasoline motors and engines including a gasoline engine serial No. 658874 purchased by plaintiff, with the permission, consent and agreement and as agent for the defendant Lamb Motoren.

8. Prior to January 18, 1990, defendant Lamb Motoren manufactured a certain two cylinder engine, 650 c.c. displacement, serial No. 658874, which said engine was distributed and delivered into the State of Minnesota by the defendant Eldon Motors, a division of Tri-State Industries, Inc., and was sold to the plaintiff by the defendant Johnson Power, Inc.

9. On January 18, 1990, while plaintiff Wayne Brown was using said engine for the purpose for which it was intended, and at which time plaintiff was unaware of any defect existing in said engine, the crankshaft thereof fractured causing injuries and damages as hereinafter set forth.

10. That said injuries and damages were a direct cause of the defective and dangerous condition of said engine which rendered the same hazardous and unsafe and which exposed persons using said engine for the purpose for which it was intended to an unreasonable risk of serious bodily harm; that said accident and the resulting injuries and damages sustained by the plaintiff were further caused by the negligent and defective design and manufacture of said gasoline engine in the following respects: (a) said engine was defective because of the design and manufacture of crankshaft mechanism; (b) because of the failure of the defendants, and each of them, to properly inspect said engine for defects; (c) because of the failure of the defendants, and each of them, to adequately test said engine for defects; (d) because of the failure of the defendants, and each of them, to provide necessary and proper warnings and instructions with respect to the use and operation of said engine and potential hazards relative to its use.

11. Defendants, and each of them, were guilty of breaches of implied warranty of fitness and purpose and breaches of warranty of merchantability of said engine and defendant Johnson Power, Inc. is liable in addition thereto for breaches of express and implied warranties of suitability for the particular purpose for which plaintiff purchased and used said engine.

12. As a result of the accident above described, plaintiff Wayne Brown was injured; has suffered pain in the past and may suffer pain in the future; has been caused to incur expenses for medical care and treatment and may be caused to incur further and like expense in the future; has been prevented from carrying on his usual occupation and activities and may have suffered a diminution of his earning capacity all to his damage in the sum of One Hundred Fifty Thousand and no/100 Dollars ($150,000.00).

Wherefore, plaintiff prays for judgment against defendants, and each of them, in the sum of One Hundred Fifty Thousand ($150,000.00) Dollars, together with his costs and disbursements herein.

_____
Attorneys for Plaintiff

Plaintiff Demands Trial by Jury.

UNITED STATES DISTRICT COURT

DISTRICT OF (STATE)

_____ DIVISION

Wayne Brown,

                Plaintiff,

  vs.

Lamb Motoren, a foreign corporation; Johnson Power, Inc., a Wisconsin corporation; and Eldon Motors, a division of Tri-State Industries, a California corporation,

                Defendants.

ANSWER AND
CROSS-CLAIM

Comes now this answering defendant, and for its separate answer to plaintiff's complaint:

1. Denies each and every allegation, statement, matter and thing in said complaint contained, except as hereinafter expressly admitted or alleged.

2. Admits the allegations of paragraphs 1, 2, 3, 4, and 6 of plaintiff's complaint, and further admits that during the time mentioned this answering defendant was a corporation engaged in the distribution of gasoline motors and engines manufactured by the defendant Lamb Motoren, a foreign corporation.

3. Specifically denies any negligence, breaches of warranty or any other unlawful or improper conduct on the part of this answering defendant, which would cause it to be legally liable to the plaintiff whether as alleged in the complaint or otherwise.

4. Alleges that if the plaintiff sustained injuries and damages, whether as alleged in the complaint or otherwise, that said damages were caused in whole or in major part by plaintiff's contributory negligence, or resulted from the improper use of said machine by the plaintiff.

5. Alleges that such damages as plaintiff may have sustained if they were not caused solely and exclusively by the negligence and want of due care of the plaintiff, were the result of negligence and breaches of warranties on the part of others for whom this answering defendant is not responsible.

CROSS-CLAIM

Further answering and for the cross-claim of the defendant Eldon Motors, a division of Tri-State Industries, Inc. against Lamb Motoren, a foreign corporation, alleges:

1. That at all times material herein the defendant Eldon Motors, a division of Tri-State Industries, Inc., served solely as a distributor of engines such as that described in plaintiff's complaint for the defendant Lamb Motoren; that is to say, that it purchased said engines from Lamb Motoren for the purpose of resale to others at the wholesale level; that defendant Eldon received said engines from the manufacturer Lamb Motoren in a packaged condition and resold them at the wholesale level to others in the same condition and packaging in which they were received from the manufacturer with no additions or changes in the product being undertaken or executed during the period of handling of said product by the distributor Eldon Motors, a division of Tri-State Industries, Inc.

2. That if it should be determined and adjudged that the motor described in plaintiff's complaint was distributed from manufacturer to consumer in the fashion described and the motor did in fact pass through the distributive corporate hands of Eldon Motors, and if it further be adjudged that there is some liability on the defendant Eldon Motors and in favor of the plaintiff, under the facts as alleged in Paragraph I above, then Eldon Motors is entitled to be fully indemnified and held harmless by Lamb Motoren for all such liability to the plaintiff together with attorneys' fees and other defense costs incurred by Eldon Motors in the defense of this action.

Wherefore, this answering defendant prays that plaintiff take nothing by his pretended cause of action, and, alternatively, prays that in the event there is liability adjudged against this defendant in favor of the plaintiff, then in that event Eldon Motors, a division of Tri-State Industries, Inc., be granted judgment of indemnity or contribution, as the case may be, against Lamb Motoren, together with its costs and disbursements herein.

_____
Attorneys for Defendant
Eldon Motors

Jury Trial Demanded

UNITED STATES DISTRICT COURT

DISTRICT OF (STATE)

_____ DIVISION

Wayne Brown,

                Plaintiff,

vs.

Lamb Motoren, a foreign corporation; Johnson Power, Inc., a Wisconsin corporation; and Eldon Motors, a division of Tri-State Industries, a California corporation,

                Defendants.

ANSWER TO
CROSS-CLAIM

Lamb Motoren, for its Answer to the Cross-Claim of Eldon Motors, alleges:

1. Denies each and every allegation in said Cross-Claim contained, except as hereinafter admitted, qualified, or otherwise duly answered or explained.

2. Admits those paragraphs numbered I and II of the Cross-Claim.

Wherefore, Lamb Motoren prays that the Cross-Claim of defendant Eldon Motors be dismissed, and that this defendant have judgment as prayed for in its Separate Answer to Amended Complaint and Cross-Claim together with its costs and disbursements herein.

_____
Attorneys for Defendant
Lamb Motoren

UNITED STATES DISTRICT COURT

DISTRICT OF (STATE)

_____ DIVISION

Wayne Brown,

                       Plaintiff,

   vs.

Lamb Motoren, a foreign corporation; Johnson Power, Inc., a Wisconsin corporation; and Eldon Motors, a division of Tri-State Industries, A California corporation.   CROSS-CLAIM

                Defendants.

Comes now defendant Eldon Motors and for its Cross-Claim against defendant Johnson Power, Inc.:

1. Alleges that plaintiff in the above-entitled action has caused a Summons and Complaint to be served upon each of the above-named defendants, and that plaintiff alleges in said complaint that all defendants are liable to plaintiff for money damages, as set forth more fully in said complaint.

2. Alleges that defendant Eldon Motors has interposed an Answer to the Complaint and has denied liability to plaintiff, all as set forth more fully in said Answer, a copy of which has been served on all parties.

3. Alleges that if plaintiff sustained injuries and losses as alleged in the complaint, or otherwise, said losses and injuries were proximately caused by the negligence and breaches of warranty by defendant Johnson Power, Inc., as set forth more fully in plaintiff's complaint.

4. Alleges that if Eldon Motors Corporation is determined to be liable to plaintiffs for money damages, it is entitled to indemnity or contribution, as the case may be, from defendant Johnson Power, Inc.

Wherefore, defendant Eldon Motors prays for judgment of indemnity or contribution, as the case may be, from defendant Johnson Power, Inc. to such sums as are awarded to plaintiff against defendant Eldon Motors together with its costs and disbursements herein.

_____

Attorneys for Eldon Motors

Defendant Eldon Motors Demands
a Trial by Jury.

UNITED STATES DISTRICT COURT

DISTRICT OF (STATE)

_____ DIVISION

Wayne Brown,

                        Plaintiff,

   vs.

Lamb Motoren, a foreign corporation; Johnson Power, Inc., a Wisconsin corporation; and Eldon Motors, a division of Tri-State Industries, a California corporation,

                      Defendants.

ANSWER TO
CROSS-CLAIM

Now comes the defendant, Johnson Power, Inc., and for its answer to the Cross-Claim of Defendant, Eldon Motors, Inc., states:

1. Specifically denies each and every allegation in said Cross-Claim contained.

Wherefore, defendant Johnson Power, Inc. prays that the Cross-Claim of defendant, Eldon Motors, Inc. be dismissed, and that this answering defendant have judgment for its costs and disbursements herein.

_____

Attorneys for Defendant
Johnson Power, Inc.

UNITED STATES DISTRICT COURT

DISTRICT OF (STATE)

——————— DIVISION

Wayne Brown,

　　　　　　　Plaintiff,

　　vs.

Lamb Motoren, a foreign corporation;
Johnson Power, Inc., a Wisconsin corporation; and Eldon Motors, a division
of Tri-State Industries, a California
corporation,

　　　　　　　Defendants.

SEPARATE ANSWER
TO COMPLAINT AND
CROSS-CLAIM

Now comes the defendant Johnson Power, Inc., a Wisconsin corporation, and for its separate Answer to the Complaint of the plaintiff
herein:

1. Denies each and every allegation, matter and thing contained in said
Complaint as to this defendant, save and except as is hereinafter admitted, qualified or otherwise explained.

2. Admits the allegations of paragraphs 3, 6, 7 and 8 except as paragraph
VIII refers to the engine in question being sold to the plaintiff by the
defendant Johnson Power, Inc., which this defendant specifically denies.

3. As to paragraphs 1, 2, 4, 5 and 9 of the plaintiff's complaint, alleges
that it has insufficient knowledge and information upon which to form
a belief as to those allegations, and, accordingly, denies same and puts
plaintiff to his proof.

4. As and for a defense this answering defendant alleges that the accident described in plaintiff's Complaint and resulting injuries and damages to the plaintiff, if any, were caused by the contributory negligence
of the plaintiff.

5. As and for a further defense this answering defendant alleges that if
the plaintiff was injured and suffered damages as a result of the negligence, breach of warranty, defective design or manufacture or through
fault of any other party named herein, then said injuries and damage
were caused by the negligence, breach of warranty, defective design or
manufacture or through fault of defendant Lamb Motoren and Eldon
Motors, Inc.

CROSS-CLAIM

Now comes the defendant Johnson Power, Inc., a Wisconsin corporation, and for its cross-claim against the defendants Lamb Motoren,
and Eldon Motors, Inc.

1. Alleges that if there was any injury or damage to the plaintiff due to negligence, breaches of warranty, defective design or manufacture, failure to properly inspect or test, failure to provide necessary and proper warnings and instructions, or otherwise, of any person other than the plaintiff, then said injury and damage were caused by defendants Lamb Motoren and Eldon Motors, Inc.

2. Alleges that in the event this answering defendant is determined to be liable to the plaintiff, this answering defendant should have judgment against defendants Lamb Motoren, and Eldon Motors, Inc. for such amount by way of indemnity or contribution as the Court should find just and proper.

Wherefore, Johnson Power, Inc. prays that plaintiff's pretended cause of action be dismissed as to this defendant, and that it have judgment for its costs and disbursements herein; and further this answering and cross-claiming defendant prays that in the event it is adjudged that the plaintiff recover against this defendant, that it have judgment against defendants Lamb Motoren and Eldon Motors, Inc. for the amount of such recovery by way of indemnity or contribution, together with its costs and disbursements herein.

_____
Attorneys for Defendant
Johnson Power, Inc.

UNITED STATES DISTRICT COURT

DISTRICT OF (STATE)

_____ DIVISION

Wayne Brown,

        Plaintiff,

vs.

Lamb Motoren, a foreign corporation; Johnson Power, Inc., a Wisconsin corporation; and Eldon Motors, a division of Tri-State Industries, a California corporation,

        Defendants.

ANSWER TO CROSS-CLAIM

Comes now defendant Eldon Motors, Inc. and for its Answer to the Cross-Claim of defendant Johnson Power, Inc.:

1. Denies each and every allegation, statement, matter and thing in said Cross-Claim contained, except as previously admitted or alleged in this

answering defendant's Answer and Cross-Claim heretofore served on the parties.

Wherefore, defendant Eldon Motors, Inc. prays that defendant Johnson Power, Inc., take nothing by reason of its pretended Cross-Claim, and that this answering defendant have judgment for its costs and disbursements herein.

_____
Attorneys for Eldon Motors

Defendant Eldon Motors, Inc.
Demands Trial by Jury.

Appendix III

Sample Forms Used in Declaratory Judgment Action for Construction of Contract

UNITED STATES DISTRICT COURT

DISTRICT OF (STATE)

_____ DIVISION

Linda A. Smith, a minor, by Clyde A. Smith, her father and natural guardian,
                  Plaintiffs,
   vs.
 Mutual Insurance Company, a corporation and David T. Black,
               Defendants.
	COMPLAINT*

Come now plaintiffs above-named, and for their cause of action allege:

1. That defendant Mutual Insurance Company is an insurance corporation which has its principal place of business in the State of Georgia.

2. That Linda A. Smith is the minor daughter of Clyde A. Smith, having been born on July 29, 1974, and lives in the latter's household at 3043 Hayes Street N.E., Madison, Wisconsin.

3. That at all times material herein the Hayden Automobile Leasing Corporation was the owner of a certain 1990 Dodge Automobile bearing 1990 (State) license number 3SG737.

*This complaint is for a declaratory judgment as authorized by Rule 57.

4. That at all times material herein said Dodge automobile was leased by the Hayden Automobile Leasing Corporation to Rent A Car System, Inc., for the purpose of subleasing to the general public.

5. That at all times material herein defendant Mutual Insurance Company had in full force and effect a certain automobile liability insurance policy issued to Rent A Car System, Inc. and Hayden Automobile Leasing Corporation, a copy of said policy is attached hereto as Exhibit A.

6. That on or about June 15, 1990, Clyde A. Smith leased said Dodge automobile from Rent A Car System, Inc. for his own use and the use of the members of his family, including Linda A. Smith. That said lease agreement was entered into at the City of Madison, Dane County, Wisconsin, and a true copy of said lease is attached hereto as Exhibit B.

7. That on or about June 18, 1990, while plaintiff Linda A. Smith was driving said Dodge automobile with the permission and consent of the Hayden Automobile Leasing Corporation and Rent A Car System, Inc. she was involved in a motor vehicle collision with defendant David T. Black at the intersection of Fairview Avenue and Ryan in Madison, Wisconsin.

8. That said David T. Black has made a claim against Linda A. Smith for money damages as compensation for certain alleged injuries and property damage said to have resulted from the accident.

9. That plaintiff Linda A. Smith is an additional insured under said insurance policy issued by defendant Mutual Insurance Company, and is entitled to the full benefits provided by said policy.

10. That plaintiffs have made demand upon defendant Mutual Insurance Company to provide Linda A. Smith with a defense to the claim of David T. Black or settle the claim, as is appropriate; however, defendant Mutual Insurance Company denies any obligation to plaintiffs and David T. Black under said insurance policy.

Wherefore, plaintiffs pray for a judgment and decree of this Court determining the rights, liabilities, duties and legal relationships between the parties hereto; that, specifically, it be determined and declared that defendant Mutual Insurance Company insures plaintiff Linda A. Smith under said policy; and that plaintiffs have judgment for their costs and disbursements herein.

_____
Attorneys for Plaintiffs

Plaintiffs Demand Trial by Jury.

UNITED STATES DISTRICT COURT

DISTRICT OF (STATE)

——————— DIVISION

Linda A. Smith, a minor, by Clyde A. Smith, her father and natural guardian, Plaintiffs, vs. Mutual Insurance Company a corporation and David T. Black, Defendants.	ANSWER

Comes now defendant Mutual Insurance Company, and for its Answer to the Complaint of plaintiffs herein:

1. Admits that at all times material herein this answering defendant was a duly organized insurance company authorized to conduct a general insurance business in the State of Wisconsin with its principal place of business in the State of Georgia; and, further, that Linda A. Smith is the minor daughter of Clyde A. Smith, having been born July 29, 1974, and resides in the latter's household at 3043 Hayes Street Northeast, Madison, Wisconsin.

2. Admits further that this answering defendant issued a certain policy of insurance to Rent A Car System, Inc. and Hayden Automobile Leasing Corporation, a copy of which is attached to the Complaint, marked Exhibit A.

3. Specifically denies that Clyde A. Smith leased said Dodge Automobile from Rent A Car System, Inc. for his own use and the use of the members of his family, including Linda A. Smith.

4. Specifically denies that plaintiffs have made a demand upon defendant Mutual Insurance Company to provide Linda A. Smith with a defense to the claim of David T. Black or settle his claim, as alleged in plaintiffs' Complaint or in any other manner.

5. Specifically denies that plaintiffs were insured pursuant to the terms and provisions of the policy of insurance issued by this answering defendant to Rent A Car System, Inc. and Hayden Automobile Leasing Corporation pursuant to the terms and provisions of the lease agreement entered into by Clyde A. Smith with Rent A Car System Inc., a copy of which is attached to plaintiffs' Complaint and marked Exhibit B.

6. Except as hereinbefore admitted, qualified or otherwise answered, this answering defendant denies each and every allegation, matter and thing in said Complaint contained, and each and every part thereof, as though more fully set forth herein at length and denied in particular.

Wherefore, this answering defendant prays that plaintiffs take nothing by reason of their pretended cause of action, and that judgment be entered on behalf of this answering defendant for its costs and disbursements incurred herein.

_____
Attorneys for Defendant
Mutual Insurance Company

UNITED STATES DISTRICT COURT

DISTRICT OF (STATE)

_____ DIVISION

Linda A. Smith, a minor, by Clyde A. Smith, her father and natural guardian, Plaintiffs, vs. Mutual Insurance Company, a corporation and David T. Black, Defendants.	ANSWER OF DAVID T. BLACK

Defendant, David T. Black, for his Answer to plaintiffs' Complaint herein states and alleges:

1. Unless otherwise admitted, qualified or explained herein, said Defendant denies each and every thing, matter or allegation contained in Plaintiffs' Complaint herein.

2. Said Defendant does not have sufficient knowledge or information to form a belief as to the truth or falsity of the allegations contained in paragraphs 1, 2, 3, 4, 5, 6, 9, or 10 and puts Plaintiffs to their strict proof thereof.

3. Defendant Black admits paragraphs 7 and 8 of Plaintiffs' Complaint herein.

4. That said Defendant has also and will in the future make claim against all interested parties for his personal injuries and his property damage.

Wherefore, David T. Black prays for a judgment and decree of this Court determining the rights, liabilities, duties and legal relationships between parties hereto and awarding unto said Defendant his costs and disbursements.

_____

Attorneys for Defendant Black

UNITED STATES DISTRICT COURT

DISTRICT OF (STATE)

_____ DIVISION

Linda A. Smith, a minor, by Clyde A.
Smith, her father and natural guardian,
                              Plaintiffs,
  vs.   NOTICE OF MOTION
Mutual Insurance Company, a corpo-   AND MOTION
ration, and David T. Black,
                              Defendants.

To: Linda A. Smith, a minor, by Clyde A. Smith, her father and natural
    guardian, and their attorneys, _____, and David Black and his
    attorney, _____.

   PLEASE TAKE NOTICE that the defendant Mutual Insurance Company will move the Court sitting at Special Term on Wednesday, the 7th day of June, 1991, at 9:30 A.M., or as soon thereafter as counsel can be heard, for an Order of the above-named Court, allowing defendant Mutual Insurance Company to serve a Third-party Summons and Complaint on Clyde A. Smith and Federal Farm Insurance Company, in order to join all of the interested parties in the above-captioned declaratory judgment action.

   Said Motion is to be based upon the files and records of the above-captioned Court, together with the attached Affidavit.

_____

Attorneys for Defendant
Mutual Insurance Company

UNITED STATES DISTRICT COURT

DISTRICT OF (STATE)

_____ DIVISION

Linda A. Smith, a minor, by Clyde A.
Smith, her father and natural guardian,
              Plaintiffs,

vs.   AFFIDAVIT

Mutual Insurance Company, a corporation, and David T. Black,
              Defendants.

STATE OF WISCONSIN

                                          ss

COUNTY OF DANE

David R. Lewis, being first duly sworn on oath, deposes and says
that he is one of the attorneys representing the defendant Mutual Insurance Company in the above-captioned declaratory judgment action.

That on or about March 14, 1991, defendant Mutual Insurance Company was served with a Summons and Complaint, a copy of which is
hereto attached and marked Exhibit "A." That said Summons and Complaint among other things, seeks declaratory relief determining that defendant Mutual Insurance Company provides coverage for plaintiff Linda
A. Smith as a result of a motor vehicle accident which took place on
June 18, 1990, between a motor vehicle owned by Hayden Automobile
Leasing Corporation and Rent A Car System, Inc., which had been
rented by plaintiff's father, Clyde A. Smith and which was being driven
at the time by plaintiff Linda A. Smith, and a car driven by defendant
David. T. Black.

That plaintiff's father, Clyde A. Smith, and Federal Farm Insurance
Company have an interest in the above-captioned declaratory judgment
action and would be affected by the declaration.

That in order for the above-named Court to grant complete relief in
the above-captioned matter, that it is necessary for Clyde A. Smith and
Federal Farm Insurance Company be joined as third-party defendants
so that their rights may be determined along with the rights of Linda
A. Smith and Mutual Insurance Company.

That any declaration by the above-captioned Court in this declaratory
judgment action would affect the rights of Clyde A. Smith and Federal
Farm Insurance Company and that Clyde A. Smith and Federal Farm
Insurance Company should be joined as third-party defendants in order
that any declaration by the above-captioned Court regarding insurance

coverage of Linda A. Smith would be binding upon all interested parties, including Clyde A. Smith and Federal Farm Insurance Company.

A copy of the proposed Third-party Summons and Complaint is attached hereto and marked Exhibit "B."

Further, Affiant sayeth not, except that this Affidavit is made in support of defendant Mutual Insurance Company's Motion to join Clyde A. Smith and Federal Farm Insurance Company as third-party defendants in the above-captioned matter.

_____

David R. Lewis

Subscribed and sworn to before
me this 26th day of May, 1991.

_____

Notary Public

UNITED STATES DISTRICT COURT

DISTRICT OF (STATE)

_____ DIVISION

Linda A. Smith, a minor, by Clyde A. Smith, her father and natural guardian,
                 Plaintiffs,
  vs.
Mutual Insurance Company, a corporation and David T. Black,
                 Defendants.
_____
 	
Mutual Insurance Company, a corporation,
            Third-Party Plaintiff,
  vs.
Clyde A. Smith and Federal Farm Insurance Company,
           Third-Party Defendants.
	(EXHIBIT B)
	THIRD-PARTY
	COMPLAINT

Comes now defendant and third-party plaintiff above named and for its cause of action against third-party defendants herein:

1. Alleges that at all times material herein defendant and third-party plaintiff Mutual Insurance Company was a duly organized and existing corporation authorized to conduct a general insurance business in the State of Wisconsin.

2. Alleges that third-party defendant Federal Farm Insurance Company was a duly organized and existing corporation authorized to conduct a general insurance business in the State of Wisconsin at all times material herein.

3. Alleges that Clyde A. Smith, third-party defendant herein, entered into a lease agreement with Rent A Car System, Inc. on June 15, 1990, and that said lease agreement was entered into in the City of Madison, County of Dane, State of Wisconsin.

4. That on or about the 8th day of March, 1991, a lawsuit was commenced against defendant and third-party plaintiff Mutual Insurance Company by Linda A. Smith, a minor, by Clyde A. Smith, her father and natural guardian, in which plaintiff Linda A. Smith, a minor, seeks to determine her rights, if any, upon a policy of insurance issued by defendant and third-party plaintiff Mutual Insurance Company to Rent A Car System Inc.; that third-party defendants, Clyde A. Smith and Federal Farm Insurance Company, a corporation, ware the real parties in interest in any determination of the rights of Linda A. Smith pursuant to the terms and provisions of the Mutual Insurance Company policy or the lease agreement entered into between Clyde A. Smith and Rent A Car System, Inc.

5. That third-party defendant, Federal Farm Insurance Company, a corporation, at all times material herein had in full force and effect a policy of automobile insurance issued to third-party defendant Clyde A. Smith; that by the terms and provisions of said policy of insurance third-party defendant Federal Farm Insurance Company agreed to indemnify Clyde A. Smith and Linda A. Smith, in addition to defending Clyde A. Smith and Linda A. Smith against any suits or claims arising out of the operation of a motor vehicle by Clyde A. Smith or Linda A. Smith, including but not limited to the claim presented by defendant David T. Black.

Wherefore, defendant and third-party plaintiff Mutual Insurance Company prays that the Court determine the rights of Clyde A. Smith and Linda A. Smith, plaintiffs, to coverage under the Federal Farm Insurance policy issued to Clyde A. Smith; and that the Court enter judgment in favor of third-party plaintiff Mutual Insurance Company in accordance with the request set forth in its Answer; and that judgment be entered on behalf of plaintiff Linda A. Smith and third-party defendant Clyde A. Smith, holding that said plaintiff and third-party defendant are entitled to insurance coverage pursuant to the terms and provisions of third-party defendant Federal Farm Insurance Company's policy, together with costs and disbursements incurred herein.

Attorneys for Third-Party
Plaintiff

UNITED STATES DISTRICT COURT

DISTRICT OF (STATE)

_____ DIVISION

Linda A. Smith, a minor by Clyde A. Smith, her father and natural guardian, Plaintiffs, vs. Mutual Insurance Company, a corporation and David T. Black, Defendants.	ORDER

The above-entitled matter came before the Court on the motion of defendant Mutual Insurance Company for leave to serve and file a third-party complaint in the form attached to the motion. Thomas Jones, Esq., appeared on behalf of plaintiffs in opposition to the motion. David Lewis, Esq., appeared on behalf of defendant Mutual Insurance Company in support of the motion.

The Court having heard and considered the proposed third-party complaint, and having heard the arguments of counsel and being fully advised in the premises,

IT IS HEREBY ORDERED that defendant Mutual Insurance Company's motion for leave to serve and file a third-party complaint is denied.

This order is without prejudice to Mutual Insurance Company or the Federal Farm Insurance Company to litigate issues between them through a third-party action or otherwise. Specifically, counsel for Mutual indicated the possibility of a dispute as to which Insurance Company has the primary coverage. That issue was not resolved by the above Order.

By the Court:

Judge of District Court

(date)

UNITED STATES DISTRICT COURT

DISTRICT OF (STATE)

_____ DIVISION

Linda A. Smith, a minor, by Clyde A.
Smith, her father and natural guardian,
                       Plaintiffs,

  vs.

Mutual Insurance Company, a corporation and David T. Black,
                      Defendants.

NOTICE OF MOTION AND MOTION

To: Defendant Mutual Insurance Company and its attorneys; and, Defendant David T. Black and his attorneys.

PLEASE TAKE NOTICE that the above-named plaintiffs, through their
undersigned attorneys, will bring the attached motion on for hearing at
a special term of the above-named Court to be held at the courthouse
in the City of Madison, Wisconsin on the 24th day of August, 1991, at
9:00 A.M., or as soon thereafter as counsel can be heard.

MOTION

Plaintiff Linda Smith hereby moves the Court, through her undersigned attorneys, for an Order accelerating the above entitled action on
the active trial calendar for trial by jury as soon as the Court's business
will permit.

This Motion is made on the grounds that the case involves a determination as to whether the Mutual Insurance Company affords liability
coverage for an automobile accident that occurred on June 18, 1990,
which allegedly resulted in injuries to defendant David T. Black. Mr.
Black has made claim against plaintiff Linda Smith for compensatory
damages. It is to the benefit of all parties to know as soon as possible
whether or not Linda A. Smith does have liability coverage under the
Mutual Insurance Policy. That an acceleration of the case on the active
trial calendar should not cause prejudice to any of the parties herein.

_____

Attorneys for Plaintiff

UNITED STATES DISTRICT COURT

DISTRICT OF (STATE)

_____ DIVISION

Linda A. Smith, a minor, by Clyde A. Smith, her father and natural guardian, Plaintiffs, vs. Mutual Insurance Company, a corporation and David T. Black, Defendants.	FINDINGS OF FACT, CONCLUSIONS OF LAW AND ORDER FOR JUDGMENT

The above-entitled declaratory judgment action came before the Court for trial without jury on (date). Plaintiffs appeared in person and by their attorney _____. Attorney _____, appeared on behalf of defendant.

The Court having heard the evidence presented by the parties and having considered the arguments of counsel and all the files, records and proceedings herein, makes its:

FINDINGS OF FACT

1. Linda Smith is a minor daughter of Clyde A. Smith, and at all times material herein resided in his household at 3043 Hayes Street North East, Madison, Wisconsin.

2. That defendant Mutual Insurance Company is an insurance corporation authorized to conduct its insurance business in the State of Wisconsin, including the issuance of automobile liability insurance policies.

3. That the Hayden Automobile Leasing Corporation owned a certain 1990 Dodge automobile which, at all times material herein, was leased by Hayden Automobile Leasing Corporation to the Rent A Car System, Inc., for the purpose of subleasing to the general public.

4. That at all times material herein defendant Mutual Insurance Company had in full force and effect the automobile liability insurance policy in question (Exhibit A) in which the Rent A Car System and the Hayden Automobile Leasing Corporation were named insureds; that said policy provides, among other things, that persons under the policy include:

"Any other person while using an owned automobile with the permission of the named insured, provided his actual operation * * * is within the scope of such permission * * *."

5. That on June 15, 1990, Clyde A. Smith leased the said Dodge automobile from Rent A Car System, Inc. to replace his automobile which was used by his family and which had been damaged in an accident on or about June 11, 1990; that he specifically informed the Rent A Car System clerk, June Wilkerson, that he needed to lease the automobile to temporarily replace a family automobile which had been damaged in an accident while his daughter was driving it.

6. That Clyde A. Smith signed a "Rental Agreement" (Exhibit B) before taking possession of the Dodge Automobile, but he did not read the terms and conditions stated on the back thereof, including:

"Further said vehicle will be operated only by renter or * * * (2) Any member of renter's immediate family provided that renter's permission first be obtained and all such operators shall be at least twenty-one years of age and duly qualified and licensed."

That said provisions were not otherwise brought to the attention of Smiths before the motor vehicle accident of June 18, 1990; that Clyde A. Smith truthfully and fully answered the clerk's questions pertaining to the Rental Agreement so that she could complete the form.

7. That on or about June 18, 1990, Clyde A. Smith authorized Linda A. Smith to operate the Dodge automobile, and while operating said Dodge automobile Linda A. Smith was involved in a motor vehicle collision with defendant David T. Black at the intersection of Fairview Avenue and Ryan Street in Madison, Wisconsin; that defendant David T. Black has made a claim against Linda A. Smith for money damages for injuries and property damage he alleges resulted from said accident.

8. That at the time of said June 18, 1990, accident, plaintiff Linda A. Smith was driving the Dodge automobile with the permission and consent of the Hayden Automobile Leasing Corporation and Rent A Car System, Inc.

CONCLUSIONS OF LAW

1. That plaintiff Linda A. Smith was operating the Dodge automobile with the permission and consent of the Hayden Automobile Leasing Corporation and the Rent A Car System, Inc.

2. That plaintiff Linda A. Smith is an additional insured under the terms and provisions of defendant Mutual Insurance Company automobile liability insurance policy.

3. That defendant Mutual Insurance Company is obligated to assume defense of the claim by David T. Black against plaintiff Linda A. Smith and pay on behalf of Linda A. Smith all sums which she may become legally obligated to pay as damages for the claim of David T. Black up to the limit of the policy.

4. That plaintiffs are entitled to recover their costs and disbursements herein.

ORDER FOR JUDGMENT

Let Judgment be Entered Accordingly.

By the Court:

_____
Judge of District Court

Dated: _____

MEMORANDUM

The facts in the above case cannot be distinguished from those in Taylor v. Allstate, 286 Minn. 449, 176 N.W.2d 266 (1970). The "Rental Agreement" does contain a limitation or prohibition to the effect that no one under twenty-one years of age is authorized to operate the leased automobile, and plaintiff Linda Smith was under age. However, the evidence clearly shows that the prohibition was not brought to the attention of the Lessee, Clyde A. Smith, nor to the attention of his subpermittee Linda Smith.

As noted in the *Taylor* case, the lessor should know and appreciate that when an automobile is leased for the purpose of temporarily replacing a family automobile, it will probably be used by members of the lessee's family, including minor children. The burden is upon the owner to make clear to his permittees or subpermittees any limitations which he desires to impose on the scope of the permittee's use of a leased automobile. An uncommunicated intent to limit the scope of consent is not effective.

In Taylor v. Allstate, supra, the lease agreement contained a similar prohibition to that in the present case, and the lessee signed the lease agreement. Nevertheless, it was not effective to preclude permission and consent to the lessee's minor son. The same is true in the present case.

This memorandum is part of the attached order.

/s/ _____
(District Judge)

Appendix IV

Sample Forms Used for Concluding Litigation

STATE OF MINNESOTA	DISTRICT COURT
COUNTY OF _____	_____ JUDICIAL DISTRICT

Georgia Watson,

               Plaintiff,

  vs.

Alvin Johanson,

               Defendant,

STIPULATION FOR
DISMISSAL

    The above-entitled action, having been fully compromised and settled,

    NOW THEREFORE, it is stipulated and agreed, by and between the parties hereto, through their respective counsel, that said action may be and hereby is dismissed with prejudice and on the merits, but without further costs to any of the parties.

    IT IS FURTHER STIPULATED AND AGREED that either party, without notice to the other, may cause judgment of dismissal with prejudice and on the merits to be entered herein.

_____

Attorneys for Plaintiff

_____

Attorneys for Defendant

STATE OF _____   DISTRICT COURT

COUNTY OF _____   _____ JUDICIAL DISTRICT

Anderson Fish Company,   DISMISSAL
                    Plaintiff,   WITHOUT PREJUDICE
    vs.
Alan B. Fredericks,   File No. _____
                    Defendant.

The above-entitled action may be and is hereby dismissed without prejudice and without further costs to either party.

_____
Attorneys for Plaintiff

_____
Attorneys for Defendant

Dated: _____

RELEASE OF ALL CLAIMS

FOR AND IN CONSIDERATION of the payment to me/us at this time of the sum of _____Dollars ($_____), the receipt of which is hereby acknowledged, I/we, being of lawful age, do hereby release, acquit and forever discharge _____ of and from any and all actions, causes of action, claims, demands, damages, costs, loss of services, expenses and compensation, on account of, or in any way growing out of, any and all known and unknown personal injuries, developed or undeveloped, and property damage resulting or to result from the accident that occurred on or about the ____ day of _____, 19___, at or near _____.

I/we hereby declare and represent that the injuries sustained may be permanent and progressive and that recovery therefrom is uncertain and indefinite, and in making this release and agreement it is understood and agreed that I/we rely wholly upon my/our own judgment, belief and knowledge of the nature, extent and duration of said injuries, and that I/we have not been influenced to any extent whatever in making this release by any representations or statements regarding said injuries, or regarding any other matters, made by the persons, firms or corporations who are hereby released, or by any person or persons representing him or them, or by any physician or surgeon by him or them employed.

I/we clearly understand that I/we are releasing _____ and that this release includes all injuries now known to me/us and also all injuries now unknown, and I/we clearly understand that this release also includes all disabilities or results which may develop in the future from injuries now known or unknown to me/us.

It is further understood and agreed that this settlement is the compromise of a doubtful and disputed claim, and that the payment is not to be construed as an admission of liability on the part of _____ by whom liability is expressly denied.

This release contains the ENTIRE AGREEMENT between the parties hereto, and the terms of this release are contractual and not a mere recital.

I/we further state that I/we have carefully read the foregoing release and know the contents thereof, and I/we sign the same as my/our own free act.

WITNESS _____ hand and seal this _____ day of _____, 19___.

In presence of

CAUTION! READ BEFORE SIGNING

_____

_____   _____(Seal)

_____   _____(Seal)

_____

RELEASE AND INDEMNITY AGREEMENT

KNOW ALL MEN BY THESE PRESENTS: That we, Robert William Grant and Gloria Jean Grant, husband and wife, of _____ County, State of _____ in consideration of the sum of Nine Thousand Five Hundred and No/100 Dollars ($9,500.00), and other valuable consideration, to us duly paid, receipt whereof is hereby acknowledged, do hereby for ourselves, our heirs, executors, administrators, successors, and assigns, release, acquit and forever discharge Patrick Mathias Ryan, Mutual Insurance Company, Richard Martin Halvorson, and Federal Farm Insurance Company of and from any and all actions, causes of action, claims, demands, damages, costs, loss of services, expenses and compensation, on account of, or in any way growing out of, any and all known and unknown personal injuries, developed or undeveloped, and property damage resulting or to result from an accident that occurred on or about June 24, 1991, at or on Highway 35W at the turn-off onto County Road No. 42 in the County of _____, State of _____.

We hereby declare and represent that the injuries sustained may be permanent and progressive and that recovery therefrom is uncertain and indefinite, and in making this release and agreement it is understood and agreed that we rely wholly upon our own judgment, belief and knowledge of the nature, extent and duration of said injuries, and that we have not been influenced to any extent whatever in making this release by any representations or statements regarding said injuries, or regarding any other matters, made by the persons, firms or corporations who are hereby released, or by any person or persons representing him or them, or by any physician or surgeon by him or them employed.

We clearly understand that we are releasing Patrick Mathias Ryan, Mutual Insurance Company, Richard Martin Halvorson, and Federal Farm Insurance Company and that this release includes all injuries now known to us and also all injuries now unknown, and we clearly understand that this release also includes all disabilities or results which may develop in the future from injuries now known or unknown to us.

It is further understood and agreed that this settlement is the compromise of a doubtful and disputed claim, and that the payment is not to be construed as an admission of liability on the part of Patrick Mathias Ryan, Mutual Insurance Company, Richard Martin Halvorson, and Federal Farm Insurance Company by whom liability is expressly denied.

In and as a further consideration of the receipt of the above amount, the undersigned hereby agree, except for attorney fees and direct suit costs, to indemnify and to reimburse or make good any loss or damage or costs that the said Patrick Mathias Ryan, Mutual Insurance Company, Richard Martin Halvorson, and Federal Farm Insurance Company may have to pay, and to hold them harmless from and against any and all demands, liabilities and charges which any of them may incur by reason of their being made a party to any lawsuit arising out of the aforementioned accident which occurred on June 24, 1991, and particularly, but not limited to any claim for contribution or indemnity made by any individual, person, persons or party against whom the undersigned made or may make any claim, claims, commence litigation or institute legal proceedings; and this release and indemnity agreement in the event of a breach thereof, may be pleaded as a defense and the said Patrick Mathias Ryan, Mutual Insurance Company, Richard Martin Halvorson, and Federal Farm Insurance Company, their heirs, executors, administrators, successors, assigns or their estate will not be required to respond in damages to us in any action whatsoever and any other proceedings of every kind, nature and description which may be brought, instituted, or taken by us and others against the said Patrick Mathias Ryan, Mutual Insurance Company, Richard Martin Halvorson, and Federal Farm Insurance Company, their heirs, executors, administrators, successors, assigns or their estate.

This release and indemnity agreement contains the entire agreement between the parties hereto, and the terms of this release are contractual and not a mere recital.

We further state that we have carefully read the foregoing release and indemnity agreement and know the contents thereof, and we sign the same as our own free act.

Date: _____, 19___.

In the Presence of:

_____   _____

                                                Robert William Grant

_____   _____

                                                Gloria Jean Grant

COVENANT NOT TO SUE

KNOW ALL MEN BY THESE PRESENTS, that Daniel Trost, Paul Trost and Thomas E. Trost, hereinafter referred to as plaintiffs, for and in consideration of the sum of Four Thousand Dollars and no cents ($4,000.00), the receipt of which is hereby acknowledged, do hereby covenant and expressly agree with The Griff Company and Mutual Insurance Company, their successors and assigns (all of whom are hereafter referred to as "Settling Parties") not to further prosecute the suit for damages by plaintiffs pending against The Griff Company in the _____ District Court, County of _____, State of _____, and agree to execute a Stipulation for Dismissal with prejudice in said action insofar as The Griff Company is concerned.

Plaintiffs further covenant and expressly agree with the Settling Parties to forever refrain from instituting any other action or making any other demand or claims of any kind against said settling parties for damages sustained by them as a result of an accident which occurred on June 22, 19___, in the Village of _____, _____.

The aforesaid consideration is not intended as full compensation for damages claimed by plaintiffs arising from said accident. However, by this covenant, plaintiffs do hereby credit and satisfy that portion of the total amount of their damages from said accident which has been caused by the negligence, if any, of such Settling Parties hereto as many hereafter be determined to be the case in the further trial or other disposition of this or any other action. Plaintiffs do hereby release and discharge that fraction and portion and percentage of their total cause of action and claim for damages against all parties resulting from said accident which shall hereafter, by further trial or other disposition of this or any other action, be determined to be the sum of the portions or fractions or percentages of causal negligence for which any or all of the Settling Parties hereto are found to be liable.

By this settling agreement the Settling Parties are hereby discharged of their liability for contribution with respect to the claim for damages of plaintiffs resulting from said accident.

Plaintiffs reserve to themselves the balance of the whole cause of action which they may have against Lloyd Koesling as a result of said accident. This covenant is not entered into nor in any way intended to release any claim or cause of action by plaintiffs against Lloyd Koesling as a result of said accident.

Plaintiffs specifically agree to hold the Settling Parties harmless and specifically agree to indemnity them from any claim, demand or cause of action by Lloyd Koesling for apportionment by way of contribution, whether such claim for contribution is alleged to arise by reason of judgment, settlement or otherwise.

Plaintiffs will effect compliance with the provision of the last paragraph by settling and compromising any recovery which they might later obtain from Lloyd Koesling, whether or not arising from judgment, so that such recovery does not exceed the amount determined by application to total damages of plaintiffs of that proportion or fraction or percentage of causal negligence for which Lloyd Koesling may be found to be or considered to be liable and thereby eliminating any claim by Lloyd Koesling and his subrogees, insurers, assigns or successors for equalizing contributions from the Settling Parties.

The Settling Parties in whose favor this covenant not to sue is executed, reserve and retain all claims and causes of action which they or any of them might have against others and, including without limiting the generality of the foregoing, any claim for contribution which they might have against Lloyd Koesling.

The payment of the consideration for this covenant is not to be construed as an admission, on the part of any of the Settling Parties, of any liability whatsoever in consequence of said accident, to plaintiffs or to any other party.

This covenant is intended to release any claim for contribution against the Settling Parties in connection with said accident in the same manner and mode as the covenant and/or release before the court in the case of Pierringer v. Hoger, 21 Wis.2d 182, 124 N.W.2d 106 (1963).

IN WITNESS WHEREOF I have hereunto set my hand and seal this _____ day of May, 19___.

In presence of

_____

_____

_____

Daniel Trost

_____

Paul Trost

_____

Thomas E. Trost

STATE OF _____ ⎫
                       ⎬ ss

COUNTY OF _____ ⎭

On this _____day of May, 19___, before me personally appeared _____ to me known to be the persons described herein, and who executed the foregoing instrument and _____ acknowledged that _____ voluntarily executed the same.

_____

Notary Public

My term expires _____, 19___.

RELEASE AND COVENANT NOT TO SUE

AS TO AUTO LISTINGS, INC.

AND JOHN RIDER

FOR THE SOLE CONSIDERATION of Six Thousand Five Hundred and no/100 Dollars ($6,500.00), the receipt of which is hereby acknowledged, I hereby fully and forever release and discharge Auto Listings, Inc. and John Rider and The Mutual Insurance Co., their heirs, administrators, executors, successors and assigns from all claims, demands, damages, actions, rights of action of whatever kind or nature whether statutory, based on contract or otherwise, which I now have or may hereafter have arising out of, in consequence of or on account of all injuries to me, including any latent injuries and all developments and results therefrom, known and unknown injuries, whether developed or undeveloped, and anticipated and unanticipated consequences of all such injuries, and damages to property resulting to me in any way from an accident which occurred on or about the 27th day of March, 1991, at or near County Road 15 and Orchard Road in _____, _____ County,

_____. In accepting said sum I hereby release and discharge that fraction, portion or percentage of the total cause of action, or claim for damages I now have or may hereafter possess against all parties responsible for my damages which shall by trial or other disposition, be determined to be the sum of the fractions, portions or percentages of causal negligence for which the parties herein released are found to be liable to me as a consequence of the above accident.

I hereby accept said sum as a compromise and settlement of all claims on account of the dispute between the parties hereto as to whether the above named parties are liable to me or not, and also as to the nature, extent and permanency of the injuries sustained by me.

I agree that in making this release, I am relying on my own judgment, belief and knowledge as to all phases of my claims and that I am not relying on representations or statements made by any of the persons hereby released or anyone representing them or physicians or surgeons employed by them.

I agree that the payment of the above sum is not to be construed as an admission of any liability whatsoever by or on behalf of the above named parties, by whom liability is expressly denied.

I further agree that any claim of whatever kind or nature the above named parties might have or hereafter have growing out of the above accident, is hereby expressly reserved to them.

This release is intended to release only the parties specifically named. The undersigned expressly reserves the balance of the whole cause of action or any other claim of whatever kind or nature not released hereby which I may have or hereafter have against any other person or persons arising out of the above accident.

As a further consideration for this release I agree to indemnify the parties released hereby and save them harmless from any claims for contribution or indemnity made by any other person, firm or corporation adjudged liable with or in addition to the parties released hereby; and the undersigned agrees to satisfy any judgment which may be rendered in favor of the undersigned, satisfying such fraction, portion or percentage of the judgment as the causal negligence of the parties released is adjudged to be of all causal negligence of all adjudged tort-feasors. In the event the undersigned fails to immediately satisfy any such judgment to the extent of the fraction, portion or percentage of the negligence as found against the parties released, the undersigned hereby consents and agrees that upon filing a copy of this agreement, without further notice, an order may be entered by the court in which said judgment is entered directing the Clerk thereof to satisfy said judgment to the extent of such fraction, portion or percentage of the negligence as found against the parties released and discharged under this release.

The undersigned acknowledges that as a result of the injuries sustained in the accident of March 27, 1991, he has incurred medical expenses with _____ Memorial Hospital of the reasonable value of $1,419.00 and that a hospital lien has been filed on behalf of said hospital and that out of the amount being paid as consideration for this release he will satisfy said lien and furnish the parties released herein a satisfaction of said lien as to said parties.

The undersigned further acknowledges that he has as an inducement to the parties released hereby represented and warranted to them that at the time and place of the accident out of which his claim arose and for which this settlement has been made, he was not in the course and scope of his employment with Auto Listings, Inc. and that he is not entitled to recover benefits under the Workmen's Compensation Law of (State) therefor. The undersigned agrees that the payments made hereunder are received in lieu of any benefits that he may be entitled to recover under the Workmen's Compensation Law of (State); for the injuries sustained on March 27, 1991. That in the event it is ever determined that he was in the course and scope of his employment with Auto Listings, Inc. at the time of the accident here involved and is entitled to benefits under the (State) Workmen's Compensation Law therefor that Auto Listings, Inc. and The Mutual Insurance Co. as their Workmen's Compensation insurer are entitled to a full credit to the extent of the payment made for the release herein given on any liability that may be determined against them under the Workmen's Compensation Law for the injuries and damages sustained by the undersigned as a result of said accident.

The undersigned further acknowledges that it is his intention to proceed with a claim and action for damages against Gary Ford, the owner of the automobile in which he was riding at the time of the accident here involved to recover such damages as he may be able to prove against said Ford and that an action has been instituted in the District Court of Hennepin County, Minnesota therefor. That in the event it is determined in said action against Ford either directly or indirectly, or as a consequence thereof or as an adjunct thereto that Ford is entitled to be indemnified for any liability that he may have as a result of said accident by any of the parties released hereby, then and in that event the undersigned agrees to satisfy and release any such claim to the entire extent thereof in consideration of the payment that has been made as set forth herein.

It is further understood and agreed, and within the contemplation of the undersigned and the parties released hereby, that the undersigned intends to pursue an action against Patrick Vickner, individually, and doing business as Vick's to recover damages as provided by (dram shop statute) for the recovery of such loss and damages as he may have sustained as a result of this accident. That the undersigned hereby agrees that the parties released hereby may have a cause of action for contribution or indemnity against Patrick Vickner individually, and doing business as Vick's under (dram shop statute) and that he will do nothing to prejudice that claim and will cooperate and assist the parties hereby released in pursuing, and perfecting that claim, and shall attend hearings and trials and assist in securing and giving evidence and obtaining the attendance of witnesses therefor.

The undersigned further agrees to dismiss the action which has been instituted in the District Court of _____ County in the _____ Judicial District on his behalf against Auto Listings, Inc., on the merits and with prejudice as to said defendant.

Signed and sealed at Minneapolis, Minnesota, this 18th day of June, 19___.

CAUTION: READ BEFORE SIGNING.

_____

James Kendall

In the presence of:

_____

_____

Appendix V

Miscellaneous Forms

UNITED STATES DISTRICT COURT

DISTRICT OF _____

_____ DIVISION

Mary Smith,		
	Plaintiff,	NOTICE OF TAKING
vs.		ORAL DEPOSITION
Robert Jones,		
	Defendant.	

To: Robert Jones and Clay Johnson, his attorney.

YOU WILL PLEASE TAKE NOTICE that the oral deposition of Robert Jones will be taken on the 7th day of May, 1990, at 10:00 A.M. at 2205 Parkway South, Chicago, Illinois, by and before a notary public, or some other officer qualified by law, and that the said Robert Jones shall present himself at said time and place for the purpose of his oral deposition.

_____

Attorneys for plaintiff

UNITED STATES DISTRICT COURT

DISTRICT OF _____

_____ DIVISION

William Smith,
         Plaintiff,
vs.
R. E. Miller Corporation,
         Defendant.
	MOTION FOR PRODUCTION
	OF DOCUMENTS
	File No. _____

MOTION

Plaintiff, William Smith, moves the Court for an Order requiring defendant R. E. Miller Corporation to produce and to permit plaintiff to inspect and copy the following documents:

Release dated June 1, 1990, signed by plaintiff for a consideration of Five Hundred ($500.00) Dollars paid by defendant and referred to in defendant's Answer.

Statement signed by William Smith on May 3, 1990, and given by him to R. E. Miller Corporation.

Defendant, R. E. Miller Corporation has possession, custody or control of each of the foregoing documents. Each of them constitutes or contains evidence relevant to the subject matter of this action as is more fully shown in affidavit attached hereto.

_____
Attorney for Plaintiff

(date)

NOTICE OF MOTION

To: R. E. Miller Corporation and Richard Jones, its attorney:

YOU WILL PLEASE TAKE NOTICE that the undersigned will bring the above motion on for hearing at a Special Term of the above-named Court to be held in the City of Los Angeles on the third day of May, 1990, at 10:00 A.M. or as soon thereafter as counsel can be heard.

_____
Attorney for Plaintiff

UNITED STATES DISTRICT COURT

DISTRICT OF _____

_____ DIVISION

William Smith,
               Plaintiff,

  vs.   AFFIDAVIT

R. E. Miller Corporation,
               Defendant.

STATE OF _____

                            ss

COUNTY OF _____

William Smith, being first duly sworn on oath, says:

1. That defendant, by and through its liability insurance company, received from plaintiff on or about June 1, 1990, the Release referred to in the Answer and said Release is now in the files of said insurance company.

2. That on or about June 3, 1990, said insurer on behalf of defendant, visited plaintiff while plaintiff was in Memorial Hospital and at that time talked to plaintiff and recorded the answers in writing and had plaintiff sign the same. Plaintiff was not at that time, nor at any time subsequent thereto, given a copy of said statement. Said statement is now in the files of defendant's liability insurer.

3. That each of said documents are relevant to the subject matter of this action. Defendant has pleaded the Release as an affirmative defense. Plaintiff, at one time received a copy of said Release, but it is now lost and cannot, after diligent search, be found. Said statement taken in writing from plaintiff on June 3, 1990, contains statements made by plaintiff while in the hospital and under the influence of drugs and relates directly to the occurrence involved in this law suit.

_____
                                   William Smith

Subscribed and sworn to before
me this 30th day of April, 1990.

_____

Notary Public

UNITED STATES DISTRICT COURT

DISTRICT OF _____

_____ DIVISION

William Smith,
 	
            Plaintiff,
vs.
R. E. Miller Corporation,
            Defendant.
	)))))))	ORDER REQUIRING
		PRODUCTION OF
		DOCUMENTS

The above matter was heard by the Court at Special Term on the third day of May, 1990, on plaintiff's motion for production of certain documents. John Doe, Esq. appeared in support of said motion, and Richard Roe, Esq. appeared in opposition thereto.

It appears that defendant has possession and control of the documents in question and said documents contain or constitute evidence material to the subject matter of this action and good cause being shown,

IT IS ORDERED, that defendant produce and permit plaintiff's attorney to inspect, copy and photograph the following documents:

Release, dated June 1, 1990, signed by plaintiff and releasing claims against defendant.

Statement, dated June 3, 1990, signed by plaintiff and pertaining to the facts involved in this case.

Said documents are to be delivered to plaintiff's attorney within ten days hereof and returned by plaintiff to defendant promptly upon completion of the photocopying.

_____
Judge of District Court

Dated: _____

UNITED STATES DISTRICT COURT

DISTRICT OF _____

_____ DIVISION

APPLICATION FOR APPOINTMENT OF

GUARDIAN AD LITEM

To the Above-Named Court:

William Johnson, a minor, applies to the Court and states:

1. Applicant's full name is William Johnson; he is fifteen (15) years old, and resides at 264 Elm, in the City of Fairfield, County of _____, State of _____.

2. Applicant's father is deceased; applicant's mother is Mrs. Sarah Johnson, residing at 23 South Front Street, Denver, Colorado; that applicant has no custodian or testamentary or other guardian.

3. Applicant is not married.

4. Applicant has, as he is advised by _____, an attorney of this Court, a good cause of action against Leo Hatfield for personal injury, which action your applicant is desirous of commencing forthwith in this Court.

5. Thomas Murphy, age forty-seven, residing at 6754 A Street, Fairfield, _____, and a salesman by occupation, is a responsible person competent to act as guardian ad litem for applicant in said action.

Wherefore, your applicant prays said Thomas Murphy, or some other competent person, be appointed guardian ad litem of applicant to commence and prosecute said action for applicant.

(date)

_____
William Johnson

STATE OF _____ ⎫
                      ⎬ ss
COUNTY OF _____ ⎭

William Johnson, being duly sworn, deposes and says that he has read the foregoing Petition subscribed by him, and knows the contents thereof, and that the same is true of his own knowledge, except as to those matters stated therein on information and belief, and as to those matters he believes it to be true.

_____

William Johnson

Subscribed and sworn to before me
this 2nd day of January, 19___.

_____

Notary Public

CONSENT OF GUARDIAN

I hereby consent to act as guardian ad litem of William Johnson, for the purposes stated in the foregoing Petition.

_____

Thomas Murphy

(date)

UNITED STATES DISTRICT COURT

DISTRICT OF _____

_____ DIVISION

ORDER APPOINTING GUARDIAN AD LITEM

On the foregoing attached Application and Consent, and on motion of _____, Esq. attorney for the petitioner,

IT IS ORDERED, that Thomas Murphy, be and hereby is, appointed guardian ad litem of William Johnson, for the purpose of prosecuting one Leo Hatfield as requested in the petition.

By the Court:

_____

Judge of District Court

Dated: _____

UNITED STATES DISTRICT COURT

DISTRICT OF _____

_____ DIVISION

OATH OF GUARDIAN

I, Thomas Murphy, do swear that I will faithfully and justly perform all the duties of the office and trust which I now assume as guardian ad litem for William Johnson, to the best of my ability. So help me God.

_____
                                        Thomas Murphy

Subscribed and sworn to before
me
this 2nd day of January, 19___.

_____

Notary Public

UNITED STATES DISTRICT COURT

DISTRICT OF _____

_____ DIVISION

(Title of Case)   **INTERROGATORIES**

                              (Commonly directed to plaintiff
                              in wrongful death action.)

Defendants respectfully submit to the plaintiffs for answer by them under oath as provided for by the Rules of Civil Procedure the following interrogatories:

1. State decedent's date and place of birth.

2. State decedent's residential addresses for the past ten years preceding his death, indicating the period of time he was at each address, respectively.

3. Describe fully all disabilities that decedent had immediately prior to the accident for which he received medical care or which affected his employability or limited his activities.

4. Describe fully the extent of decedent's formal education, including the schools attended, degrees obtained and dates of completions.

5. State the amount of income decedent reported as income in his United States federal tax returns for each of the years 1989, 1990, and 1991, respectively.

6. Describe decedent's employments during the five years preceding his death, including the name of each employer, period of time for each employment, his job title, and a description of the work he performed in each job.

7. As to each personal injury accident the decedent has had, state:

   a. the date of the accident

   b. the location of the accident

   c. the type of accident

   d. the nature and extent of injuries sustained

   e. the names and addresses of physicians who attended him

   f. the names and addresses of hospitals at which he received treatment

   g. the nature and extent of any consequential disability

   h. the name and address of all persons against whom claims were made due to the accident

8. State the name, address, age and relationship to decedent of each next of kin for whom claim is being made in this action.

9. Describe fully the pecuniary contribution made by decedent to each next of kin for whom claim is being made in this action.

10. Specify each item of special damages claimed by the trustee by showing the source of each expense, the amount of money owed or paid, and the dates of payments.

11. Describe in detail the occurrence of the accident referred to in the complaint.

12. State the medical cause of decedent's death.

13. If decedent had ever been convicted of a crime, identify the court where the judgment was entered, the date of conviction and describe the nature of the offense for which he was convicted.

14. State the names and addresses of all witnesses who have any knowledge or information about the alleged accident.

15. Identify by name, address, and occupation each person who has custody of photographs relevant to the alleged accident.

16. Identify each photograph by its subject matter and the date on which it was taken.

17. State the names and addresses of all persons from whom statements have been obtained, and indicate the date on which each statement was made.

(date)   Attorney for Defendant

UNITED STATES DISTRICT COURT

DISTRICT OF _____

_____ DIVISION

(Title of Case)   INTERROGATORIES

(Commonly directed to plaintiff
in personal injury action.)

To: Plaintiff Above-Named and _____ His Attorney.

PLEASE TAKE NOTICE that defendant demands answers to the following continuing interrogatories under oath, pursuant to the provisions of Rule 33 of the Federal Rules of Civil Procedure:

1. State the names and addresses of all persons you claim have any knowledge or information concerning the accident described in the complaint.

2. State the names and addresses of all persons you claim have any knowledge or information about the injuries alleged in the complaint.

3. List all expenses and losses you claim you incurred by reason of the alleged accident.

4. List the dates on which you were examined or treated at any hospital whether as an in-patient or out-patient.

5. List the dates on which you received any medical treatments and medical examinations at a physician's office, giving the name and address of such physician.

6. Describe fully how the alleged accident occurred.

7. List all other accidents of any kind in which you have been involved by answering the following:

    a. dates and places;

    b. type of accident such as automobile, work or otherwise;

    c. names and addresses of all persons involved;

    d. nature of injuries;

    e. doctors and hospitals rendering care and treatment;

    f. names of all persons, corporations, employers and insurance companies against whom claims were made.

8. State the names and addresses of all persons, including parties, from whom you have obtained statements or reports concerning the above entitled matter; give the date on which the respective statements and reports were obtained.

9. If you have any insurance which covers any of the expenses or losses you claim resulted from the accident in question, state the name of the insurer and the amount of the coverage afforded.

10. State the date and place of your birth.

11. State your social security number.

12. Describe fully the nature and extent of your alleged injuries.

        (date)

                                      _____
                                      Attorneys for Defendant

---

UNITED STATES DISTRICT COURT

DISTRICT OF _____

_____ DIVISION

(Title of Case)   INTERROGATORIES

                                    (Commonly directed to defendant in accident cases.)

To: The Above Named Defendants and To _____ Their Attorney.

Plaintiff in the above entitled matter requests answers to the following interrogatories in compliance with Rules 26 and 33 of The Federal Rules of Civil Procedure:

1. State the name and address of all eye witnesses to the accident referred to in the complaint.

2. State the name and address of all persons being or arriving at the scene of the accident referred to in the complaint.

3. State the name and address of all other persons who have any knowledge or information concerning the accident referred to in the complaint, including expert witnesses.

4. State the name and address of all persons who have any knowledge or information relating to the personal, social, vocational, avocational, educational or other background of the plaintiff.

5. List the names of any of the persons referred to in your answers to interrogatories 1, 2, 3 and 4 whom you have interviewed, stating the date, time and location of each such interview, the name, address, employer and occupation of each person present at the time of each such interview.

6. With regard to each person listed in your answers to interrogatories 1, 2, 3 and 4 from whom you have obtained a statement, state:

    a. The date and time each such statement was taken.

    b. The location at which each such statement was taken.

    c. The name and address, employer and occupation of the person who prepared the statement.

    d. Whether the person from whom each statement was obtained was given a copy thereof.

7. If you have secured any photographs, slides, motion pictures or other photographic or non-photographic visual representations relating in any manner to the subject matter of the complaint herein,

    a. Describe the type of visual presentation.

    b. Identify the subject matter of each visual presentation.

    c. State the date each was taken, or made.

    d. State by whom each was taken, or made.

    e. Give the name and address of the person who is currently in possession of the negatives and prints, or other representations.

8. State the name of the insurance company or companies that carry your liability insurance covering the occurrence or accident involved herein, and state the amount of coverage under said policy or policies.

9. If you have any knowledge of the plaintiff having ever sustained any injuries prior or subsequent to the occurrence which is the subject matter of this litigation, state:

    a. The precise nature of each such injury.

    b. The date each such injury was sustained.

    c. The location where each such injury was sustained.

    d. The names and addresses of the persons involved in the occurrence surrounding such injury.

    e. The names and addresses of the physicians or other healing-arts practitioners rendering medical treatment for such injury.

10. If you have any knowledge of the plaintiff having every suffered from any illnesses, diseases or disabilities at any time prior or subsequent to the occurrence which is the subject matter of this litigation, state:

    a. The precise nature of each such illness, disease or disability.

    b. The date each such illness, disease or disability was incurred, contracted or otherwise endured.

    c. The location where each such illness, disease or disability was incurred, contracted or otherwise endured.

    d. The names and addresses of all persons having knowledge of each such illness, disease or disability.

    e. The names and addresses of each doctor rendering medical treatment for each such illness, disease or disability.

11. Describe in detail the manner in which the accident occurred.

12. At the time of the accident, where were you coming from and where were you intending to go?

13. If you consumed (i) any liquor, beer or other alcoholic beverage of any sort whatsoever, or (ii) any drug, narcotic, pills or any medication of any sort whatsoever, within the twenty-four hour period preceding such accident, state:

    a. What precisely was ingested.

    b. The quantity consumed.

    c. The time and place of each such consumption.

    d. The name and address of each person observing you at each such time and place.

14. Describe in detail all conversations which took place at the time of, or following, the accident and list the names and addresses of the persons involved in such conversations and the names and addresses of all persons who overheard or may have overheard such conversations.

15. With regard to all medical reports or medical records of any type or nature examined by or in the possession of you, your attorney, your insurers, or any of their agents or employees relating to the plaintiff in this action, state:

    a. Identify each such report or record, being specific as to the date and author.

    b. State the method by which said report or record was obtained by you.

    c. Attach a copy of each such report or record to these interrogatories.

16. With regard to each expert witness that you expect to call to trial, state:

    a. The subject matter in which the expert is expected to testify.

    b. The opinions to which the expert is expected to testify.

    c. The grounds for each opinion.

    d. The facts relied upon by the expert.

These interrogatories are continuing in nature and it is specifically requested and demanded that all information coming to your attention subsequent to the completion of your answers to these interrogatories which is in any manner relevant to such interrogatories be promptly made available to plaintiff's counsel.

    (date)   _____

                                  Attorney for Plaintiff

AUTHORIZATION FOR RELEASE OF
MEDICAL INFORMATION

Patient _____ Address_____

Birthdate _____   _____

This will authorize _____ Hospital/Clinic to release

to: _____
(name/title of person/organization and address)

information from the medical records maintained while I was a patient

at _____ Hospital/Clinic during _____
(dates)

The information to be disclosed is:

_____ Discharge Summary   _____ Operative Reports

_____ Consultation Reports   _____ Pathology Reports

_____ History and Physical Exam _____ X ray Reports

_____ Laboratory Reports   _____ Other (specify)

                                   _____

The information is needed for the following purpose(s): _____

_____

_____

I understand that I may revoke this consent at any time and that upon
fulfillment of the above-stated purpose(s), this consent will automatically
expire without any express revocation. I do not authorize further release
to any other third party.

_____
(signature of patient/guardian)

_____
(Witness)

_____
(relationship to patient if signed
by guardian)

_____
(reason patient is unable to sign)

FEDERAL TAX
RETURN AUTHORIZATION

To: Internal Revenue
      Ogden, Utah

Please be advised that you are hereby authorized to disclose and make available to (Law Firm Name), and any member thereof, copies, which may or may not be certified, of the undersigned _____'s Federal Income Tax Returns for the year(s) _____-_____.

Dated: _____

                                    _____
                                    Social Security No. _____

STATE OF _____   DISTRICT COURT
COUNTY OF _____   _____ JUDICIAL DISTRICT

(Title of Case)   REQUEST FOR PRODUCTION
                                       OF WITNESS STATEMENTS

                              *   *   *

To: The Above-Named Defendants and to _____, their attorney.

In Accordance with Rules of Civil Procedure, plaintiff requests that copies of the following be made available within thirty (30) days:

All statements made by parties or non-parties concerning the above action or its subject matter.

For the purpose of this request, a statement is (a) a written statement signed or otherwise adopted or approved by the person making it, or (b) a stenographic, mechanical, electrical, or other recording, or a transcription thereof, which is a substantially verbatim recital of an oral statement by the person making it and contemporaneously recorded.

(date)   _____
                                       Attorney for Plaintiff

FILE NO. _____

WITNESS REPORT OF ACCIDENT

DATE OF ACCIDENT_____19___TIME_____—AM
PM PLACE _____

CITY_____ COUNTY_____ STATE_____

CAR A _____   _____   _____   _____
                    Make   Color   Direction Moving   Driver's Name

CAR B _____   _____   _____   _____
                    Make   Color   Direction Moving   Driver's Name

CAR C _____   _____   _____   _____
                    Make   Color   Direction Moving   Driver's Name

WHERE WERE YOU WHEN THE ACCIDENT HAPPENED?_____

IF YOU WERE IN ONE OF THE CARS INVOLVED, WHICH ONE?_____SEATED WHERE? _____

DID YOU SEE THE ACCIDENT HAPPEN?_____ SEE THE CARS AFTERWARDS?_____

COMPLETE DIAGRAM

Illustrate position of cars at time of collision:

INDICATE DIRECTIONS

SHOW STOP SIGNS AND TRAFFIC LIGHTS

SHOW CARS THUS

A   B   C

LABEL EACH STREET

STATE BRIEFLY HOW ACCIDENT HAPPENED_____

_____

_____

_____

_____

_____

WERE THERE ANY STOP SIGNS OR TRAFFIC LIGHTS FACING CAR A?_____ CAR B? _____ CAR C? _____

WERE ANY STOP-AND-GO LIGHTS VIOLATED BY CAR A?_____ CAR B?_____ CAR C? _____

WERE ANY STOP SIGNS VIOLATED BY CAR A?_____ CAR B?_____ CAR C? _____

WHAT IF ANY TRAFFIC VIOLATIONS DID YOU SEE BY CAR A? _____

CAR B?_____ CAR C? _____

PLEASE ANSWER ALL QUESTIONS ON BOTH SIDES

WERE ALL LIGHTS BURNING ON CAR A?_____CAR B?_____CAR C?_____

WHAT, IF ANY, SIGNALS WERE GIVEN BY CAR A?_____CAR B?_____CAR C?_____

WHAT WAS THE SPEED OF CAR A?_____CAR B?_____CAR C?_____

WHAT WAS THE SPEED LIMIT?_____

WAS VISIBILITY RESTRICTED FOR DRIVER OF CAR A?_____CAR B?_____CAR C?_____
   (Indicate whether rain, snow, fog, dust, trees, shrubs, buildings, parked cars)

CONDITION OF ROAD OR STREET: DRY_____ICE_____SNOW_____WET_____MUDDY_____

WHERE WAS POINT OF IMPACT ON CAR A?_____

   CAR B?_____CAR C?_____

WHAT DEFECTS DID YOU SEE IN THE CONDITION OF CAR A?_____

   CAR B?_____CAR C?_____

WHAT MARKS OR DEBRIS DID YOU SEE ON THE ROAD?_____

WHERE WERE THEY WITH REFERENCE TO THE CENTER OF THE STREET AND WITH REFERENCE TO THE CARS INVOLVED?

_____

_____

LENGTH OF SKID MARKS, IF ANY, FROM CAR A?_____CAR B?_____CAR C?_____

WHAT WAS THERE ABOUT THE POSITION OF THE CARS, OR THE MARKS ON THE ROAD, OR OTHER FACTS THAT YOU

OBSERVED, TO INDICATE WHO WAS TO BLAME FOR THE ACCIDENT?_____

_____

WAS EITHER CAR ON THE WRONG SIDE OF THE ROAD?_____

WHAT DID YOU HEAR THE DRIVERS SAY AFTER THE ACCIDENT?_____

_____

WERE YOU INJURED?_____DID ANYONE ELSE APPEAR TO BE INJURED?_____IF SO, IN WHAT CAR?_____

WHO ELSE WAS A WITNESS TO THIS ACCIDENT?

   NAME _____ ADDRESS_____

   NAME _____ ADDRESS_____

      YOUR NAME HERE:_____ AGE:_____

      ADDRESS:_____

      TELEPHONE: RESIDENCE_____ BUSINESS:_____

      DATE:_____

UNITED STATES DISTRICT COURT

DISTRICT OF (STATE)

——————— DIVISION

Anderson Construction Company, Inc.,
                   Plaintiff

         vs.   **BILL OF COSTS**

Smith Industries, Inc.,

                   Defendant

Judgment having been entered in the above entitled action on the 14th day of September, 1992, against defendant, the clerk is requested to tax the following as costs:

Fees of the clerk	$ 100.00
Fees of the marshal	21.36
Fees of the court reporter for all or any part of the transcript necessarily obtained for use in the case	N/A
Fees and disbursements for printing	N/A
Fees for witnesses	1087.15
Fees for exemplification and copies of papers necessarily obtained for use in case	N/A
Docket fees under 28 U.S.C. 1923	20.00
Costs incident to taking of depositions	N/A
Costs as shown on Mandate of Court of Appeals	N/A
Other costs (please itemize):	
Photographer's fee for blow-up of picture of grain elevator used at trial	124.11
Photographic copying fee for photographs of failed structure used at trial	107.95
TOTAL	$1,460.57

STATE OF NORTH DAKOTA
COUNTY OF BURLEIGH } ss

I certify under penalty of perjury that the foregoing costs are correct and were necessarily incurred in this action and that the services for which fees have been charged were actually and necessarily performed. A copy hereof was this day mailed to counsel for Defendant with postage fully prepaid thereon. Executed on October 4, 1992.

————————————————
                          Attorney for Plaintiff

Please take notice that I will appear before the Clerk who will tax said costs on October 18, 1992, at 9:00 A.M.

_____
Attorney for Plaintiff

Costs are hereby taxed in the amount of $_____ this _____ day of October, 1992, and that amount included in the judgment.

_____
Clerk

_____
Deputy Clerk

Sec. 1920. Taxation of costs.

"A judge or clerk of any court of the United States may tax as costs the following:

(1) Fees of the clerk and marshal;

(2) Fees of the court reporter for all or any part of the stenographic transcript necessarily obtained for use in the case;

(3) Fees and disbursements for printing and witnesses;

(4) Fees for exemplification and copies of papers necessarily obtained for use in the case;

(5) Docket fees under section 1923 of this title;

(6) Compensation of court appointed experts, compensation of interpreters, and salaries, fees, expenses, and costs of special interpretation services under section 1828 of this title."

Sec. 1924. Verification of bill of costs.

"Before any bill of costs is taxed, the party claiming any item of cost of disbursement shall attach thereto an affidavit, made by himself or by his duly authorized attorney or agent having knowledge of the facts, that such item is correct and has been necessarily incurred in the case and that the services for which fees have been charged were actually and necessarily performed."

The Federal Rules of Civil Procedure contain the following provisions:

Rule 54(d). "Except when express provision therefor is made either in a statute of the United States or in these rules, costs shall be allowed as of course to the prevailing party unless the court otherwise directs; but costs against the United States, its officers, and agencies shall be imposed only to the extent permitted by law. Costs may be taxed by the clerk on one day's notice. On motion served within five days thereafter, the action of the clerk may be reviewed by the court."

Rule 6(e) "Whenever a party has the right or is required to do some act or take some proceedings within a prescribed period after the service of a notice or other paper upon him and the notice or paper is served upon him by mail, three days shall be added to the prescribed period."

Rule 58 (in part). "Entry of the judgment shall not be delayed for the taxing of costs."

MOTION

(Title of Cause)   MOTION TO COMPEL
                                              MEDICAL EXAMINATION

Defendant hereby moves the Court for an order which requires plaintiff to submit to an independent medical examination for the purpose of diagnosis and evaluation of plaintiff's alleged injuries.

This motion is made pursuant to Rule 35 of the Federal Rules of Civil Procedure on the grounds that plaintiff has put her physical and medical condition in issue through the allegations contained in her complaint filed in the above matter, and defendant needs an independent medical examination and opinion for the purpose of evaluating plaintiff's claim and preparing his defenses.

This motion is based upon plaintiff's complaint and the attached affidavit of counsel.

(date)   _____
                                        Attorney for Plaintiff

ORDER

(Title of Cause)

ORDER COMPELLING
MEDICAL EXAMINATION

The above entitled matter came before the Court upon defendant's motion to compel an independent medical examination. A. J. Smith, Esq. appeared on behalf of defendant in support of the motion. O. P. Johnson, Esq. appeared on behalf of plaintiff. The Court having heard the arguments of counsel and being fully advised in the premises.

IT IS HEREBY ORDERED, that plaintiff shall submit to a physical examination to be conducted by Dr. I. M. Good, M.D. on September 11, 1990 at the doctor's office at 333 Pleasant Street, Huntsville, (State). Plaintiff shall submit to a general physical examination concerning her person, including a blood test and X rays. However, plaintiff is not required to submit to a spinal tap.

The results of the examination shall be reported by Dr. Good in writing, including the recorded history, his findings, and the diagnoses. Defendant shall forthwith provide plaintiff's counsel with a copy of the report.

September 1, 1990
_____
Judge of District Court

Appendix VI

Deposition Transcript

This is an actual deposition taken in connection with a personal injury claim which resulted from an automobile accident. The transcript illustrates the necessity of being persistent and detailed. Four major areas are covered, though the areas are not separated in any obvious manner: (1) deponent's background, (2) deponent's previous health and accidents, (3) the accident in question, (4) the consequential injuries and expenses. Paralegals may be asked to prepare summaries of investigations, interrogatories, and depositions. Of particular interest is the obvious lack of preparation that the deponent had for the deposition. The transcript should be read in light of the various guidelines suggested for preparing a witness to testify. As an epilogue, the defendant's insurer was able to obtain a dismissal of the case with only a nominal settlement.

Duane Johnson,

                 Plaintiff,

  vs.

Clarence A. Smith,

              Defendant and   DEPOSITION
             Third-Party Plaintiff,   TRANSCRIPT

  vs.

Carolyn Jones,

           Third-Party Defendant.

APPEARANCES

Thomas Clarke, Esq., appeared in behalf of the plaintiff.

John Fredricks, Esq., appeared in behalf of the defendant and third-party plaintiff.

Lang & Spencer, by Robert L. Lang, Esq., appeared in behalf of the third-party defendant.

DISCOVERY DEPOSITION OF DUANE JOHNSON, taken under the Federal Rules of Civil Procedure for the District Courts, at 700 Titan Building, Detroit, Michigan, on August 13, 1990, before John R. Nash, a notary public, commencing at approximately 11:10 A.M.

DUANE JOHNSON,

plaintiff, called in behalf of the defendant and third-party plaintiff, having been first duly sworn, testified on his oath as follows:

EXAMINATION

By Mr. Fredricks:

Q. Will you state your full name, please?

A. Duane Anthony Johnson.

Q. What is your birthdate?

A. One—twenty-two—seventy.

Q. Where were you born?

A. Kansas City, Kansas.

Q. Where?

A. Kansas City, Kansas.

Q. Where do you currently reside?

A. You mean in Detroit.

Q. Yes.

A. South Detroit.

Q. What is your address?

A. 1530 East 40th and a half street.

Q. East 40th and a half?

A. Yes. South Detroit.

Q. How long have you lived there?

A. About nine months.

Q. Are you married?

A. No, single.

Q. Have you ever been married?

A. No, I haven't.

Q. Do you live with anyone at that address?

A. Friend.

Q. Who?

A. Catherine Baker.

Q. What's the name again?

A. Catherine Baker.

Q. You say you are friends.

A. Well, just two-bedroom apartment.

Q. I mean you are not related in any way.

A. No.

Q. How long has she been there?

A. About a year or two. About a year.

Q. Where did you reside before moving to your current address?

A. 16th Avenue. I forgot that apartment number. It was on 20—26th and 16th Avenue.

Q. How long did you live at that address?

A. About two months, three months.

Q. Where do your parents reside?

A. At the present time 4245 Park Avenue South.

Q. And your father's name is what?

A. Donald Johnson.

Q. Are you presently employed?

A. Part time.

Q. Where do you work?

A. Hearns Auditorium.

Q. I'm having a hard time hearing you.
A. Hearns Auditorium. That's on the Detroit campus.

Q. What do you do there?

A. Work in the office. Office work.

Q. How long have you worked there?

A. This summer. Started this summer. Summer work. That's for Model City.

Q. Who is your immediate supervisor?

A. Henry Hyslop.

Q. Will you spell the last name?

A. H-y-l—H-y-s-l-o-p.

Q. Do you intend to continue working there indefinitely?

A. No. That's just summer work, you know.

Q. Will that job end then in September?

A. It ends this month some time.

Q. What other jobs have you had since August of 1989?

A. I was working at Honeywell on an assembly line, I think that was in '89.

Q. You work at Honeywell where?

A. In Detroit, Honeywell.

Q. What kind of work did you do for Honeywell?

A. Was just small work, just on an assembly line like thing. It wasn't no kind of strenuous work.

Q. For what period of time did you work there?

A. That was summer work too.

Q. What was your pay rate while at Honeywell?

A. Ten dollars.

   Mr. Clarke: You are going to have to yell a little bit louder, because I'm having a little bit of trouble hearing you, too.

   The Witness: About ten dollars an hour.

Q. (By Mr. Fredricks) Did you take an employment physical, exam—

A. No, I didn't.

Q. —before going to work for Honeywell—

A. No.

Q. —while working at Honeywell?

A. No.

Q. Did you make out an application for that employment?

A. Yes, I did.

Q. And was there any inquiry about the status of your health or physical condition in that application?

A. No, there wasn't.

Q. Okay. What was your condition, your physical condition, when you made your application to work at Honeywell? Were you having any problems?

A. The application wasn't like that, you know, as far as your health. The application wasn't—you know, it didn't ask about your health, you know, your background, nothing like that.

Q. I'm asking you now—what was your condition when you made out that application?

A. Back trouble and neck.

Q. Back and leg trouble?

A. Back and neck.

Q. And neck. Anything else?

A. That was the most—main thing at that time.

Q. Did you have to make out an application for your work when you started working for Hearns Auditorium?

A. No.

Q. Have you had any other employment since August of 1989?

A. No. I was working—last year I was working at the Children's Theatre and—

Q. Where?

A. Detroit, South Detroit. That was at—at the Mann. No, not the Mann, it's on 3rd Avenue, the Art Institute, Detroit Art Institute, and I was working for the Children's Theatre. That's combined together.

Q. How long did you work there?

A. That was summer work also.

Q. What was your pay rate at the time?

A. Ten dollars an hour.

Q. You worked forty hours a week, did you?

A. Yes.

Q. When you were at Honeywell, did you work forty hours a week?

A. Yes, it was.

Q. Did you work regularly at all of these jobs during the summer months? Did you work regularly, or did you have to miss a lot of time?

A. Well, I was getting hot pack treatments at Dr. Peterson's office.

Q. You mean after work?

A. Well, sometimes I have to go on work because his office is only open in the afternoon.

Q. Other than the times you went for back treatments, did you have to miss any time from work?

A. Yes. A little sometimes, yes.

Q. Do you have a record of what time you missed from work?

A. At home when I started I did, yes.

Q. Do you have that with you?

A. I don't have it with me, no.

Q. What chiropractor were you seeing?

A. Dr. Peterson.

Q. Thomas Peterson?

A. Thomas Peterson.

Q. I understand he is a chiropractor?

A. I beg your pardon.

Q. Do you understand that he is a chiropractor?

A. He was my doctor, I don't know what he was.

Q. I thought you said you were seeing a chiropractor. Did I misunderstand?

Mr. Lang: (nods head.)

Mr. Clarke: Maybe he was talking about therapist. Were you talking about the guy that gave you the heat and all that stuff?

The Witness: I don't know his name.

Q. (By Mr. Fredricks) Bill Freeman?

A. Yes, something like that.

Q. William Freeman or something like that.

A. Yes, I believe so. You see, when I was going to Wahlstrom I was getting treatment too before I seen him.

Q. You completed high school?

A. Yes.

Q. What high school did you attend?

A. Central, Detroit Central.

Q. When were you graduated?

A. Eighty-nine.

Q. Did you participate in sports in any school?

A. That was '88, I'm sorry. Sometimes, yes.

Q. What sports?

A. Basketball and just any—really any intramural thing. I didn't go out for—

Q. Were you ever injured in any sports?

A. No.

Q. Have you been involved in any other motor vehicle accidents other than the one of August 17th, 1989?

A. No.

Q. At any time?

A. No.

Q. Have you ever been in a car when it has collided with another car, or object, or—

A. No. No.

Q. Even if you weren't hurt.

A. No.

Q. This is the only motor vehicle accident you have ever been in?

A. Yes, it was.

Q. All right. Have you been injured in any other accidents of any kind at any time?

A. No, I haven't. Any other automobile accidents?

Q. No, no, any other accidents of any kind—

A. No.

Q. —at any time where you hurt yourself any way.

A. Well, I was just in an accident—

Q. All right.

A. —about two weeks ago, maybe a month ago.

Q. Where did the accident happen and—

A. On Traverse.

Q. What?

A. Traverse. Exact address I don't know. It was somewhere down Traverse Avenue.

Q. What happened?

A. Crossed the center line.

Q. Was this an automobile accident?

A. Yes.

Q. Oh. Well, you tell me, describe for me what—were you a driver?

A. Yes, I was.

Q. And what happened?

A. I was fixing a calendar watch and I was—the passenger was fixing my calendar watch, and she turned it—messed it up, and I looked down at it and went in the other lane.

Q. Was this a head-on type collision?

A. Yes.

Q. Did the police investigate?

A. Yes, they did.

Q. What time of the day did it happen?

A. In the afternoon, about twelve o'clock, one o'clock.

Q. It was daylight at that time?

A. Yes, it was.

Q. Who was your passenger?

A. Rebecca Parsons.

Q. Where does she live?

A. Cleveland.

Q. Cleveland?

A. North Cleveland.

Q. Where in North Cleveland?

A. I forget the address.

Q. Will you get that for me or get it to your attorney?

    Mr. Clarke: No, I'm not going to get—why don't you find out if he got hurt. If he got hurt, then I will get you what you want, but you are dinging around on a fender-bender, I suspect, and if that's where you are going—

Q. (By Mr. Fredricks) Were you hurt at all in the accident?

A. Just stitches on my lip.

Q. You struck your face against something inside the car?

A. Yes.

Q. Where did you get the stitches?

A. In the lip and also chin.

Q. Lip and chin.

A. Yes.

Q. Any other injuries in the accident?

A. And teeth, my teeth.

Q. What happened to your teeth?

A. They were all out, just about. Oh, they are all loose, you know.

Q. Lower front teeth were loosened?

A. Lower and upper.

Q. Any other injuries?

A. That was about all. I just hit the steering wheel.
Q. Have any headaches following the accident?

A. No.

Q. You haven't had any headaches since that accident a month ago?

A. No, I haven't.

Q. What doctors did you go to, for example?

A. General Hospital.

Q. Where else?

A. That was it.

Q. All of the treatment you have received was at General Hospital?

A. Yes.

Q. Have you been to Dr. Thomas Peterson since that accident?

A. No.

Q. Earlier I asked you about any other automobile accidents—

A. Yes.

Q. —and you didn't mention this.

A. Well, I didn't—you know, I really forgot about the accident. It didn't, you know, mean nothing.

Q. All right. Now, you search your mind; are there any other automobile accidents?

A. No.

Q. Do you have a driver's license?

A. Yes, I do.

Q. What's the number on it? Would you get it out and check it for me? Now, have you been involved in any other accidents of any kind? I'm not referring—

A. You mean a passenger—no, I haven't, nothing.

Q. In no sports—you have never fallen down and hurt yourself, you have never burned yourself, you have never cut yourself, you have never had any other trouble?

A. No.

Q. All right. Have you been hospitalized at any time in your life other than for childbirth?

A. Just for asthma.

Q. When was that?

A. That was—I was born with it.

Q. When were you hospitalized for it?

A. I don't remember the exact date. Last year some time. Two years before that. I stayed in the hospital with asthma.

Q. What hospital did you go to?

A. General Hospital.

Q. Have you ever made a claim against anyone for injuries other than this accident?

A. No.

Q. After completing high school you went to college.

A. Yes.

Q. What colleges have you attended?

A. Wahlstrom in Uhler, Michigan.

Q. What years did you attend?

A. Eighty-nine, '90.

Q. Did you have a physical examination at that college?

A. Yes.

Q. Did you have any treatment for your back condition?

A. Yes, I did.

Q. What course of study did you pursue there? Liberal Arts?

A. Liberal Arts.

Q. All right. Did you complete one academic year at Wahlstrom?

A. It was more or less a program like for people who aren't capable of going to college but may, you know, learn something at college, you know, if they have the opportunity to go. Do you understand?

Q. Is there a name for that program?

A. It was called Demos.

Q. What?

A. Demos. D-e-m-o something. Demos. I don't know how to spell that.

Q. What month did you start then, September?

A. Yes.

Q. And—

A. Eighty-nine, '90.

Q. What month did you complete the course?

A. I went the whole—full two years.

Q. Okay. Have you gone to another institution, college?

A. I'm going to the University at the present time.

Q. Well, you mean you have actually registered for class?

A. Yes.

Q. Will you be starting as a freshman?

A. Sophomore and junior, half and half now.

Q. Didn't you attend at Chicago?

A. No, I haven't. I seen it in the thing but I changed it. It was at Wahlstrom.

Q. I see. Did you live on campus when you were at Wahlstrom?

A. Yes, I did.

Q. Have you had your physical examination for the University?

A. Last year I did.

Q. When was that?

A. I don't know. It was at the beginning of the school year.

Q. Have you received any treatment for any physical condition or problems at the University Health Service?

A. No, I haven't.

Q. Or Hospital?

A. No.

Q. All right. Now, referring to the accident of August 17th, 1989, that happened early on a Friday morning, didn't it?

A. Friday morning?

Q. Thursday night or Friday morning.

A. Yes.

Q. Do you recall what time it happened?

A. No, I can't. It was—I think it was about one, one o'clock.

Q. Okay. It was dark out at the time, wasn't it?

A. Yes, it was.

Q. And would it be consistent with your recollection that it was about 1:35 in the morning?

A. Probably so.

Q. Who were you with that night?

A. Carolyn Jones. She was driving. And a Ruby Watts, another girl, was in the back seat.

Q. Who was the other girl?

A. Ruby Watts.

Q. Ruby what?

A. Watts, W-a-t-t-s.

Q. W-a-t-t-s? Where does she live?

A. I have no idea.

Q. Where were you going at the time?

A. Probably home.

Q. Probably?

A. Yes.

Q. Don't you remember?

A. It was probably my house. I'm pretty sure it was. See, I live about four blocks from the accident, and we were going in the direction. I believe we were. She was taking me home, I'm pretty sure.

Q. Where had you been?

A. Probably at some dance or something. At a dance.

Q. Where?

A. Downtown. I forget the name of the club. I believe we went, you know, here and there. Let's see—

Q. Did you have anything—

A. No, no, no, this was a house party. I'm sorry. It was a house party, a get-together.

Q. Did you have anything alcoholic to drink?

A. No. They didn't have anything. I'm sure they didn't. No.

Q. How about Ms. Jones?

A. No, she doesn't drink.

Q. Were you dating that night? Was this a date with either of the two girls?

A. Well, I knew Carolyn from—we grew up together, just about. Well, we went to school together, high school, grade school. She just stopped and picked me up.

Q. All right. At the time of the accident, you were riding in a Buick automobile?

A. (nods head.)

Q. And you were traveling in an easterly direction on 38th Street.

A. Yes.

Q. And the other car was in a northerly direction on 2nd Avenue.

A. Yes.

Q. Do you recall whether Ms. Jones put on her turn signals as she approached this intersection?

A. We were going straight. We were going straight.

Q. Did she put on her turn signals, or don't you know?

A. I'm sure she didn't. I'm sure she didn't, because wasn't no sense in turning, you know, that way.

Q. How far were you going to continue going straight ahead?

A. Oh, I would say we were going to my house, and I live about four blocks away on Park Avenue, and I believe it happened on 2nd Avenue. Well, I was staying at 38th and Park at that time.

Q. Well, all right. What happened? How did the cars come together, do you know?

A. No. I was hit on my side, on the right side of the car.

Q. Did you see the Smith car at any time before the collision?

A. No.

Q. How fast was Ms. Jones driving?

A. I didn't look at the speedometer. We weren't speeding or in a rush to go anywhere, you know. She normally drives slow anyways, the speed limit.

Q. Did anyone say anything before the collision occurred? Any exclamations?

A. No. Just hit. Surprised everybody.

Q. How would you describe the collision?

A. Sudden. Just happened, you know. I didn't—you know, surprised me.

Q. All right. What happened to the car in which you were riding, the Buick, when the collision did occur?

A. Seemed like it just pushed the car around in a circle, seemed like. Seemed like it just went around, you know.

Q. Are you saying the car was pushed sideways?

A. Yes. Like when it hit, seemed like I was—seemed like pain was just in my body, and I was just in pain, you know, for a second or two, and the car was just moving around.

Q. What was its position when the car came to rest?

A. It was in this way (indicating), turned like that all the way around.

Q. Well, the car had been traveling east, easterly?

A. (Nods head.)

Q. What way was it facing when it came to rest?

A. South. It might even have spun the whole time, you know, one whole time. Seemed like it was spinning a long time and sliding.

Q. Now, the other car stopped right at the point of impact, didn't it?

A. I—I thought it was down—across the intersection, I'm sure. I'm pretty sure it did.

Q. Did Ms. Jones's car come to a stop outside of the intersection? Did it continue through the intersection and—

A. It was knocked past the intersection. Spun down, you know, like, towards west, east, went down. Like it spun and sort of pushed it forward down the street in a way and spun it too. Seemed like it happened—it did happen like that. Then it came to a stop.

Q. East of the intersection.

A. Yes.

Q. Is that your testimony?

A. It went past the intersection, a little way past it, I think.

Q. So that would be east of the intersection.

A. Yes. Going towards the river, that's—yes, right.

Q. All right. So that we are clear on this, you say that the Jones car came to rest east of the east curb line of 2nd Avenue.

A. It what? Pardon me.

Q. You say that the car came to rest east of the east curb line of 2nd Avenue.

A. Yes.

Q. Okay. Now, what happened to you when the collision occurred?

A. As soon as it hit?

Q. Right.

A. Seemed like I was in pain, and seemed like I was—seemed like I was just in pain for a short time, about a second or two, and like everything had blacked out for a second or two as I was in pain.

Q. Well, did you strike yourself against anything in the car, against the windshield?

A. Against the door, that side door I believe, or probably in the corner.

Q. You what?

A. Or probably in the corner of the—not the windshield. You know, like towards—kitty-corner over.

Q. Do you remember that clearly?

A. It was—I know it was on the side, what I'm saying. It wasn't the windshield. I didn't hit the windshield at all.

Q. Did you have any accident markings on your person, any cuts, bruises, bumps?

A. Yes.

Q. What?

A. Legs—well, like everything was sore, but it was—you know, like—seemed like this side (indicating), and my legs were sore, like they were bruised and stuff.

Q. Well, Mr. Johnson, you have told me you were sore, but I want to know if there were any bumps or bruises, anything that someone else could see or feel.

A. I think it was just skinned, more or less.

Q. Skinned?

A. Skinned like.

Q. An abrasion?

A. Pardon.

Q. You mean an abrasion or rubbing of the skin?

A. Yes, abrasion.

Q. Where the skin wasn't actually broken, but it was just an abrasion of the skin, is that what you are saying?

A. Yes, I guess abrasion, I don't know. It was like—you know, it was skinned.

Q. And you are indicating that this was some place on your right arm.

A. It was on my—down here (indicating) on my chin.

Q. Now you are indicating your right chin.

A. Yes. Seemed like most of the pain was up here. Seemed like I hit the door, but my legs was hurting too.

Q. You are now indicating your right arm near your right elbow.

A. Well, seemed like my whole side was hurting, and my leg somehow was hurting too.

Q. Now you are indicating your whole right side was hurting.

A. Yes. Seemed it was a lot—I really don't know exactly—all I remember is something like my legs were hurting, too.

Q. Both legs. Is that what you are telling us?

A. I really don't remember. Just seems like it was hurting. My legs, they didn't—I didn't write it down or nothing what was hurting. It was a long time ago, and I don't remember exactly what was scratched or nothing like this.

Q. All right. You didn't notice any pain in your back or your neck immediately following the accident, did you?

A. No.

Q. The police came and investigated, didn't they?

A. Yes.

Q. And what did you tell the police about your condition?

A. Nothing. When I was walking around I thought I was all right.

Q. Did you seek any medical examinations or treatments right after the accident?

A. No.

Q. Well, didn't you go to General Hospital?

A. Yes. Well, like they were—they were busy like always, and they just took my temperature and told me to leave and—I could leave.

Q. Well, now you must listen to my questions carefully. I asked you if you sought any medical examinations. Well, you did—

A. The doctor—yes, I did—

Q. You went to General Hospital.

A. Yes.

Q. All right.

A. But I mean—go ahead.

Q. But they didn't do anything for you other than take your temperature, is that what you say?

A. No. Right.

Q. When did you next seek any medical examinations or treatment?

A. About a month or two after.

Q. Who did you see?

A. Dr. Peterson.

Q. How did you happen to go to Dr. Peterson?

A. Well, he is the only doctor that I knew over North, and I believe Carolyn told me about him because she was going there too.

Q. Who?

A. Carolyn Jones, the driver of the car.

Q. Okay. Had you ever been to Peterson before?

A. No.

Q. When did you first have any symptoms of neck problems, pains or discomfort?

A. About a month or two after when I went to see Dr. Peterson.

Q. Okay. That's when you first really noticed any pain or problem in your neck.

A. Yes.

Q. Okay. All right. When did you first notice any pain or discomfort or any problem in your back?

A. About the time when I went to see him.

Mr. Clarke: You mean you went for thirty days and you didn't have any trouble, and all of a sudden one day you had trouble with your back?

The Witness: Seemed like that.

Mr. Clarke: I don't believe that.

Mr. Fredricks: Pardon me.

Mr. Clarke: You mean you didn't have any trouble the day of the accident or the day afterwards?

The Witness: No.

Mr. Lang: Objected to as leading and suggestive.

Mr. Fredricks: Tom—

Mr. Clarke: Well, fantastic. I don't believe him.

Mr. Lang: Whether you believe him or not, that's what he said.

Mr. Clarke: I don't think he understands the question.

Mr. Lang: It's clear that he does.

The Witness: I mean it didn't hurt just one month later. It was such a long time ago, like it—problems.

Mr. Clarke: Well, they are trapping you. The way you have answered these questions, that's the end of your lawsuit. That's basically what they have trapped you into here. Now, if you understand—

Mr. Fredricks: Now, that isn't true.

Mr. Clarke: That's true.

Mr. Fredricks: The word "trap" is not at all appropriate here, Tom.

Mr. Clarke: Well, it is when it's obvious to me he doesn't understand your question, that's all.

And if you understand what you are doing, then you can answer any way you want, but I want you to understand what you are saying here. That's why I'm here, to make sure you understand your questions.

The Witness: See, it was—

Mr. Fredricks: Let's see if we can't clarify this.

Mr. Clarke: Why don't you let him answer.

Q. (By Mr. Fredricks) About the time that you first had difficulties with your neck and low back is when you went to see Dr. Peterson. Whether that was a week after or a month after, that's when you started having difficulty, and you went to see him at that time because you did notice that you were having difficulty.

A. Well, let me say—like I probably had some pain first. It was a long time ago, and I don't exactly remember how—how many days or what it was when I went to see Dr. Peterson after the accident or nothing like this. Like the pain probably came a week after, and I probably didn't think nothing of it, you know—

Q. All right.

A. —and it was probably there. I mean if a pain is just there, you don't go the same day, you see. I mean this is the way I looked at it. And from the questions you asked, you know, it was probably a month when I seen a doctor, a month or two months after when I went to see him to—

Q. But I'm asking you not when you went to see Dr. Peterson but when you first became aware of any discomfort in your neck or back, and you have said it was about a month, and now—

A. I mean I seen Dr. Peterson about a month or two after.

Q. That's what you meant.

A. I really don't even know exactly how long that was, exactly.

Q. But now it is your recollection that it was about a week or more after the accident before you first had any difficulty with your neck or your back, is that correct?

A. It was probably a week or so after I had trouble with my back?

Q. Yes.

A. I don't know exactly the—I really don't know. It probably was a week when I first felt pain somewhere.

Q. Now, do you recall if you were doing something particular, you were engaged in some activity when you first noticed this back pain where you were walking up a stairway, or lifting something, or driving a car, or—

A. I really don't remember.

Q. By the way, when you had this accident about a month ago, were you driving your own automobile?

A. No, I wasn't.

Q. Whose car were you driving?

A. The girl's car.

Q. Ruby's?

A. No.

Q. What was her name?

A. Rebecca Ann Parsons.

Q. Rebecca. It was her car.

A. Yes.

Q. Do you know who she had her insurance with?

A. No, I don't.

Q. Well, you must have talked with some insurance man—

A. Yes.

Q. —since the accident.

A. I don't remember his name though.

Q. Did he give you a card or—

A. He called on the phone.

Q. Okay.

     Tom, do you have a copy of that—did the police investigate that accident?

     Mr. Clarke: No, but if you have any authorization you want signed at all, why don't you give them to him now and I will have him check them.

     Mr. Lang: What was the name of the person you had the accident with?

     The Witness: I beg your pardon.

     Mr. Lang: What was the name of the person you had the accident with?

     The Witness: The other person. I forget her name. She was an elderly lady.

     Mr. Lang: Do you know where she lives?

     The Witness: South Detroit.

Q. (By Mr. Fredricks) All right. When you first noticed this pain in your back, or when you first noticed pain in your neck, what did it feel like. Describe it for me.

A. Just seemed like a sharp pain.

Q. Where was it located?

A. It was just a pain all over, seemed like. Seemed like I was paralyzed maybe—if that's the right term to use. Seemed like it was just—I can't even explain it.

Q. All right. Was this pain localized at any particular place in your back?

    Mr. Clarke: You better explain what localized means, you know.

Q. (By Mr. Fredricks) You know—

A. I don't—I really couldn't tell you.

Q. Was the pain in your neck localized or at any particular spot in your back? Was it on one side or the other?

    Mr. Clarke: What he is trying to say is what part of your neck— when you talk about your back, he wants to know whether it's in the middle of your back, or in the low back, or upper back. He wants to know what part of your neck or your back you are talking about.

    The Witness: When I was going to say pain, it seems like a pain all over, I—you know, I didn't stop and think of where it was at, no, or nothing like this, because at the time I was being shook around at the same time.

Q. (By Mr. Fredricks) At the time you were being what?

A. At the time of the accident, you know. There was pain, and I was being shaken around at the same time, and I couldn't tell you exactly, you know, where the pain was. It was just a pain in the head all over.

Q. You have indicated that there was some period of time elapsed after the accident before—

A. Yes.

Q. —you became aware of pain in your neck and your back. Now I want to know when you did become aware of your neck pain or your back pain, where was it located?

A. Oh, you mean when I—after the accident.

Q. Yes.

A. Yes.

Q. It was a week or more after the accident, as I understand your testimony. Tell me what you felt.

A. It was in the lower back, pain in the lower back.

Q. All right. And was it on one side or the other? Was it on your left side or right side?

A. It was down the center of my back, the spinal cord.

Q. Right in the middle.

A. Yes.

Q. Was it below your belt?

A. It was down in the lower back.

Q. Below your belt line.

A. Lower part of my back.

Q. Was it below your belt line or above it?

A. Is this (indicating) below my belt line?

Q. This (indicating) is your belt.

A. Is this my belt (indicating), below my belt, or what?

Q. Yes, that's your—you have placed your hand well below your belt line.

A. That's where it was. That's where it was.

Q. All right, fine.

A. And my neck right here (indicating).

Q. Now, was there any particular activity, or were you doing something when you first noticed this pain in your low back?

A. I don't remember.

Q. All right. When you first noticed this pain in your low back, did it limit you in any way? Were your activities limited? Were your movements limited?

A. What do you mean, limited? What do you mean, was I limited? Could I walk?

Q. Did you have to go to bed because of the back pain, or did you have to stop swimming, or did you—is there anything that it did affect you in any way?

A. Like when it hurt, I just—well, it was—it would hurt. Like when I'm sitting at school. For instance, when I first noticed it I was in school or sitting in the chair.

Q. All right.

A. And it was just uncomfortable to sit in a chair.

Q. All right. Now, this would have been at Wahlstrom.

A. Yes, it was—well, like—it couldn't have been, because I seen Dr. Peterson before I went to Wahlstrom, and he said—let's see—I don't know how—I seen Dr. Peterson before I went to Wahlstrom, I was getting therapy at the clinic before I went to Wahlstrom, and now that—when I noticed it how it acted. Then I couldn't tell, but like when I was at school when I was sitting down at the chair, I remember that, you know, because I was always turning and stuff.

Q. How does your low back feel right now?

A. Uncomfortable.

Q. Well, is there pain in it?

A. Just seemed like a slight—slight pain.

Q. Slight pain.

A. (Nods head.)

Q. Does that keep you from doing anything?

A. No. I go—I still do what I do.

Q. How about your neck, how is that?

A. It's fair. It's all right.

Q. It's okay.

A. (Nods head.)

Q. All right. You are not having any trouble with it now?

A. No.

Q. When is the last time you had any trouble with your neck?

A. I was in the hospital about last month or month—about two months ago, month and a half ago, for treatment.

Q. Which hospital?

A. Mt. Sinai.

Q. And you did have trouble with your neck at that time?

A. Yes. My neck and back.

Q. And is that Mr. William Freeman again who gave you therapy?

A. This was in the hospital.

Q. Yes. He worked at—or he—at least he did work at Mt. Sinai.

A. No, I was in traction, they put me in traction.

Q. All right. The heat packs and traction seemed to help.

A. It was all right. Like after I got out of the hospital well, last—about a week ago I drove—well, rode down to Missouri, and it was uncomfortable sitting in the car.

Q. You were what?

A. It was uncomfortable sitting in the car, you know, long distance. Like, you know, drove to Missouri.

Q. Where in Missouri?

A. Monroe.

Q. Monroe.

A. Monroe.

Q. What did you go to Missouri for?

A. To see some people.

Q. Who?

A. Some people, some friends.

Q. Who did you go to see?

A. Some friends.

Q. What's their names?

A. I forget their last name.

Q. Who did you go with?

A. Some friends. Friend of mine and his family. See, they were—I just went for the ride just to go, just to go out of town, and it was their cousins and things.

Q. Whose car?

A. Their car.

Q. And what is their name?

A. Cross. Cross.

Q. First name.

A. I forget their first name, lady's first name. I went with a family and a friend of mine my age.

Q. And what's his name?

A. Brian Cross.

Q. What?

A. Brian Cross.

   Does that make any difference who I go down there with?

   Mr. Clarke: You tell him exactly what it was, that's all. You just tell him the truth, that's all I care about.

Q. (By Mr. Fredricks) Was it on that trip then—that was the last time you had any discomfort in your neck?

   Mr. Clarke: I think he is talking about his back.

   The Witness: My back. See, I—

Q. (By Mr. Fredricks) I thought you told me it was a month ago that you last had any problem with your low back.

A. No. It was my neck.

Q. Your neck.

A. My neck is pretty much better now, but my back I still have some pain. Like I feel a slight pain now in my lower back.

Q. All right.

A. And during the trip down to Monroe, Missouri, I felt discomfort in my back on the way down and on the way back, and—

Q. And what month did you make that trip, July of 1991?

A. It was this month.

Q. August of 1991.

A. Yes.

Q. Did you seek any treatment for your back?

A. After this?

Q. While on that trip.

A. No.

Q. Did you take—

A. I was just taking hot baths and stuff.

Q. I see.

A. And I got a massage a couple times.

Q. You did?

A. Well, from, you know, his mother. She rubbed it down with Ben-Gay and stuff like that.

Q. After the trip.

A. Well, when I went down, got down to Monroe.

Q. Did you say your mother?

A. No, this—the dude's mother massaged my back when I was down there.

Q. Okay.

A. Mrs. Cross massaged my back.

Q. Have you had any military service?

A. No.

Q. Have you had a physical exam for military service?

A. No. See, I was going to school and they just gave me a deferment for going to school.

Q. Do you have a military classification?

A. No, I don't.

Q. You don't have a military identification card or anything.

A. No.

Q. Have you ever been convicted of a crime?

A. No.

Q. Did you ever see or talk to this Smith after the night of the accident?

A. No.

Q. Did you talk to Mr. Smith at the scene of the accident?

A. No.

Q. Was there anyone in the car, Ms. Jones' car, besides you and Ruby?

Q. No, just the three of us. Three of us.

Q. Do you have any plans to see Dr. Thomas Peterson again?

A. Well, I called him the other day, but he wasn't in, and I just wanted to talk to him because I haven't talked to him after I came out of the hospital. See, like when I came out of the hospital then I—he went into the hospital.

Q. He himself went in?

Q. Yes. And like I sort of tried to avoid going over to—I have just been sitting in a hot bath, hot water.

Q. You can move your neck, and your back is all right now, as I understand your testimony.

A. Yes.

Q. And it's your low back at this moment, you have slight pain in your low back.

A. Yes.

Q. Does that get worse at times?

A. At night.

Q. At night.

A. Yes.

Q. What happens at night that causes your back to bother you?

A. Seems like there is a pain all down my back.

Q. Well, what are you doing, or what position causes your back problem?

A. I got a water bed, and it still hurts.

Q. You have a water bed?

A. Yes.

Q. How long have you had that?

A. About two months.

Q. Did it seem to help at all?

A. Not really. See, first I was sleeping on a mattress with a board up under, and that didn't seem to help it either.

Q. Did someone suggest that you try a water bed?

A. No.

Q. It was your own idea.

A. Yes.

Q. Does the water bed seem to hurt your back?

A. Not really. See, it hurts once in a while at night. It didn't hurt every night.

Q. I see. So usually your back feels better during the day than it does at night.

A. Sometimes I don't notice it during the day, sometimes I notice it during the day, sometimes at nights—

Q. What are you doing during the daytime that causes you to have back problems?

A. See, I sit down, I will be working in the office in Hearns Auditorium, and that's a lot of sitting, but I still walk around, you know, to— just to walk around, move my back around and stuff.

Q. The walking around seems to help.

A. Well, it's just moving around, if it—

Q. It does help.

A. It probably helps a little bit just to get up and move around.

Q. Does it?

A. Yes, it does. But when I sit down again for about five minutes, half hour again, I can feel the pain again.

Q. The pain in your legs cleared up quite soon after the accident?

A. Seemed like that came back little bit later too, pain in the other side of the leg.

Q. Your legs don't bother you now.

A. Not right now, no.

Q. When is the last time either of your legs bothered you? Been a long time?

A. Yes. About when I was seeing Dr. Peterson, getting therapy along in that time. Not the last—it probably was the last one. I haven't seen him—

Q. For about a year?

A. No, it hasn't been that long. About three—three or four months.

Q. Have you taken any drug store medicines or—

A. Prescriptions?

Q. Prescription, medicines?

A. Yes.

Q. When is the last time?

A. About four months ago.

Q. What drug store do you get your medicine at?

A. I didn't get the medicine, this girl got it for me. It was just pain pills.

Q. Ms. Jones?

A. Yes.

Q. The girl—

A. The one I'm staying with now, she went to the drug store and got it. It was a pain pill though.

Q. Is it her prescription or yours?

A. Prescription Dr. Peterson wrote me.

Q. And when you had taken this medicine, why did you take it?

A. Why did I take it?

Q. Why?

A. For the pain.

Q. Where in?

A. My back pain.

Q. All right. Not your legs, not your neck, not for any headaches.

A. It was just—just a pain pill, Darvon. It's just for the pain. If you have pain in your leg, you know, supposed to knock it all out.

Q. The reason you have taken the Darvon is for your low back.

A. Yes, sir.

Q. All right. And that's all.

A. Yes, sir.

Q. Okay. You haven't had any particular problem with headaches following this accident, have you?

A. Yes.

Q. You have.

A. Yes.

Q. For what period of time did you have headaches?

A. Some time I had it all evening. Well—

Q. I mean for—was it a month following the accident, two months, three months?

A. I couldn't—I couldn't tell you exactly. It's—it should be in Dr.—

Q. I'm not asking for an exact period of time, I'm asking for some—

A. I really couldn't tell you. It should be in Dr. Peterson's record, because I let him know when it happened.

Q. When is the last time you recall being bothered by a headache, long, long time ago, over a year ago?

A. I still have them. Well, like when I went on that trip I had headaches going on the way down, something like a migraine headache. I remember the last time I had a terrible headache. Then again it was three, four months ago I was getting headaches, a headache, too.

Q. When?

A. About two or three months ago I was getting a headache.

Q. Did you have headaches while you were at Wahlstrom College?

A. I believe—I believe so.

Q. You don't recall now.

A. I'm pretty sure I did, because I remember getting a headache, you know, once in a while, serious headache.

Q. Like once a week?

A. No. I couldn't say exactly when—once a week or every two weeks. It was just a headache, you know, have a—a bad headache, you know, pain, headache.

Q. How often?

A. How often? What do you mean, how often?

Q. How often, when you were in college at Wahlstrom did you have a bad headache?

A. Well, I can't answer that, you know, too perfect.

Q. Do you have any photographs about the accident, connected with the accident?

A. Do I have any pictures?

Q. Yes.

A. No.

Q. Do you claim that you have lost any income as a result of the accident?

A. Work?

Q. (Nods head.)

A. Well, working, and taking the bus over there.

Q. Pardon me.

A. Taking the bus over from wherever I was at, taking a bus over to Dr. Peterson's office. And going too from Wahlstrom I was getting treatment, I had to—

Q. All right. You are claiming that you have lost some income.
A. Income and schooling too.

Q. Well, I'm not concerned about school time, I'm concerned about income right now. Do you file a tax return?

A. Did I this past one?

Q. Yes. Have you filed a tax return at any time since the August—

A. Yes.

Q. —accident?

A. Yes.

Q. Federal tax returns? You have.

A. (Nods head.)

Q. All right.

Tom, I will prepare authorizations for tax returns, and also an authorization for the accident report, and I will send them to you.

Mr. Clarke: Why don't you have him sign them now. Just sign any blank authorizations you have for any reason, because I would like to know about these things too. You can fill them in.

While you are looking, my notes show you were at the hospital for four hours.

The Witness: At General?

Mr. Clarke: Yes.

The Witness: I was there a long time just sitting.

Mr. Clarke: My notes also show you saw a doctor the next day. Who did you see the next day?

The Witness: A doctor.

Mr. Clarke: Yes, that's what this shows.

The Witness: I don't know. If it was anybody, it was Dr. Peterson, but I don't remember. I didn't see nobody at General.

(Whereupon a discussion was had off the record.)

Q. (By Mr. Fredricks) Have you ever had any injections in your neck or shoulders with a needle administered by any doctors?

A. No. No, I haven't.

Q. Pardon me.

A. No, I haven't.

Q. Have you ever had any electromyogram tests where they put a needle in your muscles and—

A. Just in the head, scalp.

Q. You have had that in your scalp?

A. Yes.

Q. And when was that done?

A. When I went to the doctor.

Q. For what?

A. When I went to the hospital for Dr. Peterson, at Mt. Sinai Hospital.

Q. And was that soon after the accident then, or when?

A. No, this was recently when I just went to the hospital about two months ago, month and a half ago, for treatment, treatments in the hospital.

Q. That was at Mt. Sinai.

A. Yes, it was.

Q. And that's the only place you have had any such tests.

A. Yes.

Mr. Clarke: I notice there is a bill here for injection something into your neck muscles; what's that for?

The Witness: What is it? What is it?

Mr. Clarke: Did it in the hospital, apparently.

The Witness: Which hospital?

Mr. Clarke: June 21st. It says injection, superior angles. Apparently into your neck.

The Witness: That was at Mt. Sinai.

Mr. Clarke: Yes.

The Witness: That's what it was then, at Mt. Sinai.

Mr. Clarke: You just told him you never had any injections. I want to know what you are talking about.

The Witness: I just seen it in the head and up here (indicating), but I don't know what he stuck down here (indicating).

Q. (By Mr. Fredricks) Do you know what I mean by a hypodermic needle, where you get a—

A. Blood thing?

Q. Yes. Needle that goes into your arm and they inject something under the skin or into the muscle.

A. All I remember is when they put pins all in the head and stuff, and—

Q. You don't remember Dr. Peterson ever injecting any needles into your neck or back?

A. No, I don't.

Q. Okay.

A. That one right there—they might have put some up here (indicating), but I don't remember.

Q. Sometimes he doesn't do it, Tom, and he records it in his records, so I'm not surprised.

Mr. Clarke: He charged twenty bucks for doing it.

Mr. Fredricks: Yes.

Mr. Clarke: I got to know, if he didn't do it, I want to know about it.

The Witness: Where was it I said those pins were at?

Mr. Clarke: I don't have to tell. We are asking you the questions. You were there, I wasn't.

The Witness: I had pins up here (indicating). Probably if they had some here (indicating), you know, I didn't feel it too much.

Q. (By Mr. Fredricks) You never had any problems and any discomfort in your throat area of your neck, have you? You didn't ever develop any pain in the front portion of your neck, did you?

A. Not that I recall.

Q. Okay.

A. Well, it was just—

Q. Just in the back of the neck.

A. You mean as far as strep throat or anything like this?

Q. No, I mean following the accident. Any injury to the front portion of your neck?

A. No, I can't—if it was, it was slight. It was just—what Dr. Peterson said it was, I don't know if it was here—you mean did I feel pain exactly right here (indicating) somewhere up in here (indicating).

Q. Yes.

A. No.

Q. Have you had strep throat or some problem like that?

A. One time, long time ago.

Q. Dr. Peterson didn't treat you for that?

A. No.

Q. You have been treated with some physical therapy at Mt. Sinai Hospital, and traction.

A. Yes.

Q. Have you had therapy or traction anywhere else?

A. At his office, at his clinic, and at Wahlstrom, downtown clinic.

Q. What clinic downtown? Was that Kennan's?

A. No. This was in Uhler, Michigan.

Q. Oh. What clinic?

A. It was at the hospital, at the Uhler Hospital down in Uhler, Michigan.

Q. But you said there was a clinic downtown in Uhler.

A. I meant Uhler Hospital, and there is a clinic there.

Q. At the hospital.

A. I believe so, yes.

Q. You saw some private doctors in Uhler.

A. Yes.

Q. Do you remember their names?

A. No, I don't.

    Mr. Fredricks: Do you have that, Tom?

    Mr. Clarke: No, except it's on the—I sent your adjuster the bill for some X rays down there, and I assume from that you can get a lead as to who ordered the X rays. I don't even know that.

Q. (By Mr. Fredricks) Right. At the present time you are engaging in all of the activities that you used to participate in and enjoy before this accident.

A. Yes.

Q. You are not claiming that you are now handicapped or prevented from doing things that you would otherwise do due to this accident?

A. Well, I—you know, I know my back is hurting, I won't be picking up something that's heavy or something. I try to use some common sense what to do and what not to do with my back.

Q. All right. But you can throw a soft ball and you can—

A. Yes.

Q. If you enjoyed ice skating, you would go ice skating, or if you bowled you would go bowling, and if you want to take a trip like to Missouri, you go ahead and do it.

A. Yes.

Q. Okay. Have you made any other trips—

A. No.

A. —out of the state or out of town since?

A. Yes. Yes.
Q. Where?

A. San Antonio.

Q. Texas?

A. Yes.

Q. When?

A. Right after school was out.

Q. And what was the purpose for that trip?

A. Just going down to San Antonio, Texas.

Q. Did you make this trip by car?

A. Yes.

Q. Who did you go with?

A. Some friend of mine. It was three in the car.

Q. Well, who were the friends?

A. Some friends I went to school with.

Q. I'm interested in names.

A. They were no kin or nothing like—

Q. Pardon me.

A. They were no kin to me or nothing like that.

Q. All right. But what were their names? Was it Ms. Jones? Was it Ruby?

A. No.

Q. Who?

A. Cooley. Cooley. They are from out of town. They are from out of town, from Des Moines.

Q. Oh, okay. Anyone else or any other trips?

A. No.

Q. How long were you gone to San Antonio?

A. Just down and back.

    Mr. Fredricks: I believe that's all the questions I have.

EXAMINATION

By Mr. Lang:

Q. Have you ever worn any kind of belt, or brace, or collar?

A. Yes. Like when I went for my—on the trip to Monroe I wore a back brace.

Q. Where did you get that?

A. At Mt. Sinai. Well, see, it was a traction belt and I just cut the things off of it and used it, just used it as a belt.

Q. How wide is that?

A. This wide (indicating).

Q. About six inches wide?

A. Yes.

Q. How many times have you been hospitalized since this accident of August of '89?

A. Just that once.

Q. And how long a time was that?

A. A week.

Q. Did the hospitalization help you?
A. Not really. Not really.

Q. How long have you lived in the Detroit area?

A. About eleven or twelve years.

Q. Did you have headaches before this accident?

A. Not that I can recall, no.

Q. You referred to migraine headaches; now, have you been bothered with migraine headaches?

A. Not like that. Not no headaches like this one. I used to have just plain headaches, you know, like cold headaches, but like these headaches is something else.

Q. How often do you get those?

A. Once in a while.

Q. How often is that? Once a month?

A. Once a month, twice a month. You know, it isn't—

Q. How long do they last?

A. A long time; about three or four hours.

Q. Do you take anything for them?

A. Yes.

Q. What do you take?

A. Aspirins.

Q. Does that relieve them?

A. No.

Mr. Lang: I have no further questions.

Mr. Clarke: We will waive the reading and signing and the notice of filing of the deposition.

* * *

STATE OF MICHIGAN ⎱
COUNTY OF WAYNE ⎰ SS.

Be it known that I took the deposition of Duane Johnson, pursuant to agreement of counsel; that I was then and there a notary public in and for said county and state; that I exercised the power of that office in taking said deposition; that by virtue thereof I was then and there authorized to administer an oath; that said witness, before testifying, was duly sworn to testify to the truth, the whole truth and nothing but the truth relative to the cause specified above; that the deposition is a true record of the testimony given by the witness; that the reading and signing of the deposition was waived by the witness and pursuant to agreement of counsel; that I am neither attorney or counsel for, nor related to or employed by, any of the parties to the action in which this deposition was taken, and further that I am not a relative or employee of any attorney or counsel employed by the parties hereto or financially interested in the action.

WITNESS MY HAND AND SEAL this 22nd day of September, 1991.

_____

John R. Nash

Notary Public, Wayne County, Michigan
My Commission Expires November 25, 1994.

Appendix VII

Review

1. Who may serve a summons and complaint in a civil action?

2. Describe the various methods available for serving a summons and complaint upon a corporation.

3. Within how many days after service of the complaint upon the defendant may he or she start a third-party action without leave of the court?

4. When may a deposition be used at trial in lieu of the live testimony of the deponent?

5. If a party wants to inspect certain written documents which are in the possession of another party who refuses to permit the inspection, what, if any, remedy does he or she have?

6. What factors must be considered in determining whether the court has jurisdiction of a particular case?

7. What consequences may result from a party's false answer to an interrogatory?

8. Define "res ipsa loquitur."

9. Define "negligence."

10. How many days notice must be given for the hearing of a motion?

11. As a practical matter, what guidelines should be followed in the preparation of interrogatories?

12. Is it ethical (proper) for an attorney to interview a witness after the witness's deposition has been noticed but before the deposition is taken?

13. May the parties stipulate to take a deposition without serving a notice for taking the deposition?

14. How soon after an action is commenced may the *defendant* serve a notice of taking deposition?

15. What are the distinctions between jurisdiction and venue?

16. What are the limitations on adverse medical examinations?

17. What is meant by general jurisdiction when referring to a court?

18. Are a parties' income tax records (reports) subject to discovery? What procedures would be employed? What would have to be shown to justify obtaining the tax returns?

19. What are the prerequisites to obtaining an adverse medical examination?

20. How does a request for admissions differ from written interrogatories?

21. When may a request for admissions be served on a *nonparty* and enforced against him?

22. What is "impeachment" as that term is used in civil litigation?

23. What considerations determine whether a party will use an oral deposition or written interrogatories for discovery?

24. Describe the proper and adequate preparation of a party for his or her deposition which is to be taken by the opposing attorney.

25. Describe at least four purposes or uses of oral depositions.

26. What is an affirmative defense, and how is it raised?

27. Define "stare decisis."

28. Define "special damages."

29. What is the function of the jury in a civil trial?

30. If a client consults a lawyer about a proposed illegal scheme which is later pursued by the client, to what extent will the communications be privileged or nondiscoverable in a civil suit by a third-party against the former client and why?

31. How many peremptory challenges does a party have in a civil case? How many challenges for cause does a party have?

32. What are the consequences if plaintiff fails to prove a prima facie case? Discuss the procedures which the parties would follow.

33. When should pleadings and other papers, used in litigation, be filed with the clerk of court?

34. When a document used in litigation is served by mail, when is the service complete, that is, effective?

35. What is an ex parte motion?

36. If the answer fails to either admit or deny an averment contained in the complaint, what is the status of the averment?

37. What are "special damages"?

38. What is an affirmative defense?

39. What happens to an affirmative defense if it is not set forth in a responsive pleading?

40. What is meant by the term "compulsory counterclaim"?

41. What is a pretrial conference, and what are the purposes of such conferences?

42. What general information should be contained in all written motions?

43. What is the purpose or function of the notice of motion which is attached to and served with all written motions?

44. What sources of information may the court consider when ruling upon a motion for summary judgment pursuant to Rule 56?

45. Why is the plaintiff precluded from inquiring into defendant's financial worth when deposing the defendant?

46. What is a "cause of action" in civil litigation?

47. How does a "declaratory judgment" action differ from an action for money damages?

48. What is meant by "res judicata"?

49. What is meant by "splitting a cause of action"?

50. What factors must exist for communications with a lawyer to be considered privileged?

51. What is a contingent fee; and are such fees ethical?

52. Describe the extent of a lawyer's implied authority in the handling of the client's litigation.

53. On what grounds or for what reasons may a client discharge his or her attorney?

54. Describe the territorial jurisdiction of the federal district courts.

55. What is "proximate cause"?

56. What is "strict liability in tort"?

57. When is a civil action commenced, that is, started?

58. If a notice of motion and motion are deposited in a United States mailbox on Saturday for service on the adverse party, but the mail is not picked up until Monday, and they are not delivered to the opposing attorney until Wednesday, what is the day from which one begins counting to determine whether adequate time for service was given?

59. If a party fails to appear at (attend) the deposition of a witness, can that deposition be used *for* or *against* the absent party when the case reaches trial? Does it make a difference whether the absent party was served with a "Notice of taking Deposition"?

60. What is a "dismissal without prejudice"?

61. If a party duly makes an admission in response to requests for admissions, when may that "admission" be used against him or her in any other proceedings?

62. What is the purpose and what are the limitations on opening statements by counsel?

63. What is an evidentiary "offer of proof" and how is it made?

64. After the jury returns a special verdict, what is the procedure for having judgment entered for the prevailing party?

65. Define "judgment."

66. What is an offer of judgment? Why is it used? How is the offer of judgment made? What are the time limitations as to when it can be made?

67. What is a special appearance?

68. What is meant by fair preponderance of the evidence in connection with a party's burden of proof?

69. What procedure would an attorney follow if he or she wanted to obtain separate trials on the issues of liability and damages?

70. What are the grounds for consolidating two or more action (cases) for the purpose of trial?

71. In a civil action, may a plaintiff force the defendant to take the stand to testify? If so, what procedure is followed?

72. How does a special verdict differ from a general verdict in its form, purpose, effect, and procedures?

73. What is an additur? When is it used? How is it obtained?

74. What are four grounds for ordering a new trial?

75. What is an affidavit of prejudice? Who signs it? What are the grounds for it?

76. What is the procedure for obtaining a restraining order, and what are the grounds for such an order?

77. What party has the right to final argument in a civil action?

78. What is the parol evidence rule?

79. What is meant by the "ultimate question of fact"?

80. Describe in general terms the procedure for prosecuting an appeal following an adverse jury verdict.

81. Who would have occasion to file an amicus curiae brief?

82. How many interrogatories may a party serve in a federal court action?

83. Is there any situation in which it is not necessary to pay a witness a subpoena fee?

84. Explain the difference, if any, between "admissions" made in answer to interrogatories, and "admissions" made during the course of a deposition, and "admissions" made in response to requests for admissions.

85. How is a substitution of parties accomplished in a civil lawsuit? (Rule 25)

86. Are insurance coverages discoverable? Why?

87. List at least four types of protective orders that a court may issue to limit discovery.

88. When does a party have a duty to supplement his or her oral deposition answers or written answers to interrogatories?

89. What is a subpoena duces tecum?

90. What grounds will permit the plaintiff to obtain the defendant's deposition in the thirty-day period immediately following service of the summons and complaint on the defendant?

91. How is a case placed on the active trial calendar in federal court?

92. If a lawyer believes that the client's recollection of the accident in question is in error, explain the extent to which a lawyer may correct the client's version in preparing for a deposition or trial.

93. What is the voir dire examination?

94. Explain the function of a "findings of fact, conclusions of law and order for judgment."

95. Define hearsay evidence.

96. What is an "advisory jury"?

97. What factors determine whether evidence is relevant to a civil action?

98. To what extent may one party require the disclosure of opinions and conclusions developed by another party's hired expert? (This question pertains to nonmedical expert opinion.)

99. What special arrangements must be made in a civil action for the deposition of a person who is confined to a prison?

100. If the parties and deponent cannot agree on the place of the deponent's deposition and subpoena is necessary to compel the witness's attendance, what are the geographical limits on where the deposition may be taken? (Rule 45)

Appendix VIII

Glossary

Action. Also called an "action at law." A claim which has been placed in suit. A lawsuit.

Accident scene. The situs of an accident before the conditions have changed, so that observations of the scene show the conditions as they were at the time of the accident.

Affirmative defense. A defense to a cause of action which bars all or part of the cause of action. The defense must be pleaded in an answer or reply to counterclaim or answer to cross-claim. The party who asserts an affirmative defense has the burden of proof to establish the defense. An affirmative defense is effective to bar a cause of action even if the claim is proven.

Bill of Particulars. A common law discovery document which a party prepares, usually pursuant to a court order, and through which the party discloses in detail the facts and circumstances which were referred to in the party's pleading.

Cause of action. A claim that is recognized by law and enforceable through the courts. A cause of action presumes a breach of a legal duty which is the proximate (direct) cause of personal injury or property damage or other loss that gives the victim the right to legal redress.

Certiorari. The name of a writ of review or inquiry. A higher court directs the lower court to deliver the court records and files to the higher court, so the higher court can review the proceedings to determine whether error occurred.

Claim. A demand for compensation or restitution due to injury, damage, or loss to person or property. A claim may be made without actually starting a lawsuit or having a lawsuit pending. A mere claim may or may not be based upon a legal right. To be enforceable in court, however, the claim must be based upon a legal right.

Claimant. A person who asserts a claim against another person, whether or not a lawsuit has been commenced.

Clear and convincing. A degree of proof which must be met to establish certain causes of action and certain defenses. Clear and convincing is more than a "fair preponderance" of the evidence, which is the most common standard of proof applicable to civil actions. But "clear and convincing" is a lesser degree of proof than proof "beyond a reasonable doubt," which is the standard imposed upon the government in prosecution of criminal cases.

Comparative negligence. A legal doctrine which requires the fact finder (jury) in a negligence action to determine the percentages of causal negligence attributable to each person involved in the occurrence. A plaintiff's causal negligence is not a bar to a recovery of compensatory money damages. If the plaintiff is found to be causally negligent, the amount of money damages recoverable is reduced by the amount of his or her causal negligence. If the plaintiff is more negligent than the defendant, however, the laws of some states preclude the plaintiff from making any recovery against the defendant. If two or more defendants are found to be causally negligent, they must share the liability for money damages in proportion to their percentages of causal negligence; however, each defendant remains separately liable for *all* of claimant's damages.

Complicity. An affirmative defense to a "dramshop" action. The liquor vendor can avoid liability to the plaintiff, who was injured by an intoxicated person, if the vendor can prove that the plaintiff was "complicit" in the illegal sale of intoxicants to the alleged intoxicated person. For example, complicity is established by showing that the plaintiff bought the intoxicants for the alleged intoxicated person and thereby participated in the alleged illegal sale.

Conclusion of law. When the court applies the law to a given set of facts, the resulting determination is called the court's conclusions of law. For example, if the facts show that a motorist violated a traffic light and the law provides that a traffic signal violation is "negligence," the legal conclusion is that the motorist was negligent. In an action where the facts are determined by a judge without a jury, the judge must report the judge's determination of how the law applies to the facts by preparing a document which contains the judge's *findings of fact and conclusions of law.* The conclusions of law determine the parties' rights and obligations and are the basis for the court's order for judgment.

Contingent. An obligation or duty depends upon the occurrence of an event or performance of an act before the obligation takes effect.

Contingent fee. A fee charged for legal services which is dependent upon the lawyer obtaining a recovery of money for the client; the amount of the fee is determined by the amount of the recovery.

Contribution. A right or obligation between parties who are jointly liable to a third person, usually the plaintiff, for money damages recoverable in a civil action.

Contributory Negligence. Negligence on the part of the plaintiff which contributed to the accident and plaintiff's injuries. Historically, it was a complete defense to the plaintiff's action in negligence against the defendant. The doctrine has been replaced in most states by "comparative fault."

Conversion. The wrongful exercise of control or ownership over another person's personal property such as to steal property.

Counterclaim. A claim asserted by the defendant against the plaintiff to obtain compensation for a loss or damages suffered by the defendant. The claim may be founded in tort or contract. The name of the pleading in which a counterclaim is asserted.

Court of record. A court in which the judicial proceedings and acts are recorded and permanently retained.

Criminal. (adj.) That which pertains to or is connected with the law of crimes, or the administration of penal justice, or which relates to or has the character of crime. Criminal justice and procedures are quite distinct from civil justice and procedures.

Cross-claim. A claim made by one defendant against a codefendant where the claim arises out of the same facts which gave rise to the plaintiff's claim against the defendants. An action to obtain relief in the form of indemnity or contribution. A defendant may seek money damages from one or more codefendants for a loss which the cross-claimant sustained, provided the cross-claimant's cause of action arises out of the same facts that gave rise to the plaintiff's action against the defendants.

Damages. (1) The harm to a person or property that arises out of the unlawful conduct of another person. (2) An abbreviation of the term "money damages." Compensation in the form of money which may be recovered in court by a party who has suffered personal injury, property damage, or, in contract actions, a loss of the bargain. The harm or loss must have been directly caused by the unlawful act or omission of another.

Declaratory judgment. A court decree that declares the parties' rights and obligations pursuant to writings such as contracts, statutes, deeds, ordinances, and regulations. A declaratory judgment may be issued even though the parties have not violated the written contract, statute, or other document which is the source of an alleged legal right or obligation. Most states have adopted the Uniform Declaratory Judgment Act, which determines when and how a declaratory judgment action may be prosecuted.

Demonstrative evidence. Physical or tangible evidence which can be brought to the courtroom and used to prove a fact or used for illustrative purposes, that is, to help a witness to explain his or her testimony. Demonstrative evidence may have been created by the transaction or occurrence which gave rise to the parties' litigation, or it may be especially prepared by a party for use at trial.

Deposition. A procedure for obtaining testimony under oath. (1) Oral deposition is a procedure established by the Federal Rules of Civil Procedure which allows any party to obtain the testimony of any party or witness for the purpose of discovering information from the deponent or to preserve the deponent's testimony for use at trial. The deponent can be compelled, under penalty of law, to testify. The procedure preserves the right of cross-examination and right to counsel. (2) Written deposition is a procedure established by the Federal Rules of Civil Procedure which allows a party to obtain written testimony of any party or witness for the purpose of discovering information from the deponent or to preserve the deponent's testimony for use at trial. The deponent may be compelled to testify. The right to cross-examination is preserved.

Directed verdict. An order by the trial judge which dismisses a claim or an affirmative defense on the grounds that there is insufficient evidence to prove the alleged claim or defense. Or, the judge determines that the claim or defense is conclusively established by the evidence, so there is nothing for a jury to decide or resolve. The order leads directly to an entry of judgment in favor of the prevailing party. The judge *must* determine that a reasonable jury could decide the facts one way. Therefore, the judge is able to apply the law to those facts to resolve the litigation.

Dismissal. The termination of a lawsuit pursuant to Rule 41. The termination may be the voluntary act of the plaintiff or by stipulation of the parties or by court order.

Dismissal with prejudice. A dismissal that precludes the plaintiff from bringing the claim at a later date against the party who has obtained the dismissal.

Dismissal without prejudice. A dismissal of a lawsuit subject to the claimant's right to bring the lawsuit again in the same court or in another court at a later date.

Equity. In its broadest and most general signification, equity is the spirit and the habit of fairness, justness, and right dealing which would regulate the intercourse of persons—the rule of doing to all others as we desire them to do to us; or, as it is expressed by Justinian, "To live honestly, to harm nobody, to render to every man his due." It is, therefore, the synonym of natural right or justice. But, in this sense, its obligation is ethical rather than jural, and its discussion belongs to the sphere of morals. It is grounded in the precepts of the conscience, not in any sanction of positive law. In a restricted sense, the word denotes equal and impartial justice as between two persons whose rights or claims are in conflict; justice, that is, as ascertained by natural reason or ethical insight but independent of the formulated body of law. This is not a technical meaning of the term, except insofar as courts which administer equity seek to discover it by the agencies previously mentioned or apply it beyond the strict lines of positive law. In a still more restricted sense, it is a system of jurisprudence, or branch of remedial justice, administered by certain tribunals, distinct from the common law courts and empowered to decree "equity" in the sense last given. Here it becomes a complex of well-settled and well-understood rules, principles, and precedents.

Expert opinion. An opinion about the effect of facts which are relevant to the parties' controversy. For an opinion to be admissible in evidence, the presiding judge must determine that the opinion would be helpful to the jury to better understand the facts in the case. The opinion must have a foundation in the record, that is, be based upon sufficient facts to be competent. As part of the foundation, the party who offers expert opinion testimony must show that the expert has the education, training, and experience to be an expert. The judge has broad discretion in determining whether the expert's background is adequate to make the witness an expert in the particular field. An opinion differs from a mere conclusion in that an opinion requires application of the expert's experience to form the judgment. Whereas a conclusion is a determination made through a process of reasoning. Where a witness makes logical deductions from the evidence, the result is nothing more than a conclusion. As a general rule, the jury is supposed to make its own conclusions from the evidence.

Ex parte. On one side only; by or for one party; done for, in behalf of, or on the application of, one party only. Ex parte are motions heard by the court with only one party in attendance.

Fiduciary. A fiduciary is a person or corporation who has assumed a special relationship to another person or another person's property such as a trustee, administrator, executor, lawyer, or guardian. The fiduciary must exercise the highest degree of care to maintain and preserve the person's right and/or property which are within his or her charge. A fiduciary must place the interests of this charge ahead of his or her own. A lawyer is a fiduciary concerning any secrets, documents, and money given by the client for safekeeping during the professional relationship. A lawyer is not a fiduciary in the handling of the client's litigation.

Findings of fact. A determination of facts made by the trial court from the evidence produced in a trial. Findings of fact are predicates for the trial court's application of the law to the facts and the court's determination of the conclusions of law.

General jurisdiction. Authority of a court to adjudicate all controversies that may be brought before a court within the legal bounds of rights and remedies, as opposed to special or limited jurisdiction, which covers only a particular class of cases, or cases where the amount in controversy is below a prescribed sum or which are subject to specific exceptions.

Grand jury. A jury of inquiry who is summoned and returned by the sheriff to each session of the criminal courts and whose duty is to receive complaints and accusations in criminal cases, hear the evidence adduced on the part of the state, and find bills of indictments in cases where it is satisfied a trial ought to be held. The jury issues an indictment if the jury determines that there is good reason to believe that a crime has been committed and the accused is the perpetrator.

Guardian ad litem. A guardian appointed by a court to assist a minor to prosecute or defend a lawsuit in which the minor is a party. The minor may be the plaintiff or defendant. The guardian may or may not be a parent who is appointed to act in the litigation for the minor. A lawyer who represents a minor could *not* act as the guardian ad litem. A guardian ad litem has ultimate responsibility for making decisions about settlement and whether the action should be maintained or dismissed.

Hearsay. Evidence not proceeding from the personal knowledge of the witness but from the mere repetition of what the witness has heard others say. That which does not derive its value solely from the creditability of the witness but rests mainly on the veracity and competency of other persons. The very nature of hearsay evidence shows its weakness, and it is received at trial only in limited situations due to necessity. Hearsay evidence is competent to prove a fact and will be received by the court in the absence of an objection.

Illustrative evidence. Evidence which does not, in itself, have probative value but which is helpful to a witness to explain his or her testimony. For example, a photograph or drawing which depicts the location of an accident may be useful for a witness to explain what the witness observed. Illustrative evidence is received at trial solely as an aid for the witness. The jury may not be allowed to take illustrative evidence to their deliberations, because the exhibit's only value is to help the witnesses describe or explain their testimony. It is not, in itself, evidence of anything.

Impeachment. To cast doubt on the credibility of a witness or exhibits by showing inconsistencies in what the witness says or the use of exhibits. Also, a witness may be impeached by showing that the witness has been convicted of a crime of a type which indicates the witness is willing to disregard the obligations of the oath.

Impeachment evidence. Evidence offered solely for the purpose of casting doubt on other evidence received by the court. It is evidence which will not, in itself, support a verdict. Prior inconsistent statements of a party, however, may be both impeachment evidence and substantive evidence.

Indemnity. Total reimbursement for a loss. Insurance is a contract providing indemnity.

Independent medical examination. A medical examination of a party to an action conducted by a physician selected by an adverse party for the purpose of evaluating the person's physical, mental, or blood condition. The medical examination is not in itself an adversary proceeding. The physician is expected to follow professional practices and procedures in conducting the examination and in making the evaluation. The right to the examination is prescribed by Rule 35. In some jurisdictions the examinations are referred to as "adverse" medical examinations.

Injunction. A court order which prohibits a party from engaging in a specified activity. A prohibitive writ issued by a court of equity against a defendant forbidding the latter to do some act which he is threatening or attempting to commit or restraining him in the continuance thereof. A court may enjoin the defendant's conduct where the harm to the plaintiff cannot be adequately redressed by an action at law with money damages.

Joint liability. Two or more parties are concurrently liable to a claimant for the claimant's entire loss. Joint liability may arise out of contract or tort. Tortfeasors may acquire joint liability by acting in concert for a joint purpose, or tortfeasors may acquire joint liability merely because their wrongful acts happen to be concurrent and contribute to an indivisible loss.

Judgment. A court's ultimate determination of the parties' rights and obligations concerning a particular matter. The official decision of a court of justice upon the respective rights and claims of the parties. The clerk of court's record of the court's declaration of the parties' rights and obligations in the particular action.

Jurisdiction. The power and authority of a court. A court's jurisdiction depends upon the court following due process of law. Jurisdiction may be limited to a specific territory or to certain types of actions or to certain types of controversies or certain classes of parties. A court's jurisdiction is necessarily limited by the authority of the body which created the court.

Letters rogatory. A formal, written communication sent by a court, in which an action is pending, to a court or judge of a foreign country or state, requesting that the testimony of a witness, who resides within the latter's jurisdiction, be taken under that court's direction and transmitted to the first court for use in the pending action. It is a means of obtaining jurisdiction over a witness for purpose of obtaining the witness's deposition. The court to whom the request is directed will have to use its subpoena power.

Liability. A legal obligation to make restitution or pay compensation. Liability may be contingent or absolute.

Mandamus. An order or writ which is issued by a court of superior jurisdiction and is directed to a governmental officer or to an inferior court, commanding the performance of a particular act which is specified in the writ. The basis for the writ is that the officer or judge has a duty to perform the act or duty and has neglected to do it or has refused to do it. A writ of mandamus may direct a lower court to restore to the complainant legal rights or privileges of which he or she has been illegally deprived.

Material. In a civil action, evidence is material if it relates to the issues raised by the pleadings. Important; more or less necessary; going to the merits; having to do with matters of substance, as distinguished from mere form.

Mistrial. A trial which has been aborted because of some defect in the proceedings which prevents the trial from being a valid or fair trial. A determination and order by the judge presiding over a trial which cancels the trial, usually allowing the case to be tried again.

Money damages. A sum of money awarded to a claimant in compensation for injury, loss, or other harm. *See* Damages.

Motion. An application to a court for a ruling or order concerning a matter of procedure or law. The term is generally employed with reference to all such applications, whether written or oral.

Negligence. An act or omission which creates a foreseeable and unreasonable risk of harm to a person or property. A person may be negligent toward another or to himself or herself.

Negligence per se. An act or omission which is declared by statute to be wrongful and, therefore, is treated by the courts as negligence as a matter of law, without any reference to the reasonable person standard and without any reference to the foreseeability of harm which the act or omission may cause. For example, the violation of a statute which prohibits the sale of firearms to minors could be the basis for a cause of action against the vendor. The sale to a minor constitutes negligence per se. The sale constitutes negligence even if the vendor believed the buyer to be an adult.

Peremptory challenge. By law and court rule, each party to a civil action has a right to remove a specified number of jurors, usually two or three, from the panel during the voir dire examination without explaining or justifying removal of the jurors. Such strikes are called peremptory challenges.

Prima facie case. A party has presented a prima facie case if sufficient evidence has been presented to establish all the elements of the cause of action or all the elements of an affirmative defense. The evidence must be sufficient to support a verdict or finding on the issue. A prima facie case may exist even though the evidence is in conflict or disputed.

Prima facie evidence. On its face, the evidence is presumed to be true unless disproved by some other evidence.

Prima facie negligence. Proof of an act or omission that is specifically prohibited by law thereby establishing that the applicable standard of due care has been violated. The act or omission is, on its face, an act or omission of negligence. The party against whom the claim of negligence is asserted, however, is permitted the right to explain and justify the violation. In the absence of some compelling excuse or justification, the fact finder (jury) must find that the conduct was negligent. An act or omission that is "negligent per se" may not be explained or justified.

Relevant. Evidence is relevant if it tends to establish or negate a controverted fact (see Rule 401).

Res ipsa loquitur. A legal doctrine by which one party may establish an inference of negligence on the part of another party. The inference of negligence comes from a showing that the accident in question was caused by an instrumentality which was in the exclusive control of the defendant; that the accident was not caused by any act of the plaintiff or some third person; and that the accident is of a kind that ordinarily does not occur in the absence of negligence.

Res judicata. A matter adjudged; a thing judicially acted upon or decided; a thing or matter settled by judgment. A legal doctrine which precludes a plaintiff from relitigating the same claim against the same defendant once the cause of action has been determined on its merits.

Restitution. To restore to a person property or a legal right which was wrongfully taken from that person or to provide its equivalent.

Settlement. An agreement between parties to a lawsuit or claim which results in a resolution of their dispute. Settlement agreements are usually made on the basis of a compromise between parties and arrived at without a judicial order or decree. Where money is paid as a result of a settlement agreement, the sum of money paid is often referred to as the "settlement." A jury verdict or arbitration award is *not* a settlement.

Sound discretion. There are certain matters concerning the admissibility of evidence and trial procedures in which the presiding judge has a great deal of latitude. The judge's decision concerning such matters will not be disturbed by an appellate court, even if the appellate court disagrees with the trial court's handling. An appellate court would have to find that the trial court clearly abused its discretion before finding that the trial court's actions constituted error which would require a new trial.

Special verdict. The jury's answer to specific questions of fact which the court submits to the jury. It does *not* require the jury to apply rules of law to the determined facts for the purpose of deciding which party is entitled to the court's judgment. The court must apply the rules of law to the facts, as determined by the special verdict, for the purpose of determining which party is entitled to judgment and the terms of the judgment (Rule 49(a)).

Stare decisis. To abide by, or adhere to, decided cases. The principle that precedent should be followed unless and until compelling reasons occur to change the rule of law.

Stipulation. An agreement voluntarily entered into between the parties concerning some aspect of their litigation. An agreement between the parties which the court will recognize and accept to facilitate judicial proceedings. Stipulations may go to matters of procedure or to substantive rights.

Strict liability in tort. A cause of action which is available in product cases. Liability of the defendant is not based upon fault. Manufacturers and vendors of products are held strictly liable in tort for injuries caused by defective products. In such cases it is not necessary to show that the manufacturer or vendor was negligent or breached an express warranty. A product is considered to be defective if it is unreasonably dangerous when used in the ordinary, foreseeable manner.

Sua sponte. When a court makes an order, without either party having made a motion to obtain the order, the court has acted "sua sponte." In other words, the court has acted on its own motion, on its own initiative.

Subpoena. A process to cause a witness, including parties, to appear and give testimony, commanding the deponent to set aside all pretenses and excuses and appear before a designated court or magistrate at a specified time and place to testify. Failure to comply places the person under penalty by the court. A subpoena may be used in connection with motions, trials, and depositions.

Subpoena duces tecum. A subpoena which directs the witness to bring and present specified documents or things to be reviewed when the witness testifies at court or in a deposition.

Subrogation. The substitution of one person in the place of another to make a claim or prosecute a cause of action. The subrogee acquires subrogation rights of the subrogor by paying the subrogor's loss under legal compulsion. The subrogee cannot acquire any greater rights than were possessed by the subrogor. For example, when a fire insurance company pays its insured for damage to property because of a fire, the insurer acquires the rights of its insured to bring a claim against the tortfeasor who caused the fire and loss; the insurance contract compels the insurer to pay the loss to the insured, so the insurer is not a volunteer in paying the loss. The insurer is limited to recovering damages in the amount it paid to its insured and is subject to any defenses which the tortfeasor had against the insured.

Substantive evidence. Evidence adduced for the purpose of proving a fact in issue, as opposed to evidence given for the purpose of merely discrediting a witness. Evidence which will support a judgment which determines the parties' rights and obligations.

Tort. A private or civil wrong which causes injury to person or damage to property. A wrong, independent of contract. A violation of a duty imposed by general law or otherwise upon all persons occupying the relation to each other which is involved in a given transaction or occurrence. There must be a violation of some duty owed to plaintiff, and, generally, such duty must arise by operation of law and not by mere agreement of the parties.

Tortfeasor. A person who commits any kind of a tort. For example, a person who was negligent and caused an accident may be referred to as a "tortfeasor." Similarly, a person who commits a battery against another person may be described or referred to as a "tortfeasor."

Transitory cause of action. A cause of action which follows the defendant and, therefore, may be commenced in any jurisdiction where the defendant can be found.

Ultimate question of fact. The conclusions of fact made by the jury from all the evidence. The conclusions which are dispositive of the claims and defenses of the parties. The fact to which the rules of law are applied so that a judgment can be rendered by the court. For example, in a negligence action, the ultimate questions of fact are whether the defendant was negligent and whether the defendant's negligence was a proximate cause of the harm and the amount of compensation to which the plaintiff is entitled.

Unilateral mistake. A mistake concerning the terms or effect of a contract made by just one of the parties.

Venue. The judicial district in which an action is brought for trial and which is to furnish the panel of jurors.

Verdict. The jury's decision based upon its determination of the facts and its application of the law to those facts.

Voidable. A contract is voidable when the contract's purpose is not contrary to law but is technically defective due to the wrongful conduct or inadvertence of one of the contracting parties. The party or parties to the contract who did comply with all legal requirements have the option of enforcing the contract or avoiding it. On the other hand, a contract which is *void* cannot be enforced by any party.

Voir dire. The preliminary examination of jurors concerning competency, interest, etc., is tested. A preliminary examination of a witness to determine whether the witness is competent to testify.

Work product. A doctrine which protects from discovery the impressions, mental processes, legal theories, and strategies of a party and the party's attorney formulated while preparing to prosecute or defend a civil action. The doctrine has been expanded to include the party's indemnitor or liability insurer. The doctrine is separate but complements the attorney-client privilege against disclosure of their communications. The doctrine has express support in Rule 26(b) of the Federal Rules of Civil Procedure.

Wrongful death action. An action at law, created by statute, that permits the heirs and next of kin to recover money damages from a tortfeasor for the pecuniary losses resulting from the decedent's death. The elements of the cause of action are established by statute in each state. State statutes also declare what pecuniary losses are compensable and the limitation, if any, on the total amount of damages recoverable.

The Thirteen Federal Judicial Circuits

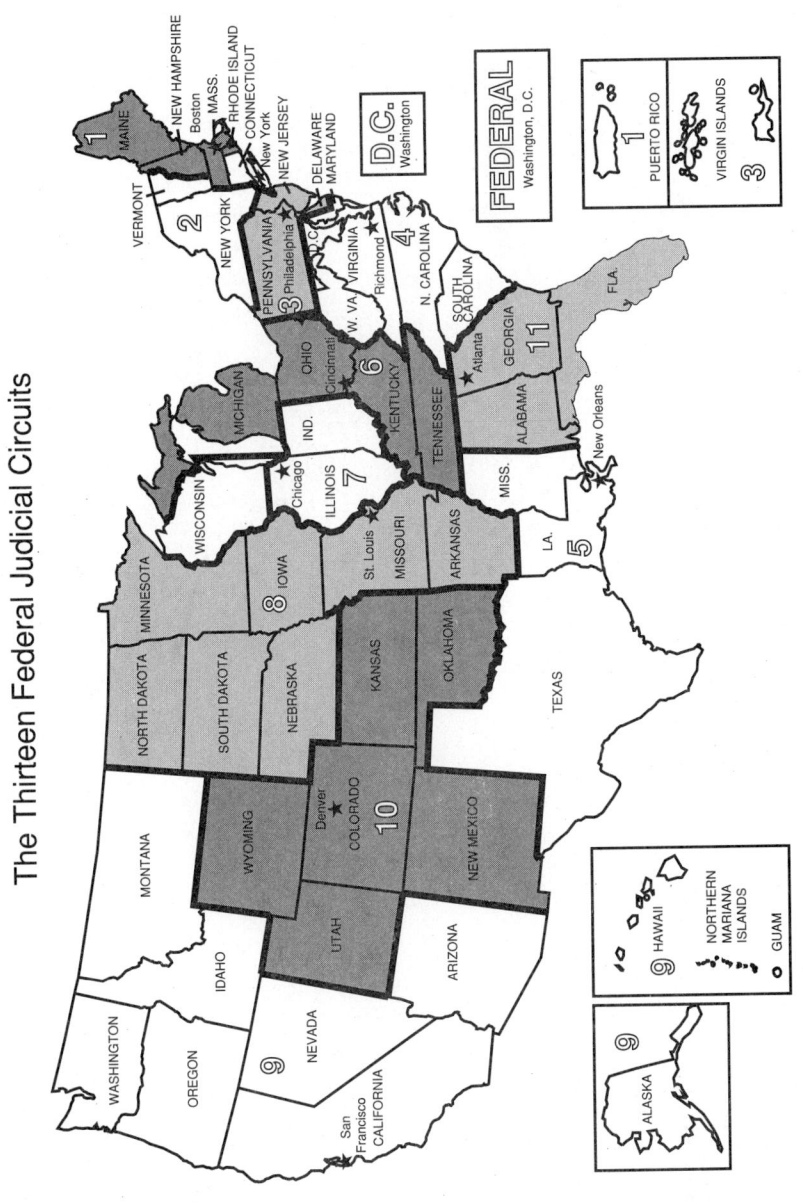

Index